Making An Impression

PRINTMAKERS COUNCIL AT **50**

Printmakers Council
Ground Floor Unit, 23 Blue Anchor Lane
London SE16 3UL
0207 237 6789
07531 883 250
www.printmakerscouncil.com

Unframed Prints and this book are available for sale from the Printmakers Council.

Published by **Imprimata**
for and on behalf of **Printmakers Council**

A CIP Catalogue record for this book is available from the British library

ISBN 978-1-906192-86-0 (paperback)
ISBN 978-1-906192-91-4 (hardback)

Printed and bound in Great Britain
Designed & typeset by Mark Bracey @ InXmedia
InX-192860-15-1 (pb) InX-192914-15-1 (hb)

Imprimata
An imprint of **InXmedia** Limited
Trident Court, 1 Oakcroft Road, Chessington, Surrey KT9 1BD, UK

Picture credits pages iv–10:

Page iv
National Open Print Exhibition Poster
designed by Harvey Daniels
provenance V&A museum

Page 2
Alistair Grant, *Fête Champêtre*
Edition 89/100, provenance RCA,
photographer Peter White

Page 3
Michael Rothenstein, *Untitled*
Edition 41/75, provenance V&A museum,
photographer Peter White

Page 4
Stanley Hayter, *Boats*
Edition 41/100, provenance Maureen Goodwin Cooper, photographer Peter White
Stanley Jones, *Essex Landscape*
Edition 46/50, provenance Stanley Jones,
photographer Peter White

Page 5
Julian Trevelyan, *Birds*
Edition 41/75, provenance V&A museum,
photographer Peter White

Page 6
Michael Rothenstein, *Blue Flowers*
Edition 11/12, provenance Caroline Streets,
photographer Peter White

Page 8
Birgit Skiöld, *Running Tide*
Artist's proof, provenance Adrian Bartlett,
photographer Peter White

Page 9
Graham Sutherland, *Cynocephalus (A Bestiary And Some Correspondances)*
Edition of 70, provenance Monica Petzal,
photographer Peter White

Page 10
John Piper, *Garn Fawr*
Edition 41/75, provenance V&A museum,
photographer Peter White

Foreword

This book presents an impressive and captivating collection of printmakers and their work. They are all contemporary artists united both by their skills as original printmakers and by their membership of the Printmakers Council (PmC). The sheer variety of subject matter, style and technique makes this a fascinating presentation of current ideas and imagery. This book also marks fifty years of remarkable influence in bringing printmaking to the fore.

Fifty years ago printmaking was very much a secondary subject in art schools and the Artist's Print was unrecognised as an art form in its own right. Those artists who made prints were firstly painters or sculptors with printmaking taking second place. The Printmakers Council played a significant role in establishing printmaking on an even footing with other fine art subjects in Art Schools. Gill Saunders expands on this theme in her engaging essay 'Motivated by desire' which asks and answers the question, why make prints? Michael Kennedy examines the history of PmC from various angles drawing attention to its huge influence and importance over the years in his fascinating essay 'A Sixties Pressure Group'.

The Printmakers Council today maintains the same ethos as its founders. An artist-run, not-for-profit organisation, its objectives are to promote the use of traditional and innovative printmaking techniques by providing information on prints and printmaking to both its membership and the public; encouraging co-operation and exchanges between members, other associations and individuals and most importantly, holding exhibitions of prints. Strongly international and welcoming members worldwide, exhibitions have been held on every continent. Within the UK, PmC has exhibited in more than ninety different locations varying from the prestigious such as The Serpentine and Barbican in London, to the very modest.

Printmaking is now at the forefront of artistic practice with both university departments and open access studios thriving. Printmaking has embraced digital technology, which sits firmly alongside traditional forms of printmaking. With an emphasis on professionalism, high standards of process and technique, a commitment to innovation and pushing the boundaries of printmaking, the Printmakers Council now highlights a broad cross section of the finest printmaking to be seen within the UK.

Margaret Ashman
Chairman, Printmakers Council

Acknowledgements

Printmakers Council acknowledges and thanks the following for their generous support of this publication:

Alan Murphy and Mark Bracey of InXmedia

Gill Saunders and Michael Kennedy for their insightful essays

Claire Jackson for her work on the Printmakers Council archive

The Heritage Lottery Fund

Christopher Marsden and Gill Saunders of the V&A Museum for their support and advice on the PmC archive now held by the museum.

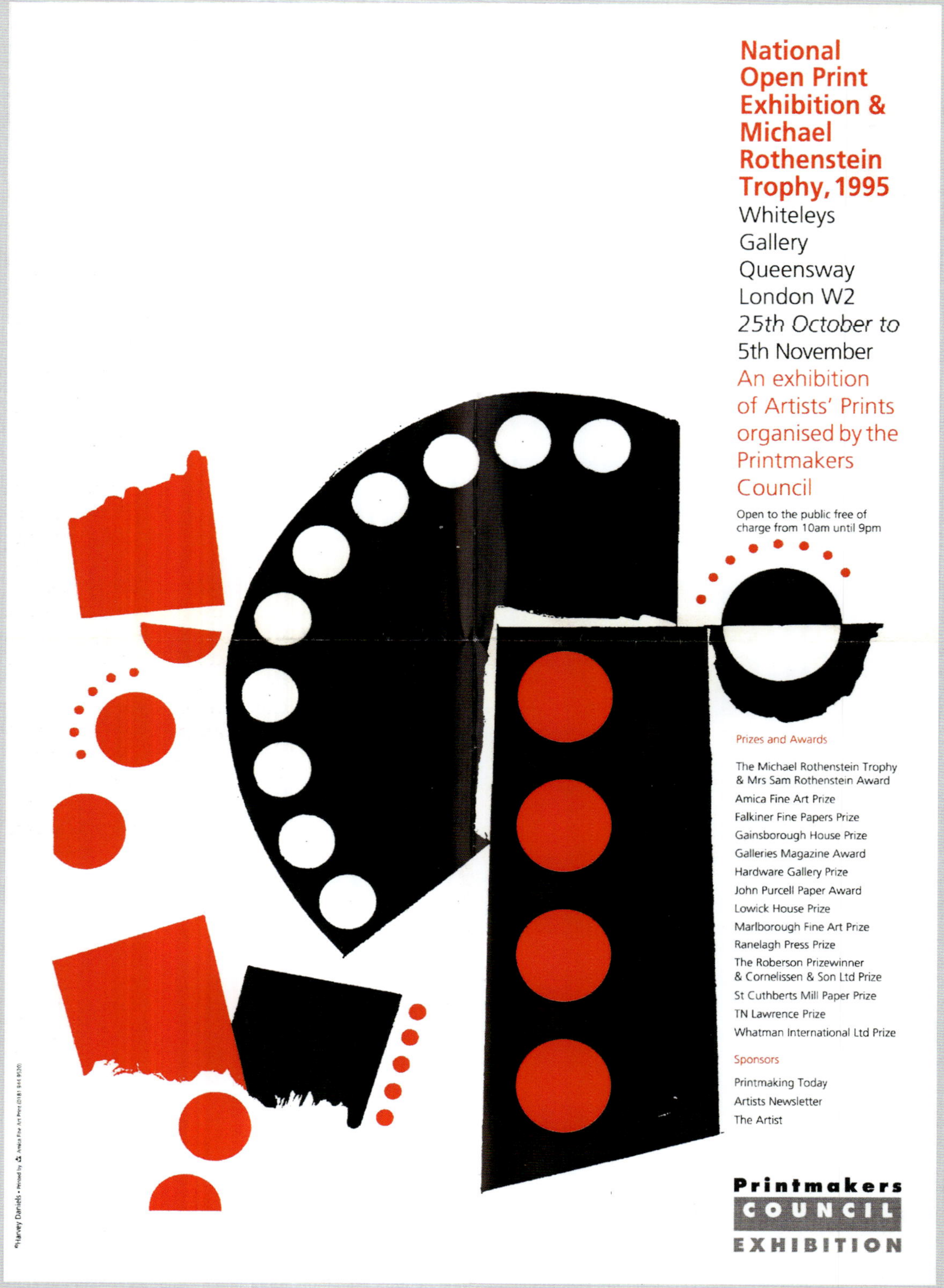
National Open Print Exhibition & Michael Rothenstein Trophy, 1995
Whiteleys Gallery Queensway London W2
25th October to 5th November
An exhibition of Artists' Prints organised by the Printmakers Council
Open to the public free of charge from 10am until 9pm
Prizes and Awards
The Michael Rothenstein Trophy & Mrs Sam Rothenstein Award
Amica Fine Art Prize
Falkiner Fine Papers Prize
Gainsborough House Prize
Galleries Magazine Award
Hardware Gallery Prize
John Purcell Paper Award
Lowick House Prize
Marlborough Fine Art Prize
Ranelagh Press Prize
The Roberson Prizewinner & Cornelissen & Son Ltd Prize
St Cuthberts Mill Paper Prize
TN Lawrence Prize
Whatman International Ltd Prize
Sponsors
Printmaking Today
Artists Newsletter
The Artist
Printmakers COUNCIL EXHIBITION

A Sixties Pressure Group:
Fifty Years of the Printmakers Council

OPPOSITE

National Open Print Exhibition Poster
Designed by **Harvey Daniels**
1995
60.5 x 42 cm

The Printmakers Council, largely the initiative of printmaker, painter and teacher Michael Rothenstein, had its origins in a series of informal meetings in the early 1960s, some of which were held at his London flat and others either at Bertorelli's restaurant or in the studio of printmaker Birgit Skiöld, both located in Charlotte Street. These meetings in turn led to the first general meeting of the Printmakers Council which took place at 7pm on 23rd June 1965 at the F.B.A. Gallery.

The primary aim was to form, in the words of one early member, a 'pressure group', while others describe it as a 'loose association', although neither description seems entirely adequate. What Rothenstein and those associated with him wanted was an organisation that would promote and encourage printmaking, especially an experimental and contemporary approach. Early members looking back point to the poor provision for printmaking both within art education and outside, and the poor status generally given to prints and printmakers. Moreover, print societies at the time were rather conservative in outlook. Stanley Jones, an early member and sometime President of PmC points out in an unpublished interview that long-established traditional print groups ensured that membership was effectively closed to printmakers who did not work in the specific discipline the society represented. It was against this background of poor status and poor provision that the Printmakers Council was formed.

The group was formally organised from the very start. At the inaugural meeting Rothenstein took the chair with Bernard Cheese as Vice Chairman. A committee was elected by secret ballot comprising Anthony Gross, Merlyn Evans, Julian Trevelyan, Birgit Skiöld, Stanley Jones, Alistair Grant and Gertrude Hermes. Subscriptions were set at seven guineas and a second meeting arranged for three weeks later on 14th July.

It is unclear why the name 'Printmakers Council' was chosen. There is a suggestion that the existence of a 'Print Council of America' – still flourishing – may have been an influence. Moreover, an annual subscription of seven guineas in 1965 was quite steep, ensuring, for example, that many postgraduate students would be excluded. The subscription level and the name together might therefore be expected to attract successful, established artists who already had some status in the wider art world. 'Council' carries with it at least some hint of authority and prestige, although it also implies 'conciliar' and 'collaborative' or 'co-operative', characteristics that continue to define the Printmakers Council. But the name has one disadvantage in that it does not slip easily off the tongue and so from the very beginning the abbreviation 'PmC' was widely used, even to the point of appearing on exhibition catalogue covers and to being used as a logo, both in the sans serif lower-case typefaces characteristic of sixties graphic design. From time to time proposals have been made to change the name, the first being recorded as early as 1971 and the most recent in 2013. None has been remotely successful; both 'Printmakers Council' and 'PmC' remain.

In addition to deciding to have a President as well as a Chairman the second meeting of the group identified a number of objectives, most of which are still pursued by PmC today. Among these was the intention to mount exhibitions, especially international exhibitions, to compile an index of printmakers, and to publish a quarterly newsletter. At the AGM of the society in 1967, Rothenstein summarised the objectives of PmC as 'firstly a service organisation providing information on materials, equipment, training, and galleries' and secondly 'as an exhibiting society'. Education was also identified as an important objective and it was decided that the third edition of the quarterly newsletter would be devoted to this topic. Issues one and two were

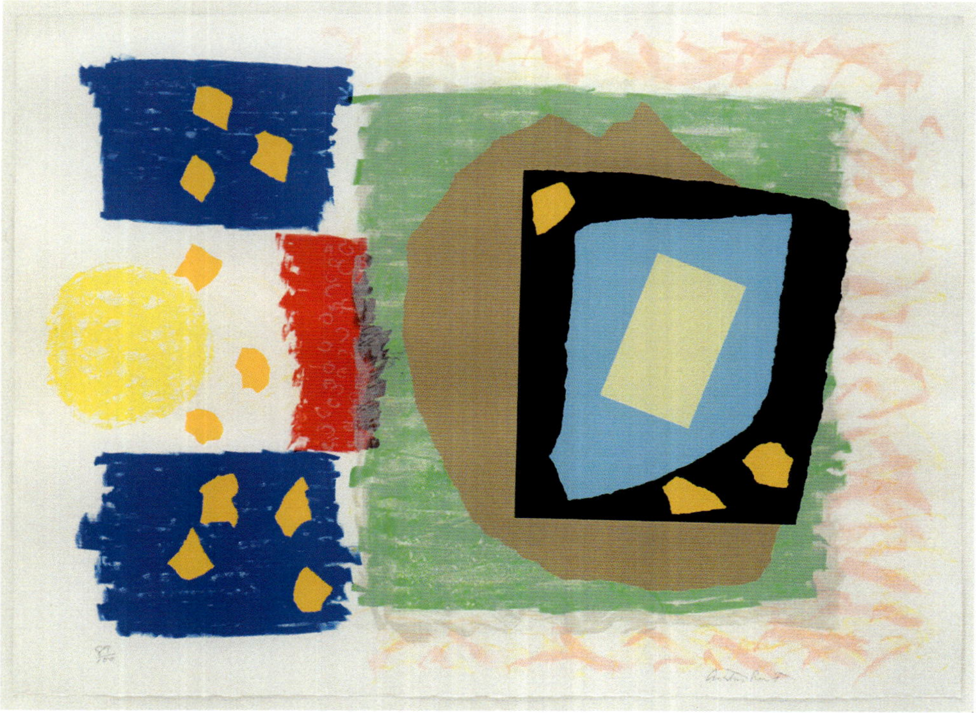

Alistair Grant
Fête Champêtre
12 Artists Portfolio
litho and screen print
56 x 76 cm
1996

to cover 'materials' and 'galleries and dealers' respectively. The meeting decided to lobby the Summerson Commission on the unsatisfactory role of printmaking in the new Diploma in Art and Design course which had replaced the old post-war National Diploma in Design. These then were to be the principal activities: to compile a database, to hold exhibitions, to publish a newsletter and to be a voice for printmaking in education.

By February 1966 the group had thirty-one paid-up members which by October had grown to fifty-five. In time, different classes of membership were debated and subsequently introduced, in particular that of honorary membership. This allowed high-profile artists to be invited to join who might not otherwise have done so. The archive evidence is incomplete but artists like David Hockney, Allen Jones, Graham Sutherland and John Piper have been either members or honorary members. Alternatively, some eminent artists would simply be invited to take part in selected exhibitions, further strengthening Printmakers Council's quest for increased status and prestige for printmaking. Membership was originally by peer election only, a principle that was eventually replaced with open membership sometime in the early 1980s.

The change caused some difficulty for founding and early members, and it still divides opinion. Although new initiatives were started, such as the inauguration of a slide index of members' work to ensure that they got something out of their membership, the reasons for the change seem to have been entirely financial; more members resulting in better financial health. However, it might also be argued that an open membership is more readily suited to an organisation devoted to encouraging printmaking as widely as possible.

In addition to creating a directory of PmC members in 1966, various other efforts have been made to place printmaking more firmly in the public eye, to increase the sale of members' work and to collect it into a permanent archive. The first was a scheme in 1969 to create a print club. Print clubs, rather like book clubs, offer a print or prints to subscribers on a regular basis. The club, with four different artists each year, ran from 1970 until 1974, and had an annual subscription of £25. At its height the club had forty-eight subscribers but it required eighty to be viable. Faced with other competing schemes it was clear that the programme could not be sustained.

In 1980 it was decided to produce a print portfolio. Published in 1980 the portfolio, organised by Joseph Winkelman, consisted of a title page and ten prints, each in a limited edition of seventy-five. Each portfolio was for sale at £300, with a discount being offered to PmC members, educational institutions, authorities or for multiple orders. The portfolio was financially successful but the exercise was not repeated.

PmC had initially been critical of the scope and content of the print collection at the V&A. One founding objective therefore was the creation of a more comprehensive national print archive. Two projects to create an archive of members' work have been attempted, the first at Exeter College of Art and Design in 1977 and the second at Scarborough Art Gallery in 1992. The Exeter project was very ambitious but funding cuts and a reluctance on Exeter's part to be legally responsible for the archive brought the project to an early close. Similarly, although some works were donated and accessioned, the Scarborough print archive came to an end soon after it had started.

The history of the Printmakers Council may be traced through its many exhibitions. Exhibitions are an ideal way to raise awareness and to promote printmaking, and they have always been

Michael Rothenstein
Untitled
Printmakers Council Portfolio 1981
seragraph
30 x 28 cm

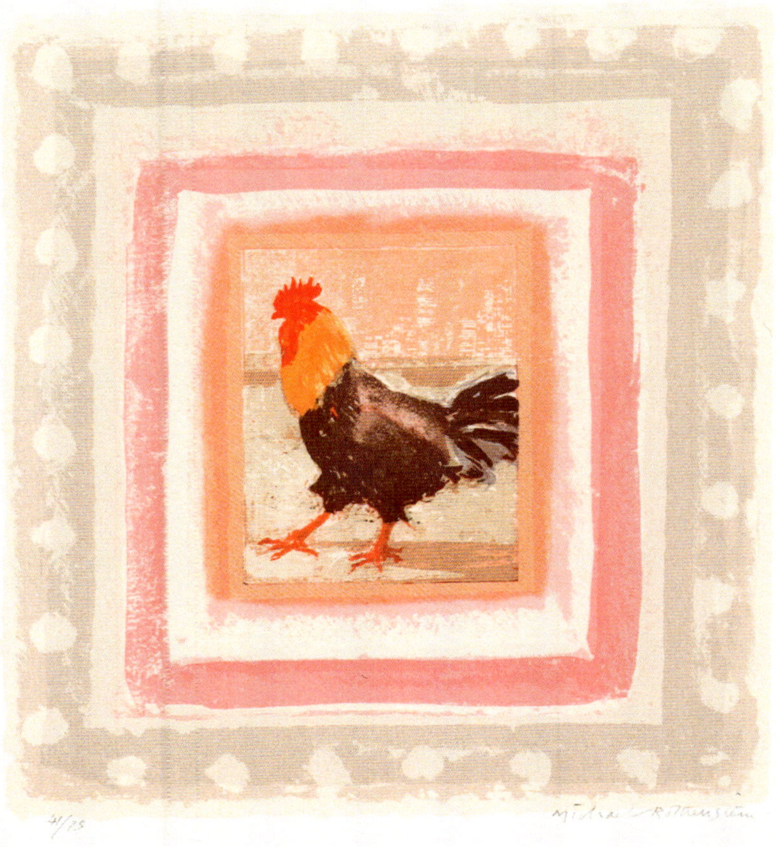

an important part of the work of the Printmakers Council. The last fifty years have been filled with exhibitions not only throughout the United Kingdom but also abroad, fulfilling one of the group's primary objectives. At a meeting on 17th March 1966 it was decided to hold the first Annual PmC Exhibition at the Grabowski Gallery from December 1966 to January 1967, with a concurrent exhibition at the AAA Gallery in New York. Just to give a small selection here, exhibitions have been held at Curwen Gallery, the Barbican, the Serpentine Gallery and the Royal Festival Hall, and in Los Angeles, Portland, Oregon, and Freemantle, Western Australia. Many of the London venues have been used on more than one occasion.

The idea for a 'miniprint' exhibition was originally considered in 1969, but the first miniature print exhibition was not held until December 1980 at the Graffiti Gallery, Great Marlborough Street, London. Writing in the catalogue Rosemary Simmons praised PmC as an organisation run 'by artists, for artists', but went on to complain that too many artists had ignored the rules of the exhibition by sending in prints of the wrong size, or by crudely gluing fragments of prints onto a larger sheet. Nevertheless, this was not to be the end of the miniature print exhibition. One lasting achievement has been the *British International Miniature Print Exhibition*. Started in 1989 by Peter Ford and other PmC members in the south west of England, in conjunction with Bristol Museum and Art Gallery and the Off-Centre Gallery, it has now been held on eight successive occasions. The Off-Centre Gallery ran the exhibition with a UK-wide touring programme four times until 2002 when it was taken on by Gracefield Arts Centre, Dumfries. The Printmakers Council took over for the seventh exhibition in 2008 and organised the eighth in 2012. The exhibition is open to all printmakers and to all print processes, and as the catalogue for the fifth exhibition notes it 'has helped to create a tradition in miniatures here in Britain that had previously been more prevalent abroad'. (Introduction, *Catalogue of 5th British International Miniature Print Exhibition, Gracefield Arts Centre*, 2003)

The debate as to what constitutes an original print has also from the very beginning engaged Printmakers Council; it was a contentious issue then as now, long before the age of digital printmaking or the advent of the giclée

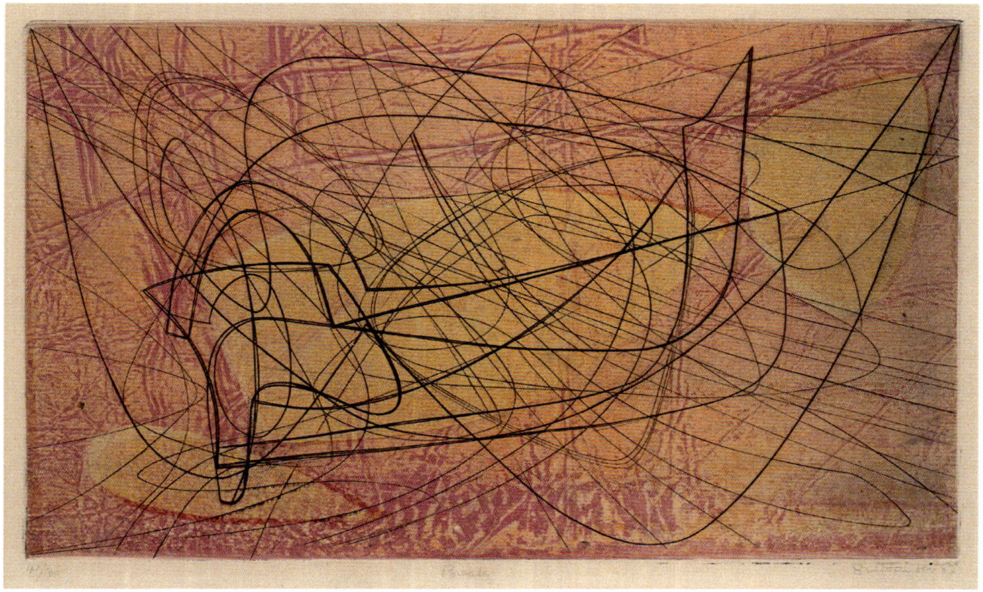

Stanley Hayter *Boats*, engraving, 24 x 40 cm, 1957

Stanley Jones *Essex Landscape*, stone lithograph, 56 x 78 cm, 1962

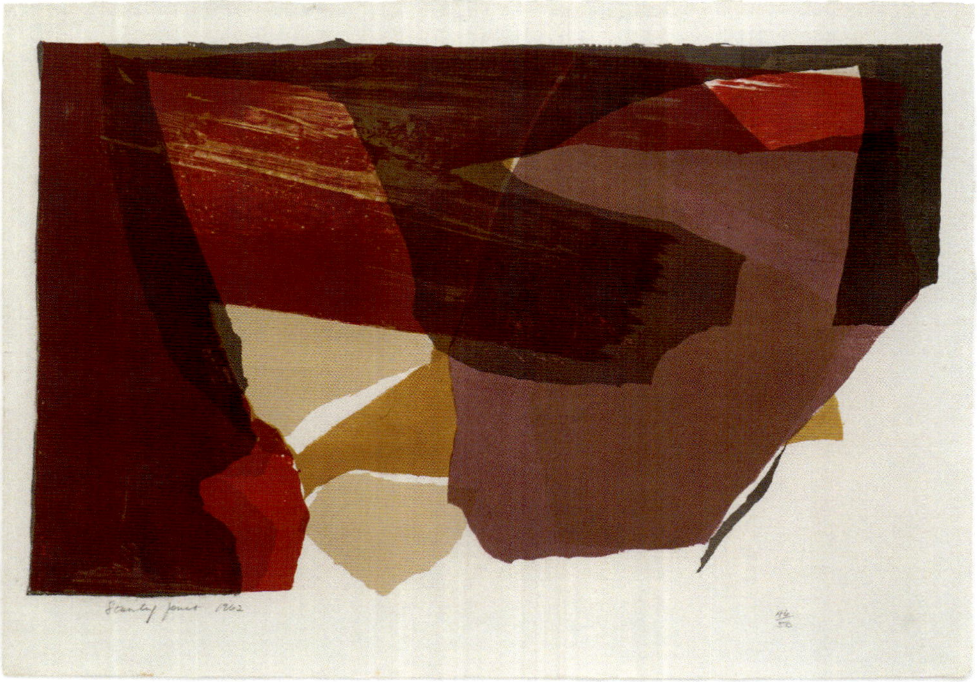

reproduction print. The catalogue for the tenth anniversary exhibition at Morley Gallery in October and November 1974 while noting 'four methods of printing, Lithography, Etching, Serigraphy and Relief', goes on to deplore perceived deceptions in printmaking where an image is duplicated using graphic means and the resulting 'print' passed off as an original. 'Imagery that was conceived in one media has been arbitrarily transposed to another and signing and dating as a mark of approval does not... elevate it from a mere reproductive process'. The author, James Burr, rightly points out that PmC has been in the forefront of an attempt to educate a 'baffled public', a struggle that continues. In 2008 PmC was represented at a series of discussions at the Fine Arts Trade Guild to agree criteria for what constitutes an original print. Although a report was published, the meetings appear to have been somewhat inconclusive. Artist printmakers know and agree what is meant by an original print; publishers and artists who make their living from producing printed reproductions often seem to have a different view.

Education too has been at the forefront of PmC activities throughout; many members have been and still are teachers as well as artists. Beginning with lobbying the Summerson Commission in 1966 the educational activities of the Printmakers Council have been varied, and in which the education of the gallery-going and print-collecting public has perhaps been paramount. Exhibition catalogues for example have regularly carried glossaries of printmaking techniques and printmaking terminology while efforts to inform the public on the nature of an original artist's print have already been noted. Many exhibitions have frequently included talks, lectures and demonstrations and have offered access to small-scale, practical classes in printmaking techniques. More formal lectures by members have been arranged from time to time, for example at the British Museum in 1986 to coincide with the PmC exhibition *Print 86* at the Barbican Centre.

Closely allied to education the dissemination of ideas through newssheets, bulletins and a magazine has also had a high priority. All organisations need to communicate with members and with the outside world, a relatively easy and inexpensive thing to do in a digital age. Fifty years ago the need was the same but the means were very different.

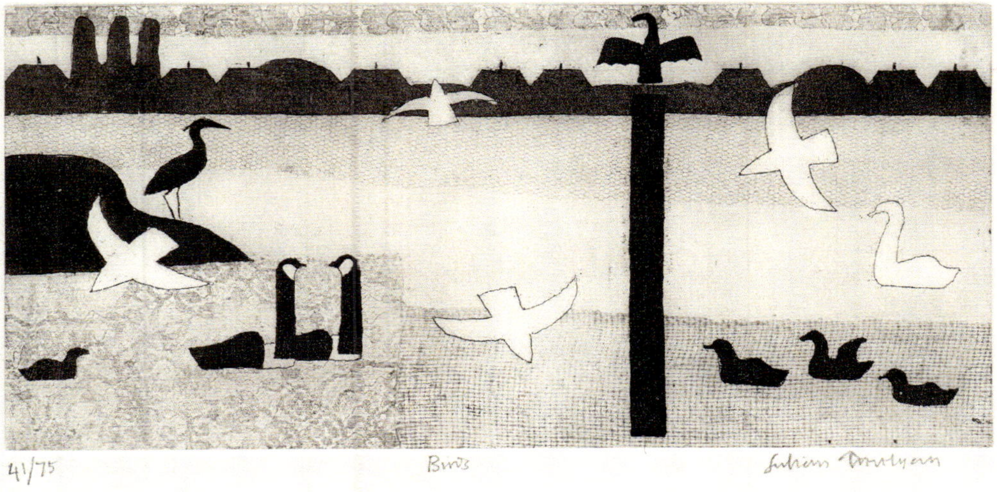

Julian Trevelyan *Birds*
Printmakers Council Portfolio 1981
intaglio, 22 x 47 cm

Two early objectives for the Printmakers Council were the publication and distribution of a magazine and a news bulletin. In 1967 'Printmakers Council Magazine', began and ran for three issues. Edited by Agathe Sorel its aim was 'to inform people in general of developments in Printmaking and related fields'. This stylish, ambitious and expensive undertaking – at one point it came complete with an original print inside – was discontinued in 1970 owing to production costs and time constraints to be replaced by *PmC Newsletter*. Originally distributed only to members this in turn was supplemented in 1982 by a regular column on PmC in the magazine *Artist's Newsletter* written by Peter Ford. Under the terms of an agreement with the magazine PmC members could obtain copies at a discount. Two years later a new publication appeared intended to supplement Peter Ford's column with the inclusion of technical and critical articles. Initially called *PmC Broadsheet* it was later renamed *Impress* and by 1997 had become *Imprint*. Still published as a quarterly magazine today, albeit digitally and continually evolving, *Imprint* offers a mix of opinion and information together with a regular illustrated focus on the work of a PmC member. Today *Imprint* and social media, together with an e-bulletin and the Printmakers Council website, upgraded in 2015 as part of the fiftieth anniversary celebrations, ensure that communication with members and beyond is both efficient and economic.

Like any organisation the Printmakers Council has had a varied history. Many documents were disposed of when the office was reorganised in 1992 creating a large gap in the archive material. Today the original objectives of PmC have been modified to suit a different age but in essence they remain intact. In contrast to 1965 many open-access print studios now exist and traditional societies are less conservative. Printmaking is no longer relegated to a subsidiary position either in contemporary art or in art education, although the advent of new technologies have challenged the notion of what printmaking *is* and the debate over the nature of an original print is still far from concluded. Educational objectives, and the continuing need for a print exhibition society, ensure that the Printmakers Council will have a role to play for many years to come.

Michael Kennedy

Acknowledgements

This is a revised and extended version of an article first published in the exhibition guide to the Printmakers Council's 50th Anniversary Exhibition held at the Bankside Gallery, London, November 2015.

I have made extensive use of the archive of the Printmakers Council in the writing of this essay. My thanks are also due to Margaret Ashman and Claire Jackson who have both provided me with much useful information and help.

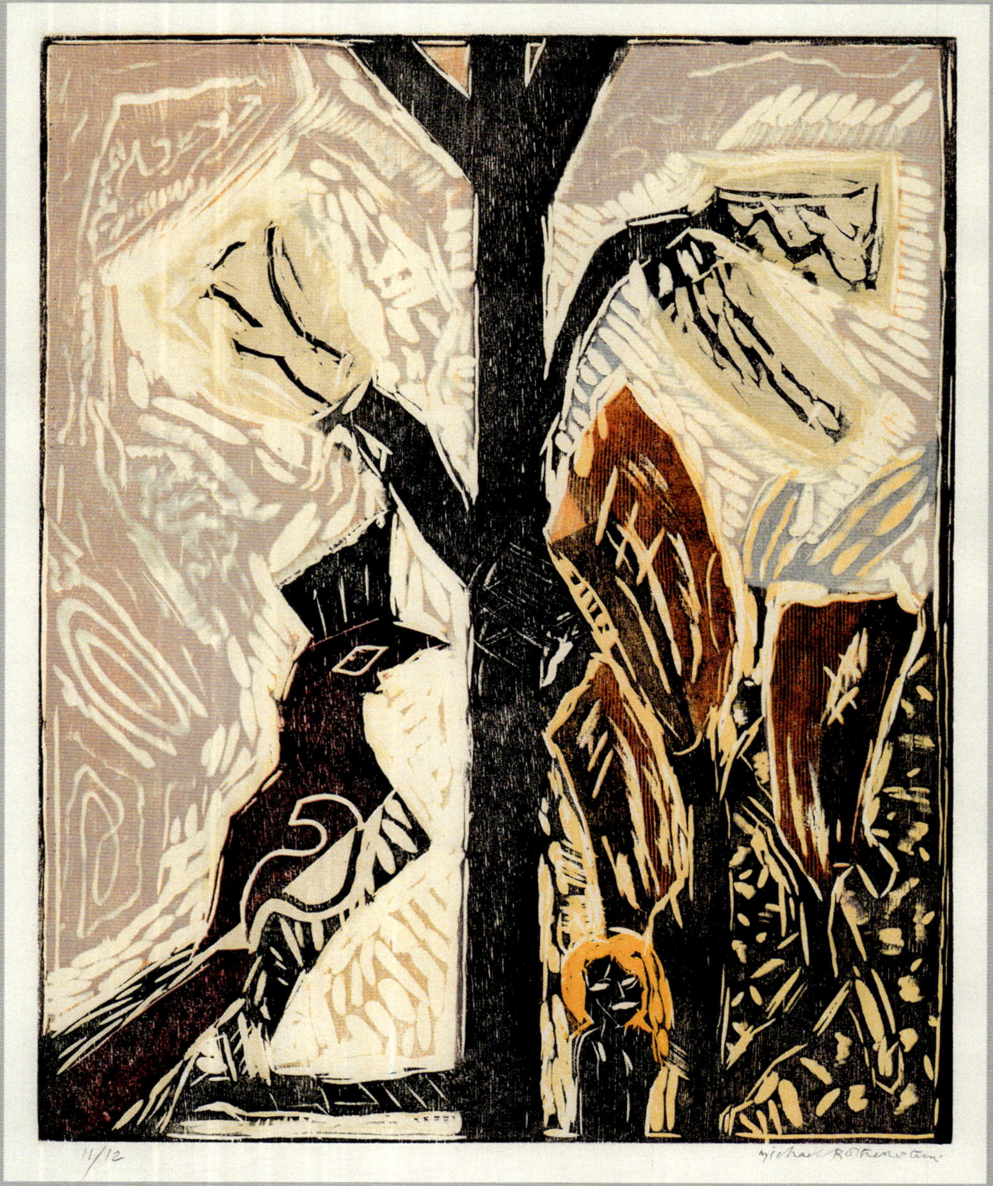

Michael Rothenstein *Blue Flowers,* coloured woodcut, 76 x 60 cm, 1991

'Motivated by desire': some thoughts on printmaking

Gill Saunders

Whilst researching the life and work of Michael Rothenstein (1908–93) in preparation for a new book, I was struck by his own estimation of his achievements and his place in the art world. A former chair of the Printmakers Council, Rothenstein was an inspiring teacher, and an innovator par excellence. His output was prodigious, and his energies were largely focused on printmaking – in his view it constituted his 'real creative life'. Over a long career his work spanned a range of print media from linocut and woodcut to photoetching, and he won prizes aplenty. But despite international renown, recognition at home was hard-won and came only belatedly. He was not elected to full membership of the Royal Academy until 1984, and although his life's work was summarised in a modest touring show in 1989/90 there was no major museum retrospective in his life time (or indeed since). This was a matter of some regret to him and in a late interview he acknowledged that his devotion to print had been limiting, in terms of career and reputation, because 'printmaking is accorded second place', and its capacity for repetition is valued above 'the creative process which engendered the print'.[1]

And this is the perennial problem for prints – and printmakers. For it is an inescapable fact that for the greater part of its history printmaking has been first and foremost a reproductive process, a means of repeating and disseminating images to share information and further knowledge. Given the weight of this history, how can the lingering prejudices and misapprehensions about print, which have contributed to this second-class status, be successfully challenged and overturned? How is printmaking to assert its rightful place as one of the most exciting and dynamic of the creative arts? In many ways this has been, and continues to be, a reiterative process, as each generation finds itself having to defend and promote prints anew.

Prints need champions – artists, curators, critics – but they also need audiences who are interested, informed and appreciative. Works in print must be made visible and accessible, and there must be occasions for prints and printmaking to be the subject of study, debate and exhibition. When museums include exhibitions of prints in their programmes, audiences have valuable opportunities to see works which are, of necessity, kept behind the scenes for much of the time, often available only to those in the know and those prepared to make the effort to visit a Study Room. And of course shows of prints by big-name artists will always draw a crowd who must then, perforce, engage to some extent with the meaning and purpose of print – as we've seen in recent years with Lucian Freud, R.B. Kitaj, and David Hockney, for example. In identifying renowned art-world stars as printmakers such exhibitions can help to recalibrate the public perception of prints, and confirm the idea that prints are original independent works of art.

The V&A's recent UK touring exhibition *Modern Masters in Print* was a case in point. By bringing together powerful images, some familiar, some not, all by well-known artists, it offered opportunities to explore and differentiate the characteristics of various processes and techniques; as such it proved to be an effective vehicle for promoting public appreciation and understanding of printmaking. Presenting this diverse range of work in print by Matisse, Picasso, Dalí and Warhol, the curators also took the opportunity to address the persistent confusion between those vexed categories 'original' and 'reproduction' that continues to bemuse the uninitiated. Artists themselves have also made attempts to explain the distinction. One of the more poetic comes from Man Ray, who said 'An original is a creation motivated by desire. Any reproduction of an original is motivated by necessity. The original is the result of an automatic mental process, the reproduction of a mechanical process. In other words: inspiration then information; each validates the other.'[2] More prosaic, perhaps, but admirable for its clarity, is the statement made by Allen Jones in 1967, in defence of commercial print processes. He asserted that the crux of 'originality' in printmaking was to conceive a print for the medium of execution and to utilize the specific qualities of that medium.[3]

Another strategy – showing prints alongside paintings, as in the recent *Late Rembrandt* exhibition at the National Gallery – serves as a valuable corrective to the idea that printmaking is merely a process of translation by which a unique work in one medium becomes a multiple in another. Indeed when we look at prints by artists who have worked extensively, if not exclusively, with print media, we see what rich potential they have found in the process. Prints by Rembrandt, Picasso, Freud – all attest to the ways in which artists exploit the specific qualities of their chosen medium, and how they find inspiration for original expression in the process itself. For Freud the shift between the painterly mode of his oils and the linear mode of etching enabled him to find a new perspective on familiar subjects, and to refresh ideas about composition, form and surface that had become entrenched by habit. He has described how etching introduced speed and urgency, as well as the 'danger and mystery' of an unpredictable outcome[4], and these qualities were just as important to him as the facility to repeat an image, and publish an edition. For the 2006 Turner Prize winner Tomma Abts, making etchings at Crown Point Press gave her 'a freedom to explore' and the opportunity to do things differently. When she was asked about the relationship between the prints and her paintings and drawings she made it clear that 'the prints occupy their own place' in which the imagery evolved directly from the etching process, and 'the technique becomes part of the work' and not merely a means of replicating the effects she had achieved in other media.[5]

OPPOSITE:

Graham Sutherland
Cynocephalus (A Bestiary And Some Correspondances)
lithograph
67.3 x 52 cm
1965–68

BELOW:

Birgit Skiöld
Running Tide
embossing & etching
21 x 18 cm
1967

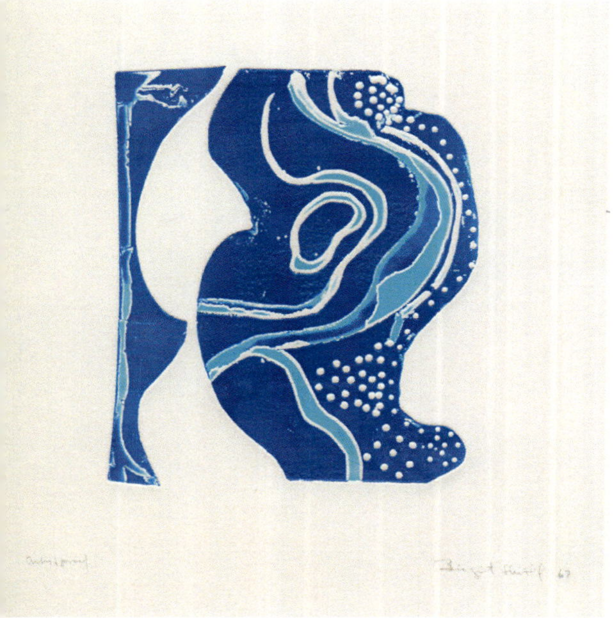

The history of printmaking has been marked by successive inventions and the arrival of new technologies, driven largely by commercial imperatives, but also by artists. What is fascinating about this history is that the innovations did not render earlier methods redundant. Instead they liberated these older methods from the constraints of reproduction and opened them up as independent art forms. When the laborious cutting of wood-blocks for printed books and broadsheets was supplanted by the engraving of a metal plate, woodcut enjoyed a new lease of life in which the expressive qualities of the medium could be exploited; once engraving and etching had lost their reproductive role to photography, artists reclaimed the processes, and societies were founded to promote 'creative' printmaking. Intended as a reproductive technique, lithography was quickly adopted for artistic purposes, and screen-printing, co-opted from its commercial origins, was instrumental in the great burst of printmaking and print publishing in the 1960s and '70s. That one-time rival, photography, was readily accommodated, and adopted as a new tool for the printmaker, and today digital technologies are further extending choice and possibility.

Printmaking is always – to a degree – experimental, with outcomes that may be hard to control or predict, and for many artists that is a key part of the appeal. Roland Penrose has described Miró at work: 'After long periods of contemplation, he would plunge into new experiments, inventing unheard-of techniques with complete and unhesitating conviction...'[6]. Working alone, or in collaboration with technicians and print studios, artists have continued this inventive engagement with print. Michael Rothenstein found inspiration in innovation at every turn, whether in printing from assemblages of found objects, etching lino, or abandoning conventional knives and gouges in favour of industrial tools and wire brushes. Unanticipated but serendipitous effects are often welcomed by the artist: for example Susan Aldworth, in her 'brainscape' etchings, found that letting methylated spirit bleed into white spirit on the plate gave a fluid organic imagery that aptly mimicked the chemical reactions in the brain that she was seeking a visual equivalent for.

It has been suggested that those of us who make prints, along with those of us who collect and study prints, are an anachronism; that we are merely nostalgic custodians of a redundant art, now supplanted by the ease and ubiquity of digital processes. The evidence tends to support a very different view. In art schools the enthusiasm for working with traditional print media is

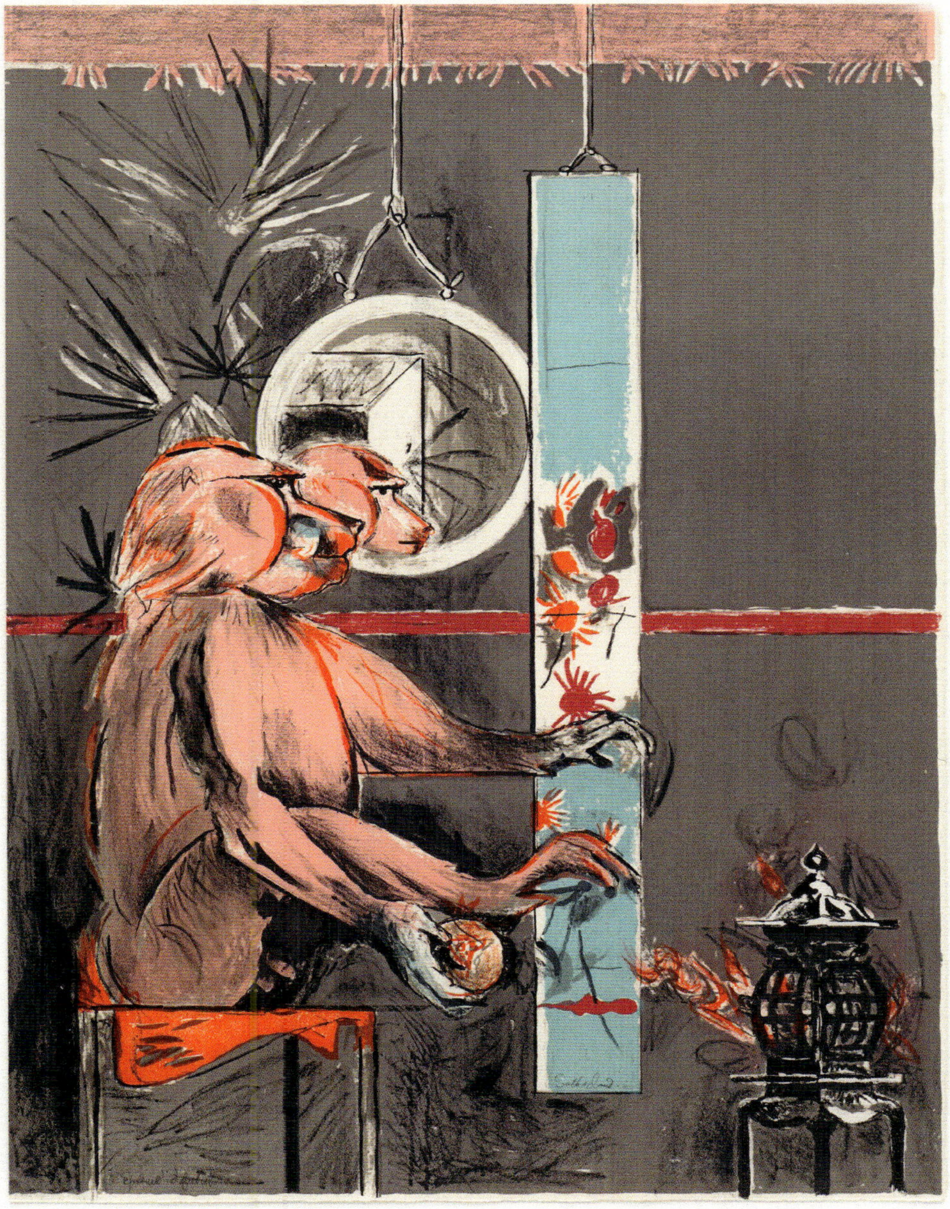

undimmed, and print studios and workshops appear to be flourishing. We can cite numerous examples of artists who may have started out ignorant or unenthusiastic about printmaking, but go on to endorse it with the zeal of the converted once they understand, through experience, the very particular qualities and capacities of the medium. Robert Rauschenberg, reminiscing about his work with print, recalled 'I began lithography reluctantly, thinking that the second half of the 20th century was no time to start writing on rocks.'[7] As we know he overcame this initial reluctance and embraced the medium with confident audacity, going on to create some of the most ambitious and impressive lithographs ever made. Likewise Ken Kiff was at first dismissive, declaring 'Printmaking – couldn't see my way into it at art school', but thanks to self-guided experiments and professional collaborations he later produced a fine body of printed work, mostly etchings and woodcuts. He described the pleasures of an intimate collaboration with process itself, where one must be 'prepared to be led, to some extent by the medium. It does feel, in stroking a stone with a litho-pencil, or cutting into copper or wood, as though you're listening to what the wood or copper or stone is saying.'[8]

Fifteen years into the 21st century, 'writing on rocks' and all the other traditional print techniques are thriving, alongside – and often in combination with – the digital processes. The rich and complex vocabulary of print is alive and well, and printmaking continues to assert its place as an independent art as it is quietly but tenaciously embedding itself in contemporary creative practice.

1. British Library National Life Stories/Artists' Lives, Michael Rothenstein interviewed by Mel Gooding, 1990, C466/02/04 [F817], side A, p.7
2. Man Ray, *Opera Grafica*, Turin, 1973, p.5
3. See *Kelpra Studio: an exhibition to commemorate the Rose and Chris Prater Gift*, London: Tate Gallery, 1980, p.18
4. Quoted in Starr Figura, *Lucian Freud: The Painter's Etchings*, New York; MOMA, 2008, p.15
5. *Overview: Crown Point Press Newsletter Fall 2009: Tomma Abts*, p.3
6. Roland Penrose, *Miró*, London, 1970, p.162
7. Quoted in Edward A. Foster, *Robert Rauschenberg: Prints 1948-1970*, Minneapolis: The Minneapolis Institute of Arts, 1970, n.p.
8. Quoted in *Ken Kiff Etchings, lithographs and woodcuts, 1984-1999*, London: Marlborough Graphics, 2002, n.p.

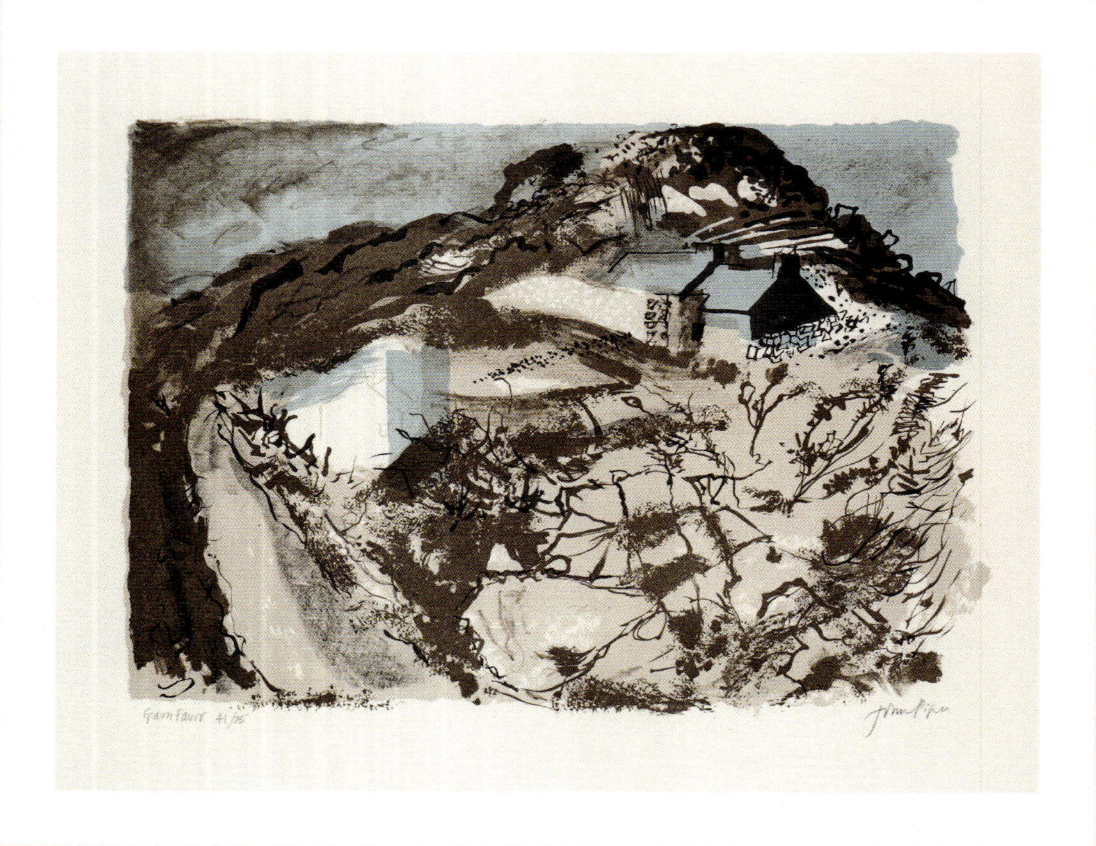

John Piper *Garn Fawr*
Printmakers Council Portfolio 1981
lithograph, 38 x 51 cm

The Printmakers

Anna Alcock
Mary Algar
Eman AlHashemi
Margaret Ashman
Stephen Asquith
Thomas Robert Baggaley
Helen Baines
Ruth Barrett-Danes
Clare Bassett
Jacki Baxter
Tania Beaumont
Helen Benson
Alison Bernal
Kit Boyd
Pauline Bradley
Jill Bray
Angela Brookes
David Brown
Dilys Bryon
Emma Buckmaster
Jess Bugler
Gavin Iain Campbell
Dawn Cole
Graham Cooke
Phil Cosgrove
Richenda Court
Barbra Cropper
Sandra Daniel
Jane Daniell
Rebecca Denton
Anne Desmet
Eleanor Durbin
Steve Edwards
Matthew J Egan
Shuxiang Jin Farrall
Peter Ford
Kate Fortune Jones
Heather G Foster
Christina France Crews
Janet French
Diane Comte Frost
Sarah Garvey
Eric Gaskell
Janette Gibson
Colin Gillespie
Anne Gournay
Lucie Green
Lisa Gribbon
Clare Grossman
Andrew D Hambleton
Pamela Hare
Eleanor Havsteen-Franklin
Martin Henley
Tessa Holmes
John Hutton
Claire Hynds
Caroline Jackman
Barbara Jackson
Elizabeth A Kelleher
Michael Kennedy
Frances Kiernan
Jenny Lagnado
Marco Lawrence
Lolana
Avril Macdonald
Gail Mallatratt
Marie-Louise Martin
Mary Martin
Biagio Mastroianni
Amanda McAllister
Julia McKenzie
Margo McNulty
Chris Mercier
Janet Milner
Paul David Mitchell
Ros Morley
Heather Muise
Stephen Mumberson
Frances Murray
Maureen Nathan
Glynis Jones Owen
Theresa Pateman
Bronwen Paterson
Sumi Perera
Monica Petzal
Helen Peyton
Robert Pugh
Venessa Pugh
Daniela Rizzi
Sarah Rogers
Dan Romer
Sue Rowling
Handan Sadikoglu
Ian Scaife
Margaret Sellars
Marilyn Simler
Ewelina Skowronska
Carolyn Smith-Shaw
Tim Southall
Francesca Souza
Carolyn Stafford
Louise Stebbing
Euan G Stewart
Jane Stothert
Nicola Styan
Julie Sullock
Anne Sumpner-Evans
Annette Elizabeth Sykes
Despina Symeou
Jasia Szerszynska
Emma C Tabor
Peter Tingey
Susie Turner
Maggie Warwick
Felicity Weaver
Caroline Whitehead
Patrick Whitehead
Cleo Wilkinson
Roy Willingham
Kate Willows
Joseph Winkelman
Mary Yazhari
Fouzia Zafar
Sisetta Zappone

Anna Alcock

I consider myself an artist and storyteller first, but printmaking is the means by which I express myself – the tones, layers and depth that the printing process imbues cannot be achieved with any other medium. I have always loved myths, legends and the stories that we tell to make sense of the world, and was fortunate enough to have the opportunity to immerse myself in philosophy, history and classics while completing my degree.

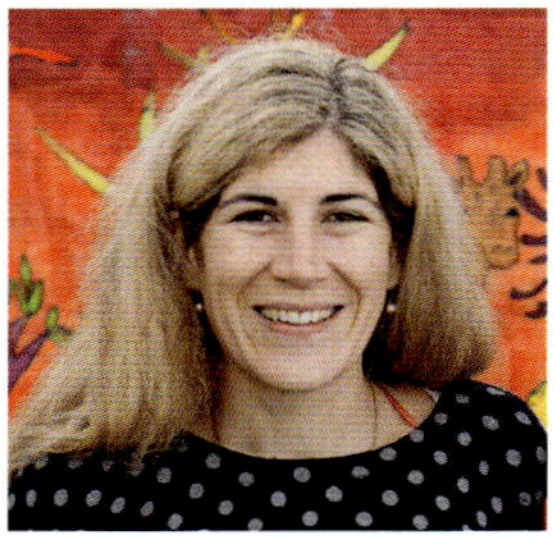

1976 Born Johannesburg, South Africa
1995–98 1st Class Honours BA Fine Art, University of KwaZulu-Natal, Pietermaritzburg, South Africa
1996 Merit Award for Painting and Printmaking, University of Natal
1998 Merit Award for Printmaking and Dean's Commendation, University of Natal
2002–04 MA Printmaking, Camberwell College of Art, London
2005–06 Chair, East London Printmakers, London
2007 Co-founded Inky Cuttlefish Studios, Blackhorse Lane, London
2008 *Signature: Works on Paper*. Curated travelling exhibition: Inky Cuttlefish Studios, William Morris Gallery, ArtSPACE Berlin, ArtSPACE Durban, South Africa
2010 *Art in the Community*, London Borough of Waltham Forest. Award for contributions towards community arts
2010 *Trust Artists* at St Paul's School, London. Exhibition in aid of University of KwaZulu-Natal UK Trust.
2010 *Inspired by William Morris*, William Morris Gallery, London
2012 *Isabella's Gift* etching. Selected artist and cover design for *E17 Art Trail: Bestow*
2012 *Mythology in London*, Tokarska Gallery, London
2014–15 Director, Gnome House Community Asset CIC, Creative Arts Space, Walthamstow

Growing up in South Africa, I attended Uthongathi, a progressive school, one of the only multi-racial schools at the time in South Africa. Following this I earned my four-year fine arts degree in 1998 from the University of KwaZulu-Natal (previously University of Natal), where I majored in printmaking, drawing and art history with a special dispensation for the study of classics. In 2004 I was awarded my master's degree in printmaking from Camberwell College of Art. In 2007 I established my art studio Inky Cuttlefish Studios.

With expressionist art a major thread in my style, I have been shaped and guided by the works of Pablo Picasso, Marc Chagall, Paul Klee, Wassily Kandinsky, Der Blaue Reiter (The Blue Rider) 1911–1914, German Expressionists, notably Emil Nolde, a key figure in the German Expressionist movement Die Brücke, the Fauvism movement, and the drawings, printmaking and painting of the peerless Rembrandt van Rijn.

My art is deeply personal and hopes to touch the soul of my audience by exploring the manipulative externalities and seemingly inextricable limits established by an insecure and rapidly shifting society and the sense many of us have of being controlled by outside forces. Much of my work is about the interpretation of space, light and darkness in their most profound senses. It underscores contradictions in the violence and dangers of our world, including mystery and sorcery, with the concomitant universal search for safety. In my work, the threat of menaces in animal form (wolves) or verbal form (arguments) is reduced by the mediation of compassionate overtures and a retreat to safety. In this light, I have engaged in exploring the human form, including the complexities and ambiguities of the human condition. My imaginative work also assesses relationships, couples, groups of people, and, not least, the vagaries of life which women confront in the complexities of growth and the changing seasons of life.

Always scrutinizing the human condition, my creative and sometimes pioneering work in several media encompasses joy, empathy, sadness and anger, often with a redemptive and empathetic conclusion. My development is an ongoing process, fuelled by my passion and experiences. Recent works reflect a shift in style and a deepening appreciation for life's joys and sorrows.

Protection, 180 x 90 cm, mixed-media (unique)

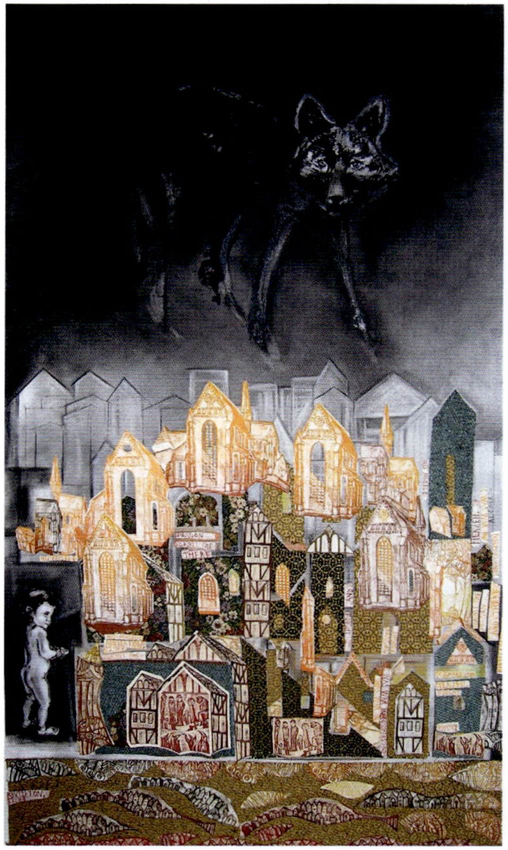

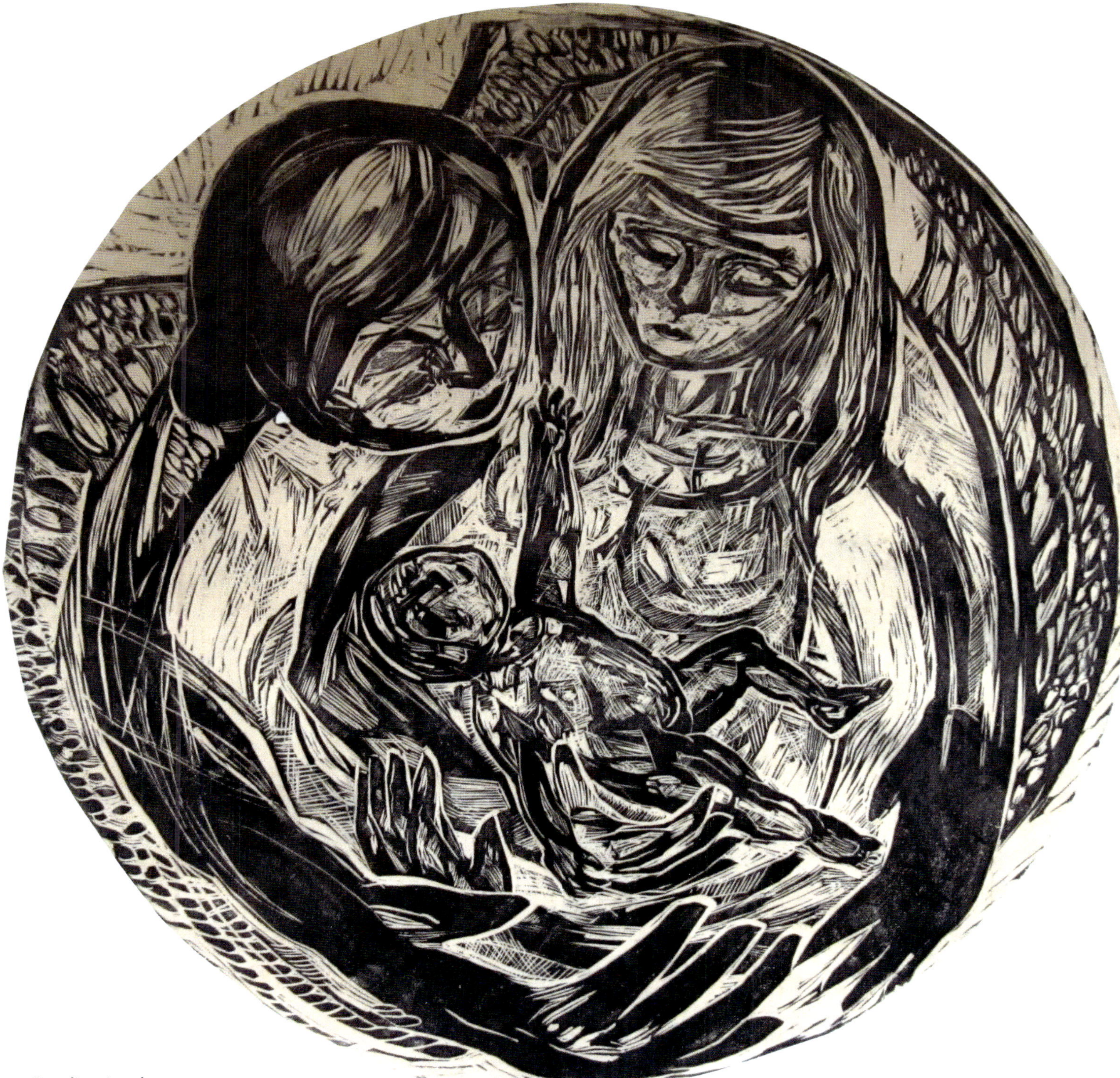

Guardian Angel, 50 x 50 cm
woodcut (edition of 20)

Mary Algar

Mary Algar is interested in abstraction and mark-making. She employs a layering technique, superimposing different forms over each other to produce her vibrant prints. She enjoyed a career of teaching art in schools and colleges of further education and has subsequently devoted her energies to her own art practice of printmaking.

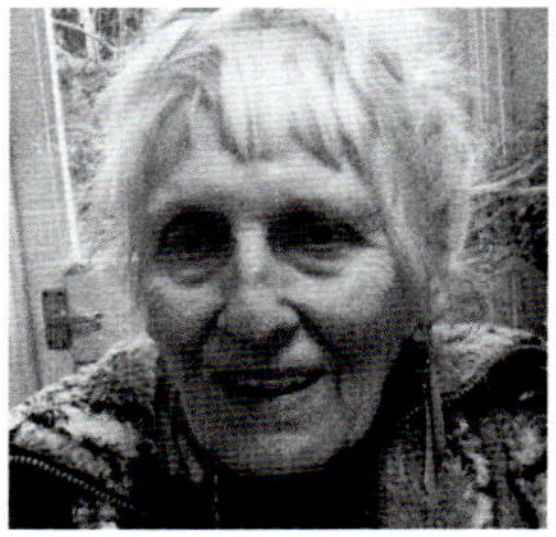

1926 Born London
1934 Boarding School, Buckinghamshire
1942 Special emphasis on art and music
1942 Scholarship to St Martin's School of Art
1945–46 Art Teacher's Diploma in Painting, Drawing & Teaching. Part-time studies at St Martins's School of Art in Lithography with John Minton. Studied Painting with Victor Pasmore and Ruskin Spear RA
1948–88 Taught Art in Secondary Schools including Mayfield, Putney; Adult Education Centres and Morley College
1988 Retired
1989 Taught studio classes at home
1990s Joined Printmakers Council

Exhibitions

1950s–1960s Royal Academy Summer Exhibitions
2000s Various Printmakers Council Exhibitions including National Theatre, Natural History Museum, Highgate Literary and Scientific Institution. Selected Art & Craft Market at St Martin-in-the-fields, Trafalgar Square. Merton Abbey Mills Market
2015 *Open Art House Studios*, Richmond *International Print Show*, Bulgaria *7 Barnes Women Artists, 70 years of My Art*, Old Sorting Office Arts Centre, Barnes, London
2015 Solo show Old Sorting Office Arts Centre, Barnes, London

As a 16 year old during the war, Mary won a scholarship to St Martin's School of art. She followed this with a diploma in Painting, Drawing and Teaching. Shortly after the war she took some part-time classes at St Martin's including lithography with well-known artist John Minton. She also remembers being taught by Victor Pasmore in the post-war years. She recalls exhibiting her work with the AIA or the Artists International Association, an exhibiting group founded in London in 1933, which began as a radical left-wing organisation, holding large exhibitions with social political themes but by the 1950s it had abandoned its political roots. Mary remembers exhibitions organised by the AIA in Soho, London, which was in those days quite a 'colourful' part of the city.

Mary uses various printmaking techniques in her multi-layered prints. She has always been drawn to lithography, as this was the first technique she was taught. At St Martin's in the '50s it would have been the traditional stone lithography, but later she got to grips with more modern variations available to the students at Croydon College in the 1980s when she taught there.

The other printmaking techniques that Mary is skilled at are etching and screen-printing. Some of her prints combine lithography, screen-printing and etching in one work.

She combines different processes to develop her images, printing forms and colours over each other to produce the desired effect. She sometimes introduces collage into the finished work too.

Although Mary's prints seem full of colour and vibrancy, she would say that colour is secondary in her work to form and mark-making. For her, line, form and marks are the things she is interested in, and the backbone of her art practice. She works somewhat intuitively, leaving some things to chance, and enjoys the serendipity of printing in layers when forms are superimposed over forms and marks sit in an interesting way over the marks below.

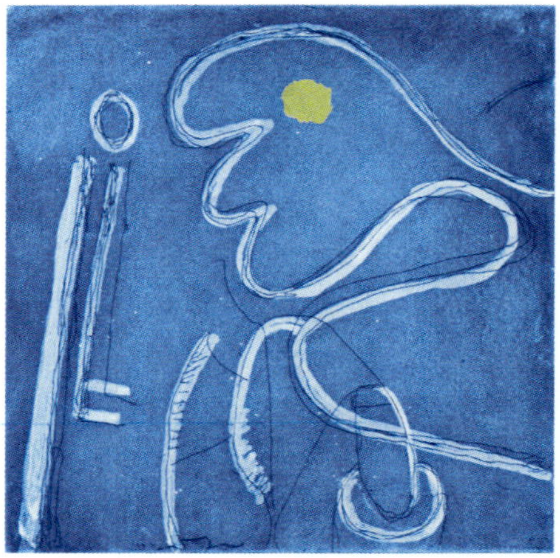

Yellow Spot, 14 x 15 cm, photo etching & collage (edition of 10)

Palm, 14 x 14 cm, screen print (edition of 10)

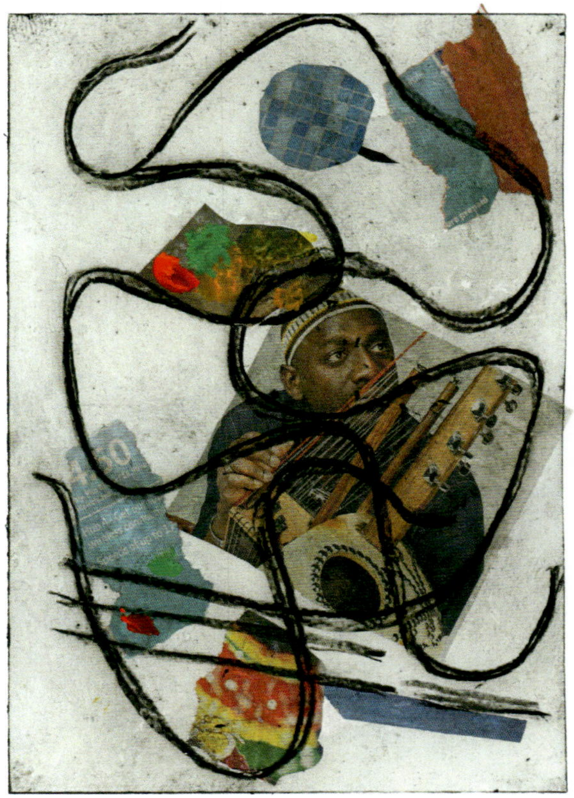

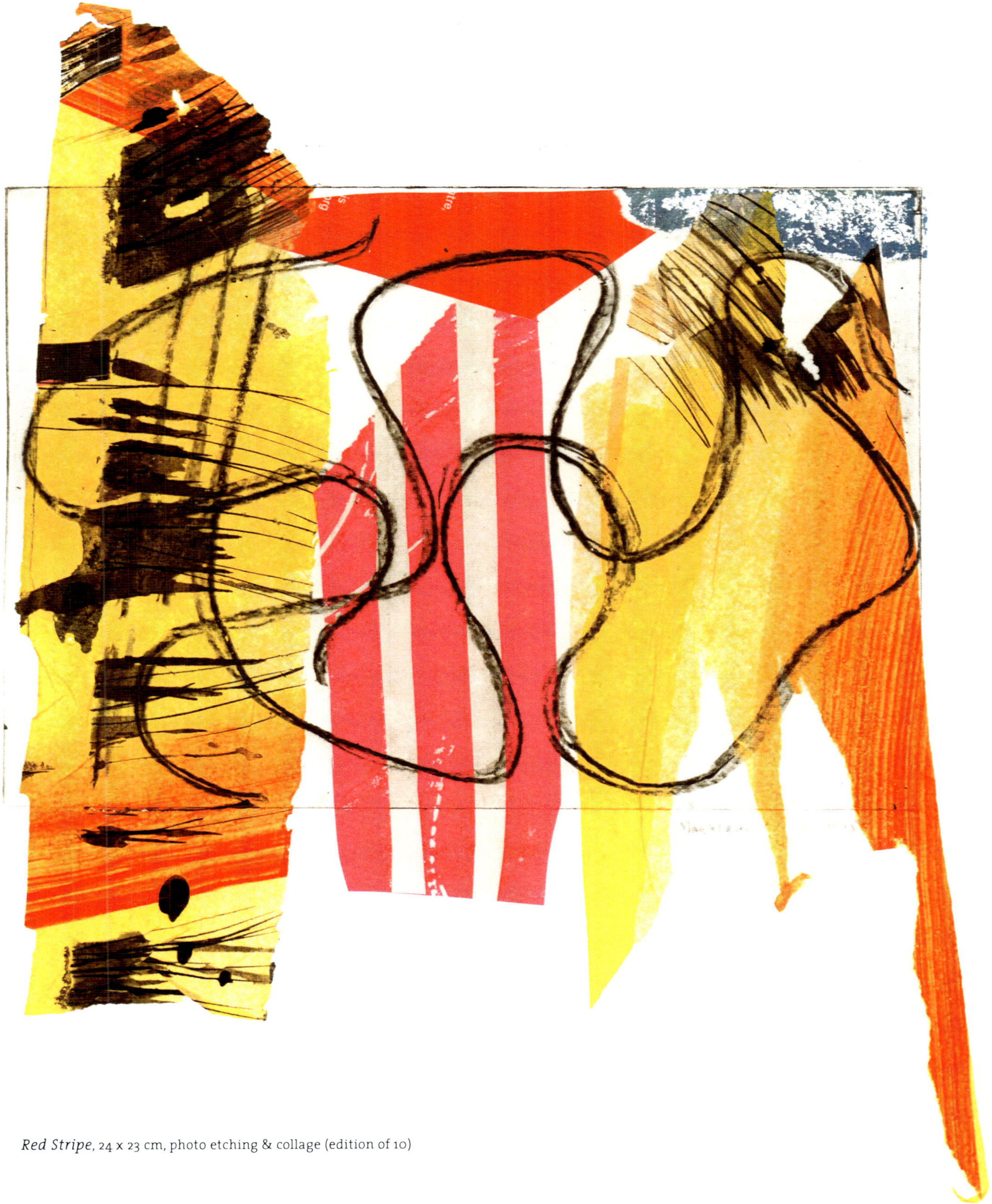

Red Stripe, 24 x 23 cm, photo etching & collage (edition of 10)

Eman AlHashemi

I discovered my interest in printmaking when I was in my second year of study at the University of Sharjah. I found the medium fascinating with great potential to experiment and explore many new things. I make my work using intaglio etched relief plates, woodblocks, rubberstamps and silkscreen.

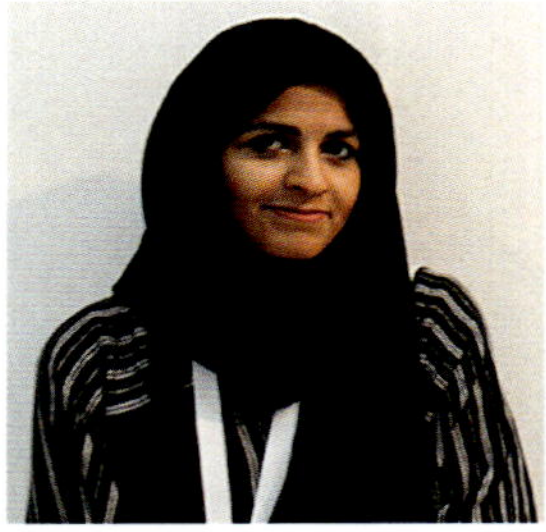

1993 Born Dubai, United Arab Emirates
2011–15 Studied at University of Sharjah, United Arab Emirates
2012 Featured in *Mawahib Talent Directory* for graphic designers, illustrators and photographers
2013 *12th Lessedra World Art Print Annual*, Bulgaria
2014 Internship at *London Print Studio*, London
2014 Featured in *Artists to Look Out For Volume I*
2015 Shortlisted for Sheikha Manal Young Artist Award
2015 Joined Printmakers Council

Having dedicated the past two years to the exploration and investigation of printmaking processes, I have developed a way of working that employs both intaglio and relief printing. The etched copper plates are printed over and over, which results in the deterioration of the plate and allows subtle change and variations that are only apparent in the prints over time. This reveals the combination of strong bold marks alongside delicate textures and tones. The process of creating the print is all important, from cutting the plate to painting on it up to constructing different forms. The two-dimensional prints are sometimes constructed into three-dimensional objects then carefully formed into precariously balanced structures. The ephemerality of the work ultimately explores the vulnerable fragile nature of things. I enjoy the unpredictable nature of my work.

I try to embrace the accidents and mistakes that create unexpected surprises by embarking on further experimentation. Unintentional effects and my management of them are an integral part of the work. This kind of printmaking is uncertain, mysterious and unpredictable. Sometimes I attempt to make perfect work by repeating the process over and over again but eventually I accept the imperfections and work with them. It all adds to the work. I like the fact that my work resembles codes and riddles that not everyone understands including myself. The combination of random, bold, chaotic marks that I try to control by layering and positioning shapes is an attempt to control and order the chaos. My work explores the contrasts between boldness and fragility, order and disorder, predictability and chaos. It's like a puzzle!

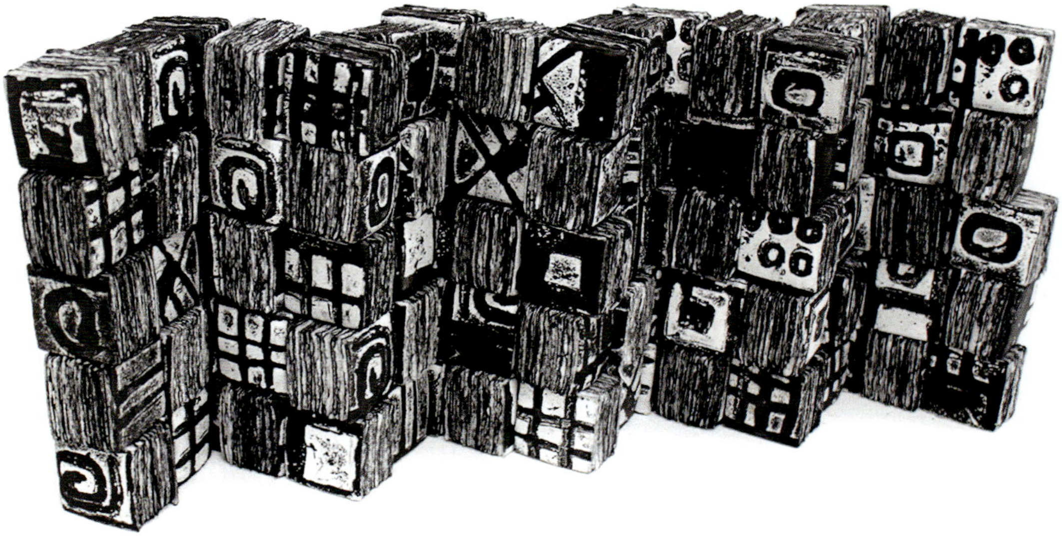

Stacked
75 x 75 x 89 cm
folded intaglio relief prints
(unique)

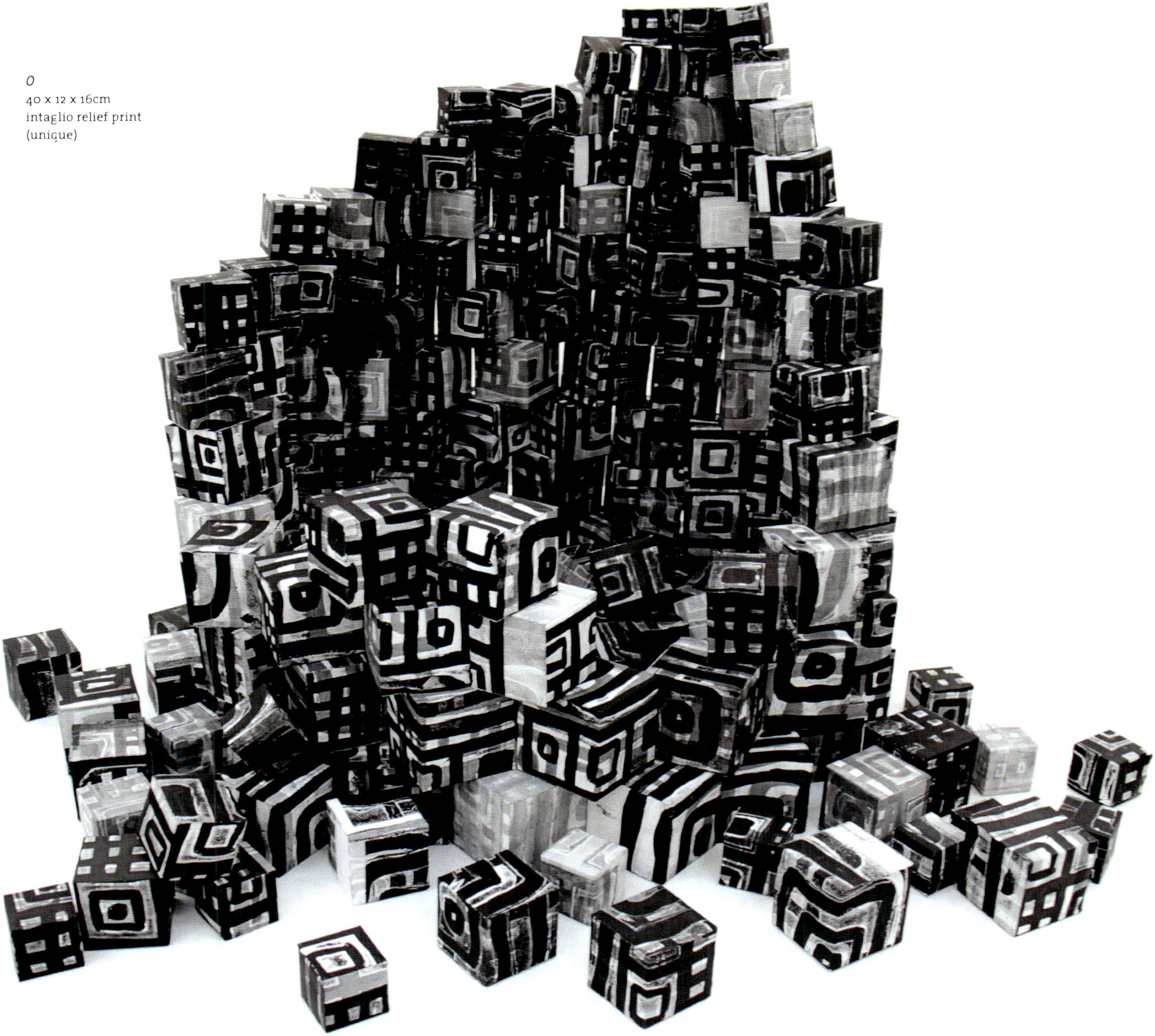

O
40 x 12 x 16cm
intaglio relief print
(unique)

Margaret Ashman

I began working from photographic images during my Fine Art Studies at the University of Hertfordshire, a working practice which continued through a Masters Degree in Printmaking at the University of Brighton. I am still excited by the potential of printmaking and particularly photo etching to transform the everyday into something transcendent.

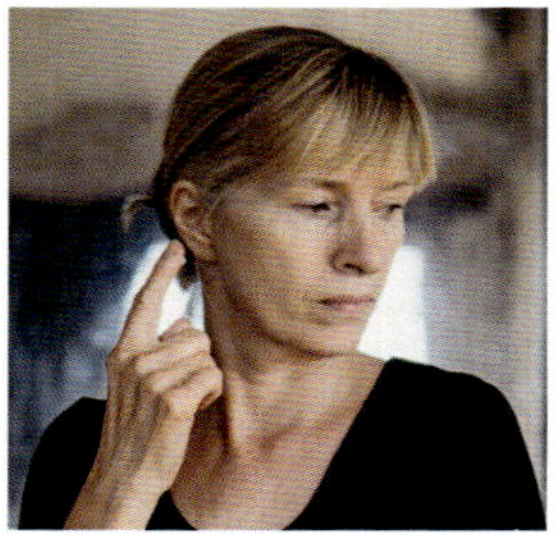

1959 Born Northampton, England
1977–80 BA Physics Oxford University
1980–84 Employed Hirst Research Centre
1998–2003 BA Fine Art, University of Hertfordshire
2003–05 MA Printmaking London Print Studio & University of Brighton
2003 Solo Show Harrow
2003–10 Elected Member of Southbank and Greenwich Printmakers Associations
2005 Joined Printmakers Council
2006 Solo shows – Harrow and Hammersmith
2007 Elected Associate Member Royal Society of Painter Printmakers
2009 Exhibited at Biennials in Liège, Krakow, Split, Qijiang, Guanlan
2010 Elected Fellow of Royal Society of Painter Printmakers
2010 Finalist, *Art of Giving* Saatchi Gallery. Exhibited at Biennials in Penang, Douro
2011–15 Exhibitions, talks & workshops at the Abbey Walk Gallery, International Print Prize winner at Guanlan Biennial
2011 Elected Chairman, Printmakers Council
2012 Biennials in Kyoto, Tokyo, Beijing
2013–14 *Parallel Print Project*, Keri-Keri, Marcilhac-sur-Célé, Nanjing, Dresden. Exhibited International Print Exhibition Shanghai
2015 Exhibited in *Good Figures*, Mall Galleries & Jerwood Gridshell

My practice is an investigation of communication through hand gesture, movement and facial expression. Much of my work is based on photographs, usually my own, of models signing or performing sign dance. There is congenital deafness in my wider family, which gave me the idea of making work from sign language. However, signing and gesture have a particular connection with all of us because of their origins as the roots of spoken language and therefore provide a firm basis for strong and resonant imagery. My chosen medium is photo etching on steel or copper plates. Ideas are painstakingly developed digitally first, then made into metal plates in the workshop. The proofing stage on the press is a vital part of the creative process during which the final print is realised.

My models have included family members, the deaf dancer and choreographer Chisato Minamimura, Sign Dance Collective artists David Bower and Isolte Avila, and visual artist Wuon-gean Ho. I have also photographed Susanna Harrington dancing Bharata Natyam, a classical Indian style. The dance features *natya* or mime, and *mudras*, symbolic hand gestures. Currently I am working on a self-portrait project in which I am the model performing a sign dance, with collaboration from Chiasato, cinematographer Emil Kunda, photographer Rachel Manns and composer Hannah Ashman. The finished work will be a short film and a series of self-portrait photo etchings. It is part of an Arts Council funded project, *Shifting Subjects*.

The self-portrait dance is based on a personal text, my diary. Using written sources as starting points is a frequent device. The poem, *A Time for Everything* found in Ecclesiastes, Philip Larkin's *The Trees*, and the hymn *Amazing Grace* are among the texts I have asked my models to turn into sign. Subsequently, I choose shots without reference to the translation of the sign, and may juxtapose them with other images creating new meanings in the finished work. I have also reconstructed the context of images by creating my own landscapes out of many different photographs of ruined and ancient buildings.

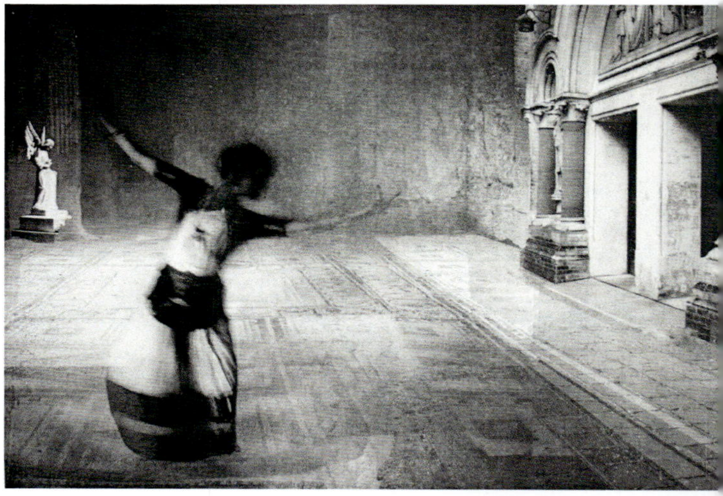

Altered Histories Highgate, 39 x 66 cm, photo etching (edition of 20)

Other sources of inspiration and content have included fragments of oriental embroideries and paintings. My interest in Chinese and Japanese art objects stems from my grandparents' collection of objects, bought in Hong Kong in the 1920s, with which I was familiar as a child. I was allowed to handle these 'treasures', which seemed to be charged with mystery and significance. It was only later that I became aware of the meanings attached to particular subjects, adding another layer of symbolism to my artworks.

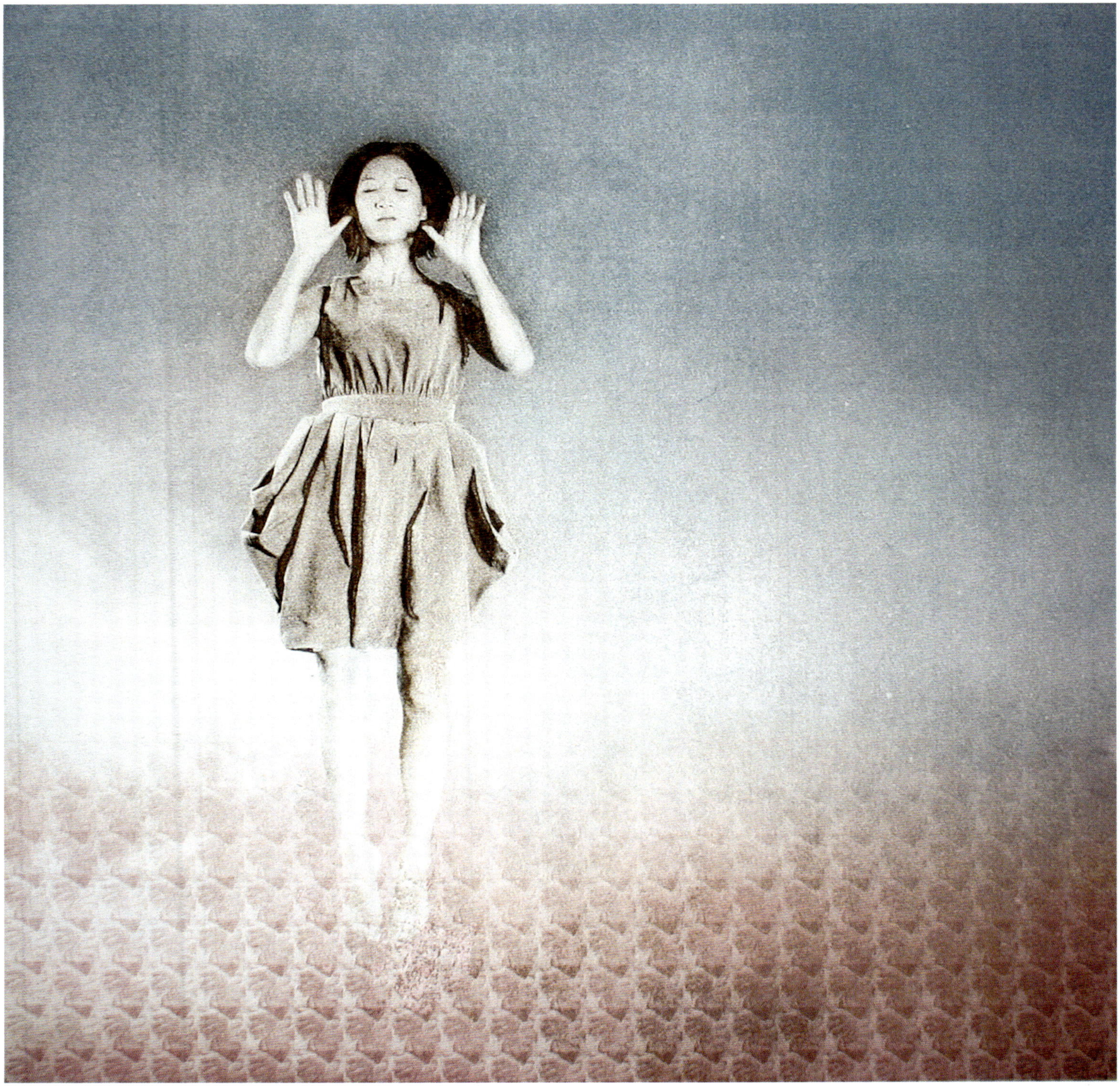

Maid of the Mist, 57 x 57 cm, photo etching (edition of 20)

Stephen Asquith

I blame my wife – for my 50th birthday she enrolled me at The Slade Summer School in copper-plate etching – and that was it, I was hooked! The possibilities offered by printmaking felt like alchemy, turning base metal into the riches of line and tone. The excitement and anticipation of pulling a print has never diminished.

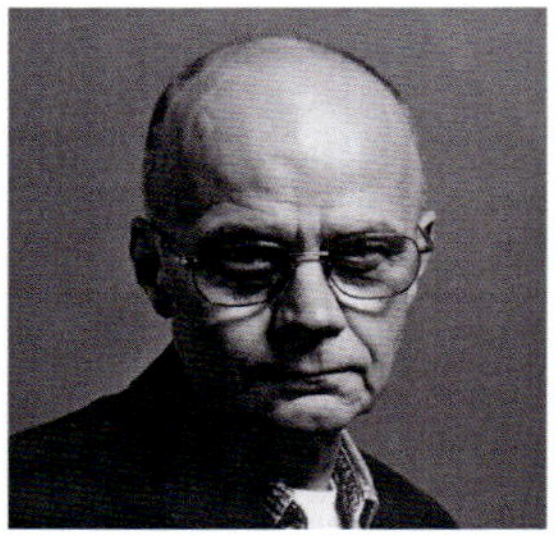

1952 Born Ballymena, Country Antrim, Northern Ireland

1971–74 Diploma Communication Design, Epsom School of Art and Design

1975–90 Worked as a model maker/animator for Clearwater Films, an award-winning stopframe animation production company based in Battersea

1990–2000 Freelance model maker and animator working mainly in TV commercials

2000–07 Director of children's TV series *Thomas the Tank Engine*

2008–09 MA Fine Art Printmaking, Anglia Ruskin University, Cambridge

2011–13 Founded Saxon Shore Press, a small open-access printmaking studio based in Whitstable, Kent. Taught courses in drypoint, etching, linocut, and woodcut.

2013 Self-employed artist printmaker

Exhibitions

2009 The Society of Marine Artists, The Mall Galleries, London

2010 Show Stark Gallery, Canterbury

2012 Solo show The Fishslab Gallery, Whitstable

My imagery involves natural forms, such as waves, cliffs, rock formations and landscapes. I have spent periods of my life living by the sea, and am fascinated by the movement of water and how to capture that fluidity onto a print. I have experimented with screen-printing to produce images of waves but I found that to achieve the tonal range I wanted, working on aluminum and etching in copper sulphate solution gave both a soft edge and the range of subtle tone I was looking for. This method though works equally well when applied to landscape – as it allows me to use a combination of fine line work and areas of soft tone, which provide a pleasing contrast.

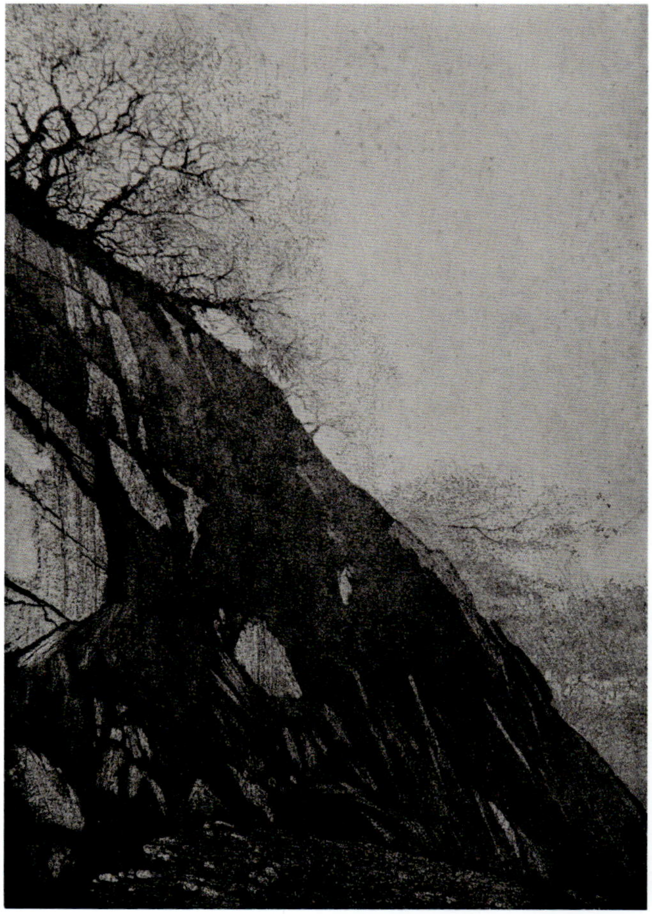

Valley to Thornton Force, 41 x 29 cm, aquatint (edition of 50)

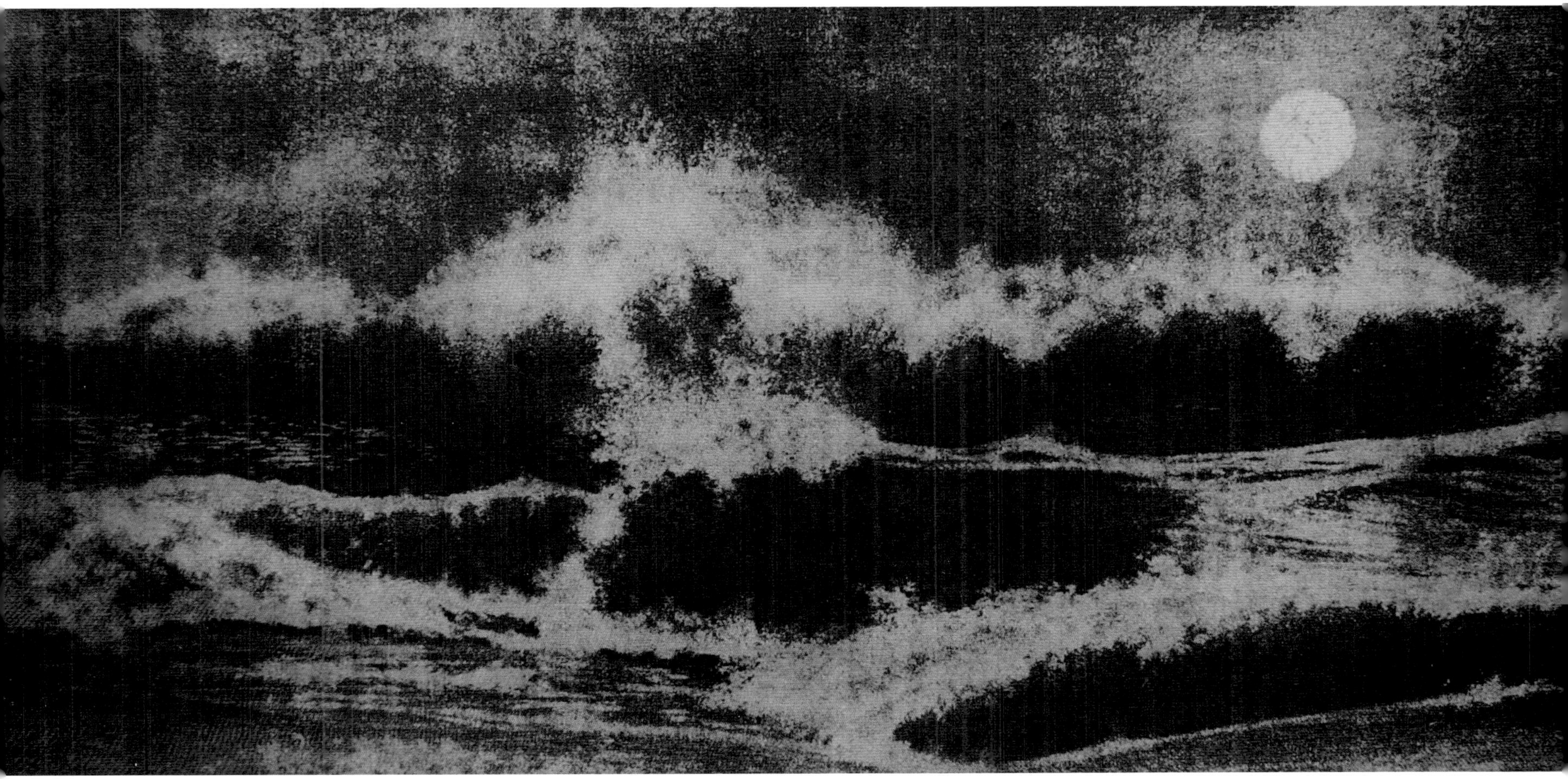

Night Waves V, 81 x 40 cm, screen print (edition of 30)

Thomas Robert Baggaley

I am a second-generation printmaker born into a highly creative family. Printmaking has surrounded me from as far back as I can remember: it was inevitable that I would develop a passion for print. I studied printmaking at both undergraduate and postgraduate levels and now teach printmaking at the University of Sharjah, UAE.

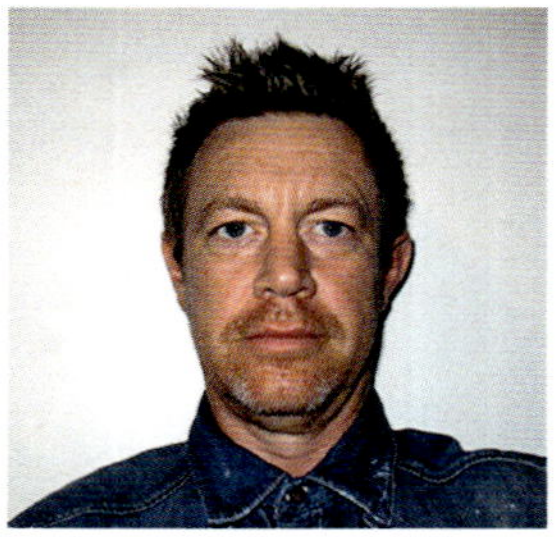

1973 Born London

Education

2002–03 BA (Hons) Fine Art, Printmaking and Bookbinding. Croydon College, London

2003–05 MA Printmaking London Print Studio & University of Brighton

Exhibitions

2010 *Royal Academy Summer Exhibition*, London

2010 *The Biennial International Miniature Print Exhibition*, Federation Gallery, Vancouver, Canada

2011 *10th Lessedra World Art Print Annual*, Bulgaria

2011 *Royal Academy Summer Exhibition*, London

2011 *Recent Prints by Vincent Leow & Tom Baggaley*, Chan Hampe Galleries, Raffles Hotel, Singapore

2012 *Lost for Words*, Printmakers Council Exhibition, UCLH London

2012 *Fourth International Miniature Print Biennale Exhibition*, Ottawa School of Art, Byward Campus

2012 *11th Lessedra World Art Print Annual*, Bulgaria

2012–13 *BIMPE VII Exhibition*, Federation Gallery, Vancouver

2013 *Brother can you spare a stack*, Center for Book Arts winter exhibition, New York

2014 *Sheffield International Artist's Book Prize*, Bank St Arts, Sheffield

2015 *Sustainable Identity*, Tashkeel Dubai UAE. *Out Of A Box. Migration.* Art*ry space Al Quoz Dubai

I have been living and working in the United Arab Emirates for the past eight years. The hostile environment of the desert has become something that fascinates me: my initial response to the hot seemingly barren landscape was not one of great joy, however over time I have realized the beauty of the place, the vast expansive waves of golden sand, the clarity of the sky at night, the deafening silence and solitude of the desert. This passion for the extreme environment I find myself living in has led me naturally to incorporate the environment in to my art practice. I have successfully cultivated a section of the desert and have taught my young children how to grow vegetables and how to compost household waste. This triggered the idea of growing something that could perhaps become art. I planted a crop of long green pumpkins, and with a lot of care and attention I produced what would seemingly become a bumper crop, only to have my excitement dashed by the devastating decimation of my crop due to the infestation of Squash Vine Bore.

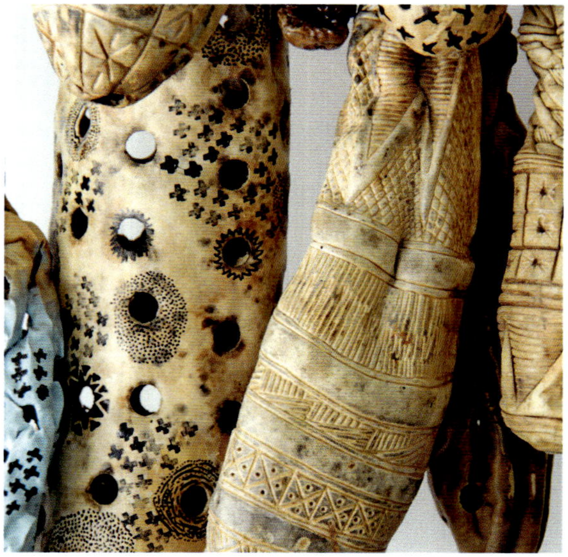

Not to be defeated, I visited the local supermarket and bought large quantities of these vegetables and spent my evenings carving patterns and shapes in to them. I then hung them from a string in the garden and let the sun do its work. I enjoyed the shrivelling and distortion of the forms as they dried. They hung for months on end in the baking sun. It became apparent to me that the deterioration of the medium began to relate to other areas of interest, the ageing process, the deterioration of life, the passing of time, ephemerality, the adornment of death, the preservation of life. I have spent many years working with a wide range of print processes striving to perfect sometimes complex, challenging techniques but at present I have loved the use of very simplistic, crude forms of printmaking. I made tiny foam stamps and began to adorn my dried shrivelled forms with print. At one time I planned to preserve them, permanently in a sarcophagus of resin.

Having reached a point where it may be the appropriate time to do this, I realize that somehow this seems wrong. So, very slowly they continue to deteriorate, turning to the dust from where they once came.

DETAIL (LEFT) AND OPPOSITE

Squash Vine Bore
110 x 150 cm
relief print
hand-stamped
mixed-media on dried pumpkin
(unique)

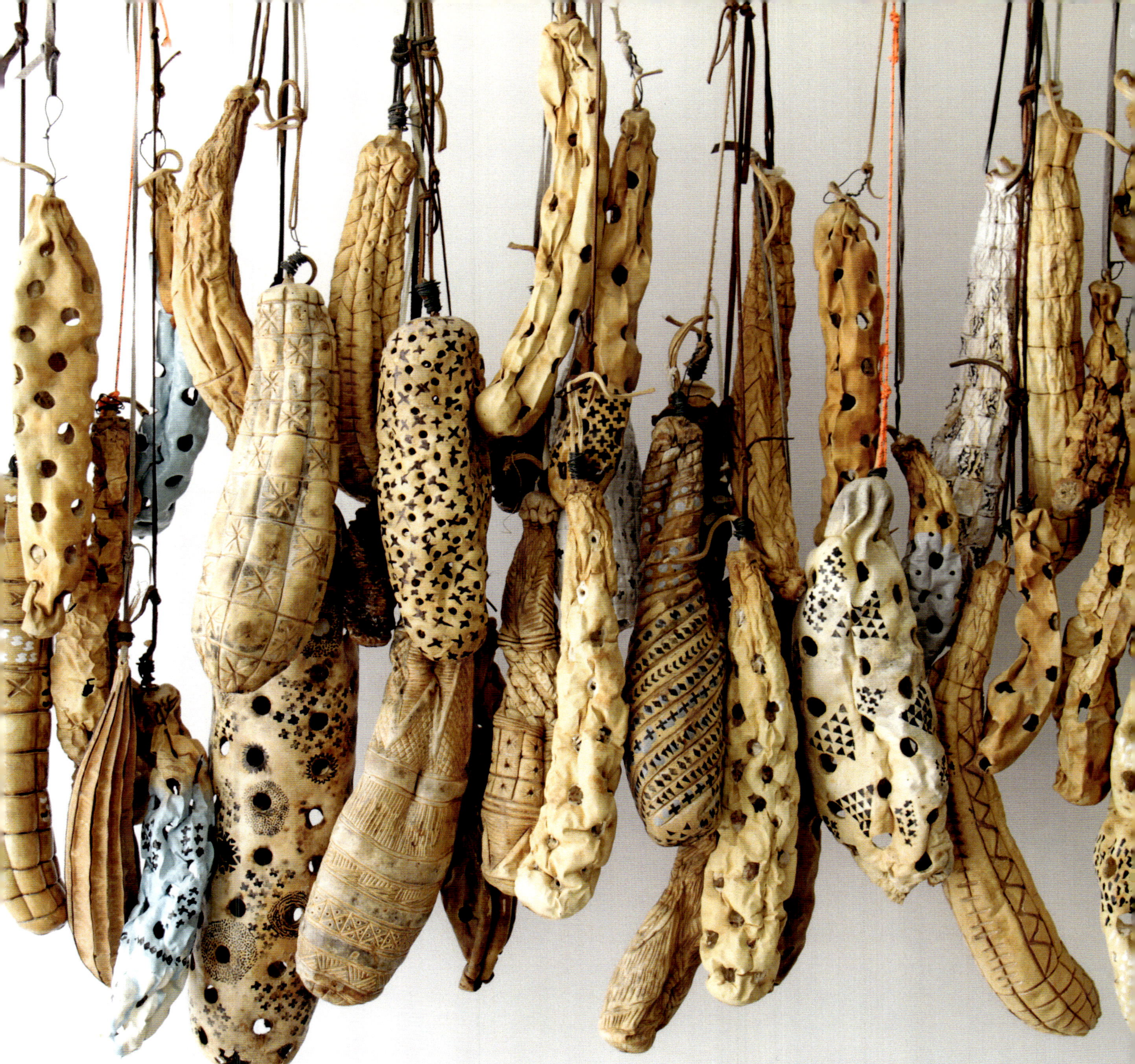

Helen Baines

I came to printmaking in 2011, having worked in design and marketing for many years. I took a screen-printing course at a local studio, as this seemed like a logical progression for a designer, and became both fascinated and excited by the various print processes and the endless opportunities they presented as a medium to convey my ideas.

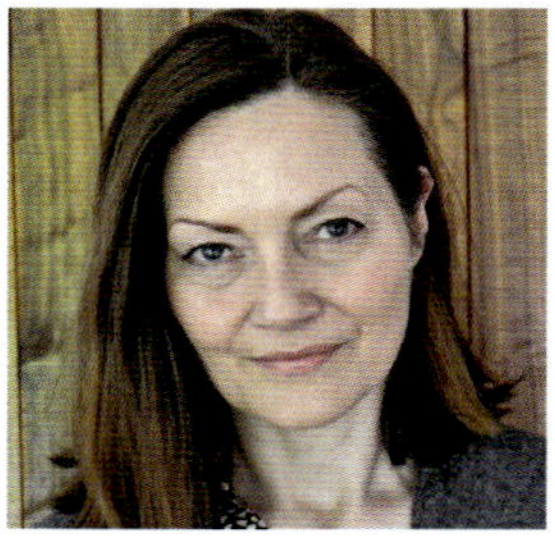

1992–93 General Art and Design BTEC Foundation, Richmond Upon Thames College

1993–96 BA (Honours) Graphic Design, West Surrey Institute of Art and Design

1997–99 Branding/Packaging designer, Fulham, London

1999–2001 Lived and worked as freelance designer in Hong Kong

2011 Started printmaking at Ochre Print Studio, Surrey

2013 Winner of Printmakers Council Student Award and Membership to Printmakers Council

2013 Winner of Printmakers Council Award at *Highgate - a Reflection in Print*, Highgate, London

2014 Commissioned to produce cover artwork for award-winning poet, Rosie Shepperd's first collection of Poems, *The Man at the Corner Table*

2014–15 Group exhibitions with Printmakers Council including *Works on Paper*, City of London Barbican Library

My work is informed primarily by the landscape, and references my broader historical and cultural interests. Although figures are not often present in my images, it is the human aspect which compels me to make a print, and by attempting to understand the definitive nature of a subject, I hope to arrive at a resolution which is more resonant or unexpected. I work from photographs and drawings, combining imaginary elements with those from memory and reality in order to bring a new focus to perennial themes.

Exploring the possibilities of form is fundamental to my practice, and I approach each piece of work as though it were a geometrical problem to be solved, reworking my drawings until I achieve a compositional harmony and balance. Perspective is flattened, angles are exaggerated and objects elevated as a means to depict the world through simplified forms and distill the spirit of a subject. Bold shapes such as shadows, which appear more tangible than the land or structures they mirror, are recurring motifs. Colour is used only to set a tone and is never representational, although it is essential to the whole and I consider its effect at length, taking many proofs in the process.

To complement my screen-printing I have recently started to experiment with collographs and carborundum. I love the expressive surface and texture that intaglio and relief printmaking offer, and the immediacy of the process compared to screen-printing. This experimental period has helped to evolve my ideas and given an added energy and depth to my printmaking.

I am particularly influenced by Modern artists, especially those of the post-war era. As a student I was captivated by the early Cubist paintings of Braque and Picasso with their collaged fragments glued on in rudimentary fashion, and it is these pioneers of Modernism who continue to thrill and inspire me today.

My work is held in private collections in Hong Kong and London.

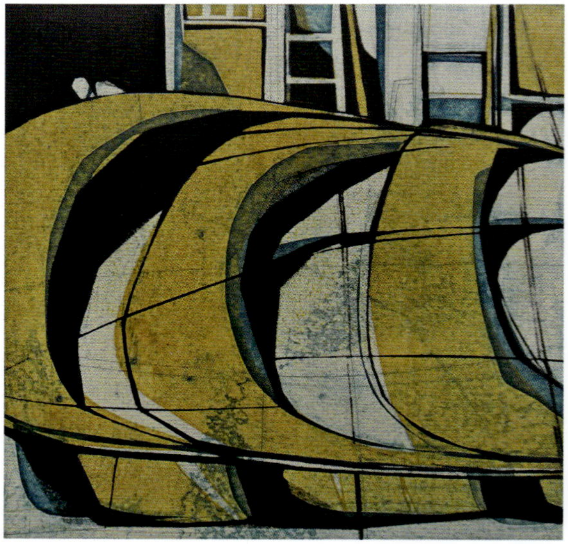

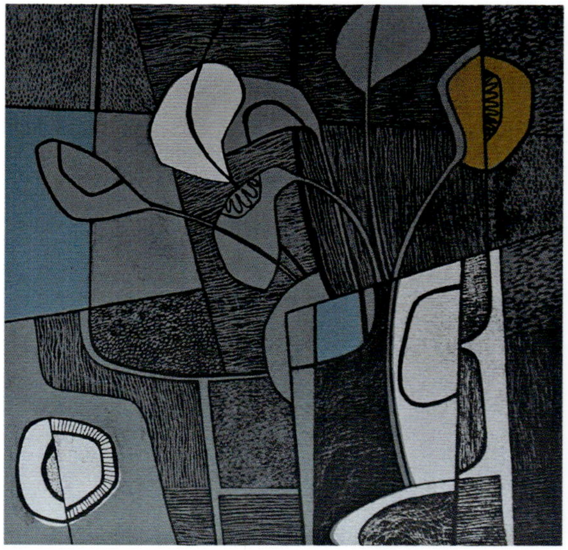

THIS PAGE:

Gondola Builder, San Trovaso, 14 x 14 cm, collograph/screen print (edition of 5)

Lillies, 18.5 x 18.5 cm, screen print (edition of 4)

OPPOSITE

Winter Vines, screen print, 28 x 29.5 cm, (edition of 10)

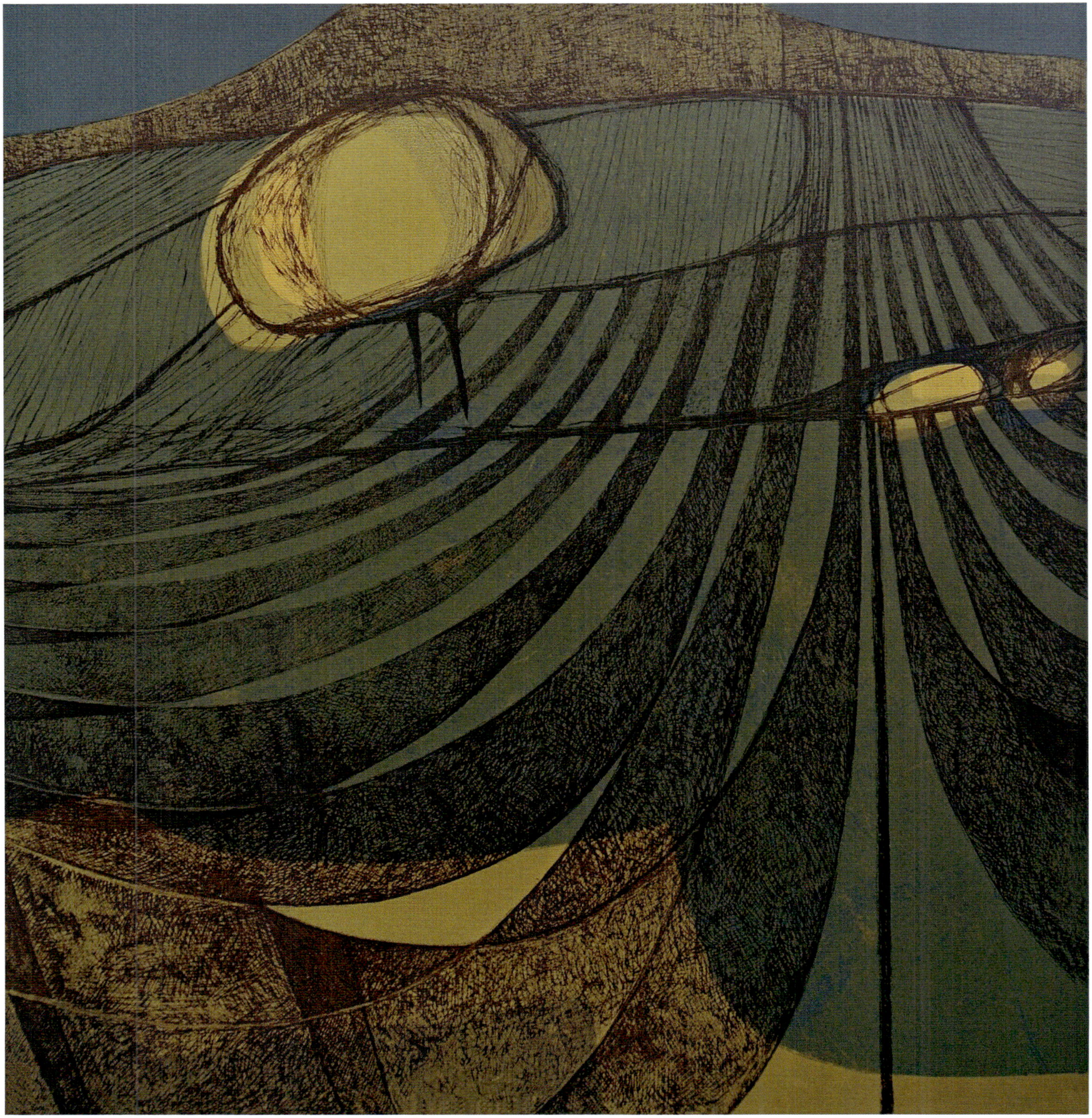

Ruth Barrett-Danes

I am both a ceramist and printmaker and my prints reflect the development of a visual language that has been synthesised from past ceramic work and my love of all things wild and strange in the landscape. My original prints use collograph and drypoint techniques that create rich surface textures.

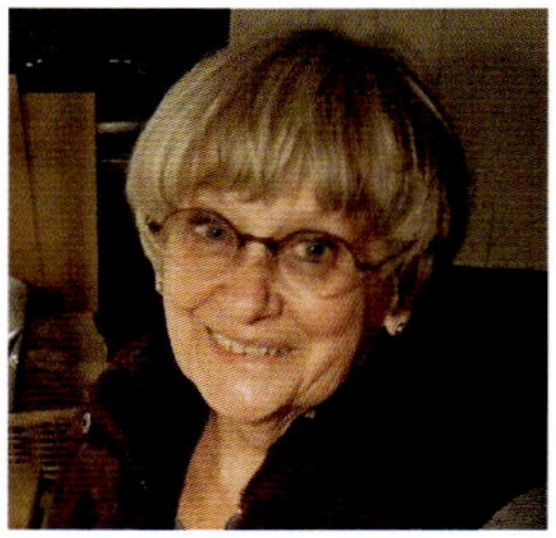

Education
Plymouth and Brighton Colleges of Art.

Recent Exhibitions

2012 *Coastal Images*, Bourneside Gallery, Dorking. *Titanic Lost Star*, Southampton Art Gallery and Museum. *Continuing Traditions*, Draw International, Caylus, France

2013 *Parallel Lives*, School of Art, Aberystwyth University. John Stripe Gallery, Winchester University. *Double Exposure*, The Wool House. Southampton. *New Horizons*, Selborne Gallery. *British Printmakers*, Twenty Twenty Gallery, Much Wenlock.

2014 *Ochre Originals* Oxmarket Gallery, Chichester. Summer Show, Bourneside Gallery, Dorking. Printmakers Council *CMYK*. *Feast of Printmaking*, Pie Factory, Margate. *Ochre Originals*, New Ashgate Gallery, Farnham. *Waiting in the Wings of War*, Royal Green Jackets Museum, Winchester. *New Art @ Baker Tilly*, Guildford, Surrey. *Divergence* Highcliffe Castle, Dorset. Printmakers Exhibition at Cranleigh Art Centre, Surrey

2015 *50 Years of Artists Prints*, Printmakers Council, Bankside Gallery, London. *PrintXchange* Artopie, Meisenthal France
PrintXchange Galerie N. Dahn Germany
Works on Paper, City of London, Barbican Library

Public Collections: National Museum of Wales. Victoria & Albert Museum, London, Ulster Museum, Belfast.

At Plymouth and Brighton Colleges of Art where I studied, the tutors, no matter what their discipline, were passionate and dedicated in their teaching and rigorous in their approach to craft skills. The knowledge I gained of process and preparation has informed all my subsequent work in ceramics and print and encouraged the possibilities of cross-fertilisation. The sensuous qualities of working in clay are there in the ways I work as a printmaker, albeit using different materials and processes.

Although the computer is a useful tool for generating and manipulating ideas quickly, it is the satisfying physicality of making and inking up a plate, the selecting and mixing of colour and even choosing the paper that excites and motivates. For me, it is an adventure in discovery that engages the mind at all stages; that constant urge to problem-solve as the print evolves, together with the interweaving of ideas and image towards a final realisation. There are false trails and failed prints but always the possibility of re-evaluation and further development. When I am sitting quietly contemplating the day's work those false trails and failed prints quite often take on another life for another day. Very little is discarded but instead is stored away ready for a later assessment.

My work is concerned with landscape and the natural world; its seasons, the weather and the creatures that inhabit it and attempts to explore the sense of belonging to a particular place at a particular time and those qualities that make it special. I now live in Hampshire though I was born in Devon and lived in Wales for over 40 years, and all of those places have insinuated themselves into my work, whether ceramics or printmaking. The images I make are a précis rather than a picture – a summing up. I find the company of other printmakers a catalyst to further explore, discover and invent, challenge and question.

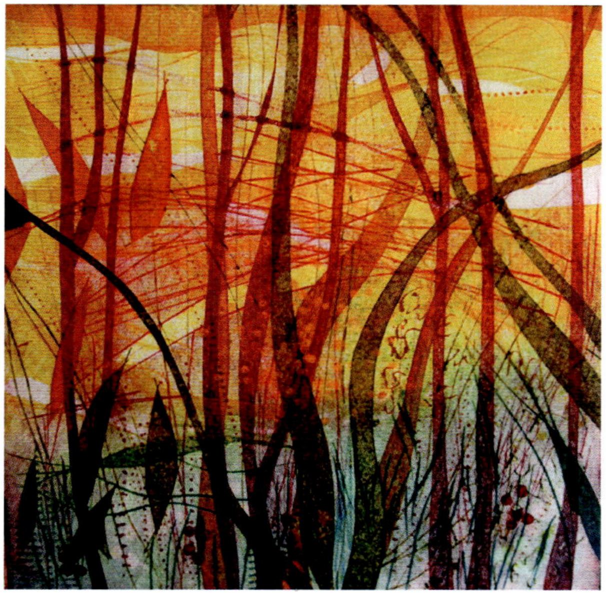

A Glorious Sunset
multiplate drypoint
and collograph
20 x 20 cm
(edition of 1)

OPPOSITE
A Winter Sun
multiplate drypoint
and collograph
20 x 20 cm
(edition of 1)

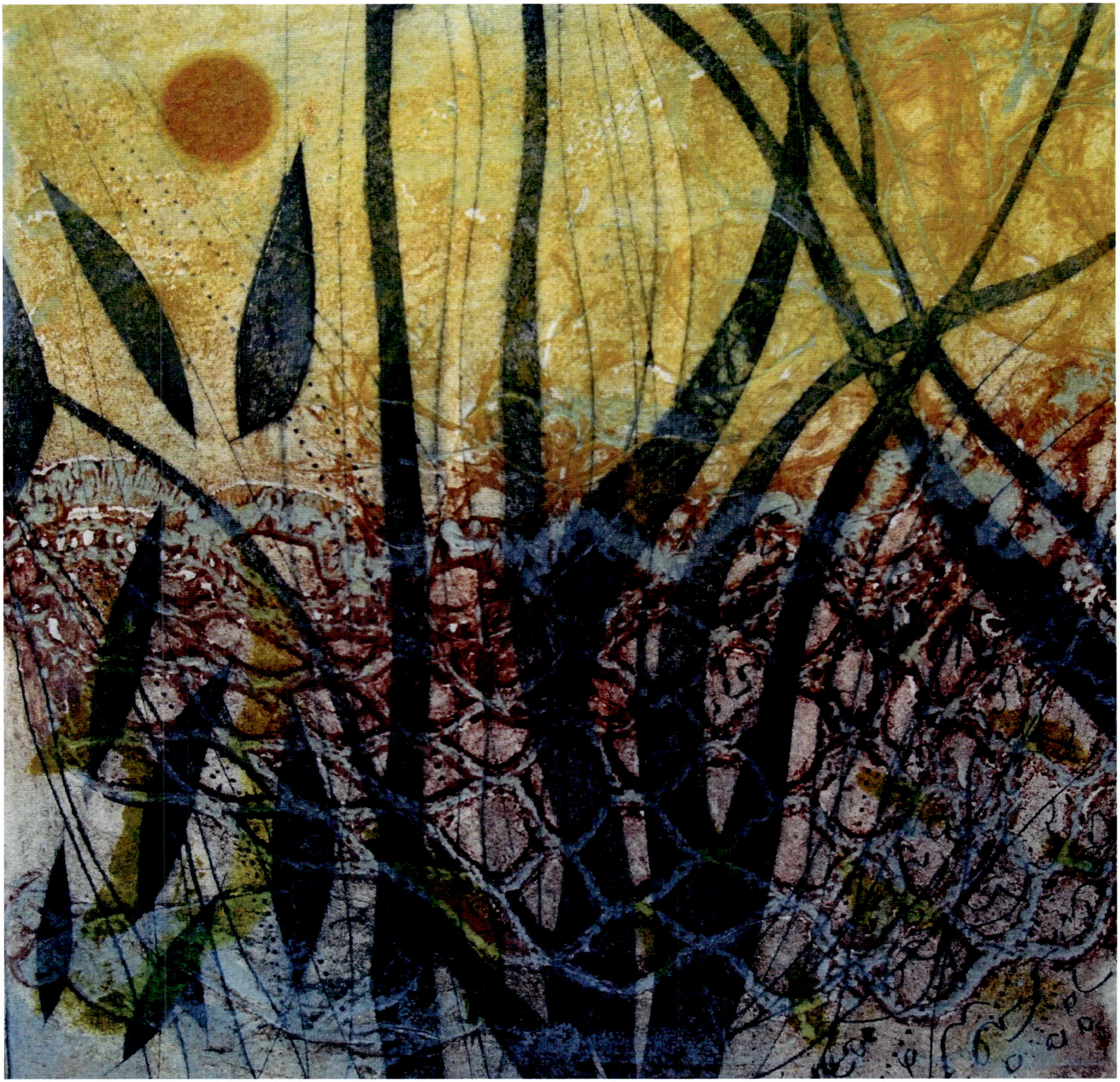

Clare Bassett

My interest in printmaking evolved from a love of drawing. I was fascinated by the way I could use printing to give drawings a further permanency. It enabled me to reproduce a drawn image and then modify it or work into it. Hence my initial attraction to lithography – a very direct form of printmaking.

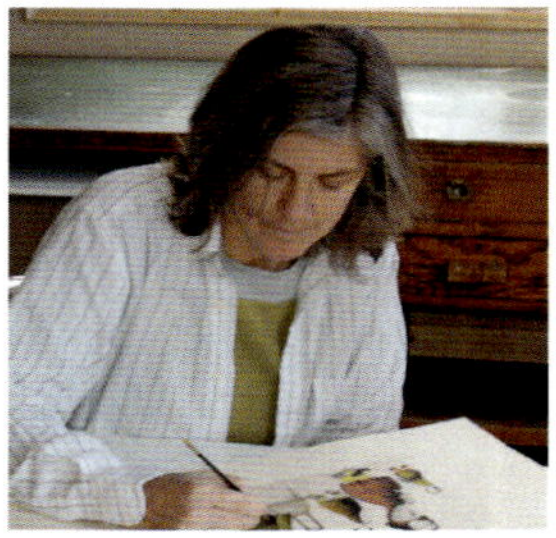

1954 Born in London, England. Brought up in Montreal, Canada. Lives in London with partner. Two sons. Studied English and Theatre at McGill University, Montreal and Warwick University. Trained in Fine Art at Goldsmiths College and Islington Institute, London. Trained in Printmaking at Oxford Printmakers.

Selected exhibitions

The Mall Gallery, London
Contemporary Print Show, London
A Woman's Touch, Singapore
Manchester Royal Exchange, Manchester
The Art on Paper Fair, Royal College of Art
Byard Art, Cambridge
New Ashgate Gallery, Farnham
Rye Gallery, Rye
Cupola Gallery, Sheffield
Affordable Art Fair, London
Montpelier Gallery, Cheltenham
Artspace, Henley
Maymie White, London
Christchurch Picture Gallery, Oxford.

Solo Exhibitions

Frivoli Gallery, London
Pyramid Gallery, York
Wiseman Gallery, Oxford
Cambridge Contemporary Art, Cambridge

Memberships

Member East London Printmakers, Member Printmakers Council
Board Member and Area Co-ordinator for Oxfordshire Artweeks 2008–2013
Associate Member of Oxford Printmakers Co-operative
Member of Oxford Art Society

My principal form of printmaking is lithography. I still work on large slabs of limestone and enjoy the tactile nature of the surface and its gritty texture. I also work on silkscreen, which allows me to complete larger images. I use TruGrain when working up the original image. This gives me the grainy surface similar to that of the lithographic stone. With both techniques I print the edition and then watercolour every print individually, giving a unique quality to each print.

My subject matter has always been figures. I love to explore human stories and events. Snapshots of life. Our lives are full of moments of opposing sentiments: of uncertainty or understanding, of indecision or commitment, of patience or frustration; but we quickly move on. I like to pause and capture some of those points in time, which we pass by so swiftly. Just by looking, we are exposed.

I look at the familiar with an unsettling glance, as well as a touch of humour. My figures are not 'knowing' people, assured in their place. For them the world is often a bit of a puzzle. Sometimes their world spirals into the dreamlike and surreal. Things are not always as we think.

I invite the viewer to become part of the moment and to question assumptions; to become part of the story. Some viewers may stand back and observe. Others may empathise and identify with those in the story.

I explore the physicality, as well as the situation, of these people. By their very solidity, they are rooted to the spot. Possibly through choice, possibly through the inabilty to act. In the lithographs, working on a piece of stone adds to the monumental nature of the figures. There is a sense of carving the images in two dimensions.

I hope that these pieces manage to stay fresh to the eye, as the discussion between the picture and the viewer continues over time, with new stories and new voices emerging.

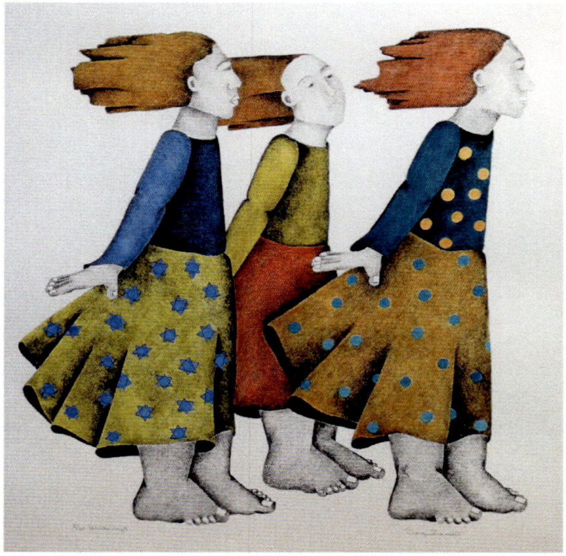

Headwind, 50 x 50 cm, screen print (edition of 20)

OPPOSITE

Lost Book, 74 x 56 cm, lithograph (edition of 5)

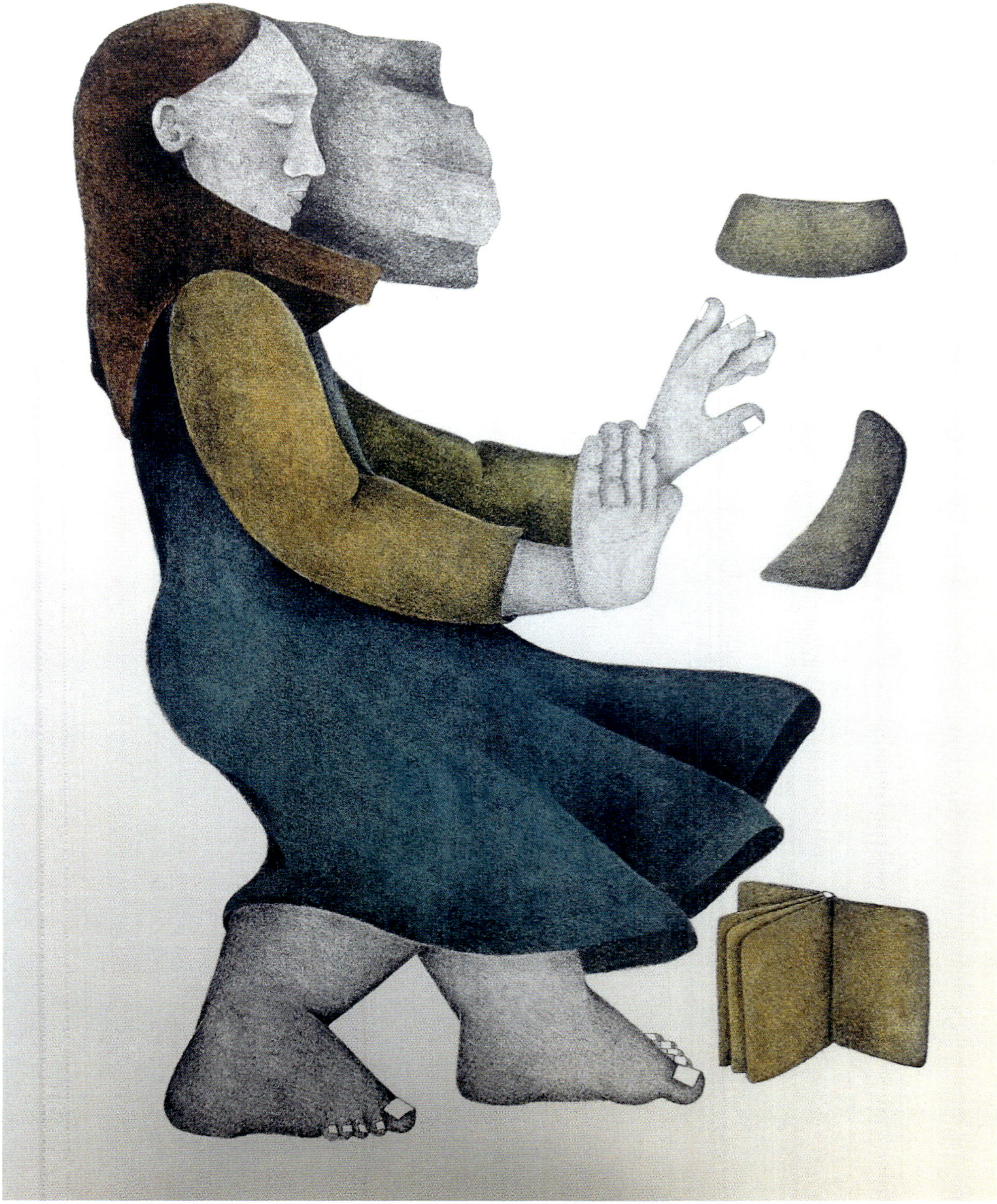

Jacki Baxter

I came to art and printmaking after ten years in the advertising industry, and that experience has informed and influenced my work. I aim to convey the beauty of everyday objects by placing them in abstract spaces, using colour and texture to enhance the forms and enrich the composition

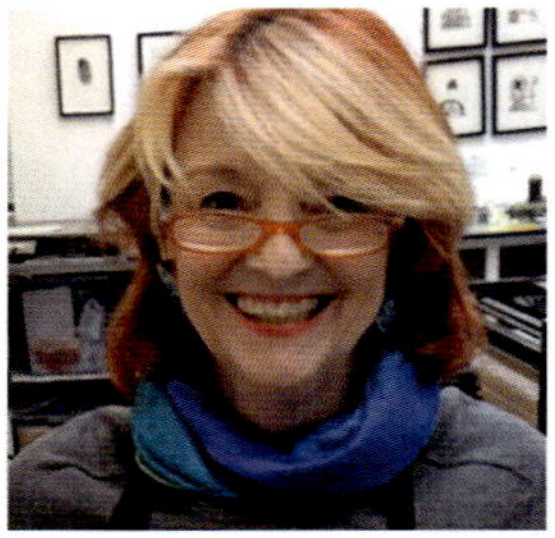

BA (Hons) Fine Art, Middlesex University
MA Fine Art Printmaking, Camberwell College of Art
2002 London Print Studio Printmaking Prize, Middlesex University
2004 *Royal Academy Summer Exhibition*. Marlborough Fine Art Prize, Camberwell College of Art. *Alternative Turner Exhibition*, Eskanzie Gallery. *100 Views of London/Tokyo*, Japan Print Association/Royal Society of Painter Printmakers, Tokyo
2005 Member of East London Printmakers
2006 Member of the Printmakers Council, elected Office Administrator
2007 *Loveletter to London*, City Hall
2008 Intaglio Print Prize, *I am 10*, Bankside Gallery. *Wonderland*, Fairy Tale Museum, Bad Oeyhausen, Germany
2009 *Wonderland*, V & A Museum of Childhood
2010 *Link*, Space Arte Ora, Foggia, Italy
2011 *Dreams*, Freud Museum, London. *7th International Mini Print* travelling show, various galleries in England
2012 *Ostrakon*, Galleria Ostrakon, Milan. *Turn, Turn, Turn*, Margate Gallery. *8th British International Mini Print*, London Print Studio
2013 *Highgate - A Reflection in Print*. *Going Underground*, Shoreditch Town Hall
2014 *Freshly Pressed*, Embassy Tea Gallery
2015 *50 Years of Artists Prints*, Bankside Gallery. Elected Member of Greenwich Printmakers. *Works on Paper*, Barbican Library

Since the earliest of times, people have created vessels to store and carry water, wine and food. A much-loved pot may be passed down through generations and through many hands, a delicate symbol of nurture and nourishment. The objects I choose to place centre stage, such as jugs, bottles, cups and spoons resonate with their own history and invite the viewer to reassess the role and importance of everyday things and spaces.

My work is loosely based within the still-life genre and inspired in part by the work of Matisse, Morandi and William Scott. A still-life creates a window which invites the viewer to reflect on the world beyond the frame, creating negative spaces which are as important as the item itself.

My prints are built in multiple layers using a combination of traditional cut lino with etched lino and handmade stencils. The stencils are my cast of characters; whether figurative or abstract, they are chosen and composed according to the individual print. Some of the stencils are carried forward into other prints, either as background surfaces or main images, providing a sense of continuity.

Distillation No 14, 24 x 24 cm, etched lino & stencils (unique)

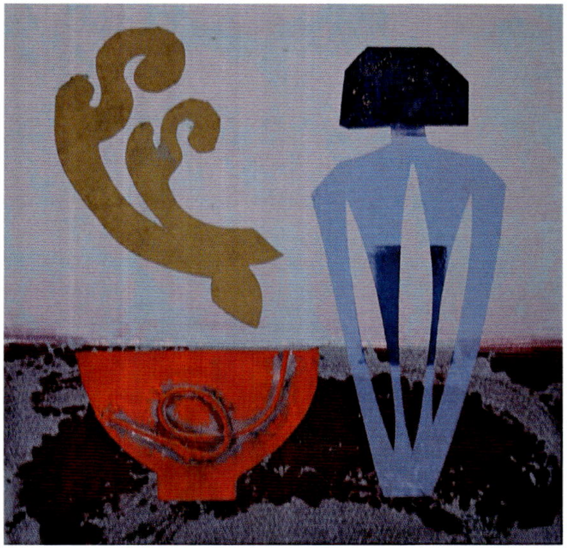

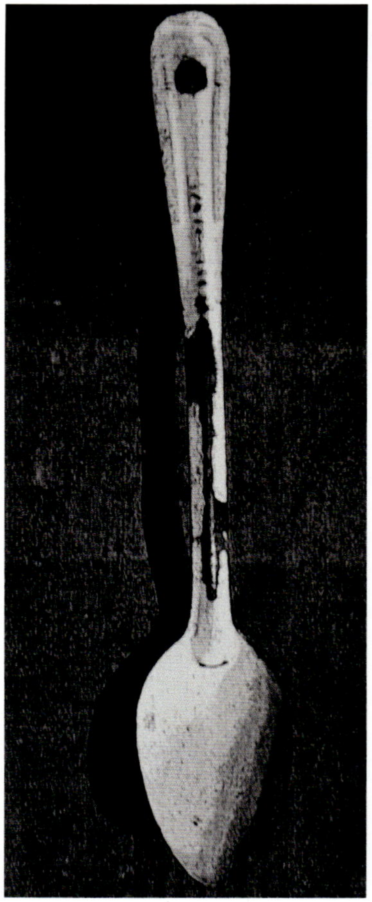

Enamel Spoon
59 x 23.5 cm
photolitho
(edition of 3)

I use oil-based ink because of its intense richness of colour which I roll on to lino and print in flat layers of background colour which are juxtaposed with various etched plates to create surfaces nuanced with colour and texture. The colour palette emerges through experimentation but always retains equal importance to the subject matter and the scale of the images. Etching lino with caustic soda leads to unpredictable mark-making and creates uniquely embellished surfaces which have an interesting sense of ambiguity.

This multi-layer method of lino printing is a process of trial and error and happy accidents. The frisson elicited by the frequently unexpected results gives me the desire to continue experimenting in my chosen aesthetic.

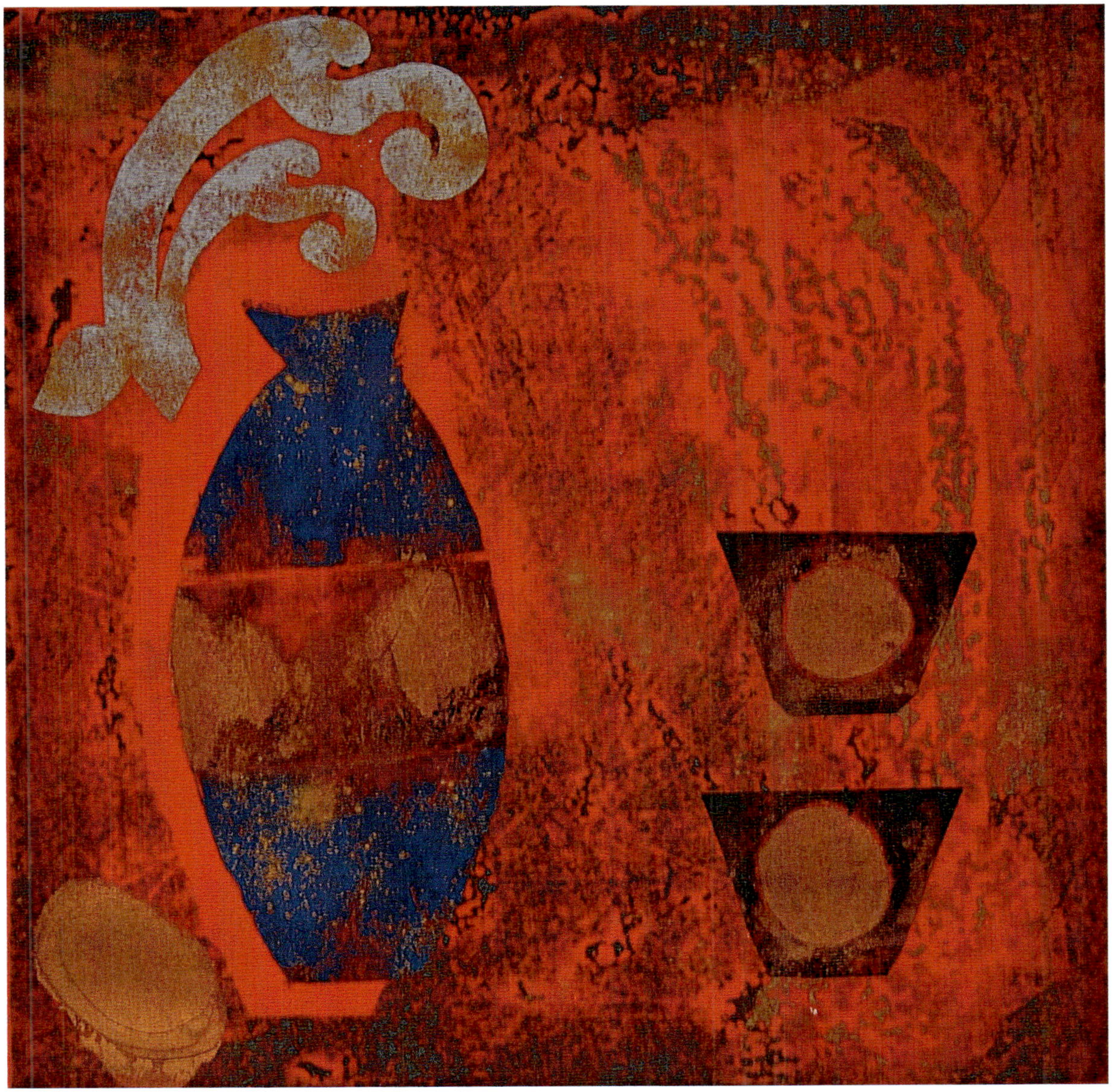

Blue & Gold Vessel, 28 x 28 cm, etched & stencils (unique)

Tania Beaumont

I am a painter-printmaker, a mixed-media artist (someone once said – 'with a vengeance'!) I incorporate painted surfaces into my prints and printed elements collaged onto paintings, to produce the narrative qualities that I like, often with subtle or hidden layers.

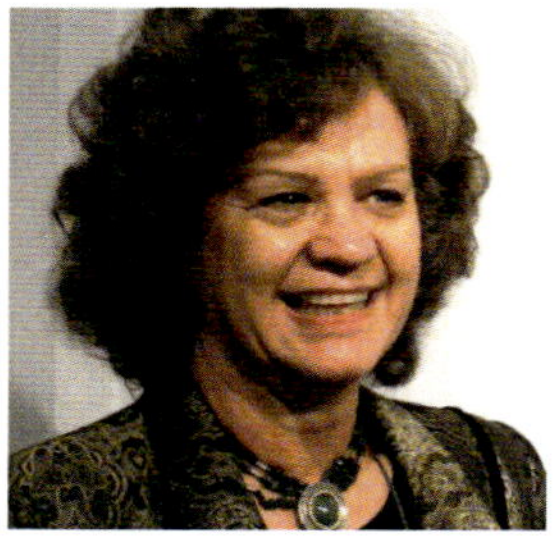

1949 Born Reading, UK

Colleges
1966–68 J.J. School of Art , Bombay
1969–72 Dip. AD (Hons) Liverpool College of Art
1975–76 PGDip Textile Design Goldsmiths College, University of London

Exhibited UK, USA, Europe, West Indies, Middle East, North Africa.
Untitled, Parallax and Palace Art Fairs, London
Member of artist-run Espacio Gallery, Bethnal Green.

January 2011 Returned home to live in West London

Having lived the majority of the past 30 years as an expatriate I have an extensive visual database from which I can produce works with narrative and ambiguity. I take inspiration from what I see around me: spring blossoms, whizzing clouds, figures at a market or station, architectural elements – and I work through these 'themes' in various media, initially through drawing but including etching, collograph, lino and silkscreen printing. Having worked as a freelance textile designer for a couple of years, pattern often still finds its way into my work.

A large collection of old documents, bought at flea markets, continues to supply interesting foundations for all manner of ideas and prints – similarly it is difficult to resist picking up discarded items in the street which may eventually be used as part of a printed 'document' or mixed-media painting.

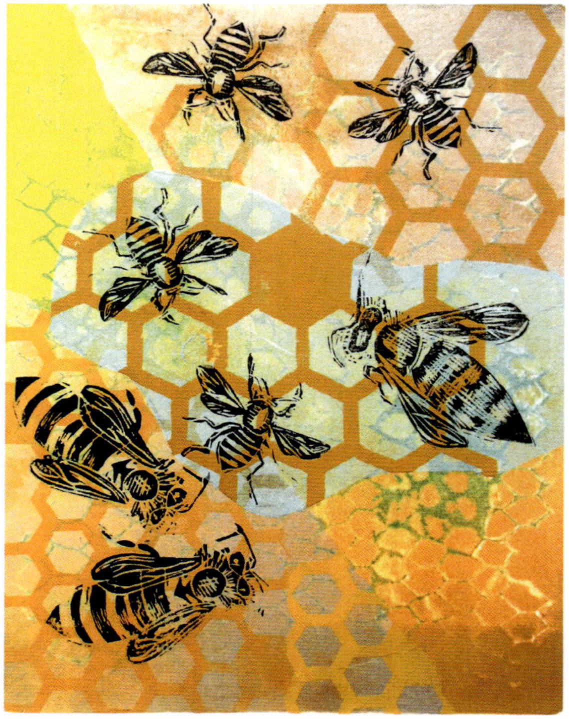

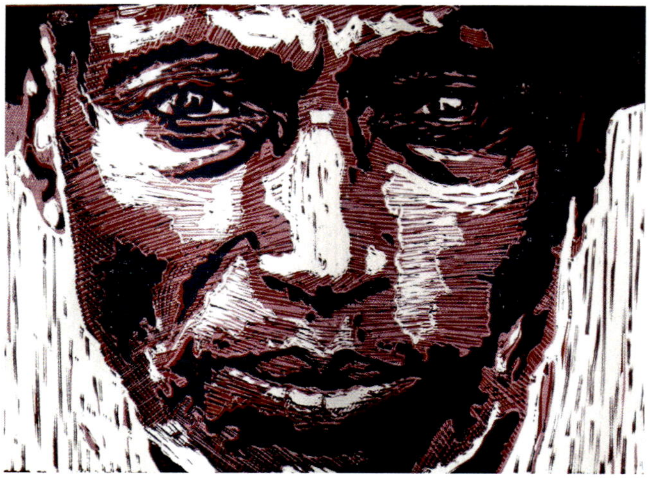

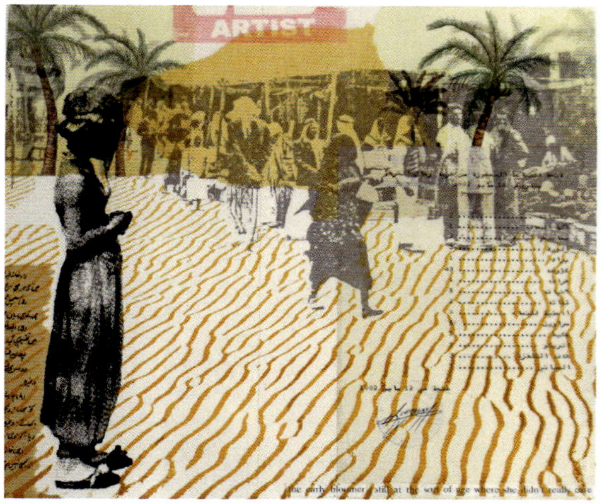

This page, clockwise from top left:

Workers, mixed-media, monoprint & chine collé
25 x 20 cm, unique

Early Bloomer, mixed-media monoprint & chine collé
35 x 30 cm, unique

Concentrate, reduction lino print, 24 x 28 cm (edition of 12)

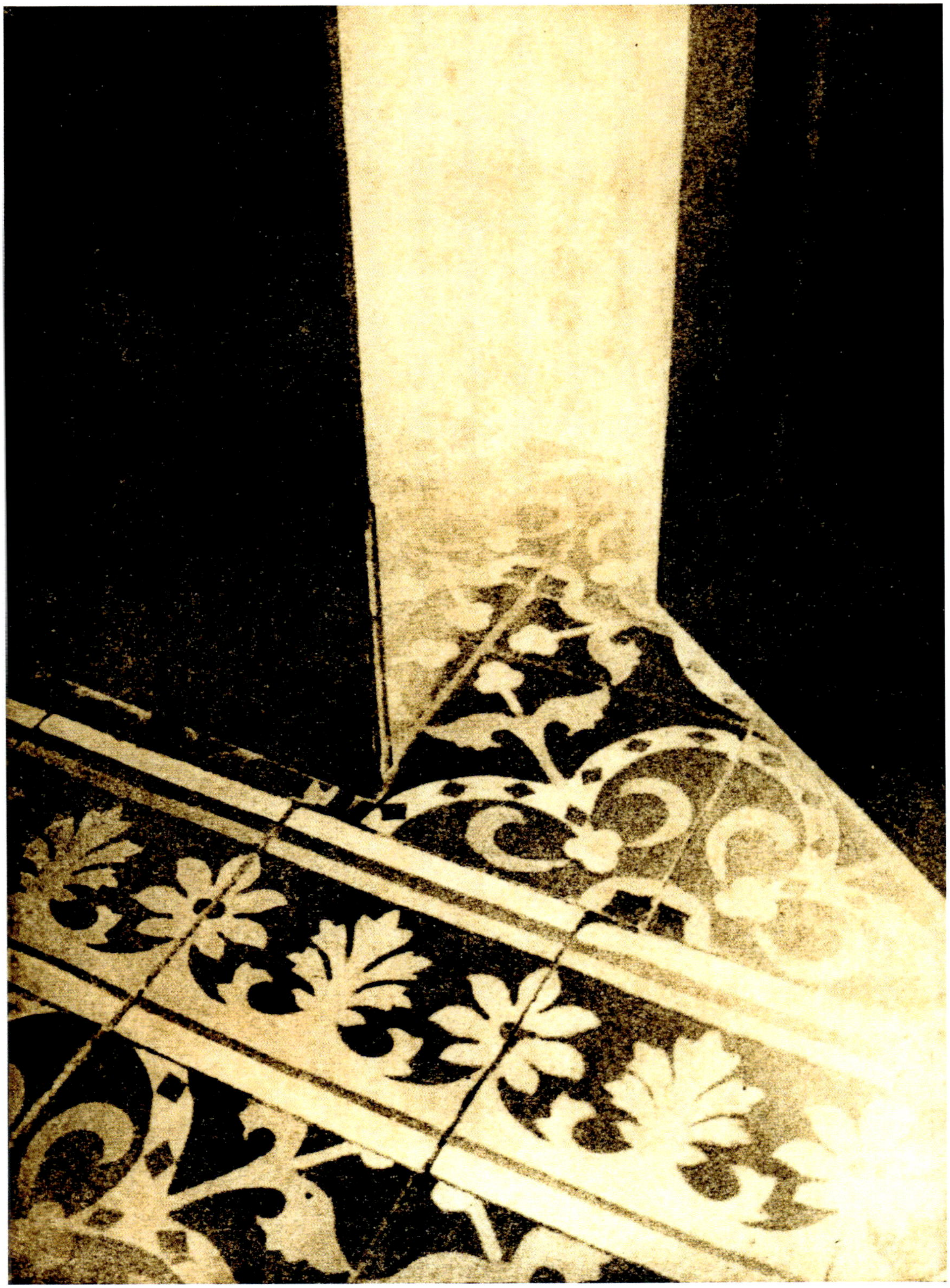

Open Door
etching
15 x 21 cm
(edition of 100)

Helen Benson

Many years ago I became interested in screen-printing and joined a class at Camden Arts Centre, Arkwright Road. Then after a long period I attended Nicola Styan's inspirational screen-printing class at the Working Men's College Camden, finding that this technique really suited – and still suits – my creative spirit. At University I continued printing on paper, but also experimented on acetate and perspex for 3D work.

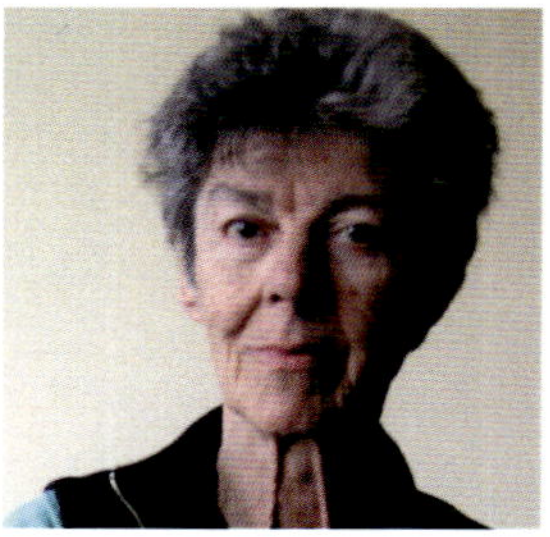

Biography

Helen Benson studied piano and cello at the Royal College of Music.

While continuing her long career as a musician she embarked upon a Fine Art course at the City Lit, London, followed by a Fine Art degree at the Cass School of Art, London Metropolitan University. She graduated in 2014.

Helen specializes in screen-printing and is a member of the London Print Studio.

Her artwork flows alongside teaching piano and cello in North London.

Exhibitions

Past group shows:

2007 Fine Art Show, City Lit 2014 Degree Show, Cass School of Art

2008 Fine Art Show, City Lit

2008 End of year show, Working Men's College, Camden Town

2012 *Salon des Refusés*, Hoxton

2013 *Whatever Next*, Mile End Pavilion

Forthcoming group shows:

2015 *Print Fair*, Espacio Gallery. Bethnal Green.

2015 *Place and Space*, Espacio Gallery

2015 *Urban Angles*, Espacio Gallery

My way of working is to have an initial image on my screen, then, as I print, ideas develop for the next layer, so I invent as I go along. I do not have a pre-conceived plan of the outcome, which means I am constantly on edge and tension is high. This can relate to musical improvisation although, strangely, I am rather a 'straight' classical musician playing entirely from the written score. Invention comes in the interpretation.

I am visually attracted by the city's huge, modern glass office blocks, which reflect each other, especially on a sunny day. These buildings give a lonely, empty feeling and yet they are visually exciting.

I use my own photographs of these buildings, transferring them to screen prints, where I experiment with layering and distorting the image. Line is a dominant influence, reflecting and drawing on the complex patterns of structures which include scaffolding, railway station roofs and city buildings by day and night. Sometimes water images and trees are juxtaposed with these structures.

I work by superimposing different shapes, which have the effect of altering the viewing angles. This is further emphasized by my use of a selective range of colours including black and white, silver and gold, which also provides structure and contrast. I am seeking to capture the interplay of the way that light, architectural features and natural elements refract on each other.

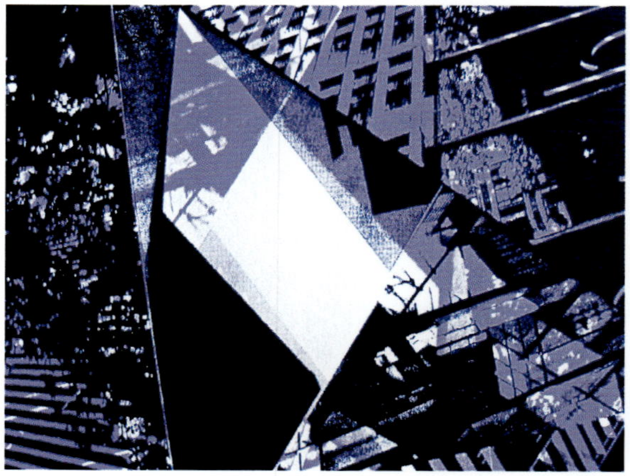

Urban Angles, No 2, 23.5 x 20.3 cm, screen print on Snowdon cartridge paper (edition of 10)

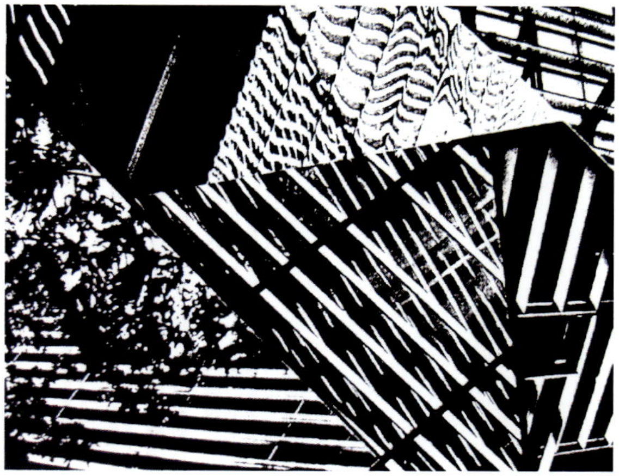

Urban Angles, No 3, 23.5 x 20.3 cm, screen print on Snowdon cartridge paper (edition of 10)

In contrast, in my 3D prints on perspex, lines contain the suggestion of movement. Viewed from different positions, the viewer has different experiences of light and shadows, reflections and distortion.

Working with acetate provides me with a new dimension. One of my projects at University was to screen-print a grid pattern onto a long roll of acetate which I then suspended, using nylon thread, from the ceiling. As it gently moved the grid lines curved into different patterns giving it a fluid effect.

One of the reasons I prefer screen-printing to other forms of printing is that I enjoy the physical gestures involved, which relate to those in playing the piano and especially the cello.

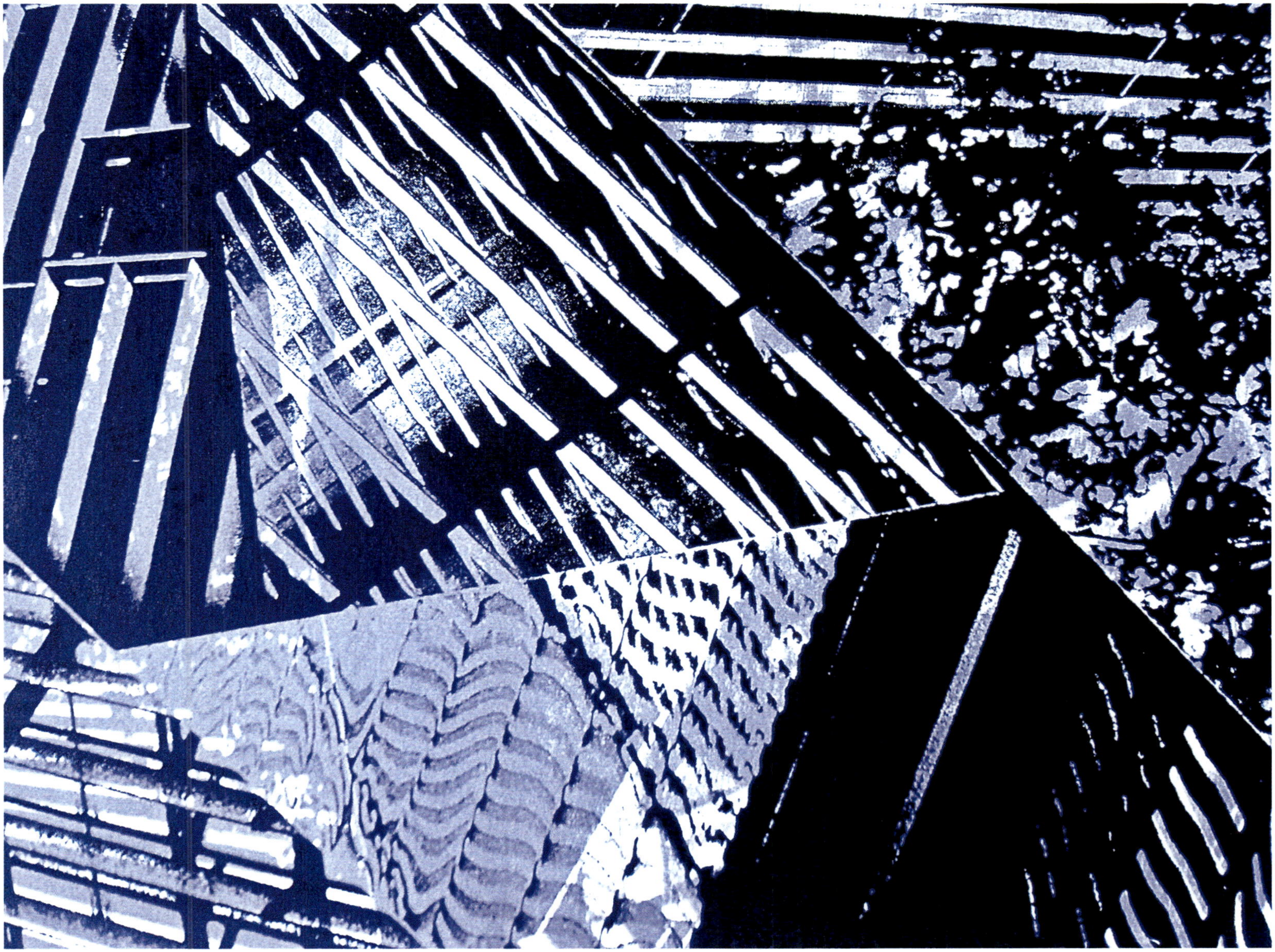

Urban Angles, No 1, 23.5 x 20.3 cm, screen print on Snowdon cartridge paper (edition of 10)

Alison Bernal

Printmaking has been a major part of my artistic practice for eighteen years since I joined a course at Morley College to inform my practice as a painter. My work is primarily concerned with the exploration of tonal values and picture space. I work with a range of printmaking techniques including intaglio, lithography, relief, embossing and monoprint. I also make artists' books.

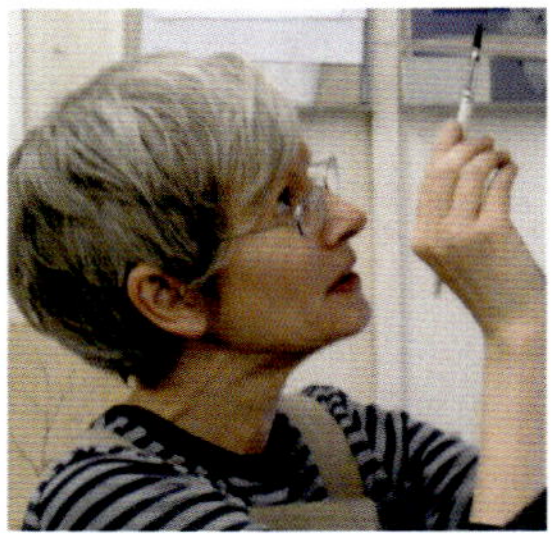

1955 Born in Britain
1977–80 BA (Hons) Middlesex Polytechnic

Recent Shows

2010 *Originals '10*, Mall Galleries
Greenwich Printmakers at The Morley Gallery
Affordable Art Fair, Battersea
16 Printmakers, Morley Gallery

2011 *Second Edition*, National Theatre
Bristol Artists Book Fair, Arnolfini
Rootstein Hopkins Drawing Exhibition
Bite, Mall Galleries
The Temple, Wanstead
PmC at the Highgate Gallery

2012 *International Mini Print*, Printmakers Council
Printathon, Formans Smokehouse

2013 *Babe*, Arnolfini , Bristol
MADE, Morley Gallery
Carte Blanche, London Print Studio
ELP Summer Show, Shoreditch
PmC at the Highgate Scientific and Literary Institution

2014 *Freshly Pressed*, Craft Central
ELP Summer Show, Embassy Tea Gallery
National Original Print, Bankside

Collections

Victoria and Albert Museum

Awards

John Purcell Paper Award 2013

Memberships

East London Printmakers;
Printmakers Council;

I first got the chance to use a press on my Foundation Course and I never forgot the thrill of transferring ink from metal to paper. It was some time until I had the time and opportunity to return to it but now printmaking has become my primary medium. From the beginning I enjoyed learning to use the new materials and tools and I eventually I realised that like all creative practices there were endless possibilities in every method. My work is often driven in a new direction by the chance discovery of a new effect while experimenting.

Before preparing any kind of plate I will draw, take photographs, make collages or monoprints to explore my ideas and imagery and I usually make prints as a series, on a theme. Previous work has included a set inspired by clouds using aquatint which gives the printmaker the opportunity to use a wide range of tones. I became fascinated by the monumental yet ephemeral nature of the movement of clouds across the sky and tried to capture some of that effect in those prints. Research at the V & A into the representation of clouds by other cultures and artists and a competition entry requiring a response to the gallery led me to embossing. This is the impression of a plate without ink and gives a surface texture to the paper.

A short course on book-making produced some small editions of artists' books based on my original source material of cloud formations. Continuing with the embossing technique I combined this with relief printing for a series based on the building of the Olympic Park near my home in East London.

My current work is inspired by Piranesi's *Carceri* (Prisons). I still go to Morley College and an exercise in restricting the printmaker to black ink only was a fruitful starting point for increasingly abstract forms and experiments using tranparent paper and printing on both the back and the front. I am now working on making prints that are embossed on both sides.

For me the exploration of the formal elements of image-making goes hand in hand with a fascination in the technical limits of materials and method.

Altocumulus, 38 x 45 cm, emboss relief (edition of 30)

OPPOSITE
Double Tracks, 28 x 28 cm, emboss relief (edition of 30)

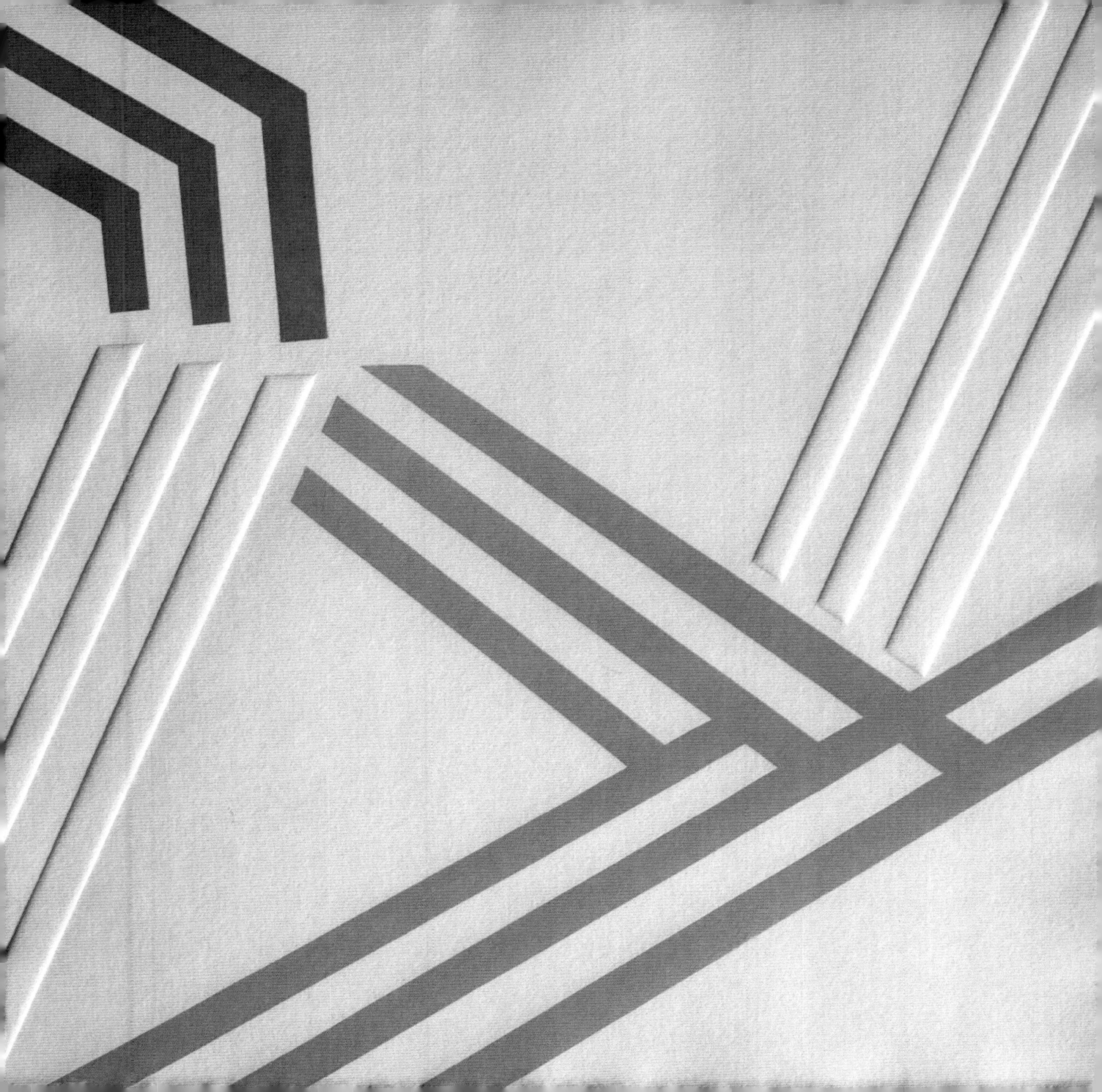

Kit Boyd

Exploring our relationship with nature and landscape, Kit's detailed etchings find refuge in the pastoral and surreal, leading you down lanes into dreamlike landscapes. He follows in the British romantic tradition, being strongly influenced by Samuel Palmer and the Neo-Romantics of the 1940s. He also works in collage and painting.

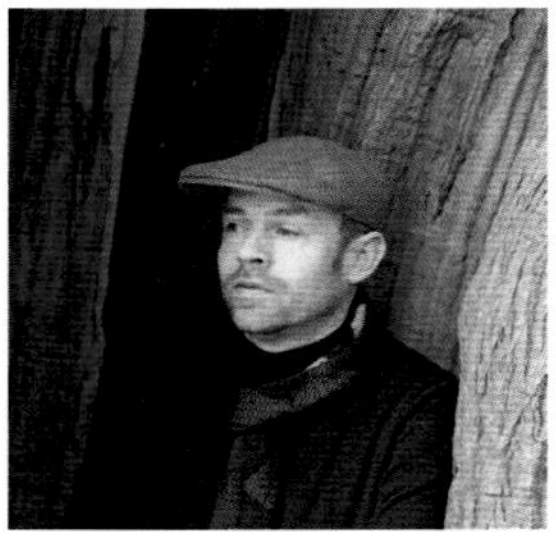

1969 Born Christopher Boyd, West Midlands
1988–91 BA (Hons) Visual Art, Aberystwyth University
1993 *A Natural Attraction*, solo show, Visage Gallery, Marylebone, London
1995 *The Discerning Eye*, Mall Galleries, London – choice of Julian Spalding
1997–2006 Works for the Campaign to Protect Rural England
2008 *Royal Academy Summer Exhibition*
2009 *Gruff and Tackleton's Winter Menagerie*, Brixton Village Gallery National Open, Chichester
2010 *Figures in the Landscape*, solo show, Brixton Village Gallery and Camden People's Theatre
2011 Joins Skylark Galleries. Takes up printmaking at Morley College. *Routes and Branches Art Trail*, St John's Wood, London. Rootstein Hopkins Drawing Award, Winner of People's Prize
2012 *The Poetic Impulse – The Etchings of Samuel Palmer*, with selections by his peers and followers, Court Barn Museum, Oxfordshire. *RE Open*, Bankside Galleries, London Joins Greenwich Printmakers
2013 *World in My Eyes* – a 20 year retrospective, Barbican. Designs dust jacket of *Dark Mountain Vol 4*. 20/21 British Art, Royal College with Rebecca Hossack Gallery. Joins East London Printmakers and Southbank Printmakers
2014 Joins Printmakers Council. *CMYK*, Pie Factory, Margate. *ING Discerning Eye*, Mall Galleries, London. Choice of Simon Martin

From rural idylls to strange metamorphoses evolving from my mind's eye, my work aims to channel the mysterious spirit of place. Green men emerge from trees, lone figures find refuge in lanes, and plantlife undergoes metamorphoses.

I'm interested in the sense of mystery that lies beyond our surface appreciation of the world, the moments of heightened perception that can come upon you when you are out alone in a landscape, the strangeness of a distant wood on a hill, the history hidden beneath your feet, the ability of landscape to give you goose pimples, the secretive domains of birds and insects, or the fleeting connection between you and a fox as you interrupt each other on a country path.

The ongoing theme of my work is our relationship to nature, whether in a realistic or surrealist depiction of our internal and external worlds. Landscape for me is often a protective womb-like place in which we can find solace, escape or a safe environment away from the information overload and overcrowding we are experiencing in the modern world, just as Palmer escaped the incursions of industrial revolution into his patch of south London by escaping to Shoreham in the 1820s.

Several of my recent etchings have been inspired directly by the visionary period of Samuel Palmer, depicting a seemingly idealised ancient vision of the countryside. However, Palmer's shepherds are replaced by a figure using modern technology, such as in the *Man on a Laptop* series, and the bucolic idyll may harbour a power station or wind farm with its associated climatic repercussions.

My move into printmaking came as a result of detailed pen and ink drawings which looked very much like etchings. While I had learned some basic techniques previously, I enrolled at Morley College in 2011 and really fell in love with the medium. I have since learnt wood engraving and stone and photo lithography, but etching remains my favoured printmaking process.

With a background as a painter in bright colours, my etchings in comparison are largely monotone. Recently I have begun hand-tinting artist proofs to make unique versions which alter the mood of a piece, reflecting time of day, geographical location or season. I feel the effect of transparent ink over the aquatint or lithographic mark has successfully deepened the tone and richness of each print. These unique hand-coloured versions seem to have found the right balance for me between my painterly background and the very detailed graphic style of my printmaking.

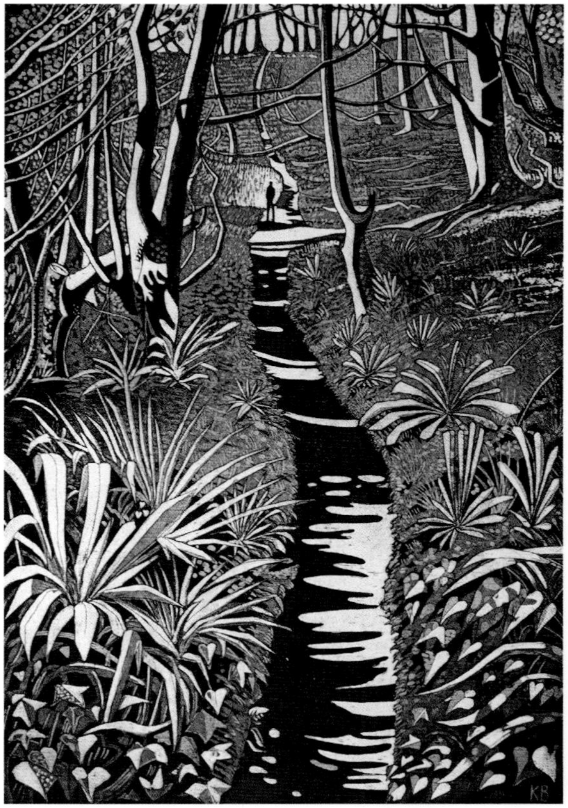

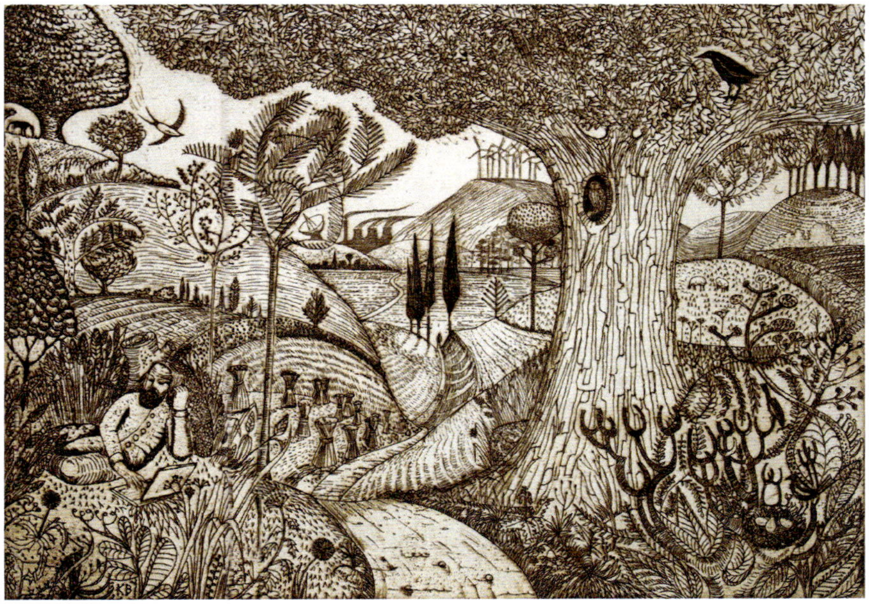

Man on a Laptop (after Samuel Palmer),
20 x 15 cm, etching (edition of 25 in sepia)

Dusk Return Red Sunset, 20 x 15 cm,
unique hand-coloured etching
(outside of the edition of 75)

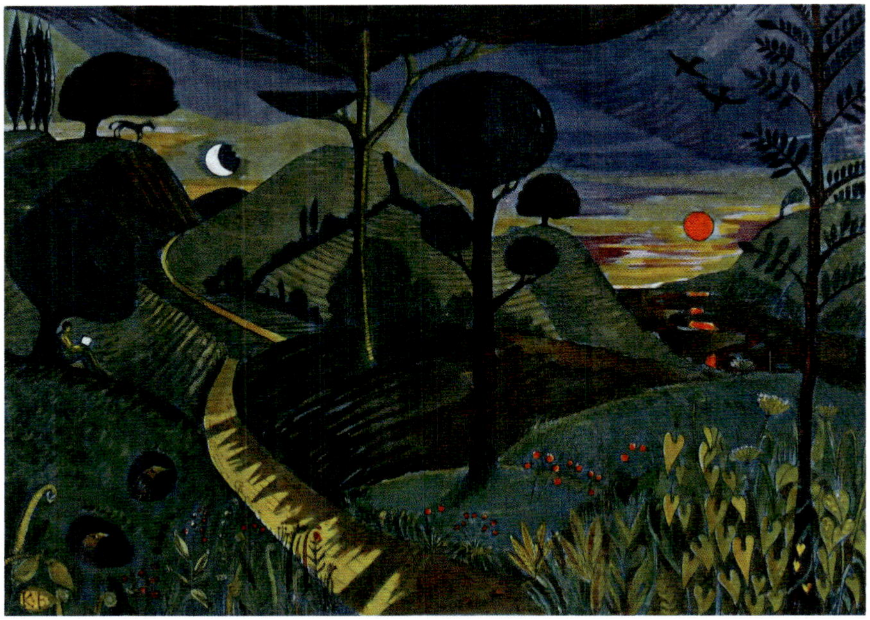

LEFT

The Way Through the Woods, 20 x 30 cm
etching & aquatint (edition of 75)

Pauline Bradley

My early work evolved through drawing and painting. In the early 1980s a Degas print exhibition at the Hayward Gallery inspired me to learn etching. Following this a Japanese woodblock exhibition at the British Museum led me to experiment more widely with printmaking. It has now become the main vehicle for my work.

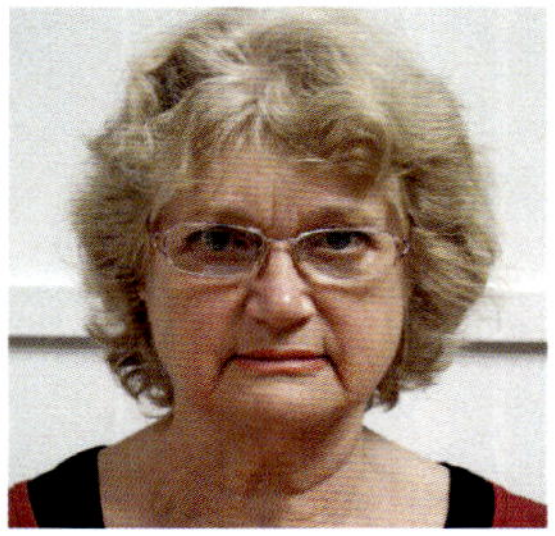

1944 Born in Wolverhampton
1959–64 Studies Painting at Wolverhampton College of Art
1965–2006 Employed as a lecturer by Wolverhampton Education Committee
1966–70 Exhibits with Arts Council Sponsored, Shropshire Artists Group
1993–98 BA (Hons) Printmaking Wolverhampton University
1994 Joins Printmakers Council
1994–96 Musée Adzak Paris
1996-97 Zella Gallery London
1998 Winner of the Mohan Kishore Agrawal Gold Medal for Excellence in Printmaking
1999 Individual participant at *The Contemporary Print Fair* London
1999 Joins and exhibits with Dundee Contemporary Arts
2006 *6th British Miniprint*
2006–15 Exhibits at Birmingham Society of Artists
2007 Joins and exhibits with East West Artists Group in London
2008 Visits and exhibits in Osaka Japan
2009 Dorf Wehlen, Germany
2010–14 Solo shows at the Tower House Gallery, Knighton
2012 Mid-Wales Arts Centre
2012–14 *MOMA Wales Annual Open*
2012–13 Best in Category Award, EWAAC
2012–present Gallery artist at Bebb Fine Art, Ludlow
2013–15 Roseangle Gallery, Dundee, DCA
2014 Jarfo Gallery, Kyoto, Japan
2014 Society of Women Artists, Mall Galleries
2015 Birnam Arts Centre, Dunkeld

I like to work in a range of media both traditional and contemporary. Since becoming a member of the internationally regarded Dundee Contemporary Arts print workshop, the techniques I have studied include all the traditional European methods and, in particular, the traditional Japanese woodblock. I will often combine these in one piece of work with contemporary techniques. Working this way, allowing for the unpredictability of print and the unexpected discoveries that occur, I find particularly exciting.

I have also studied, and continue to experiment with new methods. I have my own workshop which includes three printing presses and a special unit that allows me to expose plates with UV light.

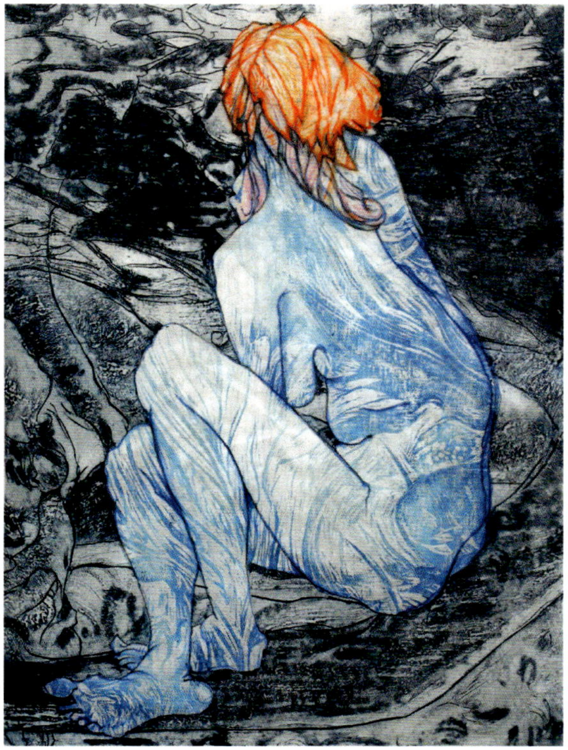

My work has its origins in the encounter with the live model, which I continue to draw on a weekly basis. Over the years I have also worked in the rehearsal rooms of professional ballet and contemporary dance companies. I have employed and collaborated with dancers and others as models, working with them in a wide range of environments including professional, individual and public spaces. These experiences have allowed me to observe the physical movements that reveal and express inner emotions. This is central to my work in creating images that explore emotional identity and aspects of the human condition, which the nude reveals more readily, where clothing conceals and can create an assumed identity.

Often images will evolve into more abstract ideas with the ultimate fragmentation of the figure into its surroundings. Natural forms are an integral part of the composition as a supporting context for the figure. I have a large collection of natural forms and use both drawing and photography to develop these images within my work.

I see my practice as the act of using visual language to find form for my personal internalised emotions which I access through a particular collaborative response to the mood and pose of the model. My work is in private collections in the UK, USA, Japan, China and France.

LEFT
Melusina 1, woodcut & collograph, 56 x 75 cm (edition of 2)

OPPOSITE
Nocturnal Light
woodcut & monoprint,
62 x 74 cm, unique

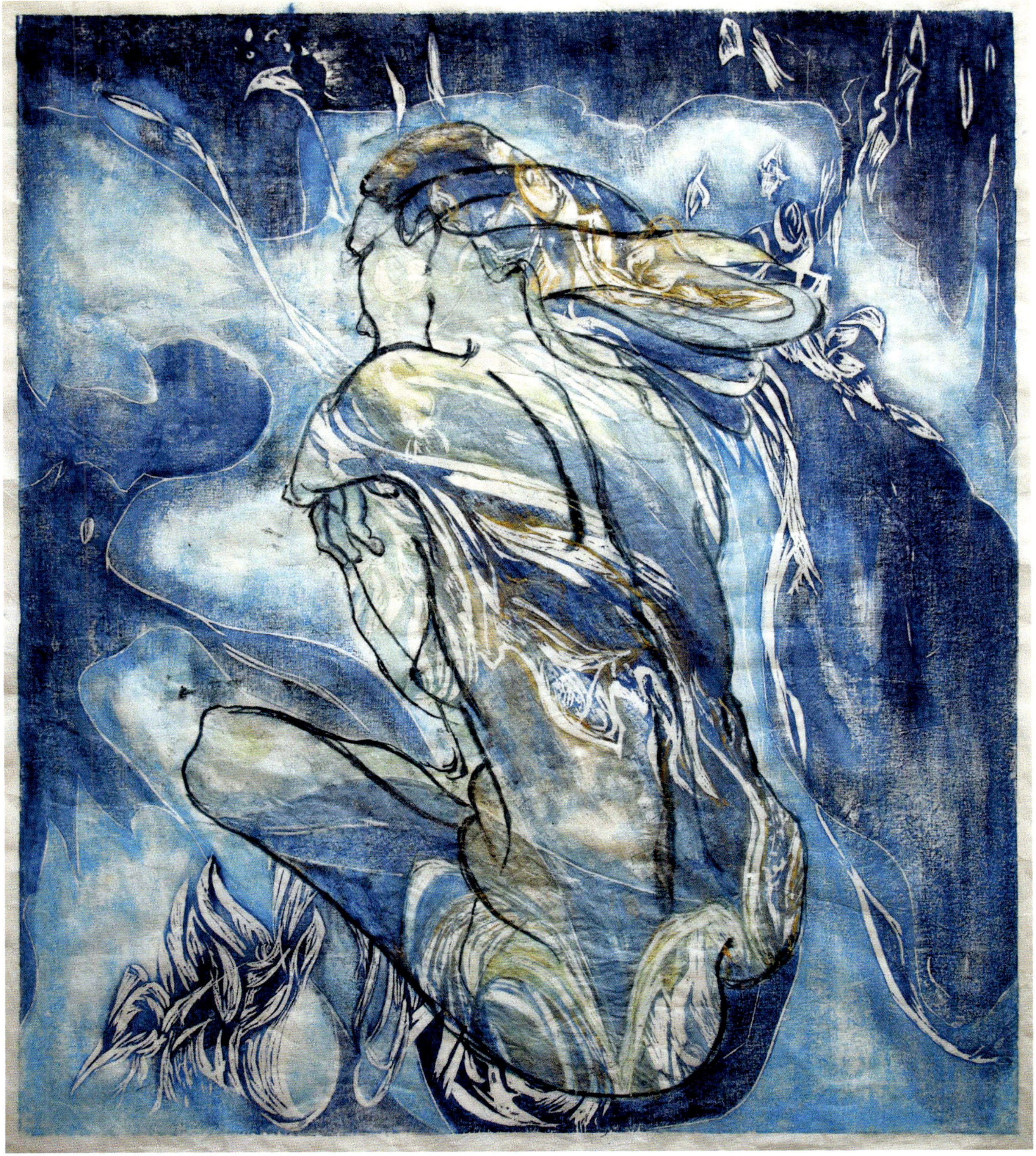

Jill Bray

Jill uses elements of landscape and man's marks on it to express her fascination with the edges of the land and the landmass. It is both abstract and referential. The texture created by collographic means, and actual collages, emphasise the relationship with the archaeology of ancient sites in Southern England. The physical manipulation of carborundum and ink mirrors the traces of land usage over many years.

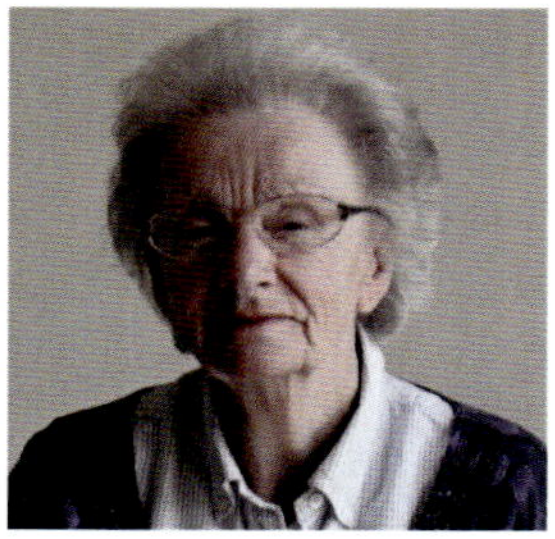

Dip Ed., Bishop Otter College, Chichester
Dip Fine Art, Southampton College of Art
Printmaking courses at Michael Honnor's Studio

Two Women Artists exhibitions
Chichester University, Southampton University, Bedales Gallery.

Open Exhibitions
Open Printmaking Exhibition, RWA Bristol.
National Print Exhibition, Mall Galleries
Art of the Printmaker, Royal Festival Hall
Contemporary Prints, Scarborough
Aspex Open (prize winner)
See the Prints, National Theatre, London
Contemporary Painting and Prints, Barbican Centre
The Half Imperial Show, Scarborough
The Big Thaw, Open, Brighton
Open Printmaking Exhibition, Scarborough
Millfield Open
Chichester Open (highly commended), Winchester University
Southampton Art Gallery Open
Red House, Christchurch
Highcliffe Castle
Oxmarket Chichester
Works on Paper, Barbican
Farnham, New Ashgate Gallery.

Work is held in private collections and at Hampshire County Arts Office, Chichester and Southampton Universities.

Member of PmC and 2d3dSouth

I studied Art and Music at Bishop Otter College, Chichester. At the time I was supposed to be more musical than artistic. However, the music tutor was useless whereas the art tutor was inspiring. Not only did Miss McCririck encourage my painting, but she was collecting Henry Moore drawings and Peter Lanyon paintings amongst others, for the College collection. I would pass these amazing images every morning and they affected me deeply.

Having finished the teacher training, I found a 3-year part-time Fine Art course at Southampton College of Art. Not only did we draw, paint and have lectures on History of Art, but in the third year we could choose to do printmaking. I was hooked.

I then had an idyllic holiday in Devon at Michael Honnor's Studio. At the time I was adding collage to my paintings. It was Michael who suggested collaging the prints and mentioned the word – collograph! I enjoyed two more holidays at his studio working from morning to late evening. Luckily, Mike Griffiths hired out his studio near Arlesford, and I took advantage of this for several years. This really made me produce larger prints as I often had the studio to myself and I could 'spread' my work without disturbing anyone else.

Then, a dear friend left me her press. Luckily I had a utility room with a solid floor so the scene was set. During the last four years I have been clearing my plan chest which was becoming overwhelmed with prints. As I was sorting the wheat from the chaff, I happened to see two contrasting prints adjacent to each other. One had a torn edge, yet complemented the other. That reminded me of cliff strata and edges of land meeting the sea, our holidays in Cornwall as children, climbing rocks to get to a remote beach. I have pushed this idea further by using torn pieces of my prints to create images that remind me of landscape and yet are also about creating a print.

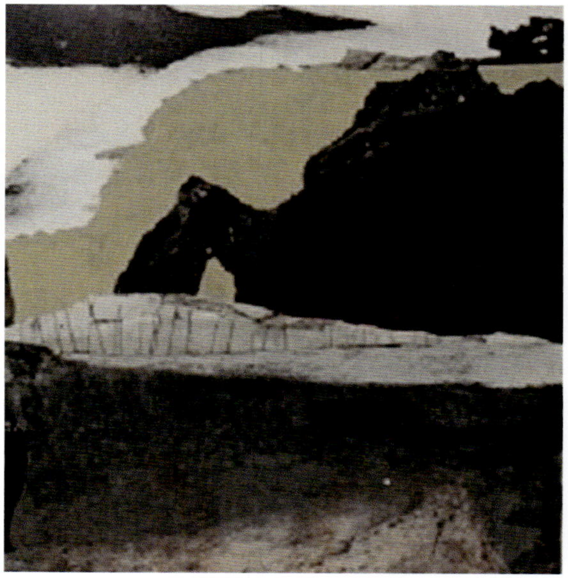

Slice 2, collage of original prints, 43 x 50 cm, unique

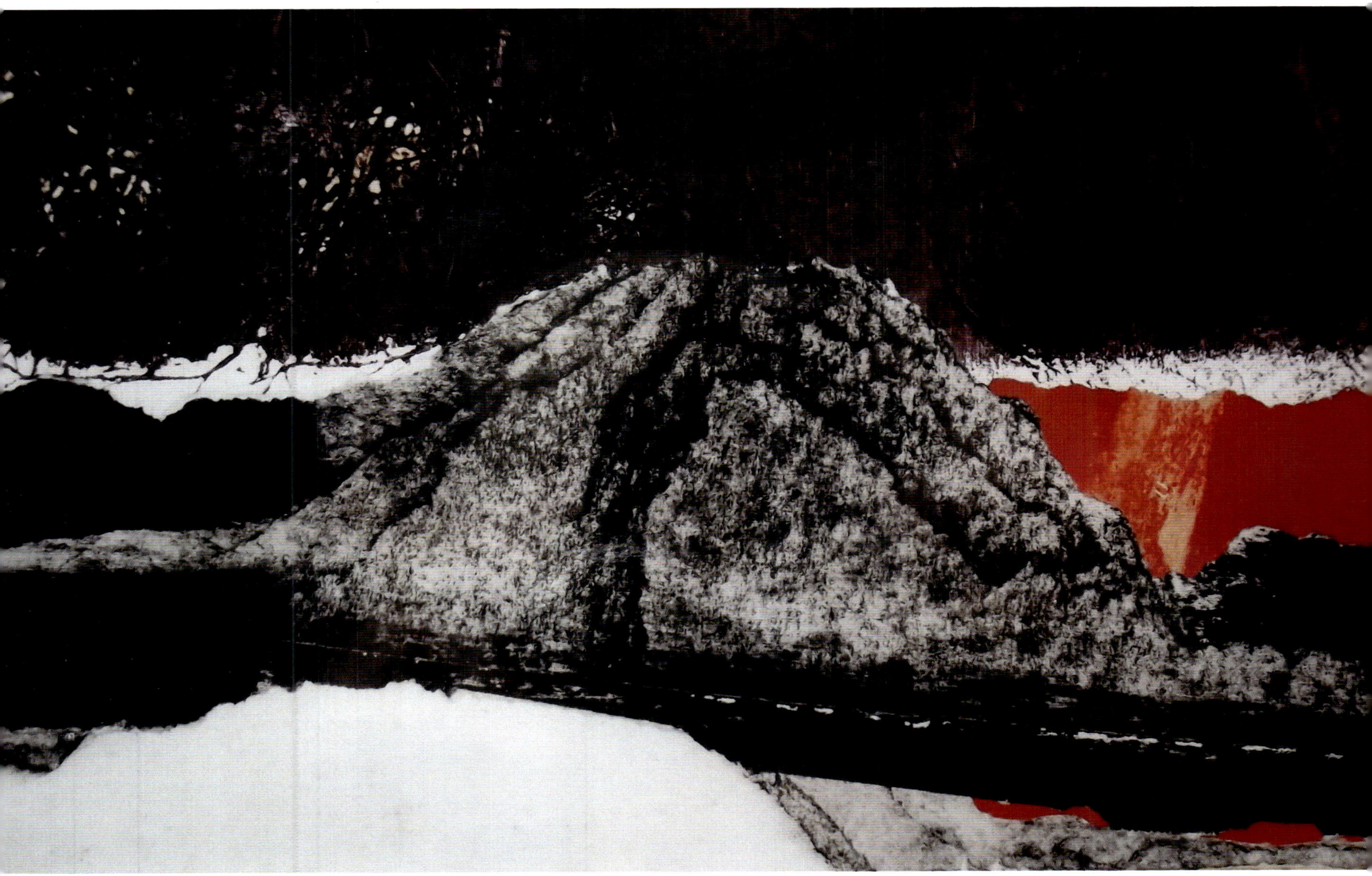

Cove, collograph and chine collé, 56 x 49 cm, unique

Angela Brookes

My first introduction to printmaking was at the Central School of Art where I was studying Ceramics. One day each week we were able to visit other departments and I chose the etching room. The whole process was a revelation to me, and I was seduced by the magical quality of ink transferred onto paper under intense pressure. I knew it would be something I would return to.

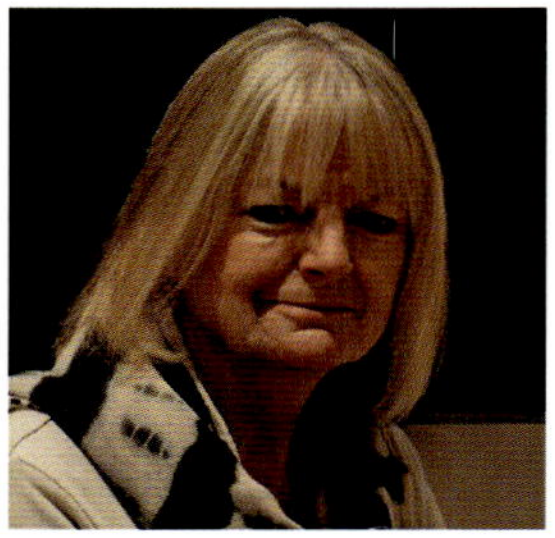

Education
1968–70 Central School of Art, London
1971–72 London University

Exhibitions
2009 *Open* Royal West of England Academy, Bristol
2009 *30 Years, 30 Artists*, The Oxo Gallery,
2009 *Lasting Impressions*, National Theatre,
2011 *Bite* Mall Galleries
2011 *Second Impressions*, National Theatre
2013 *A Reflection in Print*, Highgate Gallery
2014 *Dulwich Open*, Dulwich Picture Gallery,
2014 Prints Commissioned for Brunei Hotel London
2010–15 *SWA Annual*, Mall Galleries,
2015 Jack House Gallery, Portsmouth
2015 *50/50*, New Ashgate Gallery, Farnham
2015 *Works on Paper*, Barbican Library
2015 *50 Years of Artists Prints*, Bankside Gallery, London

Professional Membership
Printmakers Council
Greenwich Printmakers
Southbank Printmakers
National Society of Painters, Sculptors and Printmakers

Having worked with clay for most of my professional life, I now find my printmaking work is foremost in my practice. My interest centres mostly on the natural world. I frequently visit the coasts of Norfolk and Suffolk and am drawn to the vast and unpopulated open spaces and huge skies, so typical of this area. I work 'en plein air' in the fields and on the marshes working first in pastel, simply sketching and observing. These drawings are an emotional response to the subject and feed both my printmaking and my imagination. My prints explore the glory and the mystery of the landscape both rural and urban. I enjoy depicting the ever-changing effects of light and colour at different times of the day and as the seasons roll through the year. I love the reversal of all the tonal qualities of the landscape after snow has fallen, and the effect of the evening light, in all seasons, has a particular resonance for me.

I work from my own studio using my Bewick press. I have developed some unorthodox processes which suit my working set-up. My favoured printing process is etching, using soft ground, aquatint and spit-bite, sometimes using two plates. I love the qualities of aquatint, where with just a few second intervals in the acid, it is possible to create gently changing tonal values. I am captivated by the deep intensity of the ink, where the paper and the ink become one. In addition, I employ drypoint and carborundum, again often using two plates, which also produce deep rich blacks. Here the editions are smaller, often only 5–10. I like to vary the wiping on these plates, so that each print is unique, hence 'ev', 'edition variable'. More recently, I have been experimenting with colour, using two plates with dry point, carborundum and monoprint, and each print is individual. I hope to extend the use of monoprint as I find it so exciting with each print offering something different. I am also experimenting with intaglio gravure plates which provide me with yet another set of rules and further horizons to explore.

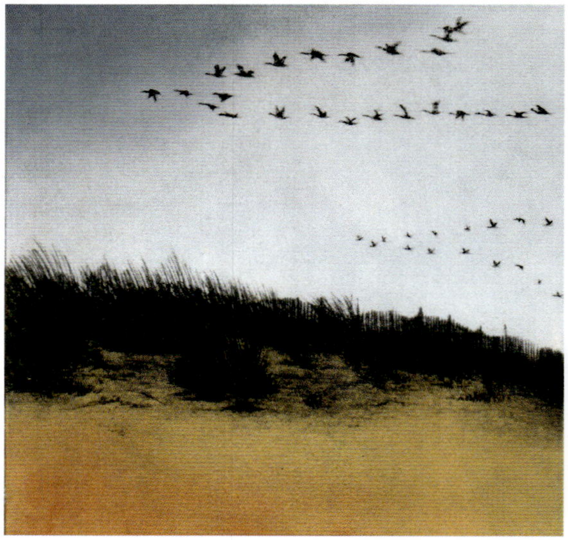

Coastal Skeins, 18 x 18 cm, intaglio gravure & monoprint (edition of 30, variable)

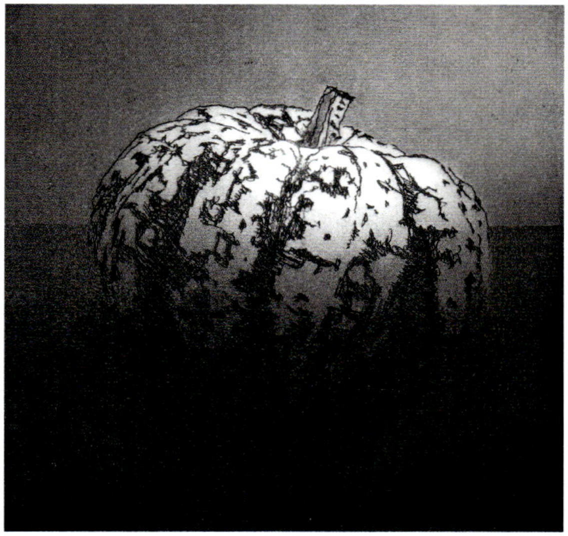

Ornamental Gourd, 15 x 15 cm, etching (edition of 40)

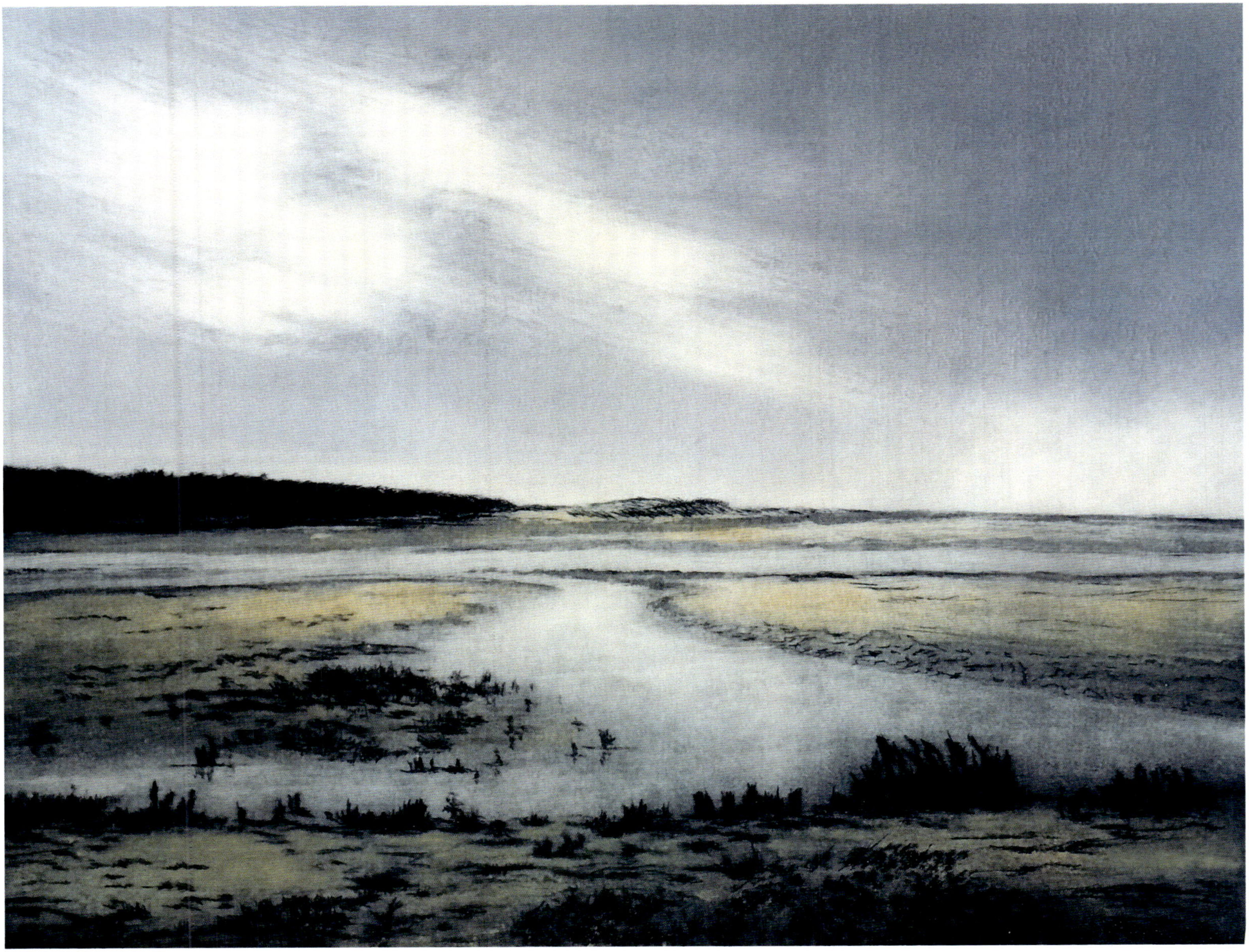

Water's Edge, 46 x 36 cm, drypoint & monoprint (edition of 10, variable)

David Brown

My first visit to Italy, in the sixties, was like an awakening, opening my eyes to art and architecture. I recorded my impressions using photography and later, intensifying the experience, by drawing. It was a natural step then, after a career as a mathematician, to use the analytical and programming skills I had acquired to produce more imaginative artworks, in the form of original prints.

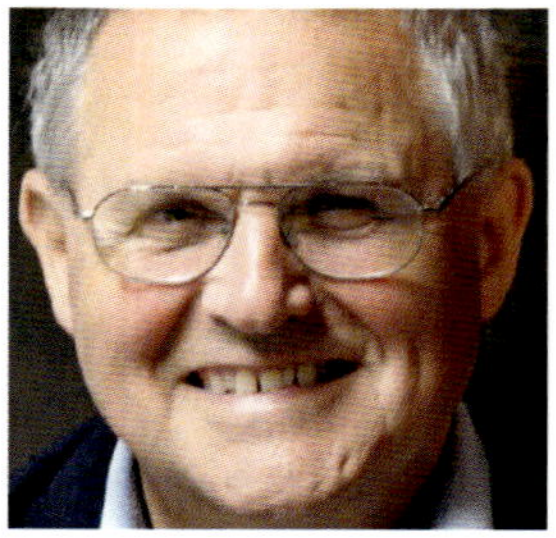

1963–66 BSc Mathematics, Durham University

1966–67 MSc Statistics, Imperial College, London

1968–2004 Career as a Mathematician working in Biology and Neuroscience

2002–06 Studied Printmaking & Art History, Cambridge School of Art

2006–14 Committee member, Printmakers Council

2006 *Originals 06 exhibition* (Open Competition) Mall Galleries, London

2006 Royal Birmingham Society of Artists Print Prize Exhibition (Open Competition)

2008 *Ropewalk Open* (Open Competition)

2008 *Eastern Open*, Kings Lynn Art Centre, (Open Competition). Thor Adam Goodall Memorial Award for Prints and Etchings

2008 *Originals 08* exhibition (Open Competition) Mall Galleries, London

2008 Royal Birmingham Society of Artists Print Prize Exhibition (Open Competition)

2009 *David Brown Prints*, Solo exhibition, Sredetz Gallery, Ministry of Culture, Sofia, Bulgaria

2009 Solo commissioned print exhibition to celebrate the Scientific Research of the Centre for Integrative Physiology, Edinburgh University

2010 Joined Cambridge Arts Movement

2013 *Metamorphosis – Abstract & Architectural Prints*, Solo Exhibition, Williams Art, Cambridge

Architectural spaces still excite me, from the serene beauty of ancient Greek temples to the edgy, nervy buildings of architects like Borromini in Rome, and our own, equally eccentric Hawksmoor, and on, further, to the work of powerful contemporary architects such as Norman Foster. Transmitting this excitement is an important motivator of my art.

Original methods for the abstracts in the *Metamorphosis* series arose from a further experience of the art of another culture: the complex Islamic patterns in the decoration of the Alhambra in Granada. I modified their systematic patterns by the use of contingent elements to soften their rigidity and regularity. Later studies of abstract form and organic pattern developed naturally out of this, and as a result of my previous professional interest in biological systems.

My digital methods (written in JAVA) are complex, and each new print entails much experimentation and development. One technique involves using the tonal density in an initial image (a photograph or painting, say) to determine characteristics of drawn marks in the final print. For example, the density, size, or colour of the marks may be made proportional to tonality in the initial image. A possible further, playful element encodes other aspects of the first (or an entirely different) image within the final print. This encoding may be minimal, or may be so cryptic that it is difficult to interpret the image in its original sense – in one recent print an image of a family group was so cryptically encoded that it was first interpreted as a storm at sea.

A further strand to my work stems from a fascination with perception – of form, of space, but particularly of colour. An undergraduate psychology course first revealed to me the peculiarities of our colour vision. State-of-the-art digital methods, together with high quality inkjet printing, allowed me to develop experimental techniques for highlighting these idiosyncrasies, and achieving more powerful colour rendering.

Some of the resulting prints contain echoes of the works of pointillists such as Signac and Seurat, and the experiments of the abstract artist Josef Albers.

Most recent has been a voyage into portraiture and our perception of ourselves – an exploration of limits, of how fragile a personality can be in its response to depiction, and the opposite, how a personality can refuse to disappear, even though its portrait hardens to granite, or all but vanishes into randomness and space.

Thirty Saint Mary Axe, 41 x 27 cm, digital/inkjet (edition of 50)

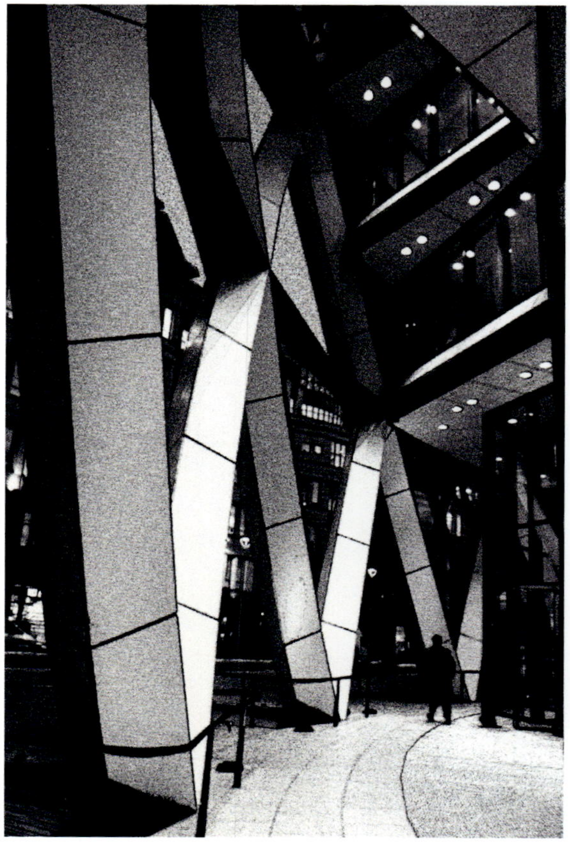

OPPOSITE:
Metamorphosis 26, 44 x 32cm, digital/inkjet (edition of 50)

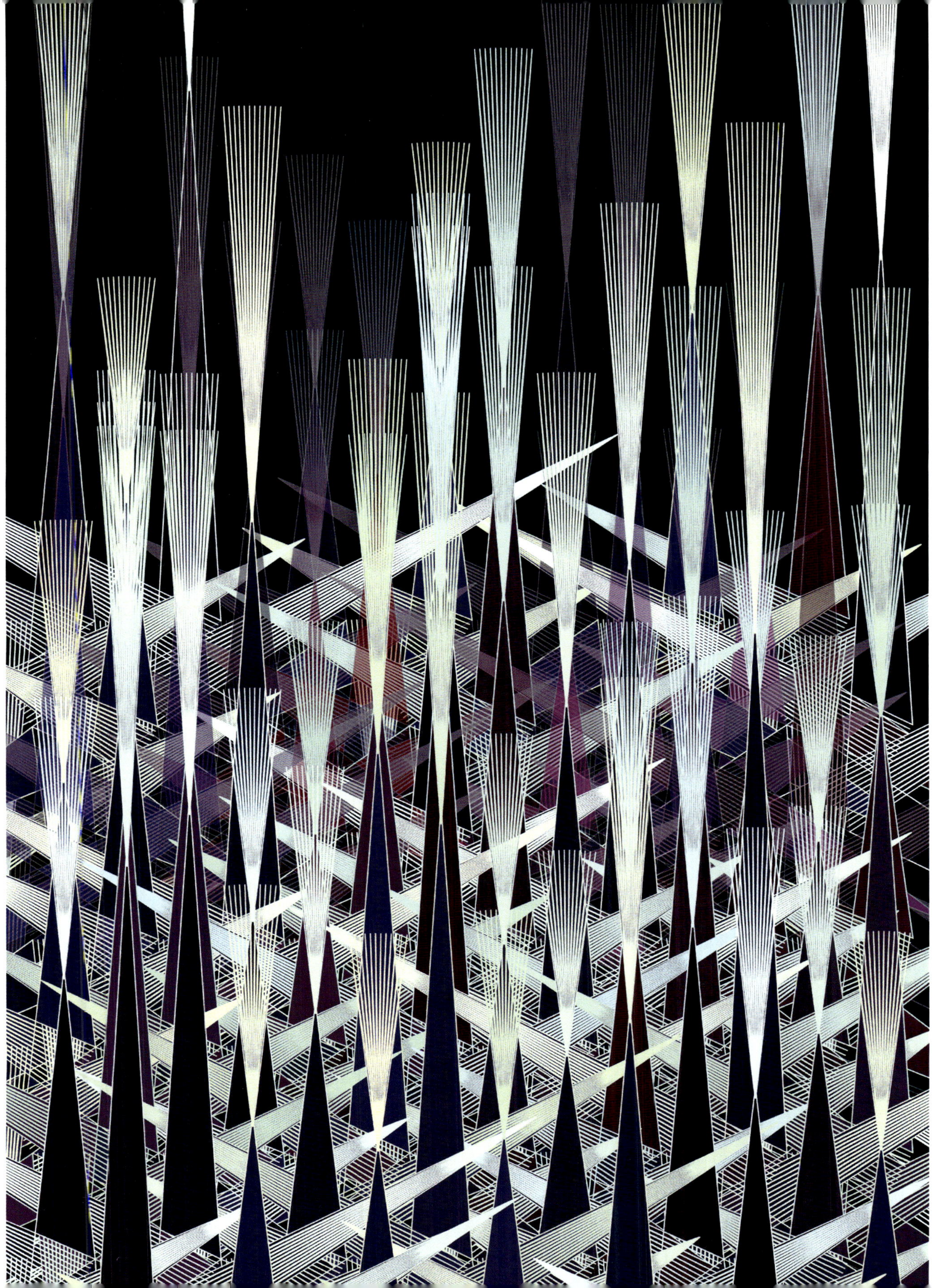

Dilys Bryon

I have made studies from Nature ever since leaving Art School, and developed these towards abstract images through painting. Studying etching and mezzotint with Mark Balakjian at Morley College, and the Hayter Method in Paris, (working from random beginnings directly onto the etching plate, and printing many colours from one plate), enabled me to pursue this rewarding process further.

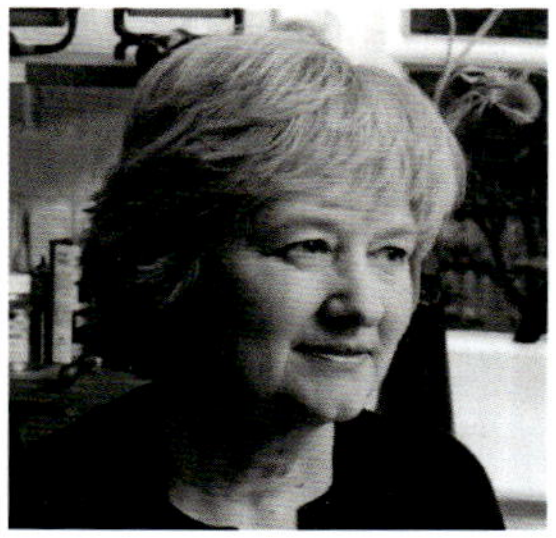

1930 Born West Bridgford, Nottingham
1947–51 NDD, Wimbledon School of Art
1951–52 ATD, London University Institute of Education
1974–78 Morley College: Etching & Mezzotint
1991 Atelier Contrepoint, Paris: Hayter Method
1997–2001 BA (Hons) French, Birkbeck College, London University
1952–54 Head of Art, Croham Hurst School, South Croydon
1965–70 Adult Education Art Teaching

Solo Exhibitions (selected)
1978 Gallery 20, Brighton
1995 Pump House Gallery, London
2014 The First Gallery, Southampton

Group Exhibitions
1999, 2000 *The Contemporary Print Show*, Barbican, London
2001 *Fresh Art*, Business Design Centre
2010 PmC at Bankside Gallery, London
2015 *50 Years of Artists Prints*, Bankside

Open Exhibitions
1985–91 Royal Society of Painter–Etchers
1985 *Cabo Frio International Print Biennale*, Brazil
1991 *Contemporary British Printmaking*, Lviv, Ukraine
1994–95 Royal West of England Academy
1995 *National Open Print Exhibition*, London
2004 *Originals 04*, Mall Galleries, London

Collections: Embragel University, Cabo Frio, Brazil. Brunel University, London. Tamar Art University, Japan

My Art School style involved objective drawing, and figure composition leading to mural paintings based on the work of the early Italian School, especially Giotto. After having a family I continued drawing, but feeling the need of a change of style, I worked on some large geometric paintings, which were bold and colourful. These led me to approach objective painting in a new way, with more emphasis on abstract qualities.

Starting to learn the processes of etching and mezzotint fed into this trend, and accidental effects became more important to me than simply reproducing drawings. Even more crucial was the practise of starting from random marks and lines directly onto the plate, a method reinforced when I studied the Hayter Method at Atelier Contrepoint, Paris, in 1991. Using multiple colours on one plate was an essential aspect of this method of printing etchings.

More recently, monoprint has become a way of using paintings and drawings made on trips to France and the West Country as a basis for prints. The process leads to a more spontaneous and simplified image than the original, as the print must be taken while the ink is still wet. Working quickly is essential, and has led me to a semi- abstract style in which I feel the influence of Post-Impressionist paintings, especially those of Paul Gaugin, Emile Nolde, and Kandinsky's Murnau paintings. Kandinsky's *Concerning the Spiritual in Art* is an important influence. These artists appeal to me because they show an art that is other than descriptive realism, an art of ideas and of the emotions.

I had become a member of the Printmakers Council in 1980, and joined the Committee in 1984, becoming Vice-Chairman in 1988, and Chairman from 1989/90. It was a way of getting to know other printmakers, especially when organising exhibitions, of which I curated a number while working for the PmC. Their first exhibition in Paris was one such, an exciting experience with good sales of members' prints.

For a fuller account of the development of my work from observational to abstraction, see *Outside Eye, Inside Eye* by Derek Banham and Dilys Bryon and *Idea and Process, A discussion of her colour etchings by Dilys Bryon*, both MGF publications.

OPPOSITE
Moonlit Cruciform, mezzotint, 17.8 cm x 15.3 cm (edition of 25)

Molten Sea and Sky, etching (Hayter Method), 29.3 cm x 39.3 cm (edition of 30)

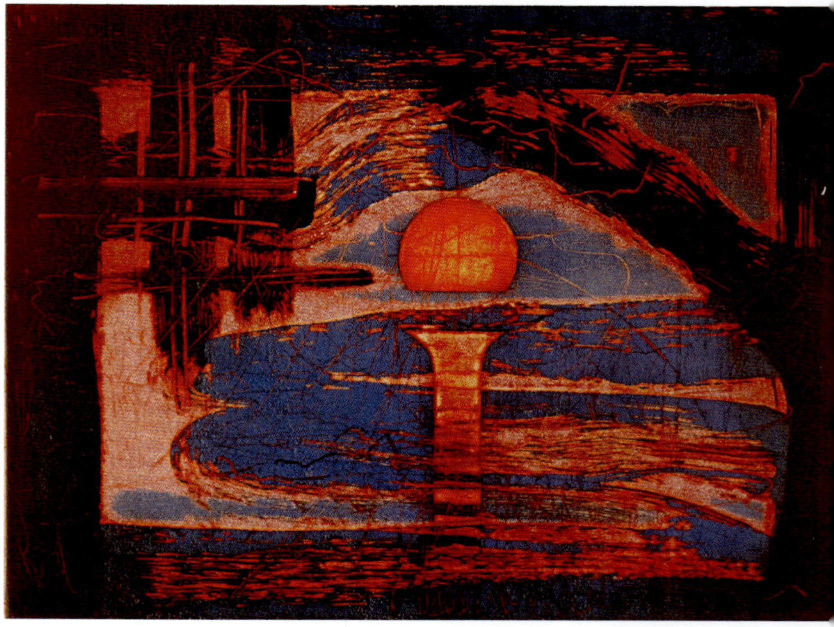

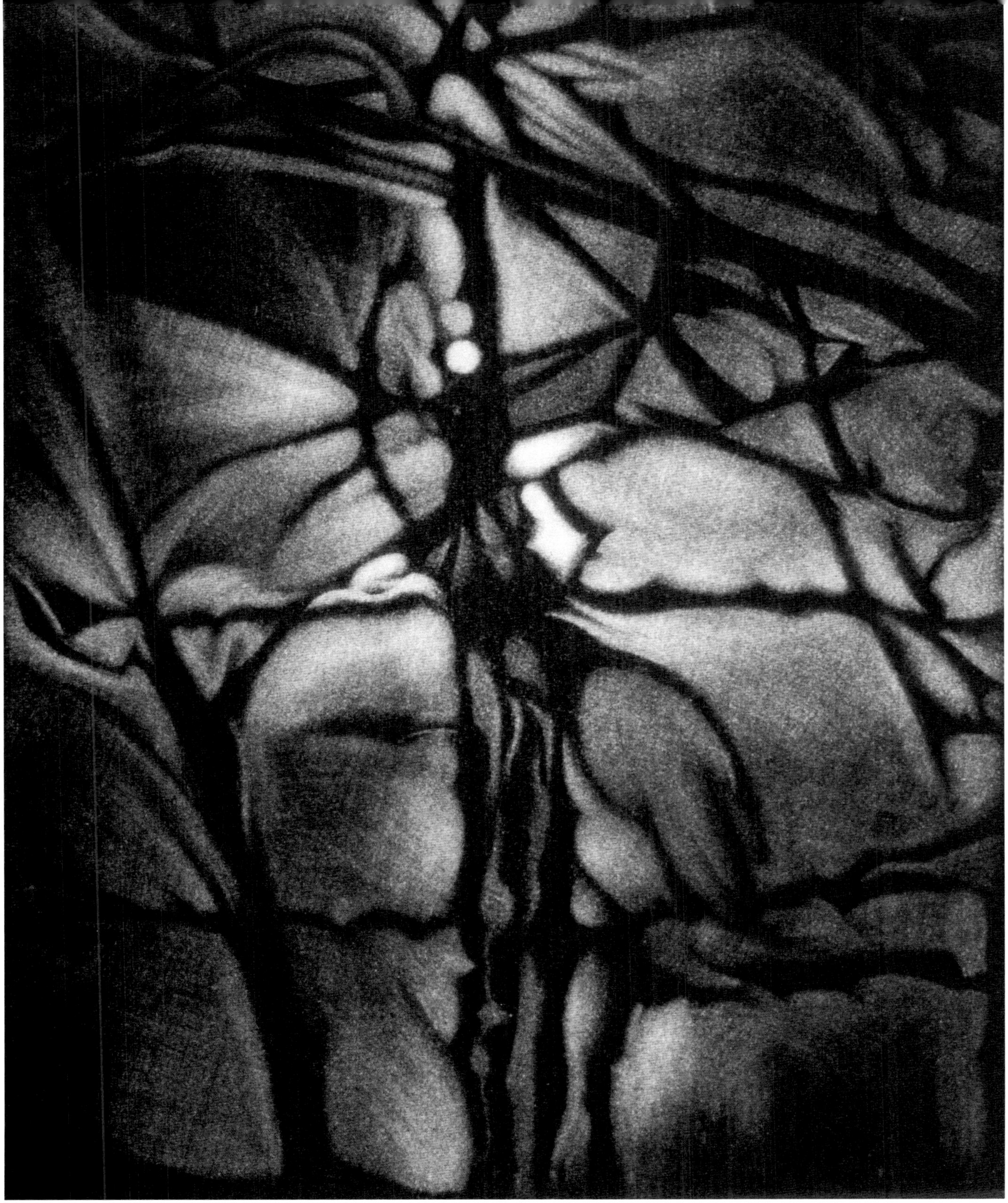

Emma Buckmaster

My prints are about the atmospheric and evocative aspects of the landscape that I encounter. I studied printmaking at the Cambridge School of Art and specialized in etching for my MA. I now work full-time from my own studio in Suffolk.

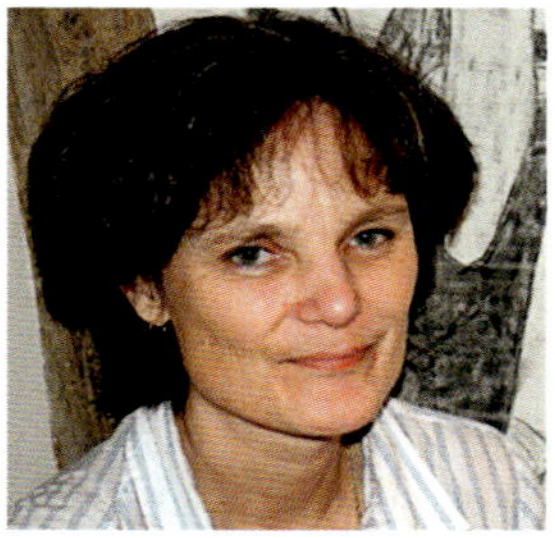

1957 born UK
1976–79 BA (Hons) Economics
2000–03 BA (Hons) History of Modern Art
2006–09 MA Printmaking, Cambridge School of Art
2009 Ruskin Gallery, Cambridge. The Forum, Norwich. Elected Member Suffolk Craft Society
2009–12 Chair (Joint) Gainsborough's House Printmakers
2010 Printmakers Council, Bankside. Peter Pears Gallery, Aldeburgh. *Re:mark*, Brighton Art Fair.
2011 *Palace Art Fair*, Fulham.
2012 Norwich Castle, *Selected East Anglian Artists. Eastern Open.* Solo exhibition Assembly House, Norwich.
2013 *Gainsborough's House Printmakers Exhibition. Royal Academy Summer Exhibition.* Solo exhibition Naze Tower. Suffolk Showcase, Smiths Row
2013–14 *8th British International Mini Print Exhibition. Art in Action, Best of the Best*, Oxford.
2014 *Cambridge City Art Fair. Liverpool Contemporary Art Fair. The Affordable Art Fair* Battersea. National Horseracing Museum, Newmarket. *The Affordable Art Fair*, Brussels. Residency at Cill Rialaig, Ireland.
2015 Tutor for Etching Course at Gainsborough's House.
2015 Anniversary Exhibition lecture for Orwell Park. Solo exhibition Grapevine Gallery. Selected *Royal Academy Summer Exhibition.*

I initially studied prints as an art historian and then I began to try the different techniques myself. Gradually the printmaking took over and when I was offered the opportunity to study part-time for an MA in Printmaking at the Cambridge School of Art, I accepted. This was a wonderful time and a group of twelve of us became friends and began to exhibit together under the name 'Re:mark.'

Whilst at Cambridge I started to use the print workshop at Gainsborough's House, which was nearer to home for me. I also joined their exhibition committee. In 2009 Janet French and I jointly took over the chairmanship of the group. We used the opportunity to raise the profile of the workshop and to organise exhibitions and monthly talks. We also introduced the Gainsborough Prize for Graduate Printmakers.

In 2012 we helped to organise a major print exhibition in Gainsborough's House selected and curated by Stanley Jones and Juliet Bowmaker, with an accompanying publication *The Coach House in Gainsborough's Garden* by Miranda Mott.

During this time, Janet French and I began a collaborative printmaking project to create a series of British Tree Portraits and we are still working together on this. We choose the trees and design the images together and then I make an etching of the tree and Janet prepares paper made from the leaves of the tree. We are slowly adding to this series. Each new portrait requires lengthy paper trials and research. We have demonstrated and spoken about this project together at Art in Action and other venues.

In 2014 I was awarded a Residency at Cill Rialaig in Ireland. This has inspired a new series of prints, leading to a solo exhibition at the Grapevine Gallery in Norfolk. I am an elected member of the Suffolk Craft Society and a visiting tutor at Gainsborough's House Print workshop.

I principally work with etching and I like to experiment with the many different techniques. For landscapes I tend to use zinc or aluminium plates but for the Tree Portraits I always use steel and nitric acid. I sometimes paint the plate using a sugar lift or I will transfer an image using photo etch resist. I tend to restrict my palette to blacks and sea blues. Most of my work is about the emotional response that we have to the landscape around us.

Isabel Blue, etching, 42 x 56 cm (variable edition of 5)

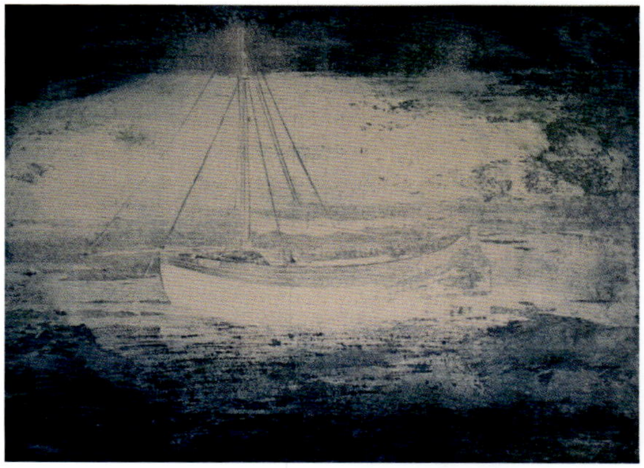

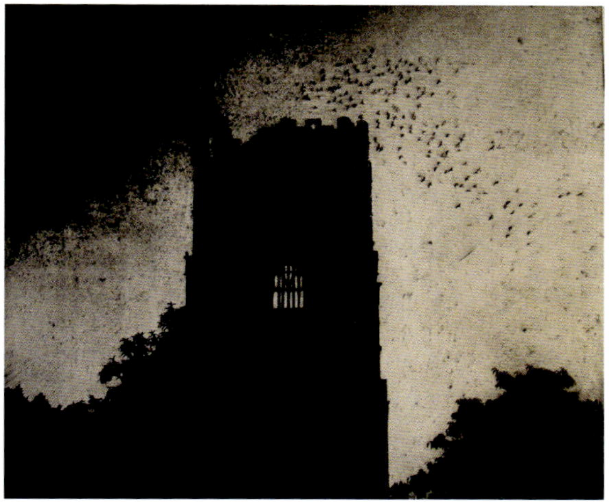

Evening, etching, 28 x 33 cm (edition of 20)

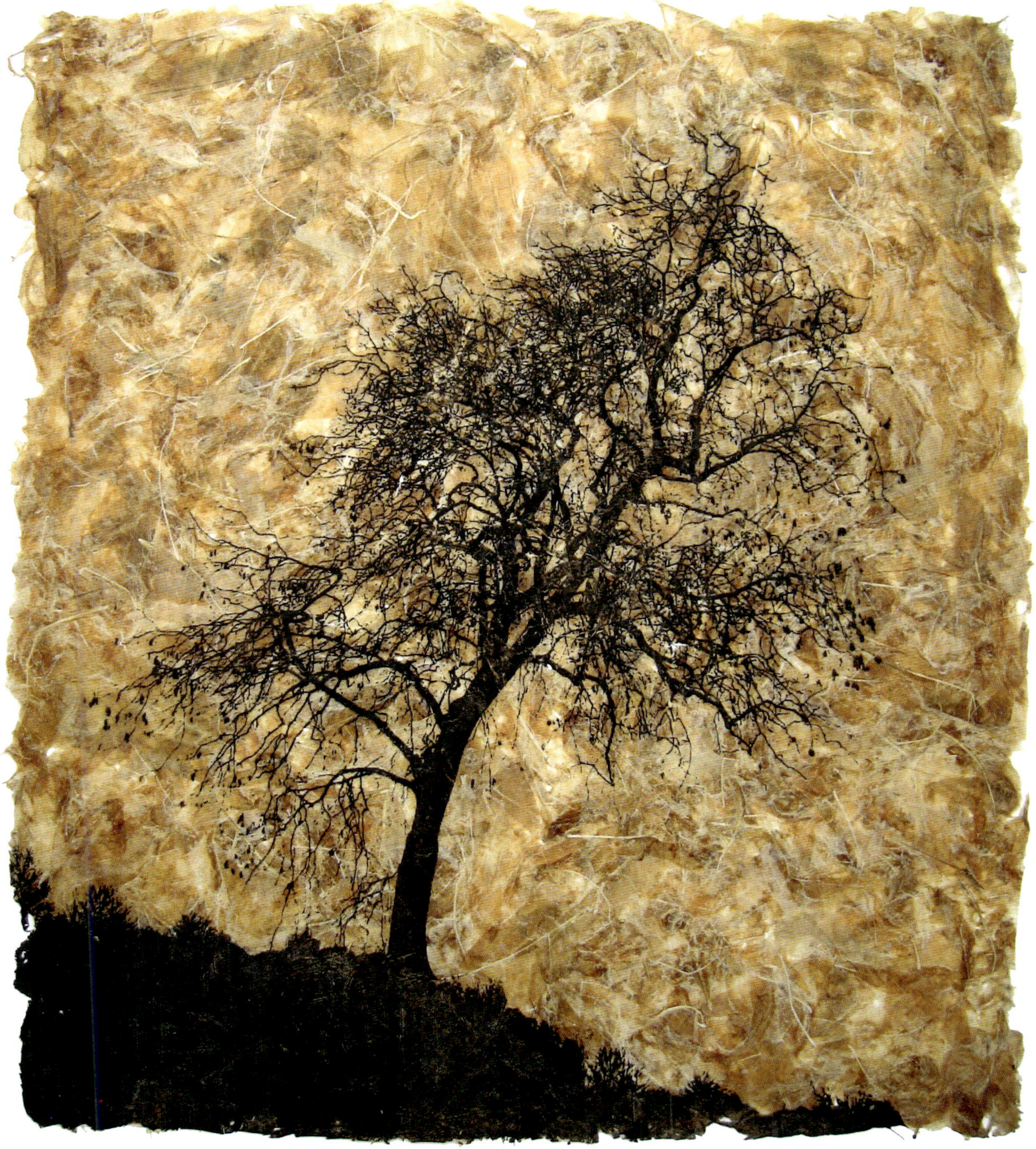

Fraxinus Excelsior, etching on ash leaves (Buckmaster-French), 62 x 54 cm (edition of 10)

Jess Bugler

Jess lives and works in Conwy, North Wales. She works in print, line and paint to grapple with life in the modern world. Her linocut prints are produced using the reduction method in very limited editions. They are intentionally intricate prints that aim to reveal the intensity and density of their subjects.

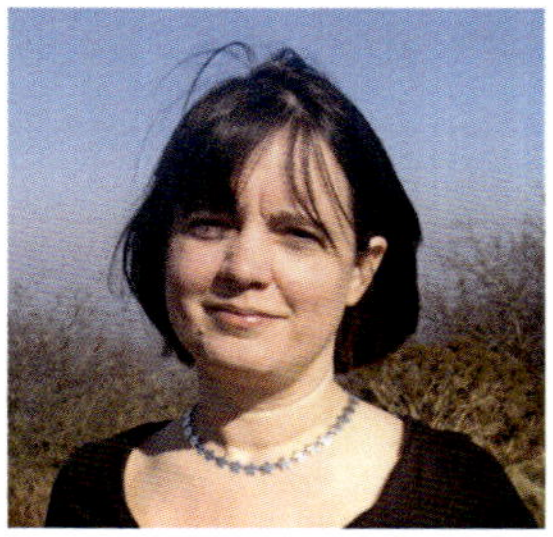

Awards

Winner of the Printmaking Today prize at the *National Original Print* exhibition 2014

Winner of the Regional Print Centre award at the National Original Print exhibition 2014

Shortlisted for the Printmaking Today prize at the *International Print Biennale*, Newcastle

Winner of the People's Choice award at *Freshly Pressed*, Printmakers Council exhibition, London, 2014.

Highly Commended in *Royal Cambrian Academy Open* exhibition 2014

Neo:Print prize 2014

Exhibitions

2014 *From Here and There: Drawings from Swansea to Colorado*, Clara Hatton Gallery, Colorado State University, Colorado USA, and Elysium Gallery, Swansea, Wales.
Gallery 22, The Market Place, Bolton
National Original Print Exhibition, Bankside Gallery, London
International Print Biennale, Newcastle, England
Freshly Pressed exhibition of new prints by The Printmakers Council in London

2015 *Caffi Celf*, Oriel Mostyn, Llandudno, Wales
National Welsh Assembly, Cardiff
Works on Paper, City of London Barbican Library
Helfa Gelf Artists, Oriel Gallery, Clywd Theatr Cymru, Mold

I explore images and ideas through drawing, painting, sculpture and printmaking in my art practice and experiment with the same theme in different mediums as I try and work through what I am trying to convey. However I seem to be continually drawn to the medium of print and in particular to linocuts. I love the strength of line that linocuts allow, and its solidity and power.

My current work is based on the war in Syria. In my prints of Aleppo and Homs I want to convey the darkness and chaos of war, where the structures of the urban landscape are distorted by bombing and emptied of people. The destructive reality. In the modern world of 24-hour news, images of Syria flick past our eyes and may briefly rattle our consciences. However I hope it is when we stop and contemplate work in the space of an art gallery that we can start to comprehend the brutality of what is occurring on a deeper level.

The absence of people is key in these images. Homs and Aleppo have been virtually depopulated by the war with ten million people displaced. The prints are records of absence and loss and the fragility of all our lives.

I have also recently made a series of clay heads inspired by Rembrandt's *Nightwatch* – then by photographing them in strong light returned them into 2D as linocuts. They gaze at me with angst now. The link with the Syrian series is not direct but they came from a similar exploration of humanity.

Today we seem to have more information than ever before yet remain busy blocking out reality. As the poet Kate Tempest writes "to really see the state of things is lethal..." it is best "just to see what we can bear... much nicer to be bathing in the glare of all that we have built to shine and soothe us... what use are eyes, at all, in times like these?"

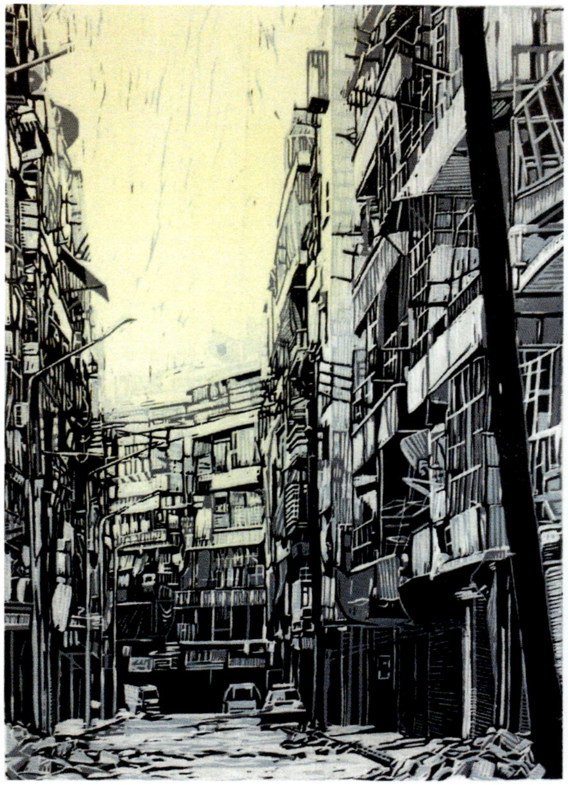

OPPOSITE PAGE

Homs II, reduction linocut, 40 x 40 cm (edition of 4)

THIS PAGE

Aleppo, reduction linocut, 32 x 42 cm (edition of 9)

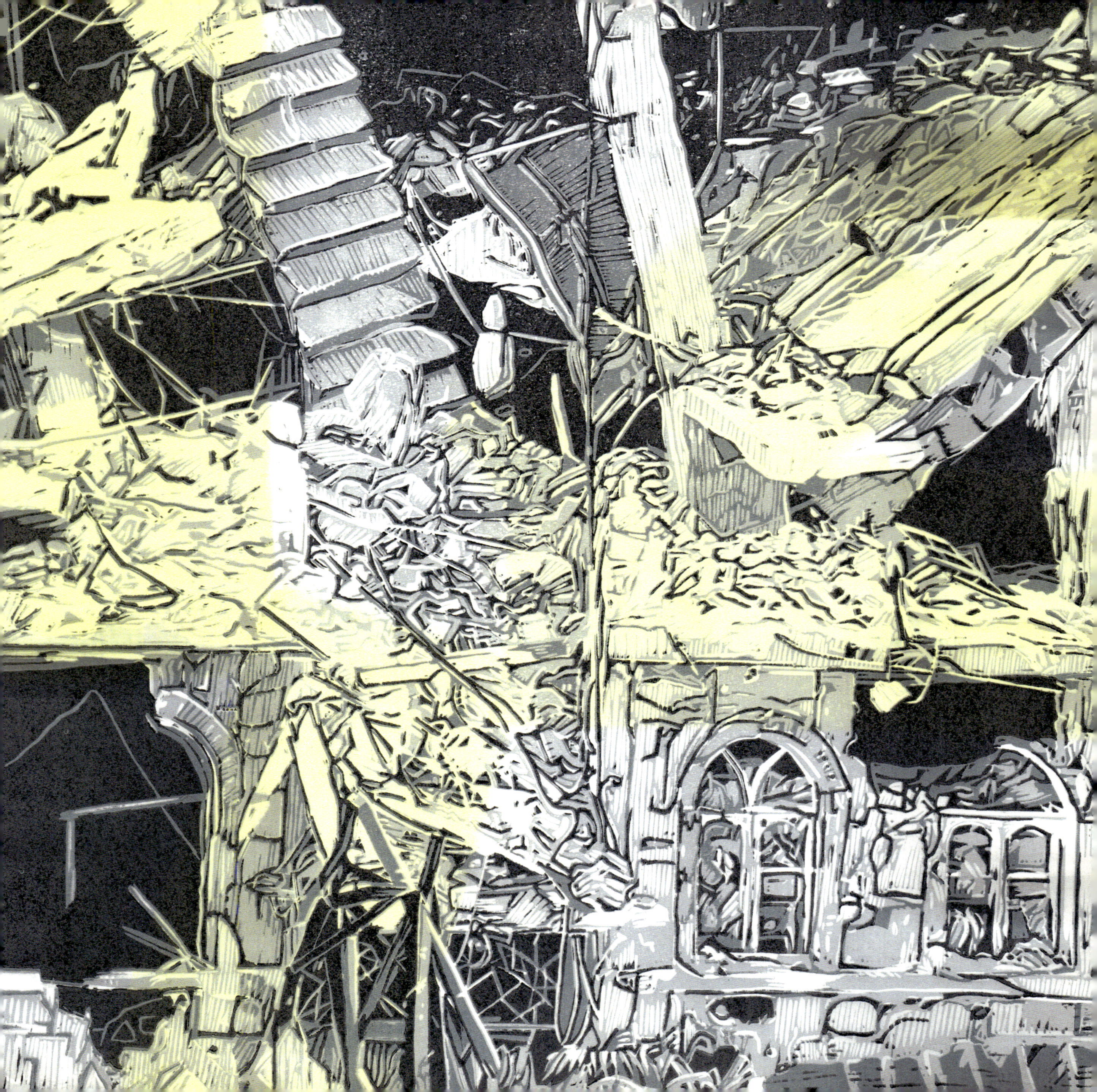

Gavin Iain Campbell

The demise of the cooling tower represents the loss of an aspect of industrial Britain from my grandfather's era. Their iconic shape may be disappearing but we should not forget cooling towers, as their form represents something just as impressive as their function.

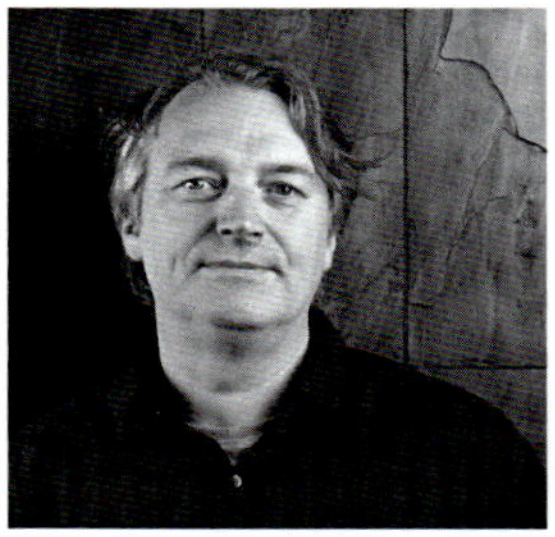

1961 Raised in Edinburgh
1979–80 Art and Design Foundation, Bath Lane, Newcastle-upon-Tyne
1980–83 BA (Hons) Fine Art Printmaking, Newcastle-upon-Tyne Polytechnic
1983 Solo show at The Netherbow, Royal Mile, Edinburgh
1983–86 Studied Finished Art and Reprographics while working in London
1983–present Employed by various printing and graphic arts companies
1989–91 Studied Intaglio printmaking at The Strand Centre, Elm Park, London
2010 Became a member of the West Yorkshire Print Workshop
2011 Joined Printmakers Council
2011–13 *Flourish*, West Yorkshire Print Workshop gallery
2013 *Royal Academy Summer Exhibition*
2014 *Art Station: Navigating Yorkshire*, Huddersfield
2014 *International Mini Print*, Seacourt Print Workshop, Bangor
2014 *Works on Paper*, Barbican Library, London
2015 *Hepworth Wakefield Print Fair*, Wakefield

For the last 16 years on my daily commute to work, I have passed Ferrybridge 'C' power station on the A1(M) and become aware of its strong significance in my life. Many of these power stations are being demolished but they still exist in clusters in the Aire Valley, Yorkshire, where power generation from coal continues. In the flat, featureless landscape around Selby they are the largest, most prominent landmarks around and you can navigate from Ferrybridge, Eggbrough and Drax power stations by sight. Most days they can be seen for thirty or forty miles but when there is a high-pressure system overhead and it is a cold, clear winter's day, their effect can be seen for a hundred miles.

For me as a printmaker, the repetitive image is a compelling one and was what attracted me to printmaking when I first attended art school. After being introduced to the industrial nature of Jim Dine, Eduardo Paolozzi and Andy Warhol's work, it was easy for me to choose printmaking as my primary artistic discipline.

To the observer an immediate impression is made by the repeating shape of the cooling towers combined with the effect they have on the atmosphere: acting as a local cloud generator and rainmaker – something I witnessed often when passing Ferrybridge – the impression is a powerful one. This power to change the atmosphere gives the cooling towers an added mythical significance and creates another interesting aspect, namely how these huge machines push an ascending cloud of water vapour into the chaos of the atmosphere. This brings me to cloud formation, something that also intrigues me. I am fascinated by how cloud patterns and shapes are made. Currently, I'm looking for ways to reproduce these effects in my etchings, and aiming to understand a bit about the chemistry and physics involved in both processes.

I recently noticed a similarity to the cooling tower in the ancient broch dwellings found in northern Scotland. Made of stone, they too are a good example of how made objects of natural materials can have their own inherent aesthetic quality and make an impression beyond their original purpose.

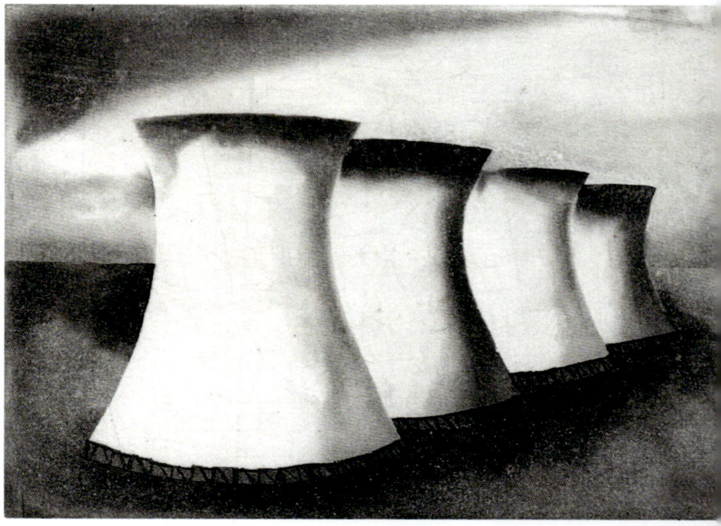

Yorkshire Power
copper-plate aquatint on
310g Hahnemuhle paper
12.5 cm x 18.7 cm
(edition of 75)

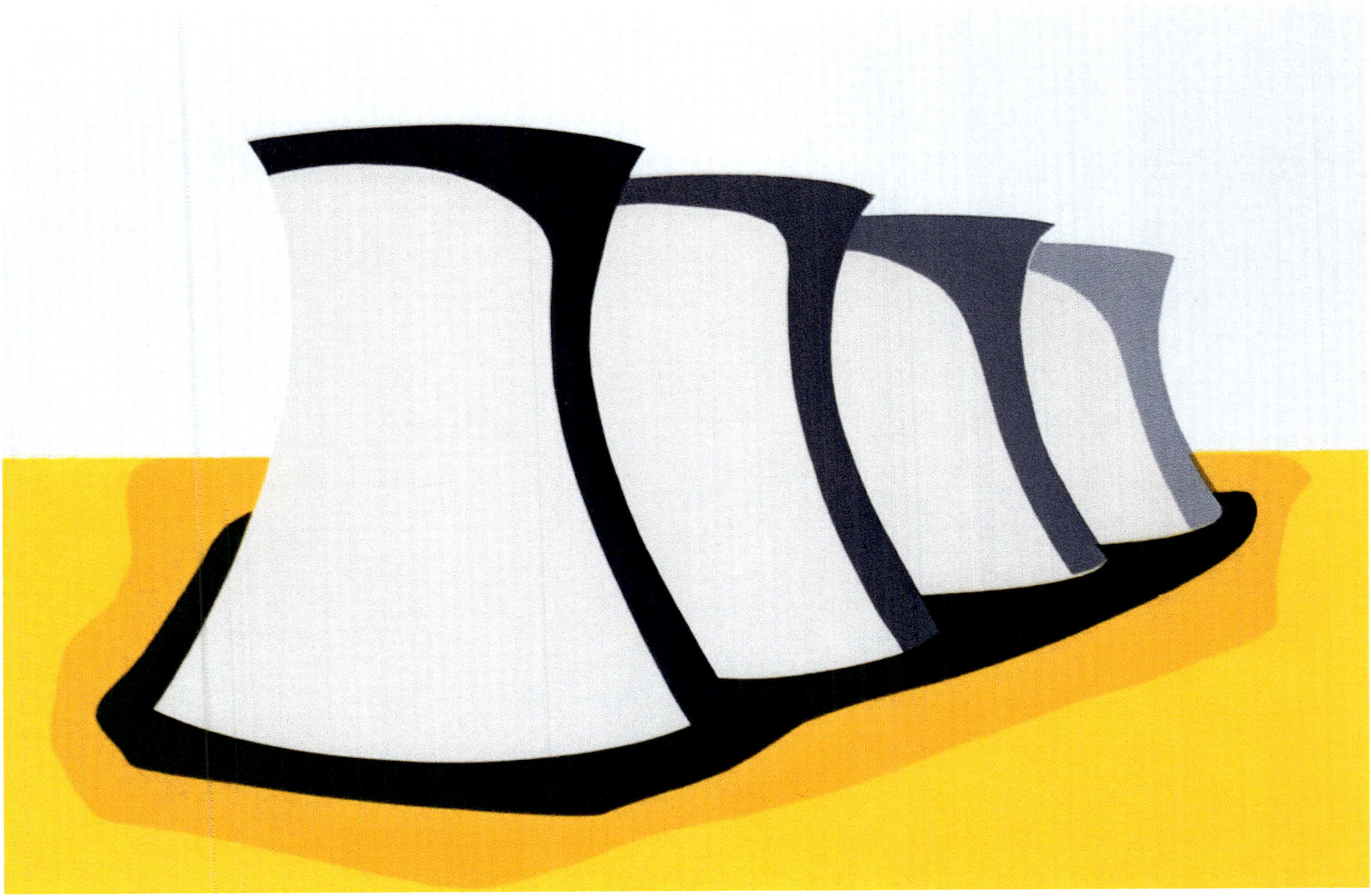

Faulty Towers, 20 x 30 cm, paper-cut stencil screen print on 300g Fabriano paper (edition of 12)

Dawn Cole

Having had a successful retailing career until 1998 I was in need of a change of direction and enrolled at college to complete a degree. Printmaking had always been an interest and I found myself drawn to it for the diversity of techniques that it offered.

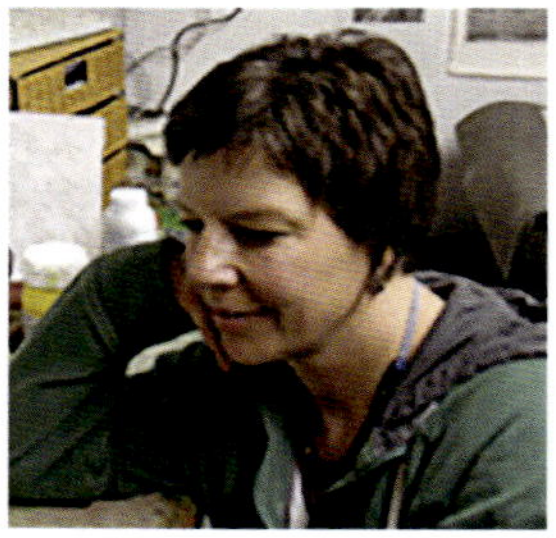

1964 Born
2003 Sculpture Commission, Kent and Canterbury Hospital
2003–05 BA (Hons) Fine Art, University of Kent
2005 Site-specific commission, University of Kent, Canterbury
2006–11 Editioner and studio technician
2009 Founder arts organisation Pushing Print
2010 *Out of Print?*, South Hill Park
2011 *International Print Biennale*, Newcastle Recipient of V&A Prize
2012 Print acquired by V&A. *6th International Kyoto Hanga Print Exhibition*, Japan. *Bite: Artists Making Prints*, Mall Galleries, London. *REOpen*, Bankside Gallery, London. Artist in residence, London Printworks Trust
Featured in book: *Artists Talking About Original Printmaking*, published by Circaidy Gregory Press.
2012–present Workshops for Turner Contemporary, Margate 2012/2014. Arts Council Grants for the Arts Award
2012–present *Resting Place* Touring Project
2013 Arts Foundation Fellowship Award for Printmaking, Runner-up.
2014 *Lace Effects 2*, International Centre for Lace, Calais. *Underexposed: Female Artists and the Medium of Print*, Studio 3 Gallery, Canterbury. *The Send-Off*, Knole House, Sevenoaks. *The Art of Remembering*, Rheged, Cumbria. *Remembering, We Forget*, Sidney Cooper Gallery, Canterbury. *Lacemakers*, Orleans House, Twickenham.
2015 *The Art of Remembering*, The Dock Museum, Barrow

My approach to printmaking I see as an exploration of the very nature of print: repetition, reversal, layering, transparency, opacity, texture, impression, process, presentation and display. Every idea, technique, material and means of display is carefully researched to ensure that each has a significance and relevance to the completed works.

My work is inspired by archives and since 2007 the archive of my Great Aunt, Clarice Spratling, a WWI Voluntary Aid Detachment (VAD) Nurse. Her archive contains a diary (written in 1915/16), a notebook containing handwritten lace patterns and remedies for ailments and photographs taken in France during WWI.

Some Poor Fellows Have Terrible Wounds, (from the *Reading Between the Lines* series) 23 x 19 cm, solar plate etch (edition of 5)

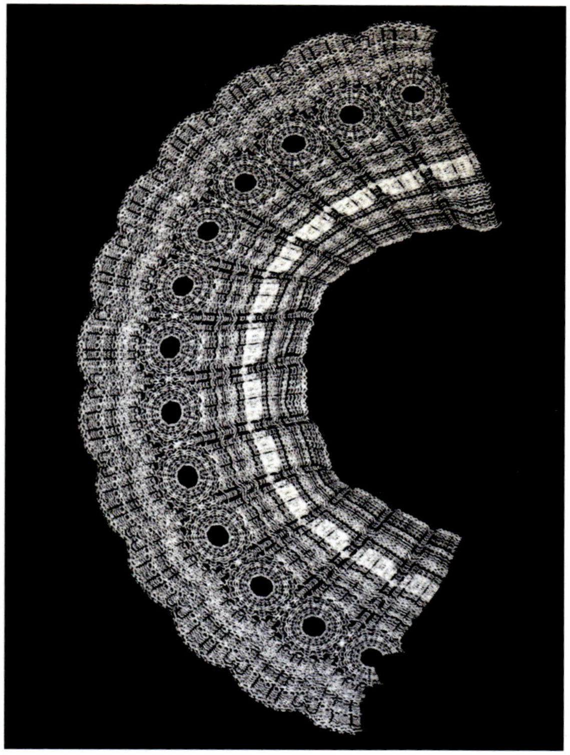

I was intrigued by the photographs, they depicted scenes of order and calm and of relaxed people taking tea, but the words in Clarice's diary were at odds with these images and described some of the horror of life in a wartime hospital.

The first body of work to come from the archive, entitled *Reading Between the Lines* began with an exploration of lace. This initial research resulted in a series of collographs entitled *Thought Patterns* and provided me with valuable research into how lace appears in two dimensions. I began to experiment with text from the diary to see if I could use it to create patterns that would resemble lace. The resulting lace designs were made on the computer, printed onto acetate and then used to make solar plates which were exposed in sunlight and then printed with white ink on Somerset Black Velvet paper.

My latest body of work entitled *The King's Shilling* is a response to the following entry in Clarice's diary:

> Sept 1915
>
> "We had not to wait long. By return of post the answer came. Would we send on our certificates, as Mrs Vaughan Johnson would have to see them before sending to headquarters saying we were fit for "nursing wounded!" This we did! As quickly as possible. A few days later we heard we had been accepted would we send the sum of 1/- to the Commandant for our badges and any little expenses during our correspondence."

At this time men were still being given the King's shilling when they enlisted into the Army or Navy and I find the idea that the nurses were paying a shilling, whilst the men were being given one, an interesting notion – one to fight, one to save. The resulting works use a combination of screen print and heat transfer to make a series of wreaths that are stitched onto vintage paper watermarked 'Handmade 1915'.

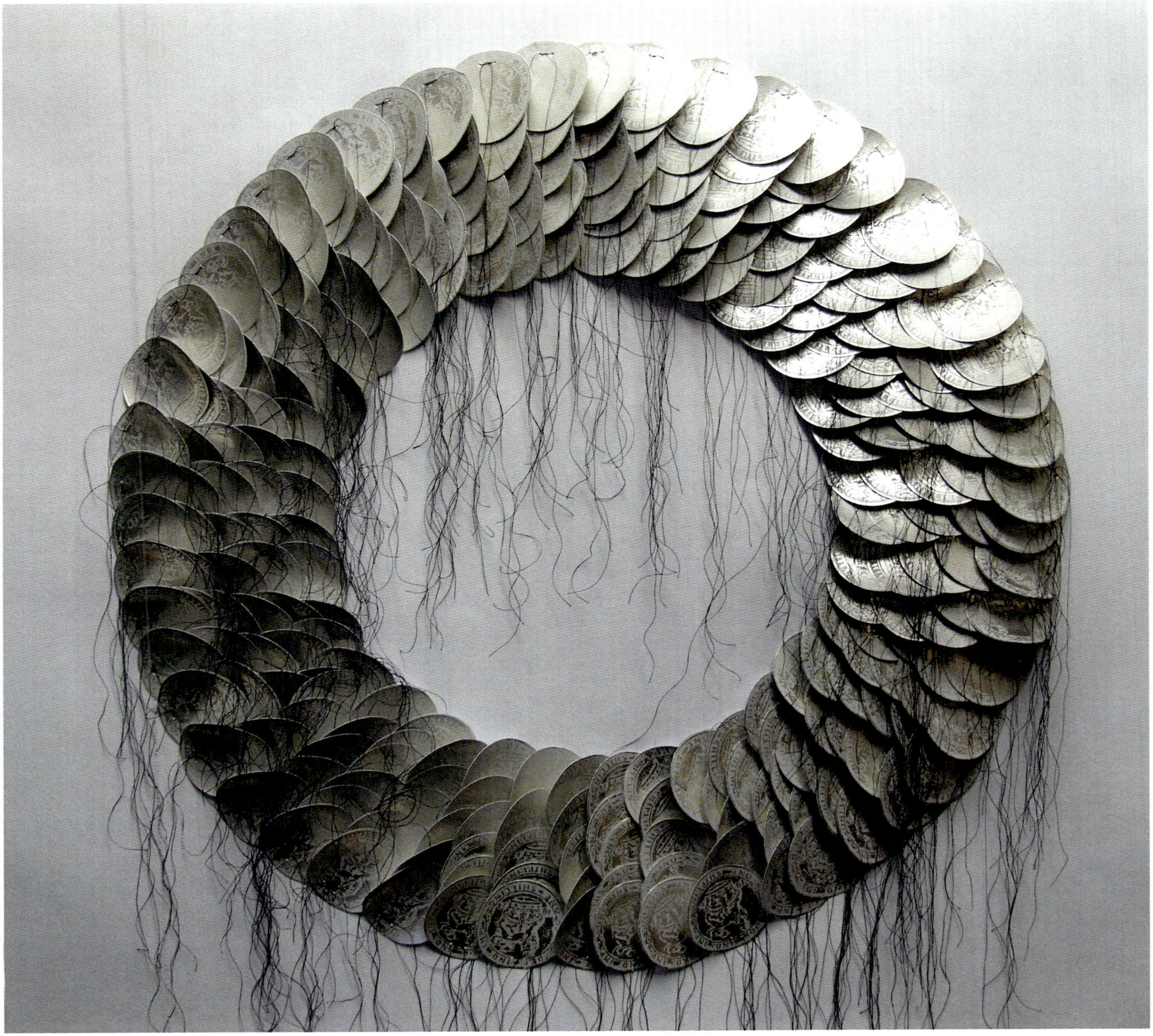

Tails You Lose, (from the *King's Shilling* series), 90 x 120 cm,
screen print, heat transfer and stitch (edition of 1)

Graham Cooke

My earliest introduction to the graphic arts was through the medium of printmaking. Throughout my working life as an artist and designer I have returned to the possibilities presented by this traditional art form as a method for exploring, refining and redefining the direction and progression of my work

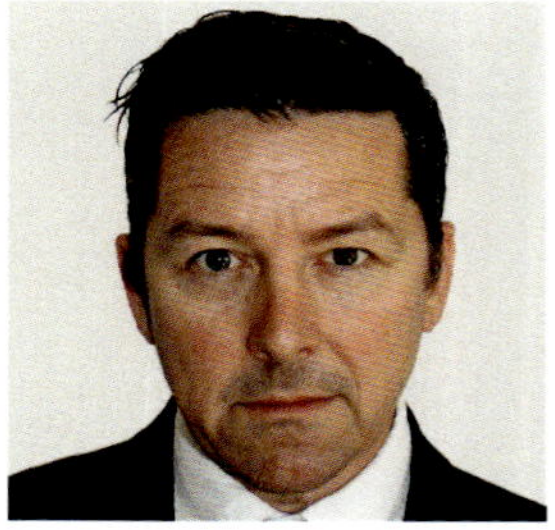

1960 Born Kingsclere, Hampshire
1978 Southampton School of Art
1979 L'Ecole des Beaux Arts Du Havre, ESADHAR, France
1980–84 Kingston School of Art and Design
1984 Scholarship Allgemeine Gewerbeschule, Basel, Switzerland
1985 V&A Museum, Boilerhouse, London
1986–92 BBC TV
1991 Gateshead Libraries and Museums, Joint exhibition with Tim Southall
1992 *Digits and Numbers*, Moscow State University, Russia
1994 Solo exhibition, Mann Gallery London
1996 *Closed Spaces*, Warwick Castle
1997 *Process Matters*, Syndicated Arts, London
1994–2001 Senior Designer Madame Tussauds
2006 *Obras Nuevas*, Galeria la Rampa, Spain
2007 *Obras Químericas*, Galeria la Rampa, Spain
2008 *Summer Open*, Galeria la Rampa, Spain
2009 Member of Gibraltar Fine Arts Society
2010 *Royal Academy Summer Exhibition*
2010 *Society of Graphic Fine Arts Annual Open*
2011 The White Room Gallery Bath, joint exhibition with Tim Southall
2012 Number Nine the Gallery, Birmingham, joint exhibition with Tim Southall
2012 *The Discerning Eye*, The Mall Galleries
2013 *Edinburgh Art Fair*
2014 *Master Etchers*, The White Room Leamington Spa
2015 *Works on Paper*, Barbican

In my early life I studied both fine art and three-dimensional design, and have subsequently followed a two-pronged career, working as a designer in film, theatre and architecture, and as a practising painter/printmaker. I endeavour to use printmaking as a complement to my work as an artist and designer, exploring ideas in one medium that can be transposed and interpreted into other mediums.

I find the process of printmaking is always a grand experiment, particularly within the traditions of intaglio. Varied disciplines are involved that require a level of exactitude, precision and craftsmanship which can elevate a simple drawing into a more intense, emotional image. However, in spite of how experienced I become as a printmaker, the pains of my endeavours are no guarantee of a successful outcome. Serendipity plays a great part in the process: sometimes the results are disasters and sometimes unexpected surprises. Each print is always a test.

I appreciate the tradition and history of printmaking, a medium that was brought to England in the late 15th century and is still just as relevant today. Because it is a medium that is so adaptable, those traditional techniques pioneered so long ago can still be explored to make something new and fresh. Added to this, its breadth allows the integration of modern technologies such as digital image manipulation and processing which I use to expand my ideas and drawings in moving towards a finished print.

Then there is the print workshop; the very heart of printmaking activity with its distinctive and intoxicating smells of turps and inks, its presses which in themselves are often antiques that have experienced the hands of other printmakers in the past, like ghosts hanging around the workshop, watching and helping to make new prints. There is also a certain alchemy involved in the process of producing prints, using simple materials, from beautiful handmade papers to dangerous and strange materials, from poisonous and volatile acids, exotic resins and shellacs to sheets of copper or zinc.

I now live between England and Spain where I am lucky enough to have a small print room, a miniature version of the traditional print workshops I describe above. Here the smells and ghosts of the past mingle with the influences of both countries in the prints that I make. My work, which is figurative, draws on my immediate surroundings as a starting point. Whether it is townscapes or seascapes, a story or a still life, I try to create pictures that work with visual illusions and trickery. Images that appear to be one thing but on closer inspection are another, implying a kind of impossible reality. The result is often quirky or has a reference to an earlier history or allegory and hopefully appeals to the eye of the spectator.

St Mary Woolnoth, 30 x 20 cm, etching and aquatint (edition of 75)

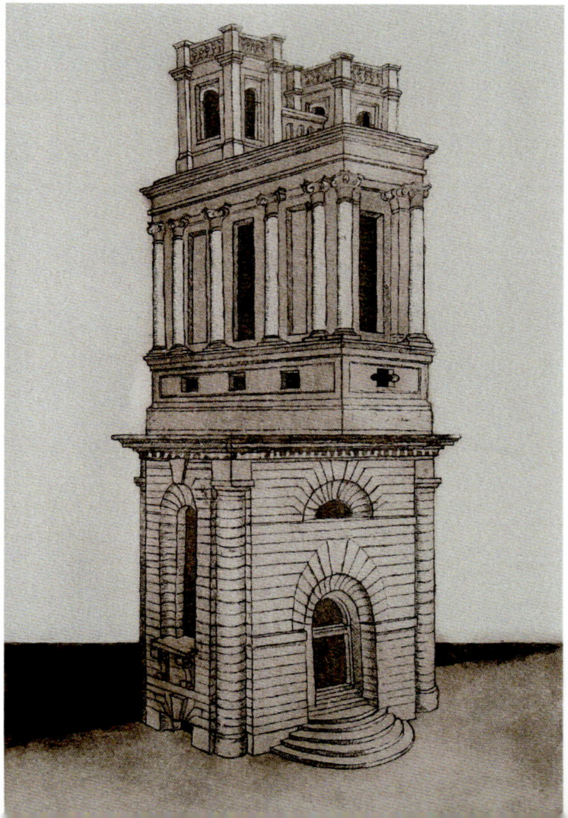

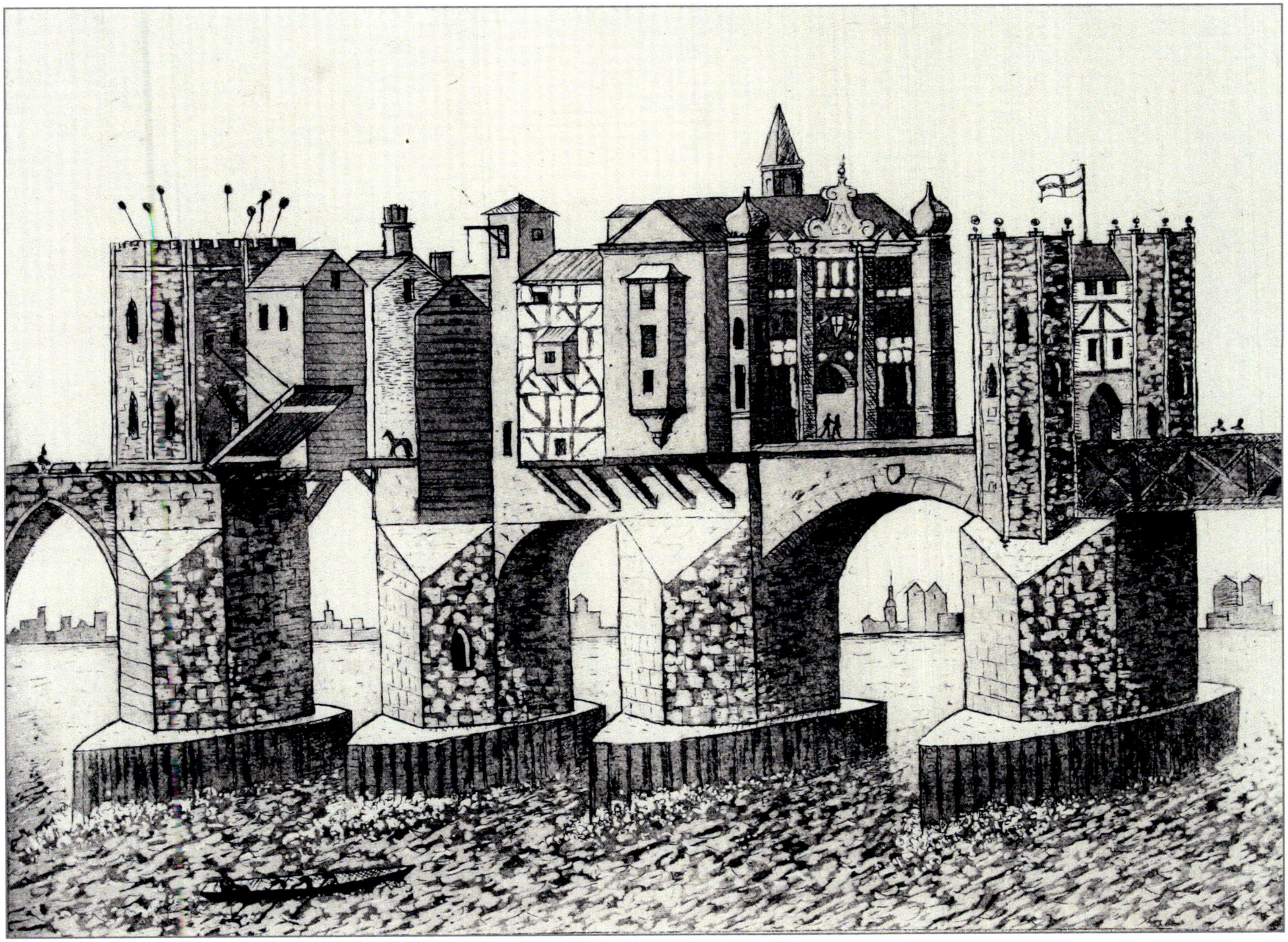

Old London Bridge, 15 x 20 cm, etching & aquatint (edition of 75)

Phil Cosgrove

My work is social and political and I am influenced by the work of Daumier, Jorge Immendorf, Steve Bell and John Keane. The work is figurative so it can be accessible to the viewer. It may not be enticing but it is a commentary on how we live today.

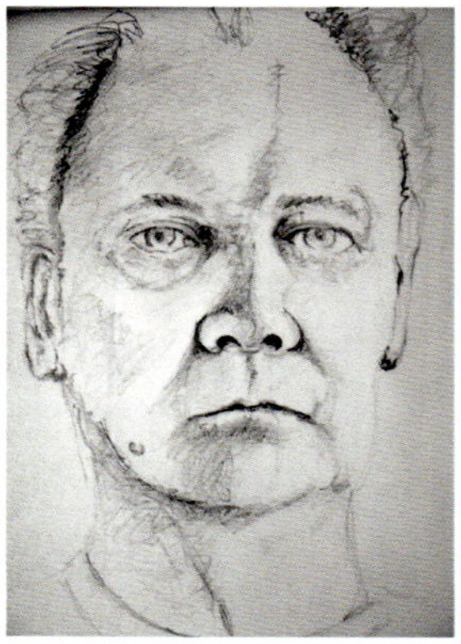

Attended Art College in Belfast (Ulster University) 1979 to 1982, Honours degree in Fine Art.

As well as working as an artist, Phil has worked on building sites and for the last 25 years has worked as a Trade Union Representative, defending employees in hearings up to Employment Tribunals, defending people when faced with dismissal or other disciplinary sanctions.

My work is mostly monoprints (monotypes) to obtain a certain mark so as to accentuate the expression in the image. Each image is unique so it can't be mass-produced. The main cartoon of the image can be reproduced at most about three times, but it depends on the print. In some prints I will draw the image on the back then roll a thin layer of paint on a piece of glass or Formica and using different pressures on the drying paint trace the image on the other side. It is a laborious task but it has developed over the years, to give me a unique image.

The work is social and political and I am influenced by the work of Daumier, Jorge Immendorf, Steve Bell and John Keane. The work is figurative so it can be accessible to the viewer. It may not be enticing but it is a commentary on how we live today.

I have had work exhibited in the Barbican, Bankside and in many other galleries as well as countries such as Germany, France and New Zealand over the years. I was exhibiting with the Young Unknowns in the late Eighties and Nineties and have been a member of the Printmakers Council for a number of years.

HBOS Bankers Club, 42 x 29.5 cm, monoprint on paper

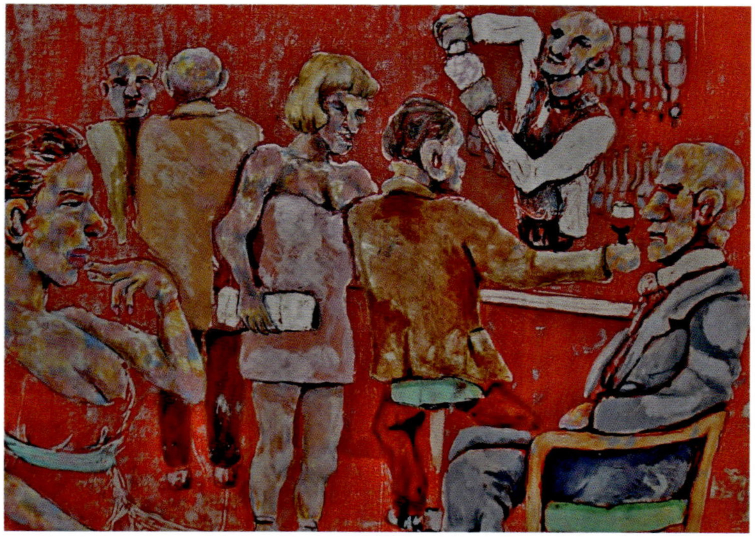

Venus, 42 x 29.5 cm, monoprint on paper

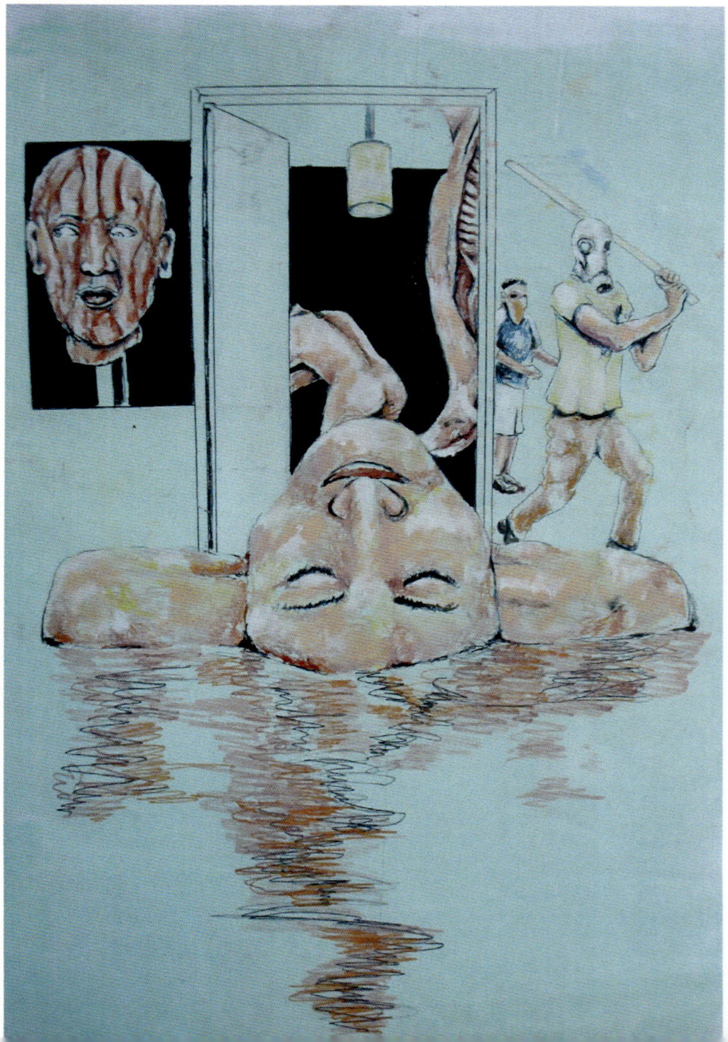

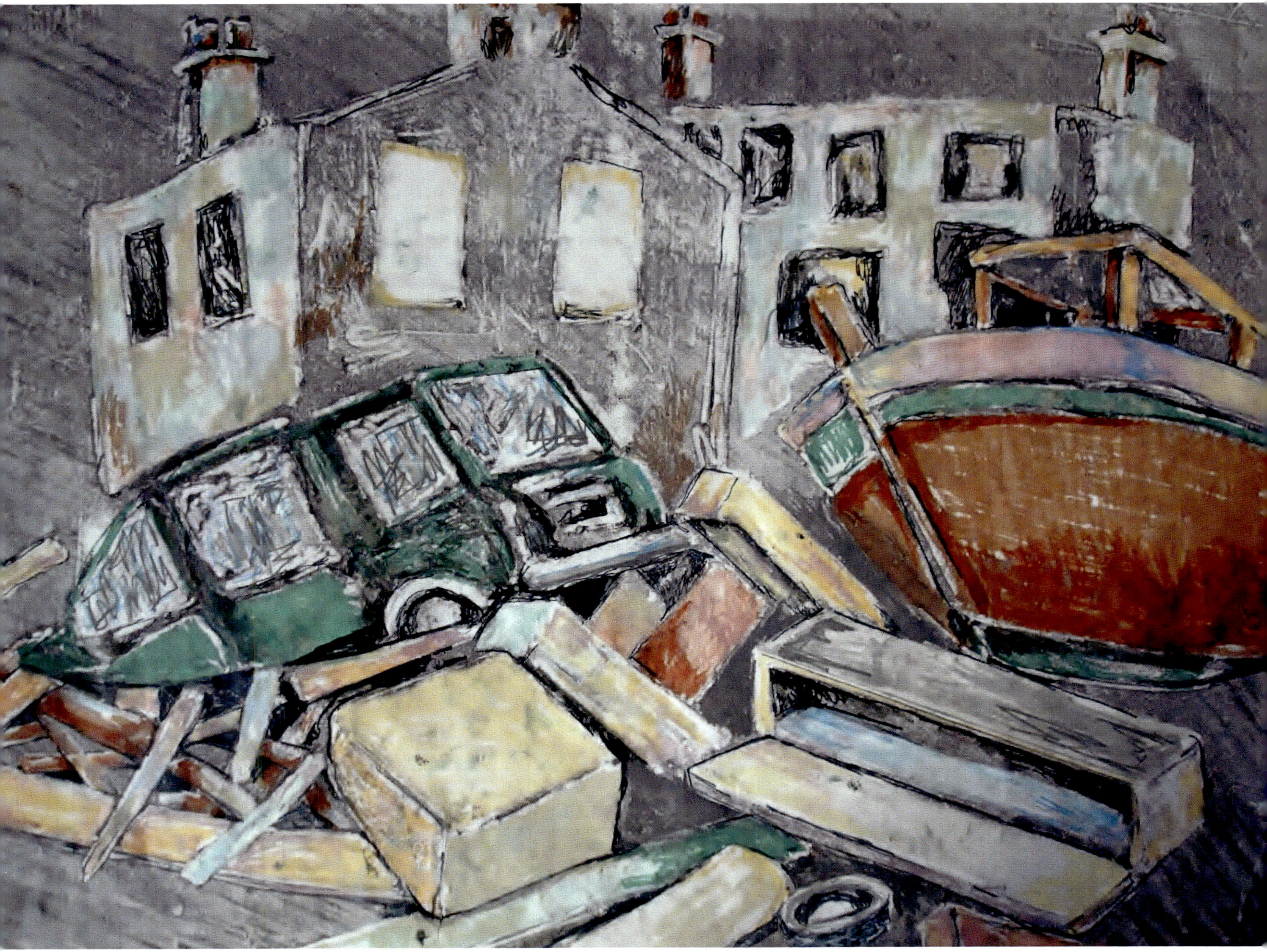

Tsunami, 47.5 x 56 cm, monoprint on linen

Richenda Court

I first started printmaking on my Fine Art and Dance degree at Brighton Polytechnic (now known as the University of Brighton). My work is figurative-based and inspired by detailed line drawings in my sketchbook which make use of subconscious ideas and thoughts. My background in contemporary dance filtrates into my prints, not so much in movement, but in the positioning of figures, hands and the occasional glance.

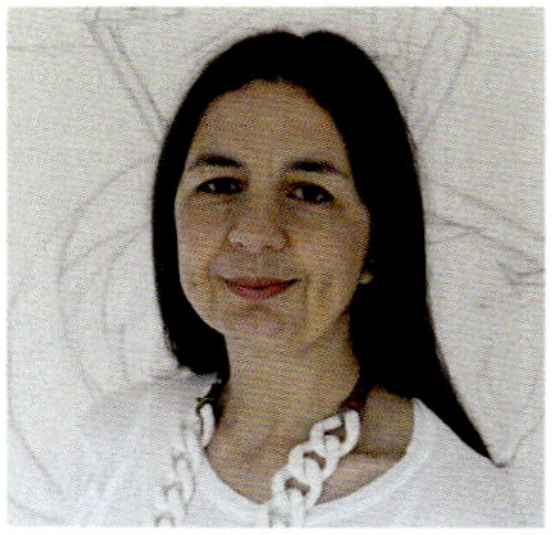

1987 Degree in Fine Art & Contemporary Dance, Brighton Polytechnic
1990 Postgraduate degree in Contemporary Dance, Laban Centre
1998 Started printmaking at Morley College, London
2006 Began teaching Printmaking as a freelance tutor
2008 First solo show at The Fountain Gallery, Hampton Court
2008 First Artist Residency at Colebrook Day Centre, Redhill
2008 Prints selected for Brook Gallery, Devon
2009 *Impact 09 Printmaking Exhibition and Conference*, Bristol
2011 Exhibited at New Ashgate Gallery, Farnham
2011 Exhibited at The Menier Gallery, London SE1 with SGFA
2011 Linocut Images published in *Learning Linocut* by Susan Yeates
2012 Artist Residency: *Dance Signatures*, St George's, Esher
2012 Winner of Olympic Poster Design for Surrey. Exhibited at Royal Albert Hall, London, and sold in Surrey galleries
2013 Became Director of Events and Relief Printmaking at Ochre Print Studios, Guildford
2014 Selected for *Printfest*, Ulverston, Cumbria
2014 Exhibited at Northern Biennale *International Print Festival*, Newcastle
2015 Became a member of the Printmakers Council
2015 Exhibited at Bankside Gallery with *LOOP*

I have always worked in fine art and dance since gaining my degree. For the last nine years, I have worked as a printmaking tutor becoming a Director of Events and Relief Printmaking in 2013 at Ochre Print Studio in Guildford, the largest print studio in the South East. Prior to this I have been an Exhibitions Co-ordinator for Surrey, an Arts Officer for Richmond and dancer/choreographer.

I've been making prints now for over 20 years, learning my craft under Richard Michell at Morley College. Richard was Birgit Skiölds' technician and an editioner to David Hockney and many other artists. I am fortunate to have been in receipt of expert advice about printmaking processes.

I still make my work at Morley and Ochre as well as in my home studio in Surrey.

Line drawings from memory are often a starting point for my work. The figures are then carefully composed and reworked to produce tonal etchings. Dance figures in my work are an unfolding, constant source of inspiration. Often in the background, they are there to represent fixed time and measurability particularly in the etchings.

Associated qualities with the image are drawn into the work with the aim of maintaining a balanced composition and consolidating it through the slow, gradual, creative processes of etching. Methods particularly favoured are softground techniques to hint and draw in on textures and tones into the final image.

As well as etchings I also enjoy making linocuts. More direct in their making, I can enjoy the freshness of carving the lino as well as the printing challenges they bring. It is a balance that works well with the slow process of etching.

For my most recent work I'm bringing together lino and etching in one image. I'm also working with a graphic designer to publish my first book of line drawings; an intimate story of a couple: their soul keepers and a subconscious journey they make under the sea.

Black Water Kings is a comment on the potential of a life, particularly a young life. The background figures portray stoic, timeless, ancestral figures overlooking our achievements and concerns.

Shadow III, 20 x 15 cm, linocut (edition of 5)

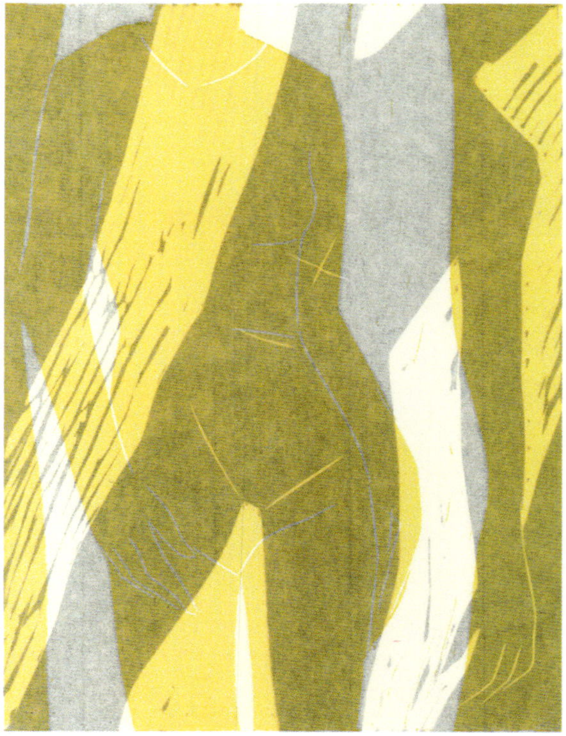

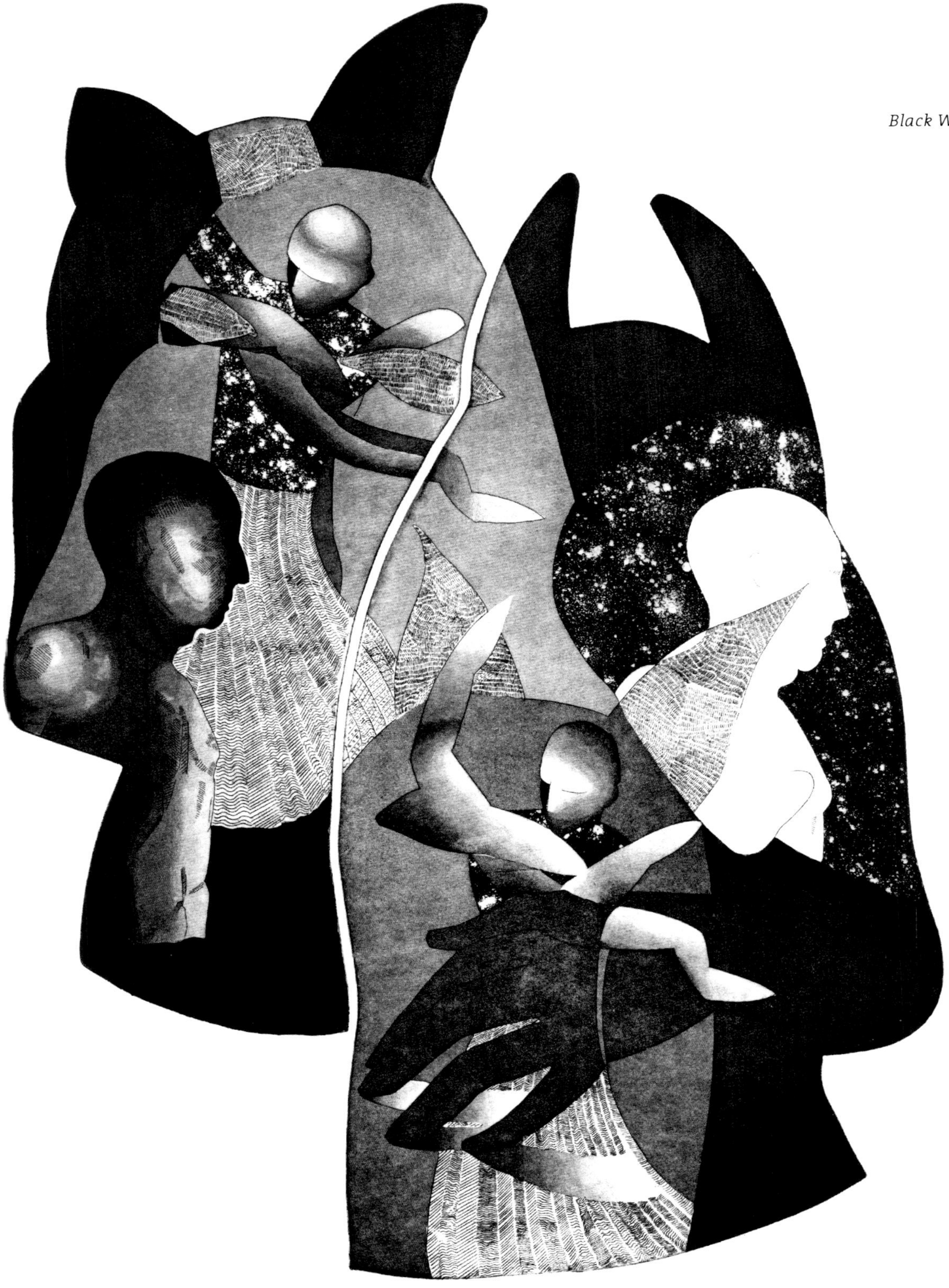

Black Water Kings, 67 x 60 cm
etching (edition of 25)

Barbra Cropper

Printmaking captures all my senses. When I ink up a plate and take it through the press there is an element of intrigue and excitement. My work is driven by my fascination for the natural world – trees, flight of birds and insects, reflections in water and the colours surrounding my Cumbria studio and in my dreams. I use my experiences of living in Africa for nine years as well as my immediate environment to inform my work.

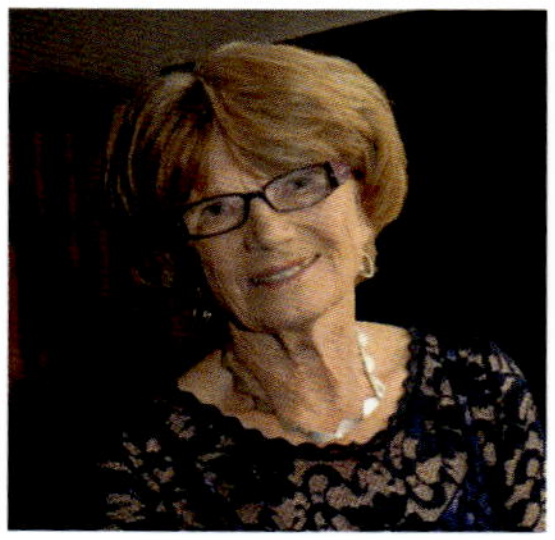

1991–99 Taught Adult Education
1994 BA (Hons) Printmaking & Art History UCLAN
1978–89 Taught Art, full-time, High School
2000–15 Talks to Art Groups, U3A & WEA Painting & Print Workshops

Exhibitions
2000–12 *Green Door Exhibitions*, Kendal. C-ART Cumbria
2000–08 *Printfest*, Ulverston
2008 Beacon Gallery, Whitehaven (PmC)
2001 Vyner St Gallery London
2002 Mall Galleries, London
2002 Manchester Academy (MAFA) John White Award.
2012/13/14 *Lake Artists Summer Exhibition*, Grasmere - Kent Valley Printers Award

Solo Exhibitions
2009 Abbot Hall Coffee Shop, Kendal
2003 Globe Gallery, Blackpool Pleasure Beach
2001 The Old Grammar Sch. Garstang
1999 Brewery Art Gallery, Kendal
1997 Grundy Art Gallery, Blackpool
1995 Harris Museum, Preston
2012/06 Brantwood, Coniston, Cumbria
2015/11/04 Lytham Heritage Centre, Lancs

Work is held in collections abroad

I am a well-known artist/printmaker in Cumbria and Lancashire. As a printmaker I have made a successful in-depth study of etching techniques looking at Picasso, Elizabeth Blackadder and Jasper Johns.

In my Lakeland studio I look at developed sketches and draw freehand on a specially ground copper plate. The plate is put in a solution of ferric chloride which bites the line and aquatint tone. The cleaned plate is inked up, covered with damp paper and taken through the press. The most exciting moment is when the paper is pulled back from the plate to reveal the first proof.

I work in monoprint and enjoy the freedom of this very painterly method. Also I like the gutsiness of cutting the surface of wood or lino for relief prints. I sketch or print in my studio each day except when I pick up my grandchildren from school. Sketching on holiday is a must and I often do small watercolours, feeding these into printmaking themes.

I hope to connect with the viewer through my etchings and other works in a way that moves them. When someone tells me they have felt a kind of emotional response, I know I have succeeded.

OPPOSITE
Follow Your Dreams, 30 cm x 30cm, etching/monoprint (edition of 2)

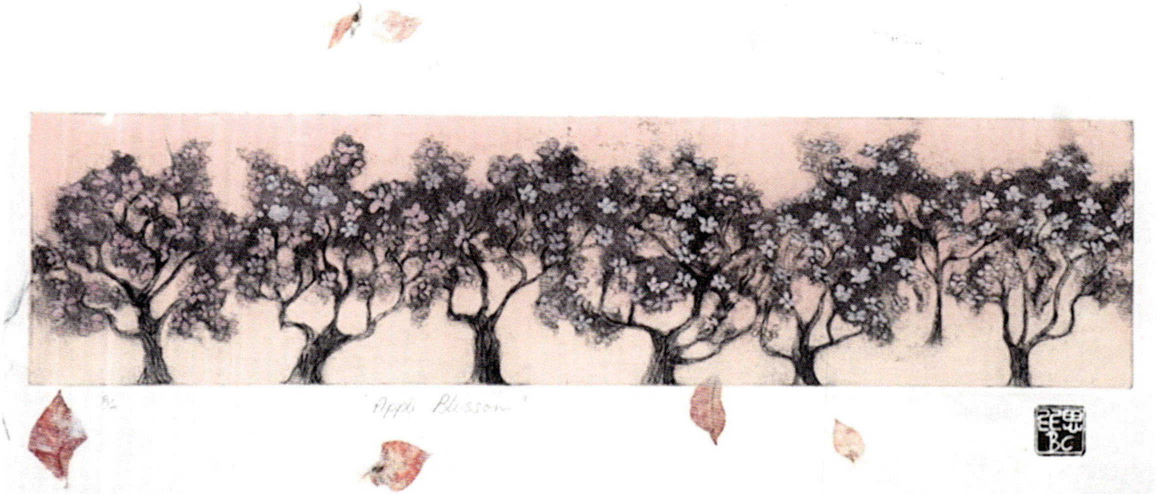

Apple Blossom, 23 cm x 40 cm, etching (edition of 7)

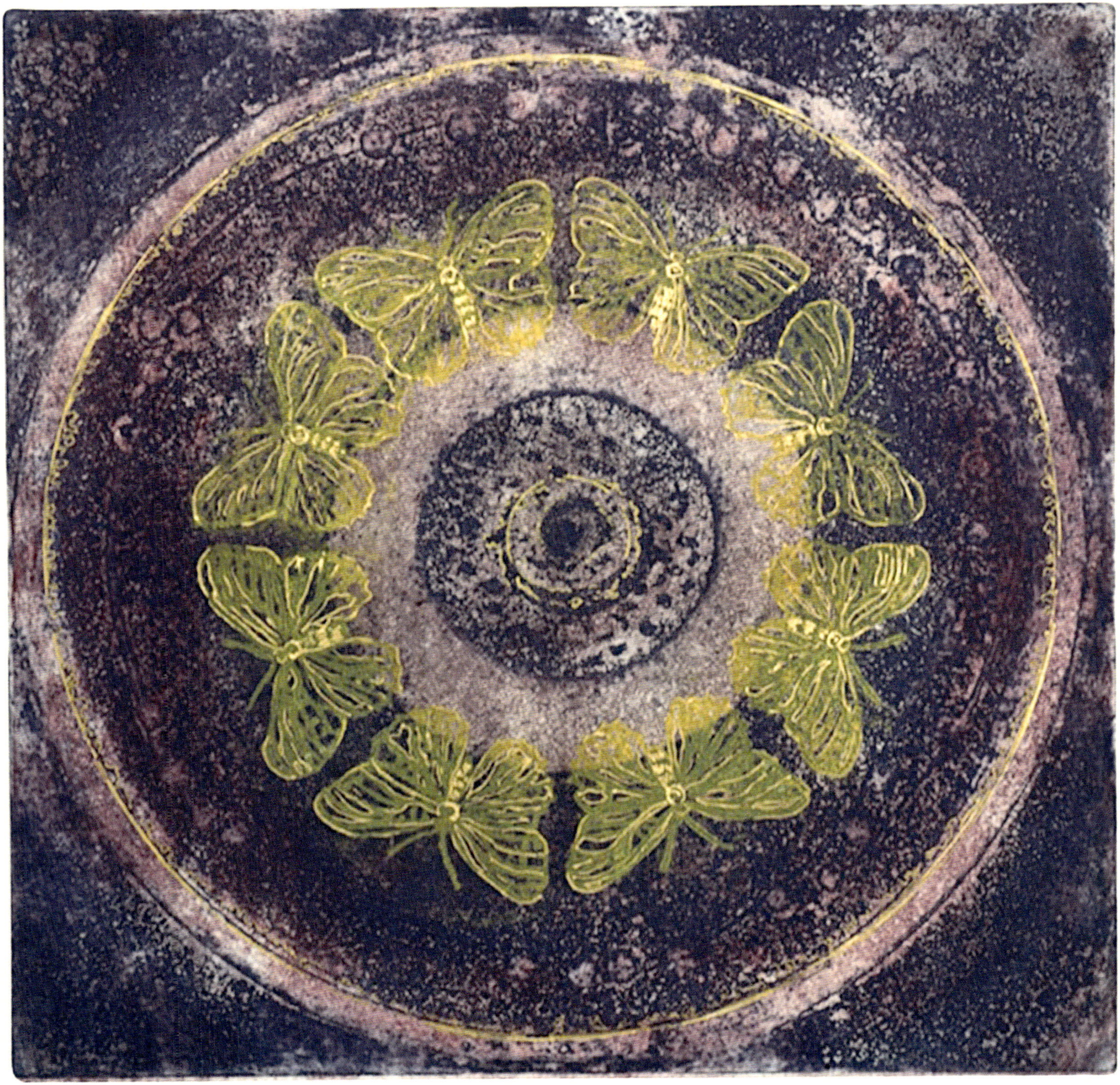

Sandra Daniel

I left Chelsea School of Art with a Distinction in Printed Textiles and continued my studies in Fine Art. Between 2003–2009 I founded desertRose, an independent design company. In 2010 I returned to college to study printmaking.

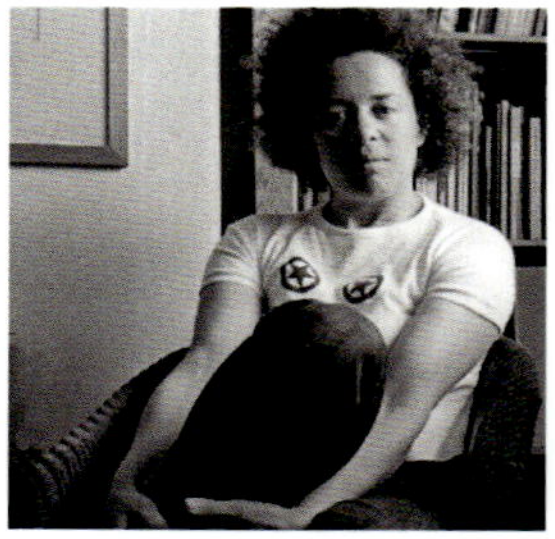

1961 Born London
1981–84 HND (Distinction) Textiles, Chelsea School Of Art.
1984–85 Life Drawing, Chelsea School of Art
1985–86 Teaching Textiles, Kingsway Princeton College, London

Exhibitions

1984 Anatol Orient London, group show, textiles. Holland Park Orangery London, group show textiles
1985 *On the Wall* London, group show, painting. Oliver & Pink London *Art in Fashion* group show, painting
1986 Crucial Gallery London *The Bedsit Collection* solo show
1988 Judd Street Gallery London. Group show, installation
2012 Kingsgate Workshop Gallery London. *Winter Print* group show The Framers Gallery, London. R K Burt Gallery London. *Works on Paper* Printmakers Council.
2013 Childwickbury Art Fair Hertfordshire Highgate Gallery London, Printmakers Council. Brighton Art Fair Kensington & Chelsea College, London group show Palace Art Fair London
2014 Christmas Art Fair, St Albans Kensington & Fulham Open Studios Brighton Art Fair *CYMK* Margate PMC. OrmeEleven *Works on Paper* Fair, Science Museum, London
2015 *Works on Paper*, PmC Barbican Library

Awards

1991 ICI Design Awards '91 *Authentic Tradition* carpet design. commendation

As a child I was fascinated by the popular illustrations of Dick Bruna's character Miffy, the flats areas of broad colour and simple forms appealed to me then as much as they do now.

Readymade objects like commercial packaging materials instantly offer me options to play with symmetrical and asymmetrical arrangements. I usually combine them with cloud formations, plant forms and other elements to evoke a sense of abstract still lifes and landscapes. Historical artefacts related to the slave trade from Africa are also feeding my current work. Words and phrases that I come across during my research give me clues for possible working titles. I am toying with the idea of titling my work with these thought-provoking words so that I can express my views about my concerns.

Structurally, I am influenced by Turkish, Persian and Indian miniature paintings. I find the use of perspective in these paintings very interesting.

My work is driven by the printmaking processes and techniques. I mostly enjoy monotypes and multiple-plate colour aquatints in combination because of the layering they allow me.

My main focus is to create a perfect balance between form, colour and proportion, it's usually one step forward and 10 steps back, this slow process gives me time to catch up with my thoughts. I am happiest working this way.

Repeating the same shapes and motifs is common in my work as I am constantly working out the best composition. I like to work on the same idea quite a few times until I believe that I have explored it enough. It's not until I lift the blanket from the press and peel back my print that I know what to do next!

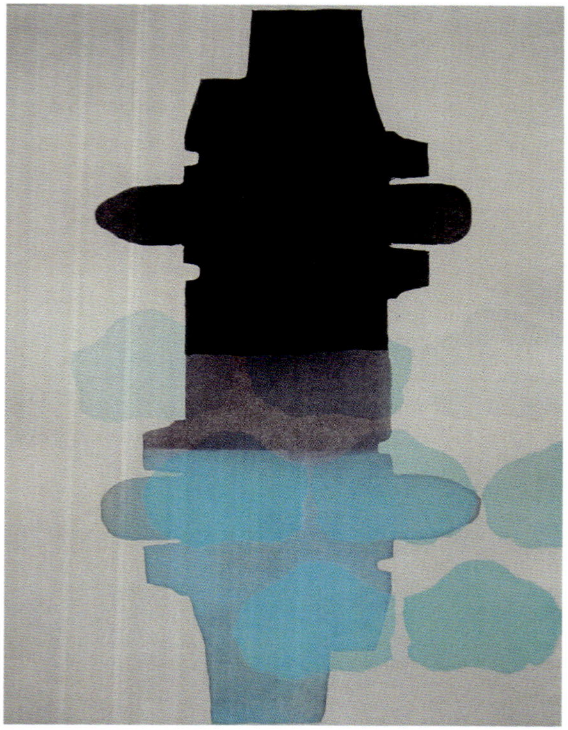

Blueprint Series New Miniatures
30 x 40 cm, aquatint, (edition of 30)

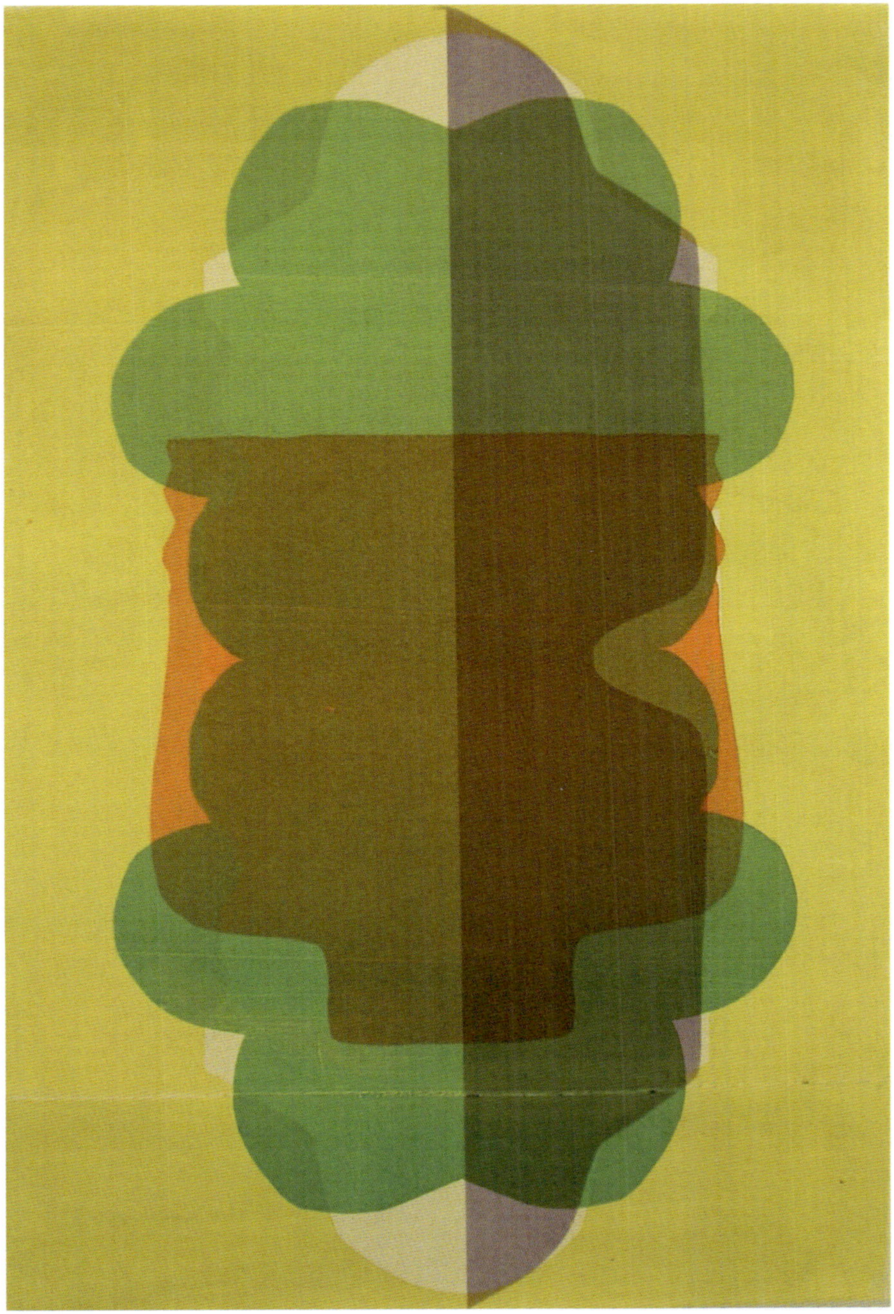

Untitled, 56 x 75 cm, monotype, (unique)

Jane Daniell

I first became interested in the printing process ten years ago when I took a course at Hampstead School of Art. I found that it lends itself to my style which tends to be fantastical as I work purely from my imagination.

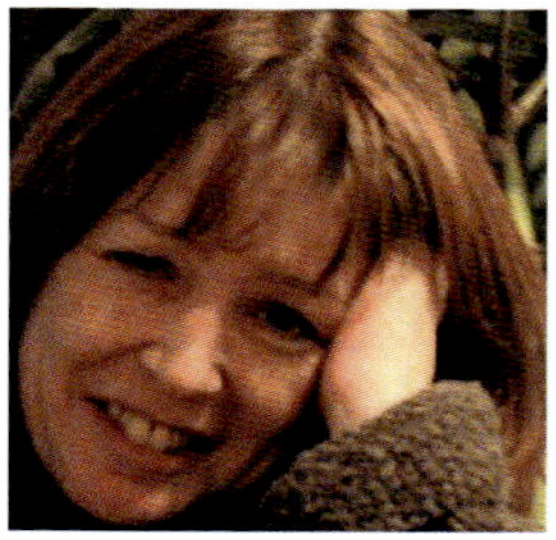

2004 *Real Art for Real People*, 1st Prize winner, The Coningsby Gallery, London W1
2005 Burgh House, Hampstead Group Show
2006 University Women's Club, Audley Square W1
2006 Printmaking Course, Hampstead School of Art
2007 Kingsgate Community Centre, London NW6
2008 Chorak, London N10 & N2
2009 (twice) Burgh House, Hampstead
2010 Hampstead School of Art Summer Show, 1st Prize winner for etching Sable d'Or London N10
2011 Joined the Printmakers Council
2011 The Printmakers Council at the Highgate Gallery
2012 Radlett Art Centre, Hertfordshire
2013 *Thou Art*, Kilburn
2013 The Printmakers Council, Upstairs at the Beccles Gallery (Public's Choice Best in Show)
2013 *Thou Art*, Kilburn, London
2013 *Microtopia*, Kilburn, London
2014 The Printmakers Council at Craft Central
Joined Southbank Printmakers
2014 *Affordable Art Fair*, Hampstead
2014 *Microtopia*, Kingsgate Workshops, Kilburn
2015 *Works on Paper*, Barbican Library
2015 Blackheath Concert Halls

Apart from my studies at the Hampstead School of Art I am largely self-taught and am influenced by Aubrey Beardsley, Arthur Rackham and more modern illustrators such as Maurice Sendak and Errol Le Cain. These artists all worked from their imaginations producing curious and beautiful paintings. Printmakers I greatly admire are Goya, Dürer, Rembrandt as well as the more recent images made by Paula Rego and Anne Desmet. There are a wealth of other brilliant works that I could mention but these, particular Rego's, such as *Mermaid Drowning Wendy*, *Flood* and *Three Blind Mice* number amongst my favourites.

I have illustrated several of Shakespeare's plays and my images have sold at various venues including The Globe, the Royal Shakespeare Company, the National Theatre and several international venues. I also, in collaboration with Shepheard-Walwyn Publishers, produced illustrations and calligraphy for *The Rime of the Ancient Mariner* and a copy of *The Night before Christmas*.

Theatre and drama have always interested me and if I had a parallel life I would have liked to tread the boards. In my work I try to express the magical and impossible in the way that it is often conveyed in contemporary immersive theatre productions, particularly through the eyes of a child – that sense of hope and of all things being possible, as well as the religious ideal of eternal possibility expressed in the Resurrection. Though not a religious person, that analogy is something I can well relate to.

The technical side of etching – the preparation of the plate, polishing, applying a ground, bevelling – takes second place to the drawing of the image which may take me several weeks. As far as I am concerned, no detail should be omitted. It is as if I am in the picture and in walking through the scene I am observing all of its intimacy and minutiae, and, like a child, find all are of equal importance to me. P.L. Travers, in her Mary Poppins stories which I read as a child, describes a baby as being born with a vast knowledge of its existence prior to birth and an ability to talk to and understand the language of birds and animals which it then loses at six months old. The children I portray are similar in that they are separate from the world as we perceive it as adults and are regarding that world through wise eyes. Having the understanding of what their world is like is something that we forget as we grow older and 'put away childish things'.

I think that, because I have not been instructed in the importance of perspective and space, I have only my own wishes as my driving force which is a sort of freedom I am lucky to have.

OPPOSITE

Taking the Fish for a Walk, 21 cm x 29.7 cm, aquatint etching, hand-coloured and printed individually on archival paper (edition of 30)

Three Friends, 10 x 10 cm, aquatint etching, hand-coloured and printed individually on archival paper (edition of 30)

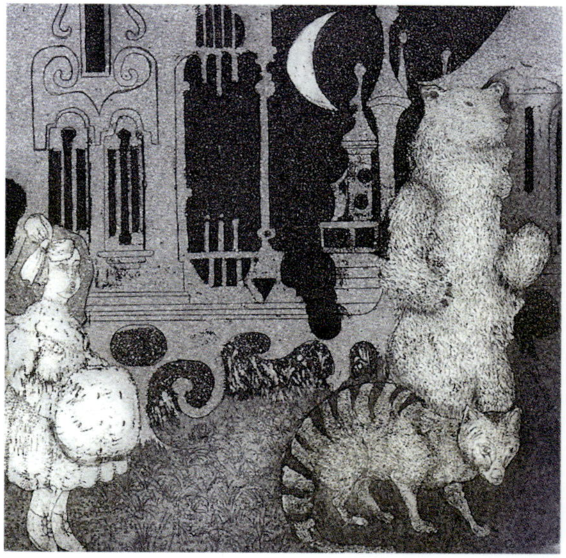

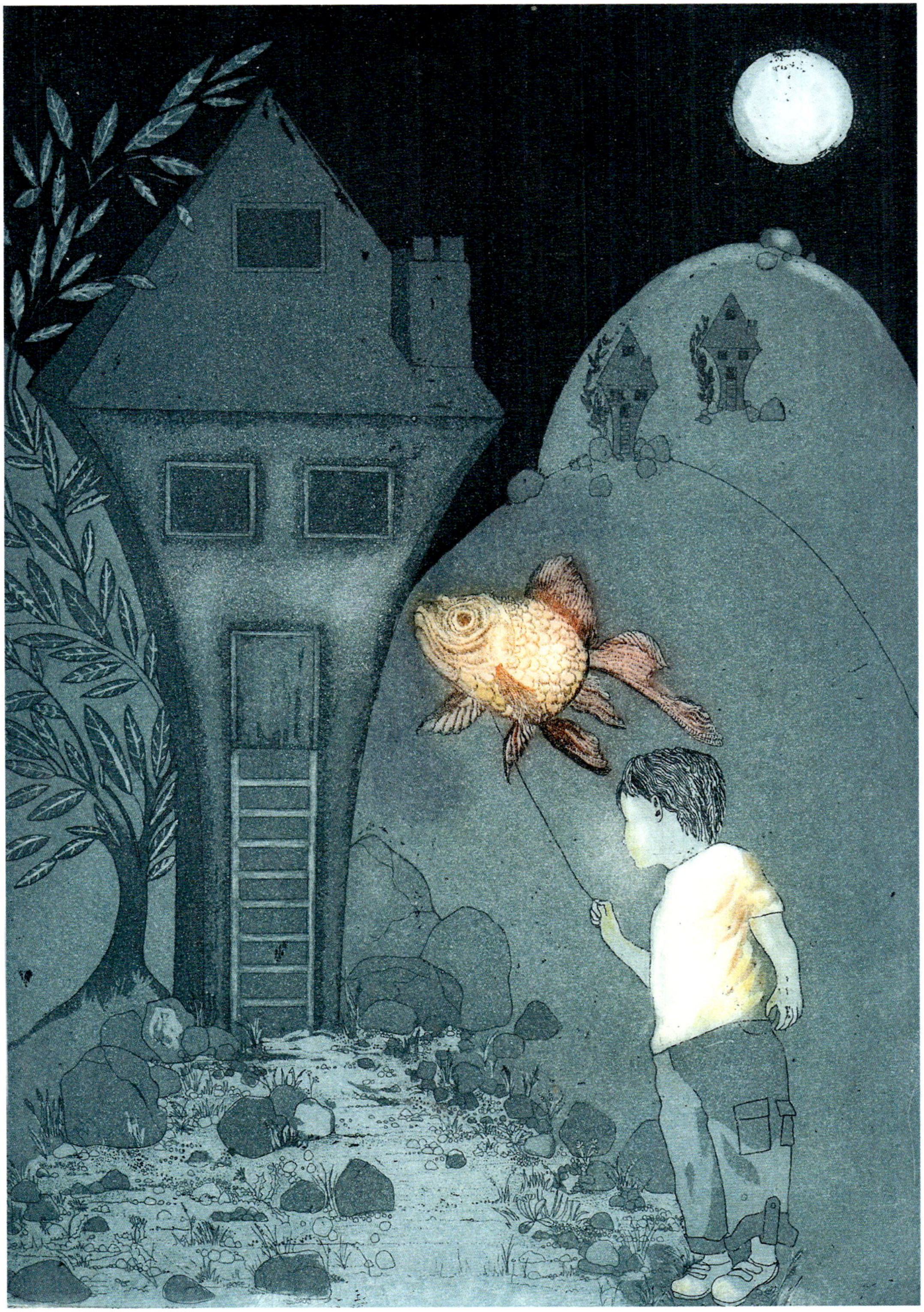

Rebecca Denton

With a background in Performing Arts, I have translated my love of storytelling and comedy into the medium of printmaking. Working from my own doodles directly onto the plate, the etching process has given me another way to illustrate. I love to combine this ancient technique with fresh and fun ideas.

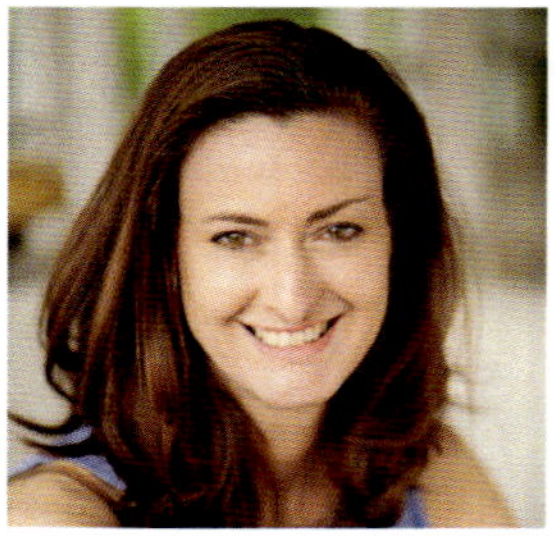

1969 Born London
1987–91 BA (Hons), Sussex University
1988 Actress, Gardner Theatre Brighton
1991–92 Tutor, North London Tutorial College
1992–94 Musical Theatre, Guildford School of Acting
1994–95 Actress (film and stage), Cabaret singer, Budapest
1995–2001 Jazz singer, Per Se Trio, London
1995–2000 RSW, Norwood Ravenswood
2001–12 Greeting Card designer, Eves Originals, Igwig Ltd
2009 Photographic producer (Jamm Creative Ltd)
2010 Printmaking, Hampstead School of Art
2011–14 Solo and group shows, North London
2014 Shortlisted for RA Summer Exhibition
2014 Group show, Southbank Printmakers Gallery, Margate
2014 Joined Printmakers Council
2015 Awarded exclusive illustration contract by Getty Images

I took up printmaking five years ago after a decade of painting and illustrating in oils, inks and watercolour.

I've always been drawn to the magical etching and linocut illustrations in children's picture books and was eager to learn. Immediately addicted to the charm and craft of these techniques, I found the fine line of drypoint etching lent itself well to my whimsical cartoons and the sketchiness of the soft ground helped create the movement in my illustrations.

Not only did I have a variety of new methods to choose from, this was also a way to create multiple prints without resorting to digital means. Although I also print high quality giclées using archival inks, I prefer the fine art etching medium where each edition is in effect an original.

Having been a performer (a singer in a Jazz Trio, an actress in comic roles), story telling and comedy play an important part in my work; anthropomorphised eccentric animals appear in odd unexpected situations, and magical dream-like settings. I enjoy playing with moral issues and ideas; they are however presented in a subtle and light-hearted way. Equality is a subtle subtext in much of my work.

My current work as a conceptual illustrator for Getty, which although very different, is a large influence: simple, graphic images which read quickly and work at any size.

I also love to create monoprints; they are a way to be spontaneous and produce a painterly print with movement, atmosphere and light. My technique has been heavily influenced by work within the world of photography. I tend to focus on the light within the image, thereby avoiding hard, obvious lines. Nonetheless the form is beautifully captured. Themes include misty London scenes and dramatic portraits and they are the perfect antidote to the etching in that they are one-offs.

What is most important to me is that a person can get lost in a picture, carried back to their childhood, be inspired or just chuckle. One of the beautiful things about art is that it can change each time you look at it and one's perception of the piece often reflects one's own personal development. So even though a print never really changes, it can still surprise you with new discoveries.

OPPOSITE
Cat Fest, 35 x 35 cm
etching & aquatint
(edition of 30)

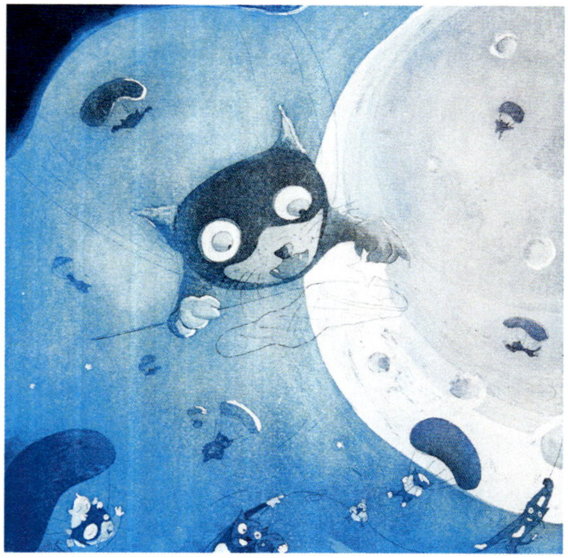

Space Cat, 38 x 38 cm
coloured etching & aquatint (edition of 40)

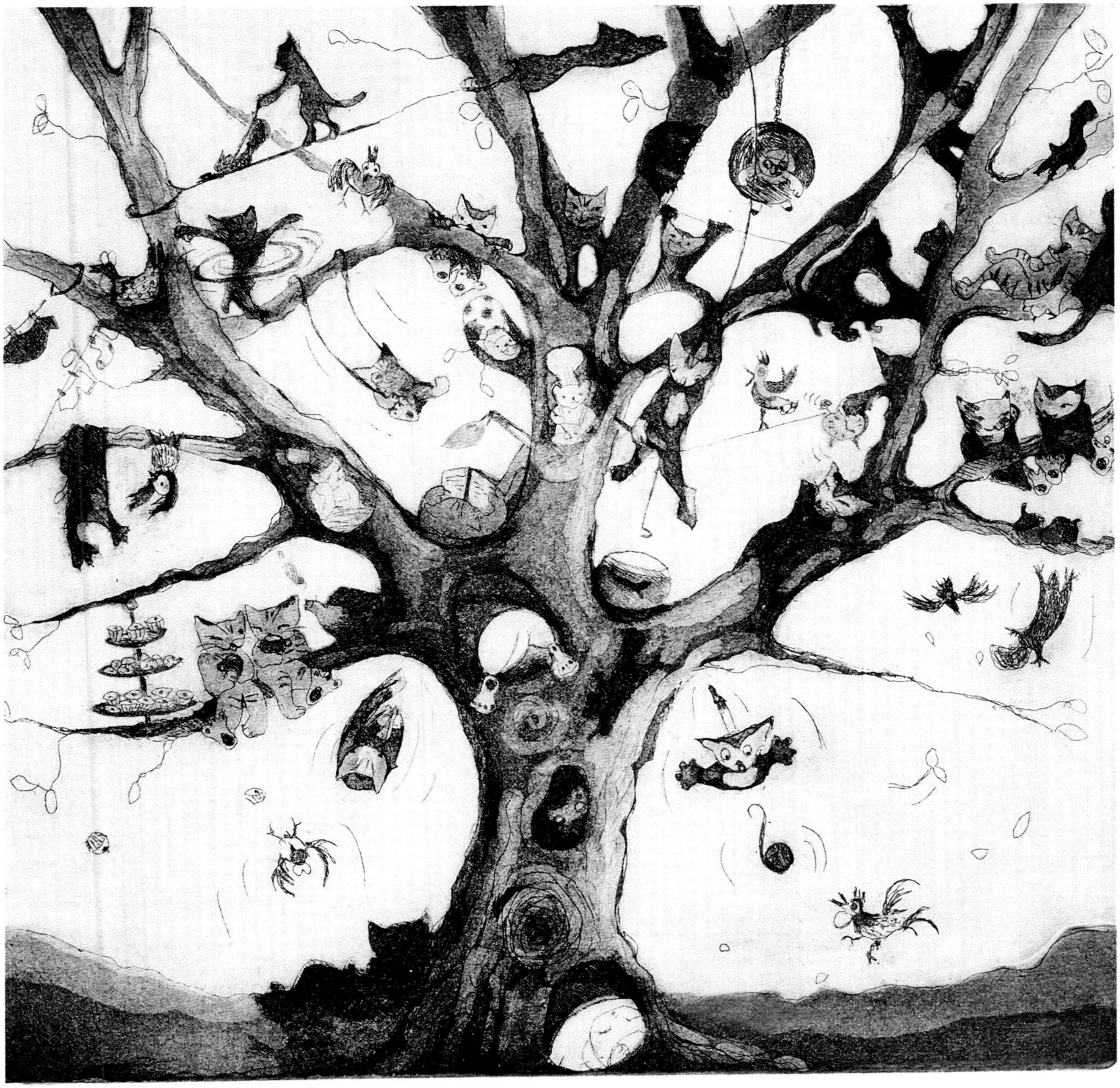

Anne Desmet

Introduced to printmaking as an undergraduate student by my tutor Jean Lodge RE, I was fascinated by Dürer's woodcuts, Piranesi's etchings, and by the 1930s graphic novels in wood engraving by Lynd Ward. I tried out many print techniques but developed a particular passion for wood engraving, linocut and mixed-media printed collage – all of which offer huge expressive potential.

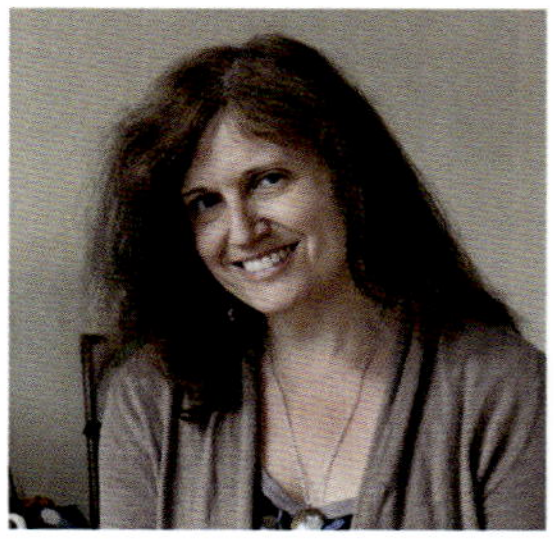

1964 Born Liverpool, UK
1983–86 BA Fine Art, Oxford University
1987–88 Postgrad. Dipl., Printmaking and Design, Central School of Art
1989–90 Scholarship in Printmaking, British School at Rome
1991 MA Fine Art, Oxford University
1987–2015 Recipient of over 30 national/international print awards
1988, 1991 Elected ARE, elected RE
1998–2013 Editor of *Printmaking Today*
2000–2010 Author of 3 print handbooks pub. A&C Black Ltd
2010–19 Honorary Fellow/Creative Associate, Aberystwyth University
2011 Elected Royal Academician (RA)
2015 Honorary Member, PmC

Selected solo exhibitions

1992 Royal Overseas League, London
1995 Ex Libris Museum, Moscow
1998 *Towers & Transformations*, Ashmolean Museum (& touring)
2008 *Anne Desmet – Urban Evolution*, Whitworth Art Gallery (& touring)
2012 *Anne Desmet – Olympic Metamorphoses*, RA Library & touring UK
2015 Long & Ryle Gallery, London
Numerous exhibitions at Hart Gallery and Duncan Campbell Fine Art, London

Anne Desmet RA RE is an established artist-printmaker specializing in wood engravings, linocuts and mixed-media collage. Her collages employ multiple fragments of proofs of her prints and other found-paper materials. These she collages into larger compositions, often on unusual surfaces – such as roofing slate, glass and ceramic mosaic and wall tiles, seashells, stones, mirror shards and convex clock glass – that relate, conceptually, to her subject matter. Her collages are suggested by and develop the largely architectural themes of her prints. She has taught printmaking in London primary and secondary schools and at undergraduate, postgraduate and public institutions including the Royal Academy Schools and the British Museum. Commissioned works include prints for the British Museum, National Gallery, British Library, V&A and Sotheby's. Her teaching and published writings have fed creatively into her art in which she endeavours to marry the rigorous technical discipline of wood engraving with a more experimental, spontaneous, yet no less carefully crafted approach to printed collage.

The focus of her work shifts between Italy (where she lived in 1989-90) and London (where she lives now). The discovery of ancient Roman ruins, medieval churches and crumbling Baroque facades juxtaposed as a potent, silent presence alongside the TV aerials and frenetic traffic of life in the modern city of Rome was a seminal experience, influencing her work ever since. Her subject matter pulls in two directions: one body of work is essentially topographical but subject to metamorphoses relating to the slow passage of time and its cycles of construction and decay. She is also concerned with urban myths, intuitive architectural fantasies and histories of urban destruction and regeneration: such as the biblical Tower of Babel, Italy's Mount Vesuvius and the Great Fire of London. She endeavours to depict both the sense of timelessness and solidity that architectural forms can convey, whilst also suggesting their impermanence and vulnerability.

Desmet's work has long been inspired by the profound stillness of Italian frescoes by Giotto, Fra Angelico and Piero della Francesca, allied with the jewel-like, detailed intensity of early Flemish panel paintings by Van Eyck and Memling. In recent years Monet's canvases of Rouen Cathedral in changing light and weather have influenced Desmet's wood engravings and linocuts: one new suite shows London's St Paul's cathedral in a sequence from dusk to dawn, while another presents New York's Brooklyn Bridge in different weather conditions: from fierce evening blizzard to crisp blue, afternoon sky.

Brooklyn Bridge - New Day,
24.6 x 17.3 cm. wood engraving, (edition of 30)

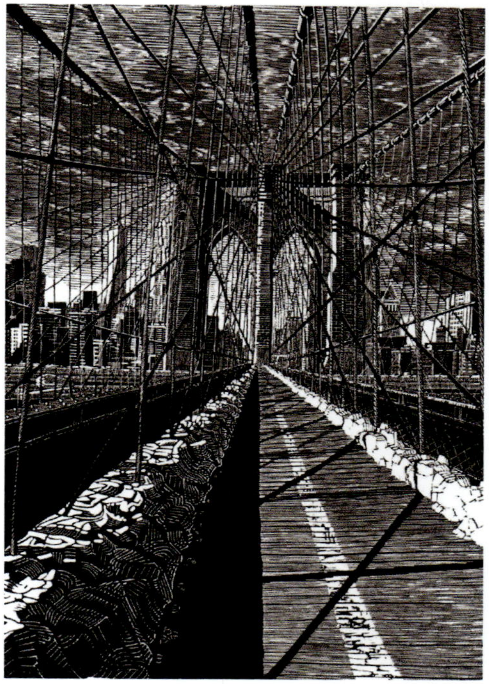

MINECRAFT
PLAYSTATION®4 EDITION

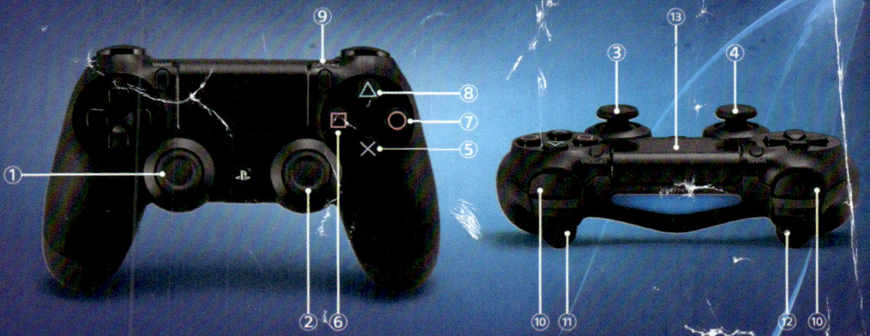

Default controls:

① Move/sprint	left stick
② Look	right stick
③ Sneak	R3 button
④ Change view	L3 button
⑤ Jump	× button
⑥ Crafting menu	□ button
⑦ Drop item	○ button
⑧ Inventory	△ button
⑨ Host and player options	OPTIONS button
⑩ Cycle held item	L1 / R1 button
⑪ Action	R2 button
⑫ Use object	L2 button
⑬ Players/invite	touch pad button

CUSA-00265
711719439417

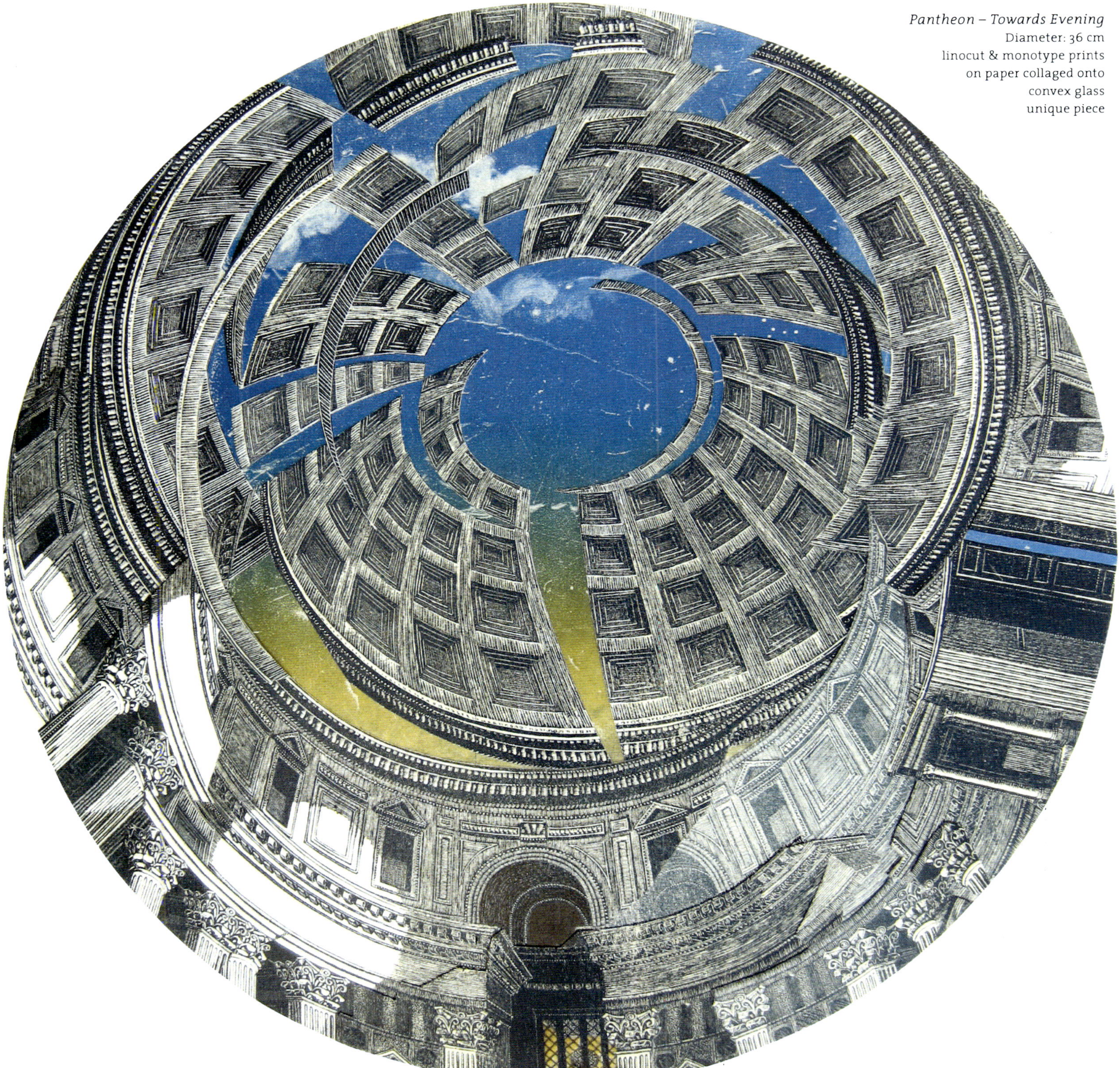

Pantheon – Towards Evening
Diameter: 36 cm
linocut & monotype prints
on paper collaged onto
convex glass
unique piece

Eleanor Durbin

Most of my work has an underlying theme of erosion with a focus on objects found in the landscape or in abandoned, destroyed man-made structures. I am attracted to the textural patterns and shapes which result from these slow, natural or sometimes violent processes. What draws me to them is the fragility, moodiness and visual beauty of what remains. The unique characteristics of etching, drypoint and linocut can be used to exploit the patterned and textural richness of my chosen subjects.

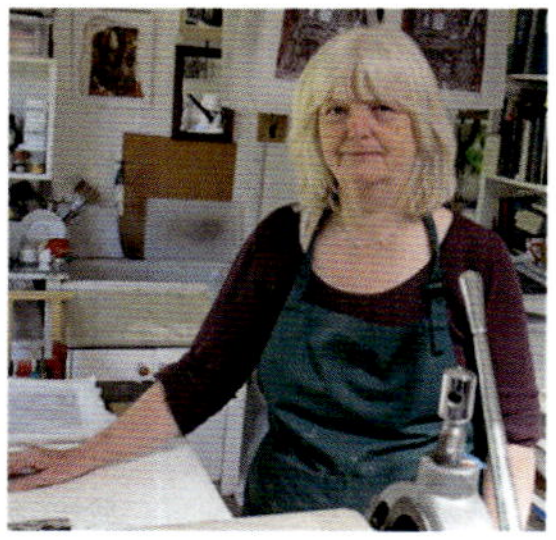

Education

1967–68 Foundation, Hornsey College of Art

1968–74 BA (Hons) Fine Art, M.Phil. Performance in Art in Britain 1963-74, University of Leeds

1975–77 Printmaking: Etching (part-time) Morley College

1977–79 Advanced Diploma Studies Etching and Lithography (part-time) Central School of Art and Design

Exhibitions

1975 *First Cleveland International Drawing Biennale*

1977 *Second Cleveland International Drawing Biennale*

1979 Printmakers Council National Touring Exhibition.

1983 RWS Bankside Gallery, London.

1986 Museum of Garden History (one-woman show)

1999 *National Print Exhibition*, Mall Galleries, London.

2001 *Originals*, Mall Galleries, London

2004 *Originals*, Mall Galleries, London

2007 *Aspects of Landscape* two-person show, Richmond, Surrey

2011 *Bite*, Mall Galleries, London

2013 *Richmond Printmakers*, Stables Gallery, Twickenham

2013 *Drawn 2013*, RWA, Bristol.

2014 *Richmond Printmakers*, Babylon Gallery, Ely.

2015 *Drawn 2015* RWA, Bristol

2015 Bath Society of Artists.

I was first introduced to the etching process during my Foundation Course at Hornsey College of Art and my fascination with printmaking has never left me. Subsequent expert teaching by Adrian Bartlett at Morley College and Norman Ackroyd at Central School of Art and Design gave me a fuller understanding of skills and the rich potential of the medium. The particular qualities of marks achieved through the different processes are as wide in potential as drawing and painting, and yet the technical procedures to attain those marks need structure and control. This combination of freedom and control offers a satisfying creative balance for me.

In 1976, on the recommendation of Adrian Bartlett, I became a member of the Printmakers Council when Michael Rothenstein was still a major presence in the group and Sylvie Turner was very active in promoting the status of printmaking in Britain. For a few years I served as New Members Officer and helped to organize touring exhibitions throughout England and Wales.

Often I find my subjects in unexpected places while on walks and I have to confess a sense of enjoyment in the quest to find a strong mood in them. For instance, I found an eerie ancient woodland near the Jurassic coast in Dorset. In the Drakensberg Mountains, South Africa, an already fragile footbridge had been further damaged by violent storms. In Cornwall, abandoned old rusting industrial fishing gear revealed beautiful colours and textures as well as the poignancy of past activity: a vast pile of abandoned old mining equipment transformed itself into noble sculptural forms. I record these sources of inspiration as drawings or watercolours in my sketchbooks and use photography as a back-up source when practically necessary. I will then choose from a range of printmaking techniques, linocuts, drypoint, collograph, carborundum to explore how to effectively evoke the particular qualities of each subject.

I have recently started making my own paper on which to print, offering me an even wider range of creative possibilities, and extending the visual qualities of the original image. Perhaps the best thing about the practice of printmaking and papermaking is the never-ending journey of exploration, anticipation, delight and discovery offered through the very nature of the processes themselves.

OPPOSITE
Dusk At Injasuthi,
Drakensberg Mountains, South Africa
66 x 40.5 cm, etching & linocut.
(edition of 6)

Old Trees On Golden Cap,
Dorset
38 x 55 cm, linocut
(edition of 4)

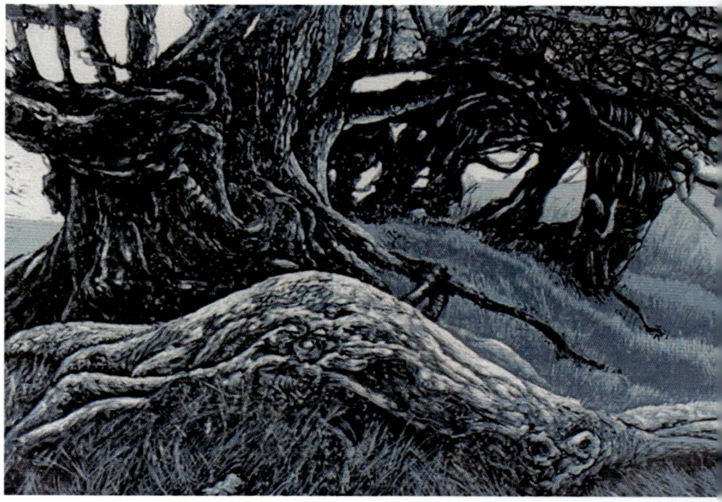

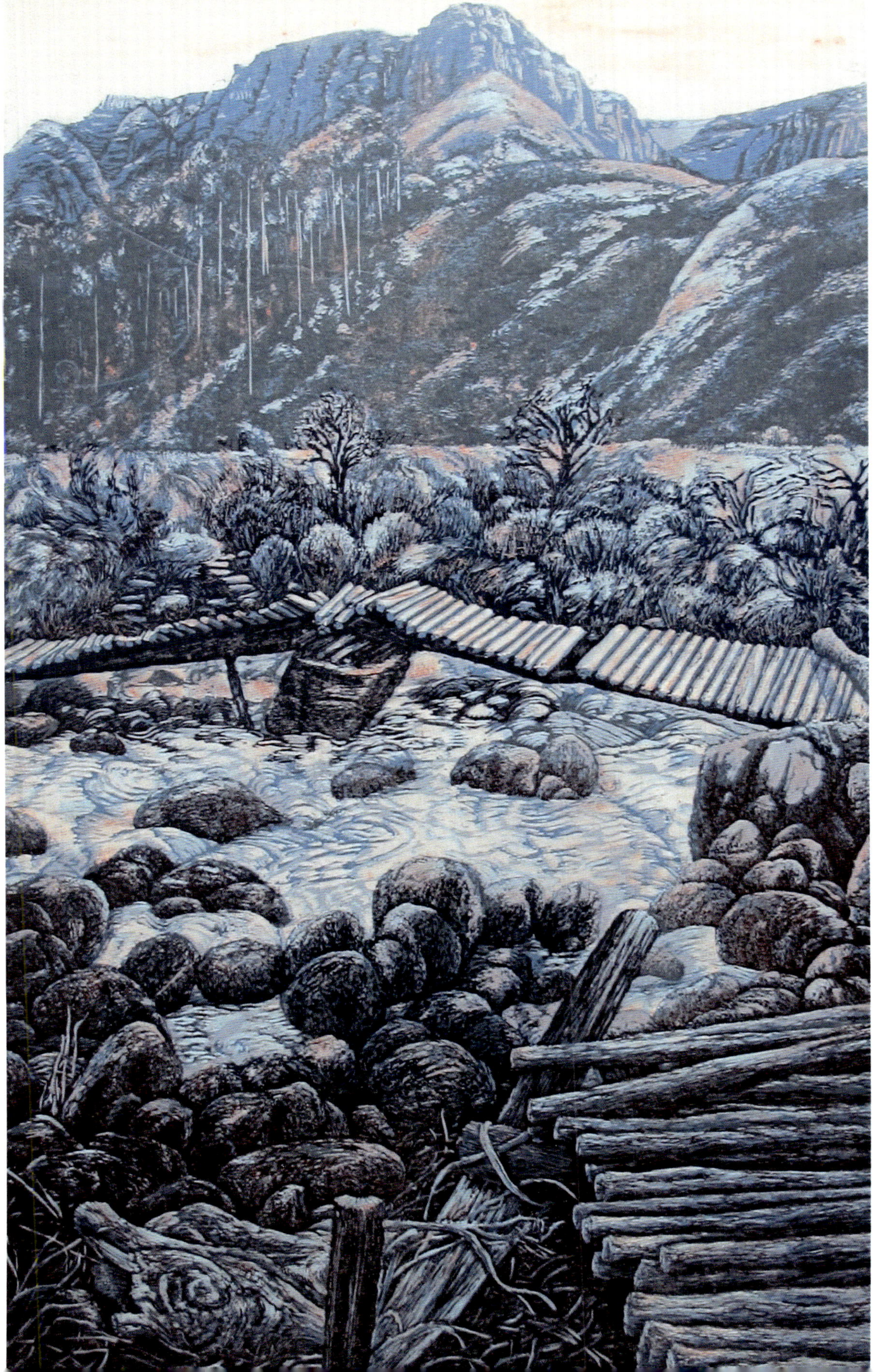

Steve Edwards

I was introduced to printmaking as a student at Camberwell School of Art and have been making prints ever since. My creative mind and the seductions of printmaking formed a bond back then which has never been broken.

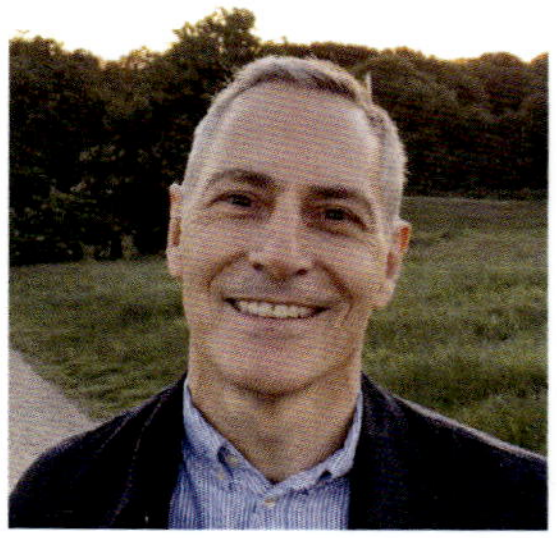

Education

1979 Foundation Course, Bristol Polytechnic
1980–83 BA Textile Design (with printmaking subsidiary), Camberwell School of Art and Crafts

Selected Exhibitions

2007 *Thin Skinned*, Waterloo Gallery
2007 *Love Letter to London*, Greater London Assembly
2008 *I Am 10*, Bankside Gallery
2008 *Wonderland*, Fairytale Museum, Bad Oeynhausen
2009 *Smokey's Tangle Lino Expo*, Oakland California
2009 *2nd International Print Exhibition*, Qijiang, China
2009 *Wonderland*, V&A Museum of Childhood
2010 *Link*, Space Arte Ora, Foggia, Italy
2011 *Big Ass Lino*, Pie Factory, Margate
2011 *Dreams*, Freud Museum
2012 *Images of The City*, Printroom at Home
2012 *Linoleum: The Cutting Edge*, Hemmingway Art Oxford
2013 *Highgate – A Reflection in Print*, Highgate Literary & Scientific Inst
2013 *Between Spaces*, Aberyswyth Art Centre
2014 *Why War?*, Freud Museum
2015 *50:50*, New Ashgate Gallery, Farnham
2015 *50 Years of Artists Prints*, Bankside Gallery, London

At college I was inspired by great artists such as Picasso, Miró and Dubuffet, who led me towards outsider art which still fascinates me today. I enjoy the freedom that those great artists and the outsiders have towards colour, mark-making and subject matter. Freedom in making is something I try to nurture in my own work.

So what is it about printmaking? For me, it is the combination of utilising the primal, creative hand/eye/brain combination coupled with the challenge of technical problem-solving that makes it so captivating. Also, it tends towards the co-operative, which I really respond to. Another aspect of printmaking that appeals to me is the variety of techniques to choose from and explore, each with their known language. At college I loved monoprinting which I found so expressive and free. Over the last few years I have returned to monoprint again and combined this freedom with a keyplate linocut block. I also practised and experimented with etching for many years, through which I started to explore more personal subject matter in my image-making. My current practice is, as ever, a distillation of all these printmaking experiences.

Around 2006 I began to make linocuts and, as a consequence, my work scaled up and became more colour-orientated. I remembered seeing an artist's work which had incorporated etched lino. The marks produced had intrigued me, so I found a recipe for caustic etch and started experimenting. I immediately liked the results, especially the combination of the more controlled cut marks with the less controllable etched marks. Another important step for me was layering multiple blocks to build an image. I use oil-based inks in order to obtain vibrant colour combinations, but also enjoy using extender in the ink to make transparent colours which I can overlay to create more complex colour combinations. Another big influence in my practice is using a computer as a tool for manipulating photography, originating imagery and planning prints.

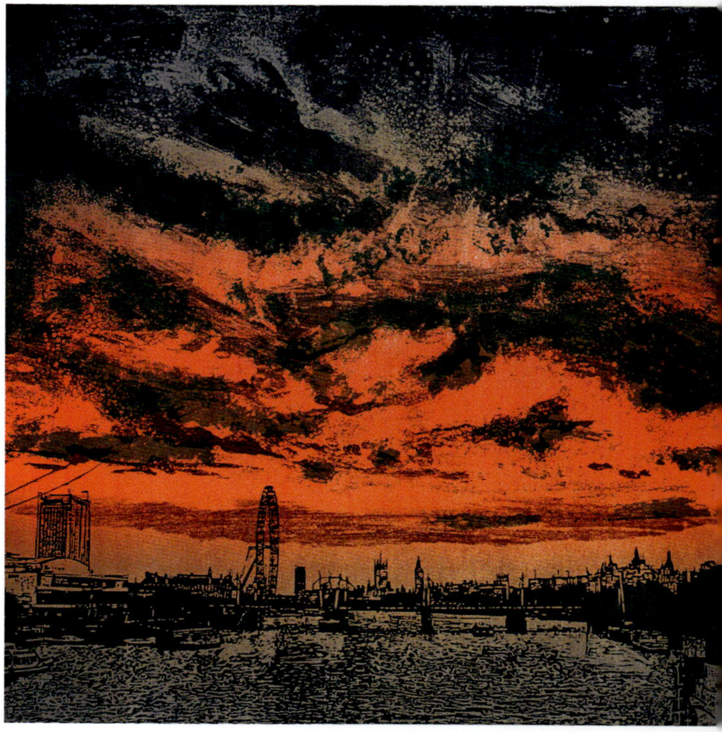

Bridge – West
56 x 56cm
etched and cut lino
(variable edition of 50)

OPPOSITE
Sunburst, 95 x 67.5 cm, etched and cut lino, (variable edition of 40)

Around this time I also started making cityscapes of London, as well as an ongoing series of ruined abbeys. These are the themes that are currently occupying my time and energy. I want these cityscapes/landscapes to be more than just locations. My aim is to capture an emotional response to these views, whether sublime or mundane, glorious or disturbing, juxtaposing the creations of man with the elemental.

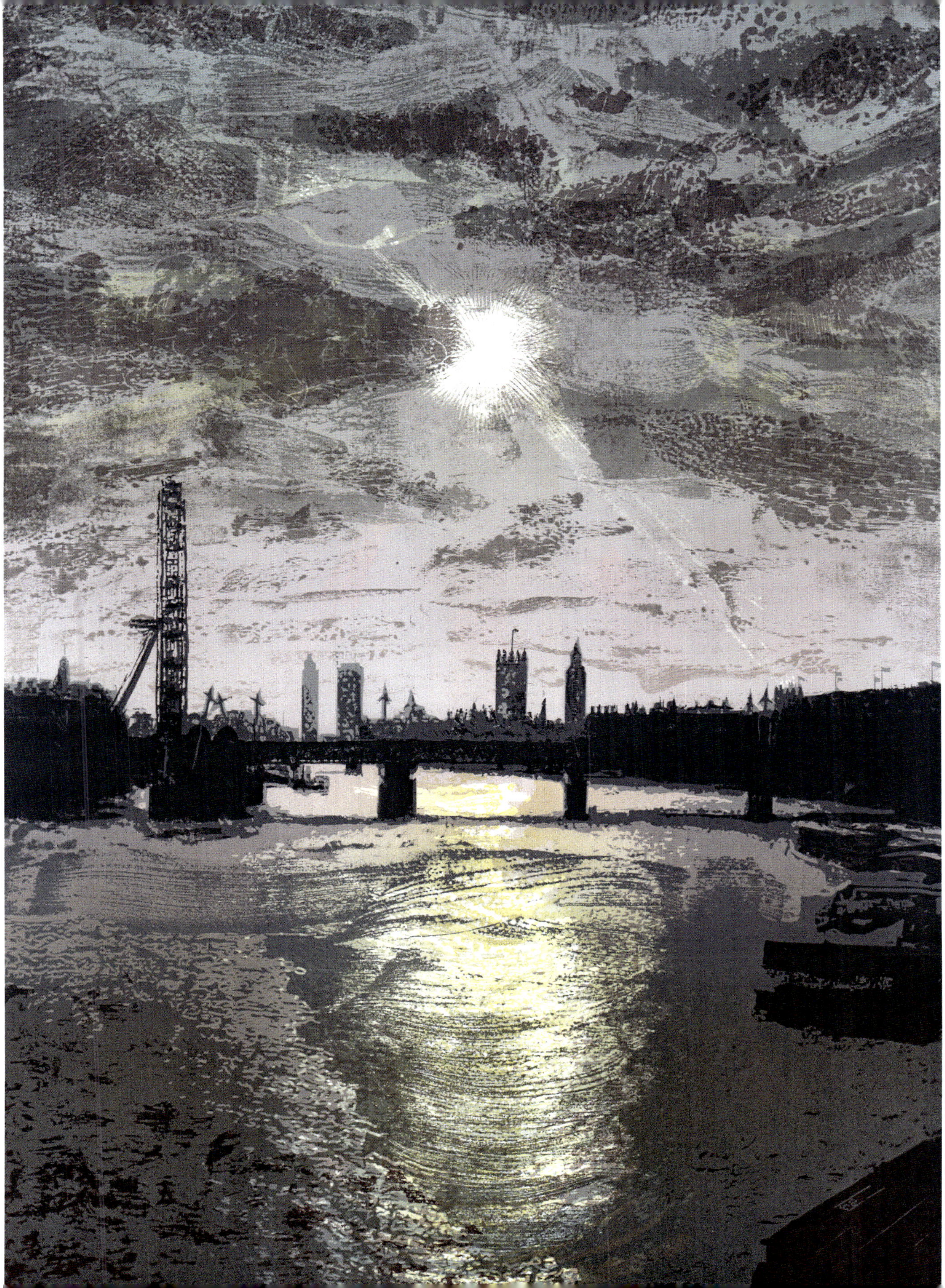

Matthew J Egan

In undergraduate school, printmaking offered opportunities to use the printed edition to explore several variations of an image. In graduate school, editioning a print became a means to participate in visual dialogues through print exchanges. My first teaching job, in a design school, encouraged considerations of combining traditional techniques and digital processes to explore the applications of printmaking.

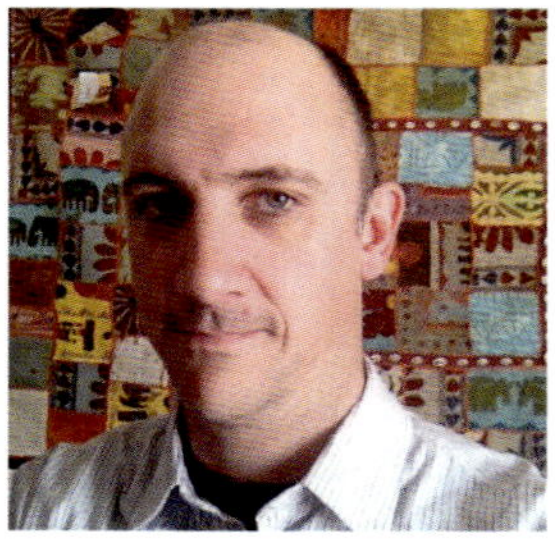

1973 Born Newmarket, Ontario, Canada
1992–97 BFA Printmaking, University of Windsor, Ontario
1996–present Member of the SGC International Printmaking Council
1996–98 Juried Travelling Exhibition
1997–2000 MFA Printmaking, University of South Dakota, USA
1998 *Contents and Contexts: Lithography after 200 Years*
2000–05 Foundations and Design Professor, American University of Sharjah, UAE
2003 *Implications of Representational Forms* Solo exhibition
2005–present Printmaking and Foundation Professor, East Carolina University, Greenville, NC USA
2008 *Minnesota National Print Biennial*
2010 *Pacific States Biennial National Print*
2011 Contemporary Print Portfolio (national collection surveying printmaking)
2011–15 East / West Portfolio Exhibitions
2012 Frogman's Print and Paper Workshop Colour Intaglio Instructor
2012 *Heavy Hitters* National Invitational Exhibitions
2012 *A Survey of Contemporary Printmaking* catalogue
2012–present Foundation Studies and Fine Arts Professor University of Sharjah UAE
2013–present *The Map is Not the Territory* travelling exhibition and catalogue
2014 *Direct Art* Magazine Competition
2015 *5th Guanlan International Print*

I find traditional hand-pulled prints to be a democratic process that promotes a visual dialogue. The process of drawing, making plates and printing layers of ink allows images to develop a sort of plausible arbitrary connection loosely based on the world we live in.

Printmaking offers opportunities to contemplate and develop imagery to consider social, political, and cultural metaphorical symbols. The image-making process reveals a plausible connection between intended and arbitrary subjects. Rather than a conclusive statement, my goal is to generate a visual language that becomes evident through the process. I am interested in the relationships and differences of the narrative and the collective story based on both present and historical events. I view printmaking as the intersection between painting and graphic design; artifact and ephemeral; contemplative and democratic; high art and low art. Recently, this has manifested itself in a series of narrative images that are often illustrative, metaphorical, formal and playful. This is an intuitive visual investigation to depict my environment and weave together events of the past and present from eastern to western hemispheres.

Through a series of hand-pulled lithographic prints I have been developing over the past decade, there is a history being developed through the collection of contemplative narrative images. Individual prints are motivated by spectacular, scary and astonishing events, by political policies, environmental catastrophes and human conditions. Many of the images reflect responses to events, while contemplating social and political situations. This often merges my perception, affected by being born in Canada, living in the United States and working in the United Arab Emirates while on leave.

My initial explorations in printmaking included drawing on the litho stone, transferring images and screen-printing colour. This has been refined to a state that mimics a commercial printing process that became influenced by teaching. Now the drawings initiate a composition for digitally produced colours, separated and printed on photo plates to support the lithographic drawings. The playful intuitive image relationships that were initially influenced by Mr Rauschenberg's Random Order have transitioned into a method of developing a suite of metaphorical allegorical prints more likely influenced by Goya's *Los Caprichos*. By combining traditional techniques and digital processes to generate colour lithographs, the process emulates the content with images that also merge the past and the present. The combination of images from media sources and fabricated drawings develop narratives ranging from historical events to contemporary issues.

Dinner Party, (*Dog Head Stew* 2 Portfolio 2015)
51 x 38 cm, lithograph (edition of 34)

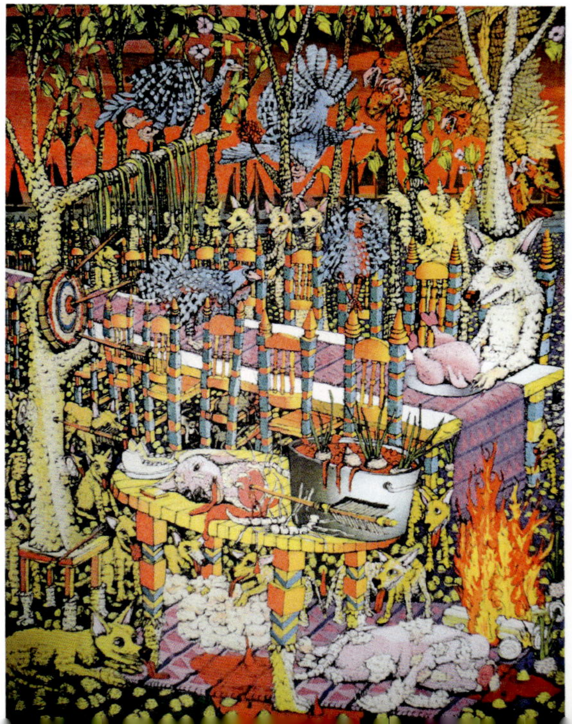

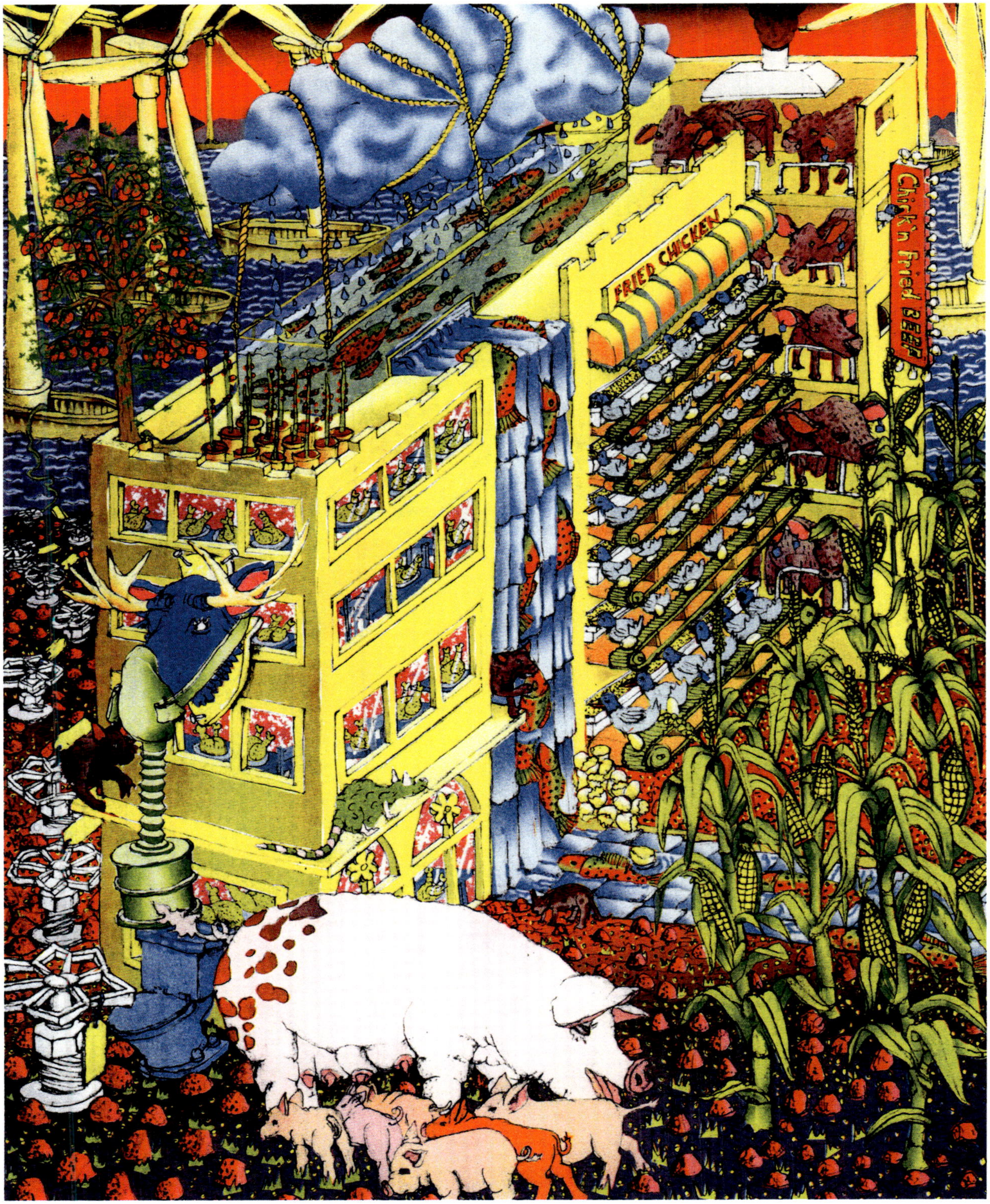

Hunters and Gatherers, (*Agritopia* Portfolio 2015)
35.5 x 28 cm, lithograph (edition of 36)

Shuxiang Jin Farrall

I became very interested in printmaking while studying at the University of East London, then Camberwell College of Arts London. I have enjoyed being a printmaker since then. My prints have been exhibited in many countries and collected by people in the UK and abroad. I use etching, lithography, monotype and linocut techniques to make my prints. I'm based in London.

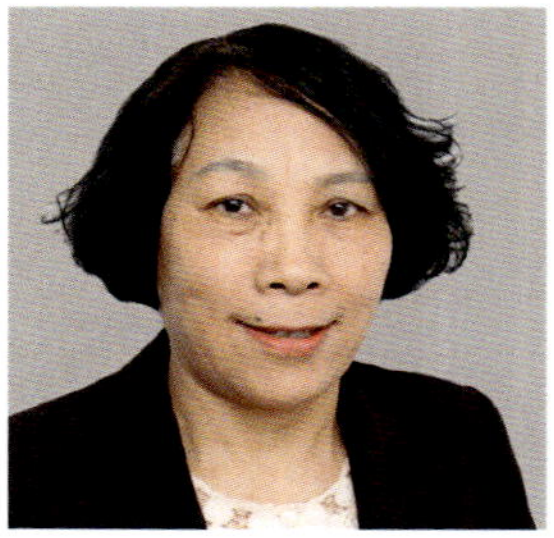

1997–2000 BA Fine, Art University of East London (UEL)
2000–02 MA Printmaking, Camberwell College of Art
2002 Joined Printmakers Council
2015 Consultant at Jinshi Gallery and Jinshijia Art and Culture Media Ltd, Tianjin China

Selected Exhibitions

2000 *Royal Academy Summer Exhibition*
2007 *International Art Fair*, Royal College of Art London
Journey - The Family Art London, Tianjin China
2008 *For Peace*, Mexico; *Loop 08*, London; Tours; London, Tokyo, South Korea
2009 *Originals 09*, Mall Galleries
7th British International Mini Print
2014–15 Cancer Research UK & British Heart Foundation Charities;
Artichoke Prints, Bankside Gallery;
50:50, New Ashgate Gallery

Awards and Public Collections

1999 Highly Recommended by Milliner Works London
2000 Purchase Prize by UEL
2002 Award by Artichoke Print studio & John Purcell Paper
Collections: UEL and Sheridan Russell Gallery London

My printmaking practice is centred on the exploration of my deepest feelings, dreams and life experiences. I work in an abstract style influenced by the natural world. Nature has always given me great pleasure and happiness, and provided me with support in my life when going through difficult times.

Many of my artworks are inspired by recollections of my childhood. I remember the fresh green grass full of dewdrops under my feet on cool, crisp early summer mornings when my grandfather would take me to see and gather mushrooms in the fields around our home. I would have a recurring dream where I would be able to communicate with the mushrooms.

These childhood memories and dreams of happiness have influenced my art practice over the years. And I have continued to study and be fascinated by mushrooms throughout my life. I have found so many different species in the fields and forests around London. In particular in 1998 during an art residency at the Hawkwood Education Centre in Epping Forest I discovered a vast array in the surrounding woodland. There I really touched, tasted and felt them, learning much more than ever before. I deeply explored mushrooms both in my artworks and my thoughts.

In my prints mushroom forms become living beings with their own feelings and thoughts. They experience a wide spectrum of emotions from joy and love to loneliness, parenthood and pain. Working with simple abstract forms surrounded by large spaces I aim to evoke powerful memories. I use soft, sharp and occasionally hard images while experimenting with a range of printing methods and techniques, informed by study at university of old and modern masters and practice over the years. I like Rembrandt, Picasso, Miró and Degas prints and their way of making prints. I want to combine the traditional with contemporary methods to make my prints. I strive to do this in a way that is new and fresh.

OPPOSITE
Dreams of Childhood, 30 x 20 cm, coloured stone lithograph (unique)

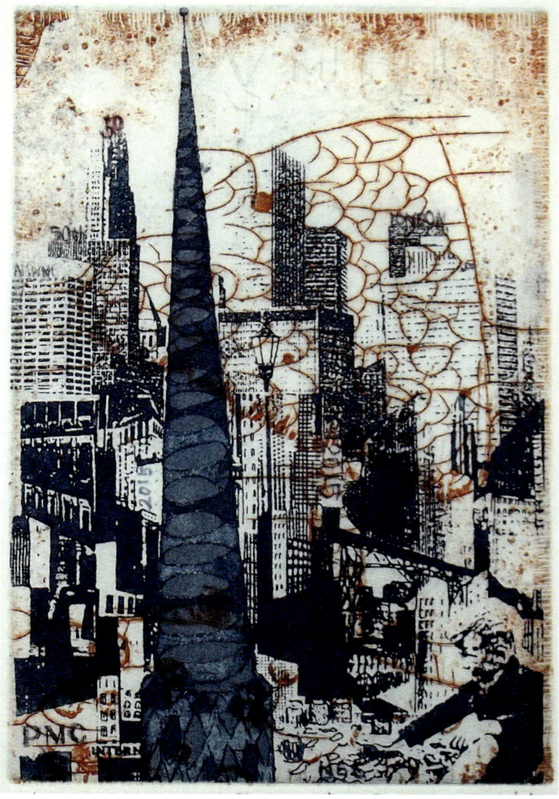

Memories, 16 x 11.2 cm, etching, drypoint, solar & monoprint (edition of 5)

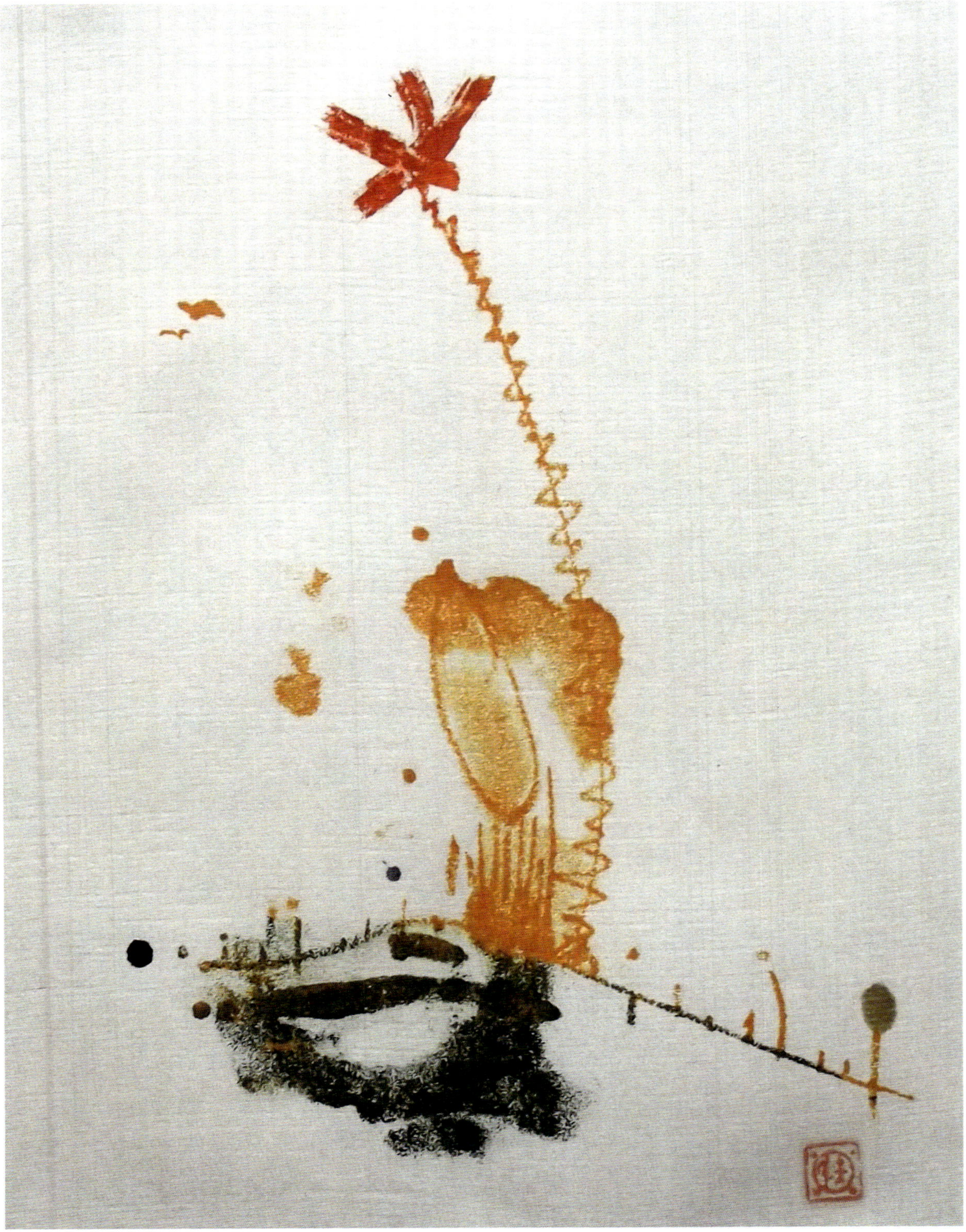

Peter Ford

My interest in printmaking began when a friend said my drawings looked like etchings. At that time I was an art teacher in my late thirties. I bought a small etching press, and between 1976 and 1994 I was a prolific maker of domestic-scale etchings and mezzotints, selling via galleries and dealers. Then I invented a new 'me' making mainly abstract images using collograph techniques combined with papermaking, another activity begun in that year.

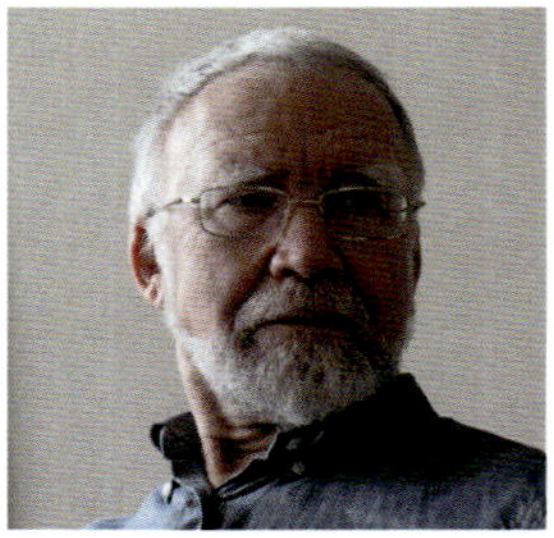

1937 Born Hereford
1960–61 Brighton College of Art and Design
1967–76 Teaching Art and English
1975 *Royal Academy Summer Exhibition*
1976 Elected PmC; Elected Senior Fellow RE
1975/85 Etchings exhibited internationally. Prizes in Spain, Korea, USA, UK
1985 First exhibited in Poland.
1987 Opened Off-Centre Gallery, Bristol, focussing on international art on paper.
1989/92 Organised *A Time of Transition, Printmaking from Russia*. Touring.
1994 *Bradford Print Biennale*. Received Openshaw Residency, Lowick House Print workshop, Cumbria.
1994 Began collographs, woodcuts and recycled paper.
1985/2014 Exhibitor in Poland – Łódź, Lublin, Warsaw, Kraków, Torun.
2001 Curator of *Made in Japan*. Bristol City Art Gallery and touring.
2004/13 Curator of 8 exhibitions at RWA including *Celebrating Paper*, 2010.
2006/13 Vice-President, Royal West of England Academy (RWA)Bristol.
2006 Prizewinner at *International Grafik Triennial*, Kraków
2007/15 Nine visits to China including personal exhibitions in Tianjin, Ningbo and Dongguan. Group exhibition participation in Beijing, Guangzhou, Hangzhou, Shenzhen and Harbin.
2008 First Prize, *Imprint 1*. Warsaw
2013 Royal Academy, London. Prize for Printmaking.
2015 Guanlan China International Print Prize; Hon PmC

In life something happens and then you can make a decision about what has happened. My attitude to printmaking is along these lines. I exercise minimal control at the beginning, then later make decisions based on what is on the plate or on the paper.

In common with many artists I find creative resources within my environment. I recollect the discovery of some painted roofing felt that was peeling away from an abandoned garden door near my home. It had nail holes and a weathered surface with a network of cracks. I cut it in half, altered it slightly, then inked, wiped and printed it using intaglio and surface ink. I was excited by the result. With some refinements this became *Equation III* and was a successful submission to the 1997 RA Summer Exhibition.

In my workshop there are trays and boxes of printable surfaces including thin wood, internal machine parts from printers and microwaves, odd unidentified things that drop off or come off. Sometimes I alter them by hammering on my anvil or change the surface with carborundum powder shaken onto white enamel or metal paint.

Another liberation of my later years is partially to abandon the habit of making uniform editions. I prefer to make a series of colour variants. When I have been obliged to make an edition, because there are exhibitions which will not accept monoprints, or because there are workshops that insist on resident artists making editions, these cloned images may lie in the dark recesses of my plan chest drawers, unloved and unseen. I can, as a last resort, recycle them into my own paper.

Papermaking has enabled me to make large designs even though I do not have a large etching press. I have managed with a converted Edwardian mangle for the past thirty five years. Modules of thick paper can be joined to make a large work in such a way that it can be folded and posted anywhere. Hence the wide geographical spread of my museum representations and exhibition history.

In printmaking now I am driven by the question 'What will happen if...?' The unpredictable nature of the outcome is the magnetic attraction. For me surprise is a key part of making and enjoying art.

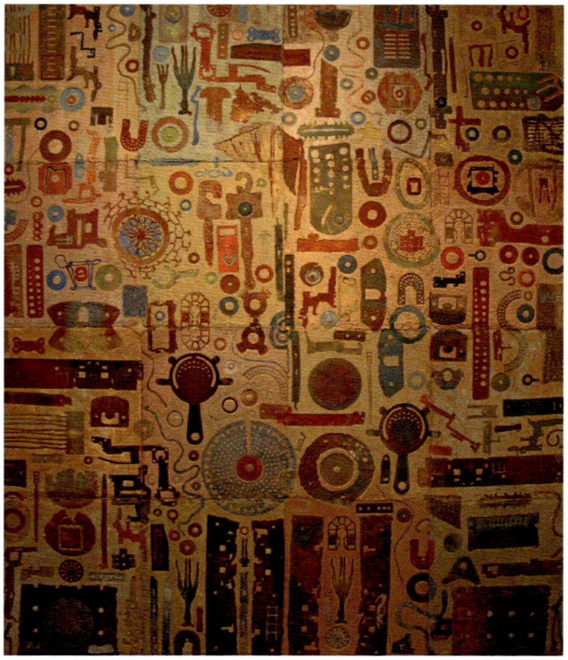

Private Collection
104 x 84 cm
relief print on handmade paper
unique

OPPOSITE
Surveillance City
140 x 139 cm
collograph on handmade paper
unique

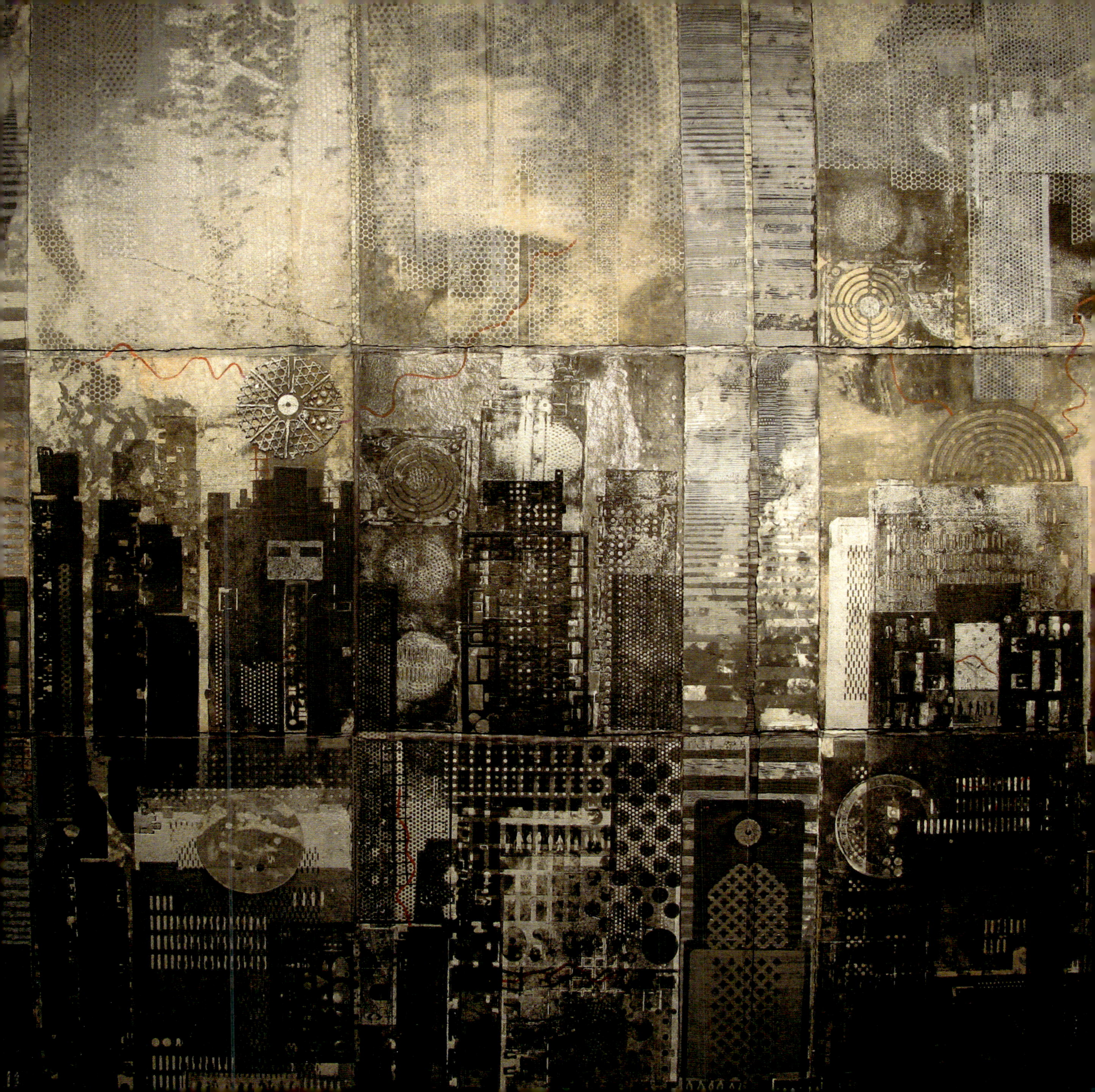

Kate Fortune Jones

After a long (and ongoing) career in the wonderful world of animation I have recently rediscovered the thrill and challenge of printmaking. As a Fine Art student over two decades ago I was fascinated by the diversity, rituals and mechanics of the different printmaking processes. And upon restarting my own art practice I was instantly hooked again, relishing the joys of working with ink, paper, rollers and presses!

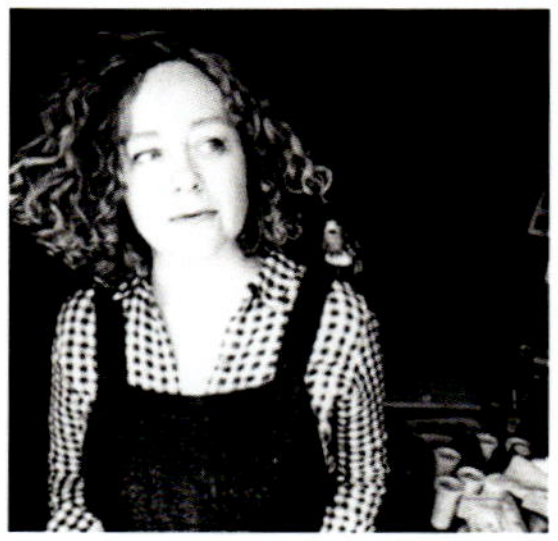

1967 Born Liverpool

1986-87 Liverpool Polytechnic Art and Design Foundation Course

1987-88 Liverpool Polytechnic Printmaking Access Course

1988-90 BA Fine Art Goldsmiths, University of London

1991-93 Postgraduate Diploma in the Cultural History and Theory of Photography, London College of Printing

1995–present Design Artist and Art Director in the Animation Industry, in Film and Television

2011–2013 Member London Print Studio

2014 Keyholder Member, Seacourt Print Studio Bangor, Co. Down

Recent exhibitions

2011 *November Ghosts of Gone Birds*, Rochelle School, London

2012 *Survival of the Fittest*, Waterworks Nature Trust, London; *Works on Paper*, RK Burt Gallery London; *Proof Perfect*, PmC Framers Gallery London

2013 *Nature through Art*, Castle Espie, WWT, Co. Down

2014 *International Mini Print*, Centre for Contemporary Printmaking, Bangor,Co.Down; *Fifty Years of Folk*, 50th Anniversary of the Ulster Folk and Transport Museum; *20:20 Print Exchange*, Hotbed Press

2015 *Works on Paper*, Barbican Library, London; Oceanographic Exhibition, Queen's University Marine Lab at the Centre for Contemporary Printmaking, Bangor, Co. Down

I have always loved drawing, and as a child would spend hours filling up sketch books. I had a keen appetite for trying out all manner of mark-making, as well as a particular penchant for pleasing surfaces on which to draw. This included, to my parents' dismay, multicoloured graffiti on pristine wallpaper, biro doodles on the smooth rubber backing of the family bath mat and the joy of repeated patterns drawn and stamped using my school eraser and fountain pen ink. The connection with printmaking is evident, as today I am still endlessly intrigued by the varied ways of applying the creative line and gesture – the potential of the duplicate, the response of the receptive surface and how these interrelate with the images I wish to create.

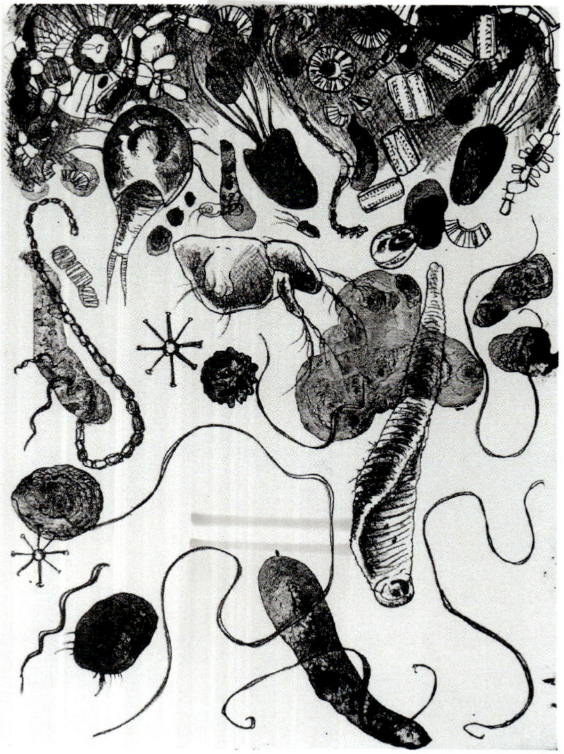

Following refresher courses at London's City Lit College and membership of the London Print Studio, I returned to printmaking after a 20 year absence. Mostly working with intaglio techniques I have gravitated toward etching, collograph and drypoint, but also employ silkscreen printing when a more graphic approach dictates. I frequently combine processes, exploring through chance and mistake as a means to investigate and broaden my printmaking 'vocabulary'. More recently I have been studying Lithography at the excellent Seacourt Print Workshop in County Down. The painterly marks and seductive drawing surface of this process appeal to my method of creative expression. Apart from traditional stone and plate, I am also exploring the possibilities of waterless lithography, using silicon with toner washes.

Central to my artwork is a focus on the natural world. A great deal of my childhood was spent outdoors – rummaging in the undergrowth, turning over stones, climbing trees, making bird hides as well as collecting curios in jam jars to study and paint. This passion and fascination for natural history has been the overriding preoccupation for my art since those early bug-bothering days. Inspired by this knowledge I continue to acquire, my work is an attempt to merge factual observations with more personal imaginary wonderings. And by employing the inherent qualities of specific print processes and my handling of them, I aim to create more abstracted landscapes, organic forms, flora and fauna which are gently odd or unfamiliar. This in turns creates a visual tension suggesting an underlying narrative of disquiet and anxiety. Issues of damage, loss and extinction are key concerns for me.

The Soup
waterless lithograph
23 x 31 cm
(edition of 10)

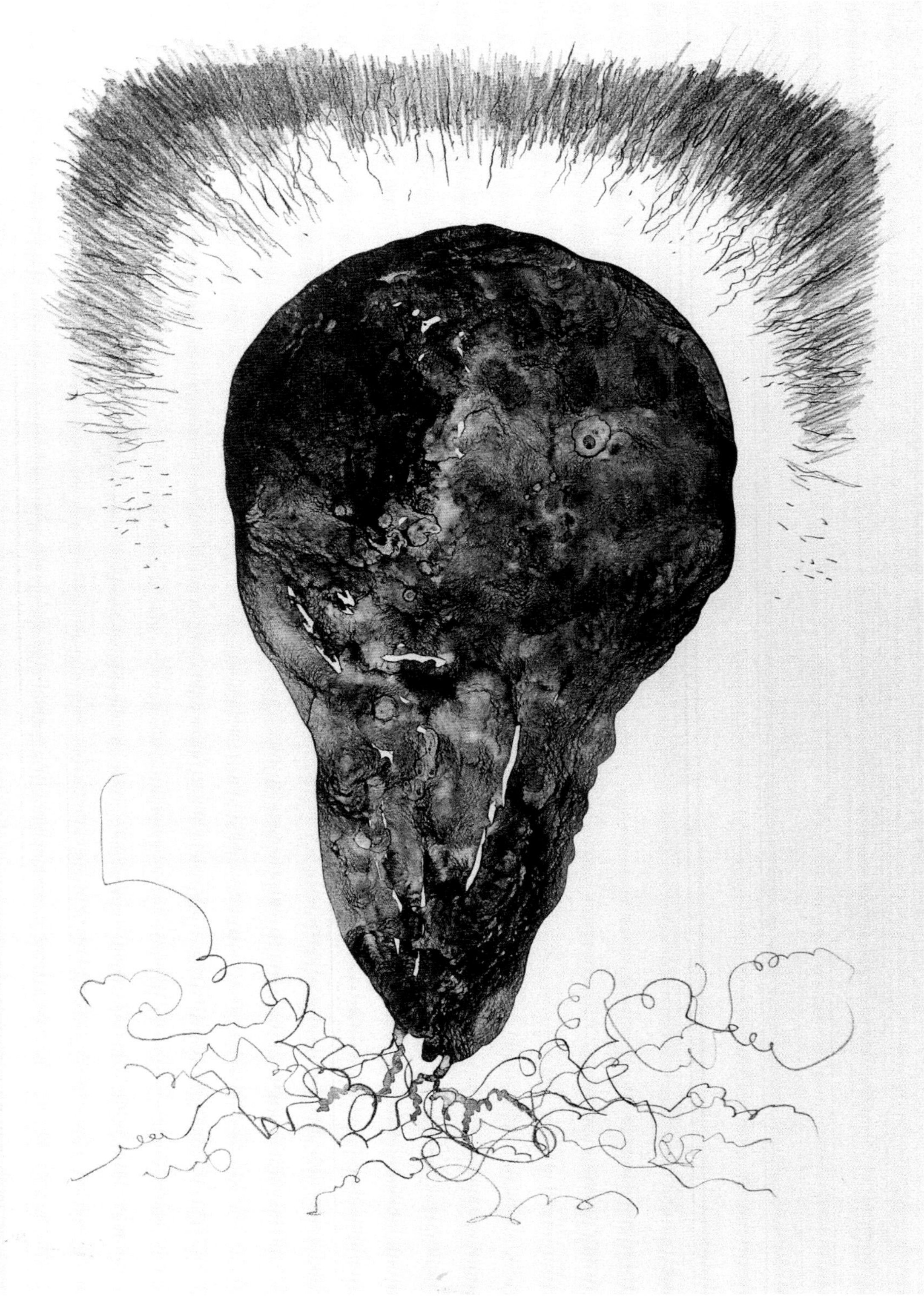

The Quarry
waterless lithograph
43 x 57 cm
(edition of 10)

Heather G Foster

Printmaking became my greatest interest after being given a piece of zinc and an etching needle by a lecturer-printmaker. Drawing has always been my first love so I took to etching instinctively. Since then I have experimented with etching in many different ways.

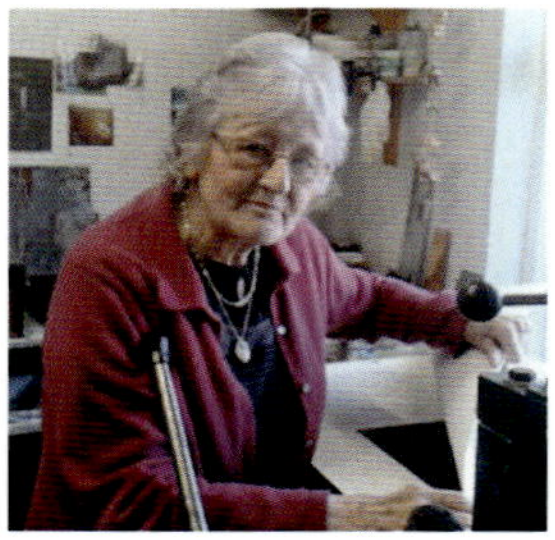

1929 Born Nottingham
1951 National Diploma in Design (Painting), Camberwell School of Art, Art Teachers Diploma, University of London
1984 Joined Printmakers Council
2000–01 Studied safe etching with Keith Howard & Freidhard Keikeben, Dumfries Arts Centre.
2001 Member, North and South Printmakers

Exhibitions

1993 *Royal Academy Summer Exhibition*
1999–2000 *Contemporary Print Show*, Barbican (North and South Printmakers)
1999/2000/2003 RWA Bristol Open (St Cuthbert's Mill paper prize)
1999–2013 Various PmC exhibitions
2002 Solo exhibition, The Vortex, London
2003–15 Various exhibitions at Mercer Open, prize winner 2003
2010–15 Open Studios Knaresborough with jeweller Chris Phillipson
2012/13 Norwalk Gallery of Contemporary Art, USA

Commissions

Murals for William Cooper Ltd Nottingham and Costain West Africa
Prints for Grantham O'Donnell Estates Ltd, Knaresborough; Rural Arts Commission, Lincs; Cawood Smithie & Co, Harrogate

Collections

Mercer Gallery, Harrogate; Pictures in Public Places, Yorkshire Arts; Scarborough Art Gallery; Musee Adzak,Paris; Tamar Art University, Tokyo, Japan

Heather trained as a painter but since she discovered etching, this became her main method of working. She also taught drawing and colour in various educational institutions from local art schools to University and latterly the International Baccalaureate – lecturer and moderator. Drawing forms the foundation of all Heather's work, be it painting or etch. Quality of light, texture and pattern together with the drama of landscape are prime sources of inspiration.

After spending time with Keith Howard and Freidhard Keikeben she changed her workshop and methods totally to safe intaglio-type methods using UV light box, ImageOn film and drawing on TruGrain. This proved a very successful way of working.

Unfortunately, since the onset of arthritis two years ago, she has had to move forward yet again, so she started to use the iPad. She still loves landscape and wanted to keep the same quality of mark-making. After experimenting with several different Apps she discovered one which gave her the way forward. After learning to use the App and an immense amount of patience, she was rewarded with the kind of print she was looking for – a different concept but equally rewarding. Her subjects are still mainly landscape as before, colour, texture, light and pattern still forming the basis of her work. These are printed professionally on fine art paper in limited editions. They can be printed to any size which makes an exciting prospect – these prints are now accepted in print exhibitions.

She has exhibited and sold in many places both in UK and abroad and hopes to continue to do so with her iPad.

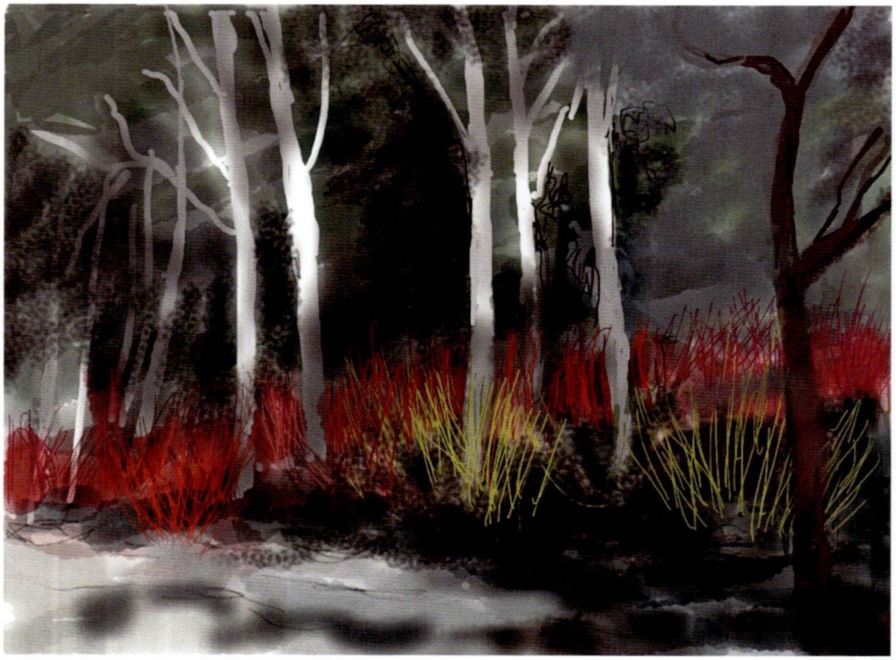

Harlow Carr, printed to desired size, iPad (edition of 50)

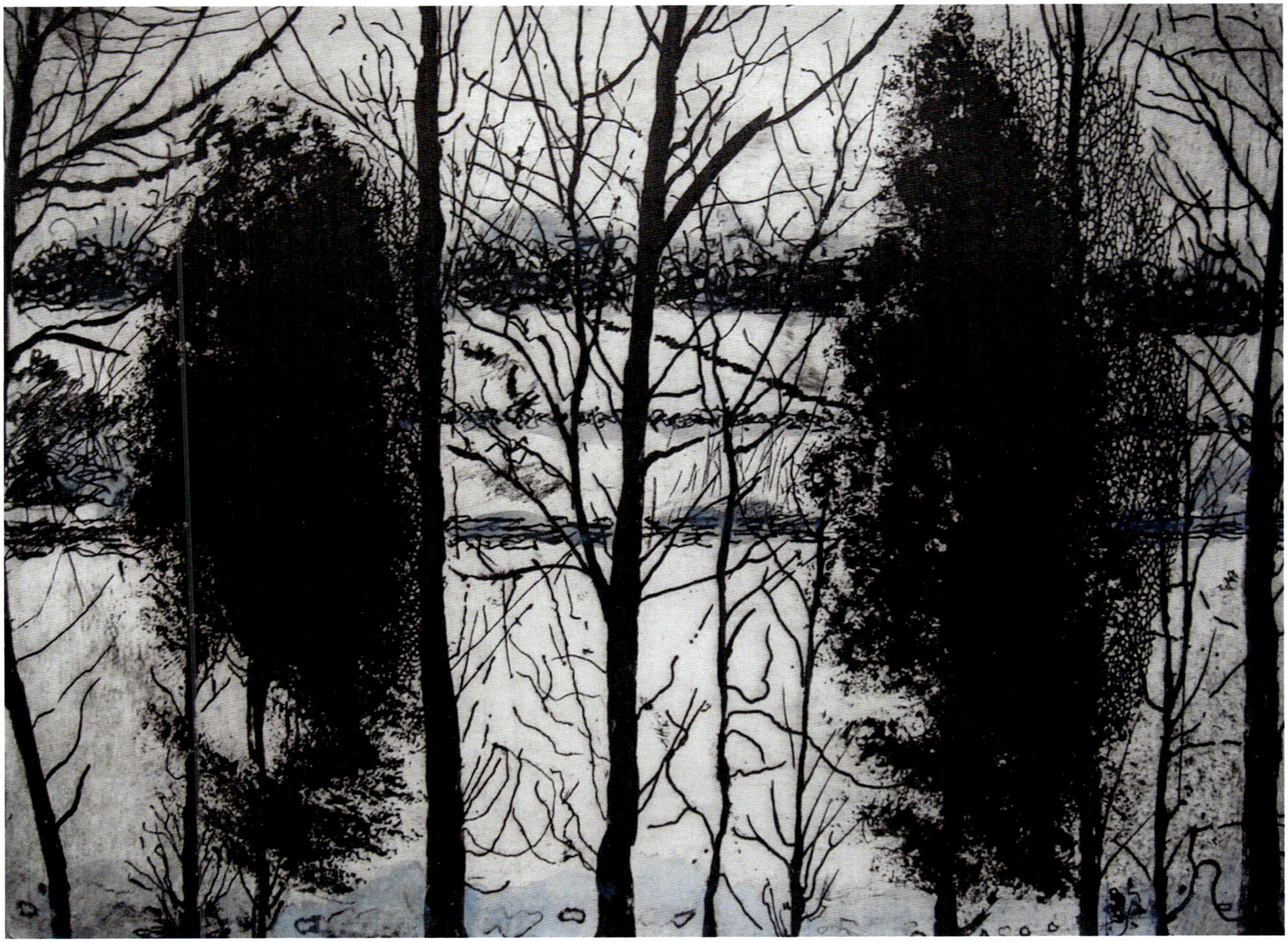

Dark Trees, 16 x 25 cm, intaglio-type etch (edition of 10)

Christina France Crews

Following a career in the design industry in France, Christina now works as an artist printmaker. She lives and works between her studio in London and Kent, returning to her adoptive country whenever possible.

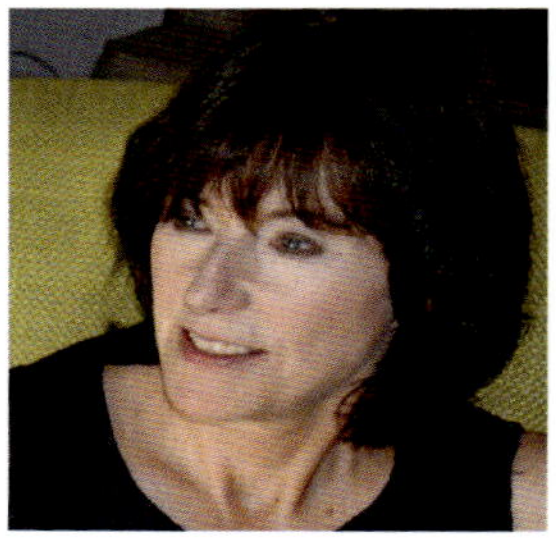

1977–80 BA (Hons) GCAD

1980–82 MA Printed Textiles, Manchester Metropolitan University

1986–2005 Designer in industry, Alsace, France

Selected recent exhibitions 2015

Generator group show curated by Saturation Point at the Kaleidoscope Gallery, Sevenoaks

NHS Greater Glasgow and Clyde Hospital Trust: Exhibition of recent acquisitions.

50:50 Online exhibition celebrating 50 years of the Printmakers Council

BAR inaugural Print Exhibition, London

Works on Paper Barbican Library

Art Market with Making Art Work, Maidstone, Kent

Group exhibition, Beaney Gallery, Canterbury, Kent

Work held in private and public collections in France, UK and the USA.

Following a BA (Hons) in Fine Art at Gloucestershire College of Art and Design, in 1980, Christina undertook an MA in Printed Textiles at Manchester Metropolitan University. Her first forays into print, were freestyle screen prints onto cutout shapes and she was commissioned by the Royal Northern Ballet company to design and produce costumes and sets for a new ballet, *Ten Easy Pieces*. Stating 'I was always drawn to the way that forms and colours could be made to dance', her work has taken many directions but has always engaged with these elements: form, colour and movement.

Her formal education was followed by a career as a designer in the textile industry in France. Christina also held academic posts in both France and the UK, including Cardiff Metropolitan University, the Higher Institute of Art and Design, Alsace, France and the Museum of Printed Textiles, Mulhouse.

Returning to her roots as a fine artist in 2010, she started experimenting with etching and learnt the fundamentals of this and other printmaking techniques at Kensington and Chelsea College. She says, "I was, if you'll excuse the pun, bitten by the alchemy of the process of etching and beguiled by its endless possibilities".

As an artist and printmaker, I work from drawings or collages which are assembled and reassembled using random actions to determine placement. The rules, or non-rules for the work are set down initially but respond to the physicality of the material and consequences of the actions taken in its construction.

Contemplating abstract languages of form, my work responds to the techniques of printmaking with spontaneity and restraint. The intangibility of the printing process and elements of chance determine the end result.

Deliberation of the haptic nature of the work is present; traces of marks made by the hand are evident or underlying.

Counterbalance, 20 x 20 cm, photopolymer etching (limited edition of 20)

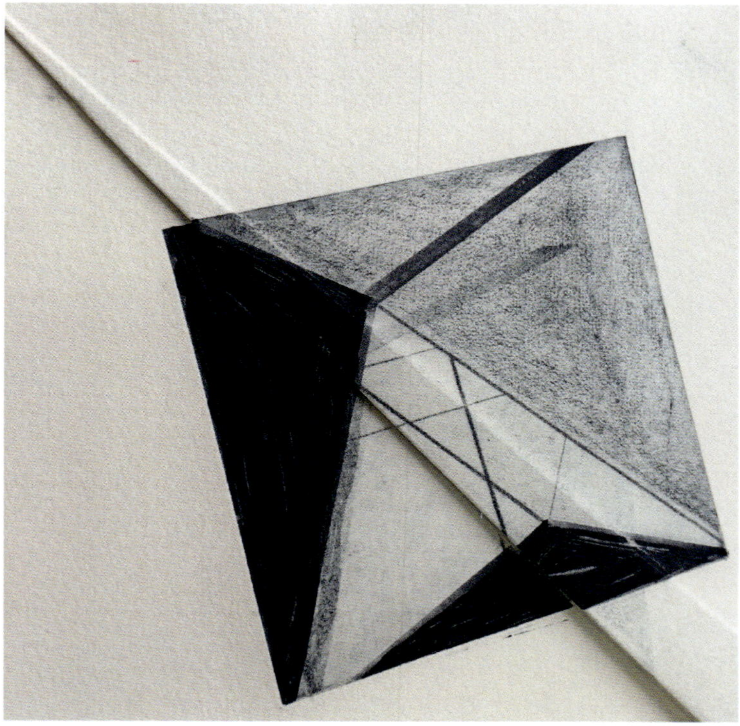

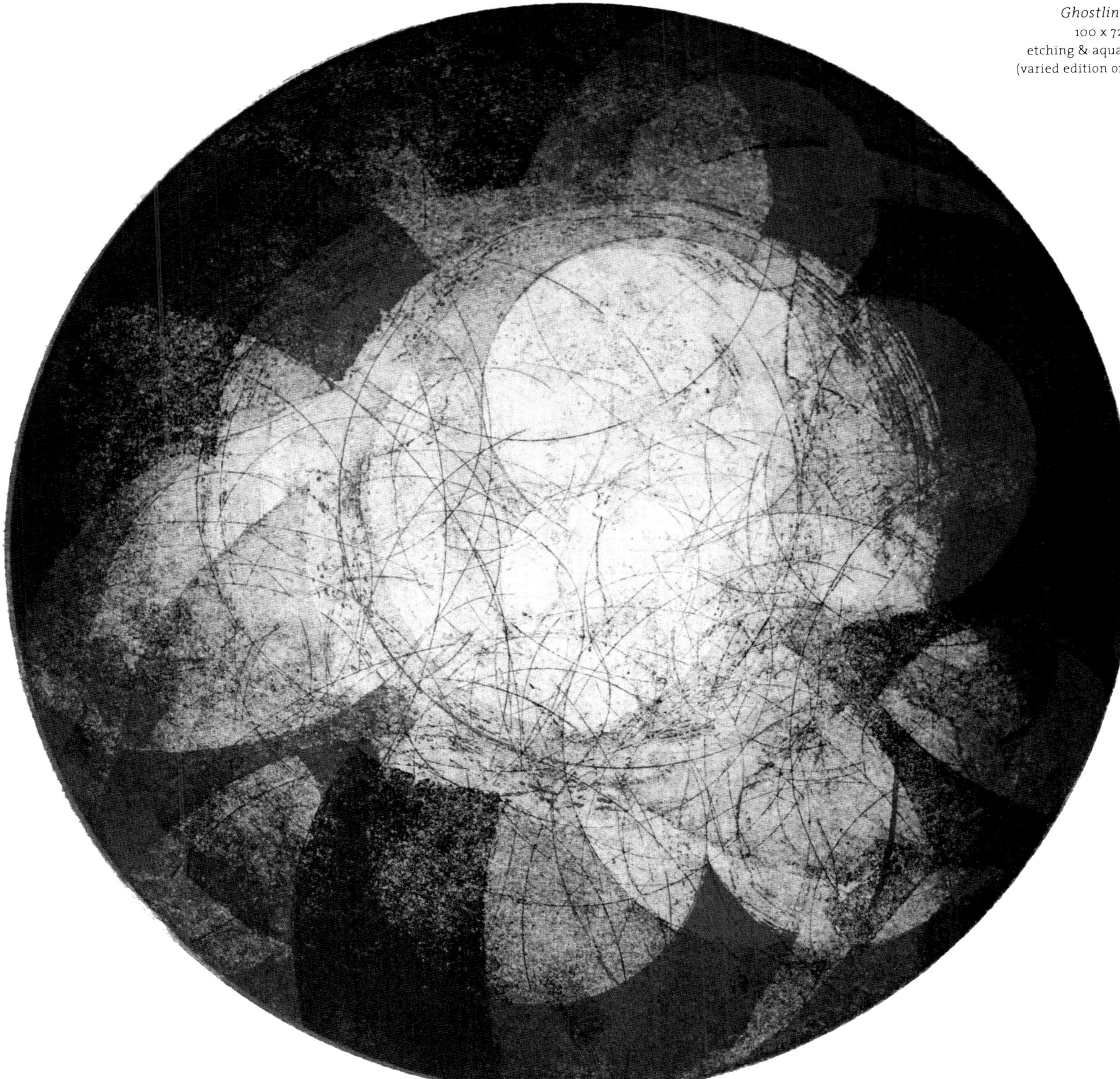

Ghostlines 4
100 x 72 cm
etching & aquatint
(varied edition of 20)

Janet French

My work explores the fragile symbiotic relationship between man and the natural environment. I work in tune with nature to create work that is testimony to my interaction with materials, conditions, seasons and weather. I transform leaves and fibres into paper on which I print images using various printmaking processes.

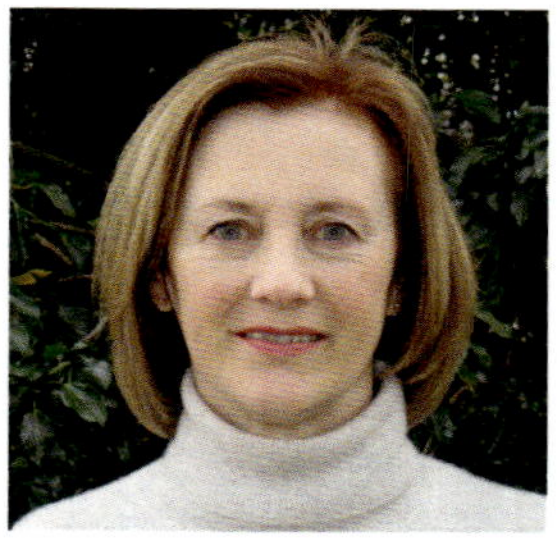

1955 Born UK
2003 National Diploma in Fine Art, Colchester School of Art & Design
2006 BA (Hons) Art & Design Fine Art, Colchester School of Art & Design

Exhibitions 2006–2012 include

2006 *Individual Perspectives in Drawing Practice*, Hay Gallery, Colchester
2007 *Oh Art*, Oxford House, Bethnal Green, London. *Down to Earth*, Pond Gallery, Snape. Fingringhoe Nature Reserve Artist in Residence including Adult/ Children's Workshops. Photographic exhibition of work produced during residency
2008 *Down to Earth*, Hay Gallery, Colchester
2012 Solo Show, Naze Tower
2009–12 Chair (Joint), Gainsborough's House Printmakers
Work in Public Collection - St. Elizabeth Hospice, Ipswich
2013 *Suffolk Showcase*, Smith's Row. *Royal Academy Summer Exhibition* *Art in Action*, Oxfordshire Demonstrating Printmaker. Artworks Annual Exhibition. Gallery in the Garden Summer Exhibition. Annual Exhibition, Cobbold & Judd. Addenbrooke's Arts. Selected Exhibition, Bath Society of Artists
2014 *Affordable Art Fair*, Brussels *Affordable Art Fair*, Battersea *20/21* Royal College of Art *Art in Action*. Oxfordshire – Demonstrating Printmaker Addenbrooke's Arts. *Hampshire Art Fair*.Cobbold & Judd Annual Exhibition Artworks Annual Exhibition Cambridge City Art Fair
2015 *Selected Exhibition*, Bath Society of Artists. Cobbold & Judd Anniversary Exhibition, Orwell Park Orangery Lecture, Orwell Park Shortlisted *Royal Academy Summer Exhibition*. Artworks Annual Exhibition. The Brighton Art Fair.

I use a variety of printmaking mediums including linocut, woodcut, Japanese woodcut and screen-print on to handmade paper which I create using leaves and fibres gathered from the local fields and woodlands, on which my images are based. The varied surfaces I am working on require different printmaking methods. I aim to create a symbiosis between print and paper by, for example, allowing the textured surface to break through the image or employing the translucent quality of the leaves by printing on the reverse and allowing the image to show through. The leaves are gathered in autumn and processed using traditional papermaking methods and techniques which I have developed to produce a continuous sheet of paper without the aid of added adhesives. It has been a fascinating journey to discover the diversity in the appearance of the paper produced from the leaves of different trees. The leaves of each tree behave differently and the process is one of continuous experimentation.

As a full elected member of Artworks I have exhibited in their annual exhibition since 2008, given printmaking demonstrations during the event and led printmaking workshops in primary and secondary schools.

While studying for my degree, I joined the Gainsborough's House Print Workshop and later went on to chair the Gainsborough's House Printmakers Committee with Emma Buckmaster. We set up monthly talks and demonstrations and organised regular exhibitions and events for members. We also set up The Gainsborough Prize for Graduate Printmakers which is now in its fifth year. During that time Emma and I began a collaborative printmaking project, Tree Portraits, which are a series of etchings of native trees printed onto paper made from the trees' own leaves. We were invited to *Art in Action* to demonstrate this project and we continue to add more trees to our collection each year.

Tilia, etching on lime leaves
51 x 43 cm (edition of 25)

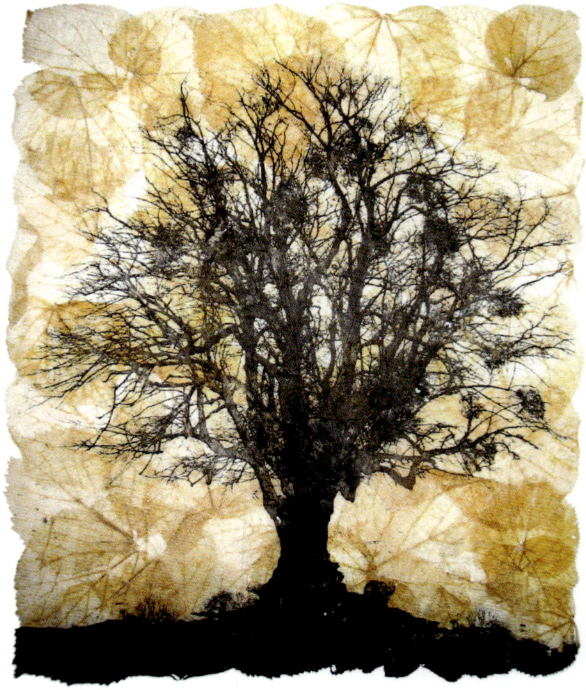

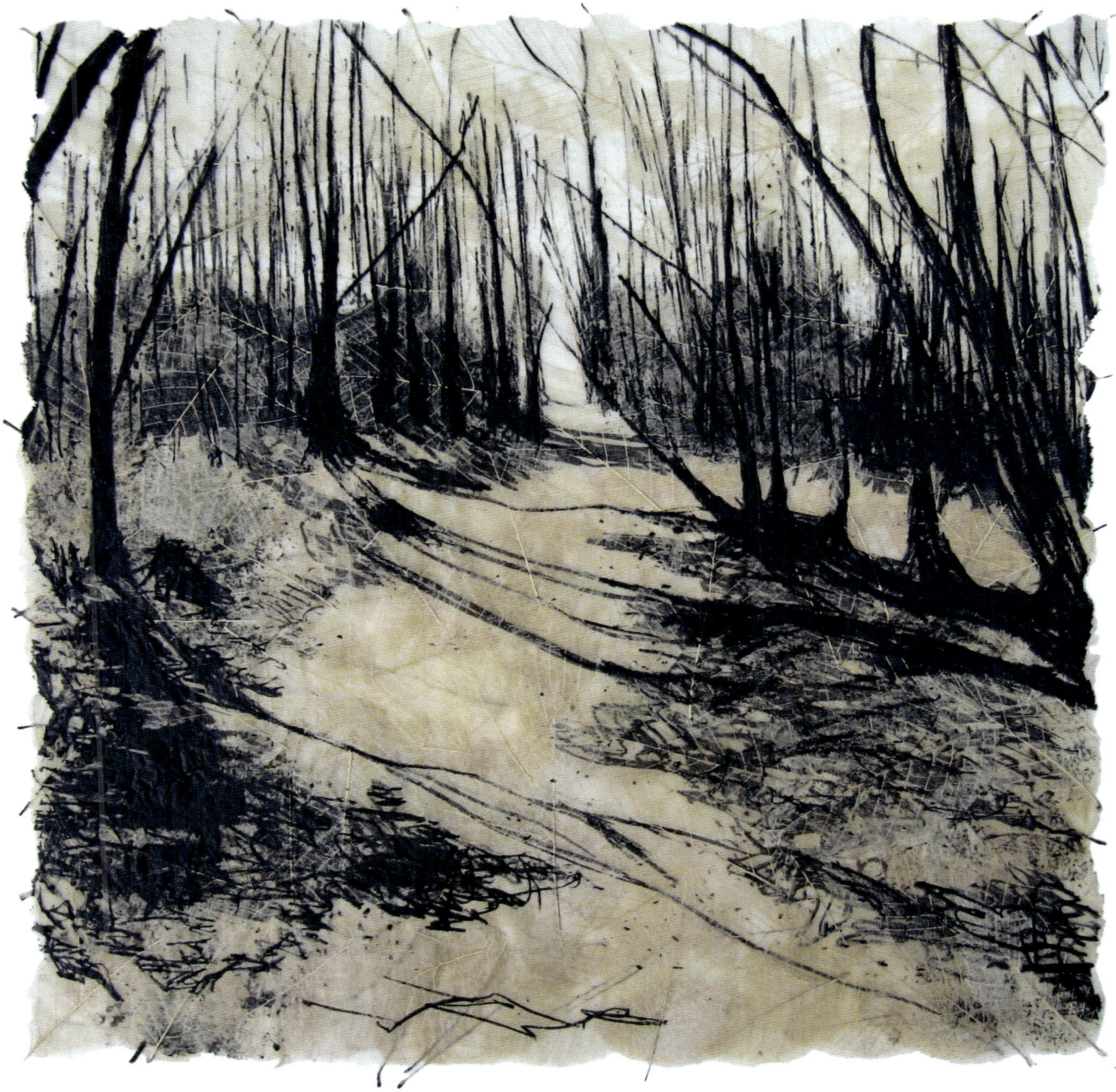

Looking Ahead, screen print on hornbeam leaves, 63 x 64 cm (edition of 7)

Diane Comte Frost

I am very inspired by my travels and the cultural differences as well as the similarities encountered away from home. I always carry both a sketchbook and a notebook and I bring my sketches and poems/notes back to the studio to provide the starting point of many etchings and mixed-media monoprints. Translating notes into a print, or a sketch into a poem, is what I find most rewarding and the reason why I always love going back to the press!

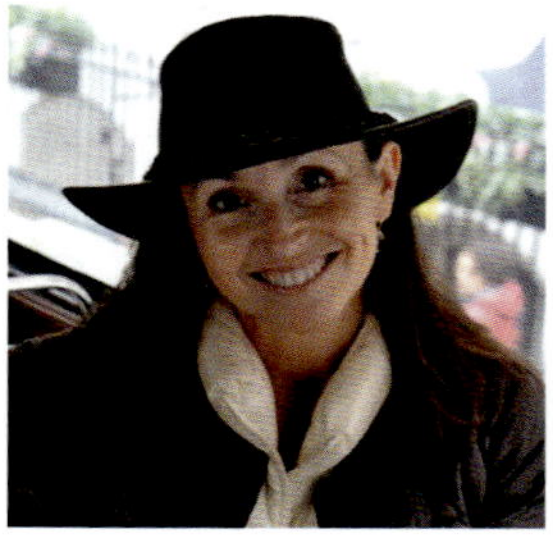

1964 Born Nîmes France
1985 BA La Sorbonne
1988 MA La Sorbonne
1989 PG Degree Communication and Media, Ecole Supérieure de la Publicité
1988–94 Worked in Advertising, Marketing and Media
2000 Dip Translation Chartered Inst. Linguists
2000 Self-employed translator
2004–05 Published in Forward Press - *Poetry Now*
2012-14 Printmaking, Kensington and Chelsea College
2013 Printmaking Award, Kensington and Chelsea College
2012/13 WLAC *Postcard Anon* Shows
2014 PmC Award
2014 Joined PmC and London Print Studio
2014 Curator and Exhibitor, *West London Original Prints Show*, Apothecary Gallery CIC
2014 Published in Flammes Vives - *Anthologie Poétique*

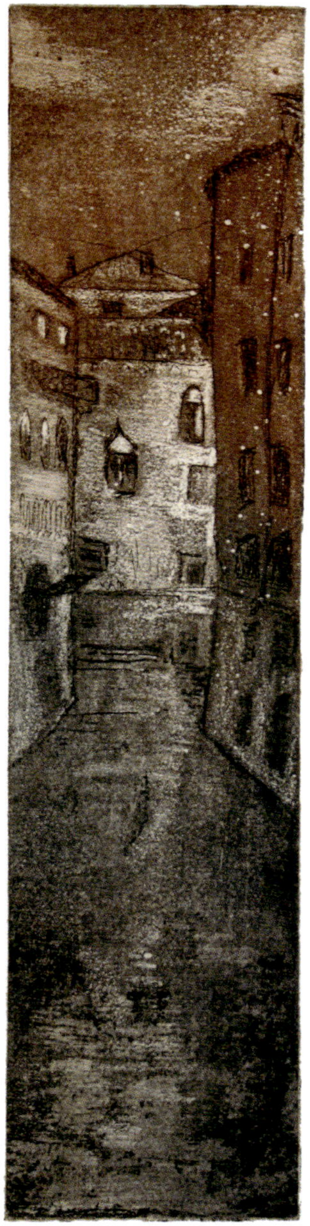

Venice II
38 x 57 cm
etching with aquatint
on Somerset paper
(open varied edition)

Coming from a background of translation and creative writing, I find my writing and my printmaking practices represent a necessary balance in my artistic expression and I am working towards finding new ways of combining the two both visually and stylistically. For me, paper and printing inks are a very exciting combination and I am looking forward to progressing towards artists' books.

I enjoy combining different techniques in the same print such as nature printing with photo etching, collograph with drypoint or lino with collograph: the various layers make for a richer fabric and I am very inspired by stories and places.

My images tend to have a strong narrative: They are fragments of a story or suggest different interpretations of the same clues. The lines of text and the lines of the etchings tend to echo each other and very often I try to mix them both.

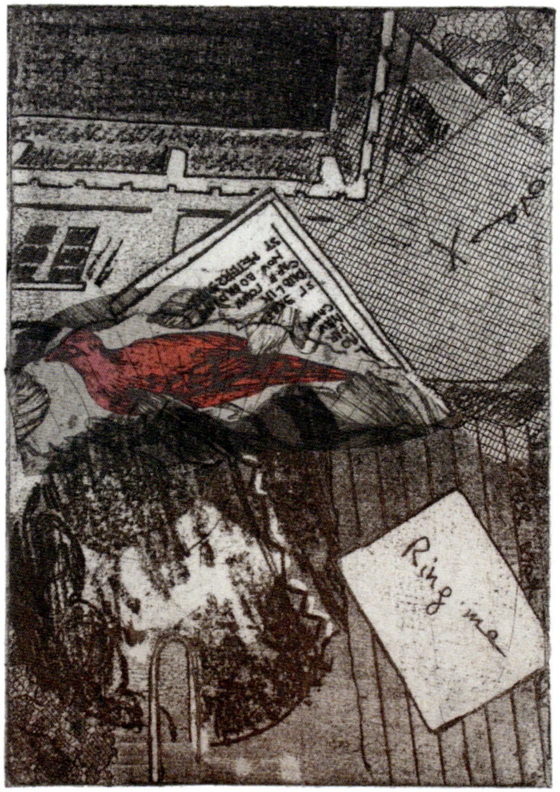

Ring me II
37 x 50 cm
etching & chine collé
(varied edition)

OPPOSITE
A Palace Full of Legends...
76 x 57 cm
etching & chine collé
(varied edition)

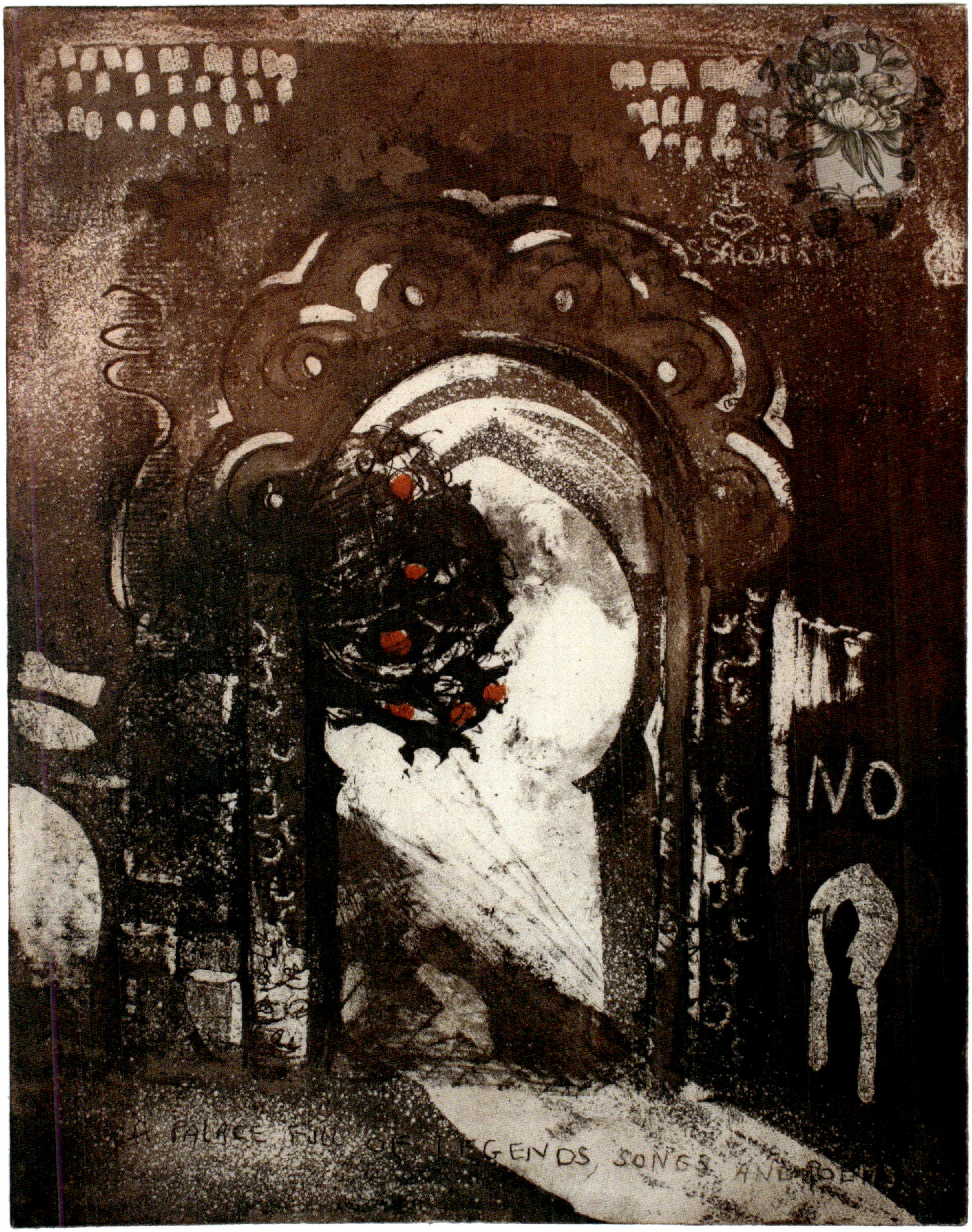
NO

Sarah Garvey

Before I began printmaking, I was making projections and films but missed getting my hands dirty. Printmaking brought my drawing practice and projections together. I enjoy combining this historic medium, so manual and unpredictable, with the colder digital technology, pushing the image back and forth until I have something 'other'. This seems a true reflection of the way I live, constantly bombarded with stills, videos and art from any period and all of the tangents and relationships this creates.

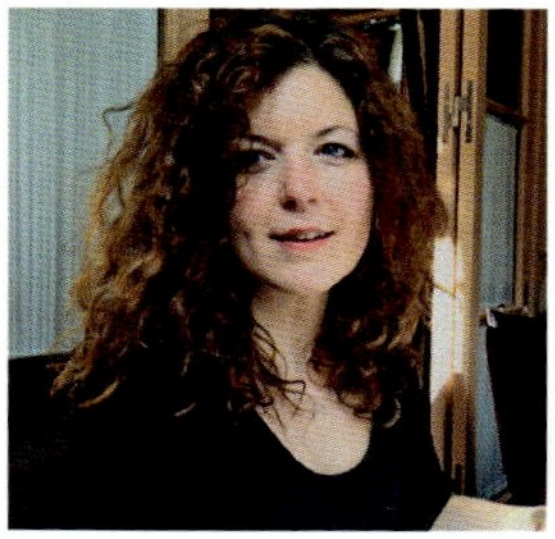

1980 Born London
1998 Central St Martins Foundation
1999–2001 Camberwell Visual Arts: Drawing
2006–10 Waterloo Gallery
CGP London Annual Open,
Supine Studios Hackney
2011 Residency, Cornaro Institute Cyprus
Printmakers Inc. Gallery at *The Affordable Art Fair*, Hampstead
Publication in *The New Encyclopedia of Watercolour Techniques*
2012 Join Printmakers Council
Lessedra Mini Print Annual
Framers Gallery with PmC
Chelsea Fringe
2013 Join East London Printmakers
Great Western Studios with PmC
Printmakers Inc. at *The Affordable Art Fair* Hampstead
Royal Academy Summer Exhibition, awarded Arts Club Charitable Trust special purchase Prize
2014 Join Barbican Arts Group Trust Studio
1 of 1 Design with Sam Hodge and John Bishcoff
Royal Society of British Artists Annual Mall Galleries
National Original Print, Bankside awarded prize from Great Art/ WLAC, Christie's Auction House/ *Art Rabbit* Haggerston Riviera
2015 *Artventure* at Wet Paint Gallery
Crouch End Open Studios

My prints are collages made from charcoal drawings, film stills, newspaper clippings, vintage and contemporary snaps which I collect and keep sometimes for years until the time is right. Often a motif is repeated through several prints. I cut, draw and mark both digitally and manually, building up the image which I often then cut again before creating a single plate to work from.

Then I ink up in layers, working from light to dark. I use large Japanese rollers to create blends and then print them cumulatively one on top of the other. Lastly the motifs are inked in black or the very darkest tone and printed over the other colours. Etching allows great subtleties of tone to be created and different colour palettes can be endlessly explored. The image evolves as I make it, rather than having a predetermined end.

My current plates are all printed on a layer of fibrous Sanwa tissue which is woven through with flecks of gold and silver leaf. This tissue creates an evident surface texture and the flecks vary from print to print. I also use chine collés (glued papers) made from ephemera such as envelopes, old music, slips, snaps, tickets and tags in older prints, bringing the collage element full circle.

The reversal of image that occurs in printmaking is significant for me, creating a mirror world to explore. I play with archetypal motifs from art history and films that I love, to build a bridge between my personal experiences and a more collective dream. I hope to make heightened sensuous projections to share in the dark.

Sing Me a Song about the Moon
40 x 28 cm, solarplate monoprint and Sanwa tissue (edition of 75)

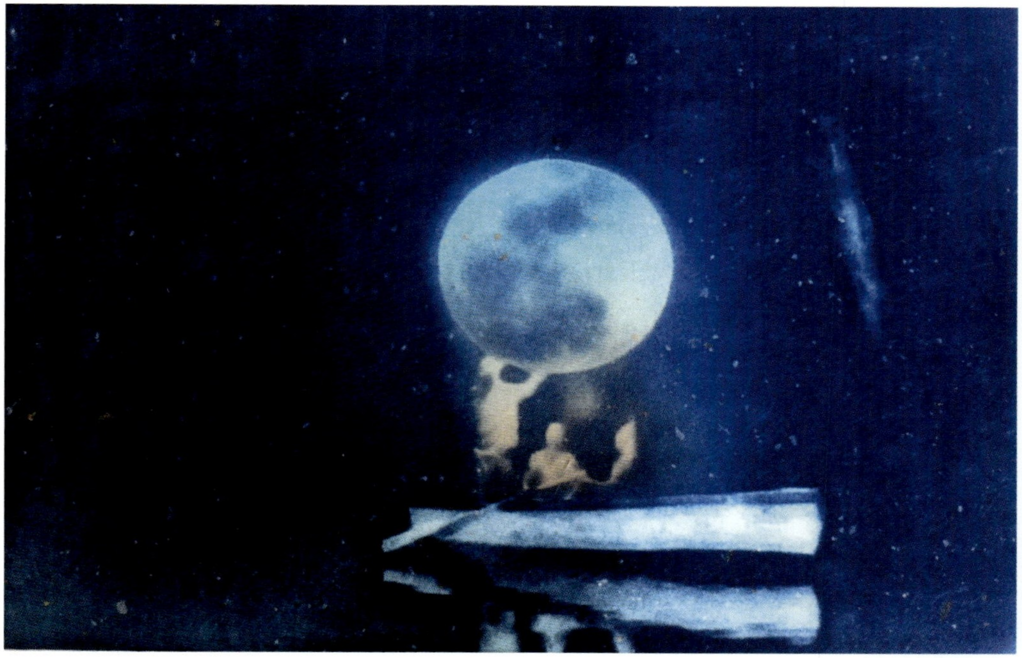

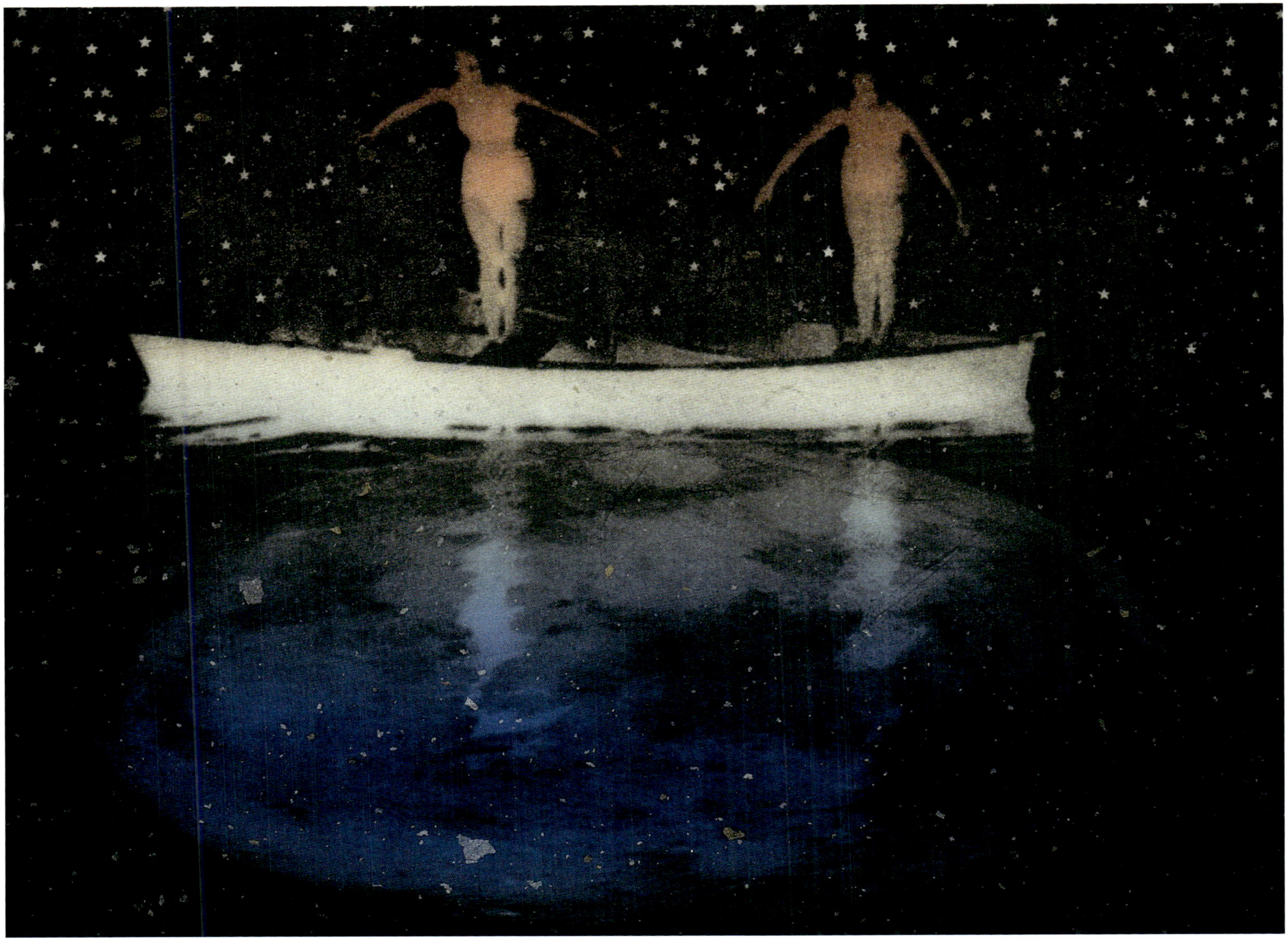

Paper Moon, 39 x 26 cm, solarplate monoprint and Sanwa tissue (edition of 75)

Eric Gaskell

Printmaking and its processes were integral to my art studies, but after leaving college they got left behind. They resurfaced in the late 1980s when a friend gave me an old galley press which led to me working in print again. I had re-caught the bug. This eventually led to buying a small press that gave me the opportunity to develop more forms of printmaking.

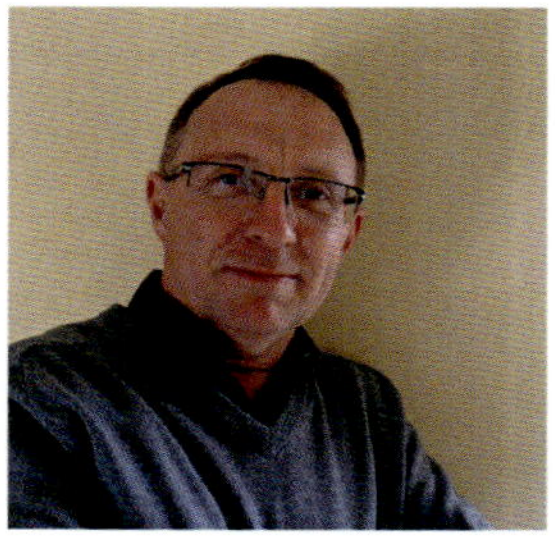

1957 Born Wigan, Lancashire
1976 Wigan College of Art
1977–80 Sunderland University
1981 Won scholarships to New York and Istanbul
1991 Alan Kitching's Typography Workshop
2007 Elected member of SGFA
2012 Elected member of GOWA
2014 Joined the Printmakers Council

Selected Exhibitions

1980, 2001 Norwich Arts Centre
1981 Middlesborough Arts Centre
1992 Pentagon Typography Gallery, London
2004 *12x12* Newcastle
2004 *Ghent Expo*, Belgium
2004 Montserrat Gallery, New York
2005 The Salon, Greenwich, New York
2005-14 SGFA, Menier Gallery, London
2008 Rugby Art Gallery & Museum
2008 Solihull Arts Complex
2009 Salisbury Arts Centre
2009 The Drumcroon Arts Centre, Wigan
2010-12 *RBSA Print Biennial*
2011 *Small Print: Big Impression*
2011 *Linocut*, Nantwich Art Gallery
2012–14 *The 8th British Mini-Print Exhibition*
2012 The Canal Museum, Gloucester
2014 *Alchemy*, Rugby Art Gallery
2013 *International Miniatures*, Quebec
2013 *Hand Drawn*, St Helen's Glass Museum
2015 Printmakers Council, Barbican Library
2015 *Works on Paper*, SGFA, RK Burt, London

My work is in private collections in the UK, Europe & North America.

The process of 'putting a picture together', along with the principle that good draftsmanship is a prerequisite of good art, was central to my college work and has never left me. So I draw – a lot – from both life and experience and over the years have filled countless drawing books. My drawing is a diary, an academic exercise and a way to work through my ideas, which can become paintings, but more often than not become prints. Drawing is my linchpin between paint and print, allowing print to influence paint and vice versa, and helps in letting ideas swap between the two mediums.

My work is colourful, structured and almost always figurative. I don't believe I have a 'style' or a fixed method and my oeuvre is quite eclectic; moving from the symbolic and iconographic work created through genealogical research to the colourful, figurative work based around the canals of the UK. Although my work comes from a figurative base I am not averse to letting it develop away from figuration toward what seems more appropriate. This works well in paint, but is far more difficult to achieve in printmaking where there is less room for error.

My preferred print method of the last few years has been the linocut; it suits my mark-making and is a good partner to my painting, allowing as it does big areas of solid colour, fine textures and strong line work. Unlike painting, in my print work I plan with more meticulous detail; here I am looking for accuracy. I work in both reduction and multi-block, often combining the two techniques. I aim to use the least number of blocks to create the most complete and complex image that I can; this often does not work and many times I start over again, regardless of how close to completion I may have been. I often spend days contemplating what the next cut will be or what effect a cut will have on other blocks. I have no sure-fire way or technique, but I always make copious notes on my proofs and blocks just in case I might need them again – which many times I do. Having said that, not having a method is often beneficial as my work always surprises me, and I hope it will go on doing just that.

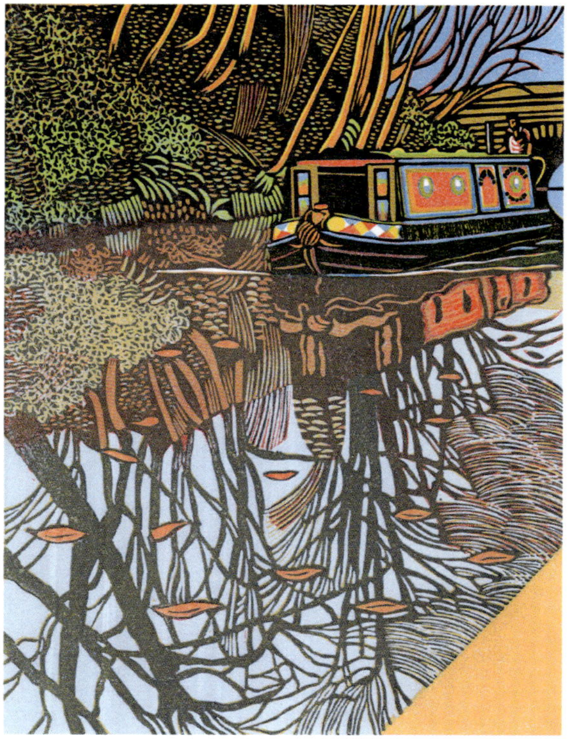

Narrowboat, 18 x 24 cm, linocut (edition of 25)

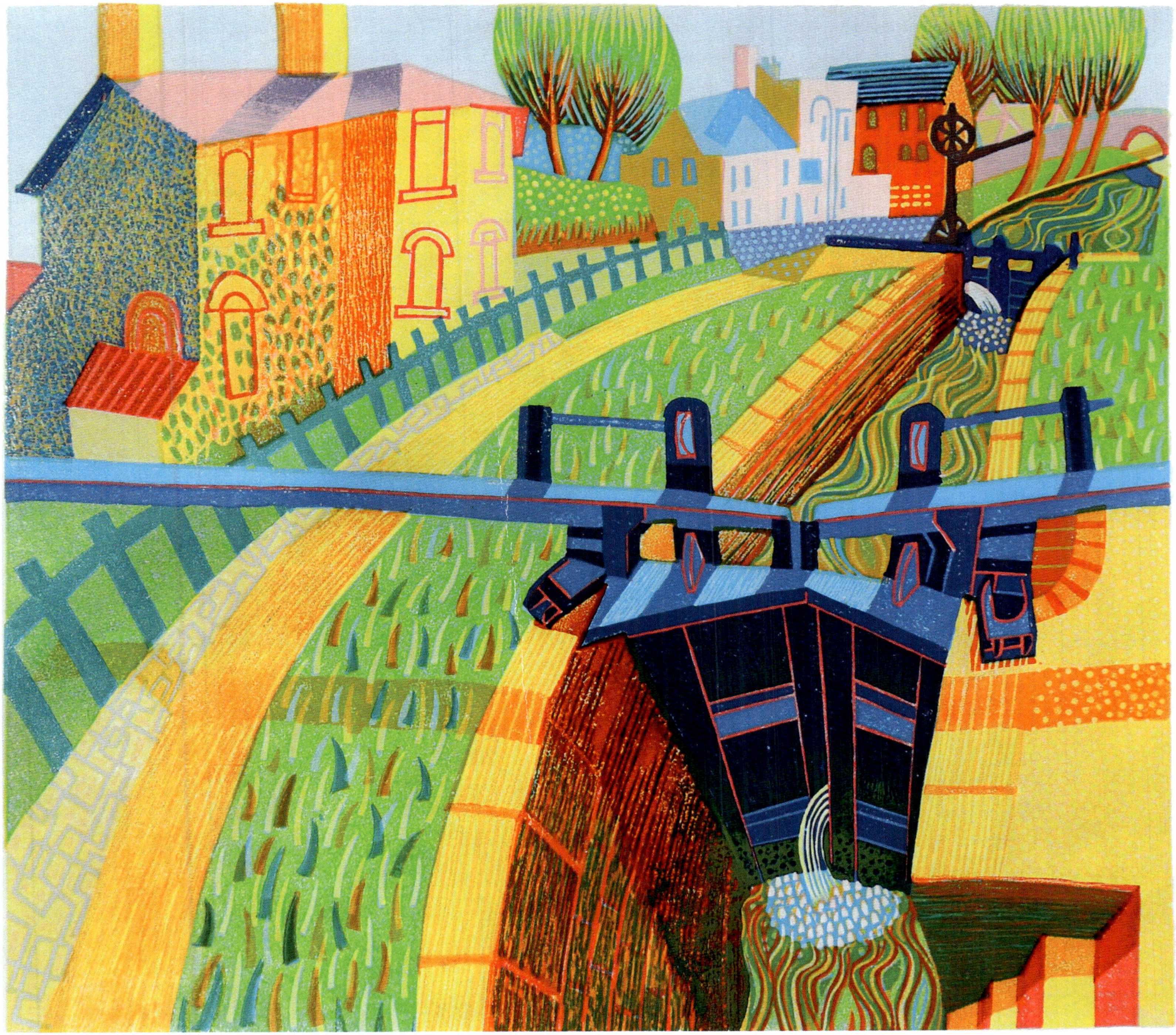

Audlem Mill, 29 x 26 cm, linocut (edition of 16)

Janette Gibson

Printmaking at The Institute has enabled me to bring together interests and influences from my textile design background, horticulture and my collection of flea market finds. The course has enabled me to develop my imagery using various printmaking techniques including intaglio, photopolymer etching, relief printing and embossing onto one surface. I enjoy the layering and juxtaposition of colour, line, pattern and texture and am often surprised by the unexpected outcome!

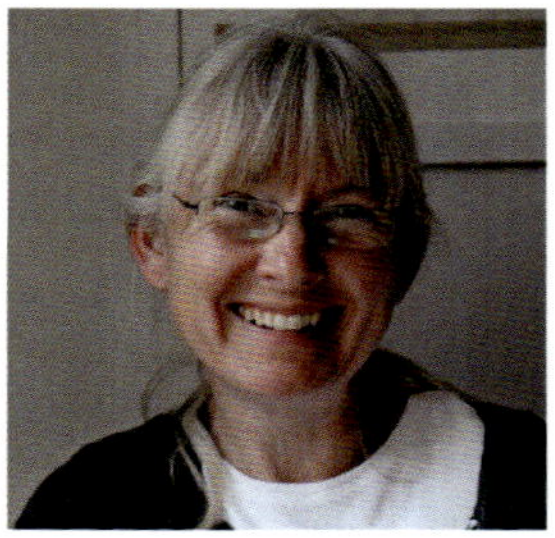

1963 Born Portsmouth, Hampshire
1983–84 Art Foundation Course, Winchester School of Art
1984–87 BA (Hons). Constructed Textiles, Middlesex University
1987–2001 Yarn Technician in Constructed Textiles Department, Middlesex University
1995–97 MA Fashion and Textiles, Middlesex University, Research into 'Paper Textiles, their history and use in Japan and Europe and the potential for future development'
1999–2004 Awarded Sir Joseph Banks Scholarship from The Economic Botany Department, The Royal Botanical Gardens, Kew. Research into the 'Classification, Conservation and Research Potential of Plant Fibre Textiles from The Economic Botany Collection'
1989–2002 Freelance Textile Designer selling prints in Europe, USA and Japan
2002–present Horticultural training, self-employed gardener specialising in mixed border planting and living willow structures.
2011–present Studying Printmaking at The Institute, Hampstead Garden Suburb
2013 Sketchbook project, sketchbook exhibited in USA
2015 *Proof*, Group exhibition of printmakers from The Institute, Phoenix Cinema, East Finchley

Whilst designing printed fabric collections I experimented with the cyanotype process on paper and fabric and I became aware of the historic use of the technique, during the early stages of photography as a method of depicting plant specimens. A short course in 'nature printing' made me realise the quality of detail that can be achieved when a print is taken directly from an object. When taking prints from plants there is a limit to the number of times a specimen can be inked and pressed and still retain sufficient detail, resulting in a short limited edition, which adds to its unique quality. Developing the idea further, I decided to produce a 'contemporary herbarium'.

Traditionally, a herbarium is made up from dried plant material. The *Indigo Herbarium* series of prints has evolved from my interest in Japanese folk textiles and indigenous plants of Japan and I have tried to replicate the many tonal ranges of indigo in my work. Plants and fabric designs are combined using multiple photopolymer printing plates with offsetting and resist techniques to produce a 'herbarium' collection of plant specimens. Each plant is used once to produce a varied edition print series which I hope has the some of the qualities of a herbarium sample. The complete collection could potentially be presented in printed book form.

The *Utensils* print series combines photopolymer intaglio and relief plates with direct print and stencil resist techniques. I have been collecting used and often misshapen household items including wire whisks, sieves and wooden implements for some time. I am attracted to their linear quality and their relationship with each other and the surrounding space, the 'negative space', which has been a source of visual inspiration when placing the image either on a flat sheet of paper or into a sketchbook. A pared-down, muted colour palette has been chosen to complement the simplicity of the outlines. I would like to develop a further collection as prints for homeware, to be applied to fabric and ceramics.

I often develop ideas by printing directly into accordion sketchbooks, working quickly and intuitively through ideas that can then be worked on a larger scale or retained in book form. Future developments will include carborundum printing to achieve a more heavily textured printed surface.

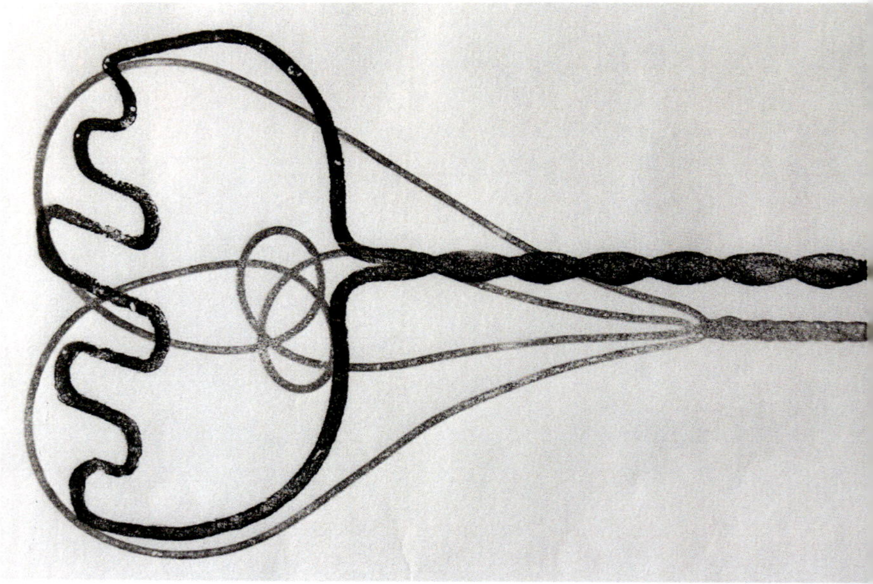

Utensils II, 30 x 45 cm, photopolymer print edition (edition of 20)

OPPOSITE

Ginkgo, 14 x 14 cm, photopolymer etching (varied edition of 50)

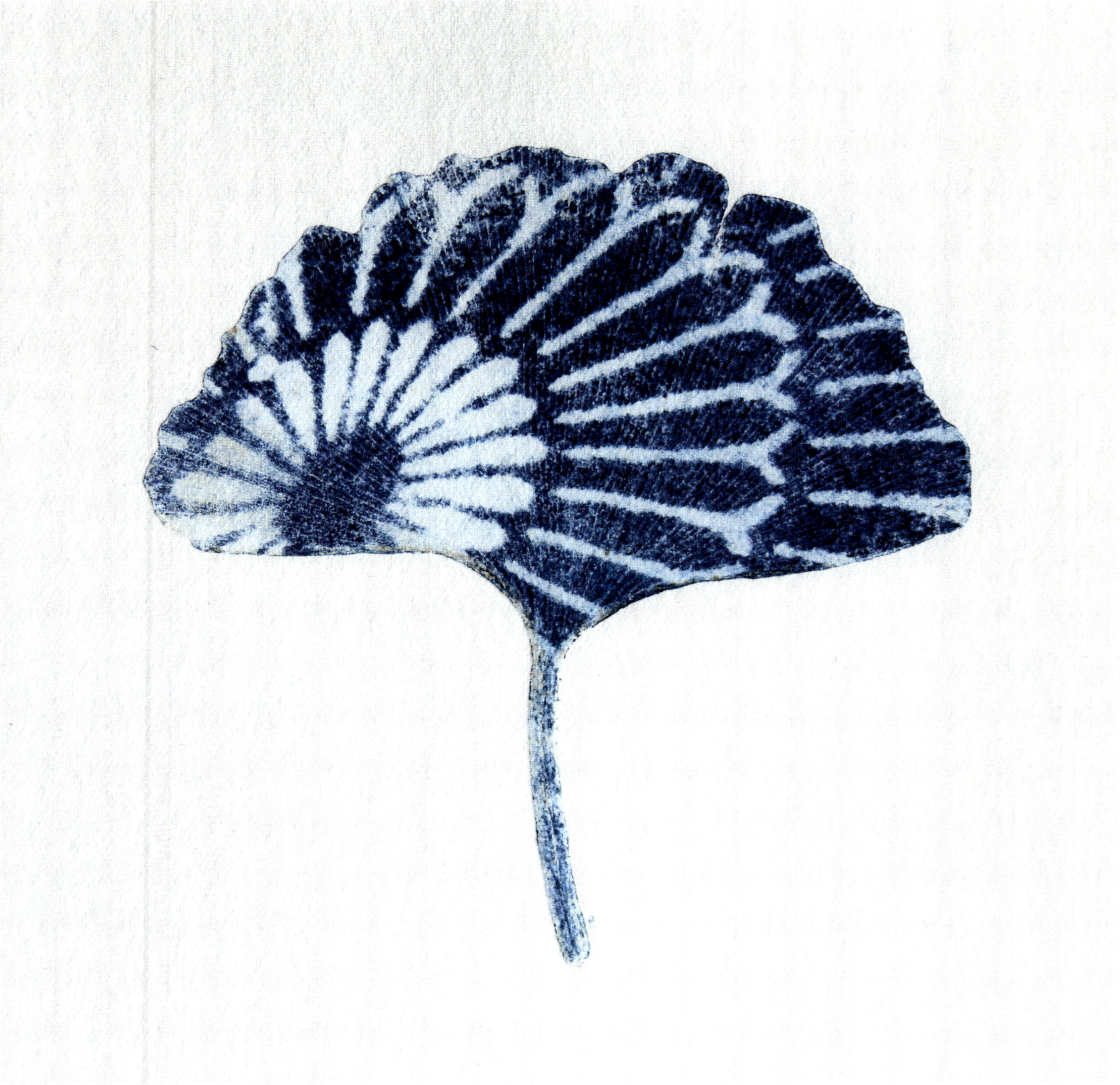

Colin Gillespie

As a student, my first introduction to printmaking was given by a tutor who taught me lithography. I remember that he wore a three-piece suit, removed his jacket for the class, carefully turned his shirt-sleeve cuffs back three folds, had forearms like Popeye – and never wore an apron. He explained that 'with printmaking, it's all about staying clean'.

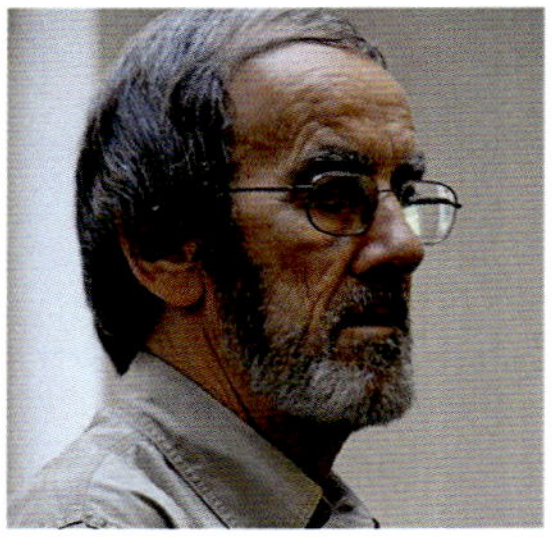

1959–62 Royal College of Art
1962–99 Lecturer, Hornsey College of Art–Middlesex University
1970–77 Course Leader, Art Teachers Certificate Programme
1977–87 Manager, Haringey Urban Studies Centre
1988–99 Course Leader, BA (Hons) Art Practice & the Community Programme
1999–2004 Development worker, *Memories* - funded reminiscence project with Community Focus Arts Organization
2000–01 Tutor, Arts & the Learning City Programme working with North London Somali Women's Consortium
2000–05 Tutor, Learning & Skills Council funded print workshops at Islington Mental Health Resource Centre
2002–03 Researcher, funded project devising North London Heritage Trails for users with disabilities
2003–04 Development worker, *My Life–Our Heritage* - funded Oral History project with Community Focus Arts Organisation
2003–04 Artist in Residence, Ealing Special Schools Project
2006–ongoing Printmaking Tutor at Islington Mental Health Resource Centre
2006–ongoing Manager, *Can I Tell You* reminiscence project

Exhibitions

Have been showing print work from 1991 to date in UK and International exhibitions.

I later realized that he was talking about 'craft' – the disciplined control of materials and process needed when making a print.

At a later stage came my first experience of using art skills for a social purpose. I became involved with a community-based environmental project that needed images. They had silkscreen facilities – but no print skills.

I was asked if I could help and it gave me a new perspective on the use of print – I enjoyed producing images that had immediate function – where content or effective communication could be quickly recognised.

This was in contrast to my early experience of selling a few 'fine art' prints – where, sometimes, the buyer would ask ' can you do more like that but in a different colour or a different size'. That made me feel uneasy regarding my role as a maker of images.

Since then I've worked in many situations, with differing age groups, where my skills as a printmaker are accepted as a means of fulfilling a need or achieving an ambition that has little to do with 'art' but has been more to do with producing a gift – a personal souvenir, a love token, commemorating an event or producing an emblem or badge of identity for the maker – all legitimate roles for print.

However, my 'own work' use of print remains strong, because it provides me with a way of making visual my thinking around ideas – which, in my case are usually concerned with some aspect of urban living.

Most of my work is related to place – identity, relationships, events, fantasies, stories or imaginings that emerge from living within an urban environment. I always seek to achieve a balance as regards time given to my own art work and the community work which takes place often using very basic facilities in Day Centres, Care Homes, Special Needs settings and so on.

I find that these two levels of working – the personal/private own work and the communal/shared activity make a good partnership: they interact with one another and help suggest new ways of using print.

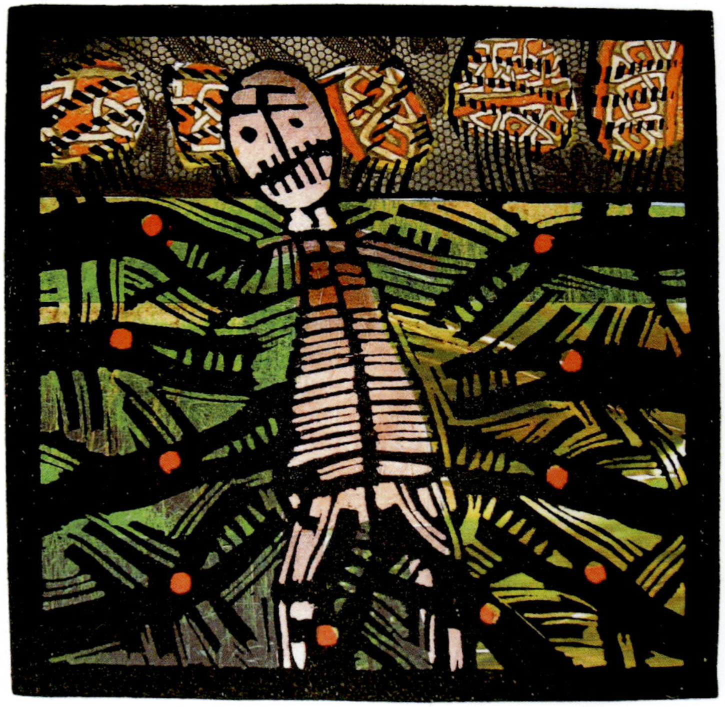

Plague, 15 x 15 cm, collage & relief (edition of 12)

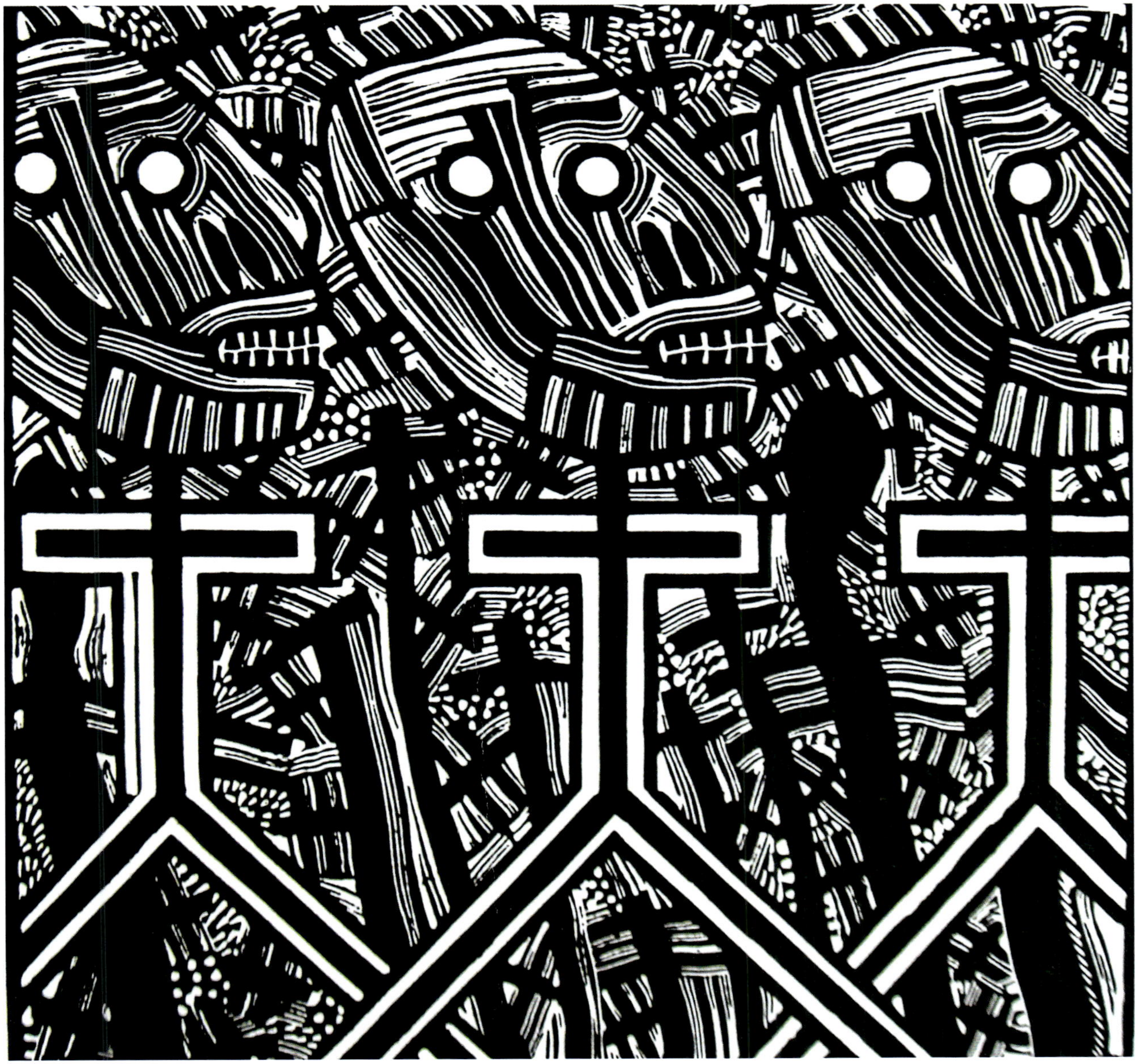

The Parade, 30 x 30 cm, relief print (edition of 15)

Anne Gournay

When I discovered printmaking at Central Saint Martins in 2007, I really enjoyed the planning and technical skills required, as well as the freedom to experiment and the forever-thrilling element of surprise – you never know what your work will look like until the first print! I decided to refocus my work on printmaking, always trying to discover new ways of exploring its endless possibilities.

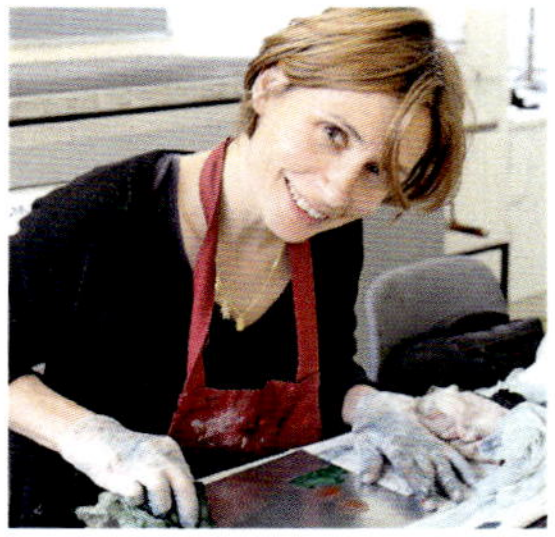

1971 Born Nantes, France
1990–94 ESCP Europe, Paris (Masters in Management)
1993–94 MBA programme at University of Toronto, Canada
1994–2004 Worked as Marketing Manager for Danone Group in France and UK
1997–2001 Art evening classes at Kensington and Chelsea College, London.
2004–06 Fine Art and Painting at Ateliers Beaux Arts de Paris–Glacière, and École des Arts Décoratifs, Paris
2007 Painting Exhibition at the Alliance Française in New York City, USA
2007–08 Central Saint Martins (Graphic Design Portfolio)
2009 Experimental Printmaking and Illustration, Central Saint Martins
2012 Member Printmakers Council
2013–present Represented by Byard Art, Cambridge.

Exhibitions in 2015 include:

Christmas Crackers, Byard Art Gallery; *50 Years of Artists Prints*, Bankside gallery; *50:50*, New Ashgate Gallery; *Affordable Art Fair*, Hampstead; *Works on Paper*, Barbican Library

Collections

V&A print collection, private collectors in the UK, France, Spain, Germany, USA, Abu Dhabi, Australia, New Zealand.

After having practised art in parallel with a marketing career, I decided to fully dedicate myself to art in 2003. I retrained and specialised in painting at the Ateliers Beaux Arts de Paris-Glacière and École des Arts Décoratifs and was selected for a painting exhibition in New York (2007). I then discovered Printmaking at Central Saint Martins and found that on many levels this medium fitted my personality. It was like when you meet someone for the first time and know immediately that you are making a new best friend!

Through solitary landscapes and close-up portraits, I explore the issues of loneliness and intimacy, in a modern world where people are very often disconnected with their real selves. In our modern age, and contrary to what still happens in some primitive societies, people have distanced themselves from nature and their own nature.

Saturated with communication, bombarded with constant stimulation, we lose touch with who we really are. By picturing empty nature (often isolated from an overcrowded urban environment), I am aiming at reconnecting us with our inner selves, giving us time and space to recollect ourselves, and think... a space to meditate.

I find inspiration in my passion for charcoal drawing and photography and aim at recreating the atmospheric images associated with these media. My screen prints are more graphic and conceptual. I use my camera as a sketchbook and rework my images many times in my head before starting the plate-making or screen-making process. Enthusiastic about new techniques, I use various forms of printmaking, from relief to screen-print, including photopolymer and traditional etchings, sometimes combining them.

L'invitation au voyage, 28 x 20 cm, two plate etching & aquatint (edition of 40)

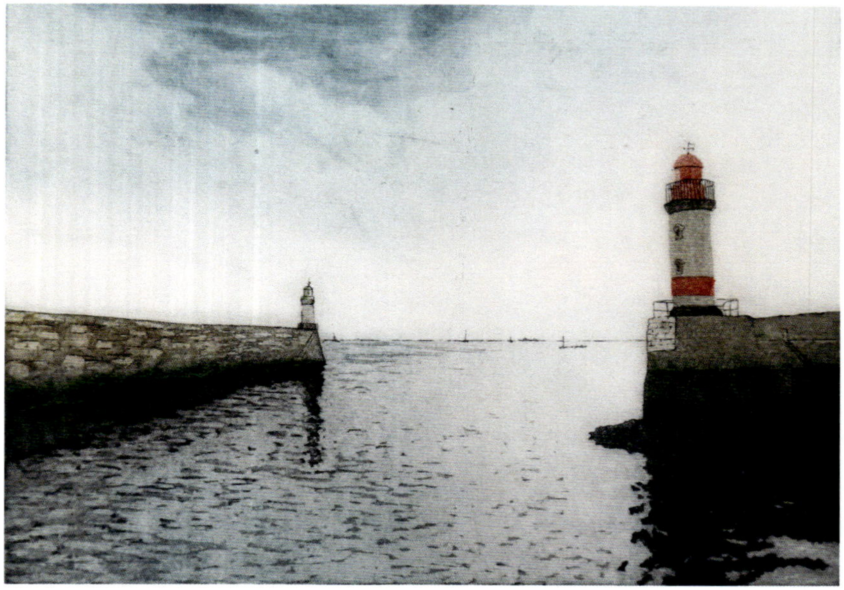

OPPOSITE
Listen to my Heart Beat II
40 x 40 cm
aquatint & solar plate
(edition of 40)

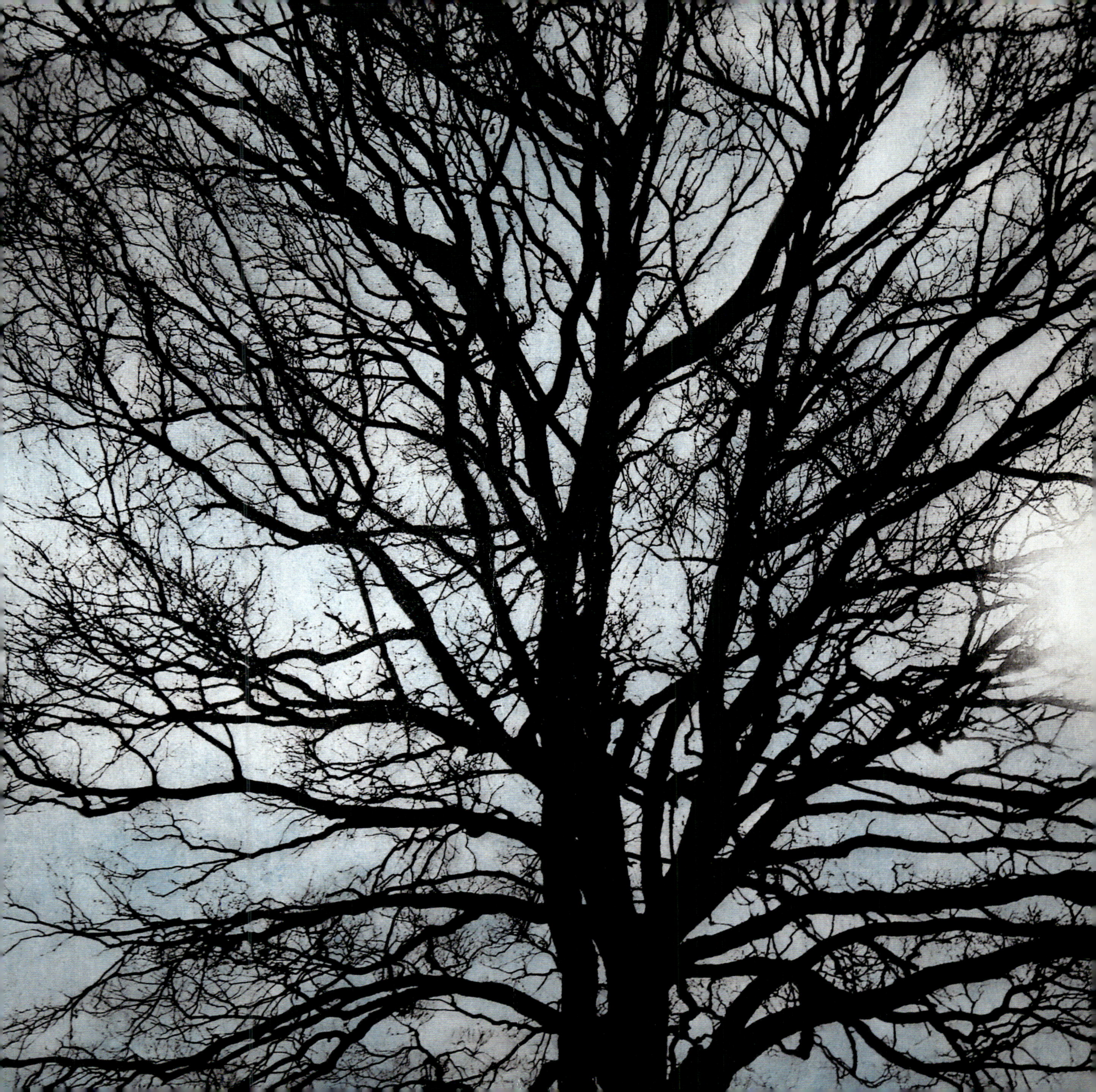

Lucie Green

A painterly approach to printmaking is central to my work. I take my subject matter from my extensive travel experiences in Asia as well as the more immediate natural environment.

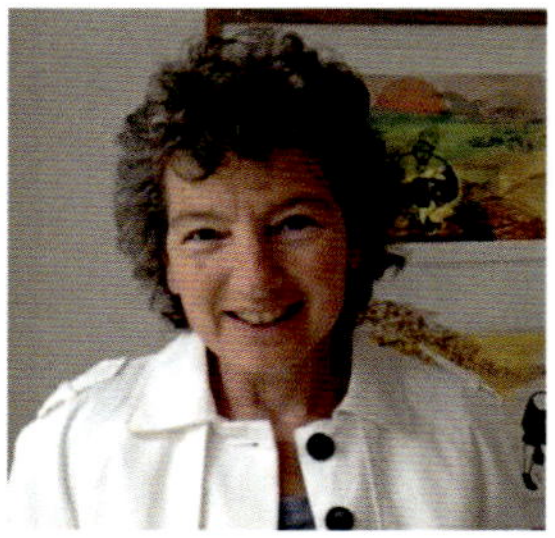

1977 BA (Hons) Fine Art Trent Polytechnic
1979 PG Dip Lib
1981–95 Working and living in Nepal, Indonesia, Bhutan and Bangladesh
2001–present Open Access Printmaking, University of Hertfordshire
2001–07 Sir John Lawes School, Harpenden
2009–present HVAF (Herts Visual Arts Forum)
2010–present BBHP (Beds Bucks and Herts Print Society)
2011–present Member Dekkle Print Studio, Hertfordshire
2011–present Member Printmakers Council
2011–present Member Southbank Printmakers

Recent Exhibitions

2013 *Printfest*, Ulverston
2013 *Southbank Printmakers Artist in Focus*
2013 *3 Artists*, Lauderdale House, London
2013 *Eastern Approaches* (Prizewinner), UH Galleries, St Albans
2014 *Seacourt Miniprint International*, Northern Ireland
2014 *Freshly Pressed*, Craft Central, London
2014 *Royal Academy Summer Exhibition*
2014 *CMYK*, Margate
2015 Weston Park (solo), Shropshire

Lucie's work is based on simple and strong images such as the group of friends sitting in the sun on a bench in Kathmandu in *Watching the World Go By*.

Lucie's overall approach is experimental, using wood and linocuts to painterly effect. These apparently freer forms contrast with the respect for craftsmanship and precision that are fundamental to her work.

The complete relief printmaking process provides a highly expressive medium through which she gains a close understanding and feel for her subject.

Colour and mood are central elements in Lucie's work which is underpinned by clear and simple forms. Major influences past and present have been the German Expressionists and Chinese woodcutting traditions.

Lucie has exhibited widely including at the RA Summer Exhibition in 2014.

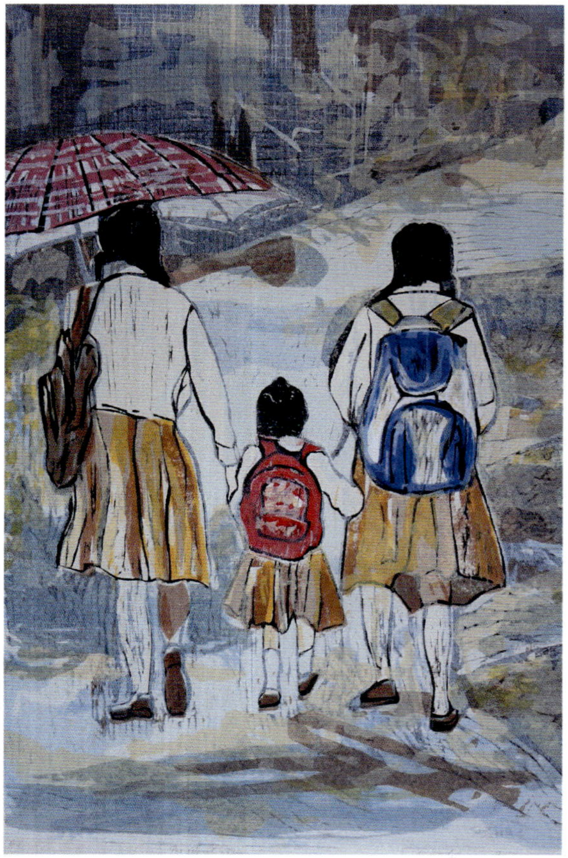

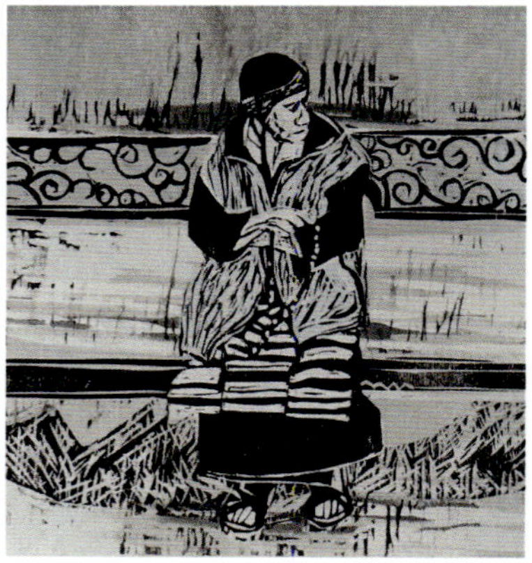

ABOVE

Watching the World Go By II, 15 x 16 cm, woodcut (edition of 15)

LEFT

The School Run, 30 x 45 cm, woodcut (edition of 10)

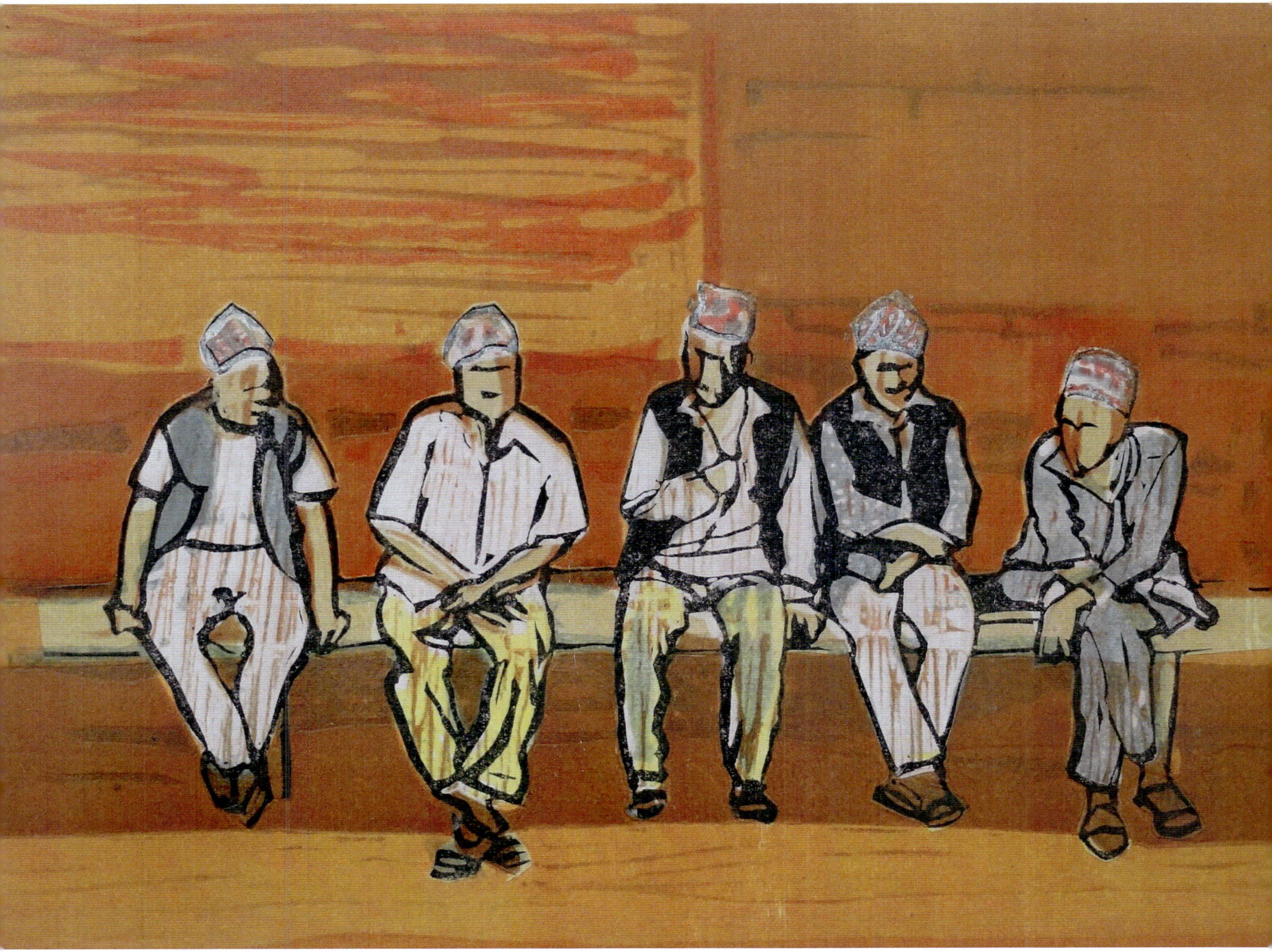

Watching the World Go By I, 30 x 22 cm, woodcut (artist's proof)

Lisa Gribbon

I left Art College at the end of the 1980s, and for the next ten years I was more involved in horticulture than art. It was the opening of Dundee Contemporary Arts, a new art centre with an open-accessed print studio, which motivated my return to making art.

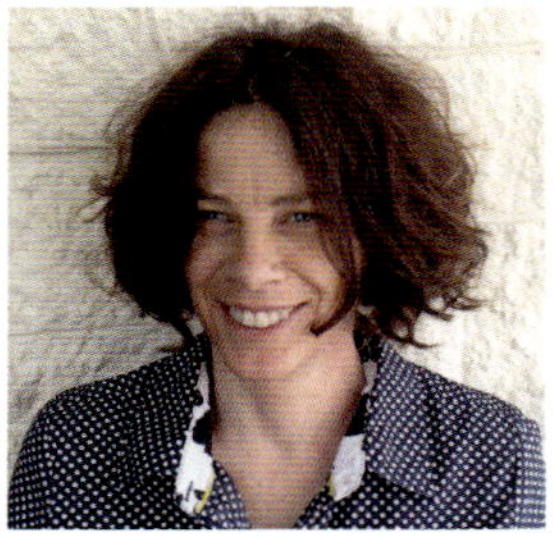

1985–89 Duncan of Jordanstone College of Art, Dundee, Scotland
1997–99 Royal Botanic Gardens, Edinburgh
1999 Join Dundee Contemporary Arts (DCA) Print Studio
2001 Creative & Technical Skills Training Bursary, Dundee Visual Arts Award
2002 'Work in Progress' Visual Research Centre, DCA
2003 'Seisar Ban' An Gaileari, Ceardlann Na gCroisbhealach, Ireland
2004 Print Residency, Clo Ceardlann na gCnoc, Donegal, Ireland
2005 Hope Scott Trust Visual Arts Award
2006 Dundee Visual Arts Award *Exchange*, Botanic Gardens, Dundee
2007 *Creating Order*, 300th anniversary of Carl Linnaeus's birth. Dundee, Fife & Edinburgh. *Remix (100)*, Baishi Institute, China
2009 *Fabric of the Land*, Aberdeen University
2010 Fife Visual Arts Award.
2011 *Maria Doyle & Lisa Gribbon*, Birnam Art Centre, Perthshire
2013 *9th Biennial Miniature Print Exhibition*, CCPC & Greenwich Art Council, USA. *Print 3*, Duckett & Jeffery Gallery, Yorkshire. The Book & Paper Studio, Dundee
2014 *Lessedre World Print Annual*, Sofia, Bulgaria. *Royal Scottish Academy Open*, Edinburgh. Joined the Printmakers Council
2015 *Tokyo International Miniprint Triennial*, Japan

Much of my work is concerned with the land, and so I prefer to use tactile printing techniques such as etching, drypoint, collograph and chine collé.

When I say the land, it is the features, whether natural or man-made, that are of particular interest. However, I am drawn to the simplicity of functional everyday objects too. I like to pare down an object to a few simple lines, so that it becomes a symbol used to represent thematic concepts and ideas. When creating a print I will often combine one or more printmaking techniques together. This method of working enables me to produce a print that is both rich in marks and textures, as each print technique has its own characteristics. My prime concern is to do with form and shape, and so I choose to work using a limited palette of colours. I see all my prints as drawings. What I really like about printmaking is the very distinctive layering quality which I believe cannot be achieved in any other artistic process.

In 2001, I greatly increased my printmaking knowledge and skills when I received a Creative & Technical Skills Training Bursary from the Dundee Contemporary Arts Print studio, which was funded by the Scottish Arts Council. This opportunity gave me a new confidence, and also provided me with a set of skills which I have used to run print workshops for a wide range of people.

Three years later I was keen to experience working in a different environment, and so I went on a residency to Clo Ceardlann na gCnoc Print Studio in Donegal on the West Coast of Ireland. There I used photography and made sketches to document the impact that crofting has had on the surrounding landscape. This documentation was subsequently used to make a number of etchings.

Throughout the years I continued to apply for visual arts awards, one of which supported the making of new work for an exhibition entitled *Creating Order*. The Book & Paper Conservation Studio at Dundee University were conserving the papers of the taxonomist Carl Linnaeus for the Linnaean Society in London. These papers were my source of inspiration for the exhibition. It was a wonderful chance to combine my background as both a horticulturalist and as an artist.

Today I have a studio space with a press in my home in Aberdeenshire. Here I am able to produce small printed works. It is a case of soaking my paper in the bath in the upstairs bathroom. However, it is important not to work in isolation so I continue to print at the open-access print studios in Aberdeen and Dundee.

Ton, 11 x 6.5 cm, collography & chine collé (artist's proof)

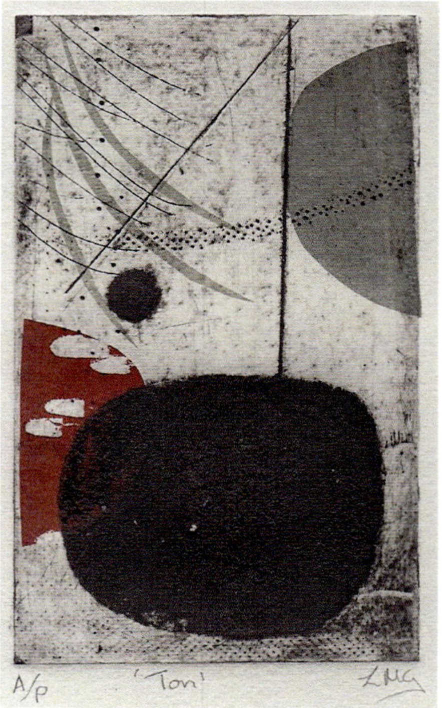

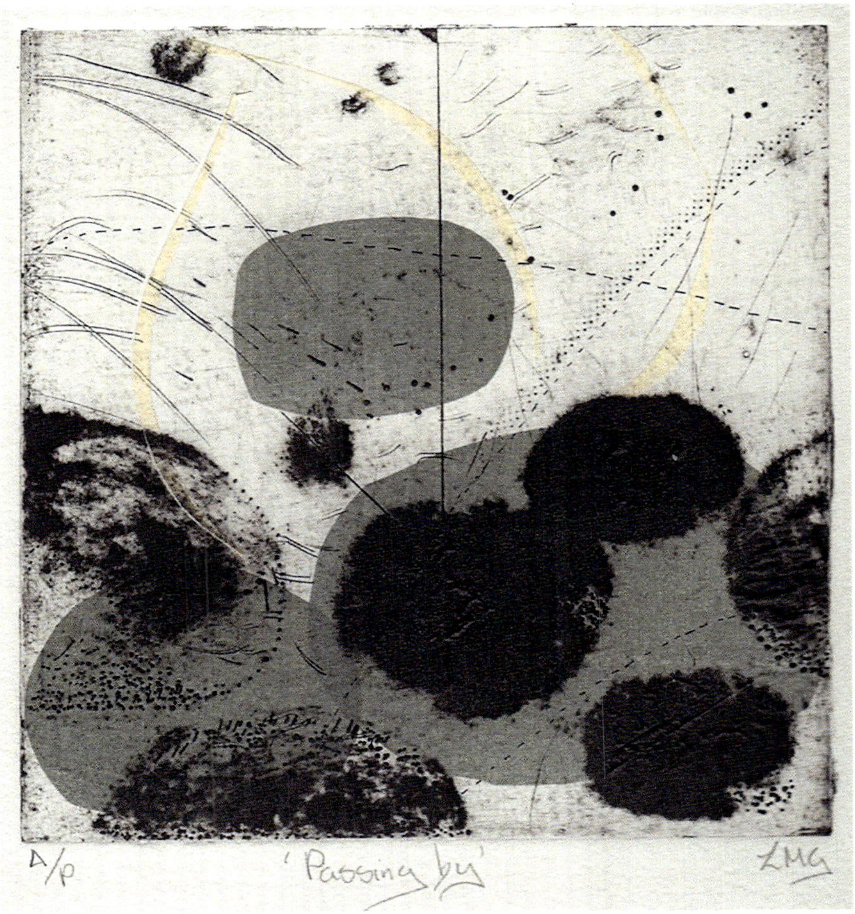

Passing by, 12.8 x 12.4 cm, collography & chine collé (artist's proof)

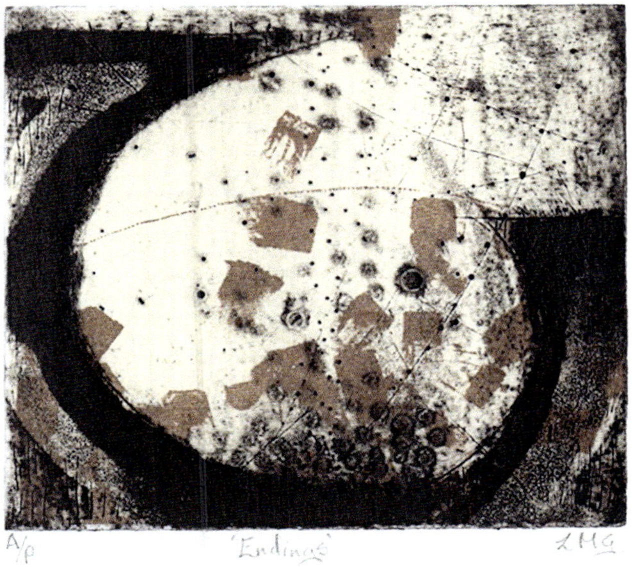

Endings, 12.8 x 11 cm, collography/toray/chine collé (artist's proof)

Clare Grossman

My involvement in printmaking derives from my connection with painting. As a painter-printmaker, my prints are often the result of a desire to produce images that encapsulate the 'essence' of a chosen subject. I use gestural experimental mark-making together with a multi-layering of colour and technique to develop works in series, each piece individual in its final result.

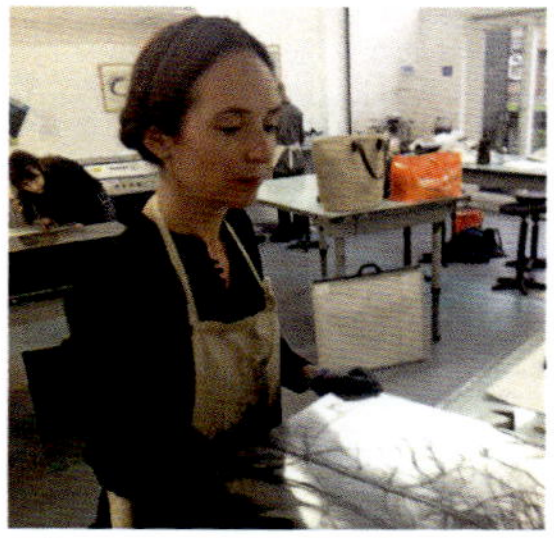

1991–93 MA Fine Art Printmaking, Camberwell School of Art

2009 *Lost Heritage*, Gallery K London, Athens & Nicosia

2011 Elected committee member Printmakers Council

2012 *BITE*, Mall Galleries
Elected member of Southbank Printmakers Gallery

2013 Solo Show, ILTM Cannes France.
Highgate - a Reflection in Print, Highgate Literary & Scientific Institution.
Photographics, Great Western Studios London.
Bainbridge Open, Embassy Tea Rooms

2014 *Multiplied*, Christie's South Kensington.
Connections, Cuppola Gallery Sheffield.
Bainbridge Open, Embassy Tea Rooms London

2015 *Fifty Years of Artists Prints*, Printmakers Council, Bankside Gallery London.
Featured Artist, London Print Studios.
Fifty Fifty, New Ashgate Gallery.
Works on Paper, The Barbican London.
Elected member of Greenwich Printmakers

Commissions & Acquisitions

The Victoria & Albert Museum; Claridge's London; Hilton Hotel Paris; Princess Noura University for Women, Saudi Arabia; King Abdula University of Science & Technology; Langham London; Care International Scotland; Raffles Makkah Palace, Saudi Arabia; DOKAEE Development Mecca; The Landmark Hotel London; The Four Seasons Hotel London; BUPA Contemporary Art Collection

The vital energy of the land and the constant movement of the skies above are often used as a personal language to convey a moment in time, a specific note on a journey travelled.

My work predominately focuses on the search for an essential energy – the 'essence' of a chosen subject or place, encapsulated in an emotional response. The very act of printmaking with its varied repertoire and moments of chance offers up a palette full of exciting and ever-changing possibilities. Working frequently with a combination of print techniques, a final piece may have many layers of overprinting. Subtle layers are built up and at times eradicated or partially hidden in order to produce results that strive to describe movement, the energy found in nature – beautiful light, contrasts of solidity against the crispness or warmth of the air; or the incredibly mysterious substance of shadows.

The juxtaposition of abstract marks set against a drawn reality is repeatedly considered and revisited using images personally experienced and recorded. Numerous studies are initially worked and reworked until the importance of the subject is pared down to an essential composition which will then be transferred over to the etching plate to begin its new process of discovery through the print practice.

The very act of printmaking, its physical directness and the visual intensity of the marks remaining on the surface of the finished piece are of equal importance as is the subject itself. The layered history of the process through to its finalisation is apparent to see. The complexity of the marks making up the journey is revealed to the viewer.

These elements are often visited and revisited with the aim of exploring the vitality and fragility of nature. It is a means of silent communication, a visual offering of those sensations, left for others to interpret.

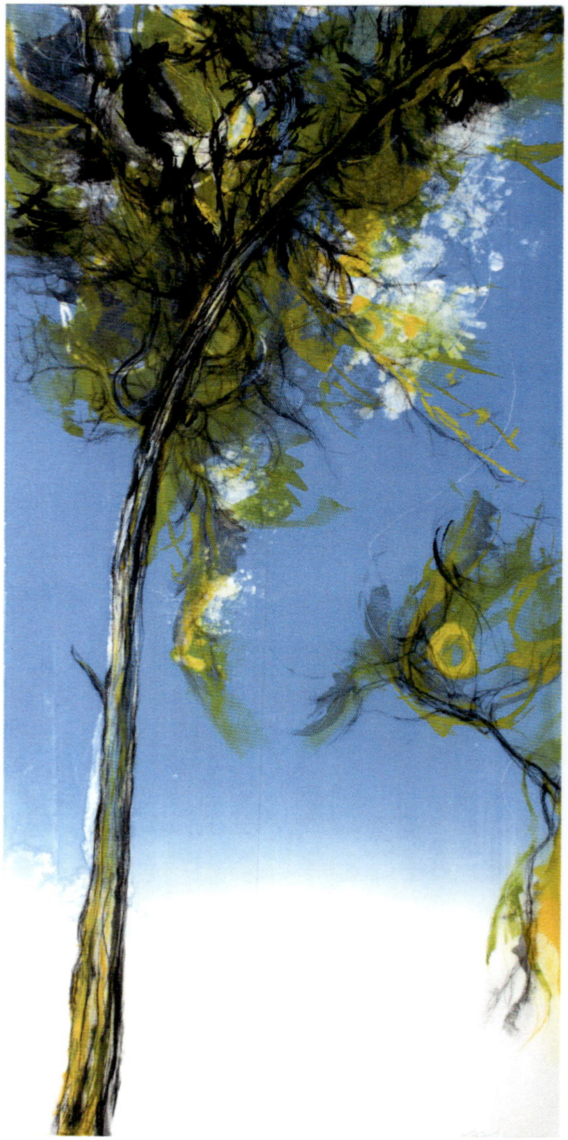

Leaning Pine, Summer Breeze No5, 35 x 73 cm
monotype & drypoint etching

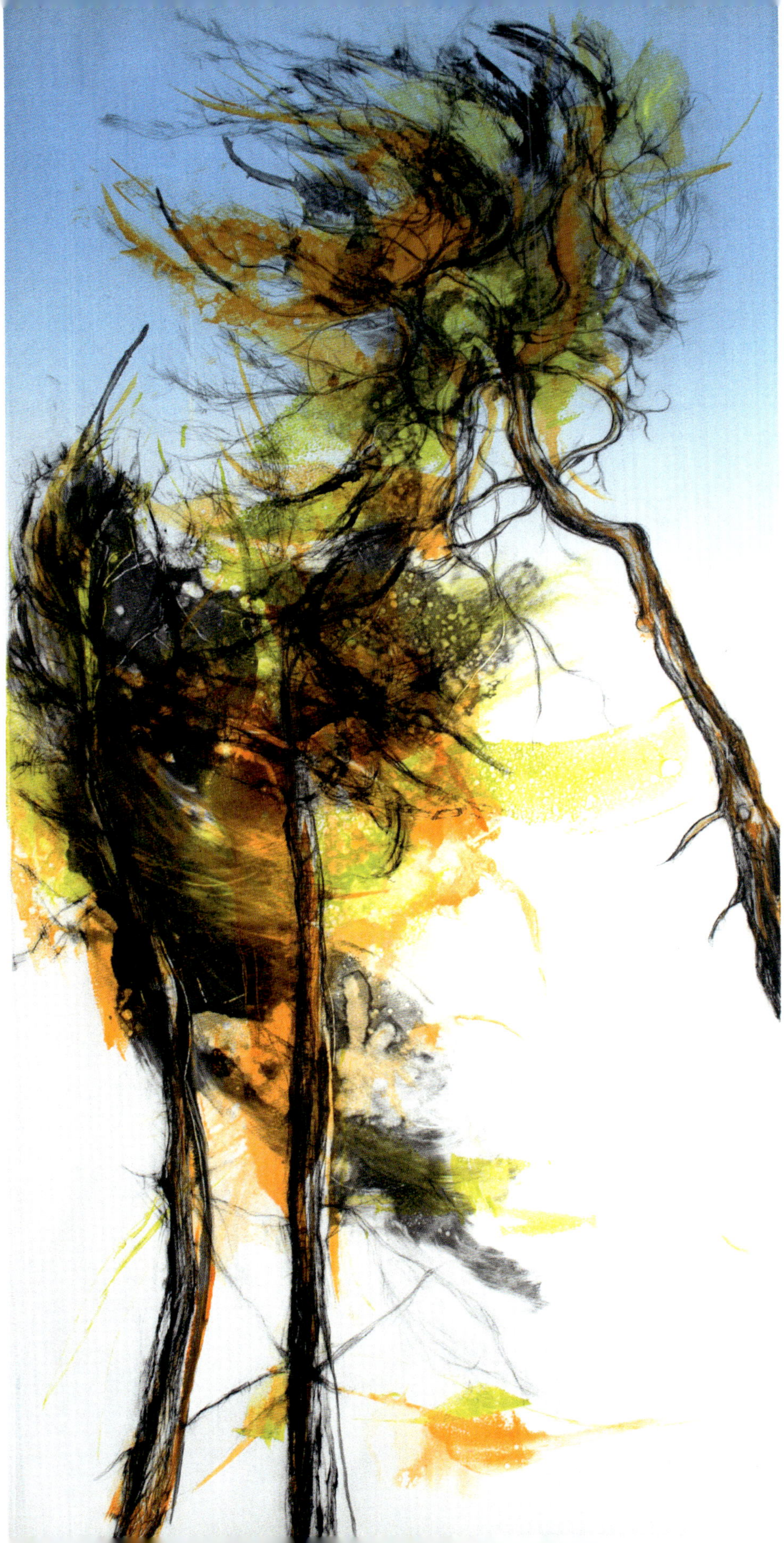

Pines Entwined, Summer Breeze N05, monotype & drypoint etching, 35 x 73 cm

Andrew D Hambleton

Printmaking is something I like to do because its processes have an exciting element of the unknown. The 'peeling back' of a piece of paper from a printed surface gives a feeling of anticipation.

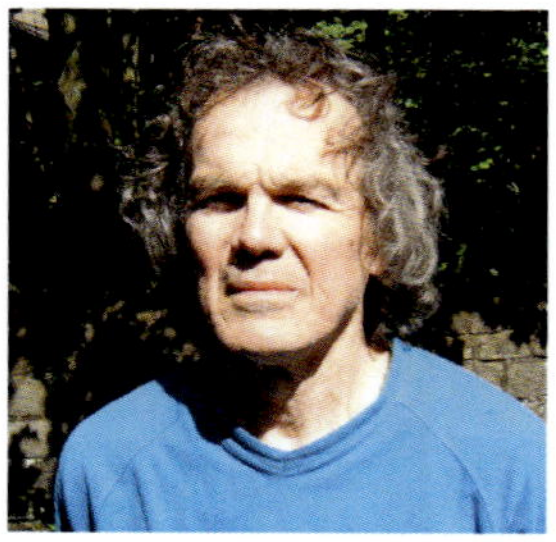

1954 Born Leek Staffordshire
1974–75 Art Foundation, Leek School of Art & Craft
1975–78 BA (Hons) Fine Art, Print West Surrey College
1979–80 MA Fine Art, Manchester Polytechnic
1980s Helped establish reformed Dundee Printmakers Workshop
1980s Visiting Lecturer Dundee, Luton, Sheffield
1990–2000 Lecturing Prison Service, various colleges
2006–present Art Teacher, Workshop Leader, print workshops and schools

Awards and Prizes

1982/83 Elisabeth Greenshields Foundation Award
1984 Artist in Industry, West Midlands Arts
1992 Cleveland Art Award
1993 Northern Art Award
1993 The Foundation for Sports & Arts Award
1997 West Yorkshire Art Award
2014 Birmingham Print Biennial, commended
2014 National Original Print Exhibition

Scholarship

Tamarind Institute USA

Exhibitions include

1983 *International Print Exhibition*, Taipei, Taiwan
1983 *International Print Exhibition*, Amarillo, Texas
2012 Water Street Gallery, Todmorden
2013 *Mini Print International 33*, Cadaqués, Spain

My interest in printmaking stems from drawing and my prints are arrived at by developing ideas through drawing or painting, often in watercolour.

Though my most successful introduction to printmaking was through lithography, I felt a lot happier making etchings, which is a process I didn't explore until I studied printmaking at MA level. I enjoyed the process of manipulating metal and in particular steel, to create tones and white/light areas. This could be achieved using oil stones, emery paper and a host of tools to make marks. However it wasn't until I moved to Scotland in 1980 and established a print workshop in Dundee that I felt what I'd learnt could be used to make etchings with more professional results. I consequently experimented with aquatint and the tonal qualities that gave effect to landscape and industrial landscapes that I embarked upon.

There is no doubt printmaking is a versatile process, whether using a direct approach offered through drypoint or woodcut or a more painterly and often spontaneous method offered in monoprint. Monoprinting has helped me see my way forward in print when I felt at a 'dead end'. It allowed me to see that interesting prints can be made from very limited means.

With the cost of materials rising and my frugal use of old copper plates and the chance marks therein, a new seam of thought and prints has arisen. We are all governed by circumstance and as artists we can't afford not to address this.

Since I began making prints all my ideas have stemmed from drawings, whether in notebooks or larger pieces pinned to my studio wall.

I work through an idea in drawing, paint and print . The prints are just one part of that family. I might turn a drawing or painting upside down and start again if I feel it's not working. This is in the hope I might be able to harness some chance marks. I also apply this process to some of my plates. However there is something special about a print framed by the paper it's printed on.

I hope what I've written here adds credence to my work.

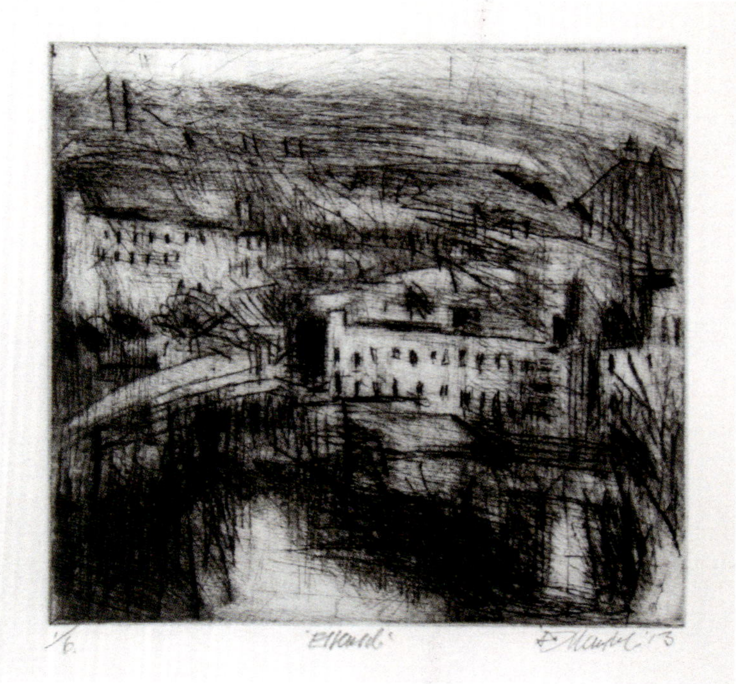

Elland, 23 x 30 cm (image), drypoint (edition of 6)

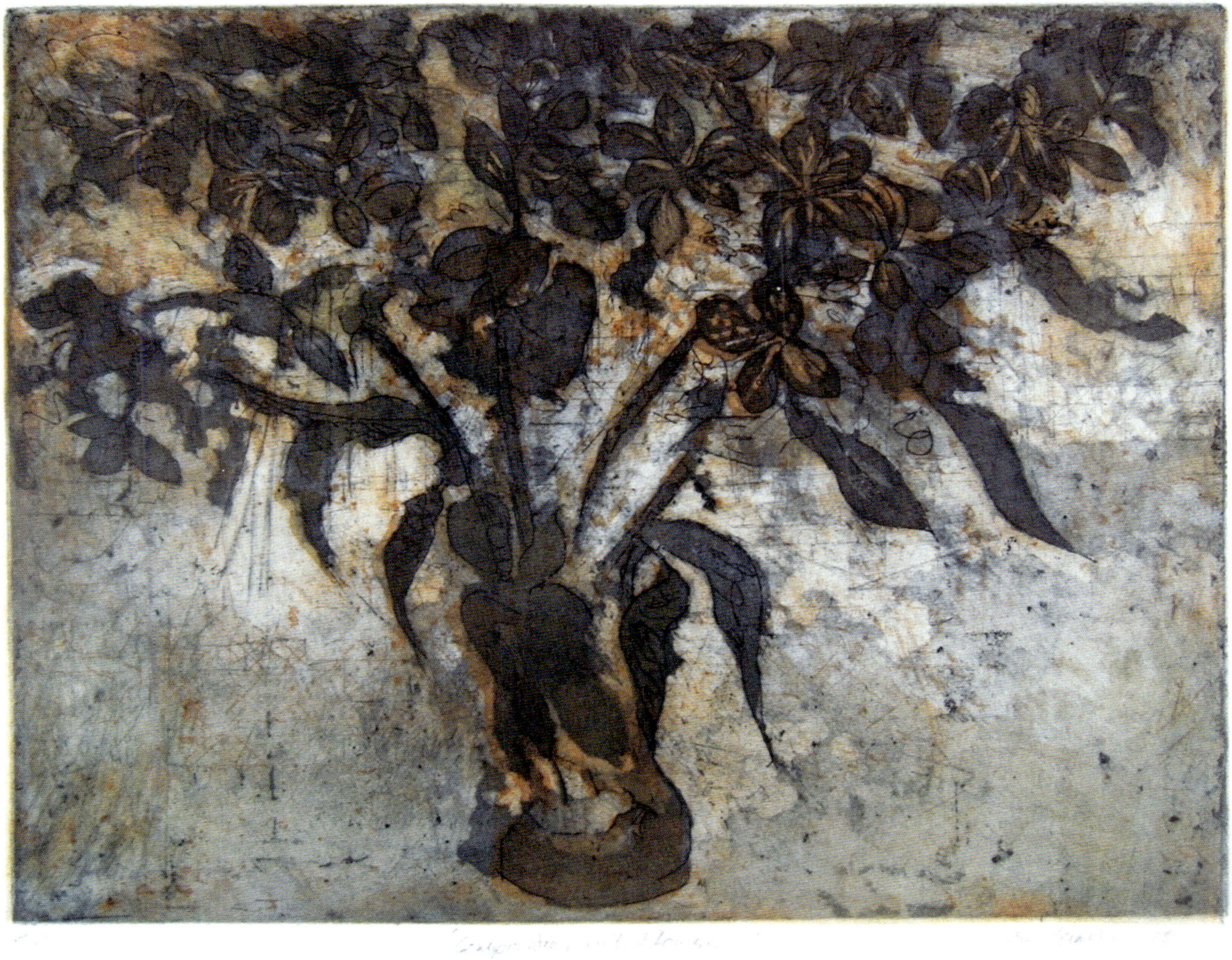

Composition with Flowers, 30 x 23 cm (image), two-plate coloured etching, drypoint, aquatint (edition of 6)

Pamela Hare

Pamela studied painting and printmaking at Portsmouth University where she obtained a BA (Hons) Degree in Fine Arts. After receiving a Postgraduate Degree from the Institute of Education, University of London, she ran art departments and lectured in multi-media art activities to a wide range of ages. More recently Pamela has participated in advanced painting and mixed-media courses at Central Saint Martins. She is also a member of East London Printmakers.

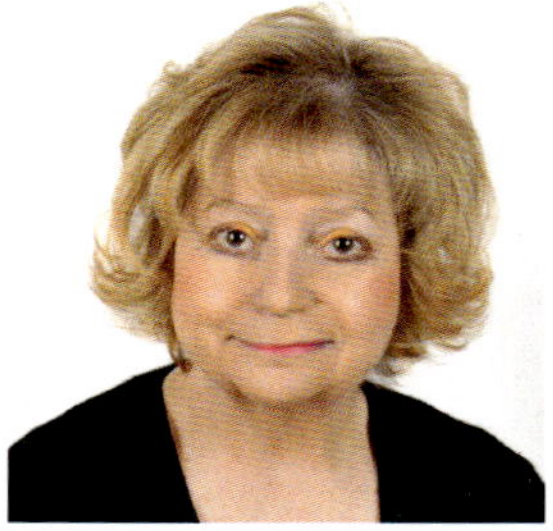

Exhibitions

2007 *Emerging Images*, Rivington Gallery, London

2009 *Personal Landscapes*, Royal Opera Arcade Gallery, London
Eleven, Bankside Gallery, London

2010 *East London Printmakers in Space*, Space Gallery, London

2010 *Dazzle London*, National Theatre, London

2011 *The Fishwick Papers*, Forman's Smokehouse Gallery, London
East London Printmakers Annual Exhibition, Triangle Gallery, London
Dreams, Freud Museum, London

2012 *Proof Perfect*, Framers Gallery, London
Affordable Art Fair, Hampstead
Pushing Print Festival, Margate Gallery, Kent
Craft Centre and Design Gallery, City Art Gallery, Leeds
East London Printathon Exhibition, Forman's Smokehouse Gallery, London
Turn, Turn, Turn, Margate Gallery, Kent

2013 East London Printmakers Summer Exhibition, Shoreditch Town Hall, London
Affordable Art Fair, Hampstead

2014 East London Printmakers Annual Show, Embassy Tea Gallery, London
Affordable Art Fair, Hampstead
Freshly Pressed, Craft Central, London

2015 *50 Years of Artists Prints*, Bankside Gallery, London
East London Printmakers Annual Show, Embassy Tea Gallery, London
Affordable Art Fair, Hampstead

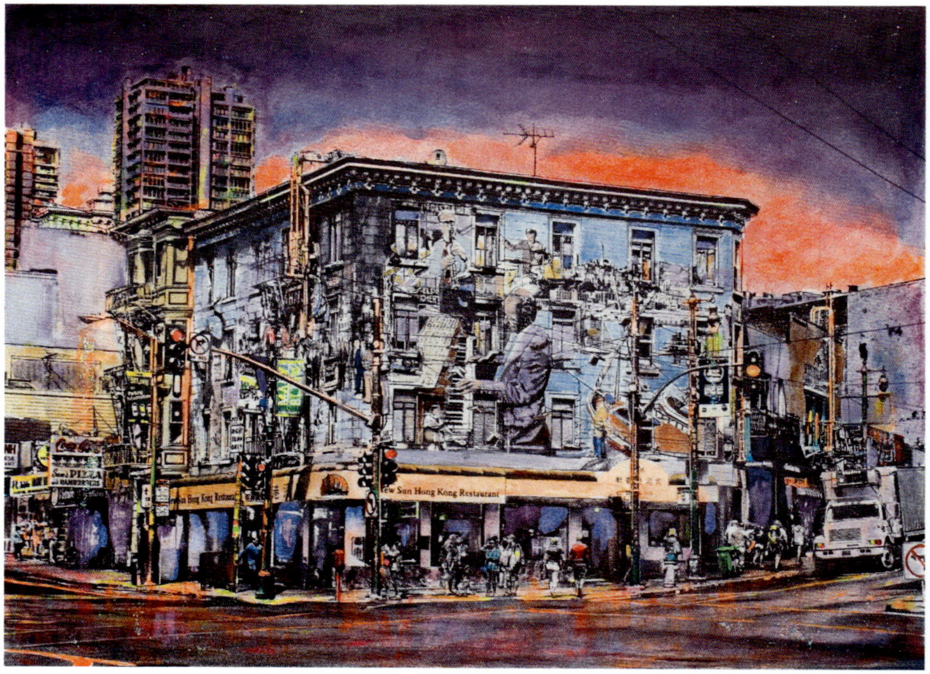

North Beach Bebop, 29 x 38.5 cm, screen print and mixed-media (edition of 15)

Pamela is an artist and printmaker living and working in Islington. She exhibits regularly in London and her artwork is held in private collections in the UK, Australia, New Zealand and France. She presents urban views of the city, including Venice, Marrakesh and San Francisco. She is influenced by the myriad richness of colours, contrasts of light and atmospheres, Georgian and postmodern styles and metropolitan histories and cultures.

Pamela's work traces the architectural fabric and ley lines connecting past to present, from church spire to glass citadel. Iconic buildings such as St Paul's Cathedral and St Pancras Station, and Regency town house rooms feature in some of her compositions.

Her recent prints of San Francisco continue this theme with an interest in its literary, cinematic and musical history. This is reflected in a panorama of Victorian houses in Russian Hill, vertiginous views of downtown buildings including a Chinatown bakery and a vibrant interpretation of the North Beach Bebop scene.

Her approach includes investigating the relationship between mono and photo-screen printed and painted shapes; the layering of pixelated and textural surfaces and contrasting vibrant colour hues with aged patinas.

Artists that have influenced Pamela include Rauschenberg, Warhol and Mara. Theoretical and cultural influences include Boorstin, Fischer, Scharf and Finch.

Brighter, 38.5 x 29 cm, screen print and mixed-media (edition of 15)

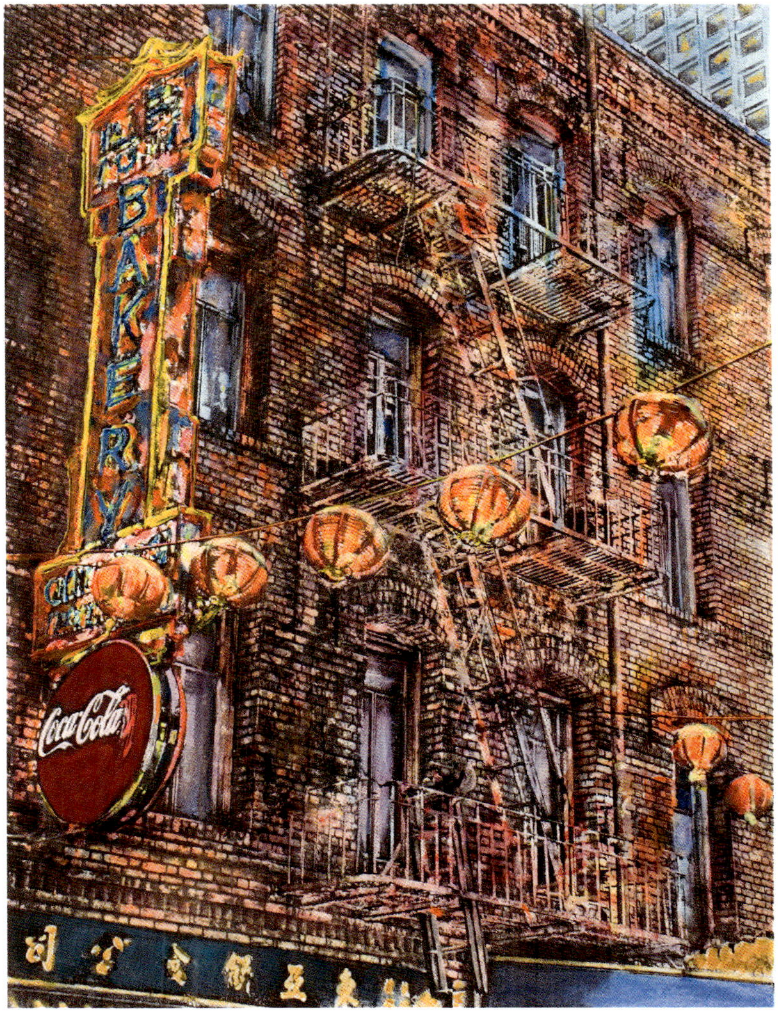

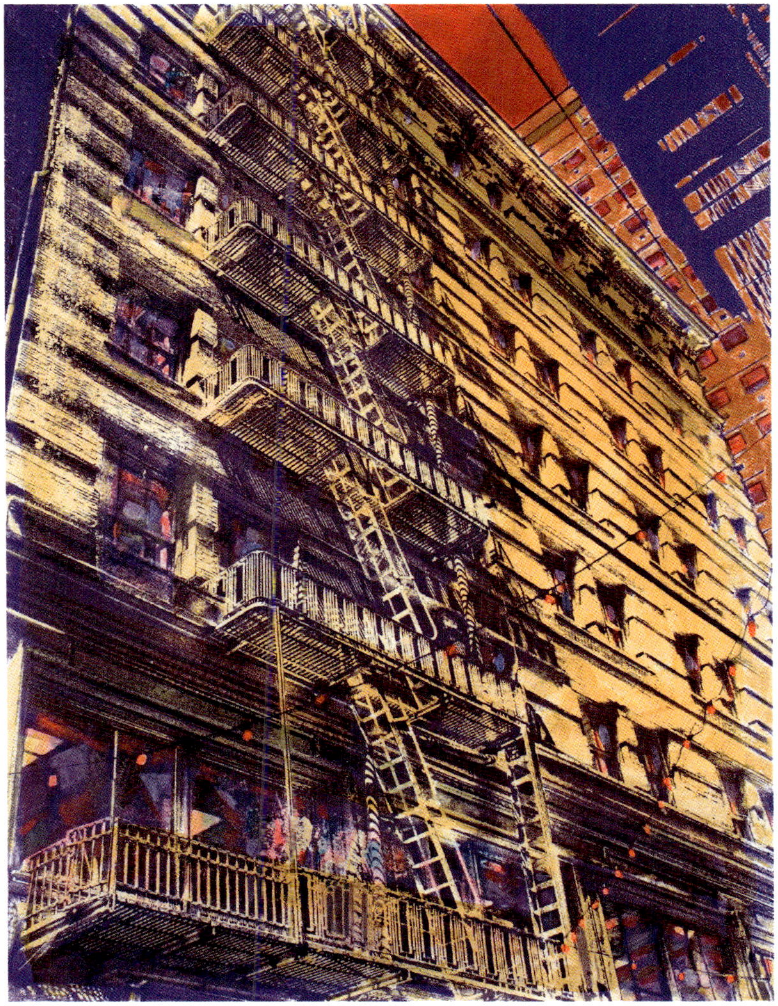

Vertigo, 38.5 x 29 cm, screen print and mixed-media (edition of 15)

Eleanor Havsteen-Franklin

My image-making has always involved an interest in re-representing the negative space and finding a language made tangible through reproduction. Being introduced to printmaking during my BA in the 1990s, I quickly realised the broad scope of printmaking, immersing myself in the etching process and working with colour. Following a PgDip in Art Therapy, working as an art psychotherapist and raising my own family I decided to return to the world of printmaking.

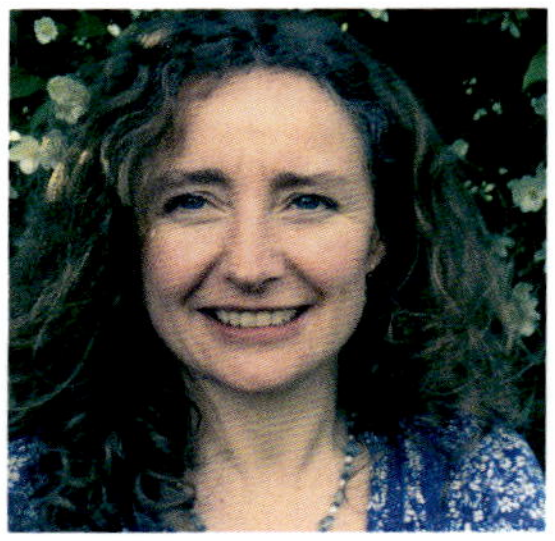

1973 Born Island of Aero, Denmark
1994–97 BA (1st Class Hons) Fine Art (major), Chester University
1997–99 PgDip Art Therapy, University of Hertfordshire
2005–07 MA Printmaking, Camberwell, UAL
2008 *The Experiment* (solo), Luton
2007–12 *Printmaking Originals*, Mall Gallery
2009 Joined the PmC, Selected for *Northern Print Biennale*, *Creekside Open*, London and *Travelling Light* with the WW gallery, Venice Biennale
2010–15 *Affordable Art Fair* with ArtDog: London, Hong Kong and New York
2012 *Inside Outside* (solo) Watford Museum. Invited to the *6th Kyoto Hanga Print*, Kyoto City Art Museum, Japan
2013 *Corpus* (solo) Pie Factory, Margate
2009/13 *Guanlan Print Biennale*, China
2012/13 Invited to *Print Biennale*, Douro
2012/14 *RE Open* at Bankside Gallery
2013/14 Residencies at Butterfly World, Herts and Hertfordshire University (AA2A)
2014 Invited to exhibit with De Queeste Art in Belgium and So Fine Art Editions, Dublin. *CMYK*, Margate
2015 Invited to *Incisioni al Femminile*, Italy *50:50*, New Ashgate Gallery, Farnham
2008–10, 2013–15 *Royal Academy Summer Exhibition*
Collections: V&A Print Collection, Guanlan (China) and private collections worldwide
Prizes: *Bainbridge Open* (2009), *BITE* (2012), *Eastern Approaches* (2012, 2013) and 1st Prize solo show *Pushing Print* (2012)
Galleries: London Print Room, ArtDog and Bircham Gallery

Initially starting with printmaking classes at Hertfordshire University in 2003, followed by an AA2A residency with them; an MA in Printmaking at Camberwell College of Art became the natural progression. This was an exciting and challenging time, leading to a consolidation of my ideas and working methods which increasingly became very 'process-led' in their approach to printmaking.

My practice has focused on etchings on copper, but also extends into digital and 3D incorporating other media such as stitching, drawing and glass. Working with etching offers exciting possibilities at different stages of the process. Initially I draw into the hard ground before the copper plates are immersed in the ferric chloride for several hours and this encourages foul biting on the copper plate. The foul biting/random marks start a dialogue between intentional linear drawing and randomness, which is pursued further by reworking the plate.

Exploring the 'surface' is an integral part of my approach and the marks, both intentional and random, make reference to subatomic happenings.

With the deeply etched plate the surface becomes textured which is suggestive of the changing textures of human contact and other living surfaces e.g. plant physiology, growth and decay. In the print *Coalesce* the surface is explored further with the use of stitching into Japanese paper, creating a tactile surface and making reference to artists such as Louise Bourgeois, Kiki Smith and Meret Oppenheim's tea cup.

The inspiration for my work is usually found in detailed drawing studies of plants, flowers, insects and other human/biological forms. I grew up on a small island in Denmark and the nature there still provides much inspiration for my work. The pre-etching drawing is central to the development of ideas, concepts and new forms, as different elements of the drawn studies are combined to create a novel object. To place emphasis on the drawn lines of the prints they are shown against the depth of a single colour background.

The idea of the multiple print is investigated by printing the same etching plate in different colours and creating a series. The relationship between form and colour is considered through a long process of testing different colours, with the choice of colours affecting the meaning and associations of the image, as with *Silva* which exist in different colour hues.

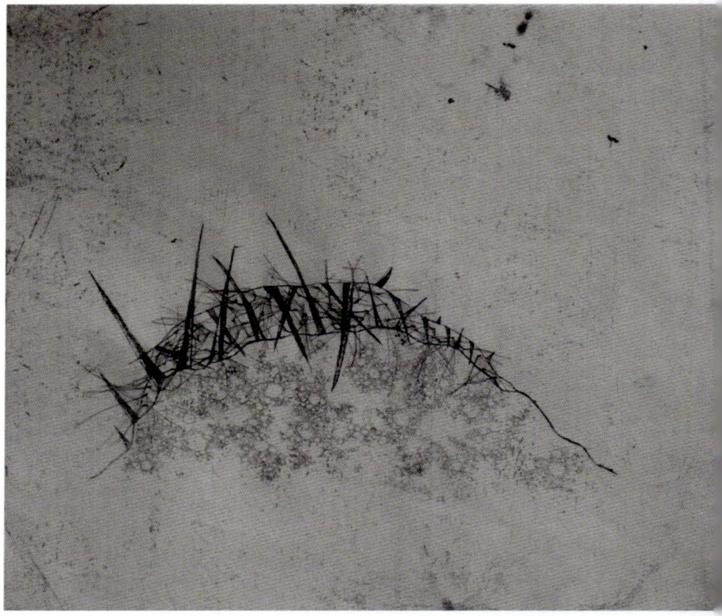

Coalesce, 37 x 43 cm, etching and thread on Japanese paper (edition of 15)

OPPOSITE
Silva III, 60 x 54 cm, etching and carborundum (edition of 15)

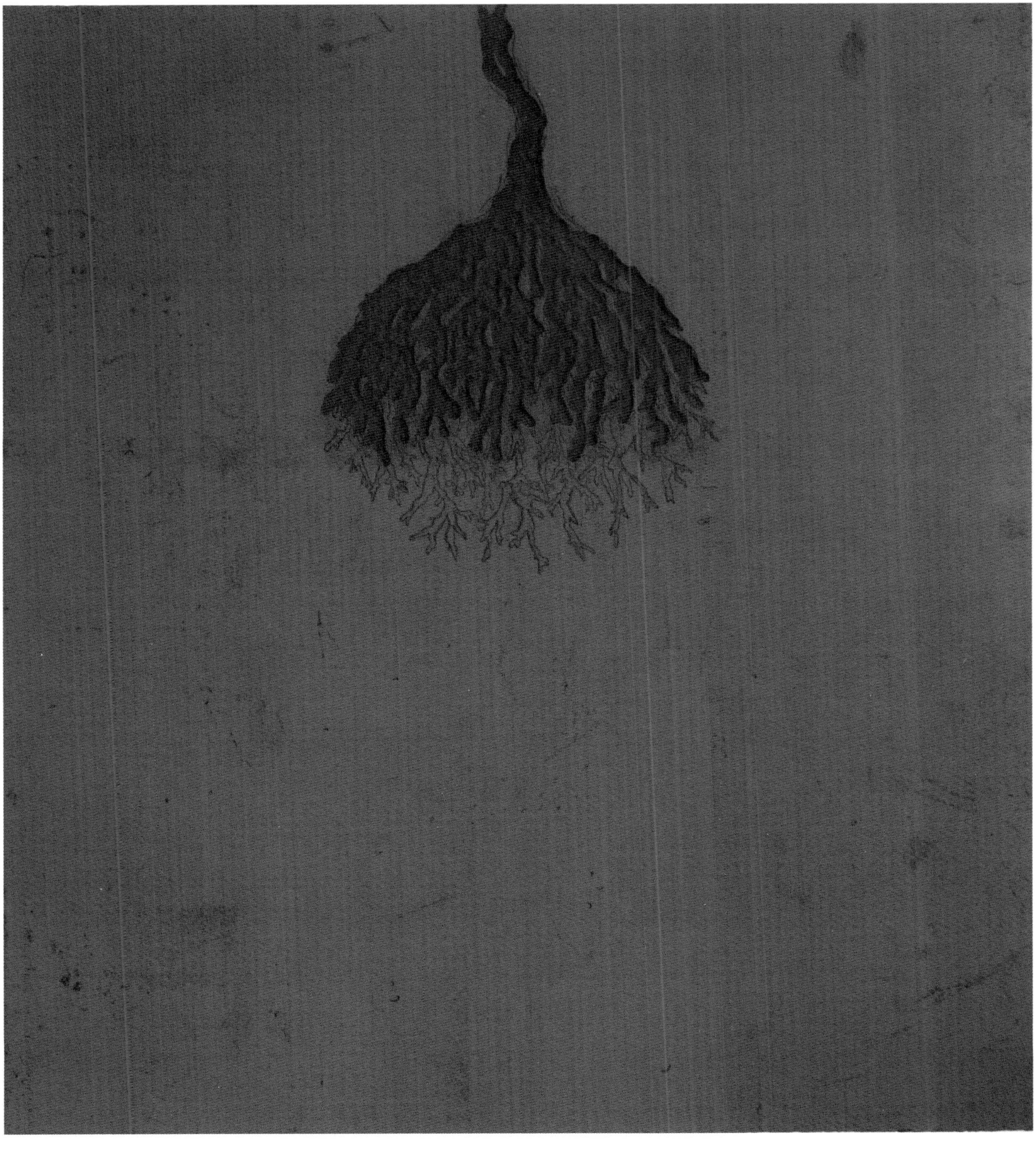

Martin Henley

I have strong memories of Winchester Art School because that was where I first studied printmaking. Then, Winchester was more of a county hub with a livestock market and strong country links. I had worked on a nearby farm during holidays and so inevitably rural, urban and local life was reflected in my image-making during my Illustration course, and still is.

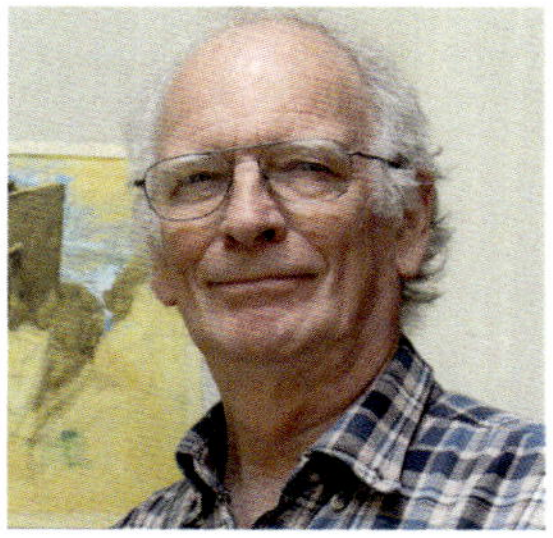

1956–61 Printmaking and illustration at Winchester School of Art and West of England College of Art
1961 Bristol University Institute of Education
1961–66 Freelance illustration, including for *The Times* Arts page
1966–70 Senior Designer at Leeds University Institute of Education
1970–94 Design and illustration practice
1980 Part-time printmaking studies at Central School of Art and Design
1994–06 Teaching and Programme Manager, Richmond Upon Thames College
From 2006 Tutor, Brunel University Arts Centre
2012–15 Part-time intaglio printmaking studies, Morley College
2013 Joined Printmakers Council

Group Exhibitions include:
1970 Leeds University Brotherton Library
2006 Art and Architecture Gallery
2011 Brunel University Beldam Gallery
2012 A4 print, Falmouth
2013/2015 RWA Drawn, Royal West of England Academy.
2014 National Trust, *Mottisfont Open*. *Royal Society of Marine Artists Open*, Mall Galleries. *RWA Open*, Royal West of England Academy. *CMYK*, The Pie Factory, Margate
2015 *MADE 2015 Printmakers*, Morley Gallery. Bath Society of Artists Open. PmC *50:50* exhibition, New Ashgate Gallery, Farnham
Collections V&A Theatre Collection, Brunel University

My tutors instilled a love of observational drawing, and inspired by Sickert's studies and etchings I would sketch local characters such as the smithy at Kingsworthy or road builders under Kingsgate. Southampton's old docks and its working ships had plenty of activities to draw, and Winchester's weathered stone, brick and flint architecture with its alleyways and back lanes was great to sketch. Some fine Georgian houses and a beautiful Victorian butcher's frontage were being demolished, and I recorded them before they disappeared. In the High Street, drawing people shopping was excellent practice for catching fleeting moments in time. I would develop these into illustrations, wood engravings, lithographs or etchings.

In London, my first commissions were drawing live theatre performances for *The Times* newspaper, and for years I balanced freelance illustration and design with teaching. I continued part-time printmaking at Central School of Art and Design and Morley College, where I explored and experimented with a wider range of intaglio processes for textural effect, such as white ground over sugar lift, all bringing ideas to life.

I usually begin with sketchbook and painting studies, often at 'off the beaten track' coastal and rural locations or in towns, seeking unusual viewpoints as well as the clutter of man-made structures alongside natural phenomena. Variable weather and fast-changing light are welcome additions because they add to the atmospherics of the study.

As changes to our landscape accelerate, I become increasingly fascinated with our vanishing heritage, and of the impact that humans have had, and continue to have, on their surroundings everywhere, from abandoned buildings to overgrown lumps and stones in the ground that once were farms, mines or factories. I am curious about the history and underlying narratives of past places and of people who lived and worked there. Revisiting subjects, I often find that they now only exist in my drawings and imagination. These dramatic scenarios, and earlier experiences, are all inspiration for my paintings, etchings and aquatints.

OPPOSITE
Botallack Mist, 26x18cm
etching & aquatint
(edition of 30)

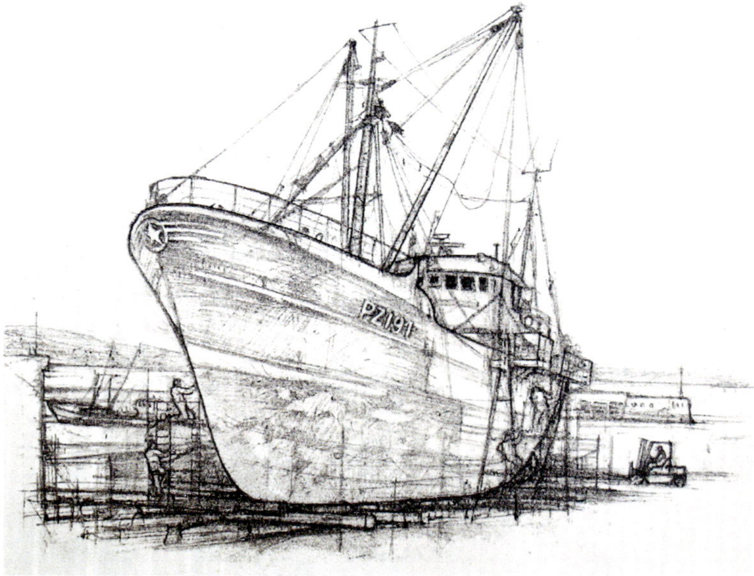

Newlyn Fishing Boat PZ191 on Maintenance Slipway
18 x 19 cm, graphite photo intaglio from in-situ study (edition of 25)

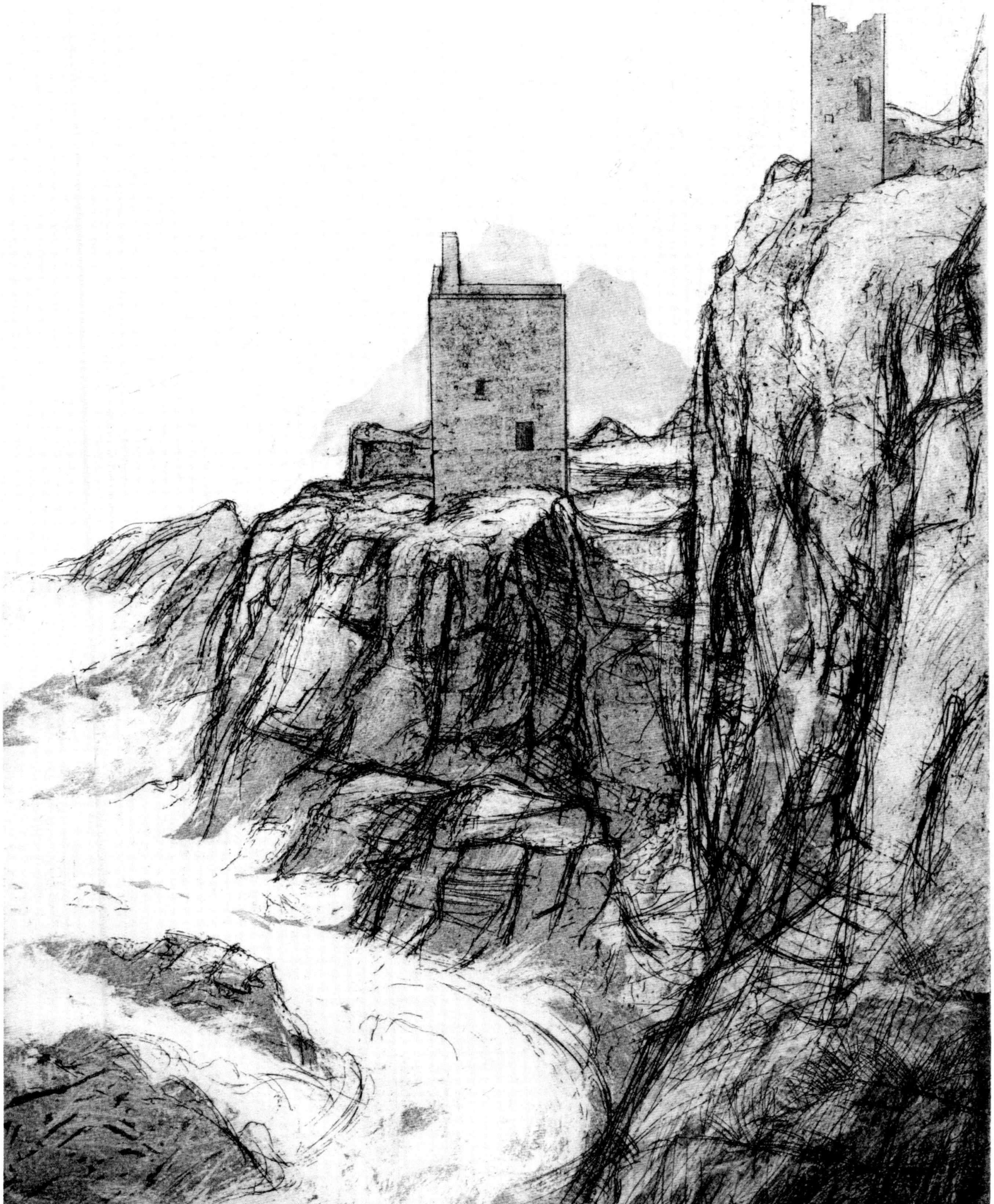

Tessa Holmes

Over 25 years ago I enrolled in a screen-printing evening class in the London Borough of Camden. In the chaos of those weekly three-hour sessions – oil-based inks, blue filler, stapled screen mesh and rickety tabletop frames – I discovered my passion. My first screen print, Higgidly Pig *was reproduced in the Hampstead and Highgate Express with the headline, 'Verve on a silk-screen'. I was hooked.*

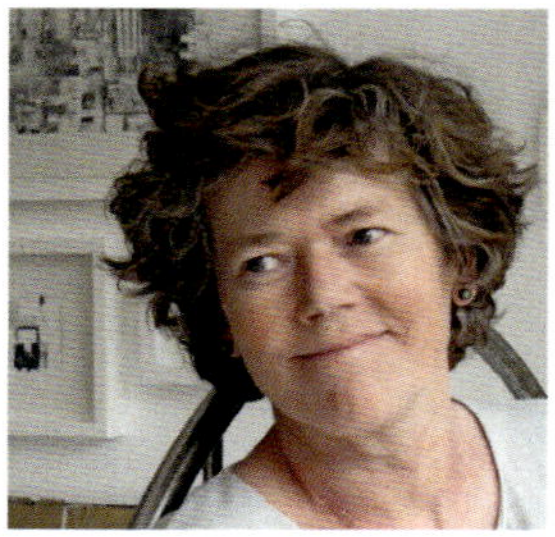

1958 Born Kent, UK

1993–96 BA Fine & Applied Art, London Guildhall University. Awarded Owen Rowley student prize

1996–98 MFA Printmaking, UCL, Slade School of Fine Art. Awarded UCL Travel Scholarship

1998–2007 Associate Lecturer, printmaking and professional development for BA Book Arts, School of Print & Publishing, London College of Communication (UAL)

2003 Printmaking residency at Scuola Internazionale de Grafica, Venezia, Italy

2007–10 Senior Lecturer, printmaking, School of Graphic Design, London College of Communication

2009 Invited artist for *Originals 09*. Awarded Curwin Print Studio Prize

1995–2015 Group Exhibitions include: Printmakers Council, *Originals*, *Affordable Art Fair*, The Foundry, Barbican Contemporary Print Show, Artichoke Print Workshop, National Print Exhibition, British Telecom, *BITE*, Dulwich Open House

2012 Solo Exhibition, Southwark Cathedral, London

Work in Collections: Government Art Collection, Ernst & Young, Institute of Directors, Manchester Metropolitan University, Stoves

I have an eclectic approach to my practice, with both subject matter and techniques. I play. I love to experiment and explore processes. Mix and match. Trial and error. And, as is often the case in printmaking, it is the chance accidents that appear which can produce the most interesting images.

I use solar plate, paper stencils, lino, screen, monoprinting and letterpress. These are all very tactile processes, which demand a level of concentration and focus. Time and patience are required in equal measure. This discipline is the perfect antidote to the frenetic life that hurls on by outside the studio door. For a time I flirted with digital prints, but soon realized that the computer, while an excellent tool, is far too removed from the true nature of printmaking. For me, part of the magic of making a print is the physical engagement it requires. It's hands-on. It's messy. It can be a struggle. It can be a thrill. I don't want to push a button and sit back in a chair. I want the heady smell of the studio: mixing inks, preparing paper, smoothing blankets...even cleaning my tools at the end of a long day!

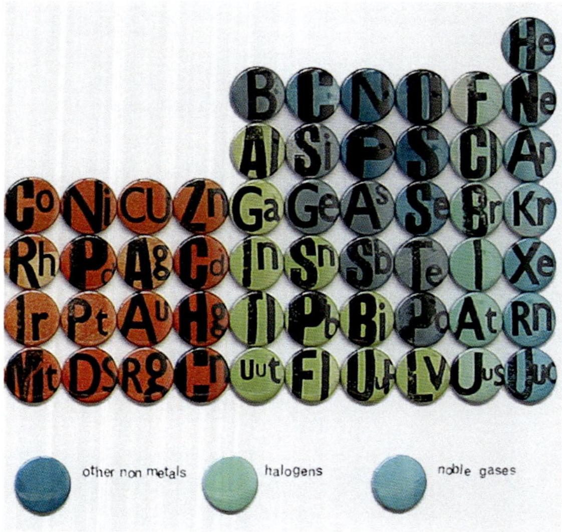

Travelling alone through the outback of Australia and deserts of America had a big impact on my practice. For many years my subject matter was rooted in a fascination with maps: contour lines, grid references, symbols and signs. My work always had a narrative: a journey to follow, a landscape to discover. After spending a lot of time in Italy, in particular Venice and Rome, architecture also became a rich source of inspiration. Still absorbed with the notion of mapping, I began to develop abstract but highly structured accounts of the urban topography.

In 2009 I moved into my own studio in Havelock Walk, Forest Hill in South East London. My work started to incorporate a more graphic dimension. Combining letterpress with recycled prints I made abstract visual grids with badges. This led me to explore classical grid patterns, reinterpreting the Periodic Table and the Multiplication Table.

In 2010 I was diagnosed with Leukaemia. My practice came to an abrupt halt. Five years of treatment has severely limited my time in the studio. However, I have carried on developing my badge prints. Making them provides a rhythm and order that I find strangely calming, even therapeutic. By contrast I have simultaneously developed an ongoing series of anarchic animal prints, *Animalgamation*. They are spontaneous, quirky and full of fun. Curiously perhaps, it is these simple images that offer the most accurate reflection of myself.

Recently I have been able to return to my studio. I have also bought a caravan on the Kent/East Sussex borders, returning to my geographic roots; back to the ethereal landscape of Dungeness, with its strange beach structures and vast lines of empty shingle. This is where my new work begins.

Periodic Table, 90 x 33 cm, mixed-media, letterpress & badges (varied edition of 118)

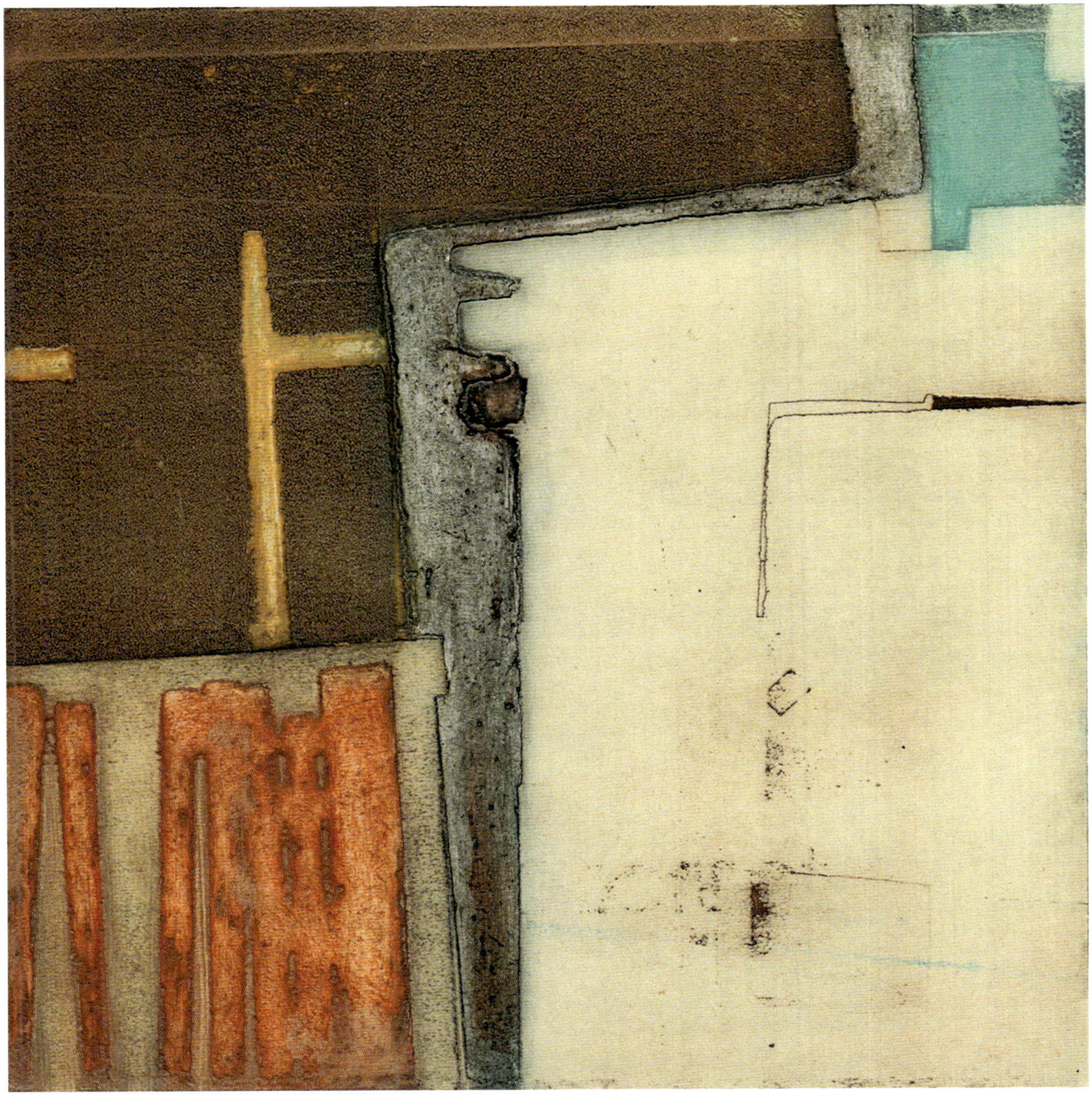

Centro Storico v1, 20 x 20 cm, solar plate etching (varied edition of 5)

John Hutton

John Hutton is a British artist living and working in France. He works in painting and printmaking. Forty years commitment to 'abstract geometric art' has resulted in a body of work which is exhibited internationally. Principles of geometry, light and scale have led him to reject subject matter that deals with representation – form and colour having its own innate reality...

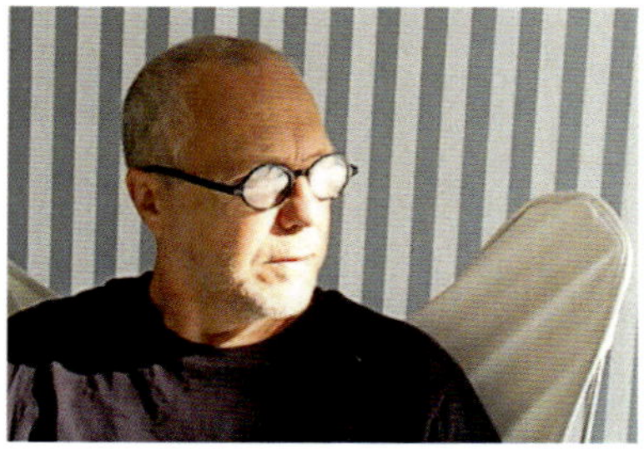

1948 Born London
Studied Watford School of Art, St Albans School of Art

Selected exhibitions

1977–93 *Royal Academy Summer Exhibitions*, London
1981 Ian Birksted Gallery, London
1981 Musée Municipal des Beaux Arts, Tourcoing, France
1981 *Contemporary British Artists*, Tokyo, Osaka, Nagoya, Japan
1981 Minsky's Gallery, Primrose Hill, London
1983 Serpentine Gallery, London
1985 The Last Wapping Show, London
1987 Patricia Knight Fine Art Gallery, London
1989 *Critic's Space 5*, AIR Gallery, London
1990 *Art of Today 3*, Budapest Gallery, Hungary
1991 *Art of the Printmaker*, PmC, Royal Festival Hall, London
1998 The New End Gallery, Hampstead, London
2000 The Metropole Gallery, Folkestone, Kent
2001 Retrospective, Folkestone Museum, Kent
2008 The Square & the Circle, Montreuil, France
2009 *Passage* La Chapelle des Jésuites, Saint-Omer, France
2010 *Souffle d'Art*, Conseil Général, Arras, France
2011 Réalities Nouvelles, Paris
2013 *Highgate - A Reflection in Print*, Highgate Gallery, London
2014 *Lux Expo*, Le Touquet Paris Plage, France
2014/15 *Affinités Abstraites 2*, Galerie Wagner, France

Collections

London Borough of Camden, British Airways, Heathrow. Conseil Général Pas-de-Calais, France. National Collection, Dainville, France. Glaxo Smith Kline, London. National Museum of Wales, Cardiff. Scarborough Art Gallery ,Yorkshire and other private collections in London, France, New York, Switzerland & Japan

Since the 1970s I have focused on geometric abstraction. My paintings and prints are created from a variety of sources and are produced through organisation, choice, trial and experimentation using simple systems of construction. I work in acrylics on canvas using flat colour within a minimalist square or rectangular format and various print media including digital printing. During research and production, chance plays a part and often new areas of investigation lead to the next series. The dynamics involved in the work reveal opposition and interplay between the vertical, horizontal and diagonal elements; based on what feels right to the eye and not just on exact mathematical theories of proportion or ideal ratios.

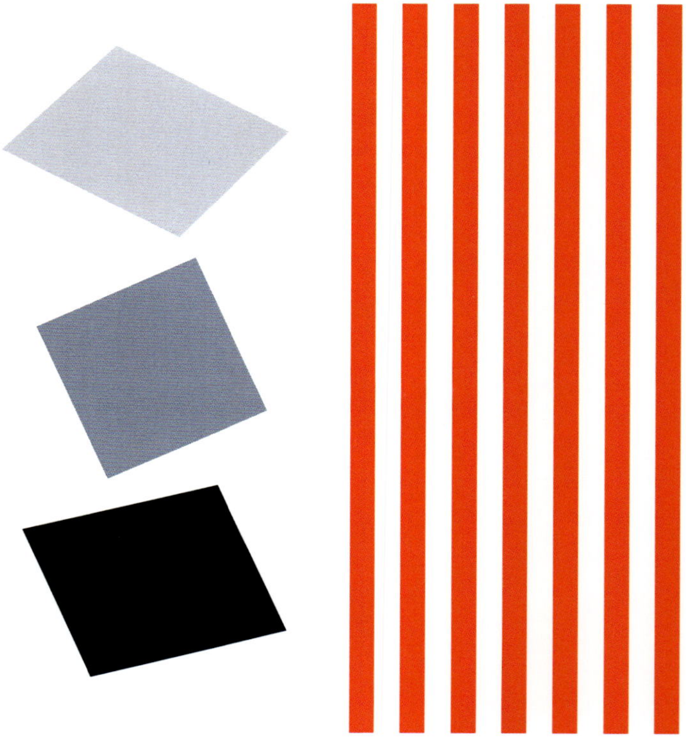

Juggler, 297 x 210 cm, digital print on paper (edition of 10)

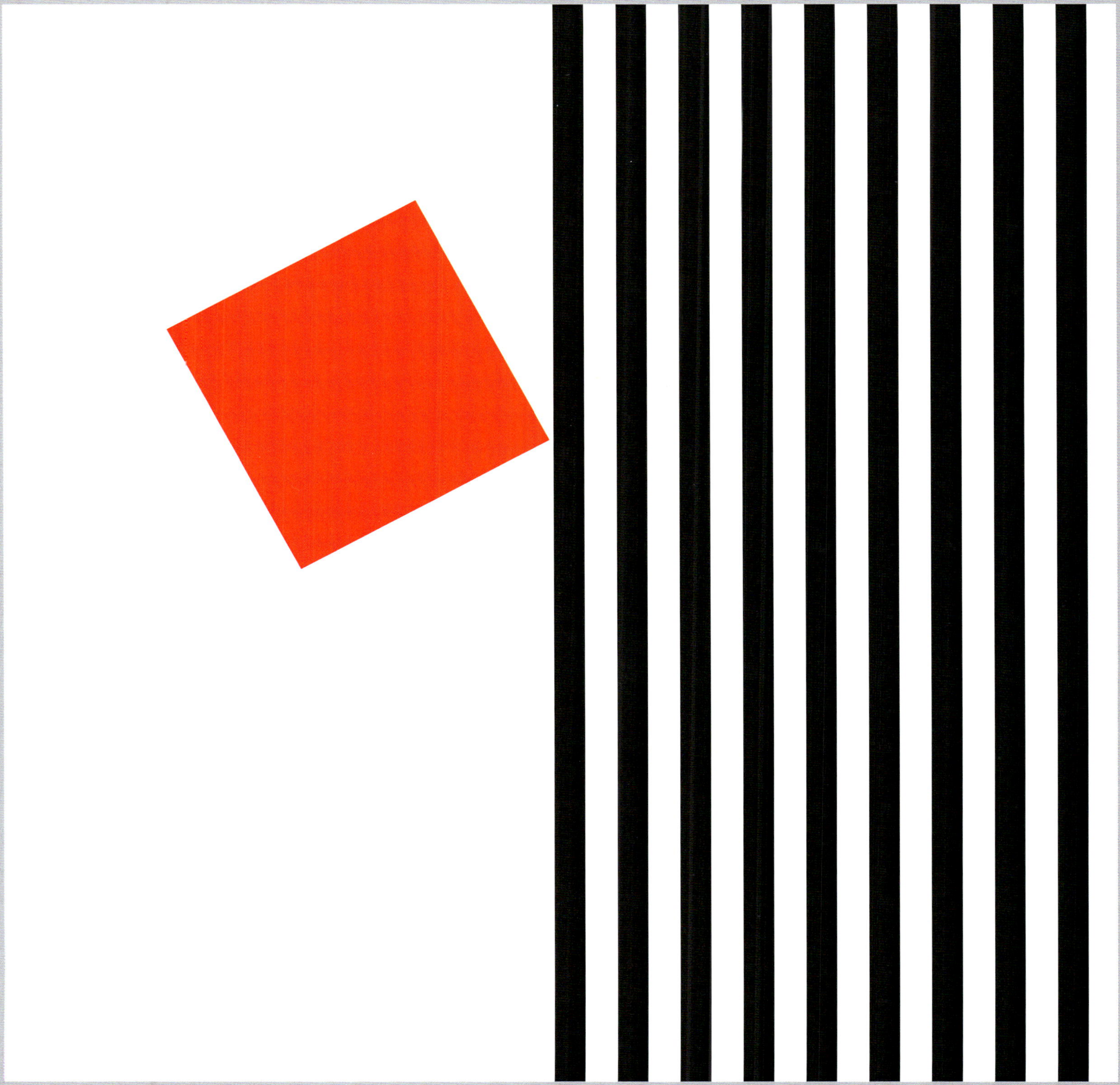

Red into Black, 210 x 210 cm, digital print on paper (edition of 10)

Claire Hynds

Claire is a London-based artist and has exhibited throughout the UK and internationally. She has work in collections at the V&A, London and the National Museum and Gallery of Wales, Cardiff. Hynds studied printmaking at the University of Wales Institute Cardiff and completed a Masters at the University of the West of England. A lecturer in Printmaking at Kensington and Chelsea College, Hynds divides her time between this and her studio.

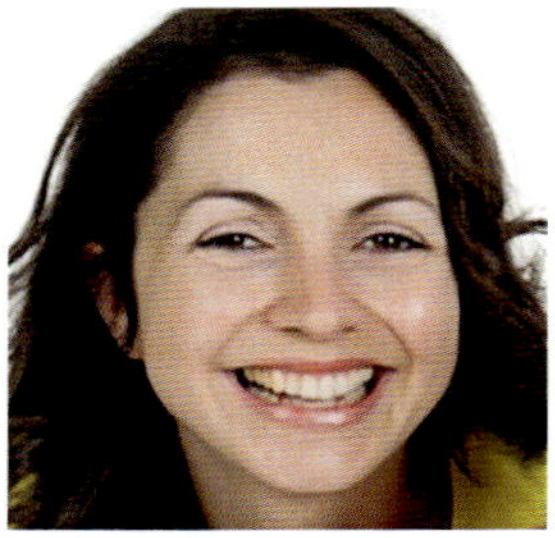

1997–2000 BA (Hons) Fine Art, UWIC
2000–2002 MA Multi-disciplinary Printmaking, UWE, Vocational & Professional Award from the Art & Humanities Research Board
2003–04 PGCE PCET, Greenwich University
2003 Member East London Printmakers
2008 *Wonderland* Touring exhibition in association with East London Printmakers, Fairytale Museum, Bad Oeynhausen, Germany, V&A Museum of Childhood, Bethnal Green, London and The Brothers Grimm Museum, Kassel, Germany.
2009 *Topographs* solo exhibition at the Turbine Gallery, Reading
Impact 2009, University of the West of England & Spike Island Print Studio, Bristol
Guns and Roses touring exhibition at Simeonskirche, Minden, Germany, Changing Room Gallery, London and La Maison de Citoyen et de la Vie Associative, Fontenay-sous-Bois
2010 *London Lives* prizewinner in exhibition at the Bankside Gallery, London
2011 *Dreams* themed group exhibition at the Freud Museum, London
2012 V&A Print of the Month
Received Printmakers Council Prize at *Printathon* exhibition by East London Printmakers
2013 *Transient Vista* solo exhibition, Stevenage Museum
2015 *Works on Paper*, Barbican Library, London

Claire Hynds' work explores the changing aspects and views one experiences when moving through an urban space. Originally inspired by the Brutalist concrete architecture of famous London landmarks such as the Barbican and Southbank Centre, Hynds begins by documenting the buildings from a range of different viewpoints. The mechanical eye of the camera lens accurately presents to the viewer the subtle angles experienced when viewing a building. This notion of viewpoint is integral to the reading of the imagery. Photographs of these buildings have been cropped, manipulated and reformed until a number of individual structures emerged. These individual plates work much like sections of a jigsaw, allowing the artist to constantly modify and reposition the composition, to tell a different story in each image. The irregular jigsaw shaped blocks are inverted, rotated and reconstructed to recreate different perspectives, inviting the viewer to engage with them on many different levels. The resulting construction forms an abstract horizon that relays a sense of encounter and transition.

In the *Barbican Series*, Hynds accentuates this further by manipulating the perspective to create work that uses a multitude of viewpoints to impart a notion of isolation and unease imposed by the often-deserted walkways and corridor of this development.

Hynds' most recent work featuring Stevenage is a natural progression from the Brutalist structures of London. A New Town development, Stevenage owes many of its architectural features to this ideology. Having grown up in Stevenage, Hynds was intrigued by the planners' utopian vision for the New Town development. She set about exploring the modern reality of moving around and living amongst these buildings. Working from imagery of the architectural features from around Stevenage Town Centre, a series of constructed viewpoints make up an imagined landscape that conveys this experience.

Hynds' work combines etching, embossing, screen print, chine collé and paper-cut to create hand-printed limited edition prints.

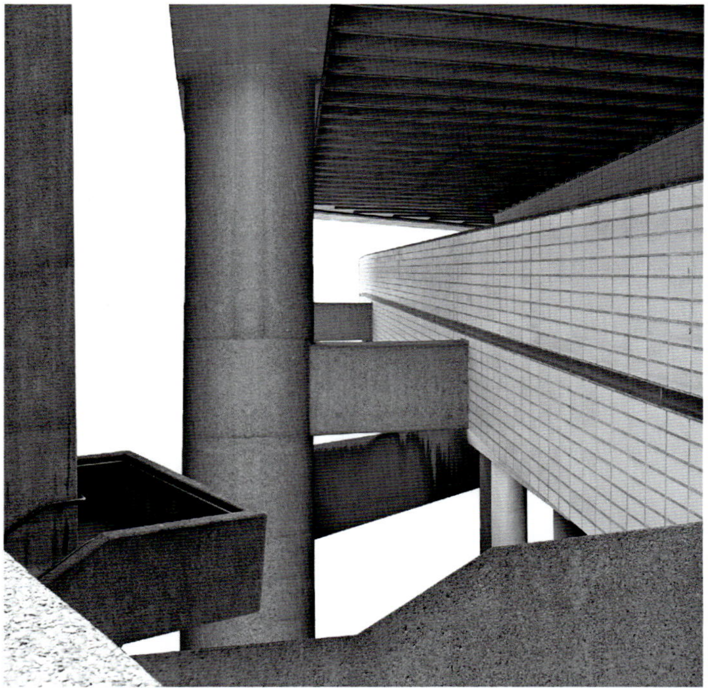

OPPOSITE
Barbican No.3, 50 x 50 cm, polymer gravure (edition of 25)

Barbican No.2, 50 x 50 cm, polymer gravure (edition of 25)

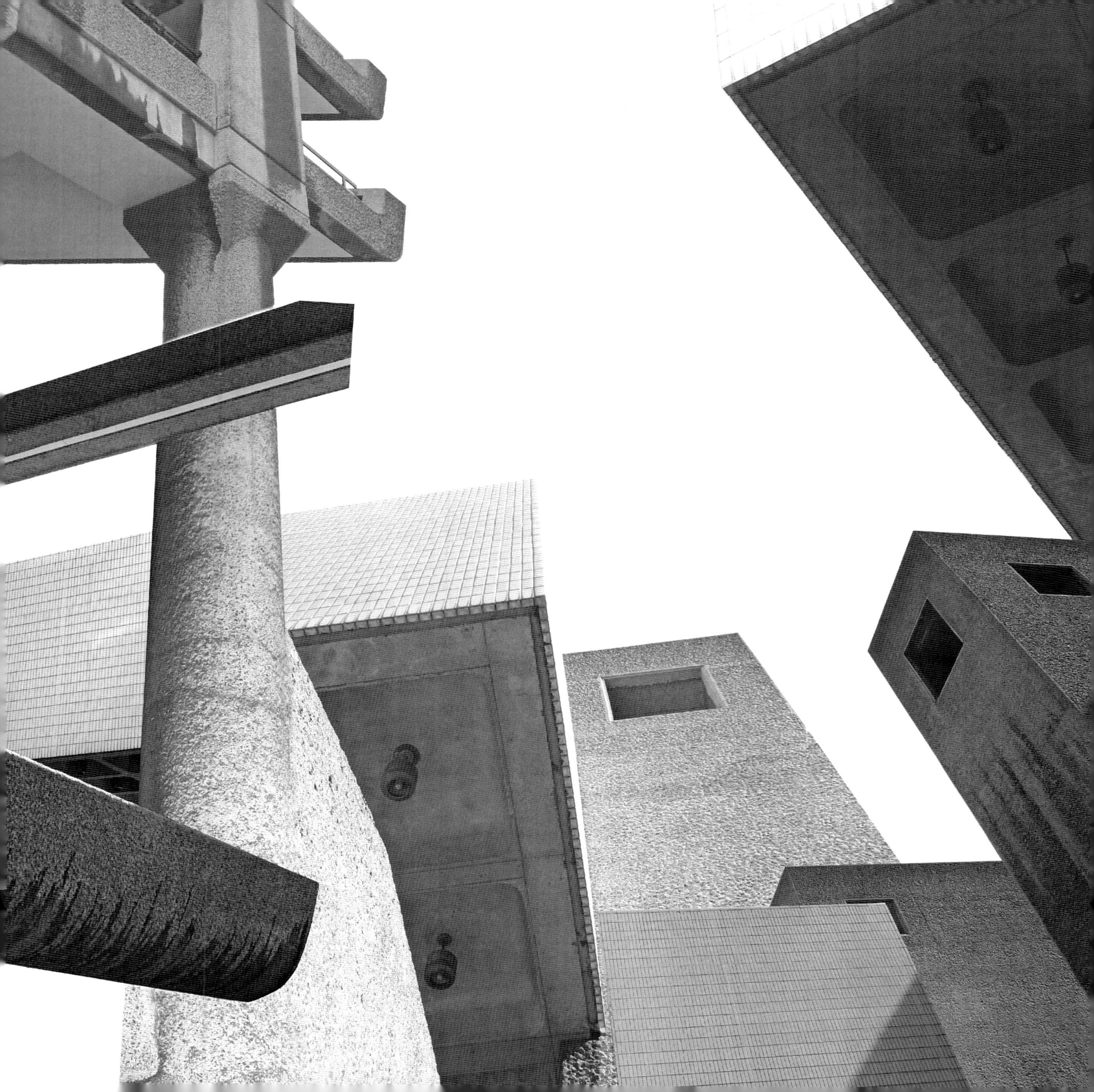

Caroline Jackman

My passion for printmaking was triggered by a truly inspirational teacher at school. I was very lucky to have access to many printmaking processes and really enjoyed lithography and monoprinting. My whole A-level was focused on woodcuts. Other influences came into play during university but it wasn't until 2007, when Ochre Print set up their print studio in Guildford, that I took up printmaking again.

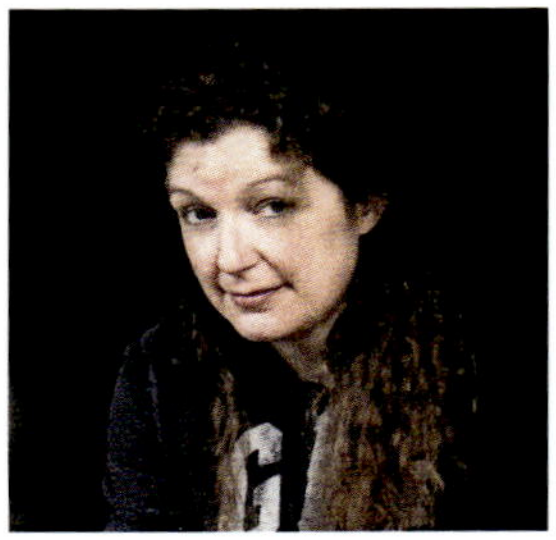

1994–95 BTEC in Foundation Studies Wimbledon School of Art, London

1995–98 BA (Hons) Fine Art, The University of Northumbria at Newcastle

2013–14 Artist in Residence, Ochre Print Studio, Guildford

Recent exhibitions

2014 *Art in the City*, Painters Fine Art Society, Painters Hall, London.
CYMK, Pie Factory, Margate
Ochre Originals, New Ashgate Gallery Farnham
Surrey Artists Open Studios
Ochre Open, Guildford. Selected Open exhibition, Jam Art Centre, Oxford
Jeannie Avent Gallery, East Dulwich

2015 *Horsepower*, equine showcase, New Ashgate Gallery, Farnham.
50:50, Printmakers Council's 50th Anniversary, New Ashgate Gallery, Farnham
Art@Work, Guildford Arts

Awards and Grants

2009 Arts Council England

2014 Printmakers Council Award, Ochre Print Studio Open Exhibition

Professional Practice

2005–13 Surrey County Council Visual Arts Officer. Surrey Artists Open Studios Coordinator

2012–14 Guildford Borough Council Arts Officer

2014–present Interim Gallery Director, New Ashgate Gallery. Freelance Arts Project Manager and workshop leader

I have recently completed a 15-month Artist's Residency for Ochre Print Studio. I devoted the time to exploring a variety of print processes (linocut relief printing, screenprinting, monoprinting and etching) and combining them. Whether the image is a success or failure, I gain so much from the techniques and this has developed my mindset, helping to inform my painting and drawing practice.

My studio is based on my parents' farm, where I am the shepherdess! I thoroughly enjoy the lifestyle of farm life, and as it is a smallholding I can keep it a hobby rather than rely on the farm for a living. As a consequence I am driven by the exploration of creatures and their characteristics, perhaps capturing a moment in time through form, colour and texture. Using a variety of processes, primarily painting and original prints, my work reflects the different nuances of each method. I am inspired by everyday occurrences, movement in animals, naivety and the subtleness of life surrounding us.

My practice includes regular commissions of portraits, in particular of horses and dogs. I thoroughly enjoy these commissions, ensuring a representation of the character of each animal and a happy customer comes from a successful piece. I am very fortunate to have returning customers and regular commissions.

During the recent Ochre Print studio residency, I took a mini residency with Andrew Baldwin, Tutor of Printmaking at Aberystwyth School of Art. It was fantastic to explore the techniques of non-toxic Baldwin's Ink Ground and its versatility with both copper and aluminium plates. I explored step etching, sandpaper aquatint, resist and spit bite and coffee lift. All great techniques, ideal to take back to Ochre to use in their soon-to-be-launched new non-toxic etching facilities.

I have become increasingly fascinated by nature, whether large or small. From recent travels to Wyoming, New Zealand and the Dolomite region in Italy, to studying spiders, insects and amphibians, the comparison of scale is fun to play with.

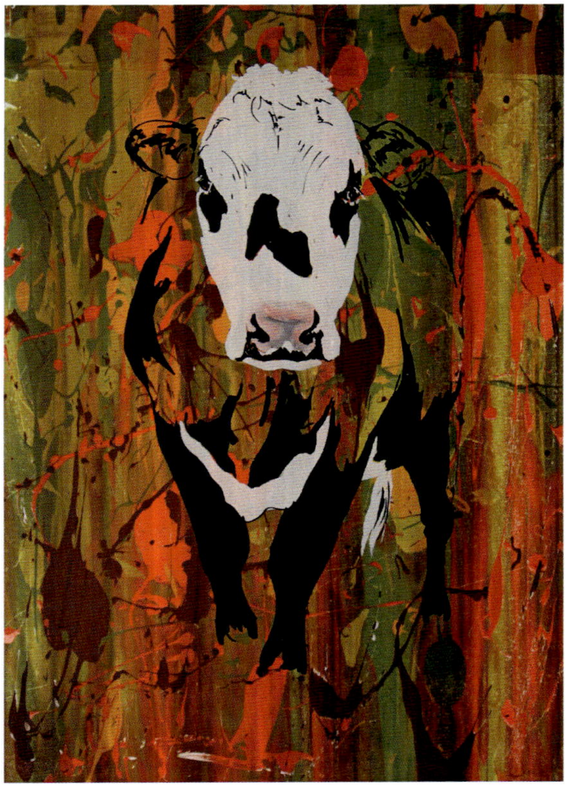

Chameleon, 70 x 50 cm,
mono screen print (varied edition of 4)

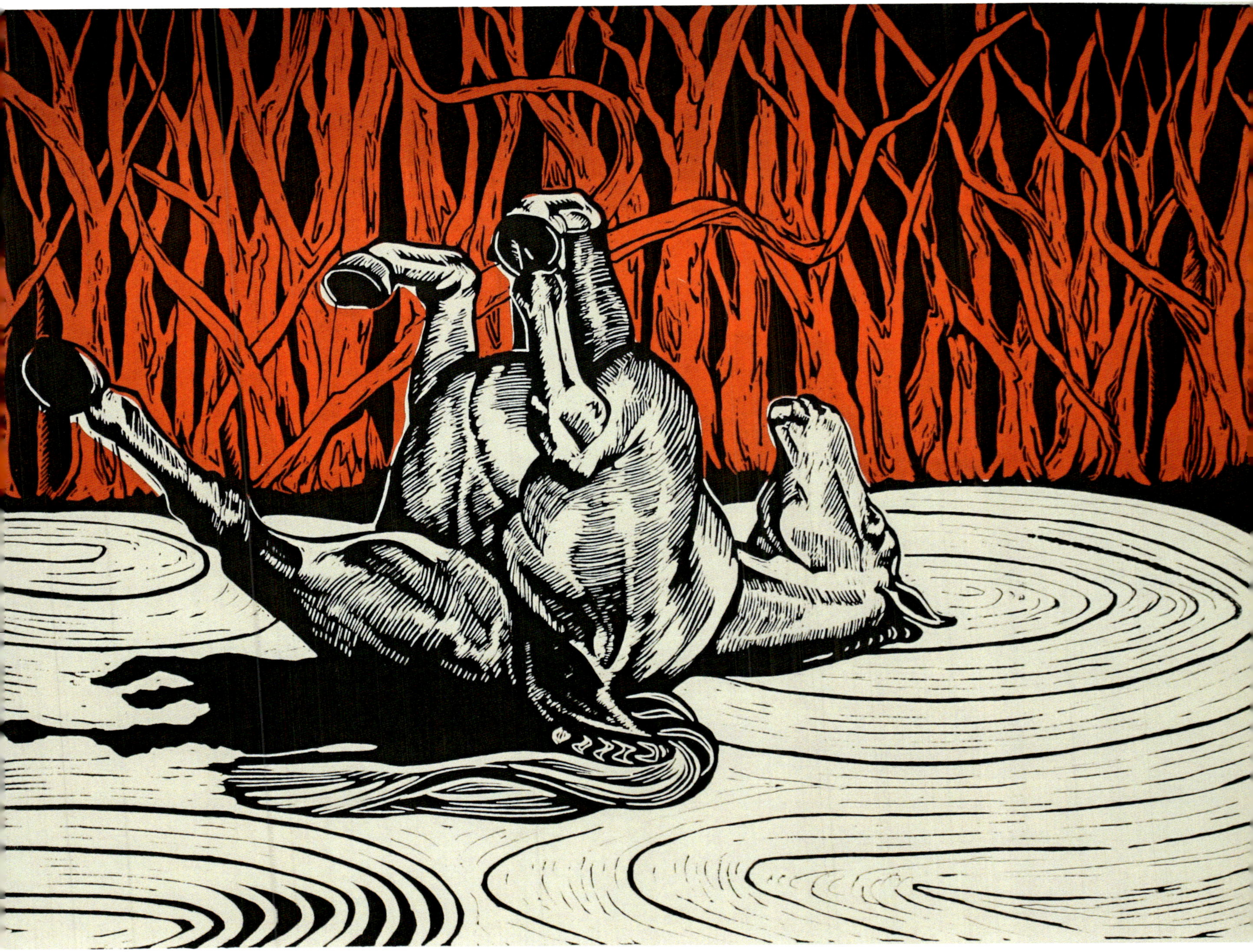

A Good Roll Heals a Thousand Wounds, 33 x 43 cm, screen print & linocut (edition of 6)

Barbara Jackson

In my print work I endeavour to capture an atmosphere using the play of light and shade, figures and architecture. I usually work in the area of etching and aquatint in which it is possible to show tonal values. Working from back to front, light to dark and timing the acid to provide the correct jumps in tone is always a test and the combination of art and craft is what I find so challenging and exciting.

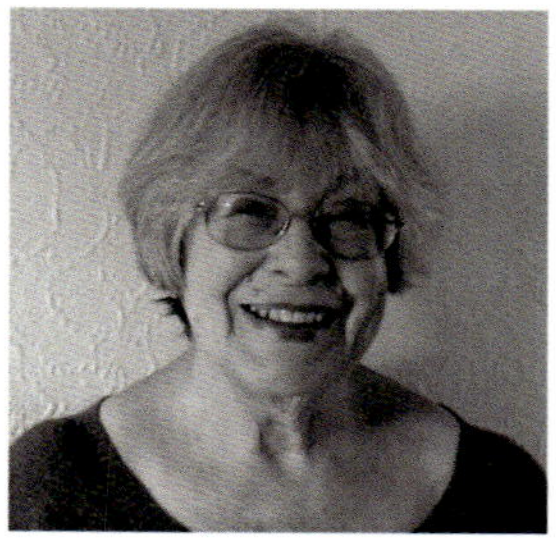

Education: St Martin's School of Art, University of London Institute of Education; validated certificate in Art Therapy

Experience: Head of Art, The English School, The Hague. Head of Art, Highbury Hill High School. Adult Education tutor in Foundation Studies - painting and drawing. Member of Printmakers Council and Southbank Printmakers Cooperative

Current Work in Galleries
Newcastle, Birmingham, London, Eastbourne

Solo Exhibitions: Four in London

Print Awards: John Purcell Award; St Cuthbert Mill Award; Birgit Skiold Prize; Artichoke Workshop Prize (all at National Print Exhibition) Prize winner - 6th British International Miniature Print Exhibition

Exhibitions:
Royal National Theatre - London
OXO Gallery , Southbank, London
2005/09/10 *Originals*, Mall Gallery London
2012 *BITE*
Pushing Print, Margate
2000/2009/2010 *Discerning Eye*, London
Landau Exhibition, Germany
2011–12 Exhibited and Demonstrated at *Art in Action*
2012–13 *Affordable Art Fair*, Hampstead
2014–15 NOA (National Open Art) Competition
2014 *Royal Academy Summer Exhibition*, three times including **2015**

Having specialised in illustration at St Martin's School of Art, I didn't feel 'comfortable' with the discipline and decided to take a postgraduate year in teaching to widen my options. I spent several years teaching Art to students of all ages and am currently running an advanced painting class.

I never abandoned my own art work and experimented with ceramics and tapestry weaving as well as painting. Then, a short course in printmaking at Central School of Art introduced me to the joy and fascination in what is essentially a combination of art and craft. I was hooked!

Printmaking links me to artists from Dürer to Paula Rego and I am full of admiration for the possibilities printmakers past and present have demonstrated in their varied techniques and imagery.

Every print I make is a battle to realise an inner vision to the best of my ability. My chosen medium is etching and aquatint where I can realise the rich tonal values and textures I like to bring to a print. It works well with the moody type of imagery, be it landscape, the city or the human condition, that I so much enjoy expressing.

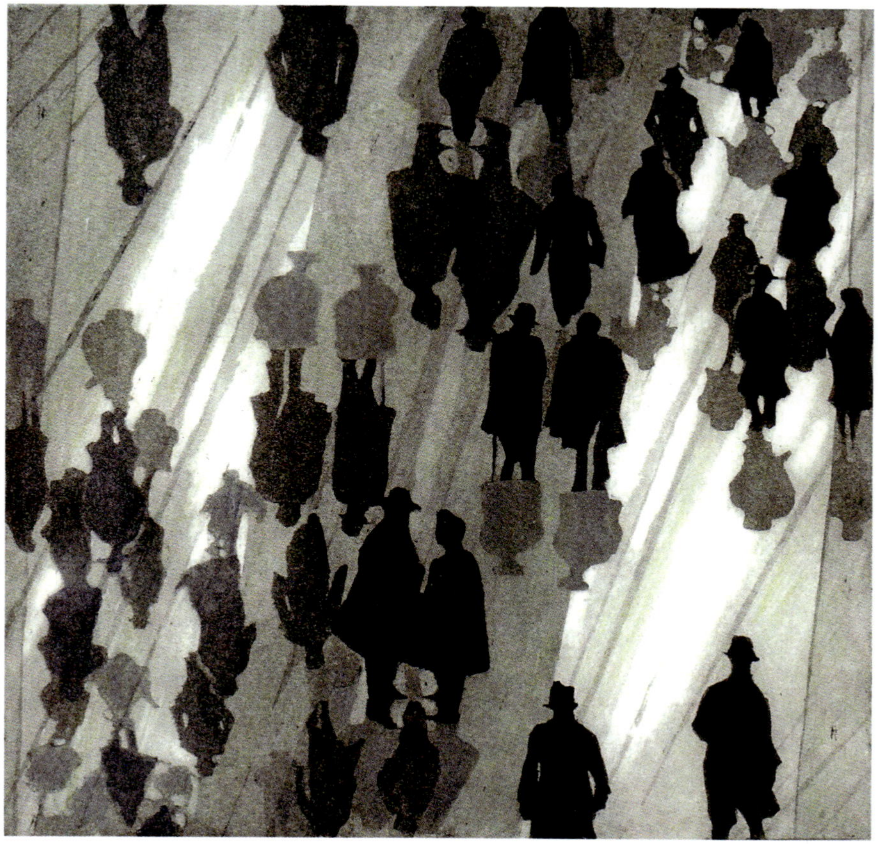

OPPOSITE
Paris Reflection
27.5 x 21 cm
etching & aquatint
(edition of 40 plus
10 artist proofs)

Transience III
18 x 18.5 cm
etching & aquatint
(edition of 40 plus
10 artist proofs)

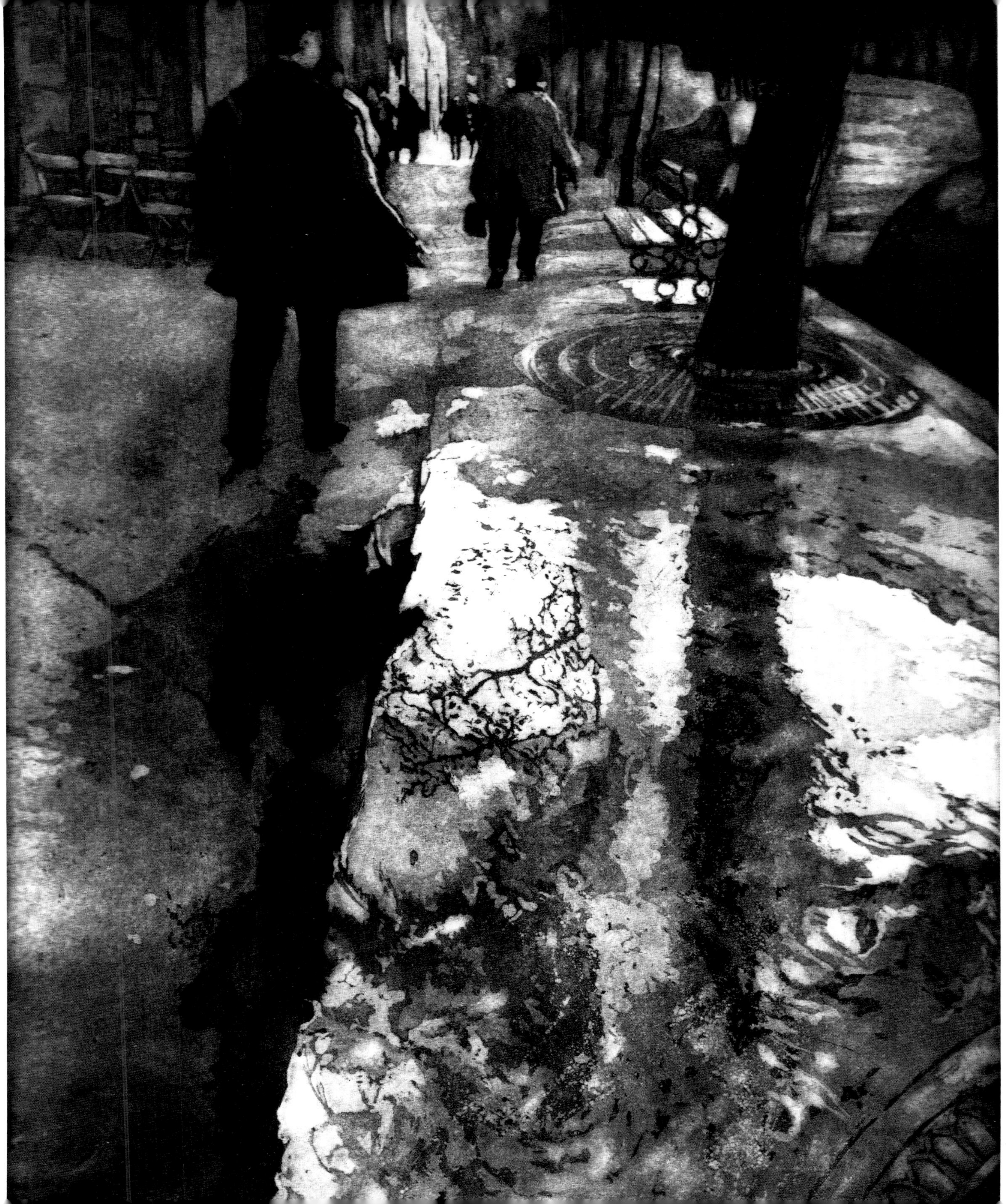

Elizabeth A Kelleher

My gap year between college and returning to printmaking became fifteen. This space was filled by teaching, initially in a primary school, before moving into special education. For eight years I worked in a special school teaching autistic children. I eventually left as the Deputy Head of this school in the early eighties to have my own children. Whilst on a family holiday in the Lake District I bought an etching by Simon Bull. This loved print of Thornton Force inspired me to return to printmaking.

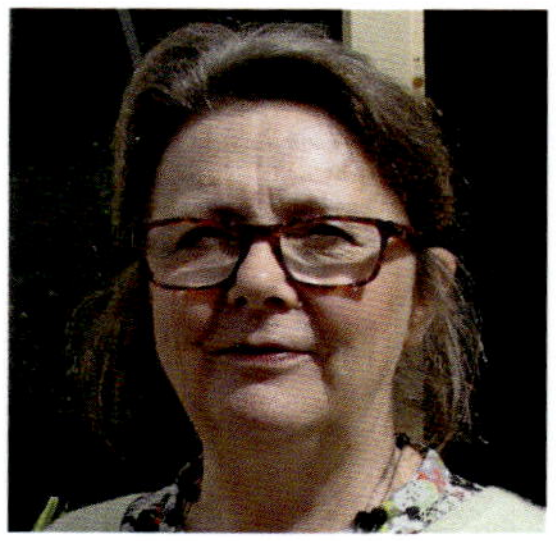

1969–72 Certification of Education in Art, St Mary's College Bangor

1972–81 Full-time teaching in Primary and Special Education

1981–87 Full-time mother of three children.

1987–99 I returned to printmaking as a member of a print workshop and to part-time teaching in Primary Education

1999 Appointed as print tutor for Kent Adult Education Service. Presently running three classes in printmaking plus a monthly workshop for the more experienced printmaker

Exhibitions

Throughout Kent at such venues as Roger Green Fine Art, Tenterton; St Andrew's Art Centre, Gravesend; The Ripley Art Centre, Bromley; The Horsebridge Gallery, Whitstable; Bexley Open Art Exhibition, Hall Place Bexley and the Sidney Cooper Gallery, Canterbury

1994, 1995, 2012 and **2014** The Society of Botanical Artists Annual Exhibition, Westminster Hall, London

2013 and **2015** Solo shows at The Sportsman gastropub, Seasalter, Kent; The Printmakers Council at Stables Gallery, Bexley; The Margate Gallery, Margate; RK Burt Gallery, London; Framers Gallery, London

2015 *Artist in the Garden*, The Tea Shop, Abergavenny

My work is in private collections in France, Spain, Ireland and the USA

Doing some research, I was extremely lucky to find out that my local adult education college, a five minute walk down the road, did printmaking. In addition it had the brilliant facility of a crèche, so I eagerly signed up!

Initially the course was run as a workshop. Then the wonderful technician Shirley Skynner, who trained at the Slade, re-honed the printing skills that I had aquired at college. Over the years the course has evolved and it is now run as a tutored class. It is at these same premises I have been ensconced for many years improving my own skills, and for the past sixteen years I have been working as the class tutor.

From just one morning class I inherited, it has blossomed into three thriving classes. My students have exhibited as a group at local art centres and as individuals in local and London exhibitions. I now also run workshops for more experienced students. My main aim is to inspire others with the wonders of printmaking. My own work is influenced by various aspects of nature, with botanical subjects being my particular favourite. Perhaps I might work initially in watercolours or sketches which I then transform into different forms of printmaking depending on the feel of the image.

My main passion is working with metal. I adore the range of tones and textures one can create with just a metal plate and some acid. Printmaking never stays still. I am always learning and building on techniques. Working with others is also inspiring as we feed off each other. These factors are what makes this medium so facinating, enthralling and addictive for me.

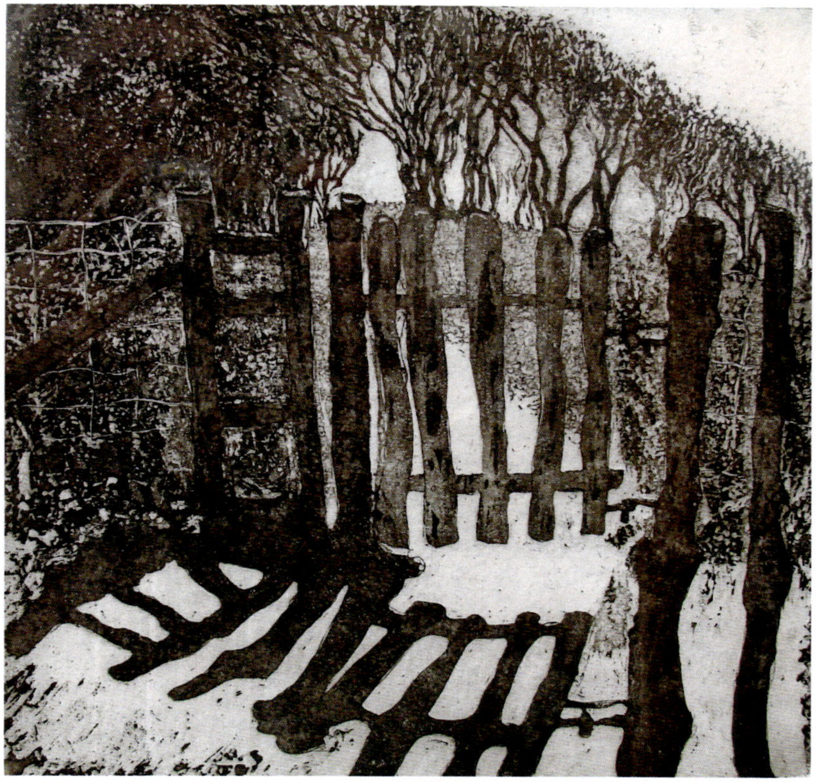

The Gate, 20 x 20 cm
etching with aquatint
(edition of 20)

The Humble Bee,
29 x 39 cm,
etching with aquatint
(edition of 20)

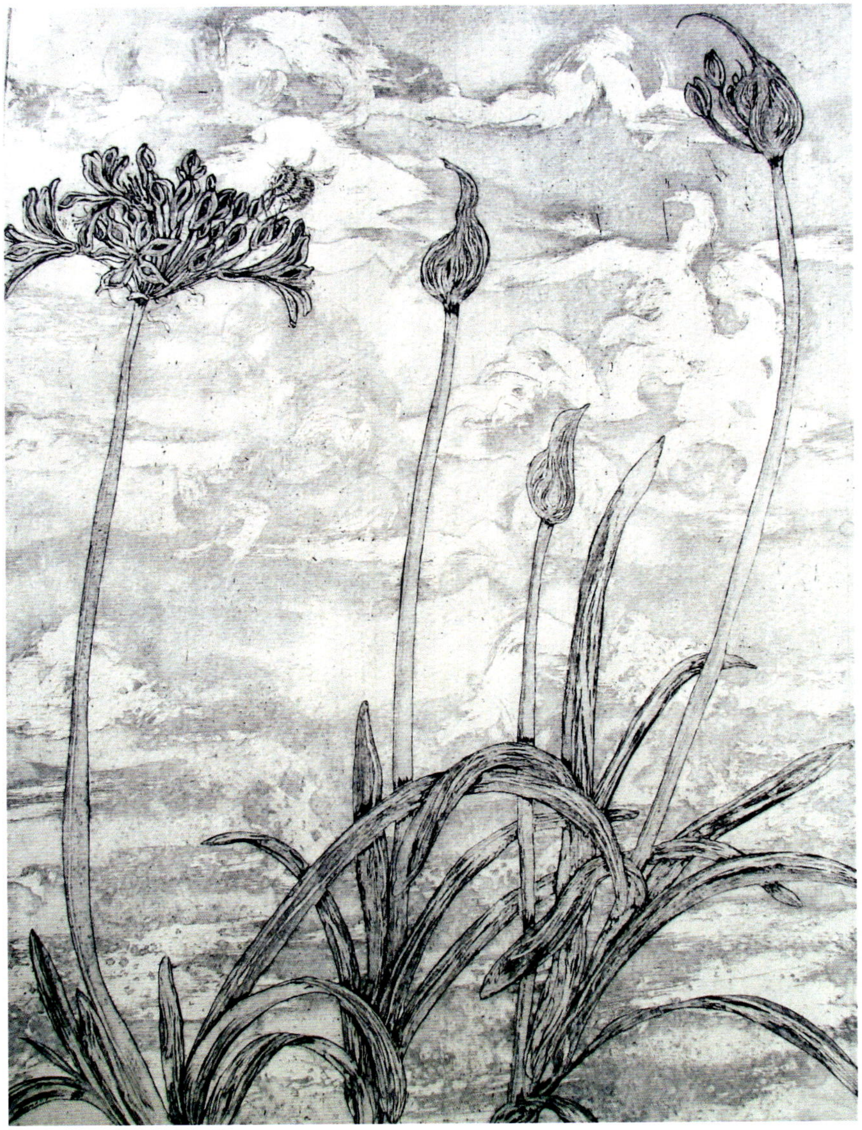

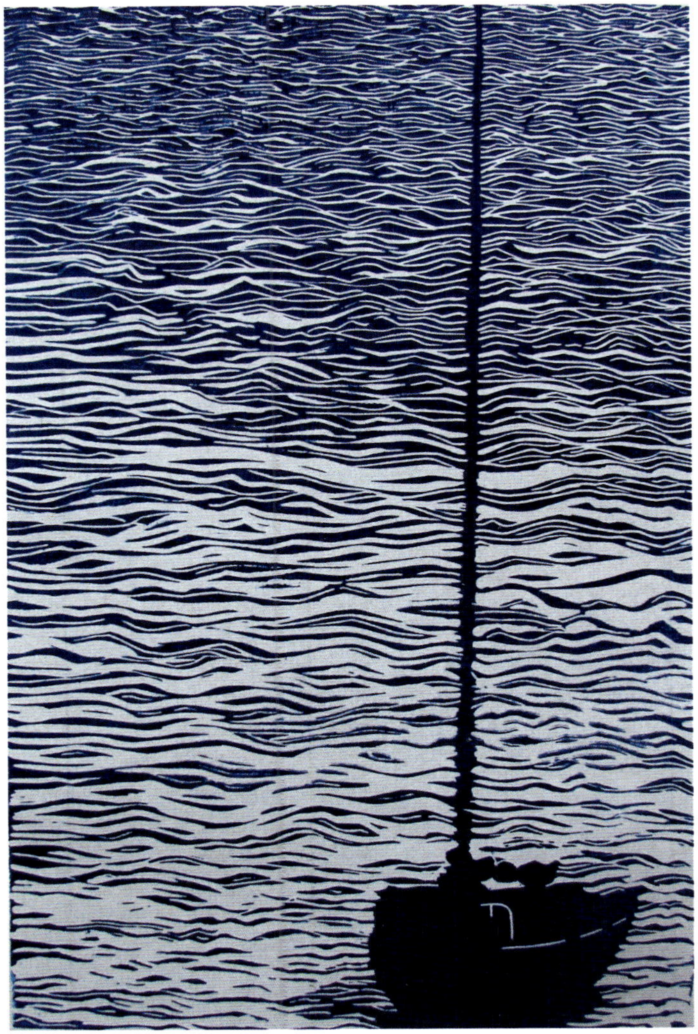

Calm,
20 x 30 cm,
linocut (edition of 50)

Michael Kennedy

I started making prints in my first year at Bromley School of Art. The Intermediate course offered a broad art and craft curriculum and this introduced me to stone lithography, which I later took as my subsidiary subject for the examination. I continued making prints, mostly lithographs, for the following two years at Ravensbourne and after that at the Slade School, where I was privileged to work with Stanley Jones.

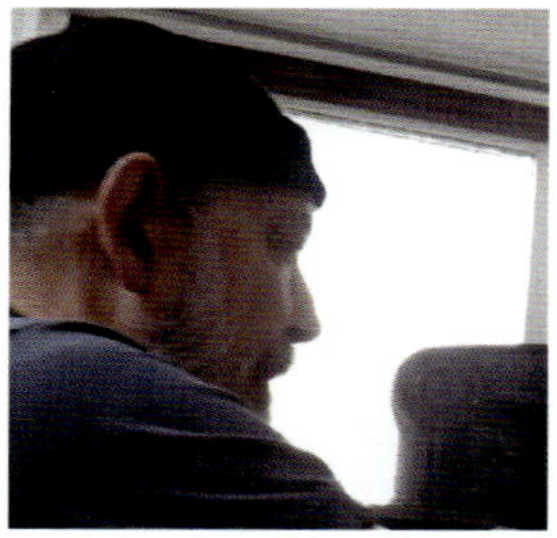

1943 Born Dartford, Kent
1960 Bromley School of Art
1962 Ravensbourne College of Art & Design
1964 The Slade School of Fine Art, UCL
1975 Teaching in Higher Education until retirement in 2003
1996 Joined Printmakers Council
2003 *British International Miniature Print Exhibition*
2004 *Royal Academy Summer Exhibition*; *Originals*, Mall Galleries
2004 *Royal West of England Academy Open Print Exhibition*
2005 & **2006** *Originals*, Mall Galleries
2006 *British International Miniature Print Exhibition*
2007 *Originals*, Mall Galleries
2008 *Royal Academy Summer Exhibition*
2009 *Royal Academy Summer Exhibition*
Royal West of England Academy Open Print Exhibition
British International Miniature Print Exhibition.
Pushing Print, Pie Factory, Margate
2010 *Royal Academy Summer Exhibition*
PmC, Bankside Gallery, London
2012 *Royal Academy Summer Exhibition*
British International Miniature Print Exhibition
2013 *Royal Academy Summer Exhibition*
2014 Joined East London Printmakers
ELP box set 2014 collection V&A Museum
2015 PmC *50:50*, New Ashgate Gallery Farnham
Fifty Years of Artists Prints, Bankside Gallery

My paintings and prints reference found and appropriated objects which are themselves often ephemeral. Images taken from books, magazines and other printed sources, together with found objects, are adapted and combined to form what I have described as 'chance encounters'. Subject matter varies: sometimes it is suggested by the various found images and the 'encounters' that result; on other occasions it is a deliberate attempt to respond to some theme or idea; often it is no more than a suggestion and the work remains 'untitled'. But there is always scope for the viewer's own perceptions and ideas so that the end result is a shared meaning, richer and more complex than a simple illustration.

Although I have made prints over the years in a variety of processes, I was fortunate some years ago to acquire an Albion press and my prints today are normally relief prints, wood and lino, which I combine with stencil. I usually start with a preliminary collage which is modified again and again. Once I have settled on a composition, it is then scaled up or down to the desired print size and further modifications made as necessary. My preferred way of working with stencil is to cut apertures in thin card with a scalpel or a Stanley knife. These are placed in register on the print surface and ink is then carefully applied using a stencil brush. The method requires little or no equipment but it does demand a lot of patience and skill. I like the combination of flat stencilled shapes with cut lino shapes, sometimes in combination with the characteristic textures that relief printing can achieve. For me, printmaking continues to be a major activity, not at all subsidiary, but equally important alongside painting.

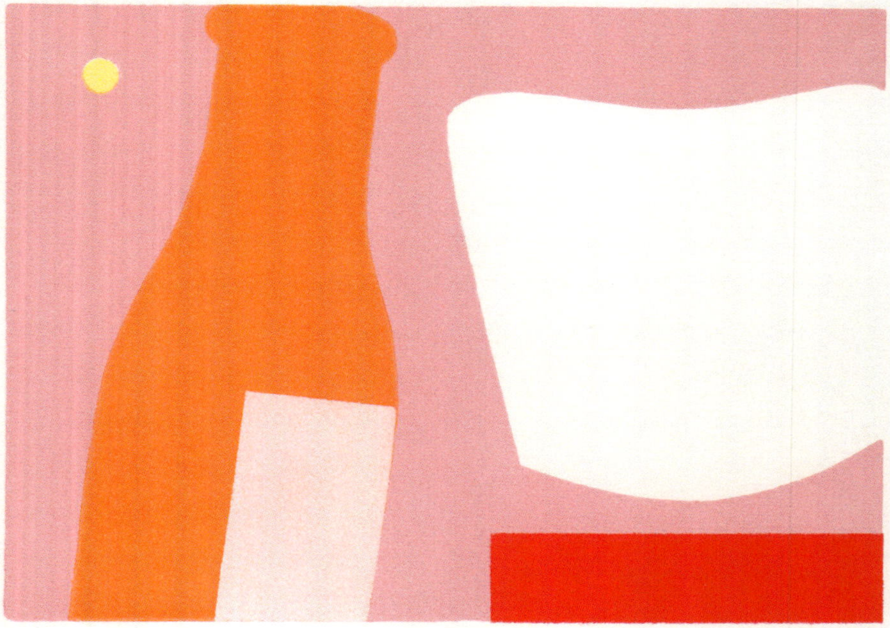

Objet Perdu
10.5 x 15 cm (image)
linocut & stencil
(edition of 38)

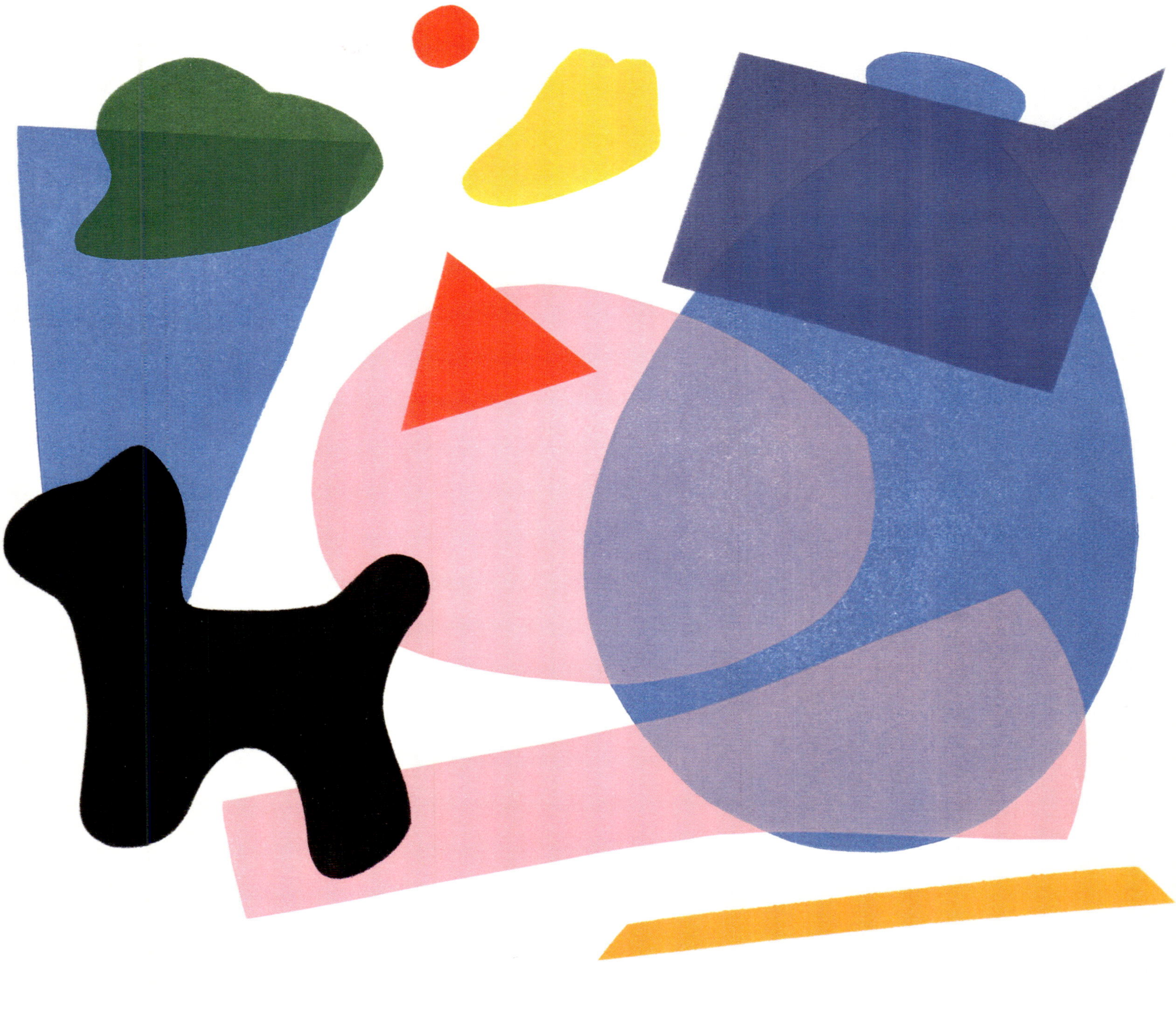

Untitled Still Life, 26 x 32 cm (image), linocut & stencil (edition of 5)

Frances Kiernan

I love everything about printmaking – the rhythm, the methods, the pace, even the cleaning up – it's a meditative process for me. It was in 1965 at Ealing School of Art that I first hand-set some type and printed a poster on a lovely old proofing press. I was hooked. Fast forward fifty years… I'm still printing and I still love it.

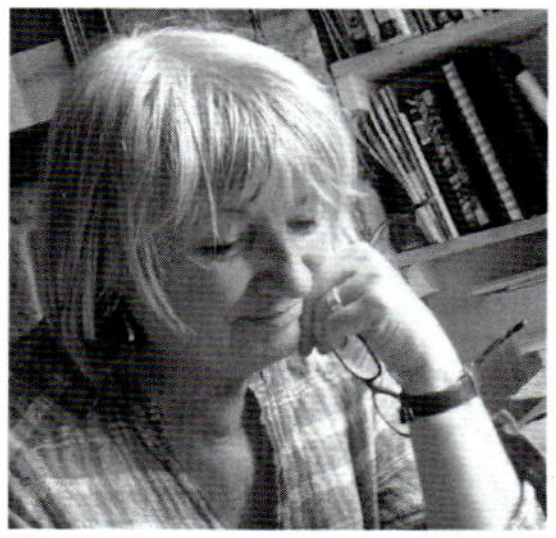

1946 Born Marylebone, London
1965–68 Typography & Design, Ealing School of Art
1968–2002 Designer/art director
2002 MA Fine Art, Wimbledon School of Art
2003 ICA Gallery, London. Artists' books
2004 MA show. Video installation *Impressions* 4:33mins
2005 Lauderdale House, London
2006 Joined Designer Bookbinders
2007 Short Film Festival, Limehouse, London. Collograph in *Intaglio* Thames & Hudson
2008 Joined Richmond Printmakers
2009 Collographs in *Aria*, Sudeep Sen, Atlas Arts
2010 Artist in Residence at Sanskriti Kendra, New Delhi, India
2010–11 *The Enchanted Palace Exhibition*, artist books installation, Kensington Palace
2011 Nehru Centre, London
2013 Stables Gallery, Twickenham
2014 Joined Printmakers Council
2014 *Artists' Books*, Riverside Gallery, Richmond
2015 *50:50* Printmakers Council, New Ashgate Gallery, Farnham *50 Years of Artists Prints*, Bankside Gallery, London

Collections

V&A Museum, Kensington Palace, Kew Palace and Sanskriti Foundation in New Delhi

Landscape, memory and language influence the work I make and continue to be a critical area of research. Man's effect on the landscape and the effect that the landscape has on Man informs my work. The traces we leave behind and the history of patterns they create led me to look at the work of poet John Clare who documented the effect of place and people when the Enclosure Acts granted local landowners permission to fence the open fields. In my current work I print separate plates to represent the division of land and link the plates with thread to acknowledge the time when people worked and walked freely on what was once common land.

I like to record the natural textures, shapes and patterns around me through observational writings, sketches and photographs. These are developed, revised and often cropped so that the final work may be quite unlike the original image. An etching plate is my choice of surface but as concept determines the medium, the matrix changes accordingly. Thread and cloth have become an integral part of my printmaking practice and continued investigation into the use of materials has given me an increased interest in textiles, construction prints and sculptural forms. Looking at the detailed structure of cloth, and printing onto cloth, moves my work into a new direction, with mark-making still at its centre.

Having spent a large part of my life involved with type, design and print, it is not surprising that book art features in my practice. I combine image and words in traditional print processes and new media. Collaborations with writers provide the opportunity to make new work and to challenge the way in which the work can be made.

I enjoy sharing my skills with community groups, children and adults through my work with outreach projects. I have devised and delivered print-based and book art workshops with the Historic Royal Palaces, Strawberry Hill Trust, Kew Gardens, Chelsea College of Art, Orleans House Gallery and literary festivals.

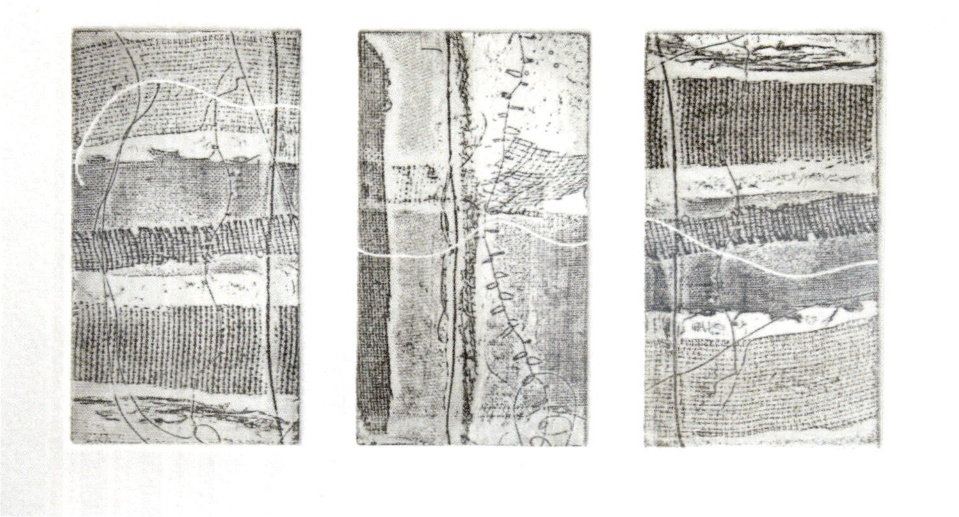

Surface Light 3
14 x 7.5 cm
etching
(variable edition of 10)

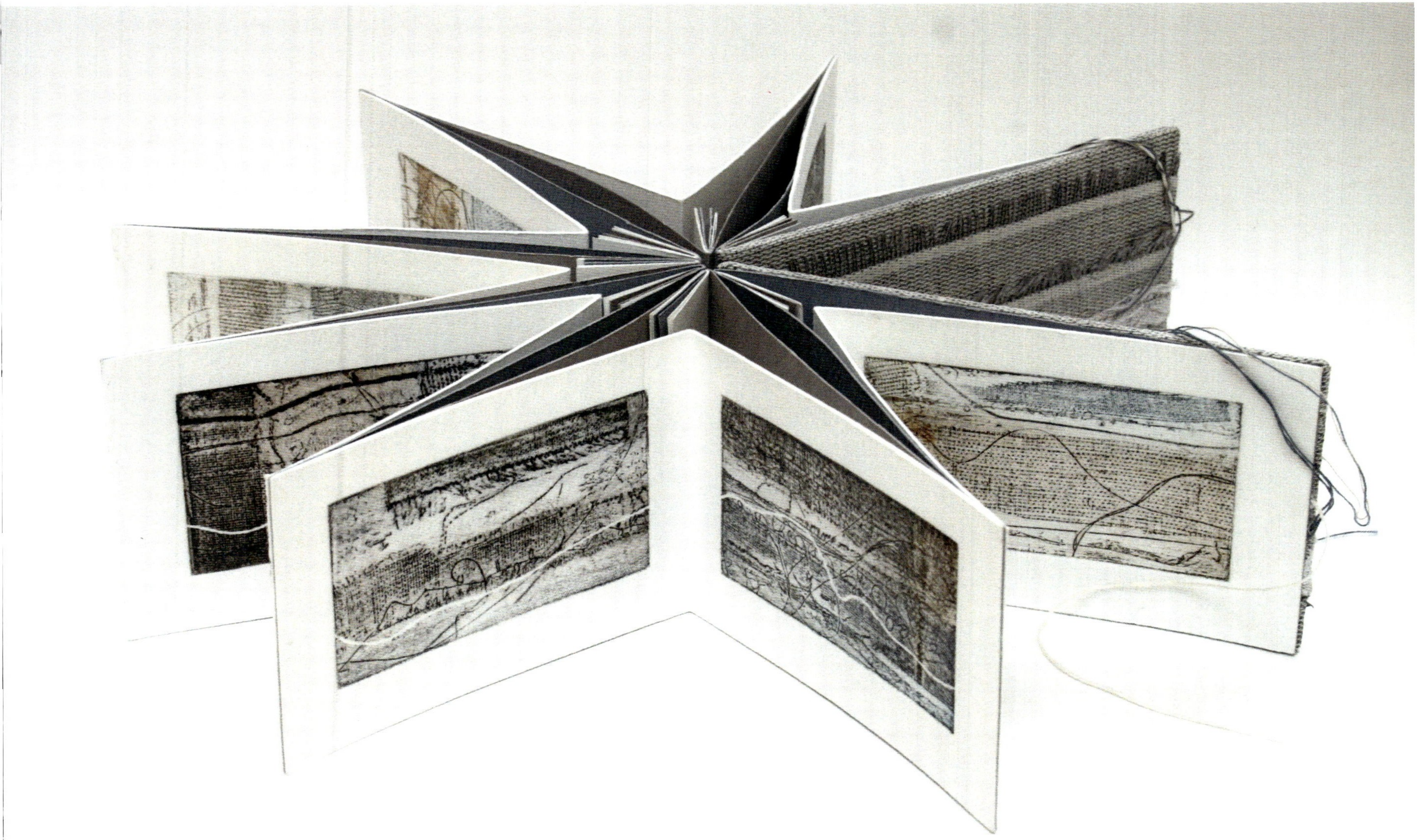

Surface, Artist Book
pages: 14 etchings, cover: linen, canvas, stitch, screen print
12.5 x 6.5 cm closed, 25 x 25 cm cpened
(edition of 2)

Jenny Lagnado

Jenny Lagnado studied Painting and Drawing at Camberwell School of Art and the Royal Academy Schools. She turned to printmaking seriously after seeing the work of Eric Ravilious which immediately inspired her to learn the art of wood engraving and lino printing at Morley College. Here a whole new world of print possibilities opened up. At the same time she explored more painterly methods through creating large monoprints and collographs, enabling her to bring colour and drama into her work.

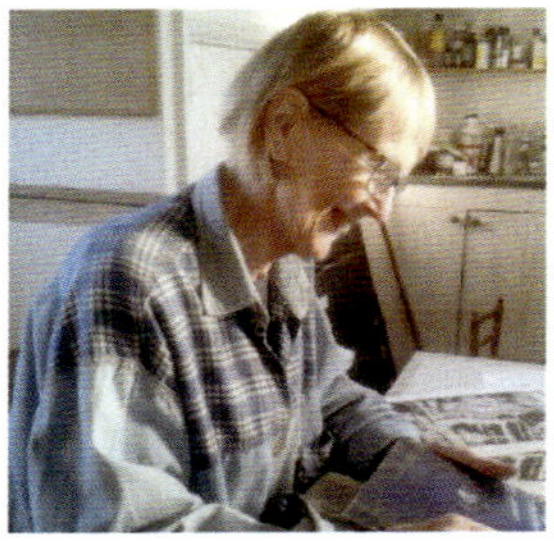

Professional memberships
The Artworkers Guild, elected member
Printmakers Council, selected member
Royal Academy Schools Alumni (RASA)
Richmond Printmakers, selected member

Teaching
Jenny has had a lifelong teaching career in the Adult and FE college sector where she has been committed from the start to setting up pioneering classes to encourage women who had missed out on their education to enrol on college courses. These courses which enabled men and women to go on to universities and art schools became known as Access to Art and Design.

Between 1978 and 1982 Jenny was in Zambia teaching art in a girls' school which considerably enriched her concepts of both art and life.

Some years ago Jenny discovered the North Coast of Somerset and its wonderful limestone formations. These rocks, worn down by time and the relentless pounding of the sea, reveal a particular identity which has proved to be a continuing source of inspiration. Jenny's aim is to make images that suggest through line, shape and colour the intense experience of looking at and remembering these inspirational places. She is fascinated by the infinite potential of colour in etching which has led her, in a way, back to painting.

Jenny Lagnado has been exhibiting her prints since the 1990s. Almost the first exhibition for which she was chosen was *Impressive Women* at the London Print Studio, which was curated by Deanna Petherbridge, the well-known writer, curator and art academic. From then until 1999 she showed her monoprints and wood engravings at the Royal Academy and in Open print exhibitions. A major exhibition was with the PmC at the Natural History Museum. She was one of the several print artists chosen to work there for three months. She later developed her practice to include etching which is now her major method of printmaking. She exhibited etchings at the Centro Modigliani in Florence, and Martins Gallery in Cheltenham, collaborating with poet Paul Christmas. Both exhibitions were with the RA Schools Alumni. She has exhibited with the PmC in various venues including the National Theatre. She joined Richmond Printmakers in 2007 with whom she has exhibited extensively.

Jenny's work has been chosen for the new West Middlesex Hospital, a curated collection founded by the King's Fund. She also has work in the Newcastle Art Gallery and was awarded the Agrawal Silver Medal.

A solo show at Putney School of Art in 2000 was later followed by a two-person show in 2002. Her favourite gallery is the Art and Architecture Shop in Kew where she has exhibited in several four-person shows.

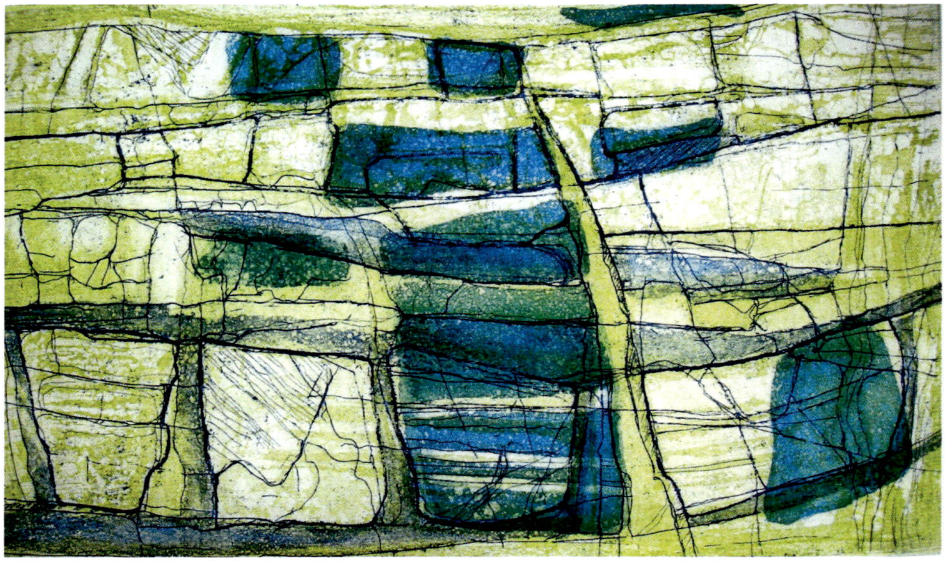

Landscape near the Sea, etching, 16.5 x 28 cm (edition of 8)

Lilstock Beach, etching, 41 x 29.5 cm (edition of 10)

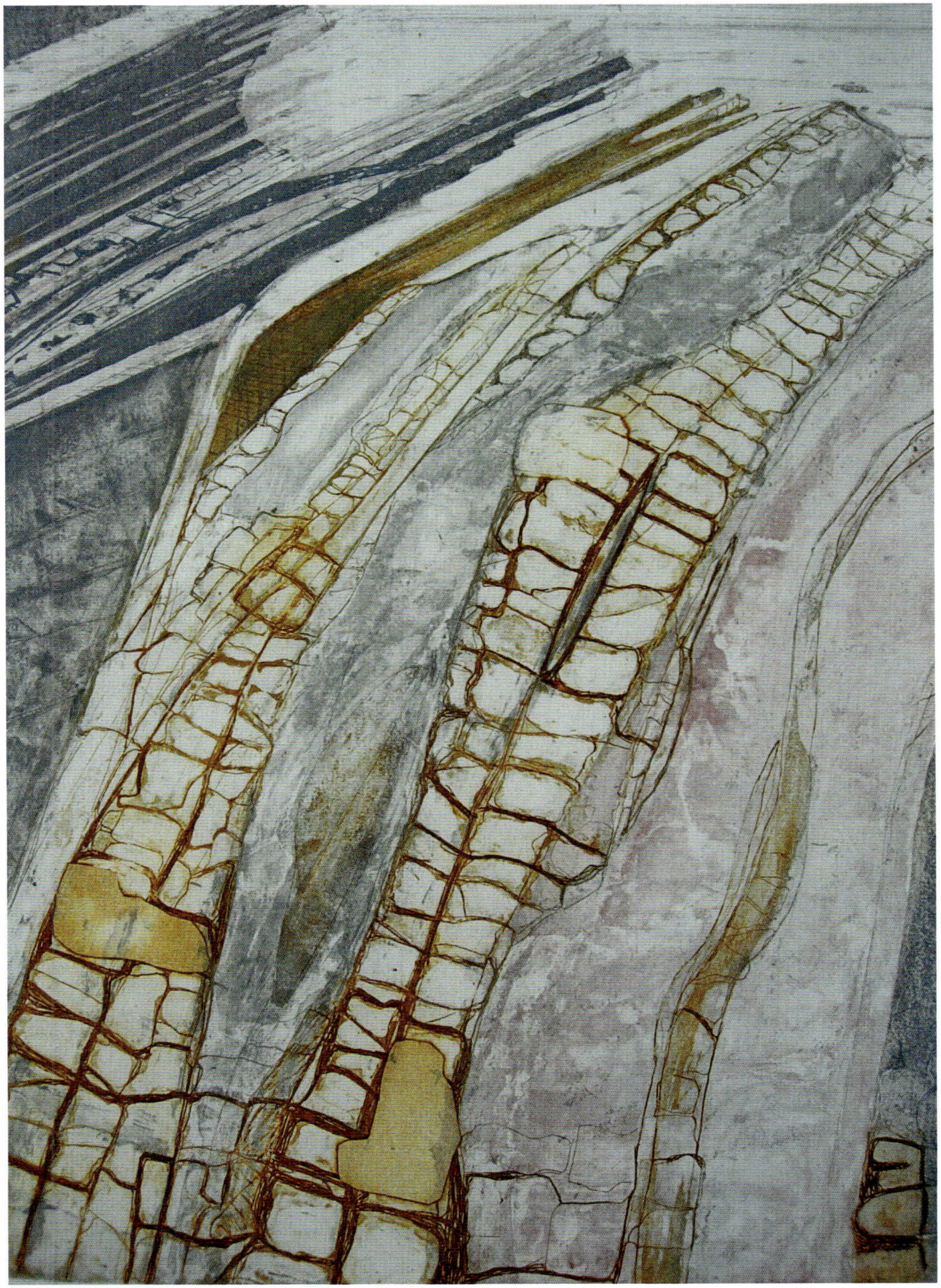

Marco Lawrence

Screen-printing is my passion and my profession. My practice as a printmaker involves the roles of illustrator, designer and tutor, as well as working in collaboration with other artists. I particularly relish the medium of screenprinting because it has all the rigours of a precise and exact trade and all the rewards of creative endeavour.

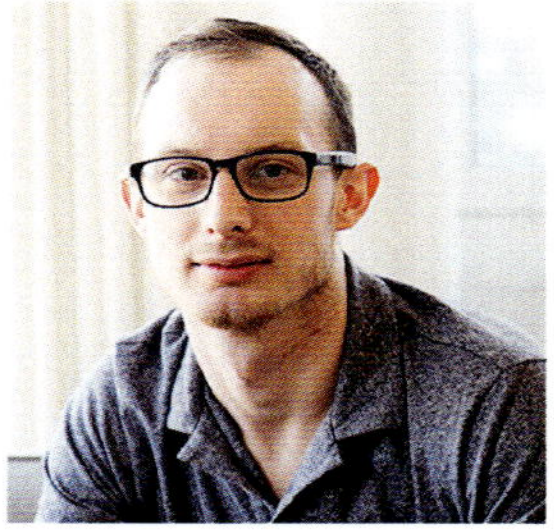

1984 Born Norfolk
2002 Queen's Prize for Excellence in Art & Norfolk Scholar for Outstanding Academic Achievement
2003–04 Diploma, Norwich School of Art & Design
2004–07 BA (Hons) Fine Art Printing & Drawing, Leeds Metropolitan University & La Universidad Complutense de Madrid
2008 Observational Draftsmanship & Portraiture, The Prince's Drawing Trust, London
2009 Advanced Screen-printing, Camberwell College of Art, London
2010 Studio Technician, Print Club London
2011 Print Assistant, London Print Studio
2011–15 Lead Tutor, Print Club London
2012–15 Head Printer, Print Club London
2012 Group exhibition, Wieden + Kennedy, London
2013–14 Screen-printing Course Leader, The City Literary Institute, London
2013 Exhibition with Bob Gill, founder of Pentagram and D&AD
2013 Colour mixing & Pantone matching, Screentec Ink Laboratory, Stoke
2013, 14 Printing & supervision of production of all works for Film 4 *Summer Screens* exhibitions, Somerset House, London
2013, 14, 15 Selected finalist for *Secret 7"* exhibitions for sleeve designs for Public Enemy, Massive Attack & Diana Ross
2015 Subject of the documentary *Chasing the White Whale*, a study of a master craftsman's relationship with his trade
2015–present Studio Manager, Lower East Side Printshop, New York

As a creative, knowing that I can make something that is objectively and absolutely correct and accurate is tremendously satisfying.
The screen-printing process shares many of the same elements as other trades, such as joinery or cabinet-making: there's a definite right way to approach it and if you diverge from that you will not get the results that you require. There are many, many stages that you have to go through to achieve a successful screen and subsequently an accurate print, each step of which needs to be given thorough care and attention.
Ultimately though, all of this precise work and concentration is geared and angled towards producing a creative object. As a result, it has all the satisfaction of artistic expression whilst at the same time being grounded in a formal structure.

Constantly working with this unforgiving medium, with its potential for pitfalls and mistakes, resigns you to the reality that there will be many days when you achieve nothing at all, or even indeed damage work that you have produced in the past. However, if you can be comfortable with that knowledge it need not prevent you from being experimental and taking risks.

All visual art is a form of communication; if you can convey the argument, comment or observation successfully, arguably it might not matter how cleanly you execute the work. However, as the voice in that communication you must be satisfied with how it is phrased and formed. How much care you take over the production, and how precise you strive to be is clearly a personal preference. In my practice I strive for complete control.

The obvious, tangible effort that the printmaker makes to create the work with exquisite care gives the print another layer of meaning and hopefully makes it that much more satisfying for the audience to enjoy and interact with.

OPPOSITE
Spin, 50 x 70cm
screen print (edition of 20)

Nahuatl, 50 x 70 cm
screen print (edition of 20)

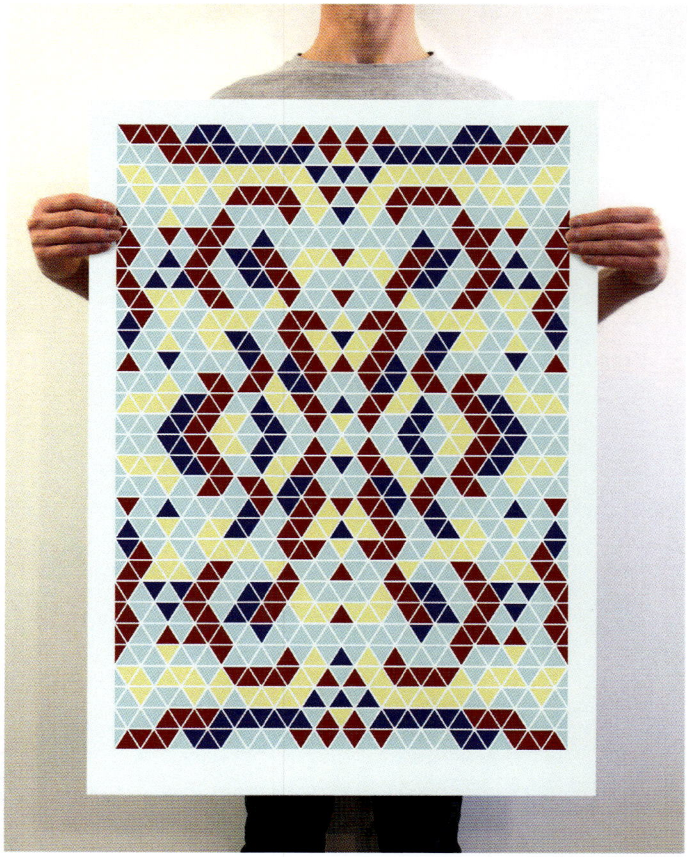

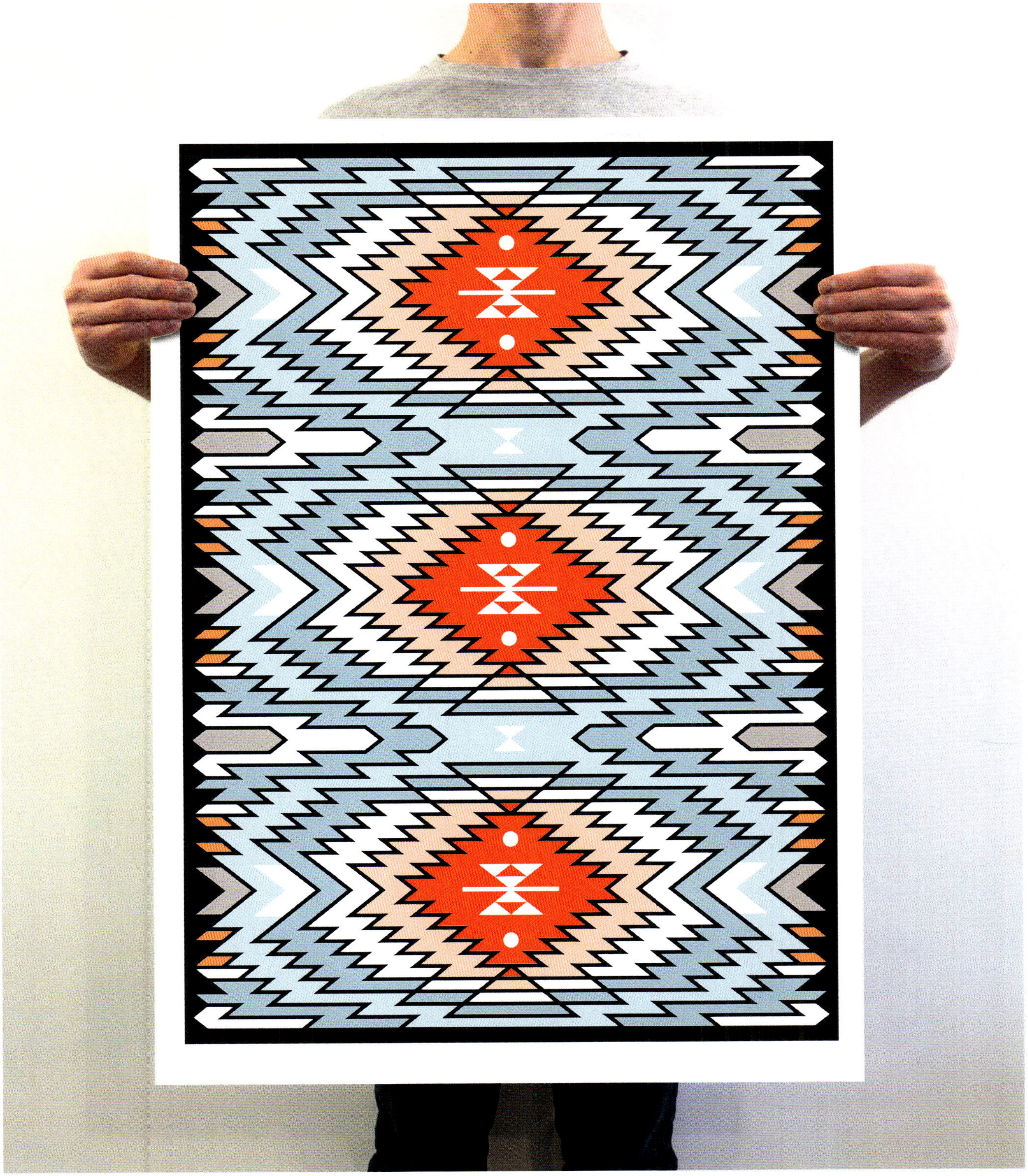

Lolana

Lolana is a painter and printmaker living and working in London. Her work was exhibited at solo shows in The Houses of Parliament in 2013 and 2014. She has had a number of exhibitions and has also produced commissions and studio work. Her paintings are in private collections worldwide.

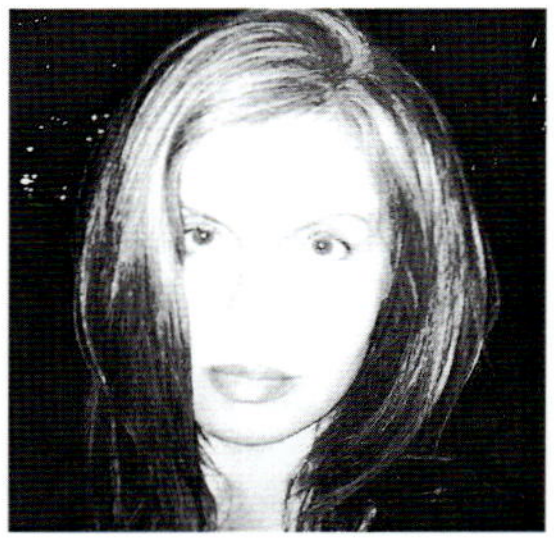

Education
BA (Hons) University of Belgrade

Memberships
Printmakers Council
East London Printmakers
London Print Studio

Gallery: Saatchi Art

Selected Exhibitions

2013 The Houses of Parliament, The Serbian Medieval Art
Sea Angel solo show, London,
The Hurlingham Club 57th Annual Art Exhibition, London
The Chelsea Gallery Printmaking Exhibition, London

2014 The Houses of Parliament *Art and Democracy* solo show, London
Chelsea Old Town Hall Exhibition, London
Celeste Prize
Longlisted for painting/drawing prize, Milan
Open Studio Breza, Belgrade

2015 Wetpaint Gallery Imprint Exhibition, Cirencester
The Hurlingham Club 59th Annual Art Exhibition, London
Menier Gallery Rare Art Exhibition, London
Minerva Gallery *Light and Shadow* solo show Belgrade
10x10 Charity Auction, London

Lolana explores the themes of solitude and liminality using symbolic concepts and a variety of media such as acrylic, collage, intaglio prints and etchings, creating her unique, variable printmaking editions and distinct mixed-media figurative art. Her influences are many. In printmaking her greatest inspirations are Rembrandt's prints and etchings. Surrealist fantasy and Expressionist subjectivity are influences too and, to a greater extent, contemporary Magic Realism. Her work has been praised for its powerful expressiveness and for conveying a profound emotional story.

"The central tenet of my art is the edge of reality, myths and consciousness, seeking to reveal the sacred harmony of life in human and animal form."

Lolana's interest in art developed early and while at art college her work won prizes and featured regularly in college exhibitions. She continued her studies at the University of Belgrade where she served as Editor, producing illustrations for the student magazine. Upon graduating with honours she furthered her art studies at University of the Arts, London. Lolana has worked in graphic design where she created successful art projects for award-winning organisations and publications before returning to the roots of her interest in fine art and printmaking.

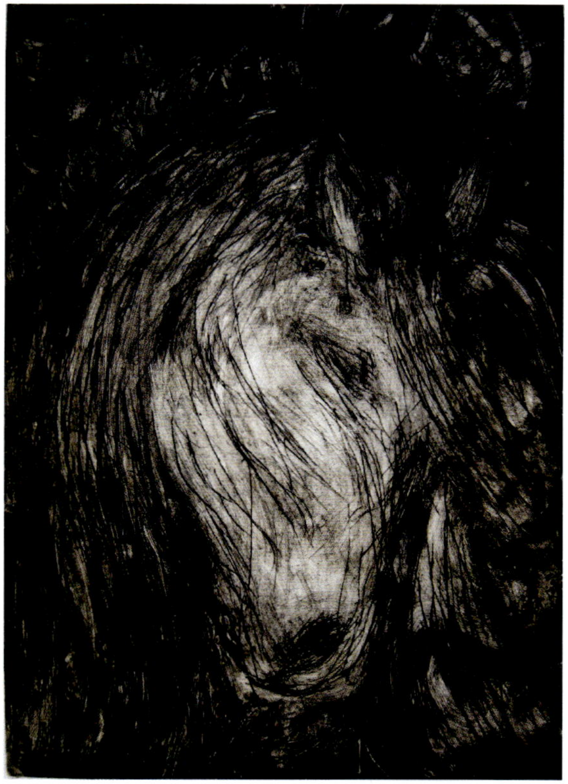

OPPOSITE
Sea Angel
65 x 48 cm
intaglio collograph/acrylic V.E.
(edition of 10)
private collection

Head of a Horse
53 x 38 cm
intaglio drypoint V.E.
(edition of 50)

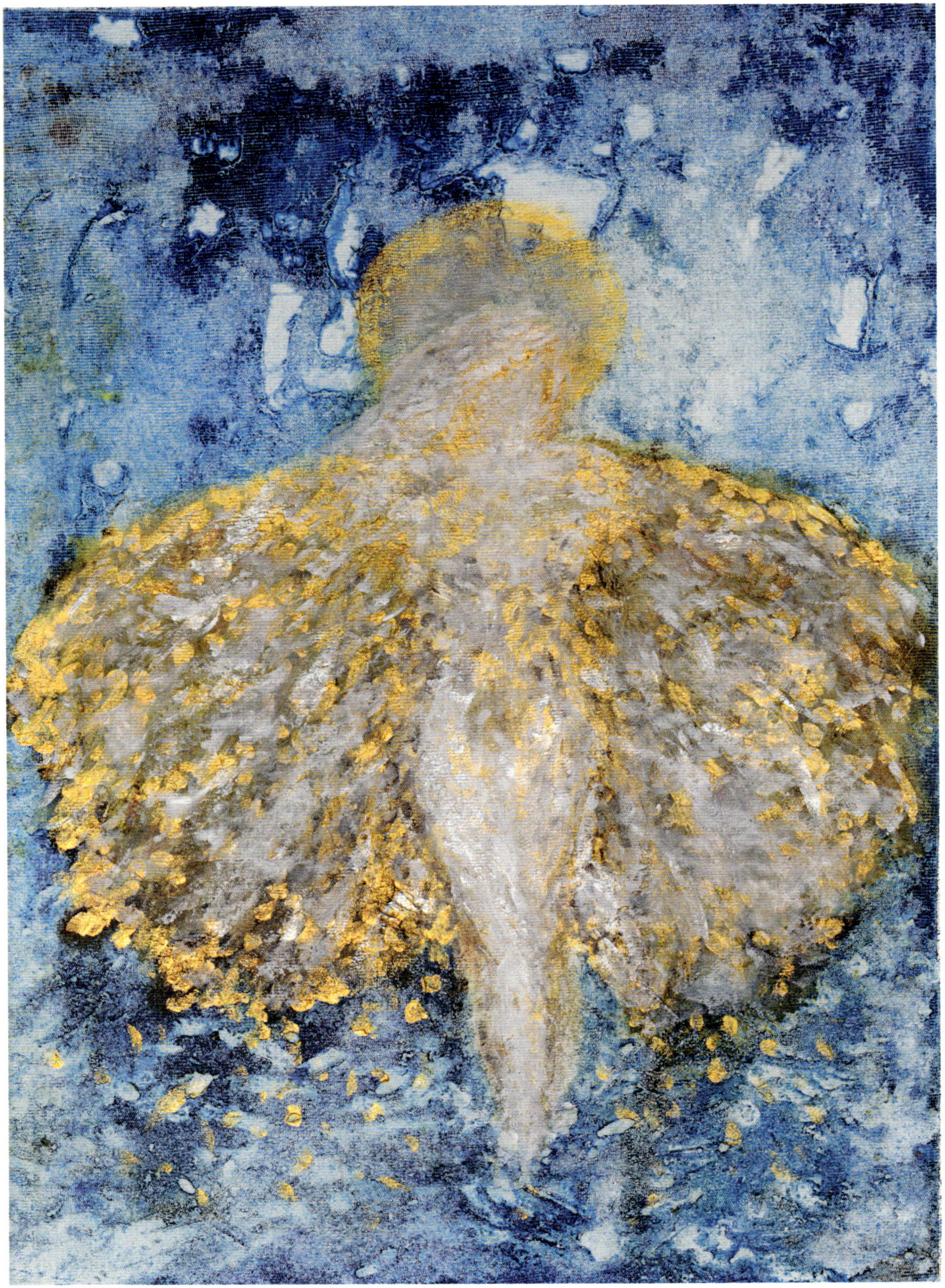

Avril Macdonald

Firstly came a fascination with the process of photopolymer etching, which is always an adventure. Different days, different temperatures, varying exposures: each ink mixture and numerous methods of application led to surprises, a solicited chance, and unexpected images. Later, etching in the more traditional sense, using acid, sugar, scribes, stop-out, etching needle and drypoint, then photo etching, followed…

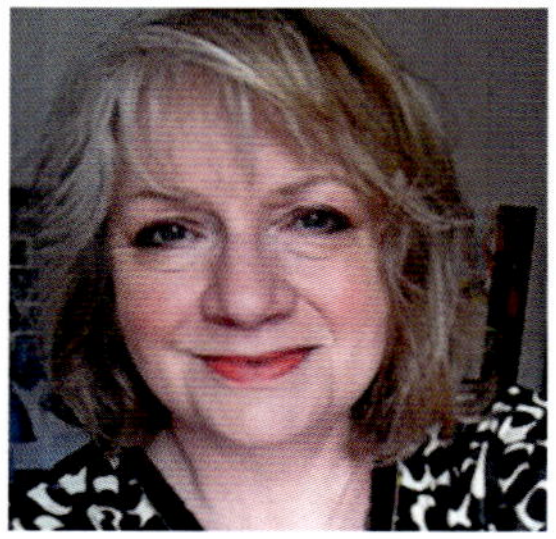

1955 Born Glasgow
1973–76 Textile Design, Scottish College of Textiles, Galashiels; ATI (Design), De Montford University, Leicester
1976–98 Journalist, PR consultant, newspaper editor, Corporate Communications Director, photographer (Scotland and London). Elected Council Member CBI (London).
1998 Elected Fellow of RSA.
1998–2010 Set up PR and Public Affairs Consultancy, Macdonald Wynne Davies.
2007–13 Solar Plate Etching, and other printmaking courses, The Institute, East Finchley
2008 Group show Burgh House, London
2010–14 Annual East Finchley Arts Festival, London
2010–15 Joined Islington Art Society, biannual shows, London
2011 Solo show, The Haberdashery, London
2011 Group show Kingsgate Workshop
2012 Joined Printmakers Council
2013 Group show with Printmakers Council, *Photographics*, Western Studios, London
2013 Joined East Finchley Artists Open (EFO), annual Open House and group shows (London)
2014 Exhibited group show Arts Depot Open (London)
2014 The School of Creative Arts, University of Hertford, Printmaking

I like the hands-on, kinaesthetic experience and also working by subtraction, so enjoy making monotypes by working backwards and removing colour, rather than adding.

An extra dimension, the third dimension, comes from collography and textures made by chine collé. Of course there is an endless and fascinating array of paper supports from which to choose.

My subject matter is frequently about place, I aim to show the sense of a place and to share its intrinsic beauty and, if possible, convey the memory of how it made me feel on the day that I was there.

My prints are always of places where I feel a strong emotional connection, such as the Northern Orkney Isles and the Western Isles – the Outer Hebrides – where my mother and father respectively were born and grew up.

I have spent much time in these places and continue to visit and experience a longing when I am not there for the sight, sounds, and smells that are etched deep in my own memory.

These places are wild and remote but are like nowhere else in Britain. In Orkney, north of mainland Britain, the stones there are our direct connection with the ancient pre-history of Northern Europe. The Outer Hebrides, west of the mainland, also has ancient stones and is the last landfall at the edge of Europe, facing the North Americas and sharing with that continent the Atlantic shores and beaches.

Closer to home, the places in London that continue to inspire much of my work include my local wood where I have depicted trees in a solar plate etching. The image from which this was made was a photograph taken on a very still and misty morning, too early for many people to be around, and in which the hubbub which can be London was silent, shrouded in the fog.

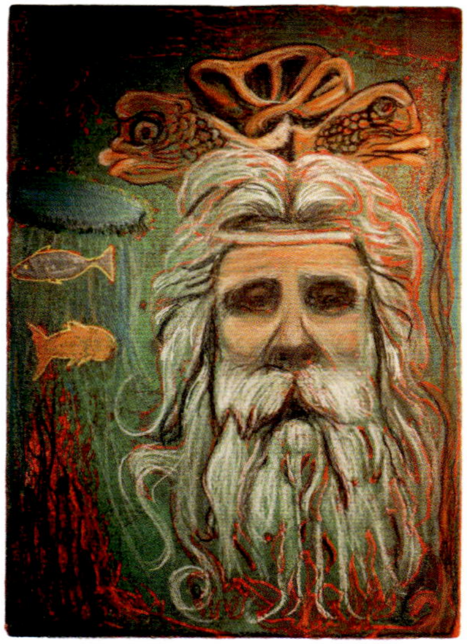

Old Father Thames 20.5 x 29 cm
sugar-lift etch overlaid with pastel (unique)

Old stones are to be found all over our nation. Indeed, old stones are all that is left of the 12th Century Augustinian priory in Haverfordwest in Wales – no-one was there that day, just the sound of bees in the herb garden, a breeze through the trees and dappled light in the shade.

Another source of fascination is the River Thames and the ancient and much built-over part of London that is the City of London. Again, the history is in the stone – in sculptures such as those on the old City of London Magistrates Court on Queen Victoria Street where remote deities surmount the windows on the Victorian edifice. Is one a representation of Mithras, the god to whom the nearby Roman Temple of Mithras was erected? Is this where Old Father Thames originated?

His likeness was inspiration for an etching using sugar lift and the resultant subtractive print in solarised, reversed colour itself inspired further embellishment with colour in pastel.

One common thread shared by my prints is that of light – on landscapes, buildings, trees – and of its absence, providing texture on stones, grass and branches.

Another is the longing for place, so eloquently expressed in Welsh by the word 'hiraeth', for which there is no direct translation in English.

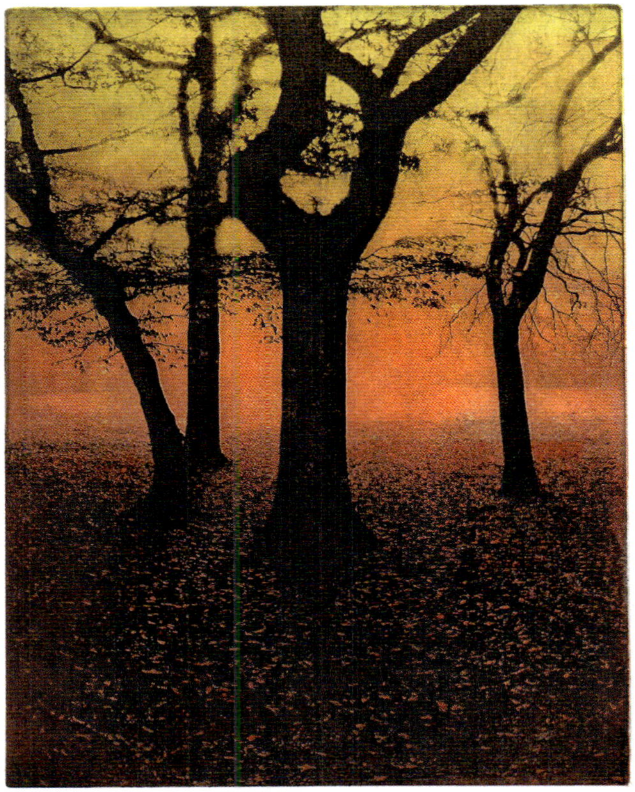

Cherry Tree Wood, solar plate etching, 18 x 23 cm (EV edition of 50)

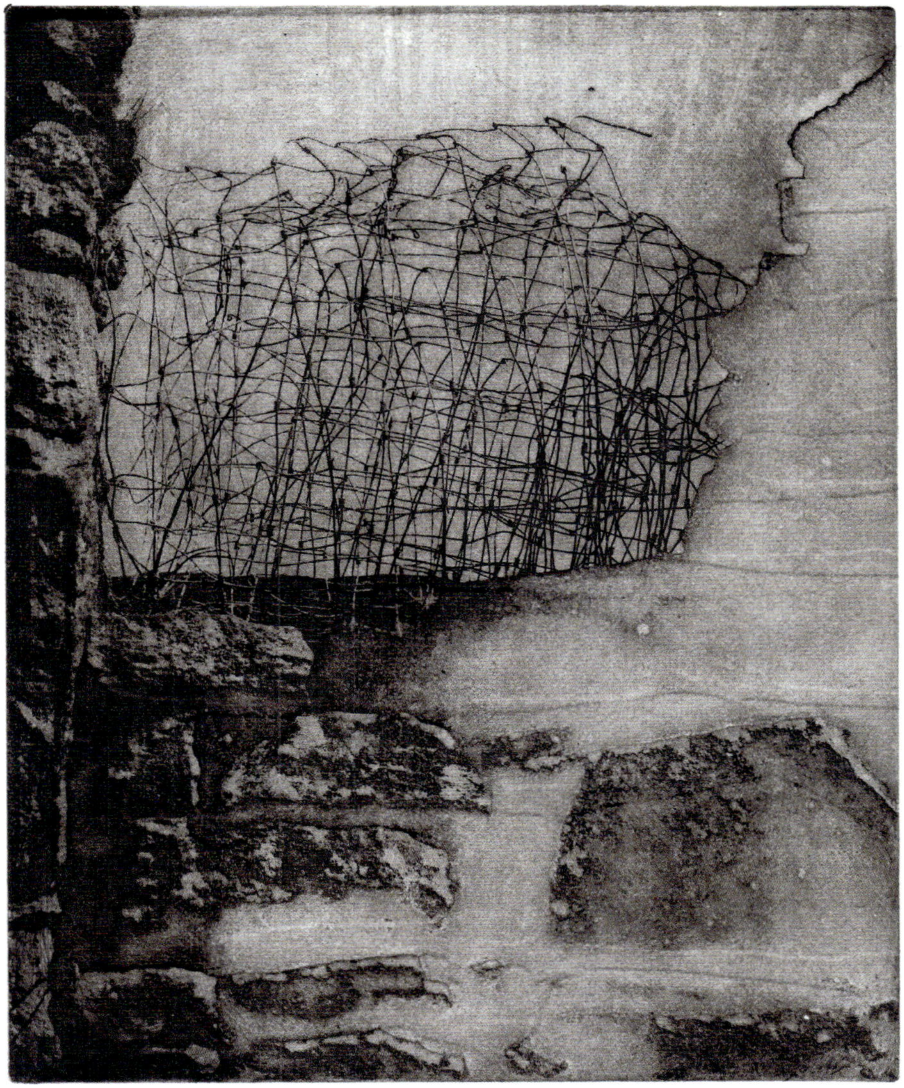

Sheep Fank, North Uist
solar plate etching and collograph
21.5 x 26.5 cm (EV edition of 50)

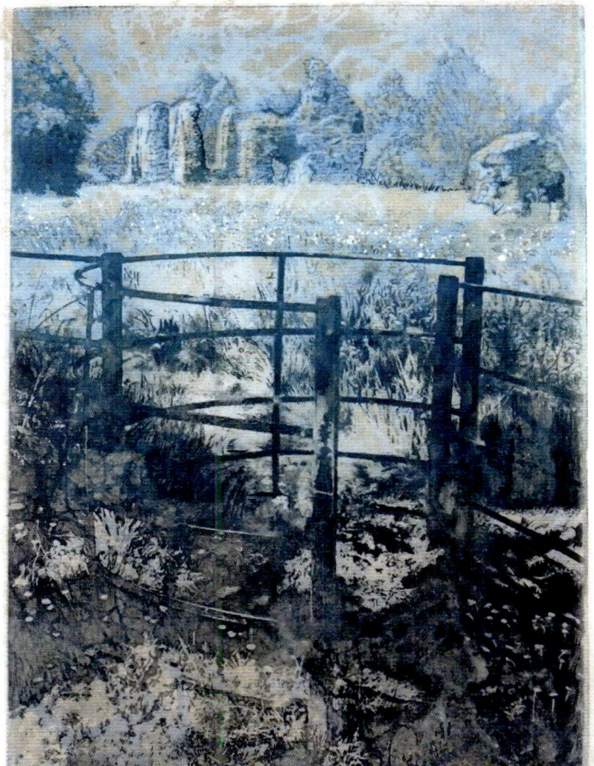

Priory Meadow, Haverfordwest
solar plate etching and chine collé
29 x 41 cm (EV edition of 30)

Gail Mallatratt

For me there is something truly magical about printmaking – the moment that the paper is pulled off the press, an image appears that is a surprise, unique from the drawing, cutting and rolling up that went into it. My method of choice is reductive woodcutting where my background in drawing and interest in historical figurative subjects come into play.

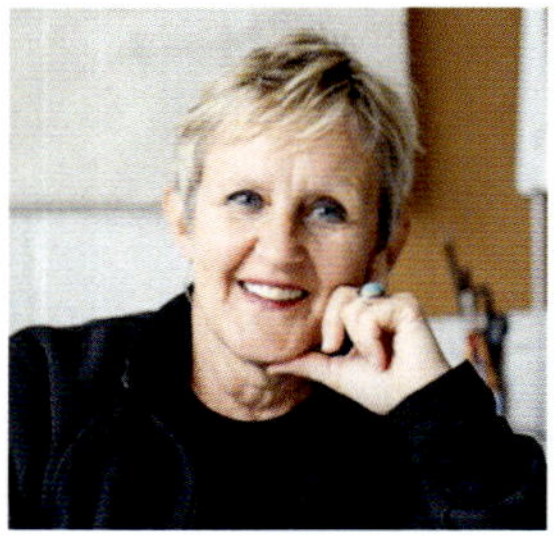

1947 Born San Francisco, California USA
1966–69 New York University and Stanford University
1973–79 BA Graphic Design St Martin's School of Art, London
1980–87 Senior Designer Allied International Designers
1987–93 Freelance Graphic Designer
2006–09 MA Printmaking Camberwell School of Art UAL
2008 *Drawn Together*, Prince's Drawing School, Redchurch Gallery, Shoreditch
2009 *Discerning Eye*, Mall Gallery, London
2009–14 LOOP Exhibition, Bankside, London
2012 *Originals*, Mall Galleries, London
2014 *Royal Academy Summer Exhibition*
2014 Group Show, Loughborough Gallery, Brixton, London
2015 *Naional Original Print Exhibition*, Bankside, London

As a descendent of the 'Forty-niners' – immigrants who travelled on the Oregon Trail to California in search of gold – I am fascinated by their story. I began to use printmaking to revisit their experiences.

I have made two sets of relief prints – the first named *Gold Fever Seized My Soul* (a quote from a miner) expresses the isolation of single miners digging in a shallow stream. The later ones – *Making Nowhere Somewhere* (two are reproduced here) – go further to portray the experiences of opening up the continent: cutting down trees, building log cabins, finding fuel, and so on.

For me, the most important thing is that the work be 'alive'. This is accomplished with drawing and colour. I choose a piece of wood, draw on it, and begin cutting into it, mindful of the grain and composition. I begin printing, respond to the printed paper, cut more on the wood, print again and so on. During this process I am mindful of the juxtaposition of colours and how they work together to build an image. I believe that all of my experiences play into this process and take influence from my favourite artists – Gauguin, Bonnard, Kirchner, and Rembrandt, among others.

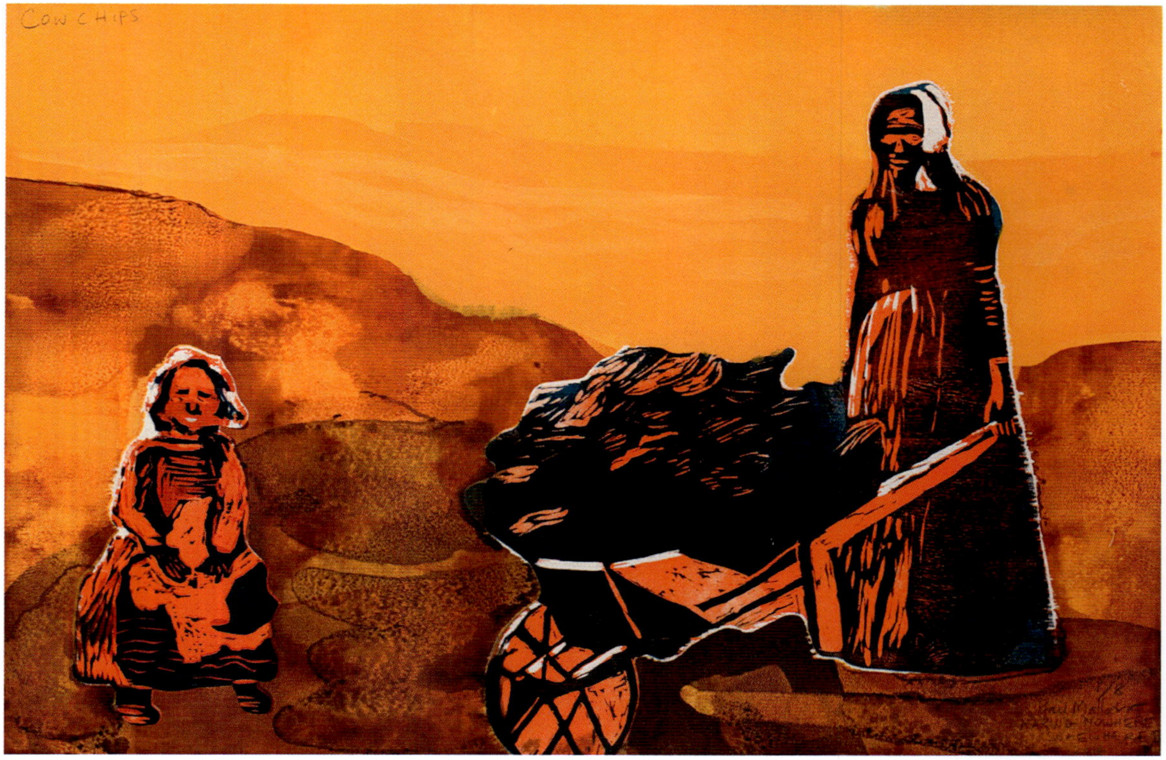

Making Nowhere Somewhere - Gathering Cow Chips for Fuel
70 x 50 cm reductive woodcut
(edition of 7)

Making Nowhere Somewhere - Building a Log Cabin
50 x 70 cm, reductive woodcut (edition of 7)

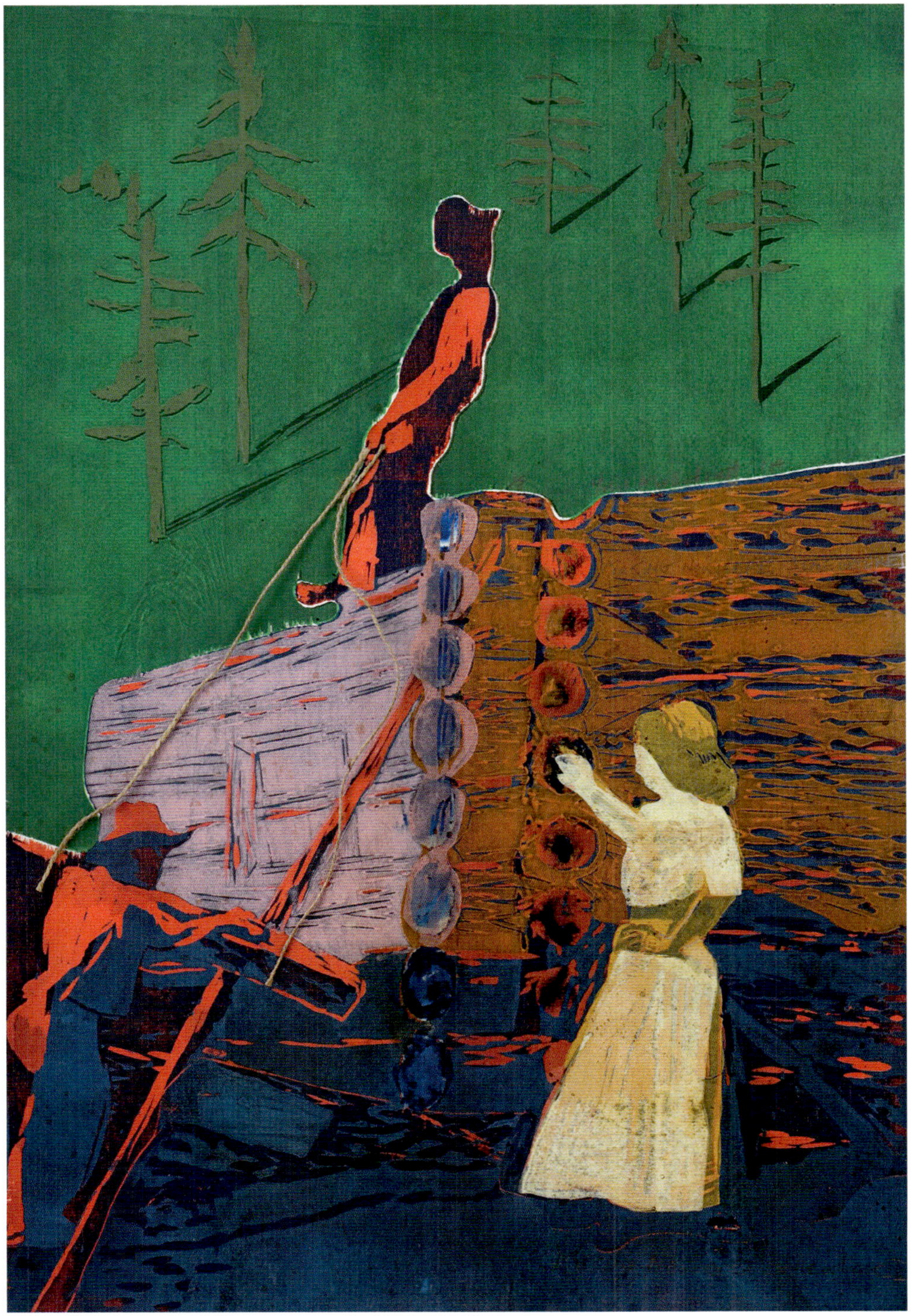

Marie-Louise Martin

As I had always enjoyed drawing, I was completely smitten by printmaking, particularly etching, from the moment I stepped into the print room of the National College of Art and Design, Dublin in 1978. Immediately after my degree I joined the newly established Black Church Print Studio, serving as a board member for many years. I work there still, as well as in my own studio. I never tire of the endless possibilities of printmaking.

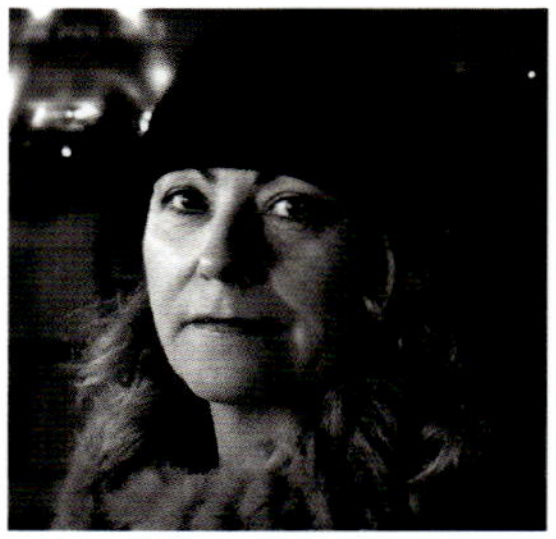

1960 Born Dublin, Ireland
1978–83 Fine Art, NCAD Dublin
1983 Joined Black Church Print Studio (BCPS)
1990–98 Served as a director BCPS
2005 Residency at Ballinskelligs, Co. Kerry
2009 Elected to Watercolour Society of Ireland
2014 Joined Printmakers Council

Solo Exhibitions

1986, 1988, 2014 United Arts Club, Dublin
1999 Claremorris, Co.Mayo
2000 *Fifteen Summers*, Antrim Castle, N. Ireland
2000 The National Concert Hall, Dublin
2004 *Tuscan Diaries*, Hallward Gallery, Dublin
2007 *That was then*, Limerick Printmakers Gallery
2009 *A Year's Passing*, Antrim Castle, N. Ireland
2010 *Making Space, a retrospective*, BCPS

Selected Exhibitions

1985–2015 Royal Hibernian Academy (invited 2007, 2010, 2014)
1987–88 Royal Academy
1987, 1999 *Miniature Print Exhibition*, Cadaqués, Spain
1987–2012 Royal Ulster Academy
1989, 1994 *British Miniature Print Exhibition*
1990 BP Oil (Europe), Young Artists Competition
1993 *International Print Exhibition* Netherlands
2002 International Print Exhibition, Ljubljana
2007 BCPS 25th Anniversary Show
2008–15 *Annual World Art Print*, Lessedra, Bulgaria
2011–12 *A4 International Print Competition*, UK

Prizes

1988 Claremorris Open Exhibition
1989 Royal Hibernian Academy
2001 & 2003 Royal Ulster Academy

My work over recent years has been time-based, with the subject matter being the investigation of the effects of time on the landscape. I live part of each year in a hill town called Radicondoli, in Italy: a rural location, where many of the farming practices remain unchanged for centuries. I am interested in the changes made by nature and man on this landscape through the advancing seasons. I spend my time capturing these changes through photography and drawing, making notes and exploratory drypoint prints. Some of the natural changes are quite subtle, taking their time to become manifest; others, like ploughing and the planting of different crops make a spectacular impact on the patterns within the fields. Even in the depths of winter, these long-harvested crops influence the patterns and shapes overlain by drifted snow.

Another aspect of this rural setting that interests me, are the woods. There is a surprisingly large area under wood; the trees are mainly a variety of oak and birch, which are harvested for firewood. Particularly inspiring is the play of light through foliage or bare branches: watching as it shifts and changes through the day, months and the full year seems to deepen connections to these places. Exploring the different light, patterns of shade and the stark or muted shapes is a compulsion; and a welcome break from the beating sun of summer.

I don't have access to a printing press in Italy so I collate materials I have gathered there and, returning to Dublin, I work further on drypoint prints and etchings. In 2010 I set up a purpose-built studio immediately adjacent to my home: this space gives me the freedom to evolve the ideas and images I bring back. I express new meaning and delve deeper into the thoughts, emotions and reactions to the landscape I have recently been in.

I have also made a small number of 'artist's books.' These books – based on specific lengths of time: a week, a month, or a year – draw directly on my sketched notes and diary entries. They incorporate flowers, leaves, dried seed heads and other materials I have brought back to my studio. I trap these, after drying, within Japanese tissue paper and chine collé to construct the end-papers: the books are presented concertina-like, opening out to two metres or more in length.

OPPOSITE
Leaving Civinnini, etching, 48 x 34 cm, (edition of 45)

Summer Storm - Monteriggioni
etching, 50 x 53 cm (edition of 45)

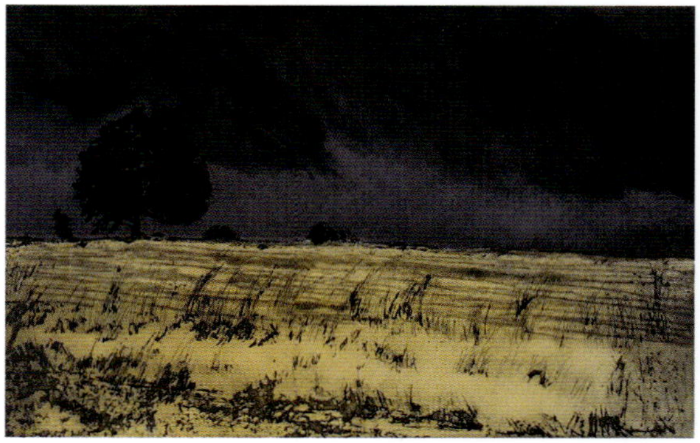

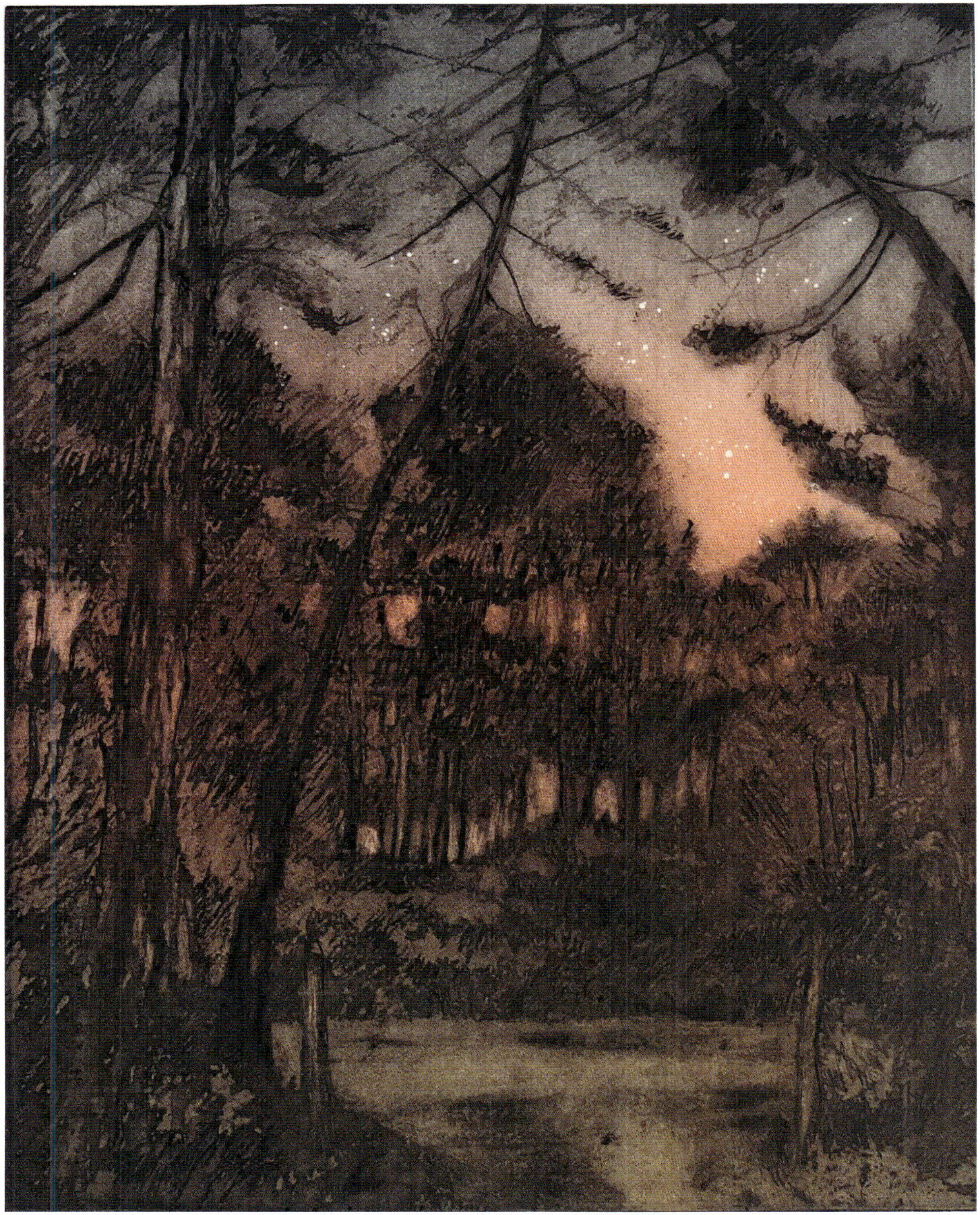

Mary Martin

After A-level and Art Foundation I studied Fine Art Printmaking at Brighton University from 2011–14. From here I went on to work and study at Draw, a vibrant drawing community in the heart of Brighton. I continue to work and study at Draw, (whilst holding together various other part-time jobs to pay my rent!) Recently I've started teaching drypoint and monotype printmaking in secondary schools as well as at Draw and have loved seeing my students start to get the printmaking bug!

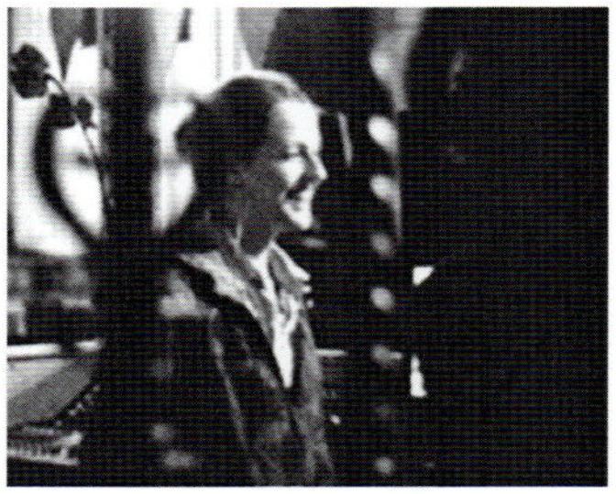

Education

2010–11 Art Foundation diploma, Ferndown College of Arts

2011–14 BA Fine Art Printmaking, Brighton University

2014–15 Draw Atelier, Brighton

Exhibitions/Shows

2012 *First Impressions* 1st year show, The Clarendon Centre, Brighton

2013 *Transitions*, 2nd year show, Grand Parade Gallery
Brighton Fringe Festival, Brighton Dome
Bourach, joint exhibition as part of a three-week residency at Cawdor Castle, Scotland

2014 *Fire in the Cabin*, Gallery 40, Brighton
Show graduate exhibition, Grand Parade
Student showcase, Spring Heritage Centre, Havant
The Grand Drawing Circus, The Old Market, Hove (as part of The Drawchestra)

2015 *Fugitive Art*, Artists' Open Houses, Brighton
The Grand Drawing Circus, The Bosco Theatre, Brighton
#makebikeportraits exhibition at the Levis Instameet, Amsterdam
Level 5, Atelier Drawing Year exhibition, Gallery 40, Brighton

Teaching

2008–2011 Classroom assistant for GCSE and Art lessons

2013–present Drawing tutor at Draw Brighton for Life Drawing Classes and hen parties

2013 Leading print workshops for children

2015 Taught printmaking at secondary schools in partnership with Brighton university and Widening Participation.

Printmaking is simultaneously the greatest and most frustrating thing I've ever dedicated myself to. The body of work represented here embodies my love of observational drawing, coupled with the beautifully addictive process of etching from which I became, for a while, inseparable.

> *"Go, said the bird: human kind cannot bear very much reality..."*

Close observational drawing of dead animals is for me an intense meditative process. There is a precious sliver of time between death and decomposition when the animal appears to be resting on the edge of life. It is that long moment that I seek to capture and honour.

The animals were all found or given to me, carefully gathered from the ground where they died. I drew them from direct observation, rendering their still forms over intense hours of close study. The process was completed by a dignified burial.

Etching lends them a permanence and stability. The physical process of scratching into metal leaves an indelible mark which suggests immortality, and the facility to print multiple images preserves a beauty which would otherwise rot away.

My art is an attempt to pay close attention to creatures that in reality are vulnerable, short-lived and yet mysteriously beautiful. I find some common ground with an older, Victorian attention to the natural world, and with the carefully posed yet emotionally charged portraits of the photographic pioneer, Julia Margaret Cameron.

Death is hard to bear. I have chosen to engage with a reality that we usually, if uncomfortably, ignore, but I attempt to do so in a way that respects the grace and integrity of these animals, even at the moment of their deaths.

Through this process I hope to evoke...

> *"what might have been and what has been... which is always present."*

Quotations are from *Burnt Norton, The Four Quartets*, by T.S. Eliot

Rat, 38 x 56 cm, etching (edition of 10)

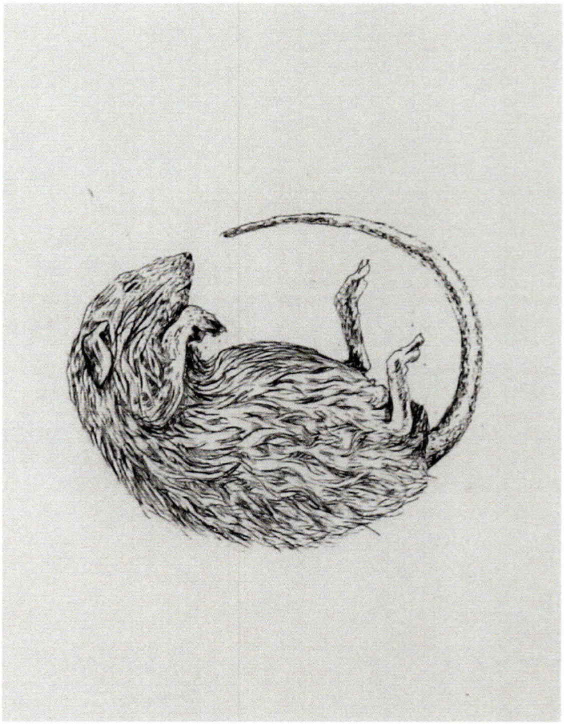

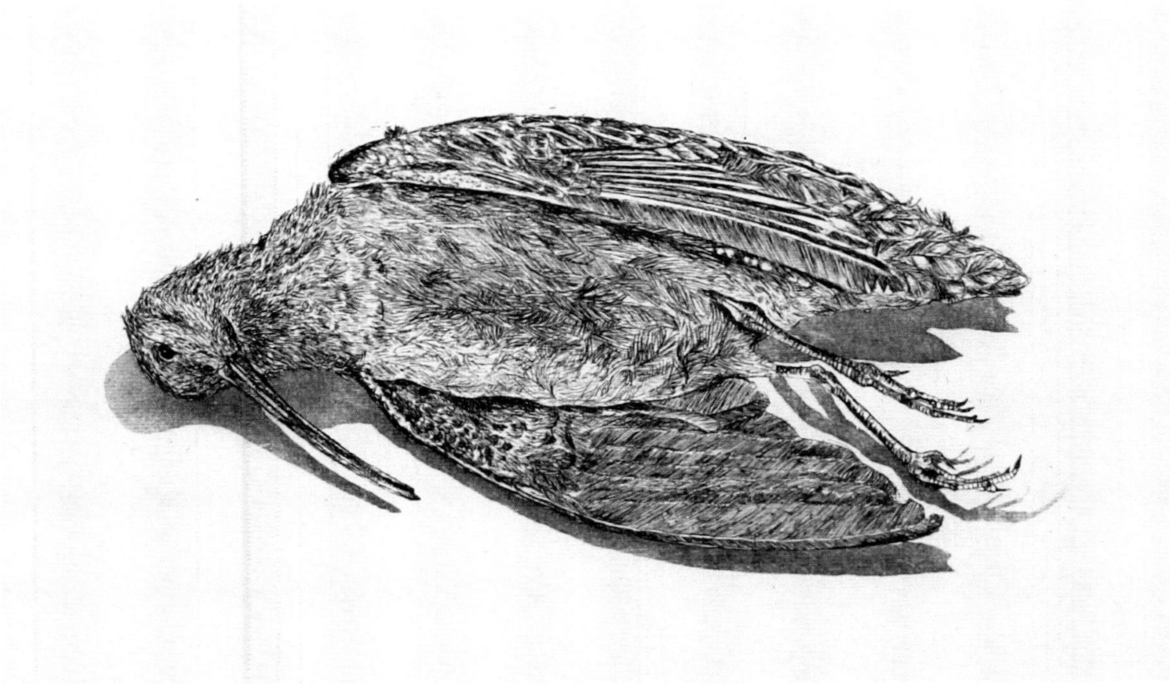

Snipe
38 x 56 cm
etching
(edition of 10)

Squirrel
38 x 56 cm
etching
(edition of 18)

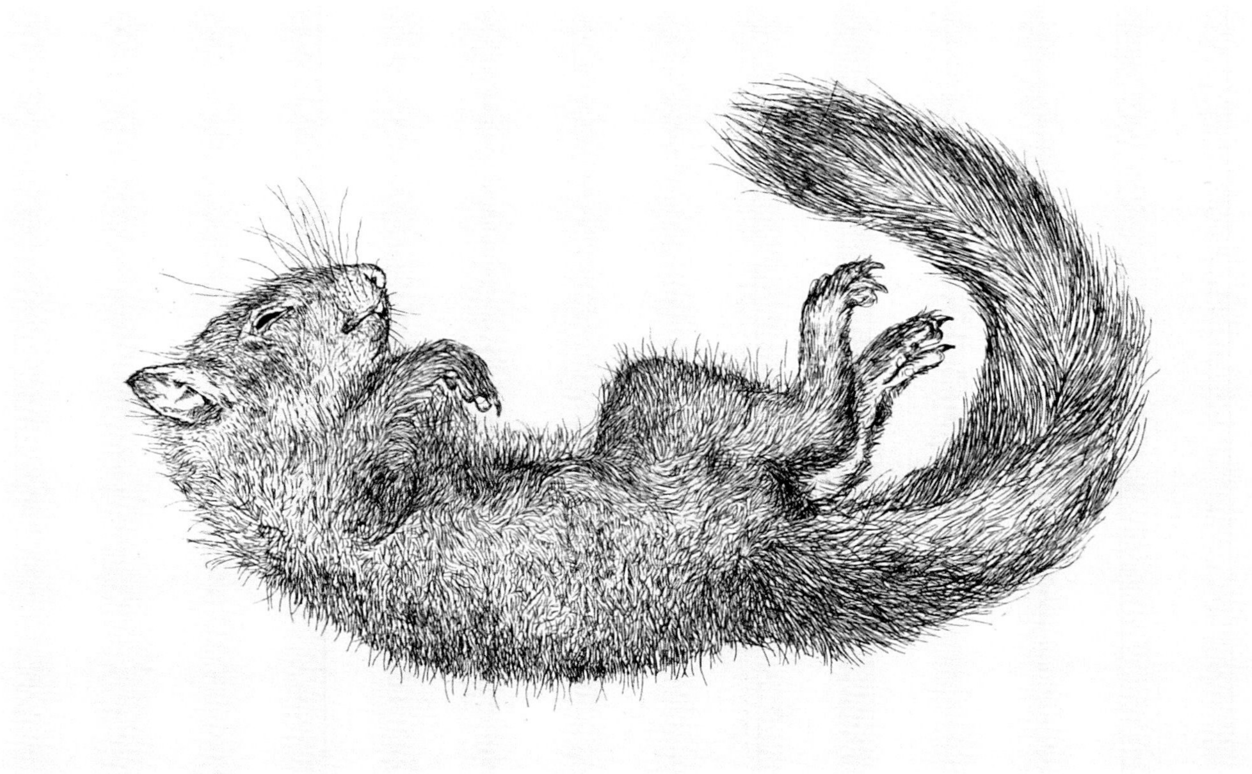

Biagio Mastroianni

I first became interested in and attracted to printmaking when I studied Illustration and Graphic Design at the Hochschule für Gestaltung und Kunst in Lucerne, Switzerland. I started with monoprinting, drypoint, etching with hard and soft ground and aquaintint on copper plates. In London I learned various techniques like screen-printing, collography, photo etching, wood and lino cuts and multi-colour printing.

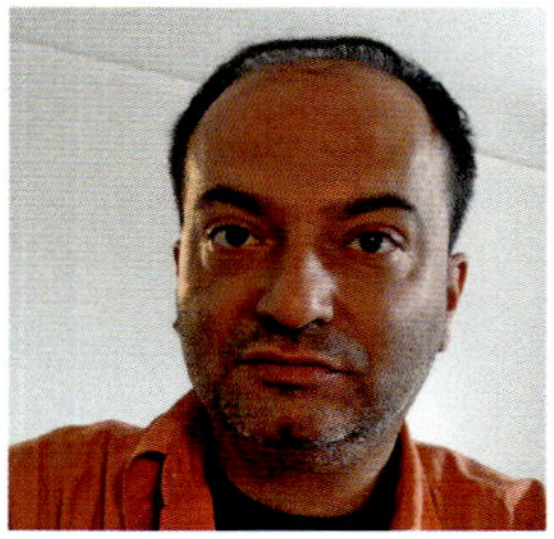

1969 Born Lucerne, Switzerland

1992–99 Hochschule für Gestaltung und Kunst, Lucerne

2000 Solo Show: St Raphael Gallery, Burlington Arcade, London; The Grove Gallery, Ealing Broadway, London

2001 Performance, Dance & Painting, Audiovisuals Culture Fund Swiss Embassy, London

Solo Shows and Audiovisuals for Dance Performance: Gallery Arlecchino, Lucerne

Deli-Bar Gallery, Barbican, London

2004 Joined Printmakers Council

2002–11 Solo Shows: Castello Svevo, Bari, Italy. *La Smorfia* in collaboration with the General Consulate of Switzerland, Naples, Italy. Grant - Swiss Arts Council CCS, Pro Helvetia, Milan, Italy. The Wine Gallery, Chelsea, London. Italian Cultural Institute, London. Brushfield Street, Spitalfields, London. Gallery das Ding, Lucerne

Group Shows: London Print Sudio, London. Kunstverket Galleri, Oslo, Norway. OXO Tower Gallery, South Bank, London.
Barbican Arts Group Trust, London
A and A Gallery, Richmond, London.
Fumetto, Comic Festival, Lucerne

2012–13 Group Show: Museum of American Illustration at the Society of Illustrators and Publication in the Annual Book *Illustrators 55*, New York

Solo Show: TuttiArt Gallery, Lucerne

2014–15 Group Shows: Ruskin Gallery; WMC Crowndale Road, London.

Biagio Mastroianni was born in Lucerne in 1969. After his education as a photolithographer he studied visual communication at the Lucerne University of Applied Sciences and Arts and gained a degree as an illustrator. Biagio works as an illustrator, painter and printmaker in Lucerne and London. His work, including illustration, painting, drawing and many kinds of printmaking has been shown in exhibitions not only in London, but as far afield as New York and Switzerland. Moreover, he illustrates in publications like *Horizon* magazine London, *The Naked Punch* magazine, *Neue Zürcher* and *Zeitung Zurich*, for the Swiss Red Cross, Bern and the company Feltbrook Ltd London. He has collaborated in audiovisual installations for theatre and dance performances in Zurich. His work has been published in several books including *International Contemporary Artists I.C.A. New York*.

In Naples, people who are about to buy lottery tickets ask dream interpreters to convert all their experiences during the day and their dreams during the night into numbers.

Biagio has especially created and constructed an etchings series with chine collé, in a rich and fascinating narrative exploring the mystical subtleties of the numerological systems of 'La Smorfia' and juxtaxposing these with the stark, and harsh realities of London urban life.

He employs a wide range of print techniques to depict present-day dramas (the credit crunch, climate change) and create illustrations inspired by Roberto Saviano's *Gomorrah*, Italy's 'Land of Fires', places and people as well as a cat series.

He has always been fascinated by trying new print techniques and he has taken short coursesin printmaking in London at Ormond Road, City Lit, Working Men's College, Central St. Martins and London Print Studio. However, etching technique is always the process that allowes him the clearest means of expression of his ideas. His next step is to experiment with combined print techniques and also to use fabrics and collage elements, to gain more structure and subject matter.

The compositions of the prints *Food Cultures in a Big City* and *London Stories* are based on sketches of people from different cultural backgrounds. Biagio started drawing and characterizing the people, their clothes and gestures and their dishes in relationship to the surrounding architecture in and outside their buildings.

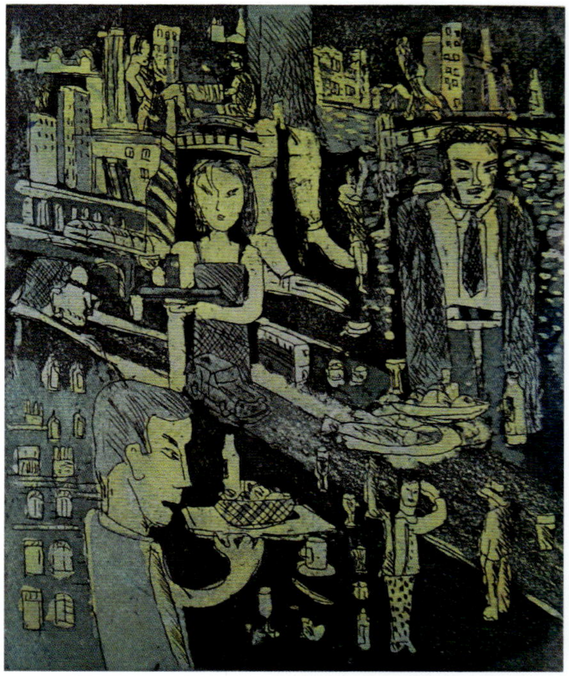

Food Cultures in a Big City, 15 x 18 cm, etching and aquatint, (edition 10)

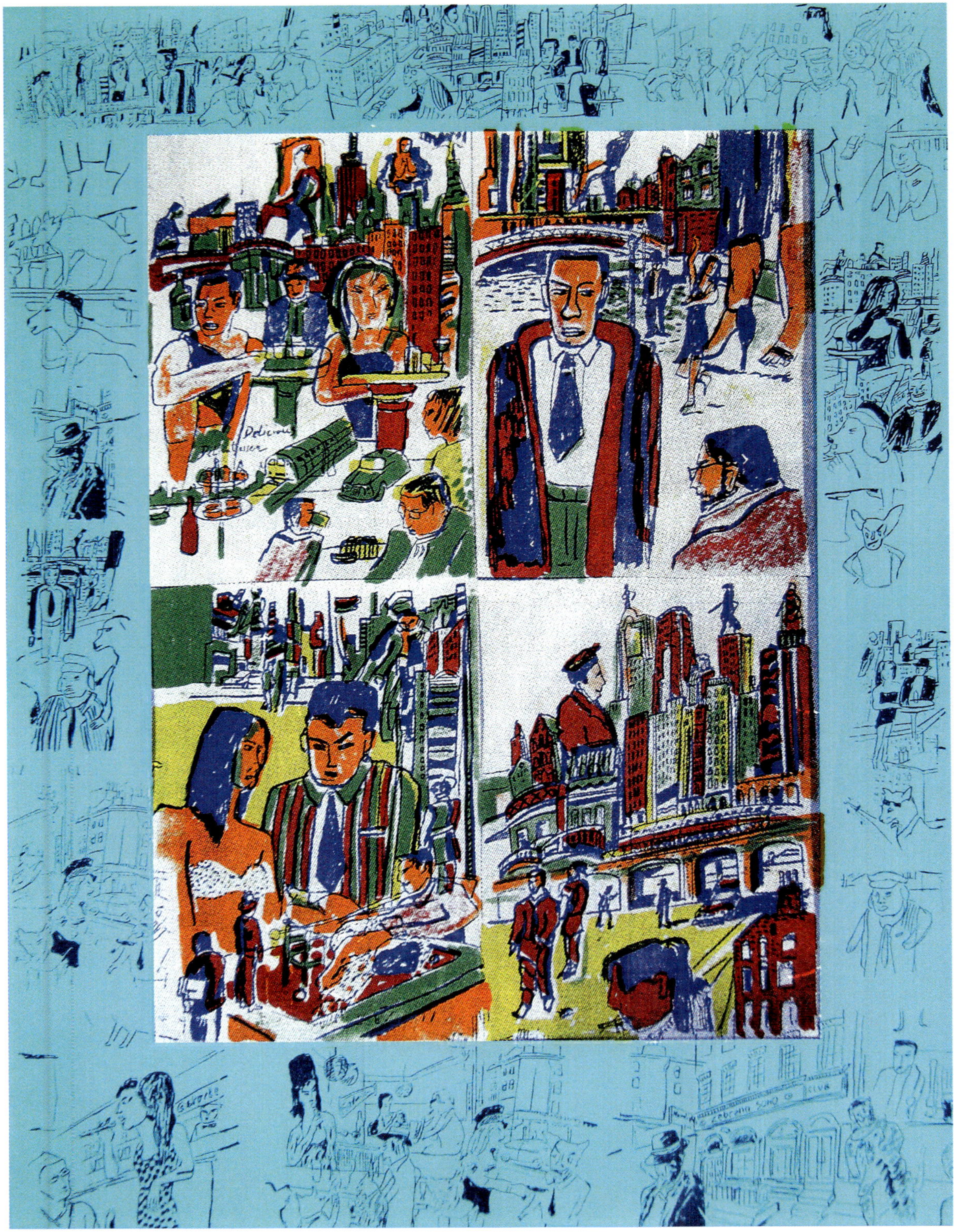

London Stories
30 x 42 cm
screen print,
(edition of 7)

Amanda McAllister

Making has always been an important activity in my life. Initially I used printmaking as an extension of my painting while I was at Chelsea School of Art, experimenting with all the traditional techniques, I then began to develop these skills with an MA in Printmaking. Since then I have continued to use printmaking as a primary art form.

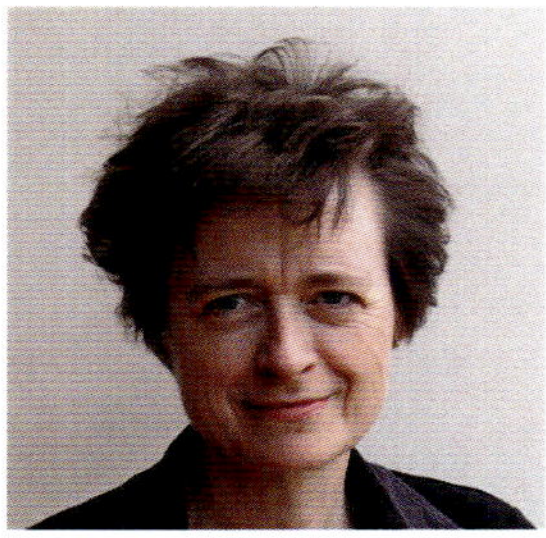

1962 Born Rugby
1981–85 Studied at Chelsea School of Art for a degree in Painting, followed by an MA in Printmaking
1985–86 Printmaking Studio Demonstrator, Sunderland Polytechnic.
1986 *A Portfolio of Prints*, Angela Flowers Gallery, London
A Painterly Approach: Artists in print, The Northern Centre for Contemporary Art, Sunderland
1986 & 88 Northern Arts Visual Arts Award
1986–94 Lecturing part-time at Sunderland University
1987–88 Co-organiser of *Open to Print*, a National Printmaking Competition touring exhibition
1988 Solo exhibition Hill House Gallery, Alnwick
1989–90 Exhibition Organiser at Sunderland University
1989 *Charlotte Press 89*, The Bishopsgate Institute, London
A Show of Feeling, Wilson Hale Gallery, London
1990 *Contemporary Masterpieces from Five Corporate Collections*, Harris Museum & Art Gallery
1992 Solo exhibition, Vicarage Cottage Gallery, North Shields
1993 *Three Dimensional Printmakers*, The Bonington Gallery, Nottingham
1994 *Pieces of Eight*, NE8 Group Show Bede Gallery, Jarrow
1996 Northern Print Award & Northern Print Show, Hatton Gallery, Newcastle Upon Tyne
2012 *Pushing Print*, The Pie Factory, Margate
2014 *Exploring Boundaries*, Neo Artists Gallery, Bolton
2014–15 Selected artist for Rednile Project, Gateshead
2015 Member of the Printmakers Council

Collections

Northern Arts, Deloitte, Haskins and Sells, Rogue and Northern Print

I am a painter-printmaker based in the North East of England. The diverse landscape of this area – rural, urban, industrial and coastal – is a predominant source for my work. Exploring the exterior and interior spaces I move through in daily life, my work reflects the changing quality of light and the shadows that are created. I am inspired and interested by large man-made structures to the small detail, and textural elements seen in the local environment. I use drawings, photographs and written notes as a starting point, abstracting and reducing forms to simple geometric shapes juxtaposed with gestural and textural marks. I later reflect upon these references, relying also on memory and the subconscious absorptions of imagery. I then make collages and small paintings on paper that are a further source for my prints. My work fluctuates between pure abstraction and its border, where elements are more recognizable. I use traditional forms of printmaking (silkscreen, intaglio and relief) alongside computer-generated images. My prints are not planned, they evolve, the element of chance and accident are embraced. Sometimes I combine different techniques or collage prints together.

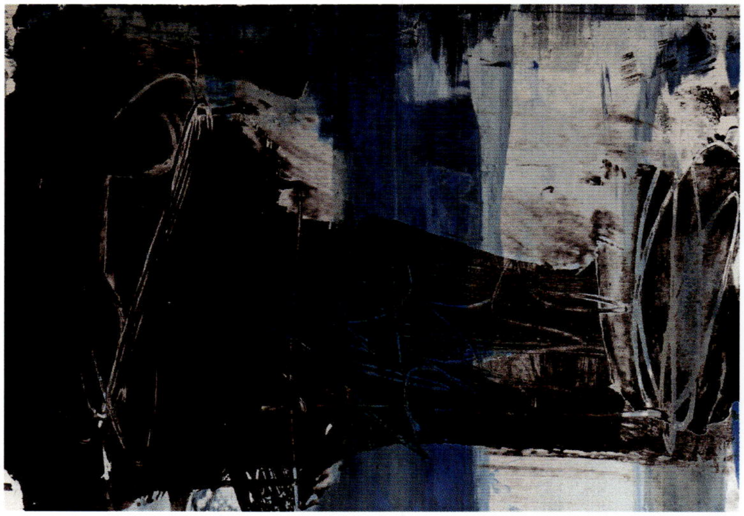

Marking Time I, 30 x 42 cm, silkscreen (monoprint)

I create digital prints by transforming binary code that describes the colour and brightness of each individual pixel into something real, making an object in its own right. Using Adobe Photoshop to manipulate the scanned work alongside Illustrator and Serif Affinity Designer and Photo programs, I draw directly within the programs to construct the prints. I work instinctively, reacting to the relationship of one area to another. I also use a tablet where I can draw directly on the screen, using a number of apps, such as SketchBook Pro, Artflow, Serious Paint and Infinite Painter. Images are built up layer by layer, removing, exposing and obscuring elements. The prints are printed with pigmented inks on fine art paper.

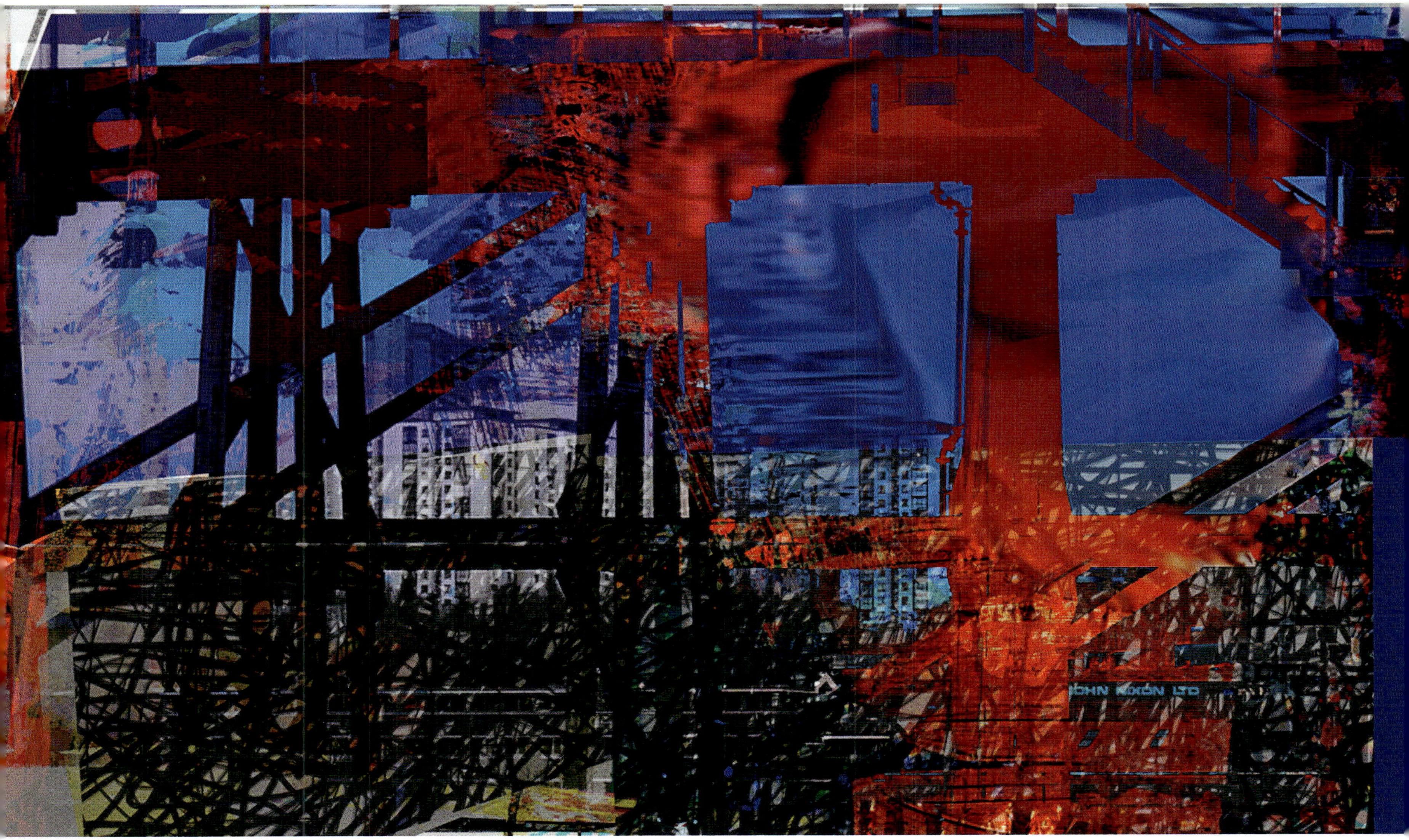

The Staithes VI, 33 x 48.3 cm, digital print (edition of 10)

Julia McKenzie

I am based in London and studied Fine Art at Camberwell School of Art. My work is primarily drawing-based, layered with paper cuts and collage. I use a lot of maps and atlases in my work, it helps anchor my work with a sense of place through their colour, text and symbols. I also produce limited-edition screen prints and etchings.

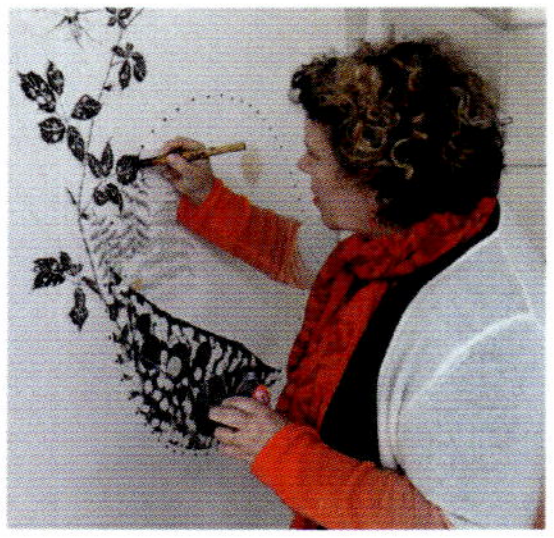

2010 Selected for *Pushing Print* Margate
2011 *The Ghost of Gone Birds*, Rochelle School
Bicentenary Friends exhibition, Dulwich Picture Gallery - awarded second prize overall
2012 *Bite*, Mall Galleries
London Calling, Tehran
Dulwich Festival Open Studio
Snap!, SLWA at the Bankside
The Space Between, Vyner Street Gallery
2013 *Offline* print fair, Embassy Tea Gallery
Curious Books, Studio 73, Brixton Village
Pushing Print, Margate
Wild Britain, Jam Factory, Oxford
Sidney Cooper Gallery, Contemporary Print Fair
I Followed the River and Came to the Sea, group show at Creekside studios
Bainbridge Open Print Show, Embassy Tea Gallery
Dulwich Festival - artists' open house
Tehran Calling, London Print Studios
Pattern and Print group show at the Jam Factory, Oxford
2014 Winter show - Stone Wall Gallery, Berwickshire
Capital City, Orso Major Gallery
Inspired by... Morley
Bainbridge Open, Embassy Tea Gallery - awarded Intaglio Printmaker Prize
Spring Forth, Noverre Gallery, The Assembly House Norwich
2015 Selected for 5th Sheffield International Artists Book Prize, Bank Street Arts Sheffield
50/50, New Ashgate Gallery, Farnham

I am really interested in broken, lost or discarded fragments of nature or man-made objects found immediately around me. I draw things found on the beach and on my travels through the countryside. I look for bones, plants, beetles and birds found outside my studio at home. The journey between my house and studio each day reveals new objects, animals and observations that helps maintain a relationship with my environment and the nature that can be found there. I like residues and husks of animals, plants or minerals that have survived long enough for me to find and examine. I celebrate the fragile, forgotten and the broken, I find them beautiful.

Drawing is the starting point to everything I produce. Holding and examining the things I see and find is really important to the process and experience. Being able to draw directly onto an etching plate, or being able to take rubbings and imprints of textures that will enhance the drawings naturally lends itself to printmaking. Drawing is about being in the moment, and that immediacy and spontaneity should try to be preserved and conveyed in the final work, even if the processes to make it are painstaking.

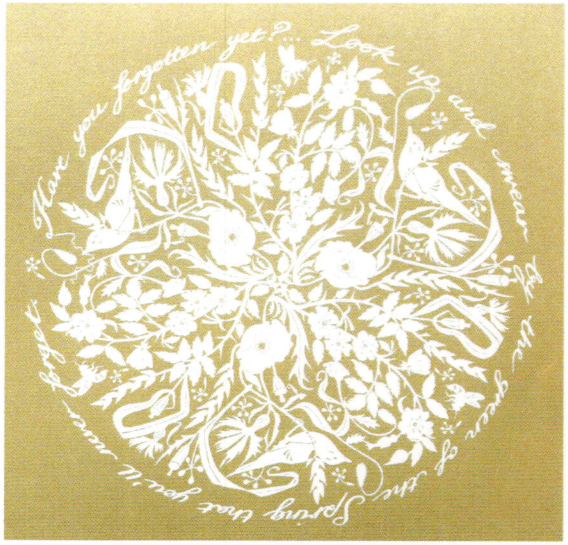

Aftermath, 32 x 32 cm, screen print (edition of 20)

In 2013 I was commissioned by the Imperial War Museum to create a design for remembrance for the 100-year anniversary of the First World War. I created an eternal spring in the round with words from the poem *Aftermath* by Siegfried Sassoon. I also have had an atlas page drawing acquired by the British Library to add to the national collection of antiquarian maps.

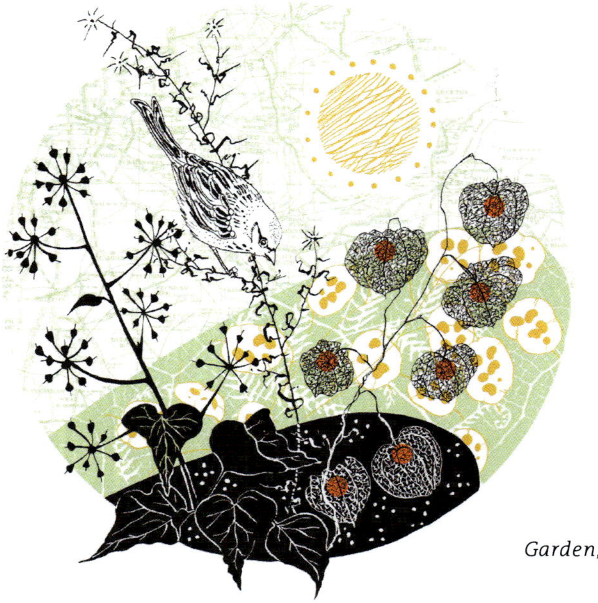

Garden, 32 x 32 cm, screen print (edition of 30)

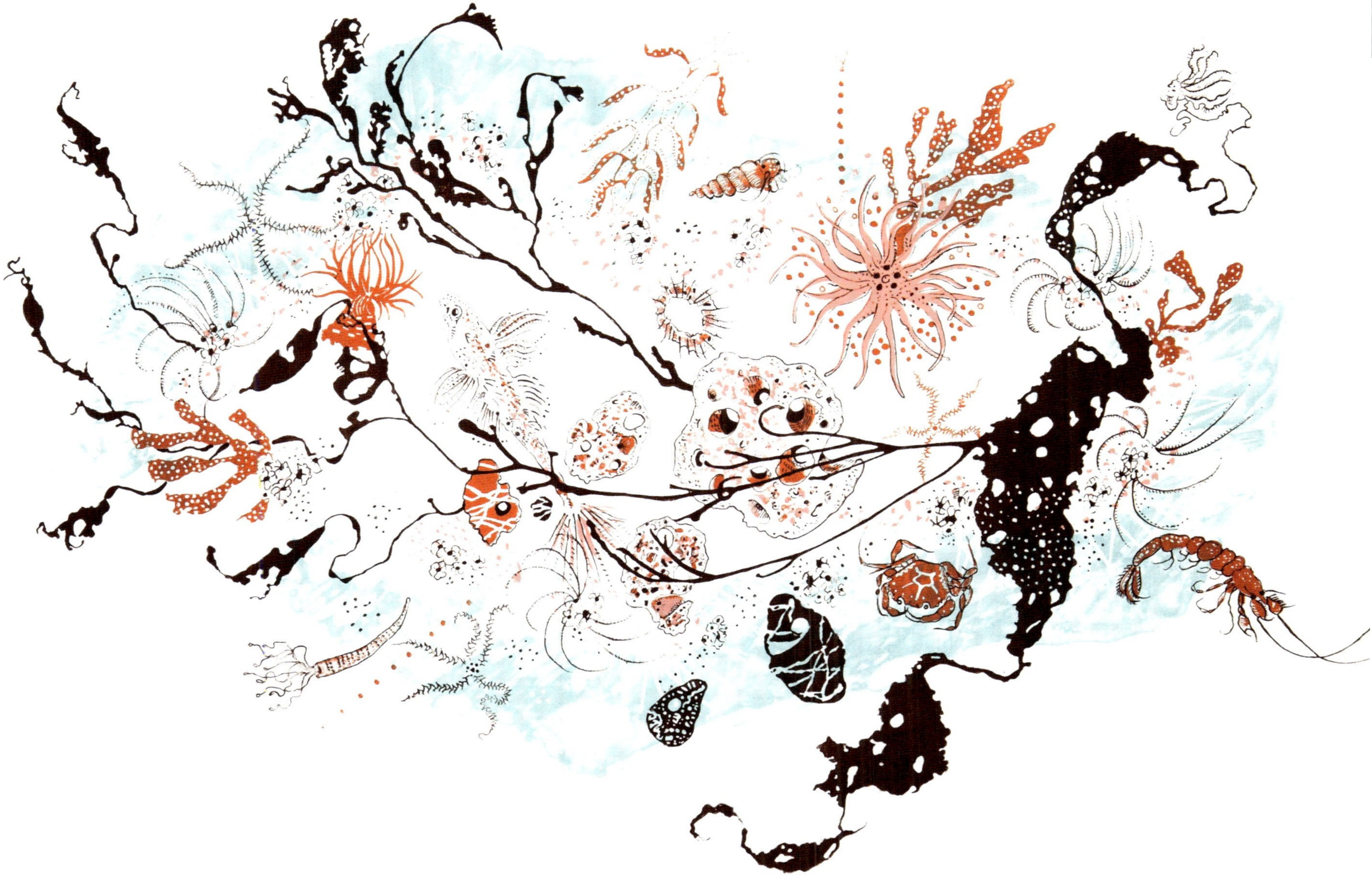

Botany Bay, 66 x 44 cm, screen print (edition of 30)

Margo McNulty

My printmaking career started when I enrolled on a Fine Art course at the Galway-Mayo Institute of Technology, followed by an MA in Fine Art Print at the National College of Art in Dublin. In the past few years, my work has concentrated particularly on etching, though I have also experimented with a range of other media including photography, lithography and video. Currently, I am based in Co. Roscommon where I work both as an artist and part-time lecturer.

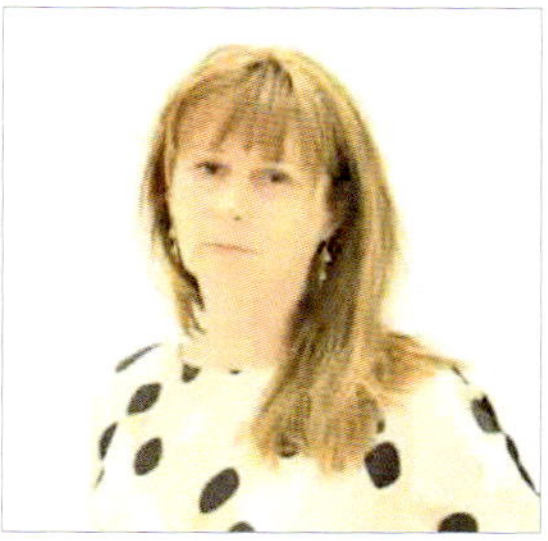

Recent Group Exhibitions

2009 *Aquila*, Rhenania, Cologne, Germany
2011 *Inside Out*, Graphic Studio, Dublin
2011 *Bite*, Mall Galleries, London
2012 *Strange Days*, Ballina Arts Centre, Co. Mayo
2012 *Claremorris Open Exhibition*, Claremorris, Co. Mayo
2012 *Bite*, Mall Galleries, London
2012 *Impressions*, Galway Arts Centre, Galway
2014 *Space and Place*, The Lab, Foley St. Dublin
2014 *Gravity*, Aba Teangai Dooagh Achill, Co. Mayo
2014 *Here Now*, RVAF, Boyle, Co. Rosommon
2014 *A Natural Selection*, Galleri Astley, Uttersberg Sweden
2016 Graphic Studio, Dublin

Residencies

2001 The Museum of Country Life, Castlebar, Co. Mayo.
2005 Custom House Studios, Westport Co. Mayo.
2009 Trade residency in Roscommon working with the artist Daren Almond
2015 Künstlerhaus, Schwandorf-Fronberg, Bavaria, Germany

Collections

Office of Public Works
Folklore Section in University College Dublin
National Gallery of Ireland
Museum of Country Life, Castlebar, Co. Mayo

My work deals with hidden history, memory and place, and with aspects of everyday life and experience. I often revisit these themes and am influenced by geography, agrarian culture and certain traditions inherent in Irish culture. Professor Luke Gibbons, Maynooth University, described my work as follows:

> "In one of Margo McNulty's images, shadows leave blots of ink outside an open window with a crumpled curtain: it is not clear whether a cat has made its escape, or a phantom limb is casting a menacing presence. In other images, paint awaits a finishing touch as abandoned tins are left on the shelf, and thin coatings peel off damp walls. Progress has come unstuck, discarded machines succumbing to rust and corrosion, extinct species once they no longer work."

Professor Gibbons has captured the essence of my work, which concerns itself with episodes of chance, the intersection of personal and public histories and how these histories and meanings can be embedded in material objects.

Jump, 55 x 75 cm, lithograph (edition of 6)

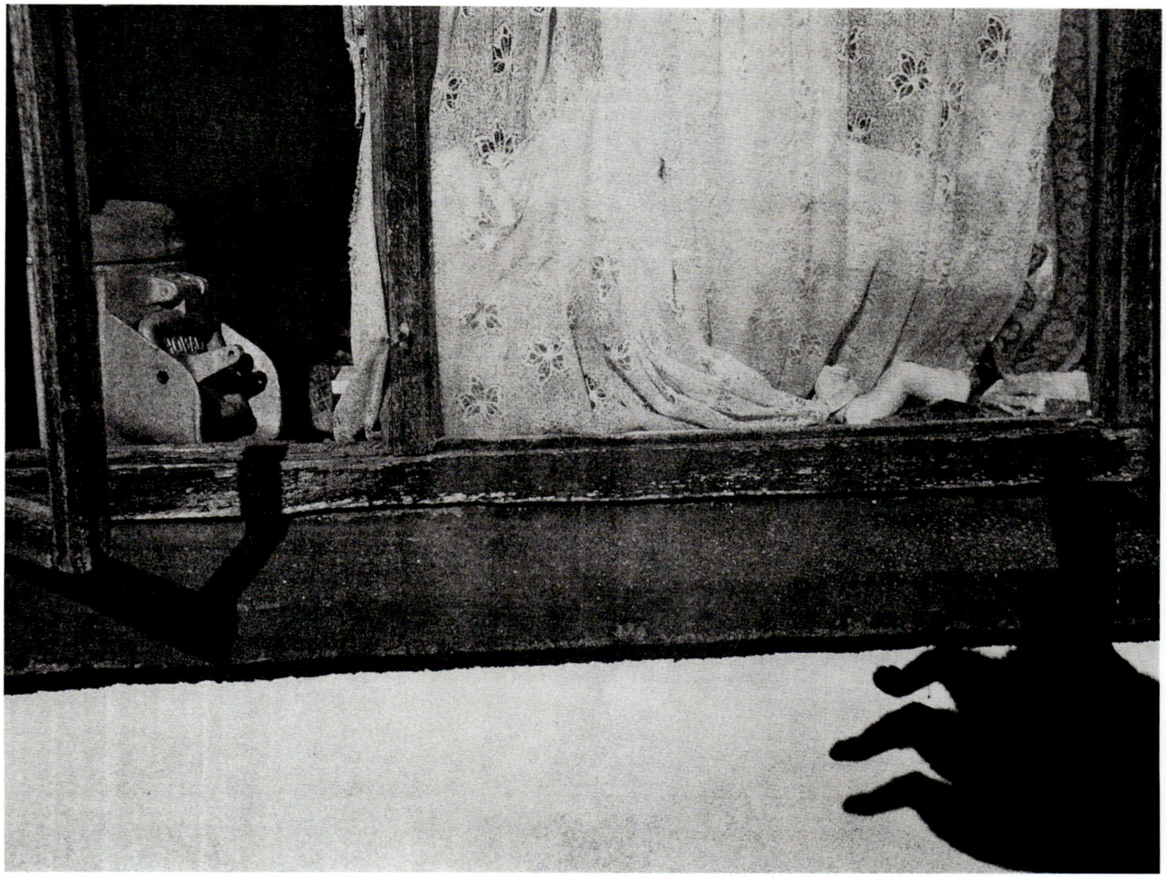

Still-Life, 23 x 30 cm, photo etching (edition of 10)

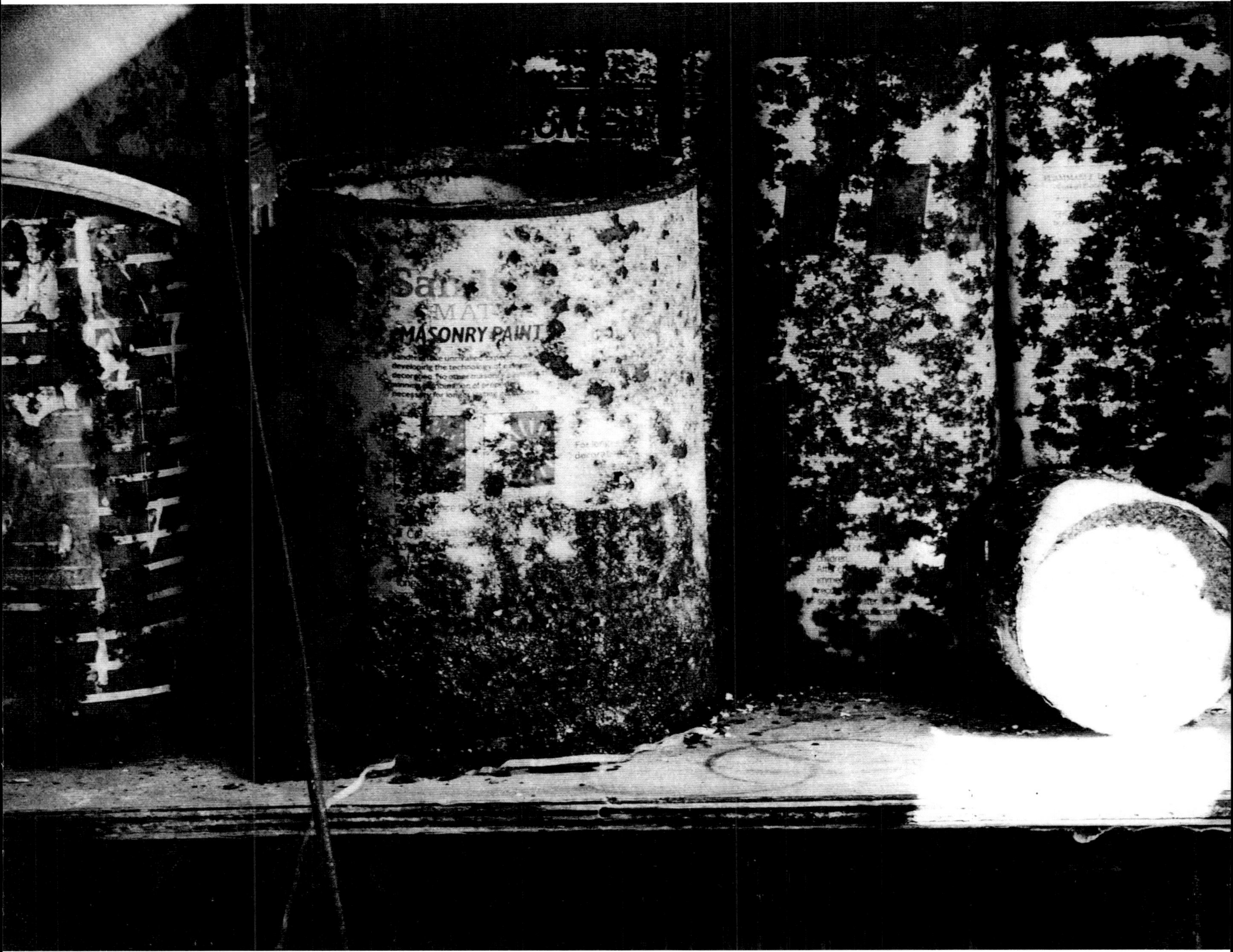

Chris Mercier

I would describe myself as a multidisciplinary artist with an interest in the nature of process and processes. I think of myself as a maker of artifacts that unfold procedures and a maker of procedures that generate artifacts. I like to explore, observe and document the repertoires of objects and processes.

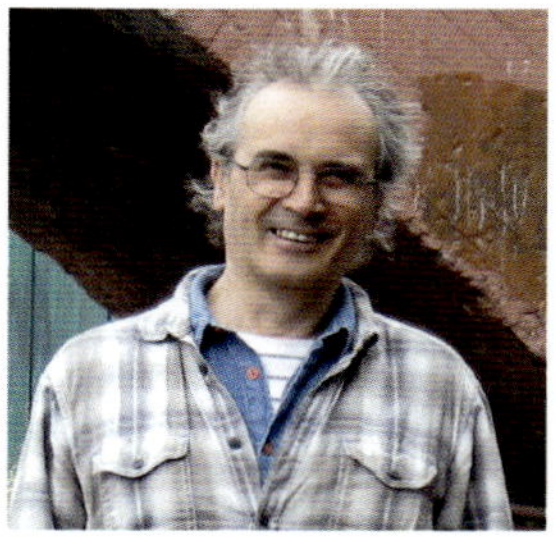

1951 Born England
1970 Art Foundation, Berkshire College of Art
1990 Founded Printmaker Studio, Reading
1991 Joined Printmakers Council
2009 BA (Hons) Fine Art, University of Reading
2009 Carter Memorial Prize (sculpture)
2009 Mary Dyson Award RGA
2012 MA Royal College of Art, London
2012 Paintings for Hospitals Award
2014 Joined OpenHand Studios, Reading
2013–15 Part-time tutor at University of Reading (I of Ed) & Henley College Oxon

Selected Exhibitions:

2012 *Lost for Words*, PmC – UCLH Arts London.
RCA Degree Show, Battersea, London
Reincarnation, London Design Festival, London Print Studio
Works on Paper, PmC, R.K. Burt Gallery
Multiplied, RCA Graduates, Christie's, London
2013 *Hot Off The Press*, Curwen Gallery
Casual Ties, TinType Gallery
In-Print-Out, Künstlerhaus, Vienna
Unfold, London Print Studio
2014 *CMYK*, PmC, The Pie Factory, Margate
2015 *Print As A Verb*, OHOS, Reading
365 Dessins, Galerie d Anieres CH

My recent work focuses on the frontier between analogue and digital technologies. An 'in-between' place that I describe as "a zone to be explored, where print as an artist's medium can falter or be reborn as it comes up against the digital vehicles of dispersion". Currently I am making work that explores process and the repertoires of objects and their articulation through motion and time.

I have worked as a screen-printer, editioning work for other artists for many years, and on reflection I now find myself questioning all the formalities of the archetypal printmaker's practice. I am wary of the ghettoisation of the 'printmaker' and printmaking processes.

However, I do find it extremely interesting how different artists are drawn to use print in their practice. The fecundity of print can be seen as a strategy for the dispersal of ideas and the broadcasting of images. A more conceptual and provocative alternative I feel, to the obvious commercial use of the multiple.

The mark-making possibilities of different print processes are obviously also something that draws me to choose one print process as opposed to another. I seem to find that I continue to use the languages and artifacts of 'print' and replication. The alchemy of process informs my work.

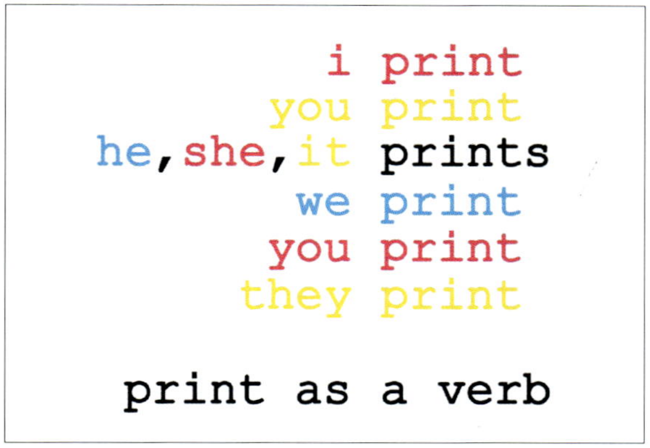

I cannot escape my history !

In the process of producing images that relate to the basic ideographic structures, the line and square, the dot, spiral and circle, I have produced work that requires to be performed, or requires the viewer to interact with it in some way. I am also exploring other early but timeless technologies such as weaving, which like 'print' have been integrated into our society and lifestyles and are also used to disperse imagery and ideas.

I am intrigued by the device of metonymy when used in visual imagery. Add to that the viral image and the virtual image, both companions to the digital age and to the internet.

I am very conscious of the way an artwork can exist on two planes, the real and the virtual, existing perhaps in a dormant mode until the virtual unfolds, replicates and performs.

The relational objects that I make, I hope provoke interactivity. These are features that I like to include. This introduces the concept of the assemblage as a coming together of the maker, the piece and the viewer. The performativity of an artwork is something I seek.

In replication, repetition, folding and multiplication there is a meditative dimension that can be found for example in Buddhist mantras. This I feel is made manifest by the early development and success of printing in oriental societies where repetition is seen as a way to achieve enlightenment. Then in European societies the French word *plier* links this idea of replication and multiplication to the concept and activity of folding, made evident in the structure of the book. All these things to me seem intrinsically linked.

Print As A Verb, 30 x 40 cm
screen print (edition of 25)

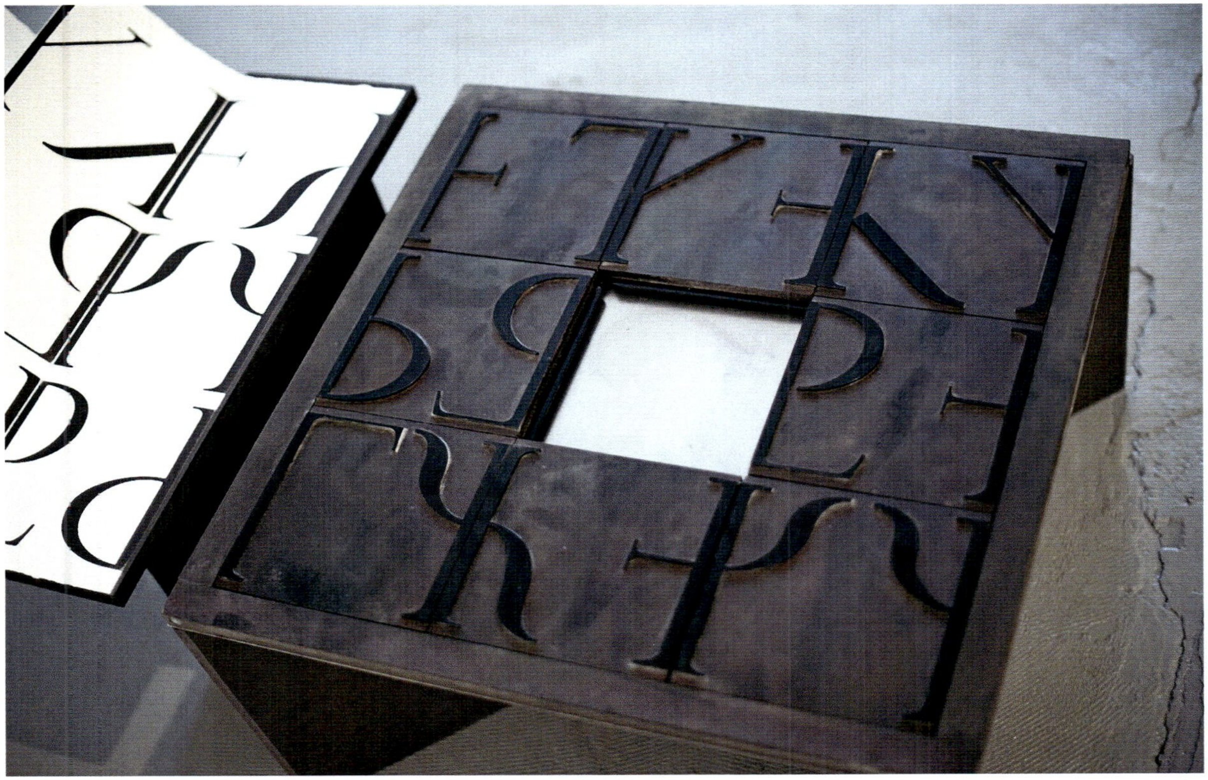

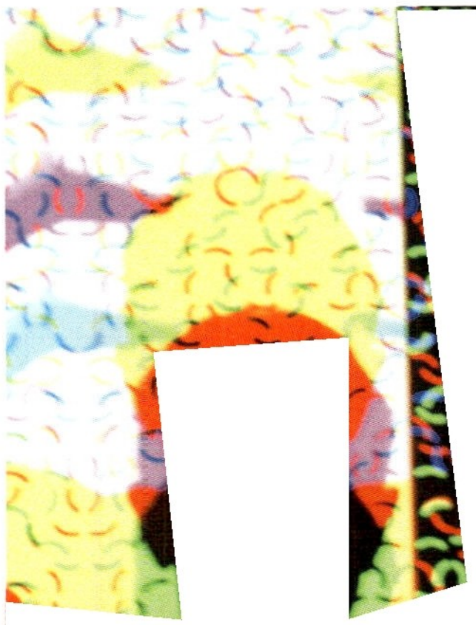

Abjad Articulator 2012
unique printing assemblage
(variable matrix and codex)

Time Prism
animated RGB projection
(3 projectors).

Janet Milner

After a long career in design and illustration I felt that I wanted to have the opportunity to discover new ways of working that could potentially help enrich my artistic creativity, and this is why I chose to embark on the MA Printmaking course at Camberwell. My interest in printmaking goes back to the early 1980s when I made my own screens and began printing my designs onto fabrics to make clothing.

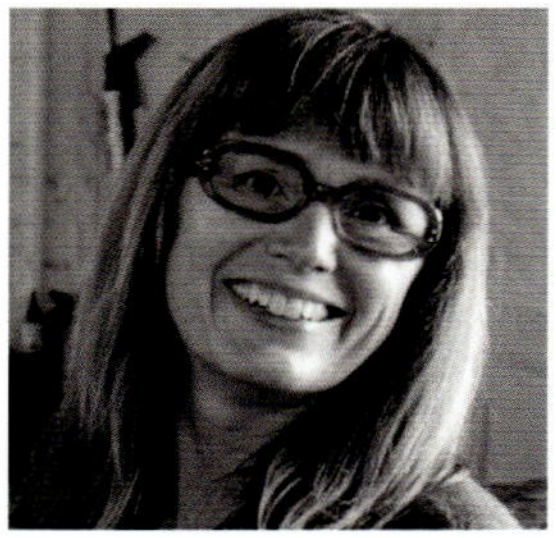

1958 Born Mirfield, W. Yorkshire
1981 BA Printed Textiles, Liverpool Polytechnic
1983–98 Janet Milner (creator & wholesaler of my own printed products)
1990 Developed a bespoke Janet Milner ceramic & textile bathroom range for Liberty (London) which led to working with Conran Shop, Heals and other retailers worldwide.
1990 Illustrations & merchandise commissioned by Warehouse (UK retail) for nationwide Christmas window display.
1998–2013 NPW (international giftware company): graphic design & product development
2012 MA Printmaking Camberwell UAL

Recent selected group shows & art fairs:
2013 London Graduate Art Festival *Pushing Print*, Margate
2014 London Art Fair. London Original Print Fair. Bainbridge Open. *Royal Academy Summer Show*. *National Original Print Exhibition*, Bankside Gallery. *NOA 14* Somerset House. London Print Studio Members' Summer Show. Christie's *Multiplied*.
2015 London Art Fair. RWS Contemporary Watercolour Competition. Painter Printmakers, The Keeper's House, Royal Academy. London Original Print Fair. *50:50, Celebrating 50 Years of the Printmakers Council*, New Ashgate Gallery
2014 Joined Printmakers Council
2015 Joined LOOP artists in Print
Member of Artichoke Print Studio

I am an artist who draws and paints, and so I am naturally interested in, and enjoy experimenting with, all types of direct painterly printmaking techniques, but it is the monotype technique that has become an important part of my art practice.

I work in an intuitive way, and like to make lots of work quickly and freely so that I can edit and select the most successful pieces. I discovered that the immediacy of monotyping suited the way I work whilst doing my MA at Camberwell. I now work primarily with watercolour monotypes, enjoying also the opportunity the medium offers for layering and accidental mark-making.

I use my monotype prints to inform the rest of my printmaking. I have gone on to develop some of them into screen-print editions. The screen prints are completely new artworks, and because they aren't direct copies, the challenge for me is to capture some of the freshness and spontaneity of the original monotype.

I choose to celebrate ordinariness and elevate it into something special by presenting throwaway remarks and objects in unexpected and intriguing ways. At present my work is predominately text-based. I make records of my own experiences, memories, thoughts and some of the random things that I collide with in everyday life. My artworks play on, and also reflect a fascination that I have with, the commonality of clutter and the mundane experiences that surround identity and being human.

The works featured are part of an ongoing body of work titled *Unremarkable Sentences*.

OPPOSITE
A Pizza Fell on her Foot, 58 x 76 cm
watercolour monotype (unique)

Doing Nothing, 42.5 x 53.5 cm
screen print (edition of 25)

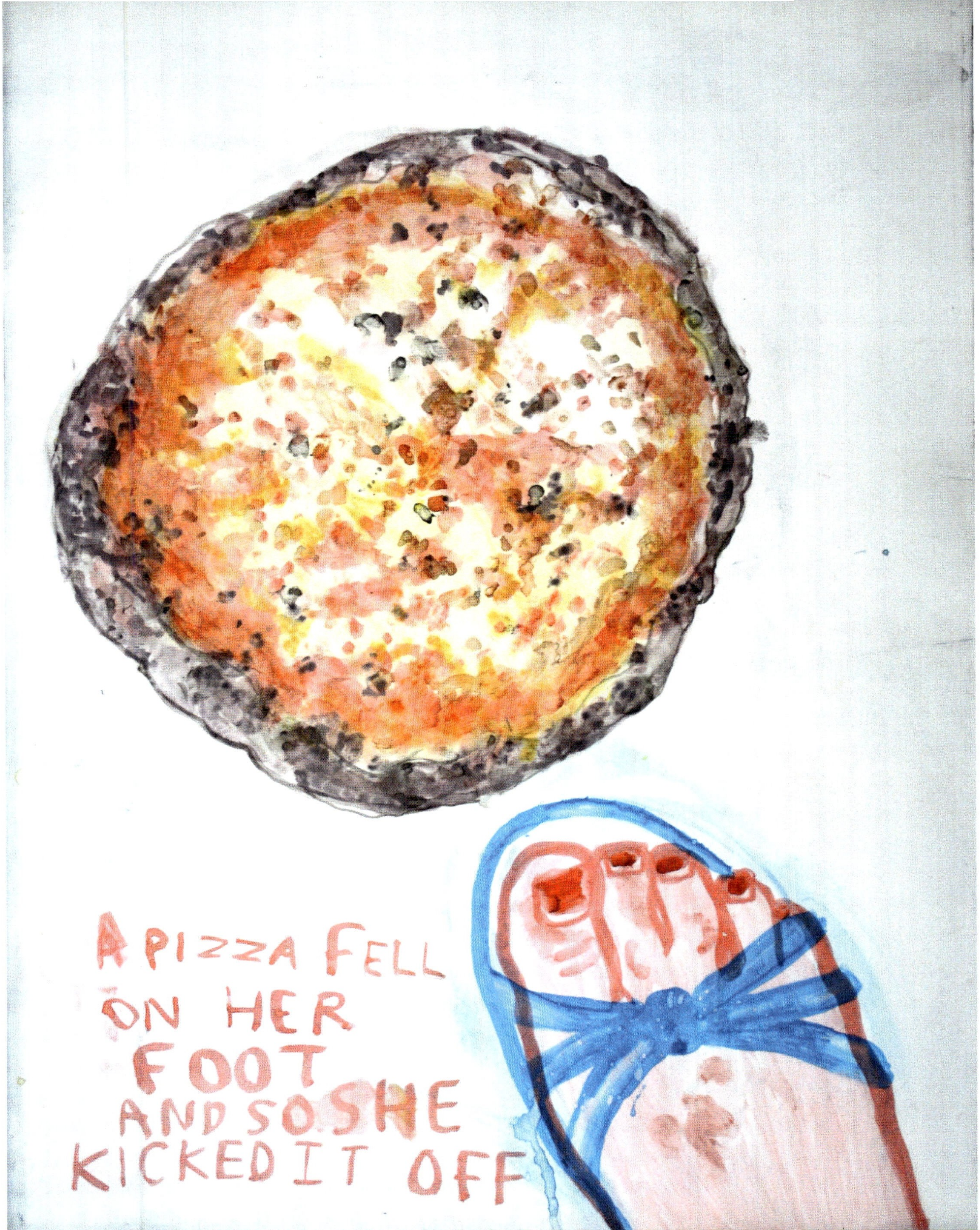
A PIZZA FELL
ON HER
FOOT
AND SO SHE
KICKED IT OFF

Paul David Mitchell

My initial experience of printmaking was studying at Aberystwyth University under Alistair Crawford. His inspirational style of teaching really engaged me with the subject and I haven't stopped making prints since. I was lucky enough to study in New York at Pratt which was a great experience. I met many artists from different countries who greatly influenced my work and ideas.

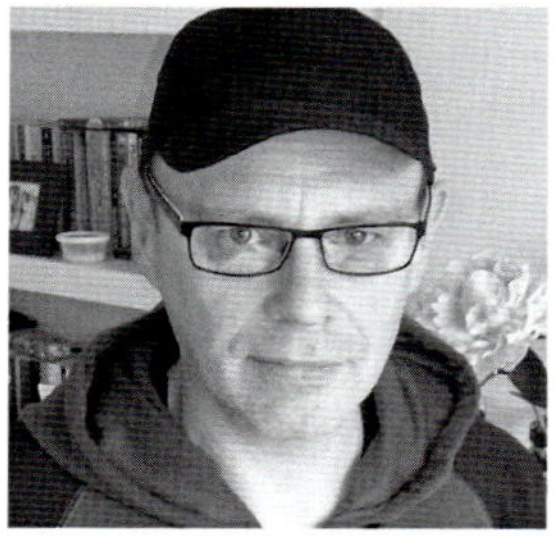

1968 Born Sussex

1989 BA (Hons) Visual Art University College of Wales, Aberystwyth

1991 Exhibited in the UK, France and the US, including *Print Europe*, Barbican, London
Studied in New York at Pratt Institute.

1994–99 Designer and art director at BBC,

2000 Master's in Psychoanalytic studies from Tavistock Centre, London

2001–12 Art director at Haymarket Group PPA, BSME industry awards.

2004 PgDip in Psychodynamic counselling from Birkbeck College, London
Freelance art direction and design.
Associate member of the Higher Education Authority (HEA)
Visiting lecturer at University of Bournemouth and Kingston University.

2014/15 Teaching at Morley College, London

2015 MA Fine Art, Kingston University
Member Printmakers Council

Selected recent events

One White Wall – The Power to Last. Solo show, Project Space, Kingston University, London

It's Finished Now, collaborative publication. Kingston University, London

Signature Art Prize 2015, Finalist

Staging the Life Class (through Maradona). Event, Dorich House, London. With Cullinan/Richards.

Coda – Group show, Platform Space, Kingston University, London

Black Mountain College – A Happening Thing. Workshop/seminar, Kingston University, London

My work explores the interrelationship between the audience and art objects within spaces. These spaces can be viewed as potential sites of an event that has happened, or is about to happen.

I am strongly influenced by both critical and psychoanalytic theory and at the moment my work derives from stories, some of which I have heard about, some of which I have experienced myself.

I use both self-generated and found images. I manipulate the pictures both manually and digitally. I also make object-sculptures. I'm very interested in the materiality of the work and the exhibition space.

A lot of my work involves using multiple images because I'm interested in exploring how the use of these multiple images can work together to create some sort of new rhythm – resulting in a feeling of an uncanny resonance.

I'm also interested in ideas around the ambiguity of communication; what we choose to say and not say, choose to remember and to forget – leave out, turn a blind eye to; and events we imagine, embellish and edit.

In my text pieces, I'm interested in the text as material and use the fragmentary and illusory quality of screen memories for inspiration. This is reflected in my interest in playing with language and meaning and exploring the 'signal to noise' of the message.

I hope my work engages and challenges people and opens up possibilities for reflection and thinking.

Blueprints for a Better Life II, 59 x 84 cm, giclée digital print on fine art paper (edition of 50)

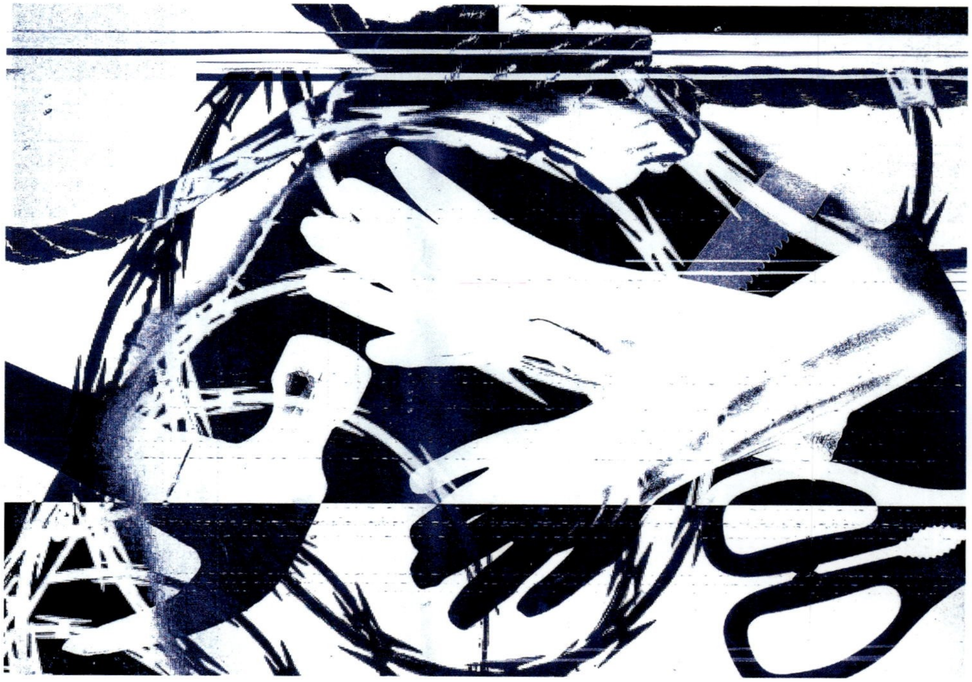

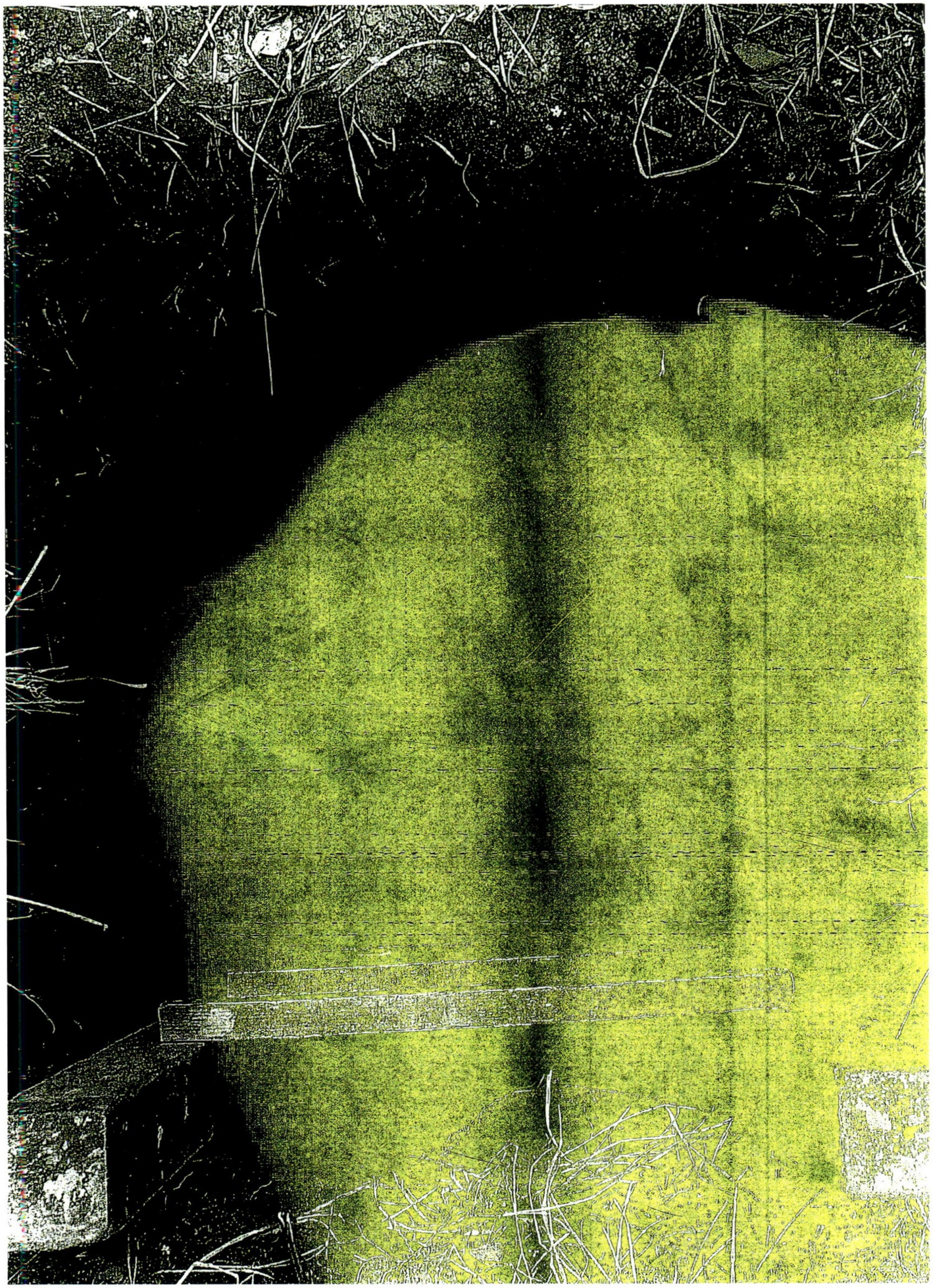

An Illegal Urban – Taipei City
84 x 59 cm
giclée digital print
on fine art paper
(edition of 50)

Ros Morley

Some years after studying for a degree in Fine Art (Painting) at Camberwell, University of the Arts, I started a short etching course in 1994, which led to my spending one day a week over 13 years printmaking (lithography and etching), at the University of Hertfordshire. In 2009 I successfully completed a Master's degree at Brighton University and the London Print Studio.

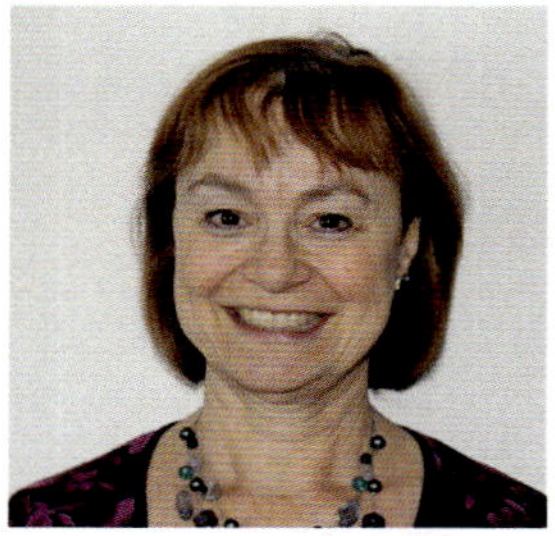

1951 Born North London
1974 BA (Hons) Fine Art Painting Camberwell University of the Arts
1975 PGCE University of London (Whitelands College Putney)
1975–95 Extensive teaching experience in colleges and schools
1995–2007 Printmaking Open Access, University of Hertfordshire
2004 Group show Lauderdale House, Highgate
2005 Solo show (paintings and prints), Wolfson College, Oxford University
2008 *Wish You Were Here*, Riverside Studios Hammersmith
2009 *Half Way There*, Brighton University
2009 MA Printmaking & Professional Practice, University of Brighton and London Print Studio
2009 Joined PmC committee
2009 co-organiser *8th British International Mini-Print Exgibition*
2010 *Printmakers Council at Bankside*, Bankside Gallery; Recent prints by PmC, Stables Gallery, Bexley
2010 *Hot Off The Press*, Curwen & New Academy Gallery
2012 *Proof Perfect*, The Framers Gallery
2013 *Highgate - A Reflection in Print*, Highgate Literary and Scientific Institution
2013–15 Selector, PmC Awards, Camberwell
2014 *Freshly Pressed*, Craft Central *CMYK*, Margate Gallery
2015 *Works on Paper*, Barbican Library

Work held in publicly and privately including Oxford and Brighton Universities

I have always adored and been influenced by the work of Matisse; also more recently, by Barbara Rae's sumptuous brightly coloured atmospheric multi-layered landscape screen prints .

During my MA studies I did a few short courses at Edinburgh Printmakers which further inspired and helped me learn new techniques such as etching with photopolymer, plus working with non-toxic etching.

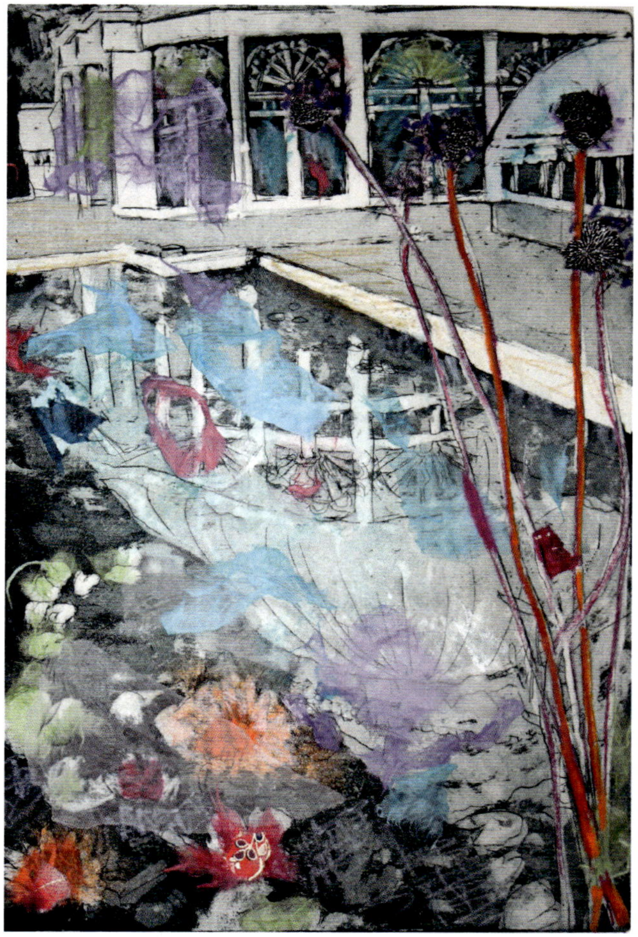

I have found my printmaking has enhanced and broadened my teaching experience over the last twenty years.

In the last six years I have mostly concentrated on etching and aquatint, with chine collé. This has been a good backdrop to introducing colour through the addition of Japanese patterned and tissue papers, torn into small pieces, which are added in to the design during the printing stage.

I like to work fairly spontaneously and if things don't at first seem to work, I'll find ways to further build up the print by hand, to achieve a better result. I often find I need to add some more colour once the design on the copper plate has been inked up and printed on to the paper. I sometimes use coloured crayons and pencils to add a bit more definition.

I have always loved landscape. I love tuning in to nature around me. I aim to express through printmaking, something of its magical, colourful and expansive atmosphere, often including reflections and distortions in water. I am mostly inspired by travel to visually new places; landscapes that hold an element of surprise and beauty. In the past this has included sites in Morocco, India, Italy and Spain.

I have always adored strong bright colours – recently I have been incorporating this more into my prints.

I have also recently done some collographs (which I love working on) – as they are a great platform for gorgeous rich multi-layered colour and texture.

My aim is to bring a slice of the beauty of nature into the hearts of the viewer in an uplifting and joyous fun way!

New York Botanical Gardens 2, 54 x 45 cm etching/aquatint (plus mixed-media), (edition of 10)

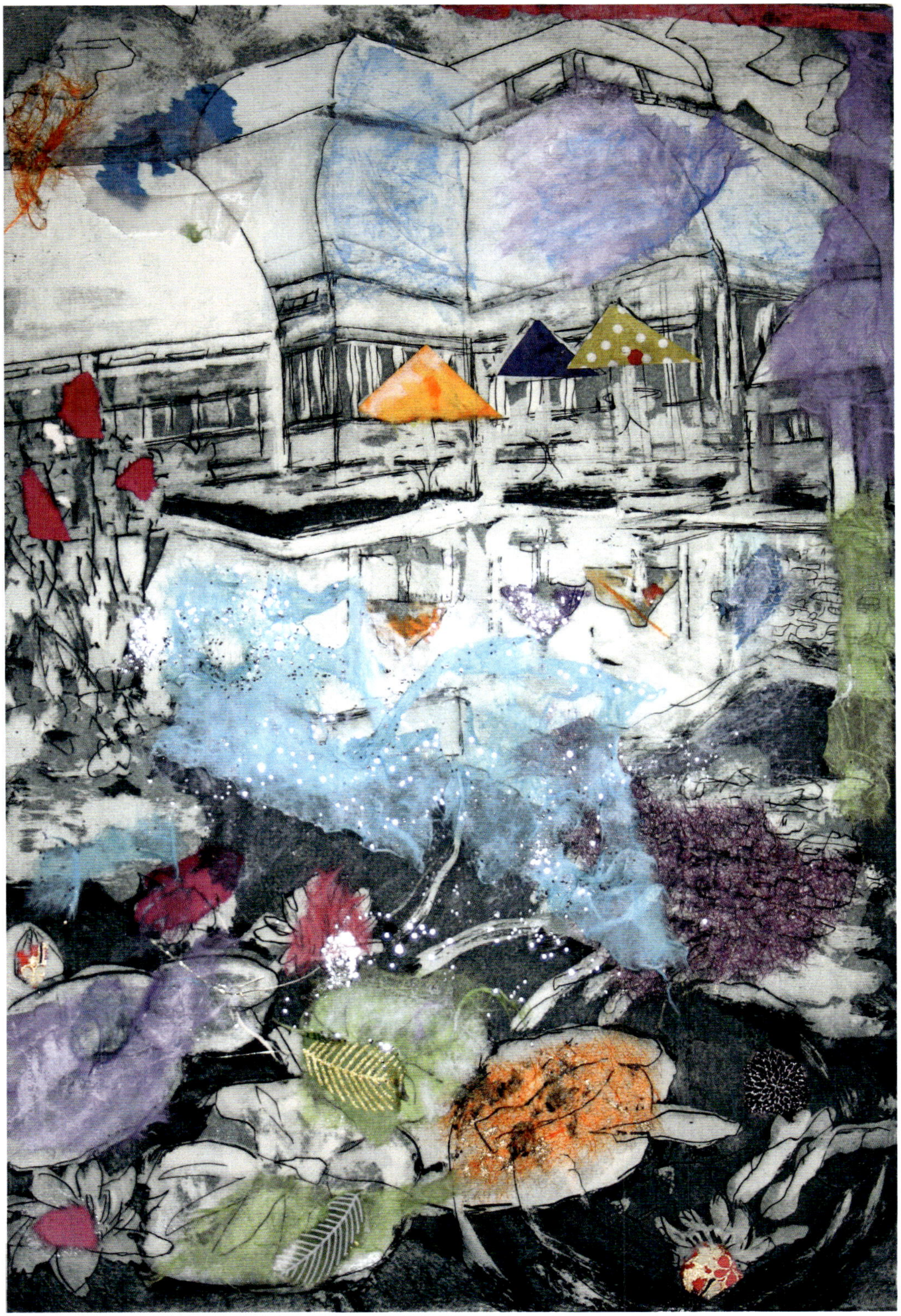

New York Botanical Gardens 1
54 x 45 cm
etching/aquatint
(plus mixed-media)
(edition of 10)

Heather Muise

I love the sense of community that printmakers seem to foster wherever they are in the world. This sense of kinship and cooperation with fellow artists has always been what attracted me to printmaking in the beginning, and it is now something I try to share and foster in my students. I try to use printmaking as a method to build bridges between Arab and Western artists and cultures.

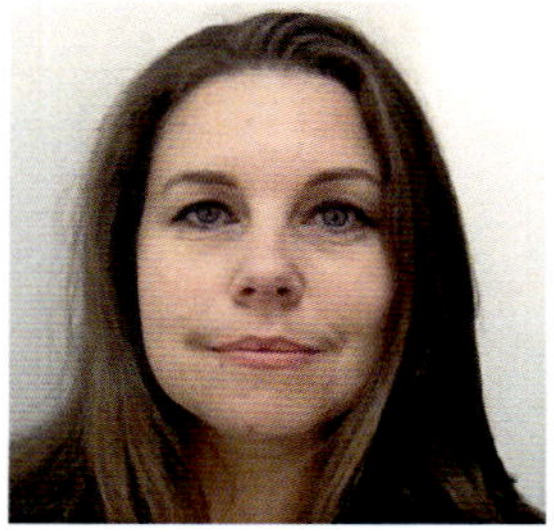

1971 Born Windsor, Ontario, Canada
1990–96 BFA with Honours, University of Windsor, Canada
1997–2000 MFA Printmaking, University of Tennessee, USA
2000–15 Exhibited work in Europe, Australia, North America and the Middle East
2000–05 Initiated Printmaking Area at Zayed University, Dubai, UAE
2003 Solo exhibition at Sharjah Art Galleries, Sharjah, UAE
2003 *What We Were Not Taught*, panel presentation at SECAC Conference, Raleigh, USA
2003–06 International Board Member of Southern Graphics International
2005 *Demographics*, a collaborative printmaking project at Impact Conference, Berlin, Germany
2009 *International Embrace*, a panel presentation at Southern Graphic Council International Conference, Chicago, USA
2010 Began teaching printmaking and drawing at East Carolina University, USA
2010 Co–organizer of *Print Summit 2010*, a printmaking symposium at East Carolina University, USA
2012–14 Taught printmaking and drawing at American University in Dubai, UAE
2012 *Evolution of Printmaking in the UAE*, paper given at Forum for Teaching Studio Art in the UAE, Dubai, UAE
2014 Organizer of *Relief Summit 2014*, a printmaking symposium at East Carolina University, USA
2015 Member Printmakers Council

The role transformation and change play in the universe, whether purely accidental, (as in the case of mutation driven by environmental responses, caused by mistranslation of information), or driven by a more imaginative and alchemical impulse, compels my work.

My work draws from many sources: alchemical texts and woodcuts, Russian prison tattoos, tarot cards and other arcane symbols. I like to use arcane, codified and symbolic imagery that conjures up the ideas of magic, imagination and possibilities that may or may not exist in our world, as a way to suggest to the viewer, rather than to narrate.

I use commercially produced stencils, architectural tools, tracing, copying, scanning, photography, Xerox machines and other forms of image reproduction to create images. By allowing matrices and image reproduction techniques to alter, translate, or degrade the image information I allow certain transformations, changes and mutations to happen and propagate in a life cycle of their own.

I am also a great fan of irony and dark humour. In my latest series of prints I examine the Avian Influenza and other viruses and our fear of them through humour, irony and a pseudo-spiritual, scientific lens.

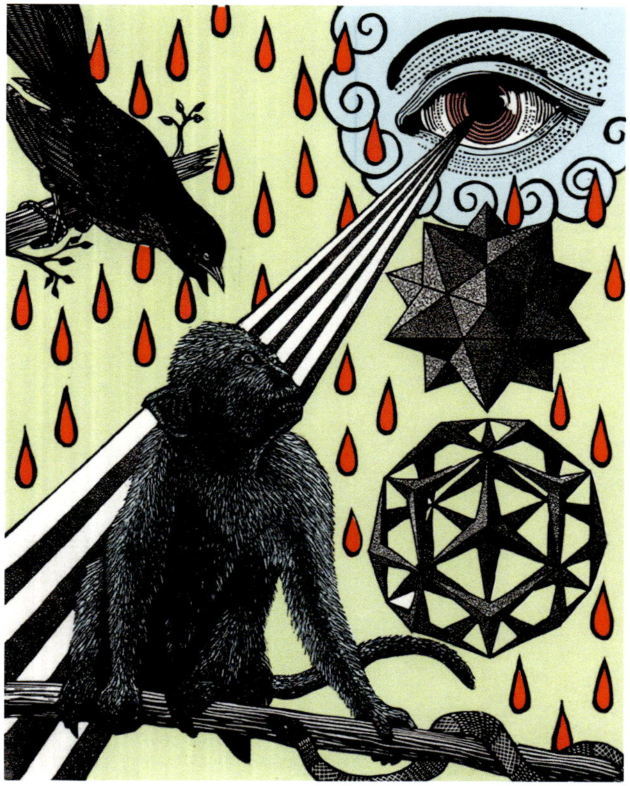

Ebola: the Annunciation
20 x 26 cm
relief and silkscreen
(edition of 10)

The Tears of Sleeping Birds, 24 x 30 cm, relief and silkscreen (edition of 10)

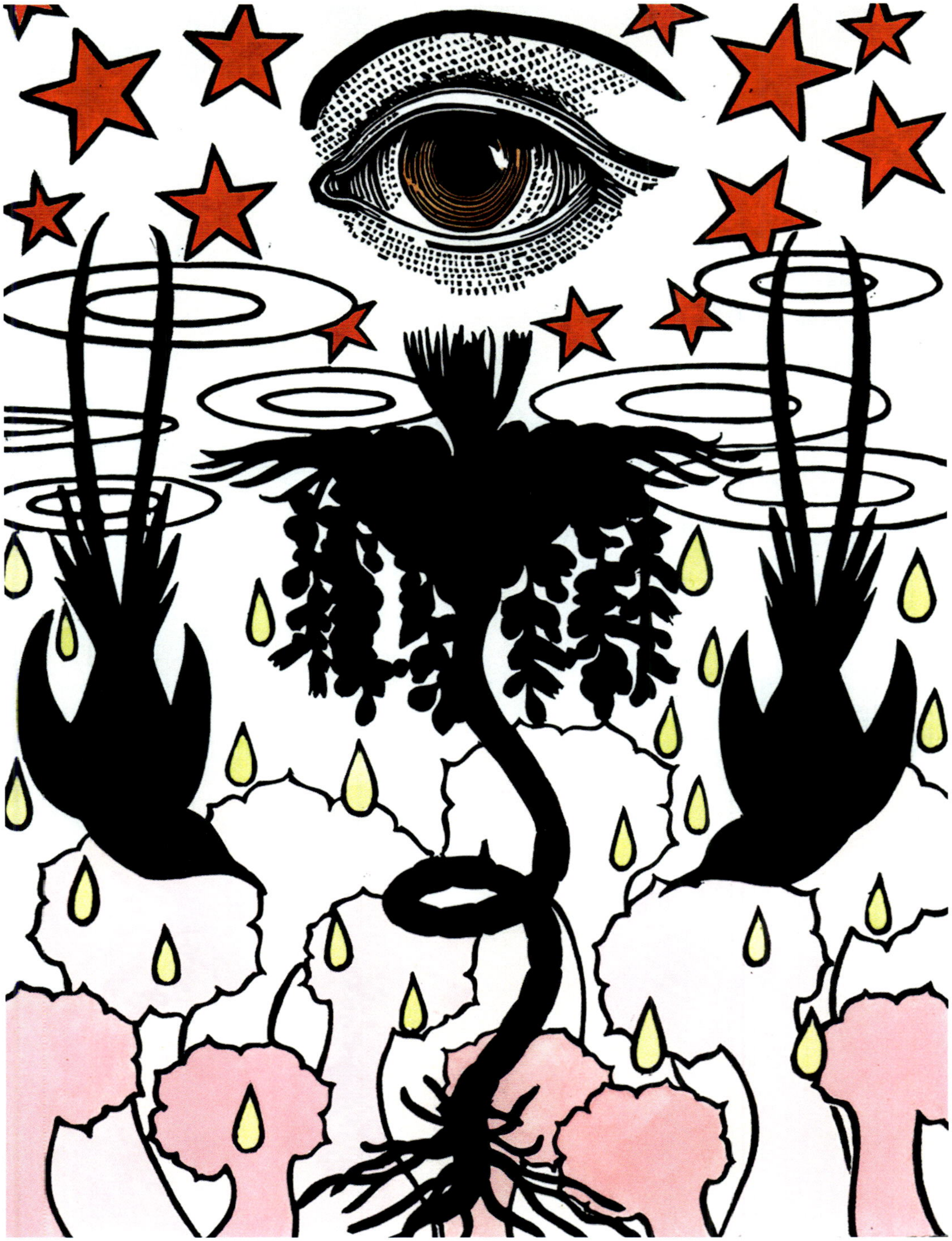

Stephen Mumberson

I been involved in printmaking for over forty years. My earliest prints were relief process which has remained the backbone of my work for all those years. Training at both Brighton Polytechnic (now Brighton University) and the Royal College of Art has extended my practice to cover silk screen, etching and lithography. In recent years I have worked with 3D printmaking.

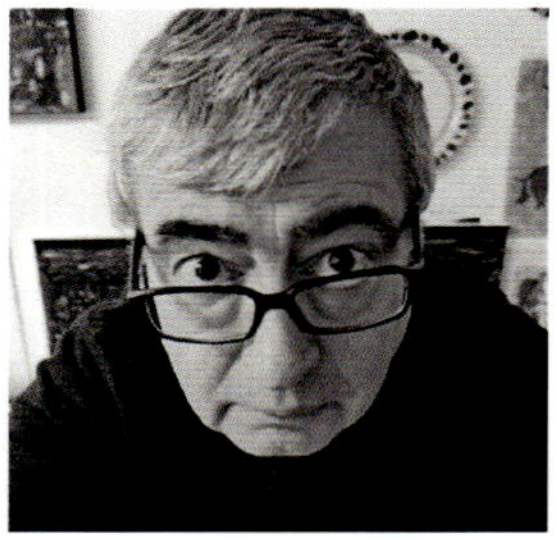

1955 Born England
1977 BA(Hons) Fine Art (1st) Brighton Polytechnic
1978 Specialist Printmaking Distinction, Brighton Polytechnic
1981 MA(RCA) Royal College of Art , London

Teaching

Reader in Fine Art Printmaking Middlesex University London
2014 Associate Professor Middlesex University London

Exhibitions

2011–12 One-person display at The 3rd China International Animation Copyright Fair Dongguan City, China
2012 Gold Panda cartoon contest – Silver Medal winner
2013 Wrexham International Print
2014 Gold Panda cartoon contest – Copper Madal China
2014 20th Ankara Cartoon Festival, Turkey – one person show / festival trophy.
2014 *Combinations* – group print show Seacourt, Bangor, N. Ireland
2015 2nd Cartoon Africa International Biennial - 3rd place winner
2015 *Behind the Barcode*, Toulouse, Paris, France & United Nations, New York, USA

A long-term desire has been to be able to print on three-dimensional surfaces or unconventional materials. My early extended practice was carried out using relief processes and printing either directly or by attaching printed tissues to a surface. This connected well with other areas of my work in painting, collage, drawing and the production of casted metal and clay sculptures. Over these years I returned to travelling, attending print workshops in France, Germany, Finland and Africa. Drawn graphic work also led to invitations to China in recent years which opened up new subjects, and new approaches to my artwork and teaching. During these years I found myself working within printmaking, graphic drawing work and collage as an interchangeable practice. This open approach has informed my teaching in printmaking and fine art. Though in recent years I have been involved in using digital means to produce work, I found it very important to support more traditional means. Much has been lost through both cuts and lost printmaking experience. Hence my support for maintaining lithography, typography and etching as experience that every undergraduate and graduate should engage in. There is no reason that should prevent digital and traditional means of printmaking from being intermixed and connected. For fine artists printmaking is valued for the particular qualities in the production of a work not just as a means of creating multiples.

In recent years at Middlesex University I had the opportunity to work with a 3D Printer. It has been a hard road, with the software aimed at engineers rather than artists and discovering how easy it is to lose a drawing by not paying full attention. The slightest mistake and a day's work is easily lost. Given time, I mastered a basic understanding. It is a strange world for my generation where what you draw virtually becomes a solid printed object. It is a fusion of sculpture, printmaking and drawing, seemly magical but very rational, (particularly when things go wrong). As with many traditional printmaking means, those not prepared to learn and gain the skills needed see it as simple! 3D printmaking is for anyone used to using their mind, hands and eyes. It is a challenging printmaking approach.

OPPOSITE:
Clock, 11 x 12 x 7 cm, 3D monoprint

BELOW:
Hex Circle, 221 x 8 x 6 cm, 3D monoprint

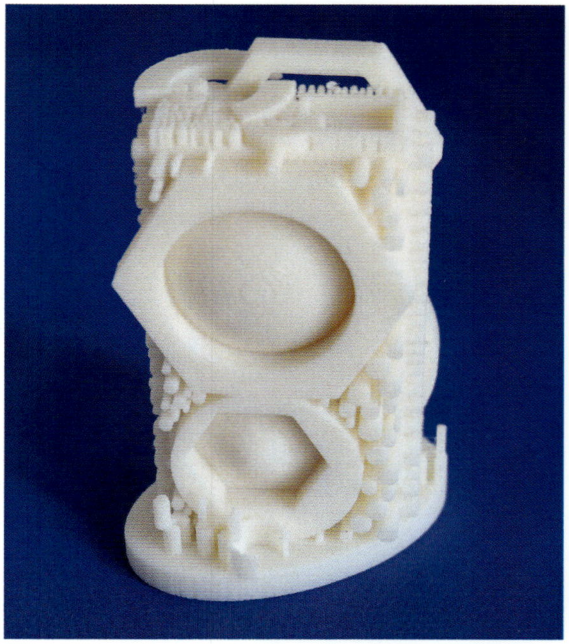

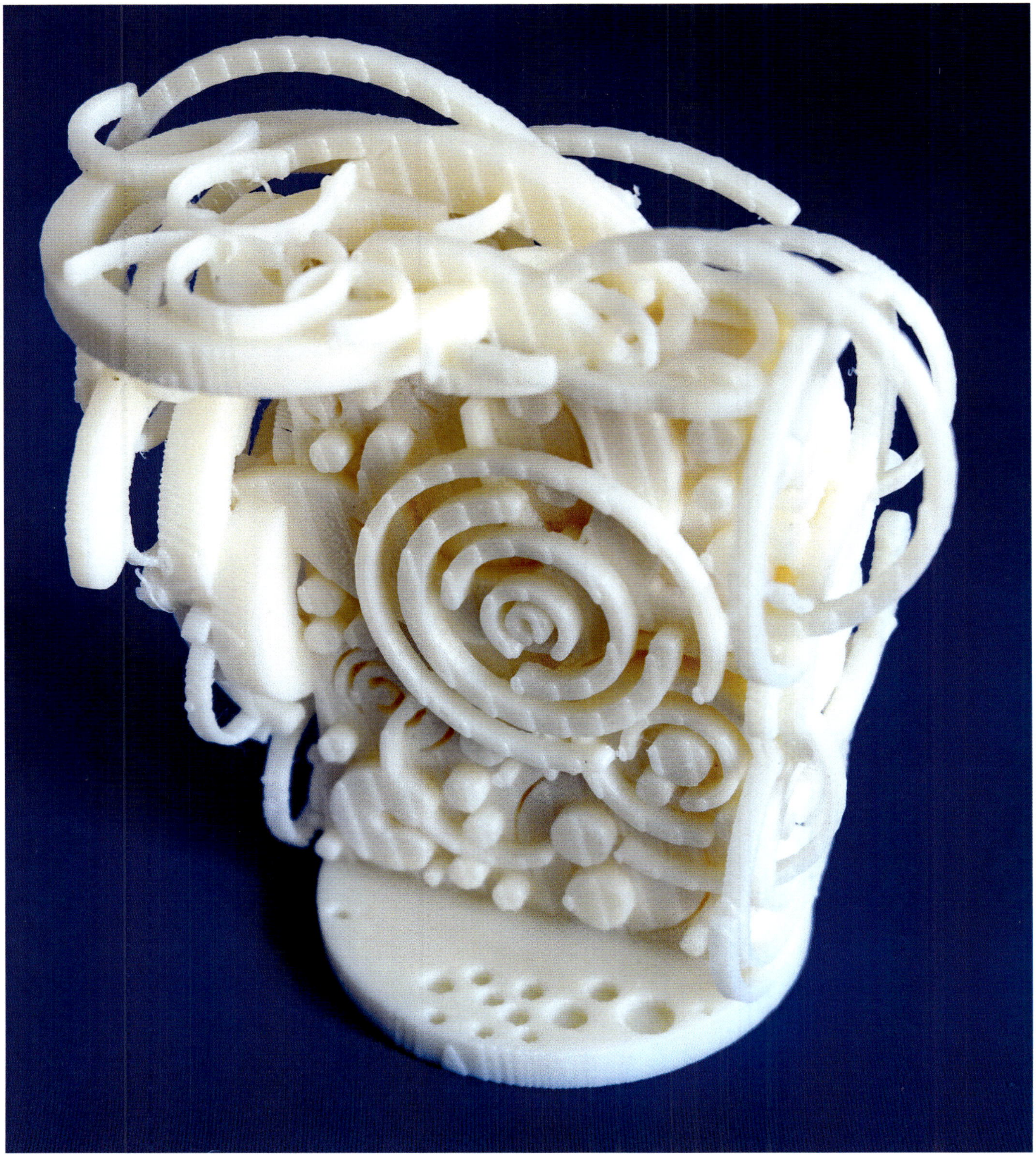

Frances Murray

Working with both small and large-scale monoprints, Frances uses intaglio, relief and carborundum to make work which draws on elements of the physical landscape. These are largely made as a series and use juxtaposition, colour and grid forms as metaphors for inner histories and spaces.

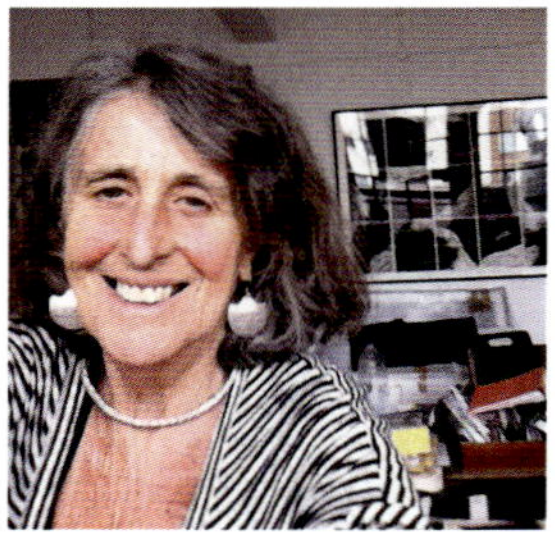

Born Uruguay. Studied at Oxford University (BA Modern History).

1989–99 Sir John Cass; London Guildhall University BA Fine Art; Ontario College of Art, Canada; Wimbledon School of Art; Camberwell College of Art, MA.

Selected Exhibitions:

1997 Pitshanger Gallery, London

1998 *International Triennale*, Lahti Museum, Finland
Salon des Graphiques, Curwen,London

1999 *London Contemporary Print*, Barbican

2000 Sarah Myerscough Fine Art, London

2001 National Theatre, South Bank, London

2002 Madelyn Jordan Fine Art, New York.

2003 Royal London Hospital, Whitechapel

2004 *Art on Paper*, Royal College of Art

2005 Jill George Gallery, London
Art London, Chelsea, London

2007 *Form*, Shirley Crowther Contemporary

2008 *Koridoor*, Istanbul Contemporary Art

2009 Pushkin House,London

2010–11 Freud Museum,London
London Group Open
Bite, Mall Galleries
RE Open, Bankside Gallery

2012 *Works on Paper*, Science Museum, London (Award)

2015 *i-contemporary*, Hampstead
Affordable Art Fair
20/21 International Art Fair, Royal College of Art

Initially made as part of a folio or journal, the prints use visual and written notes made over time to convey both symbolic human association and metaphorical landscape. Born in Uruguay and trained in the UK, Frances works from her East London studio, a member of both Space, East London Printmakers and the Printmakers Council. She curates, works to commission and exhibits widely.

Work is held in the public collections of the Bank of England, Merrill Lynch, the Hannah Peschar Sculpture Garden, Scott Bennett New York, Rosenberg and Estis NYC, with site-specific work for Independent Franchise Partners, London, Area 2, Helengreendesign.com, Artefact, Inside Space, Collett-Zarzycki, Workplace Arts, Fox Linton, Studio Mark Ruthven, XS Space, Brooklyn, Clifton Interiors, Tina Wilkinson Design,and commissions for private collectors in the UK, USA, Japan, Jordan and Switzerland.

OPPOSITE

Wall Notes 16 Installation, 140 x 140 cm, carborundum and relief (monoprint)

Untitled 1, 87 x 116 cm, intaglio and relief (monoprint)

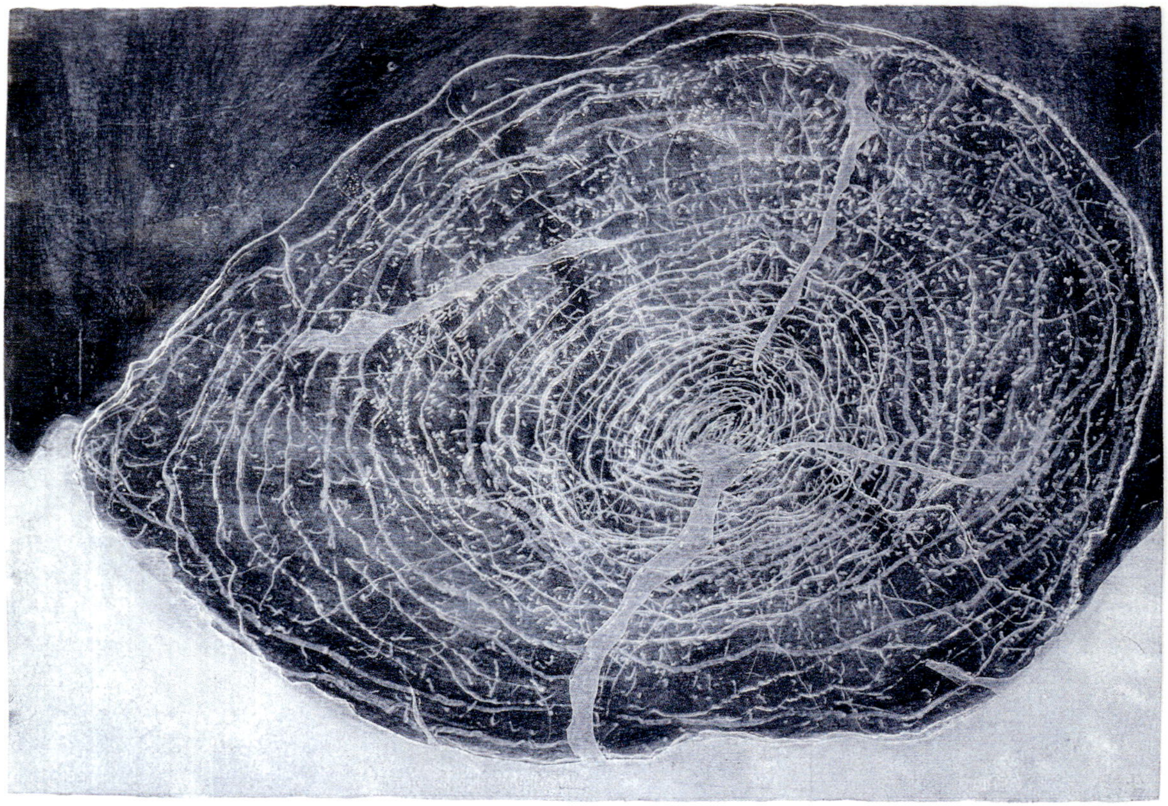

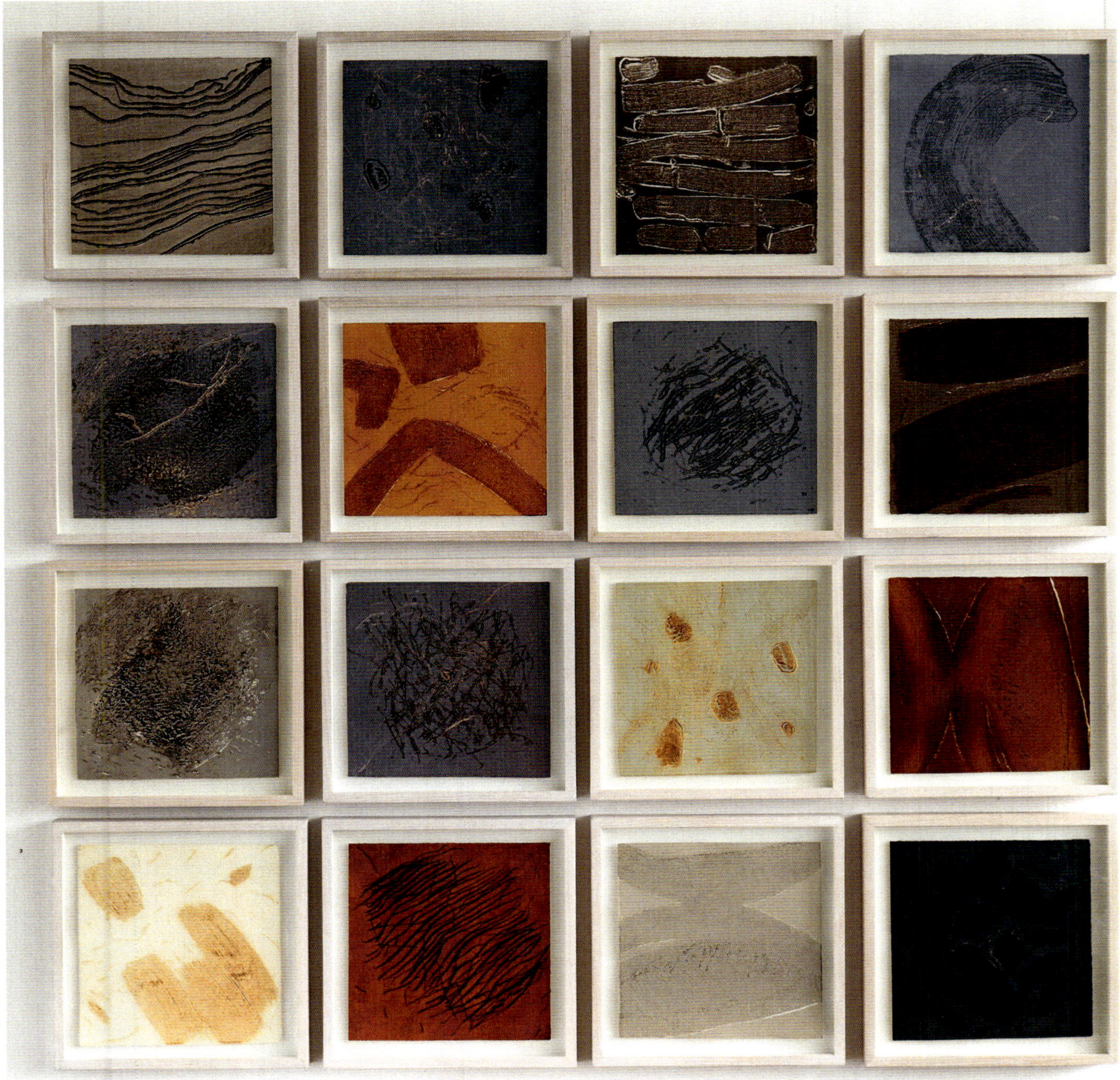

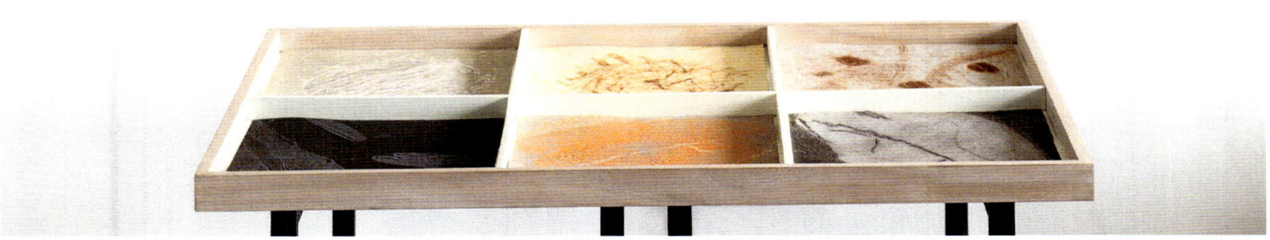

Maureen Nathan

While working towards a Portrait Painting Diploma at The Heatherley School of Fine Art, time spent in the print room led me to explore the possibilities of printmaking in relation to portraiture. Relief printing excited me: the strong connection to German Expressionist print work with its striking graphic shapes appealed and I also enjoyed the physical aspect of creating an image from wood or lino.

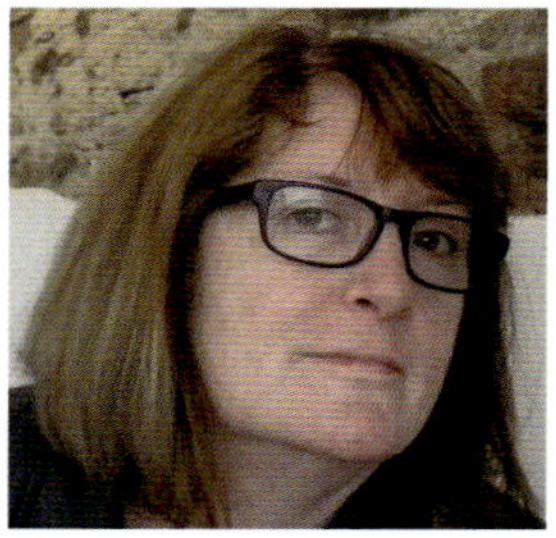

1954 Born Vancouver, Canada
1974 Emigrated to England
2006 *Royal Academy Summer Exhibition*, London
2010 *Perspectives*, group show, The Little Gallery, Beaminster, Dorset
2011 Selected for The Rootstein Hopkins Drawing Exhibition, London
2011–13 Heatherleys School of Fine Art, Chelsea, London. Diploma in Portrait Painting
2012 Royal Society of Portrait Painters Annual Exhibition, Mall Galleries, London
2013 Selected for The Rootstein Hopkins Drawing Exhibition, London
2014 *Year of the Horse*, Proof Gallery, Toronto, Canada
2014 Group show Gallery 50, Toronto, Canada
2014 *Portrait*, Espacio Gallery, London
2014 *National Open Art Exhibition*, Somerset House, London
2015 Joined Printmakers Council
2015 *Rev It Up*, celebrating Women's History Month, Espacio Gallery, London

My art practice is based on drawing, a fundamental part of image-making, whether painting or printmaking. I work figuratively and mark-making is the visual language that I use to express myself. Over time I have realised that it is also the way that I deal with the context of my life. This gives my art a more personal significance rather than a public one, at least initially, while still in the studio stages. The meaning in my work is personal before it is public and rendered primarily through my relationship with it. My art allows me a dialogue with myself, a way of working things out, to place myself in relation to the world I live in.

I am drawn to relationships between people and the narrative that exists when people engage with one another and often when they don't. Lack of engagement can work like the negative space in a composition, highlighting the emotion in the narrative even more. Cross-cultural exchanges have been a theme I've explored recently as a result of spending time in different neighbourhoods from my own in London. My current work is based on the theme of illness, its impact on relationships and the emotions that facing up to mortality can induce.

My favourite printing method to date is linocut. I draw with cutting tools straight into the lino, sometimes using sketchbook drawings as reference, but most often from life with the subjects or motif in front of me. The act of manipulating the material by hand while creating the composition and the active creation of the image give me a great deal of pleasure. The magic moment of pulling the first print is always exciting. I enjoy learning about using shape and form through the medium of printmaking to create depth and weight in an image, and find that it translates into a clarity in my painting work too.

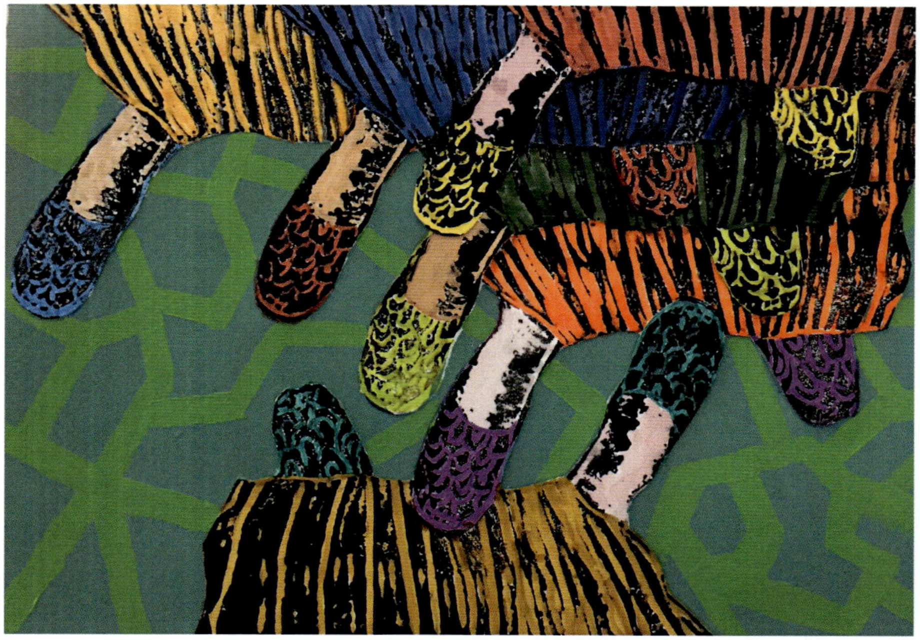

Casbah, at the Medina,
200 x 150 cm,
linocut, collage, ink and paint,
(edition of 1)

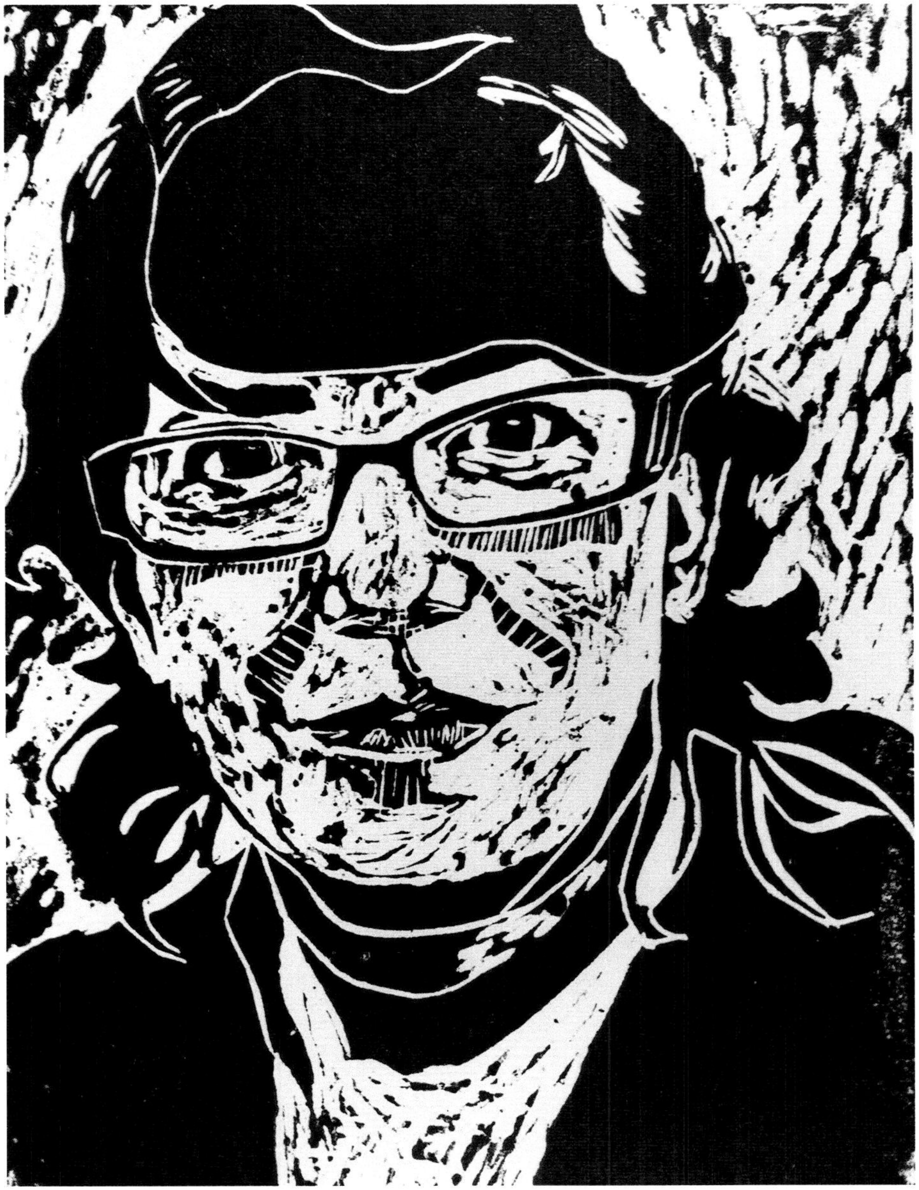

Zoraida
15 x 20 cm
linocut
(edition of 6)

Glynis Jones Owen

As a sculptor and printmaker, I am excited by the practical and direct approach required by the two disciplines. Exploring the links between them offers endless possibilities. The transfer of an idea from the three- to the two-dimensional fascinates me in the search to discover ways in which a concept can suggest new directions.

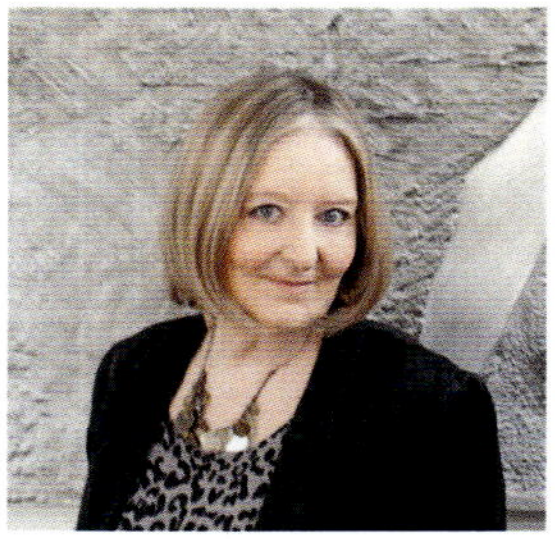

1945 Born Gravesend, Kent
1966 BA Fine Art, Portsmouth College of Art
1967 ATC University of London, Goldsmith College
1967–95 Teaching in schools and colleges, private classes
1976–82 Authored three books on Sculpture Techniques, Batsford
1976 Associate, The Royal Society of British Sculptors
1990 Fellow, The Royal Society of British Sculptors

Print Exhibitions

2002–03 *Fresh Art*, Business Design Centre
2003 *Originals 04*, Mall Galleries
2003 *Royal Academy Summer Exhibition*
2008 *Printroom*, Hampstead
2013 *Affordable Art Fair*, Hampstead
2013 *Verge Art Fair*, New York
2014 *Affordable Art Fair*, Singapore
2015 *Royal Academy Summer Exhibition*
2015 *Affordable Art Fair*, Battersea, Brussels, Hampstead
2015 *Works on Paper*, Barbican Centre, London

Public and Private Commissions include

Jacqueline du Pré Music Building, St Hilda's College, Oxford. Tate Modern Education. Covent Garden Piazza (Jubilee Building). Teaching Awards Trust

Print Collections include

Lloyds Building, ING Barings Bank, Financial Risk Management, Tony Wilson, Nick Mason (Pink Floyd) and Annette Mason.

While studying for my degree in painting and sculpture, the appointment from the RCA of a new Head of Printmaking created an exciting, new dynamic in the department. This awakened in me a lifelong fascination with printmaking, in particular linocuts, and much of my spare time on the course was spent in the printmaking department.

I grew up in West Sussex and Hampshire where the silhouette and chalk contours of the South Downs formed the backdrop of my formative years. My earliest attempts at carving and mark-making started with random lumps of chalk, found lying around a local quarry. The undulating lines, curves and textures of the landscape felt part of my identity. This formed an influence and visual reference that later translated into a pared-down imagery where a theme of 'figure in landscape and landscape in figure' underpinned much of my work.

My attraction to sculpture came through an excitement with the process of making, responding to the material and the ways in which a concept could be developed through the intrinsic qualities of surface, texture and form. Lino and woodcuts share similar attributes in the direct, decisive approach of cutting line and creating texture using a range of cutting tools. This cross-fertilization between the two disciplines is a vital part of my practice.

Moving to London in 1984, the excitement and pace of living in a capital city brought a new and stimulating visual resource. My work focused on taking recognizable figurative elements and losing their identifiable detail as with faces in a crowd or a pixelated screen.

In parallel to working on my own sculpture and prints, I was also undertaking large-scale public and private commissions. In 2007, an approach from a London architect resulted in an exciting collaboration that took my own work in a new and unexpected direction. In the search for the elements outlined in the architect's brief, requiring an abstract solution based on landscape imagery, I worked from graphite rubbings taken from surfaces around St Ives. Using varying grades of grit and sand, rather like a caustic etch in lino, this approach evolved into line, texture and burnished areas, cast as an aluminium relief panel.

The research involved in realizing this architectural installation changed the direction of my practice. Taking elements of the dimensionality of sculptural bas-relief, my focus is now printmaking.

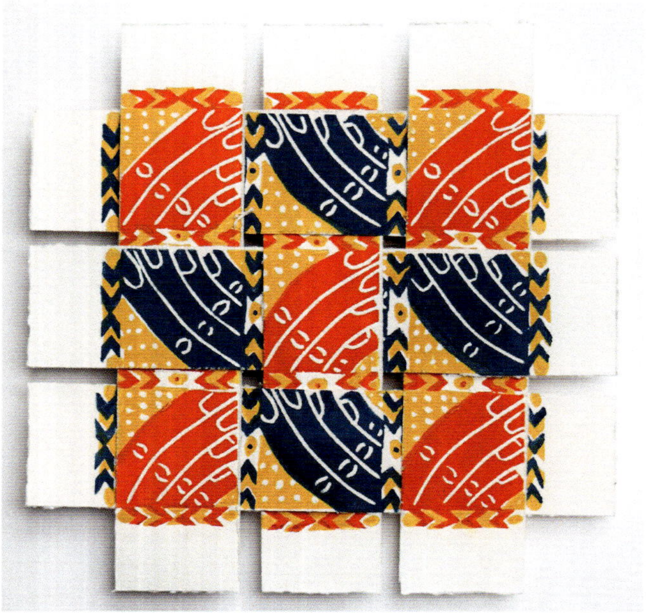

Weavatouch, 17 x 17 cm, linocut (edition of 10)

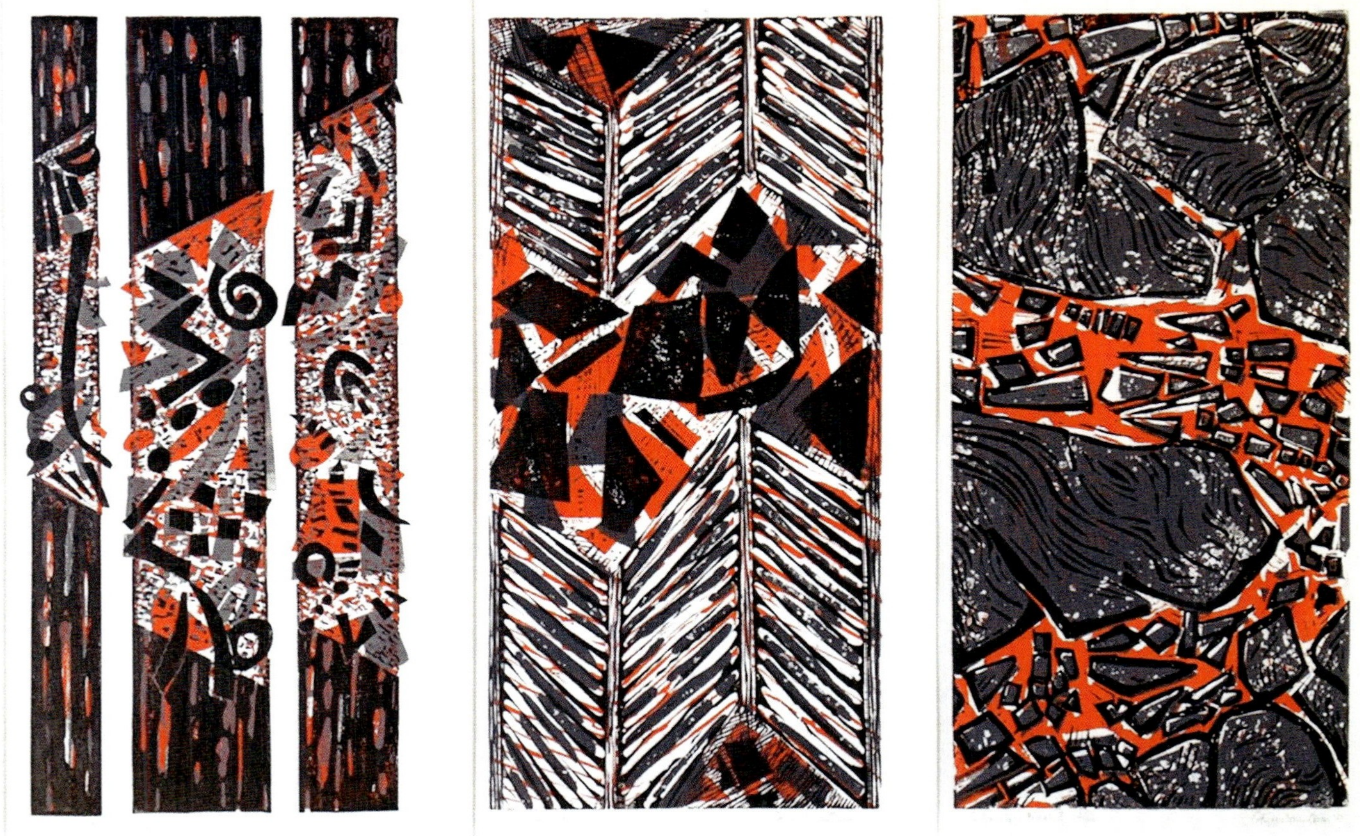

Sedimentary Shift (triptych), 60 x 100 cm, caustic etch linocut (edition of 20)

Theresa Pateman

After completing a degree in Fine Art, including the study of printmaking, I worked as a freelance illustrator using linocut and monoprint. After a brief sojourn into silkscreen printing, I started editioning for artists and etching at Morley College, which suited my love of line, tone and reinvention. I have a studio in Kingsgate Workshops, Kilburn.

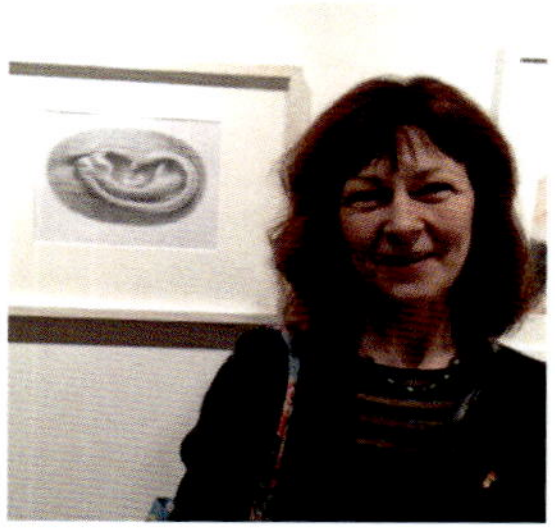

1962 Born Hannover, Germany.
1978–80 Foundation Art & Design, Thurrock Technical College
1980–83 BA Fine Art, Coventry College of Art & Design
1999 Boxed set of Millennium prints with GPA (collection V&A)
2000 Joined Southbank Printmakers
2002–present HSA Tutor Printmaking
2002 Artist Collaboration *A Slice of Ireland*, mixed-media show, London, (Collection at the Metropolitan University)
2004/2013 Solo shows at the Barbican Library
2005 *5th Miniature Print Show*, Bankside Gallery
2006 Curated *The Romantics*, The Millfield Art Centre, London
2007 Curated show, The University Women's Club, Mayfair
2007–10 Institute Arts Centre East Finchley, Tutor Printmaking
2008 Artist Collaboration *Mothers & Daughters*, drawing & mixed-media show, London
2009 Curated joint show for HSA & Institute Printmaking Students, Burgh House, London
2010 Pop–Up Shop, *Printmakers Inc.*, Woburn Place, London
2011–14 *Affordable Art Fair*, Hampstead Heath
2012/14 *Royal Academy Summer Exhibition*
2013/14 Co–curated *Microtopia*, miniature mixed-media shows, London
2014 Zilla Bell Gallery, Thirsk
2015 Coventry Drawing Prize Show, Rugby

In a recent exhibition based on the senses I was interested in exploring misperception and what triggers our interest in something. It appears that it all comes down to our earliest sense memories.

I take as my subjects everyday objects seen, heard, tasted, touched and smelt, choosing the most familiar take on a magical potency. From a printmaking perspective I love the glowing colours and textures that inks can create on paper. I work in a variety of printmaking media, but have a preference for soft-ground etching.

I was always interested in drawing and illustrating. My earliest memory is of drawing a bee which caught the attention of a teacher, and I suppose her encouragement started me off. It's wonderful to be allowed to sit, muse and create stories around what you are making. Printmaking satisfies my graphic instincts, but it is a strange life, not for the faint-hearted. Once entered, the artist finds a complex world of alchemy; although there are rules, strange things can happen even when the rules are followed to the letter. Your choice then is to go with it, or start again.

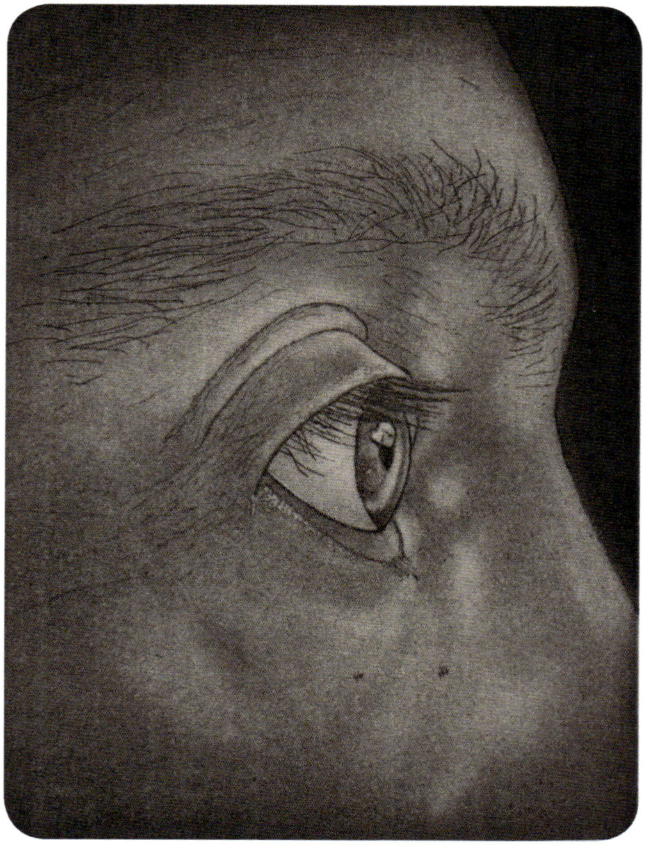

Sensibilia, 11 x 15 cm etching (edition of 50)

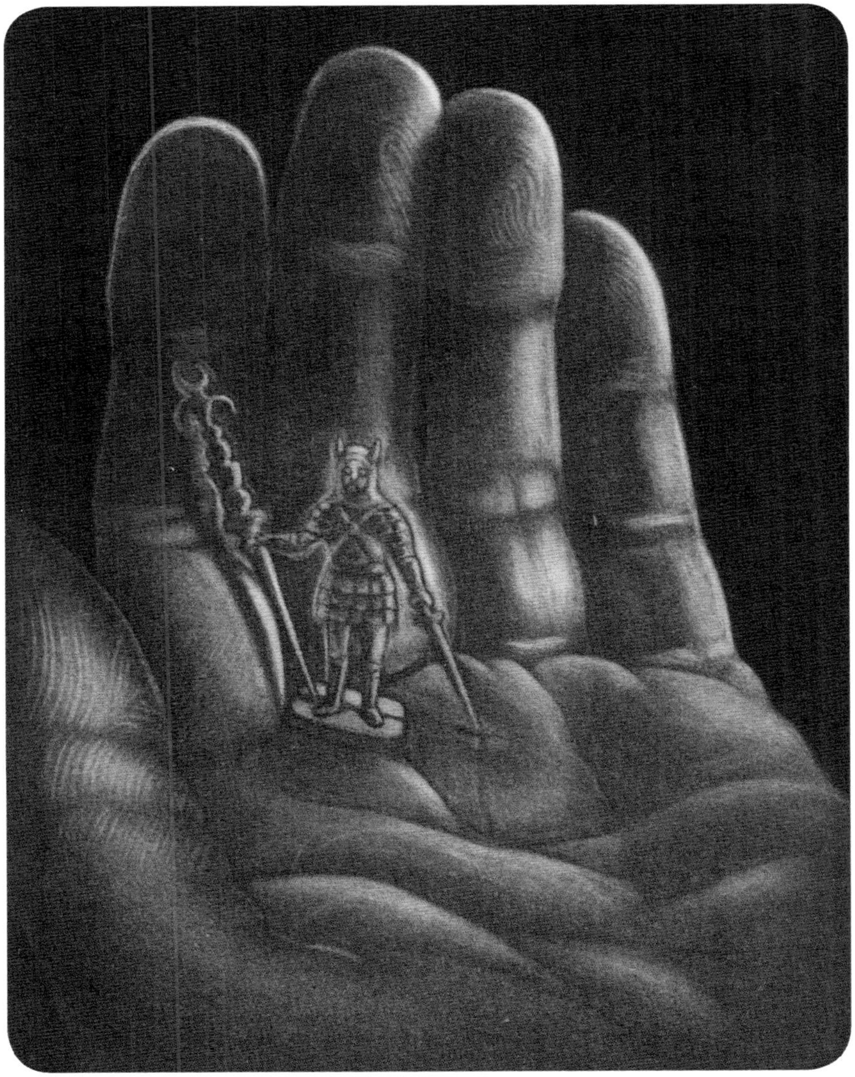

Ouch, 11 x 15 cm, etching (edition of 50)

There, there, 11 x 15 cm
etching (edition of 50)

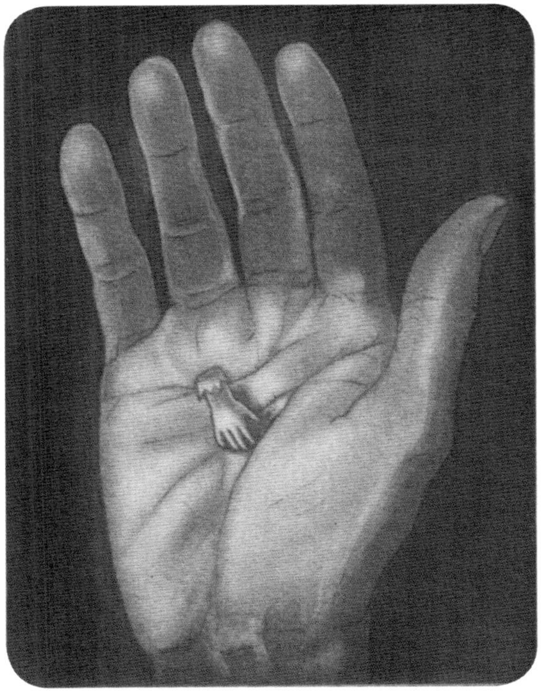

Bronwen Paterson

I have a multidisciplinary interest in art. This ranges from computer-generated graphic work to hand-constructed drawings and paintings. A combination of these can be seen in my work. I build up layers; some clearly thought-out, forming the initial base onto which I work and others spontaneous, leaving room for coincidental accidents. It is this surprise element that printmaking offers which excites me most.

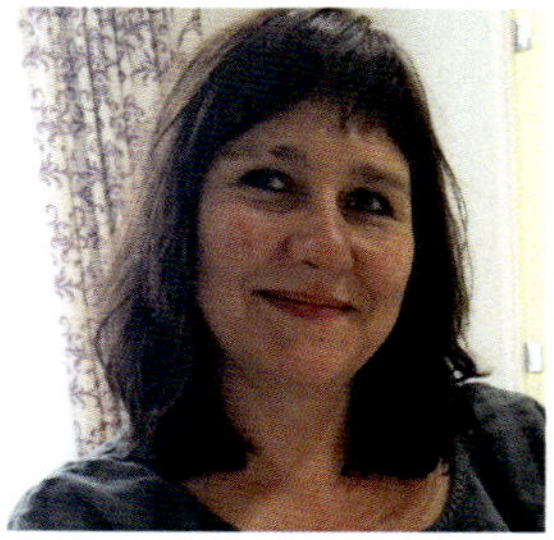

1969 Born Johannesburg
1997–99 Graphic Design Diploma studies, Technikon Witwatersrand, Fine Arts studies, University of Witwatersrand
2010 BA Surface Design, London College of Communication
2012 Joined Printmakers Council
2013 Joined London Print Studio & East London Printmakers
2014 Joined Southbank Printmakers

Exhibitions
2008 *Interprint*, Upper Street Gallery, LCC
2009 *FDA Surface Design* Exhibition, Upper Street Gallery, LCC
2009 *Free Range & All I Want for Xmas*, The Old Truman Brewery
2010 *New Designers*, Business Centre
2012 Kingsgate Gallery, West Hampstead
2013 *Mesh*, The Phoenix Cinema
2013 *Affordable Art Fair*, Hampstead
2013 London Print Studio Summer Exhibition
2013 *Microtopia*, Kingsgate Studios
2013–14 Pint Shop & Byard Art Cambridge
2013–2014 Byard Art, Cambridge
2014 *Multiplied*, Christie's, London
2012–15 *Affordable Art Fair*, Hampstead
Exhibited in many PmC Exhibitions

Collections
Victoria and Albert Museum

I grew up in South Africa. It is a place close to my heart and in the majority of my work I attempt to encapsulate images and memories from my past. These have a deep resonance for me. An example of this can be seen in *Ends in Tears*.

My subjects generally stem from the natural world and my objective is to raise nature to an almost religious or spiritual level. I get much inspiration from skulls and bones, more specifically the patterns and forms found in nature.

In *Orbit*, one of a series of bone studies, I have used the work as a meditation on the fragility of life. I have explored the objects from various angles illustrating the beauty of their form, shape and texture. In my opinion, a bone is a metaphor for existence. Although stripped of flesh, it symbolizes the very quintessence of life. Bones are mystifying, secret and silent. They hold memories and stories. By suspending them in space I hope to immortalize them and emphasize their celestial and ethereal quality.

I also get much pleasure in looking for and finding random objects, something not ordinarily valued by others. I can then exploit these and illuminate their visual potential. This forms another stimulus for my work as is demonstrated in *Found Fragment (Blue Mosque)*. Found objects can range from fragments of Old English pottery to a seashell or a wasp nest. I print and paint these small, beautifully patterned items on a grand scale thus emphasizing their overlooked beauty. I also like to explore the object in relation to its shadow. It is my view that the shadow holds as much weight and significance as the object itself and this gives the object status and validity. In summary, the essence of what I try to convey through my work is that beauty can be found in everything, we just need to take a closer look.

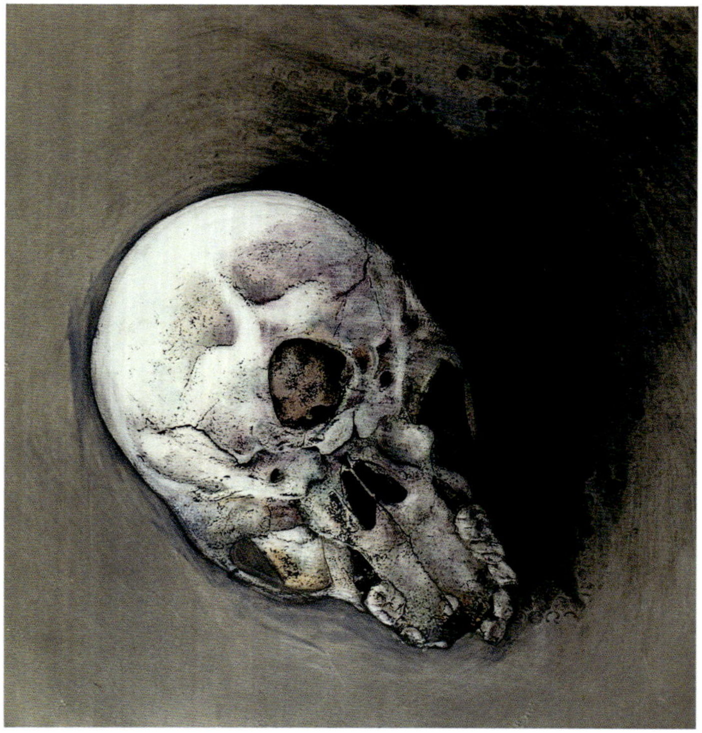

Orbit, 56 x 61 cm
screen print and monoprint
(unique)

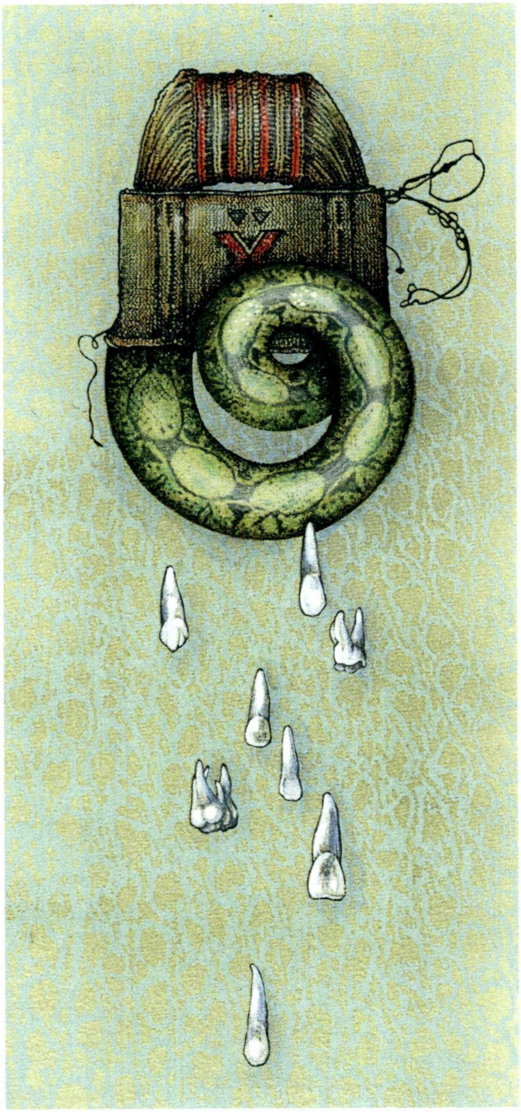

Ends In Tears, 41 x 18 cm
hand-coloured screen print
and monoprint
(variable edition of 3)

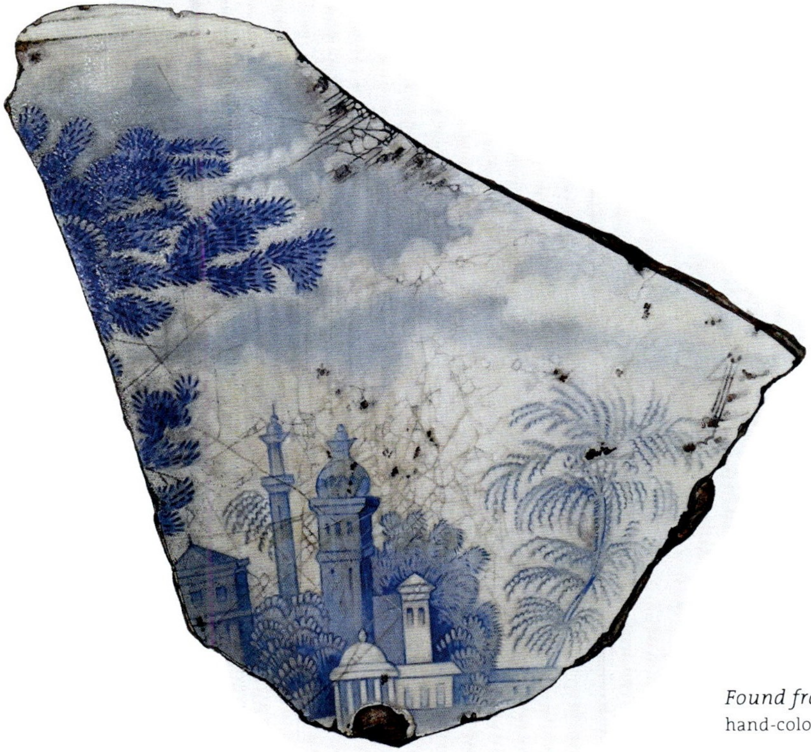

Found fragment (Blue Mosque), 52 x 48.5 cm
hand-coloured screen print (unique)

Sumi Perera

My multi-disciplinary artistic practice crosslinks traditional and contemporary techniques to generate hybrid prints that form artist books, mixed-media assemblages and installations. Printing plates are rotated and often overprinted to create different permutations. The final editorial control is usually reversed, by offering the viewer/reader the option to rearrange the sequence of pages, or to realign print modules in different combinations.

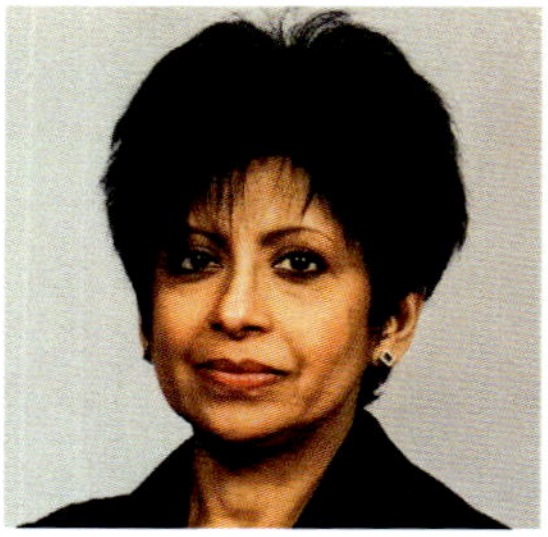

1956 Born Sri Lanka
1983 MBBS Faculty of Medicine, University of Colombo, Sri Lanka
1994 & **1996** MSc & MPhil London School of Hygiene and Tropical Medicine
2004 MA Camberwell College, University of the Arts, London
2005 Birgit Skiöld Award ICA, London. Grand Prize 1st International Bookarts Competition, Seoul, South Korea
2008 1st prize at *SHELTER*, Boston, USA
2009 Best Overall Book Design Prize (NPB) & 1st Prize Complete Book – Soc. of Bookbinders International Competition & Conference SCU Award, Australia
2011 1st Prize *Rootstein Hopkins Drawing Exhibition*, London
2012 Prize & Award at *DRAW 12* London Intaglio Prize *Printathon*, London
2014 The Arqadia & Intaglio Print Award at *DRAW 14* London
2015 *Prix de Print USA* Incline Press, Dave Gordin Award, Society of Bookbinders International Conference
Public Collections: Tate Britain, V&A Museum, Ashmolean Museum; Yale Centre for British Art, USA; Guanlan Museum, China; Sakima Art Museum, Japan; Bibliotheca Alexandrina, Egypt; British Library; SCU Collection, Australia; Iraq National Library, Baghdad; ULUS Collection, Serbia; National Taiwan Museum of Fine Arts, R.O.C; Grafisk vaerksted-Naestved, Denmark
Exhibitions: Royal Academy, ICA London, Whitechapel Gallery, Barbican

I have been printmaking since the age of three, an avid vegetable stamper. I grew up within a 'make do and mend' culture where recycling was encouraged. Perhaps this explains my desire to re-generate multiple images from a single plate.

The artisanal qualities of process are as important as the conceptual elements, and sometimes even overrides the final product which is often left intentionally 'unfinished'. Printmaking allows me to experiment and preserve all the raw stages (proofs) that no other technique offers. The evolution or 'events' are documented as variations on the theme, preserving and presenting almost all 'pulls'. Sometimes, seemingly parallel projects converge and form hybrid products. The theme of a series would generally dictate the technique, process and materials that I choose: for instance in *Cast Offs* (a series on knitting), ten strips of discarded metal (offcuts) of varying widths (to mirror different yarn thicknesses/needle gauges) were used to construct different knitted garments. This composite print was acquired for the Guanlan Museum Collection, China (2008). Sandblasted and etched glass sheets were the prototype relief plates used for the series *Shattering The Glass Ceiling* (Freud Museum, 2011). Vintage clip-on white collars were the inspiration for mezzotints for *Top 10 WCC [White Collar Crime]* an artist book, acquired for the Tate Britain & Leeds Library Artistbook Collection (2015 & 2014). Lithography was used for a series on translation/transcription/transliteration inspired by the Rosetta Stone. Maps and photographs of cracks/gaps on the underground were used to devise *Mind The Gap*, initially a 50-metre installation at Bankside, which was recreated in the Shoreditch Townhall Basement for the exhibition *Going Underground* (2013). The etching plates were reunited and placed within their respective niches and prints.

Often the work is site-specific. The most recent series is titled *IO-OI* [Inside Out - Outside In] and was designed for the Museum in the Park, Stroud, the West Yorkshire Print Workshop, Bankside Gallery, and the Embassy Tea Gallery (2015). Architectural plans of my house, the sites and road maps were incorporated for this series.

I have several ongoing collaborative projects that involve participants from many different countries, which will be showcased at the Centre for Fine Print Research, Bristol in 2016: *Perception* (exhibited at the Helen Keller International Award, 2007-), *Carbon Footprint* (exhibited at Carbonart, City Hall, London, incorporating footprints from a global database. 2008-), and *Work In Progress* (initiated by James Joyce's *Finnegans Wake*, shown at the exhibition: *James Joyce & Company*, Hadjigeorgakis Kornesios Mansion, Cyprus and the Bankside Gallery, London, 2014).

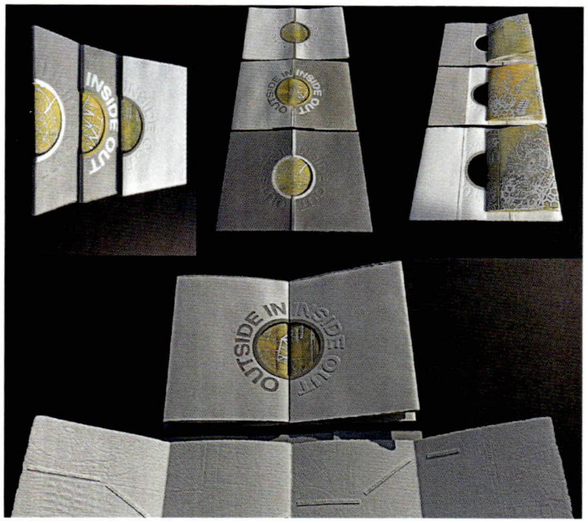

IO-OI [Inside Out - Outside In]-an artist book trilogy
etching, aquatint, embossing & stitch

Lines Exploring Space Outside The [Building] B(l)O(cks)X [XII], relief embossing & stitch

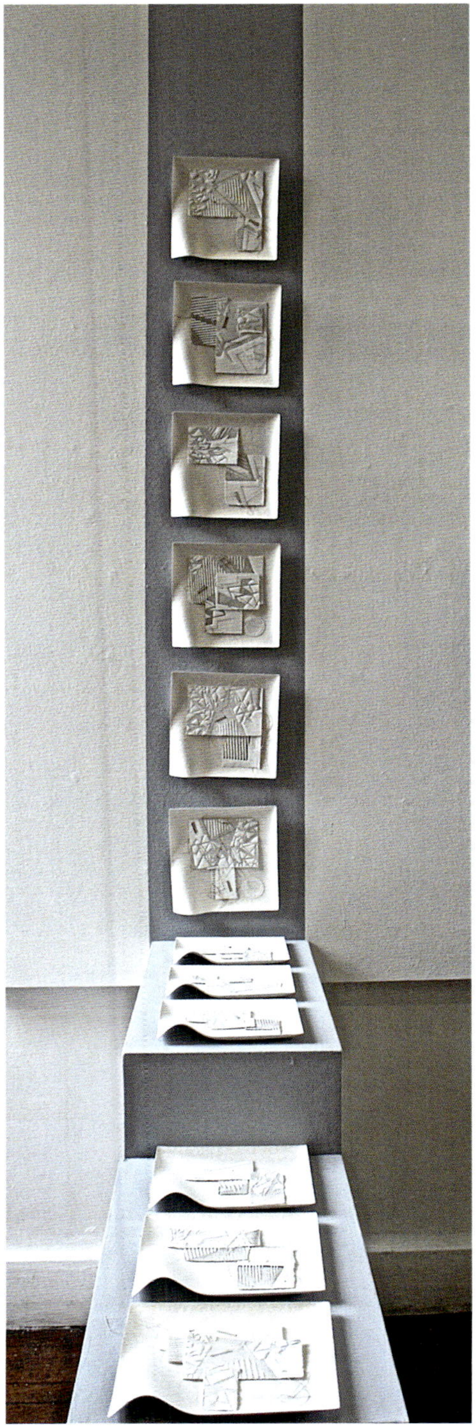

Inside Out-Outside In, etching, aquatint, embossing, stitch & incision

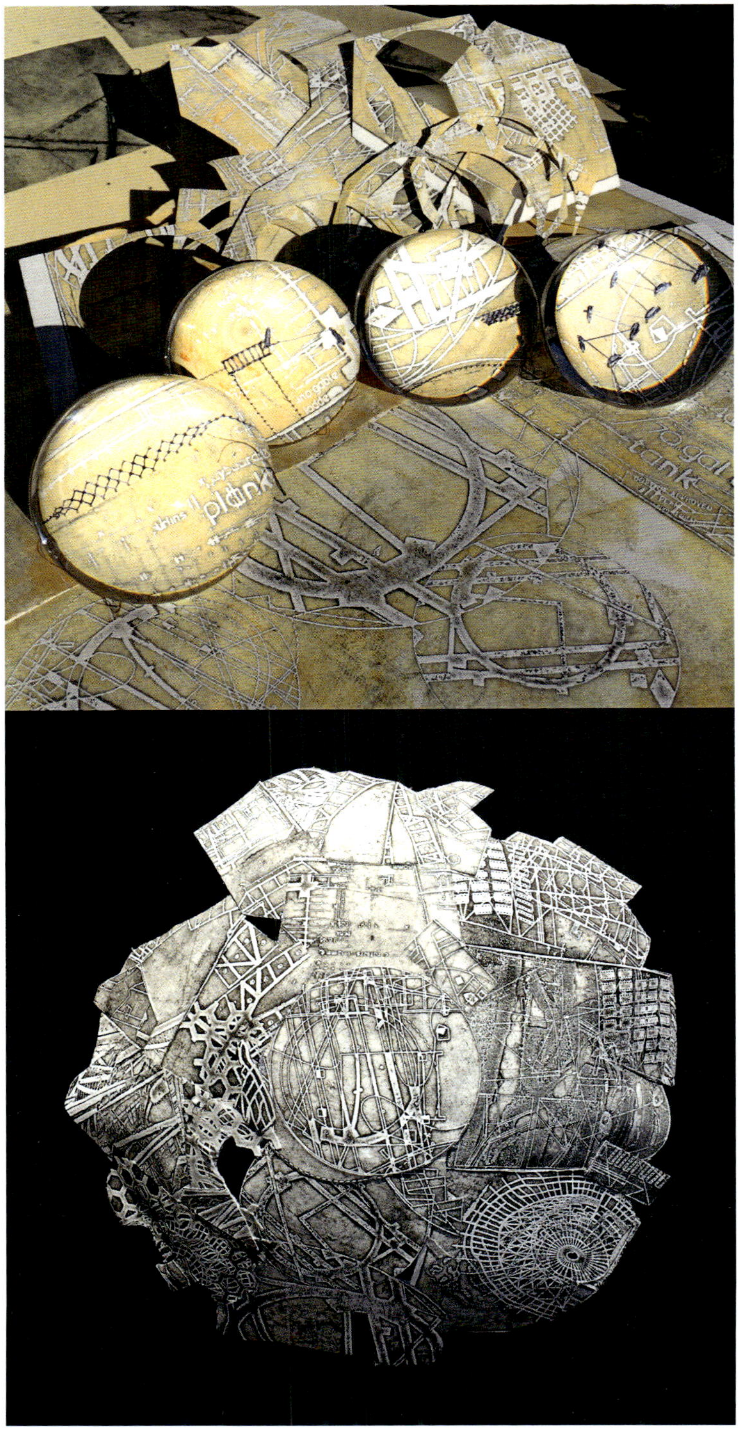

Monica Petzal

Monica is a painter, printmaker and art historian whose visual practice considers questions of history, memory and narrative. Concerned with the problematics of war, asylum seekers and reconciliation, she seeks to make visual histories which reflect both the personal and the political.

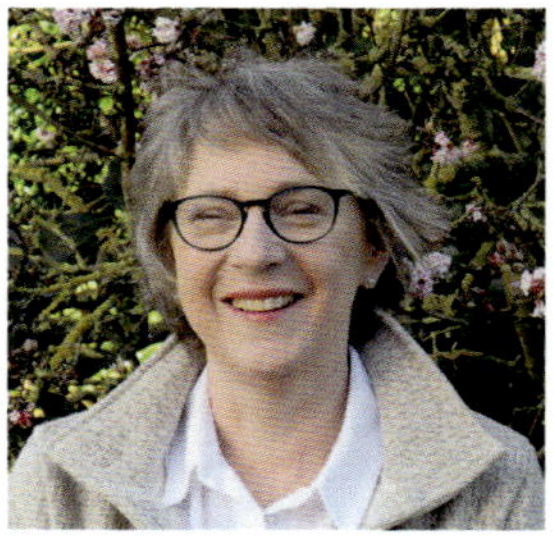

1953 Born London
1976 BA Fine Art Painting, Kingston University
1977 MA History of Art, University of Sussex
1981 MA Fine Art Painting, Royal College of Art
1990 Fellow, Royal Society of Arts
1992–2006 Director, Foundation for Women's Art
2001 MA Printmaking, London University of the Arts, Camberwell
2006 Owner, Printroom Gallery
2008 Selector for *7th British International Mini Print Exhibition*
2008– PmC Committee
2009 Selector for *Originals 09*
2010 Invited artist selector for *Originals 10* and *Pushing Print* in Kent
2014– Trustee, The Dresden Trust

Recent Group Exhibitions

2012 *Lost for Words*, UCLH Arts
2012 *British Printmaking Japan*, Kyoto Museum, Japan

Solo Exhibitions

2013 *Indelible Marks*, The Dresden Project, Printroom, London
2015 *Indelible Marks*, The Dresden Project, Dresden, Germany
2015 *Indelible Marks*, The Dresden Project, The Herbert Museum and Art Gallery, Coventry
2015 *75/70*, The Coventry Dresden Towers, Coventry Cathedral

Collections

New Hall College, Cambridge (Murray Edwards)
Sugar Quay House, London
Victoria and Albert Museum, London

Since 2012 Petzal has been working on The Dresden Project. The Dresden Project – *Indelible Marks* is an ongoing reflection on her maternal family. Made to further understanding and reconciliation, the project explores a rich family archive, contemporary historical documentation and the artist's own experience through the medium of print. The exhibition, shown in Dresden in 2015 as part of the 70th commemoration of the bombing of the city by the Allies, forms part of the 75th commemoration of the bombing of Coventry with an exhibition at the Herbert Museum in conjunction with an installation by the artist in Coventry Cathedral.

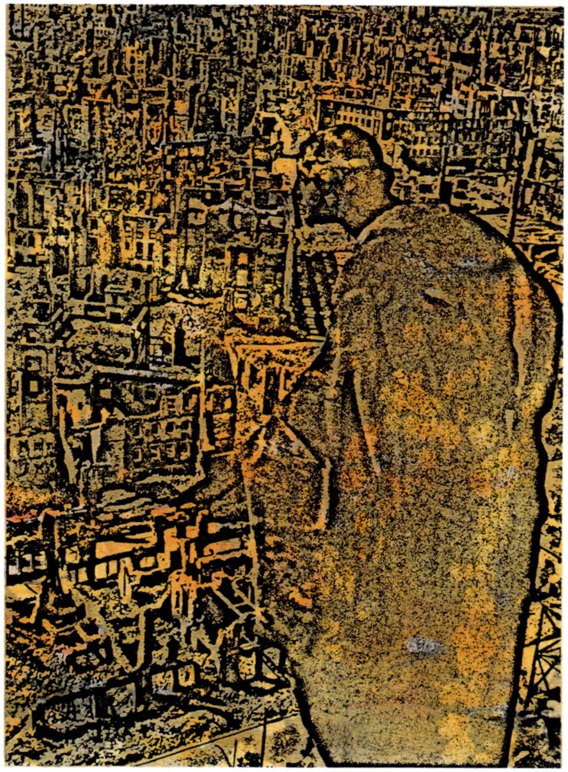

Dresden Destruction Series No 1
from a suite of 6 prints
60 x 42 cm
lithograph over monoprint
(unique)

The project was conceived in London and largely made at the Grafikwerkstatt Dresden. Worked mostly in photolithograph printed over painterly monoprint, the prints are created as one-offs or small variable editions. Woodcuts are printed in small editions.

Petzal is active as a gallerist running Printroom, a gallery specialising in contemporary printmaking and dealing largely in younger artists. The London gallery 2006–2014 now operates privately from Suffolk, at selected art fairs and online. She has curated/selected numerous exhibitions, including: *7th British International Mini Print Exhibition* 2008; *Originals 09*; and was invited to be artist selector for *Originals 10* and *Pushing Print* in Kent 2010. In 2012 she was the co-curator with Rebecca Salter of *Process and Innovation, British Printmaking Japan* for the Kyoto Museum, Japan.

13th February 1945 No 4
27 x 27 cm
lithograph over monoprint
(unique)

12th February 1945
62 x 88 cm
lithograph over monoprint
(unique)

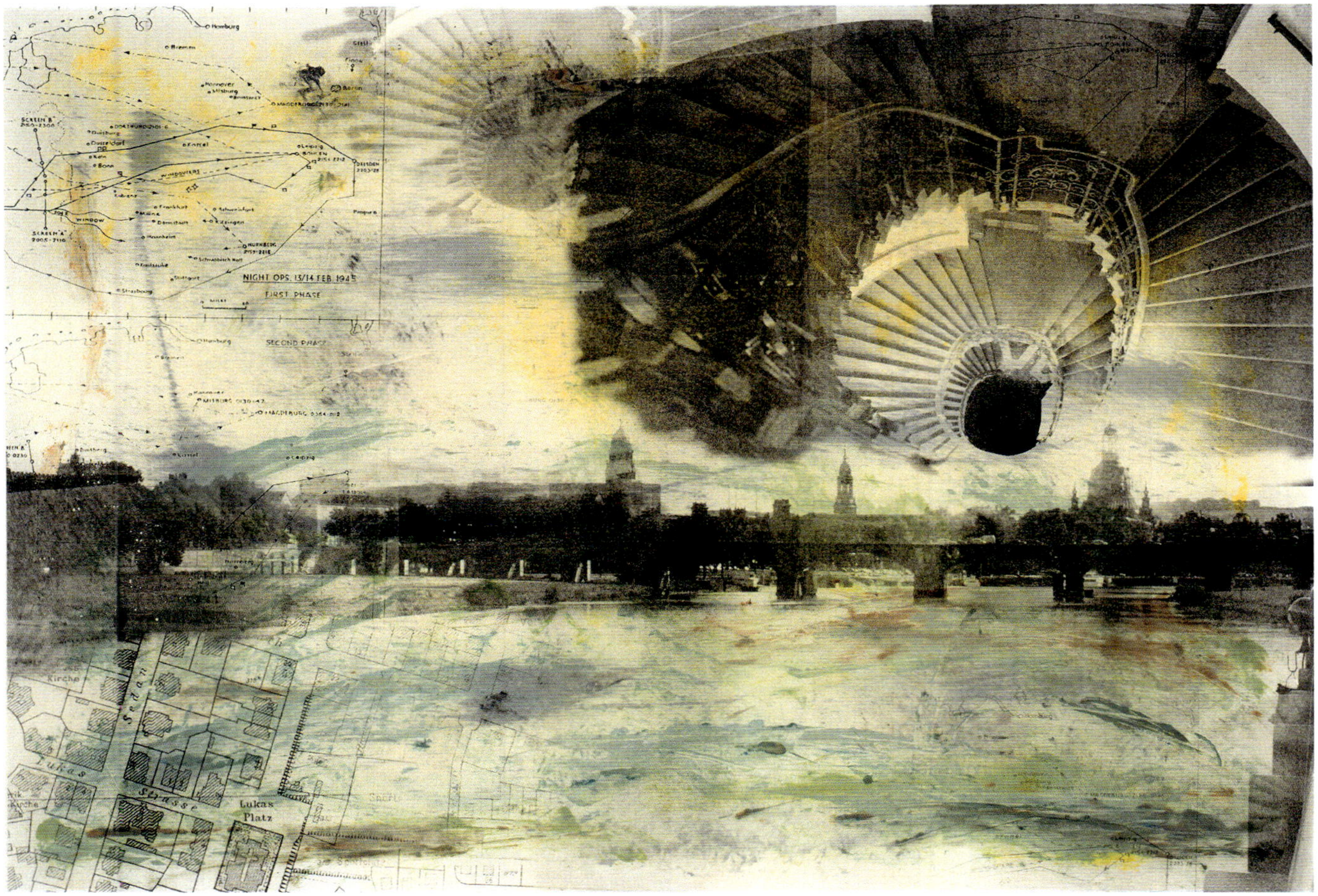

Helen Peyton

I am the Director and Artist in Residence of Smart Gallery (Social Museum & Art Gallery), where I invite the public to temporarily loan objects that they would like to see in my museum. My reduction linocuts are a direct response to these artefacts and inspire my ongoing love of objects, their stories, histories and association to our emotions.

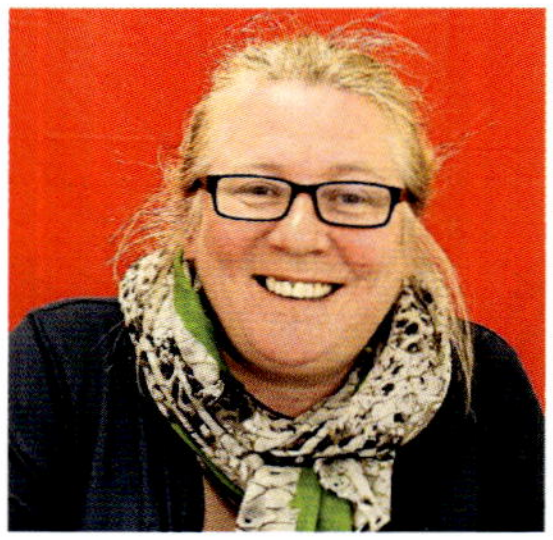

1993 Foundation Studies, Harrogate
1997 BDes (Hons) Printmaking, Duncan of Jordanstone College of Art, Dundee
1997 Royal Scottish Academy, Edinburgh
1999–2007 College Lecturer at Craven and Bradford Colleges
2003 Book - *Looking Up in London* (sole photographer credit) Wiley Academy
2003 Book - *Looking Up in Edinburgh* (sole photographer credit) Wiley Academy
2004 Book - *Fabulous Food Shops* (shared photographer credit) Wiley Academy
2005 Book - *Pub Scene* (shared photographer credit) Wiley Academy
2005–08 Creative Director of Visual Arts, Grassington Festival
2007–present Director of Granary Arts
2009–14 Artist in Residence Craven Museum & Gallery, Skipton
2009 & **2011** Mall Galleries, London
2011 & **2012** *Royal Academy Summer Exhibition*, London
2012 Filmed for ITV's *The Dales* and taught Adrian Edmondson to draw
2013 Cartwright Hall, Bradford with judges' commendations
2014–present Director and Artist in Residence Smart Gallery, Artist Ambassador Leeds City Art Gallery
2014 Book – *Low Tech* (shared print credit) Lawrence King
Flourish Award, West Yorkshire Printmakers
2015 Turner Prize nomination
Creative Practitioner at The Hepworth Wakefield

It was my residency at Skipton's Craven Museum & Gallery that sparked the inspiration for Smart Gallery. I had been Artist in Residence at the museum for six years, producing linocuts inspired by the collection. Using the museum's 1850s Britannia printing press I had become a kind of living exhibit, talking to people and helping them explore the printing process, as well as showing them things in the museum that were inspiring me.

From this participation with the public evolved the realisation that often what the public enjoys is different from what museum curators expect them to enjoy. For example, people would admire the Victorian dresses and appreciate the workmanship in them, but they wouldn't engage them. In contrast, when it came to the 1950s New World Cooker exhibit, people would suddenly talk animatedly about the memories it evoked... This realisation started my fascination with what the public might want to see in an exhibition, if they had the chance to choose.

So was born the idea for Smart Gallery, my unique concept of a social museum and art gallery which is created and curated by the public. All items are loaned to the museum for the duration of the exhibition, and literally anything will be considered for inclusion and display. With an assortment of artefacts that ranged from a six-year-old child's Chinese white rabbit sweets to a handbag made out of an armadillo, sourced on Charles Darwin's round the world voyage on the Beagle in the 1830s, to a ship's oil lamp that was given to an elephant so it could play football at night, there was an eclectic and fascinating variety of items amongst the 1200 exhibits and I was its artist in residence, responding to the artefacts using linocuts. It was hailed a critical success in Skipton with the artworks winning the Judges' Award at Flourish Printmaker of the Year 2014, as well as a Turner Prize nomination.

I am Artist Ambassador at Leeds Art Gallery and one of the few living artists that the gallery is still collecting. It means that my distinctive reduction linocuts are hanging among what has been described as "probably the best collection of twentieth-century British art outside London".

I have just been appointed Creative Practitioner at the Hepworth Wakefield, a prestigious opportunity and one which gives me unfettered access to the works of one of the world's most prominent artists.

Lino-reduction printing is time-consuming but it gives me such a thrill to see the artwork slowly emerge in the way I envisioned it and encourages the sculptor in me, the fine artist and the colourist. It's a superb medium for exploration. You can never fully master it and it will always drive your imagination.

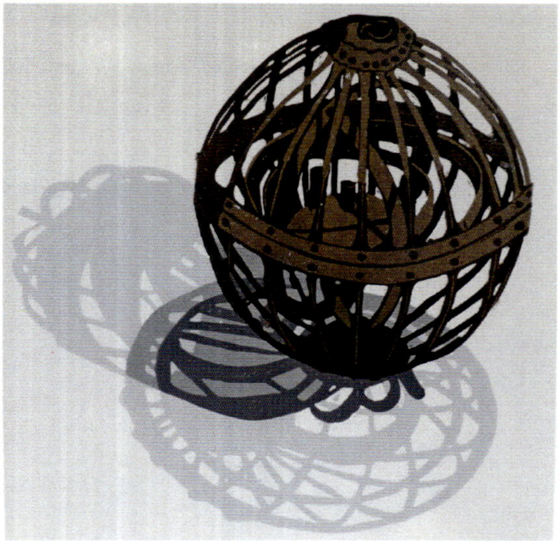

OPPOSITE
Bobbins, 30 x 30 cm
reduction linocut (edition of 15)

Elephant ball, 30 x 30 cm
reduction linocut (edition of 20)

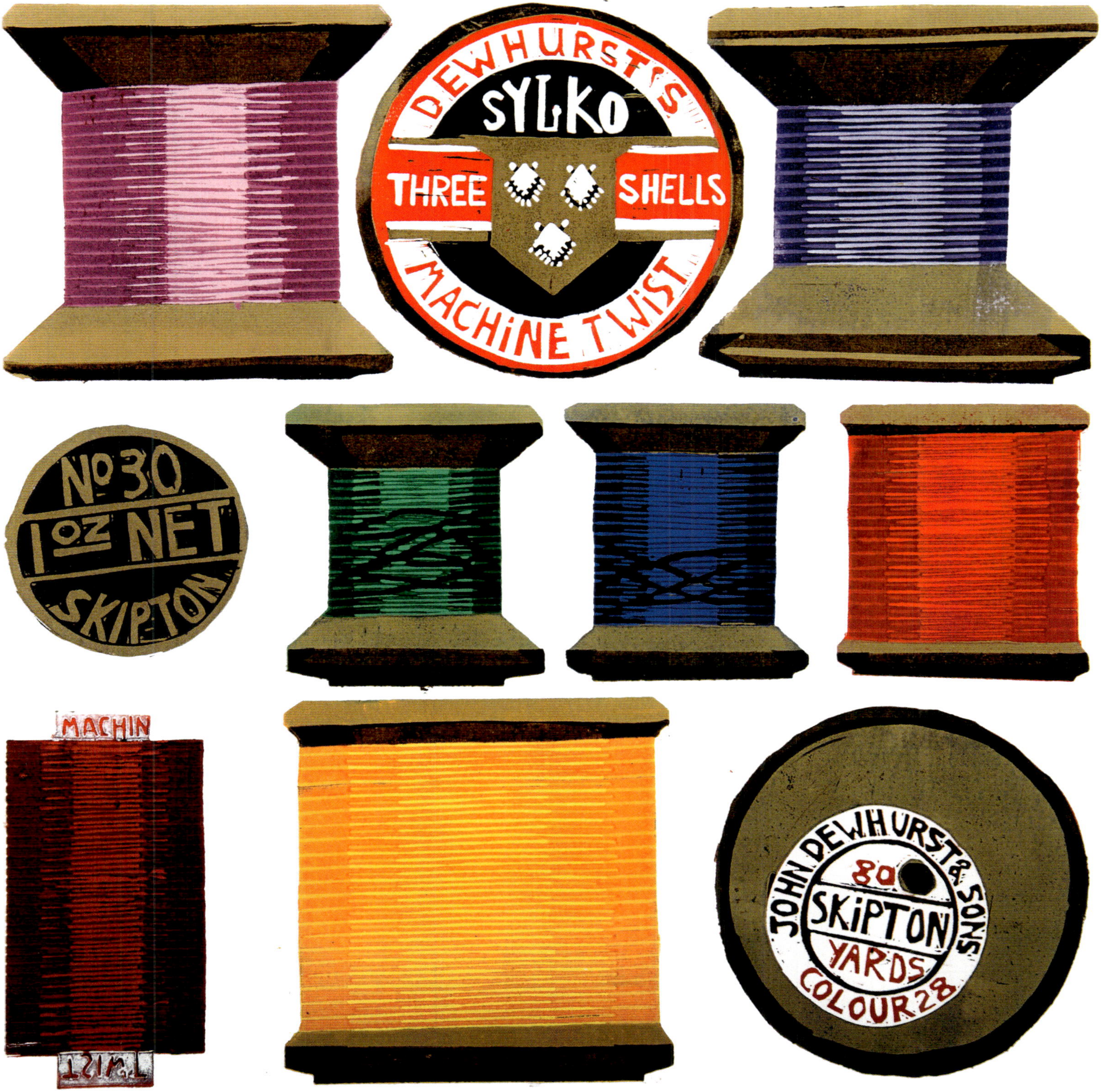

DEWHURST'S
SYLKO
THREE
SHELLS
MACHINE TWIST
No 30
1 oz NET
SKIPTON
MACHIN
JOHN DEWHURST & SONS
8a
SKIPTON
YARDS
COLOUR 28

Robert Pugh

Robert first saw prints by Degas, Bonnard and Picasso after leaving school and was strongly influenced by them before going to Art School at Byam Shaw. He made prints there and developed this further in evening classes at Morley College and Camden Arts Centre. Printmaking has become the central part of his work in the last five years. He makes prints at bip-Art in Brighton and also has his own press and etching equipment.

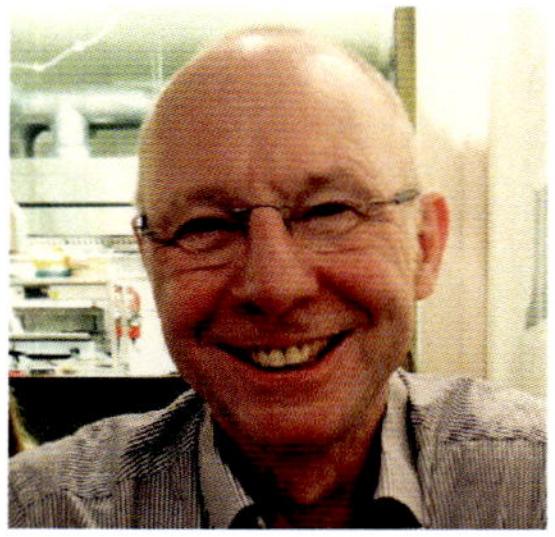

1950 Born London
1980 London Diploma in Art and Design (Distinction), Byam Shaw School of Art
1983–84 Printmaking Morley College
1985–87 Printmaking Camden Arts Centre

Mixed Exhibitions

1974, 1983, 1993 *Royal Academy Summer Exhibition*
1975 *Not the Royal Academy*, Chenil Art Gallery, London
1982, 1983, 1985 Portrait Award Exhibition, National Portrait Gallery
1986 Open Exhibition, Whitechapel Gallery
1986 *Figurative Paintings*, Jablonski Gallery, London
1991 Royal Institute of Oil Painters Open Exhibition, Mall Galleries
1993 British Transport Open Exhibition, Mall Galleries
2012–15 Brighton Independent Printmakers (bip-Art), *Affordable Art Fair*, Battersea
2013 East London Printmakers, Firefly Bookshop, Hackney
2014 *Works on Paper*, Barbican Library

People fascinate me and have been the subject of many of my paintings and prints. Sometimes I make landscapes, but there is always a human experience in them.

For some time I have wanted to make images of people that makes you feel their experience. *Squeeze* is one of them. I looked at a lot of images and found a photograph of a performance by Marina Abramovic. This was the starting point: the photograph made me remember and relive the discomfort of squeezing past somebody. I discovered that the performance itself was more complex. Visitors to the exhibition had to squeeze past Marina Abromovic and her partner, who were both naked. There was not enough room to go past them 'straight on' so the visitor had to go sideways facing one or the other. So there was an element of sexuality in the work. I like the way that the image initially looks like a straightforward experience but contained deeper, partly hidden, levels that develop the sensation of squeezing past a stranger.

Etching is an ideal medium for this kind of work because of its scale and the intensity of the marks. It enables you to develop images of a range of human experience and the fact that it is a multiple and not a unique, precious object makes its subject more accessible.

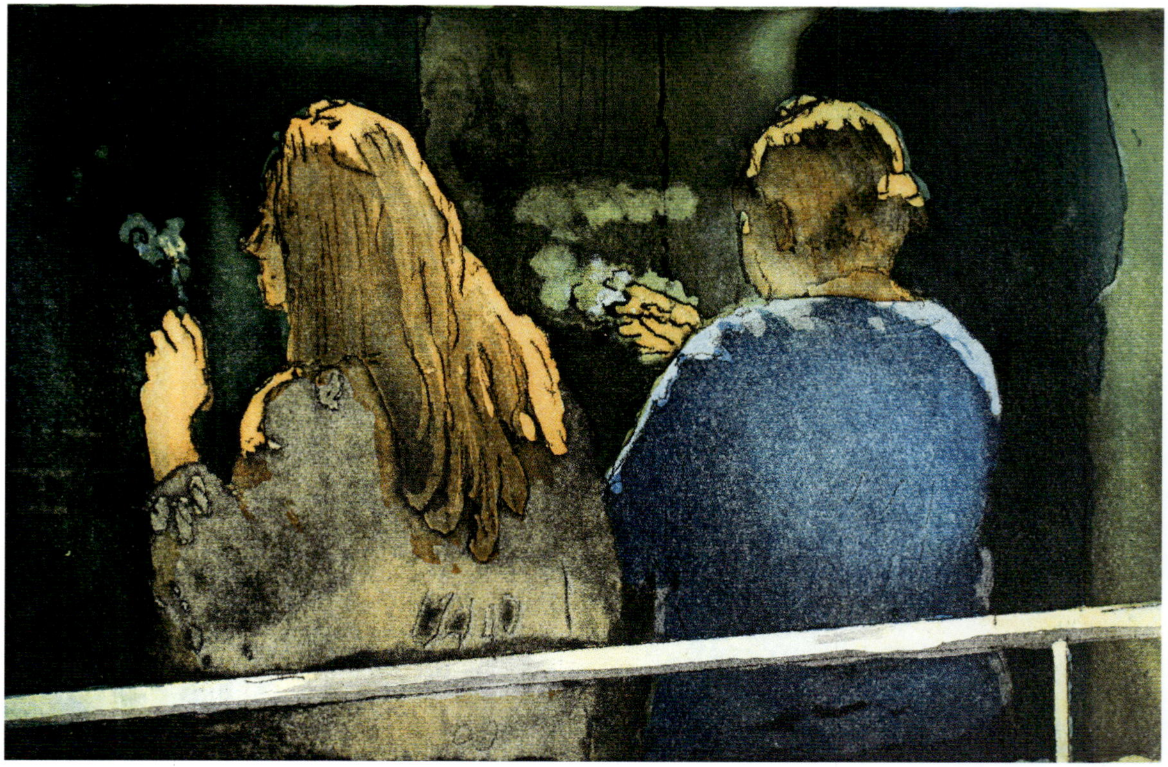

Smokers, 20 x 30 cm, soft-ground etching and aquatint (edition of 30)

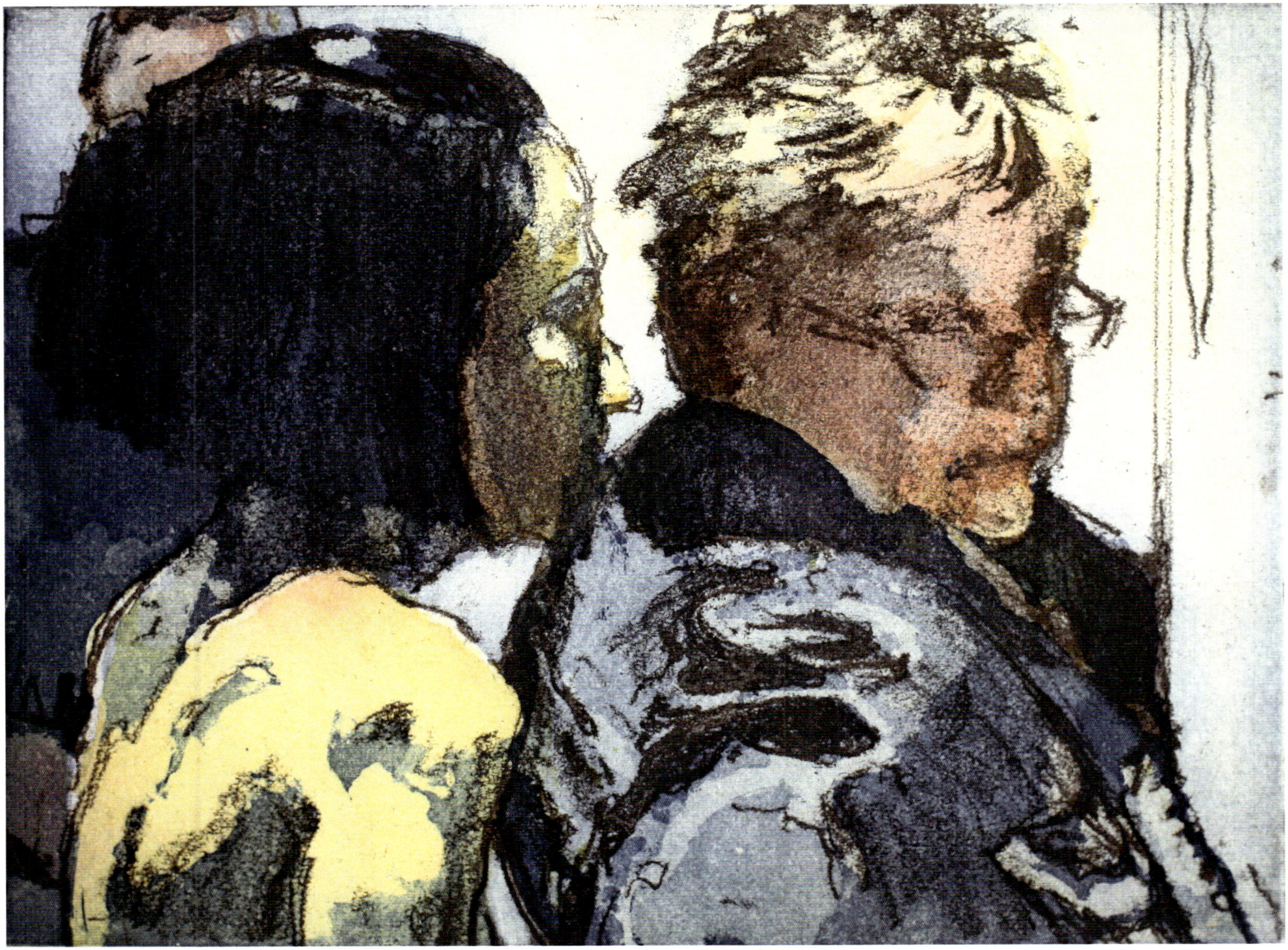

Squeeze, 15 x 20 cm, soft-ground etching and aquatint (edition of 30)

Venessa Pugh

I was attracted to printmaking because in addition to drawing I enjoy working with metal. I had explored using acids on metal when working as a jeweller and enameller and I already knew that I would like handling tools and machinery like an etching press. The prospect of being able to combine traditional skills with newer technology continues to present an interesting challenge.

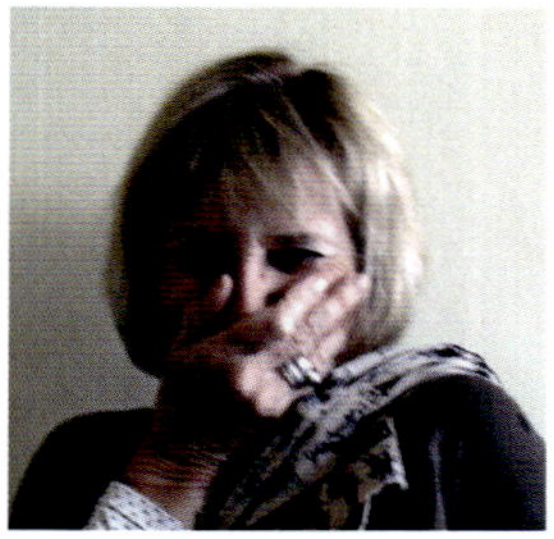

1949 Born Cardiff
1967–70 BSC (Hons) Psychology, University of Bristol
1971 PGCE, University of Bristol
1977 MA Urban Education, University of London
1982 City & Guilds Diamond Mounting, Sir John Cass Art College
1997 Art Foundation, Tottenham Technical College
2002 Fine Art course, The City Lit

Selected Group Exhibitions

2010 Mersea Arts Society, Mersea Island Museum; PmC, Highgate Gallery
2011 Cuckoo Farm Printmakers, Digby Gallery, Colchester; *Dreams*, Freud Museum; Vyner Street Gallery; *Kochi International Print Triennial*, Ino-Cho Paper Museum, Japan
2012 *Fields of Vision*, Orleans House, Twickenham; *Proof Perfect*, The Framers Gallery, Windmill Street; *Turn, Turn, Turn*, Margate Gallery; *Printathon*, Forman's Smokehouse Gallery
2013 *Not a Drop*, art event at 47 Tanner Street *Magical Mystery Tour*, The Upstairs Gallery, Beccles; Cuckoo Farm Printmakers, Benham Gallery; *Going Underground*, Shoreditch Town Hall; *Highgate - A Reflection in Print*, Highgate Literary and Scientific Institution
2014 *Freshly Pressed*, Craft Central, Clerkenwell *CMYK*, Pie Factory, Margate Summer Shows, Embassy Tea Gallery

Collections

Victoria and Albert Museum, Japanese Paper Museum, Kochi.

Printmaking appeals to artists like me who like to mess about and are happy to find that the end result is something of a surprise. I like the way the material I am working on interacts with the artist's intentions during the process of making. A particular knot in the grain of the wood, or an unintended scratch in an aquatint means the original design becomes adapted in unpredictable ways. The end result can be exciting and infuriating in equal measure.

Printmaking like jewellery is a craft as well as an art and both have a fascinating history. I like to experiment with different processes and materials and find that looking at other artists' prints and trying to decide how they were made is an addictive pastime. The social nature of printmaking and being in a studio with other artists is also a real bonus.

My subject matter is mainly landscape-based and I work both from sketchbooks and photographs, although I use the latter as a way of reminding me about a place and its unique atmosphere rather than as direct source material. I have spent a considerable part of my working life teaching refugees and their children and I am always moved by the personal reflections of people for places which mean a great deal to them and which they have left behind.

April in Minato-Ku, 22 x 14 cm, etching, (edition of 5)

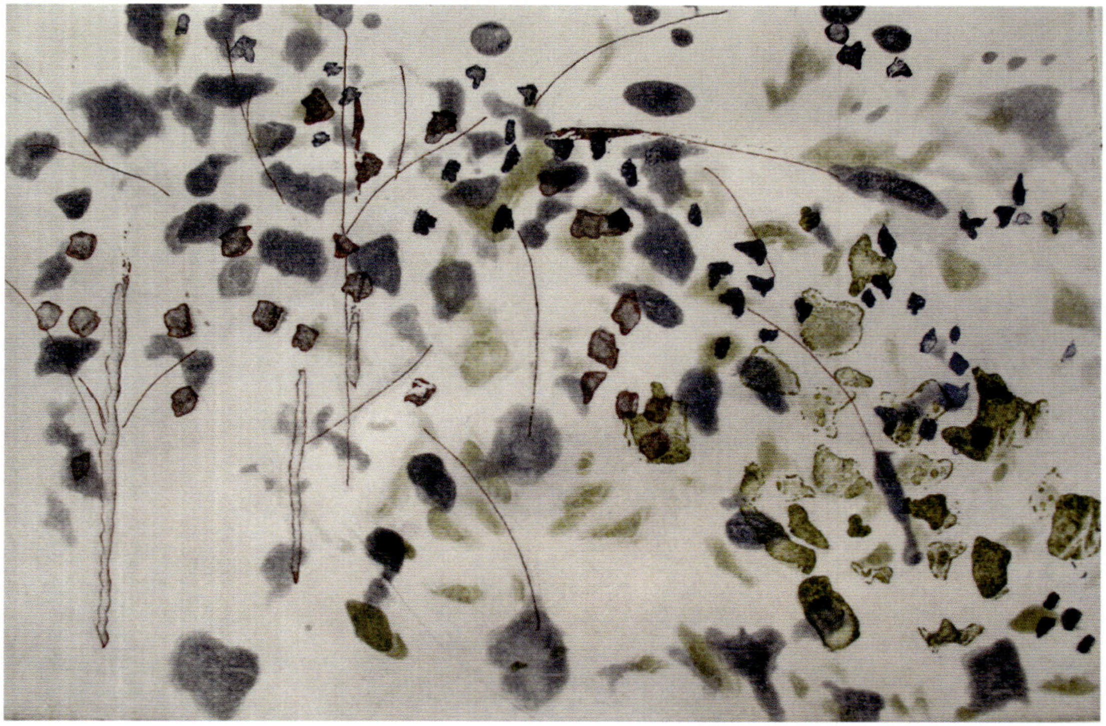

Still Waters, 18 x 18 cm, etching (edition of 10)

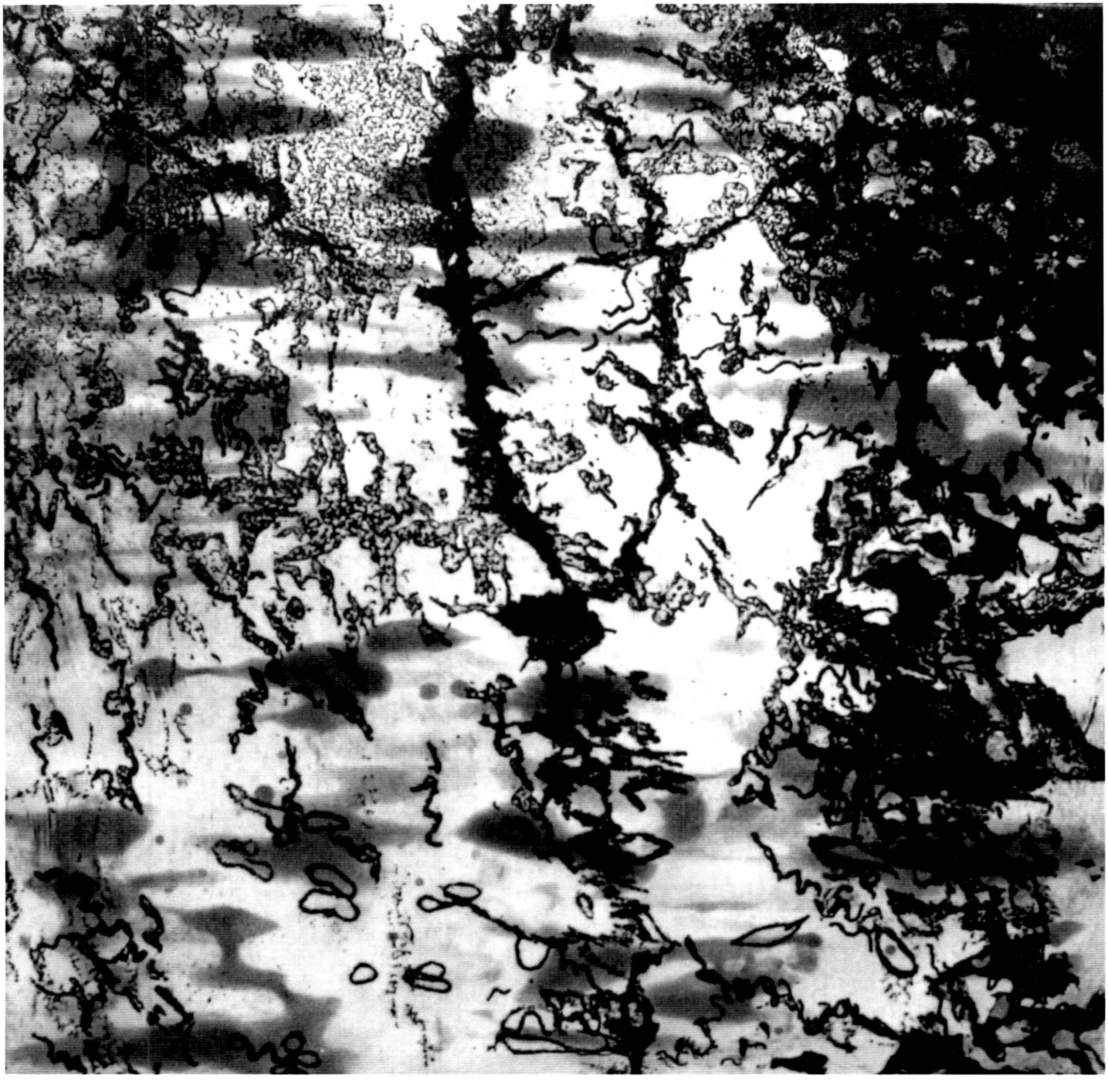

Daniela Rizzi

Daniela has been a PmC member since 1997 and was a committee member for fourteen years. Printmakers Council has been of crucial importance to her practice as an artist as she was encouraged to develop and grow as a printmaker. She is extremely grateful to Sheila Sloss, former driving force and chair of PmC, who sadly is no longer with us, for her help and support.

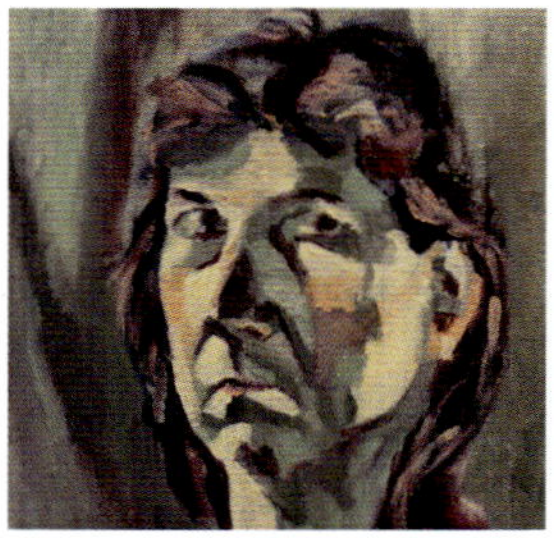

Daniela Rizzi's practice includes printmaking, painting, drawing, photography and mixed-media. She discovered silkscreen printmaking in the late eighties and has never looked back. Since then she has been working with printmaking techniques such as monoprinting, linocut, collograph, drypoint and etching.

The work evolves through the process of working and as such is intuitive, and part of it progresses with certain definitive ideas. Use of strong colour, formal and informal aspects of image-making and personal concerns define her artwork.

She exhibits regularly and has work held in the Victoria and Albert Museum and private collections. Daniela is a member of the Printmakers Council, East London Printmakers and a studio member of the Barbican Arts Group Trust.

1963 Born Italy
1991–94 BA(Hons) Fine Art Middlesex University
1995–96 PGCE Art & Design Middlesex University
1997–99 MA Printmaking Camberwell College of Arts
1997 Joined Printmakers Council
Michael Rothenstein Trophy Prize Winner
Solo Exhibition Chelsea and Westminster Hospital
1999 London Print Studio Prize Winner
PmC Open Biennale, Atrium Gallery London
Impact, Spike Island Artspace, Bristol
2001 Solo Show at Windsor Arts Centre, Windsor
The Royal National Theatre London
2002 Solo Exhibition at Egallery Luton
2003 *Fresh Art*, Islington Design Centre London
2004 The Society of Graphic Fine Art 83rd Annual Open Exhibition, Hotbath Gallery Bath
2005 *Art in the City*, The Geffrye Museum London
2006 Solo Exhibition at Crescent Lodge Dental Practice London
2007 *Here and Now*, Lauderdale House London
2008 *Presence of Place*, The Beacon Whitehaven
2010 Printmakers Council at Bankside Gallery London
2011 Joined East London Printmakers
2011 *Untitled*, Vyner Street Gallery London
2012 *Lost For Words*, UCLH London
2013 *Going Underground*, Shoreditch Town Hall London
2014 *CMYK*, The Pie Factory Margate
2015 *Works on Paper*, Barbican Centre London

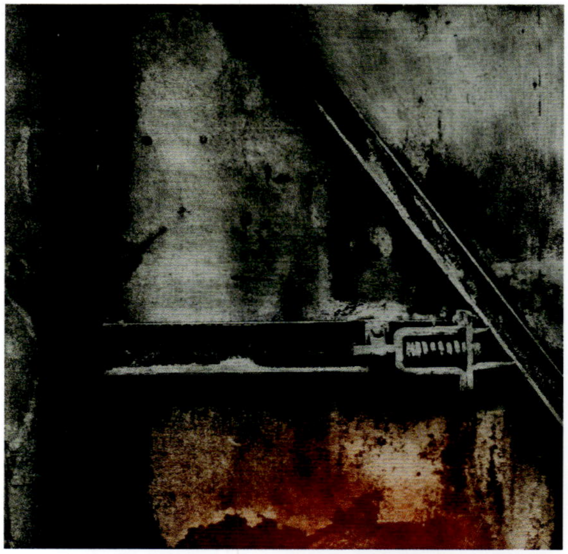

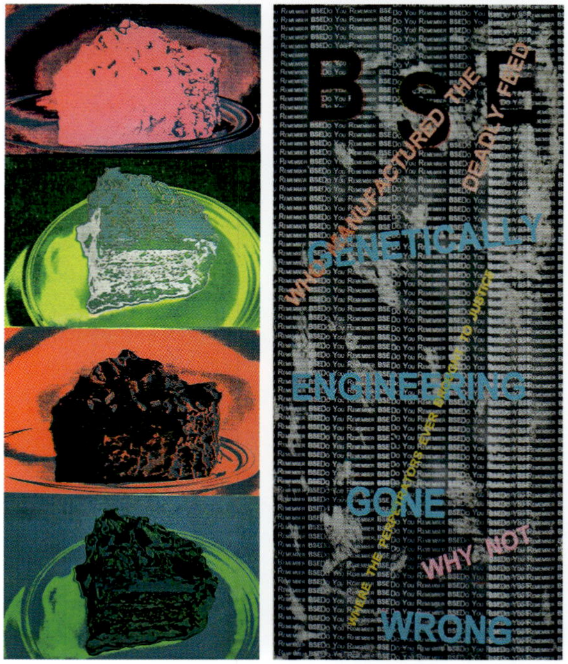

THIS PAGE: TOP

Last Journey, 30 x 30 cm
photo etching (artist's proof)

BOTTOM

X-BSE (Sponge Cake), 170 x 150 cm
silkscreen on canvas diptych
(unique)

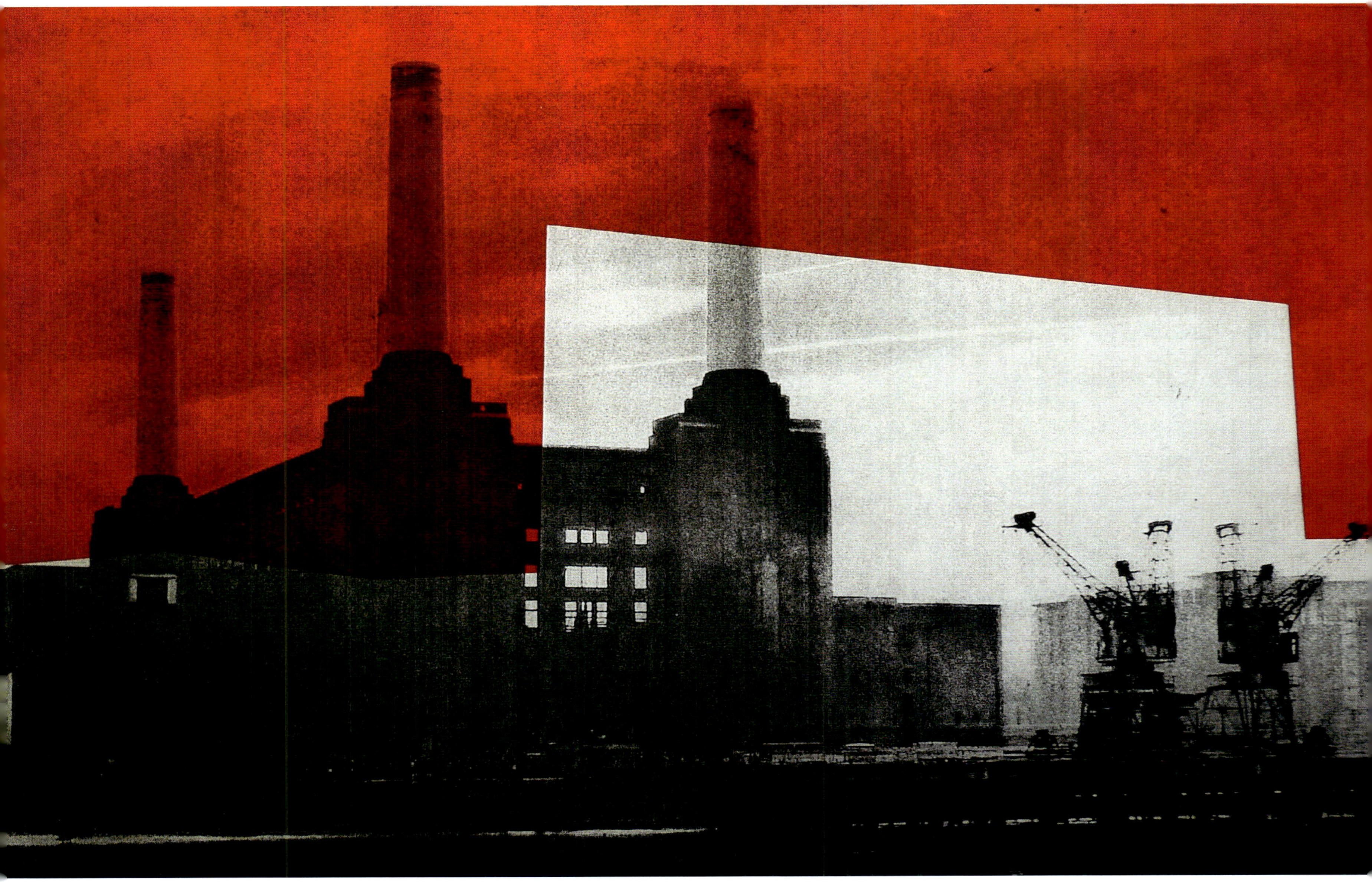

Battersea Power Station II, 36 x 58 cm, photo etching with collograph (artist's proof)

Sarah Rogers

As an artist I like to use imagery and observations from what I see as the presented, saleable world and reconfigure them into a world of experience. My work expresses an atmospheric, slightly disconcerting world. I'm interested in the obstinate side of life, sometimes difficult; moments often hidden.

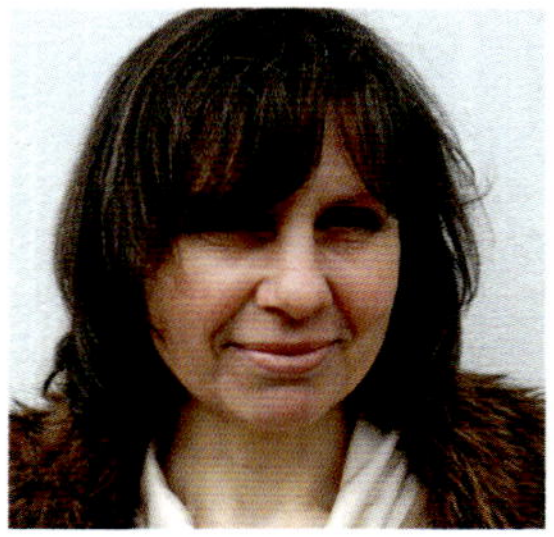

1960 Born Delamere, Cheshire
1983 BA (Hons) Fine Art/Textiles, Goldsmiths College, London

Solo Exhibitions
2014 *Perfect/Imperfect*, Aras Inis Gluaire, Ireland
2015 *Recent Works*, Newtownbarry House Gallery, Ireland

Selected Group Exhibitions include
2006/08/12/14 Royal Ulster Academy, Belfast
2008/12/13/14 *Eigse*, Carlow Visual, Ireland
2009/13 *Royal Academy Summer Exhibition*
2011/13 Ruth Borchard Self-Portrait Competition, Kings Place, London
2011/13/15 Royal Hibernian Academy, Dublin
2013 Jerwood Drawing Prize, London
2013 *Circulation*, Monster Truck, Dublin *Photographics*, PmC, London
2014 *BIMPE VIII*, Vancouver, Canada

Public Collections
A Natural Selection, The Botanic Gardens, Dublin
Strumpet City, Graphic Studio Gallery Archive, Dublin

Grants and Awards
1986 Arts Council of Great Britain
2013 Oppenheim-John Downes Memorial Trust

The starting point of many of my prints is the collecting of images from magazines, mainly women's magazines and usually centred around the home: *Kitchens and Bathrooms*, *Ideal Home* and so on. My attention is drawn usually to a specific image because of the idea of the space that is conveyed and this may resonate with certain memories. The attraction is something instant and if I'm lucky I'll try to hold on to those feelings throughout the making of a print.

The ancient saying of, "throw out your heart and spend your life chasing it," somehow captures the conditions under which my prints are made.

Using cut-out images, often quite small, is like playing. One is using miniatures of the actual world. The printed image has been a source of fascination for me since I was a child. I am still amazed and delighted by images being reduced to varying sizes of dots which can be printed in the four printers' colours.

My work is rooted in drawing and observation. Once I begin to convert a printed image into a photo-polymer plate, I am able to create an atmosphere from which a drawing can begin. I keep sketchbooks of moments I've seen in everyday life.

I'm interested in how to convey moments where one perceives the intention of an individual or group, but there is no outward expression as such yet... for instance, when walking past a group of people in a supermarket one feels a certain threatening atmosphere, or senses the fears of a housewife, an overly proud family or a despairing teenager.

Working with the process of intaglio printmaking and especially the making of the plates allows me to work out ideas in a very different way to working with paint or other ways of drawing. I think this is because there are always the moments where, however much you've worked it out, the process is out of your hands. This gap allows time to take certain risks.

When the plates are immersed in the acid, the ancient transformation that occurs adds a mystery to the making of images that I find irresistible and intriguing.

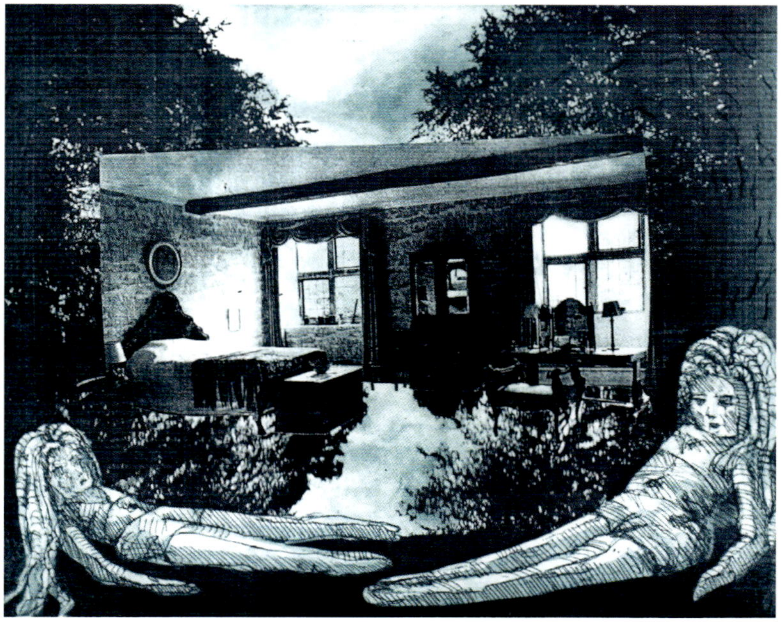

At Bay, 16 x 20 cm
etching (edition of 70)

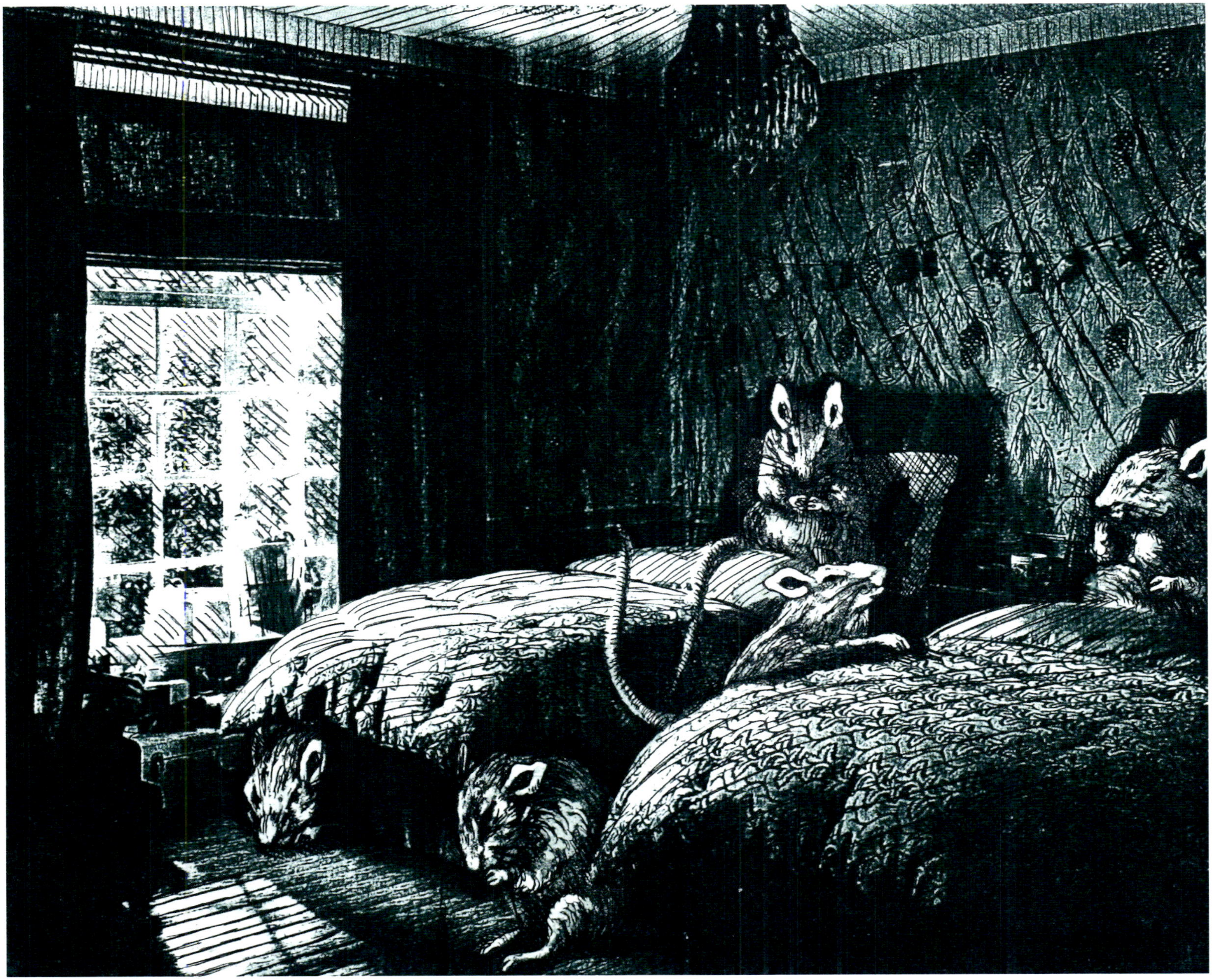

A Little Bedtime Story, 17 x 20 cm, etching (edition of 100)

Dan Romer

Dan has been producing vibrant, innovative art for over 25 years. The London-based printmaker and designer initially focussed on traditional screen printing, but has now developed additional media and expertise to include cutting-edge digital reproduction – often used to great effect in conjunction with other techniques. His work has been described as "a celebration of life", "sophisticated and multi-faceted" and "harmonising science and nature in perfect synergy".

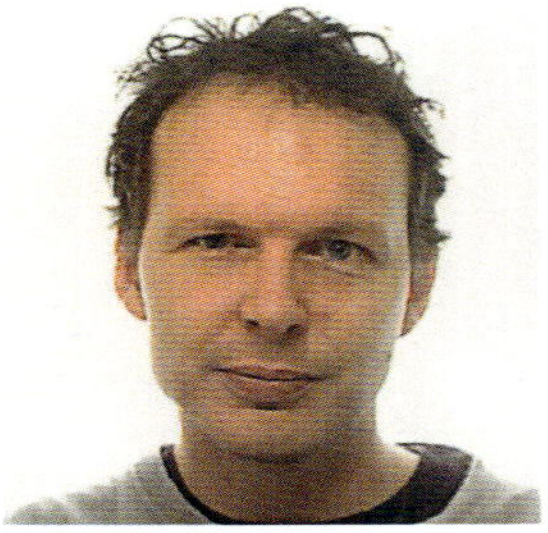

1969 Born Monmouth
1987 Art Foundation Gwent College of H.E.
1988 HND Ceramics West Glamorgan Institute of H.E.
1992 HND Screen-printed Surface Design University of the Arts London (LCP)
1994 Advanced Graphics London - Fine art printmaker
1994–2015 Various PmC exhibitions
1996 Screen-print studio set up for own work
2001 Advanced Graphics London - Fine art printmaker
2005 BA Screen-printed Surface Design University of the Arts London (LCC)
2006 University of the Arts London (LCC) Teaching various courses in screen-printing
2008 University of the Arts London (LCC) PG Cert in Learning & Teaching
2010 K2 Print Studio - Fine art printmaker

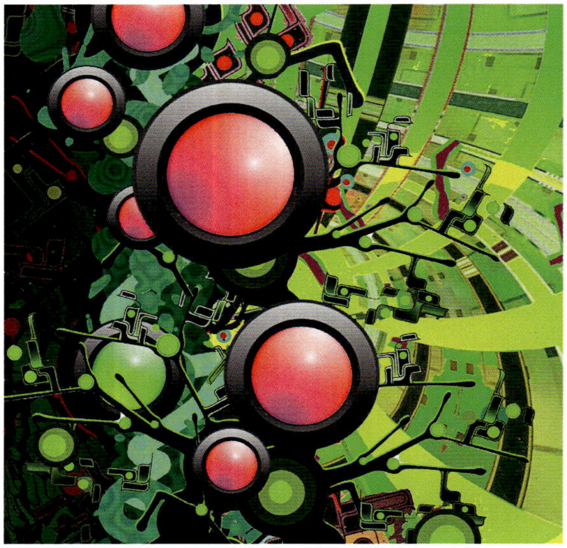

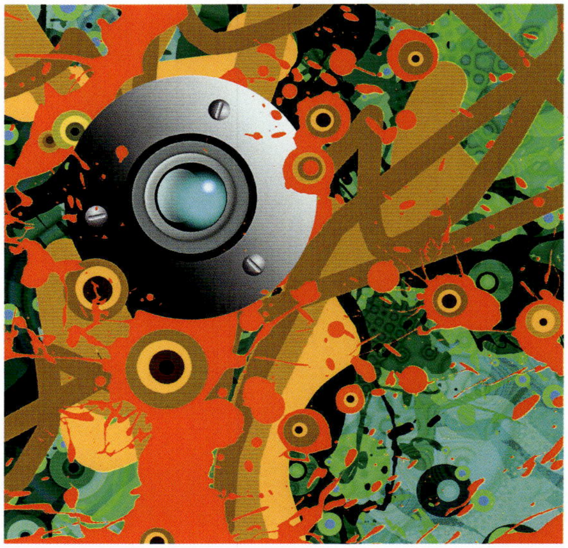

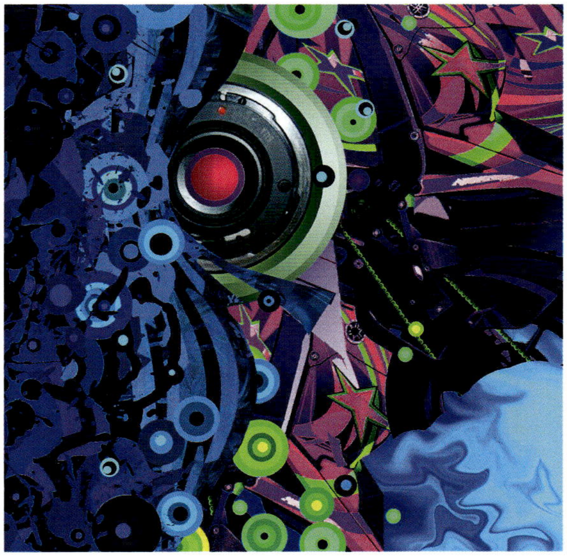

My work is inspired by the meeting point of the mathematical and the organic, reflecting the fact that it is possible to view life as an endless combination of possibilities, colour and shape. In short it's about chaos and order – and the transition from one state to the other and back again. My work seeks to represent the contrasts and similarities that are all around us.

THIS PAGE CLOCKWISE FROM TOP LEFT

Space pop 12, 90 x 90 cm, archival digital print on canvas (edition of 25)

Space pop 6, 90 x 90 cm, archival digital print on canvas (edition of 25)

Space pop 9, 90 x 90 cm, archival digital print on canvas (edition of 25)

OPPOSITE

Space pop 2, 90 x 90 cm, archival digital print on canvas (edition of 25)

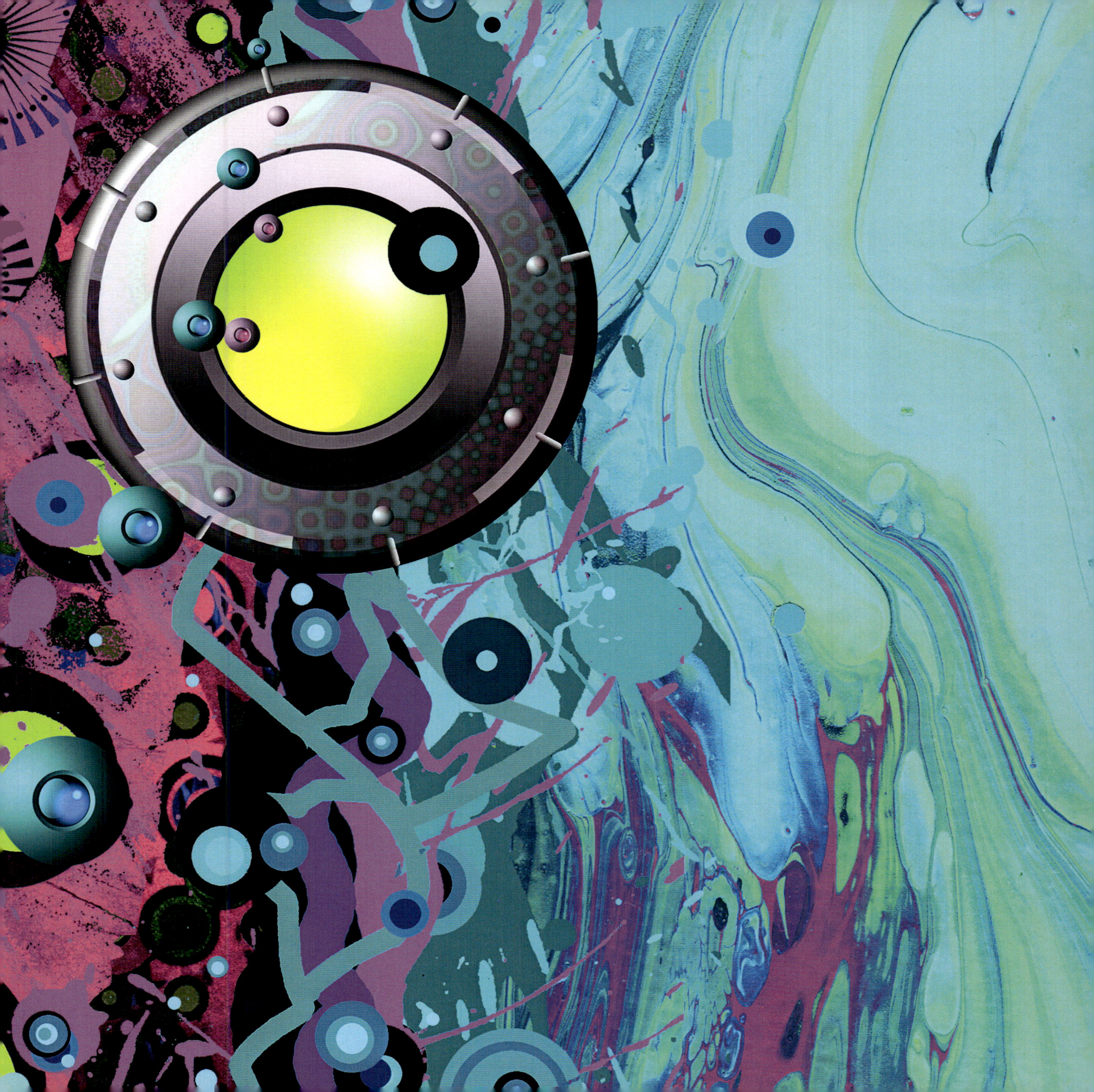

Sue Rowling

I trained as a Textile Designer at Winchester School of Art and worked for many years in the fashion industry producing print designs before specialising in design trends and colour forecasting. My career took a new turn after I completed a printmaking course with imagery applied to paper instead of cloth.

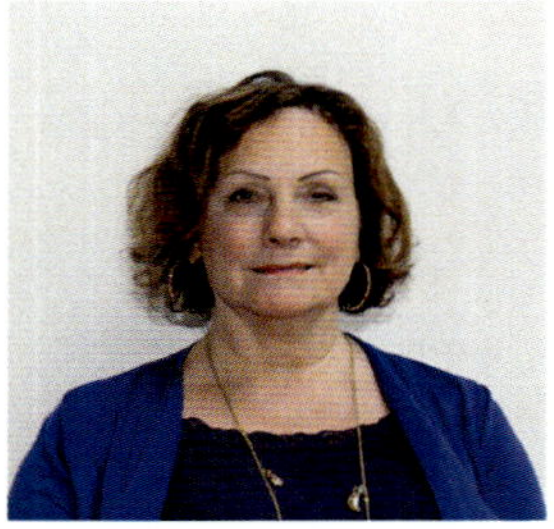

1952 Born Welwyn Garden City Herts
1975 Textile Design and Fashion, Winchester School of Art
2001 Applied Printmaking, London College of Printing
2002 Elected Greenwich Printmakers
2008 Elected St George's Art Committee
2014 Joined Printmakers Council
2014 Elected National Society of Painters, Sculptors and Printmakers

Group Exhibitions
2004 *National Print Show*, Mall Galleries
2005 *Colour*, Will's Art Warehouse
2006 Greenwich Printmakers, Highgate Gallery
2009 *30 Years 30 Artists*, Oxo Gallery
2011 *Second Impressions*, National Theatre
2014 *Art for Youth*, Royal College of Art
2014 National Society of Painters, Sculptors and Printmakers, Meunier Gallery
2014 *Prints for Presents*, Morley Gallery
2015 *Sixteen Printmakers*, Jack House Gallery

Collections
Royal Bank of Scotland
The Foreign and Commonwealth Office
British Medical Association
St George's Hospital
Croydon University Hospital

I am not a traditional printmaker as everything I do is a one-off. I love the freedom of producing painterly prints. My inspiration can be anything from a rugged landscape to an urban setting, but it is always the colour that informs the work.

As a starting point I enjoy mixing up pots of acrylic paint with the printing medium in order to work quickly when I am ready to print. There will be one or two paler ground hues, several mid-tones, a few darker colours and an accent or highlight tint. Using a silk screen l paint straight onto the mesh and print many grounds with a soft blade squeegee which will form the first layer of a series of unique monoprints.

At this stage they are too flat and each will go through many changes to achieve the required depth of colour and textural mark-making. Every print is then manipulated to create multiple layers by drawing into while still wet, scraping away or overprinting. I use paper stencils to block out areas or neat screen-printing medium for a translucent quality.

To some extent I can control or predict the colour merges and blends that develop but there is constantly an element of surprise. I love the atmospheric quality and depth that this method of experimental printmaking achieves. I will often paint into a print or add collage.

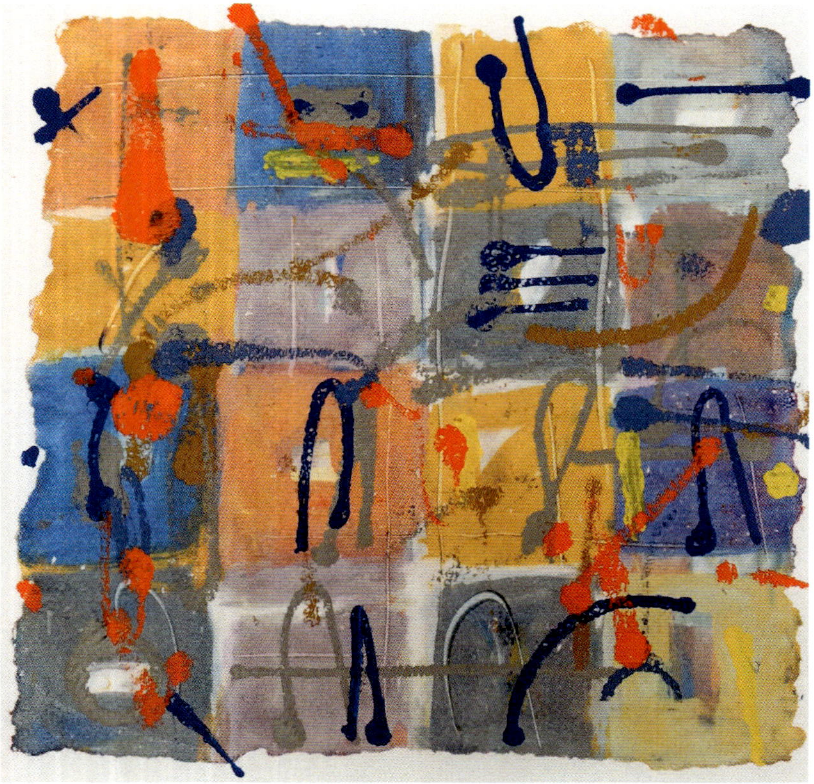

OPPOSITE
Light Moves
50 x 50 cm
mono screen print with collage and hand painting
(unique)

Graffiti
30 x 30 cm
mono screen print with collage and hand painting
(unique)

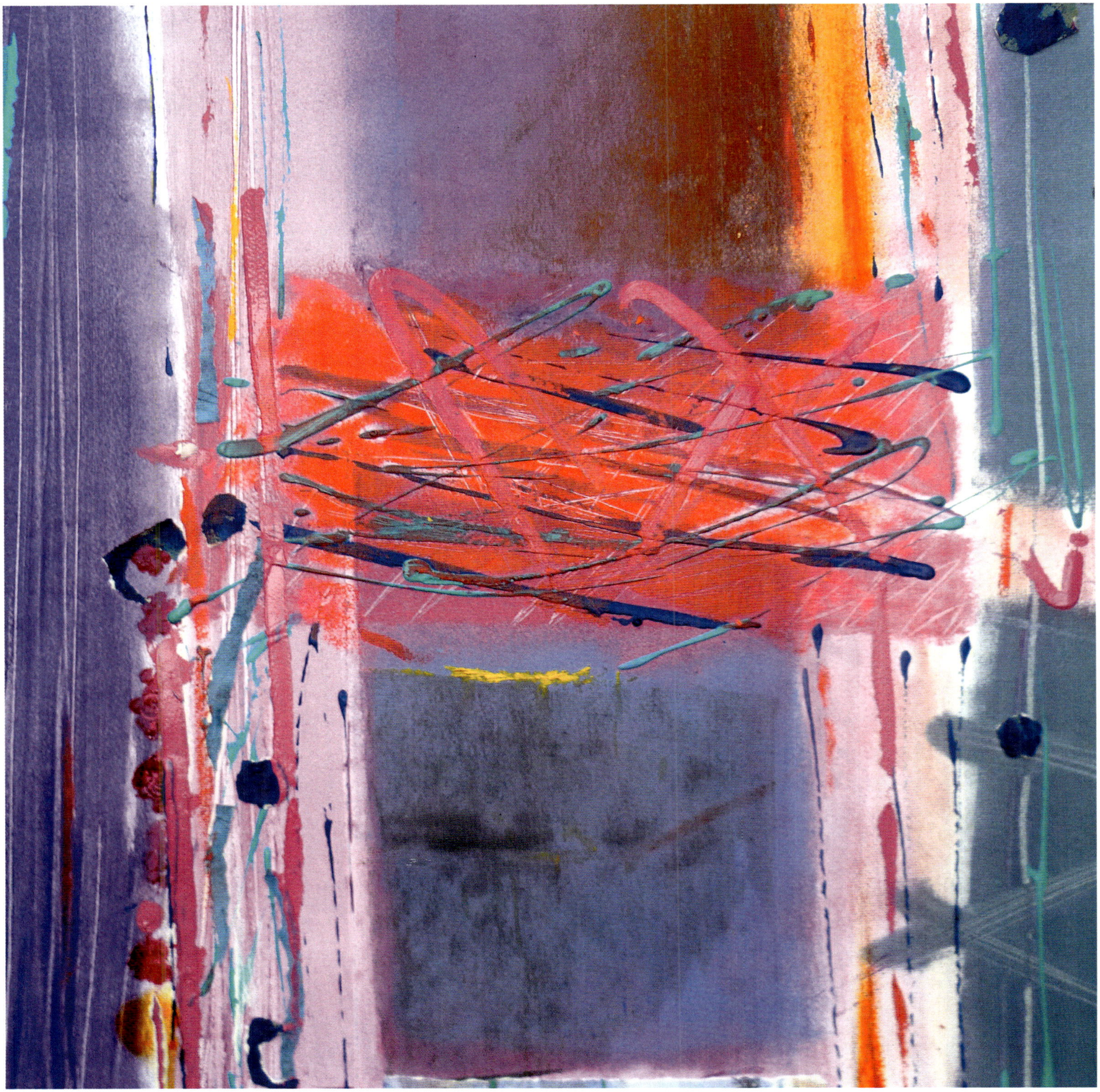

Handan Sadikoglu

I was introduced to printmaking during my first year at Cambridge School of Art, as a way of expressing ideas. I was enthralled by the diversity of the endless possibilities and their effects on different surfaces. After experimenting with various techniques, I ended up using mainly etching.

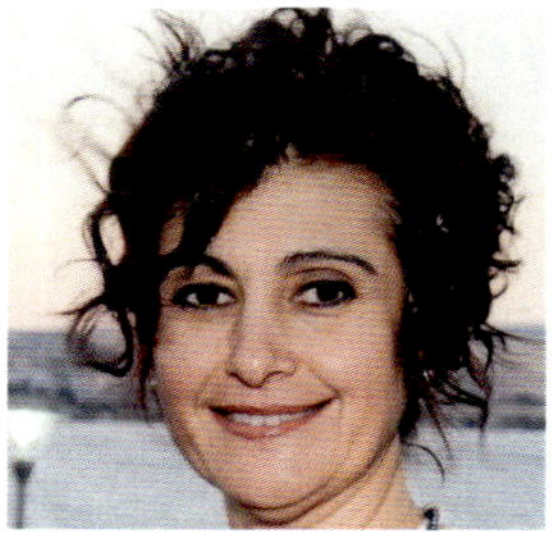

Born Ankara Turkey
2003–06 BA (Hons) Fine Art Printmaking. Cambridge School of Art, ARU
2007–09 MA Visual Art. Camberwell School of Art, UAL
2005 Cambridge University Astronomy Garden, Cambridge
2008 *7th British International Mini Print Exhibition*, touring UK to 2011
International Printmakers, Denbies Wine Estate Gallery, Surrey,
2008 Member Ochre Print Studio
2009 Member and Treasurer of Printmakers Council
2009 *Impact 6*, Bristol
Surrey Artist Open Studios, Guildford
Inside Out, House Gallery, London
2010 Printmakers Council, Bankside Gallery, London
2011 RWA 159th Autumn Exhibition, Bristol
PmC, Highgate Literary and Scientific institution, London
Vyner Streeet Gallery, London
2012 *Turn, Turn, Turn*, Margate Gallery, Kent
8th British International Mini Print
Street Gallery, UCH, London
LOOP, Bankside Gallery, London
The Framers Gallery, London
Bite, Mall Galleries, London
2013 *Royal Academy Summer Exhibition*
Photographics Great Western Studios, London
Highgate - A Reflection in Print, Highgate Literary and Scientific Institution, London
Collections include:
Tate Britain, Artist Book Collection, British Libraries Special Collection. Camberwell School of Art, University of Arts London

Handan's work investigates her own position between the cultures that she has been exposed to. They affect her perception of the world almost invisibly. She aims to create a visual dialogue that establishes a bridge between cultures, times and spaces. She implements this by working with architectural images, geometrical symbols and their combination with text.

In this series she combines an architectural image that is reminiscent of memories of Anatolian architectural tranquility with the philosopher M.C. Rumi's poem.

> "Come come again, whoever you are, come,
> Heathen, fire worshipper or idolatrous,
> Come even if you broke your penitence a thousand times
> Ours is the portal of hope, Come as you are."

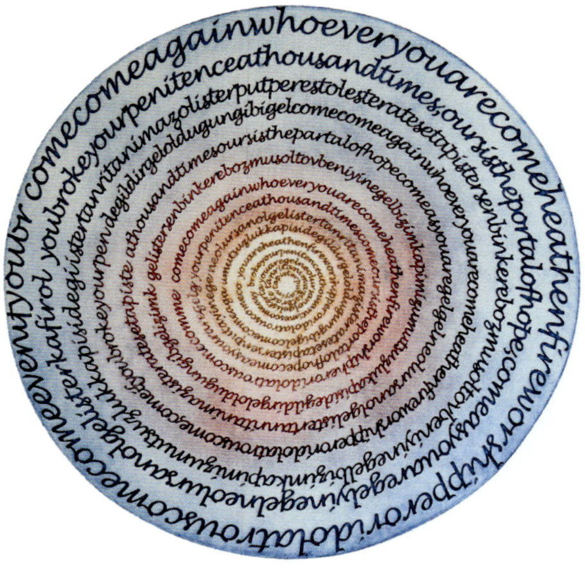

Come Again, 32 x 32cm
etching (edition of 10)

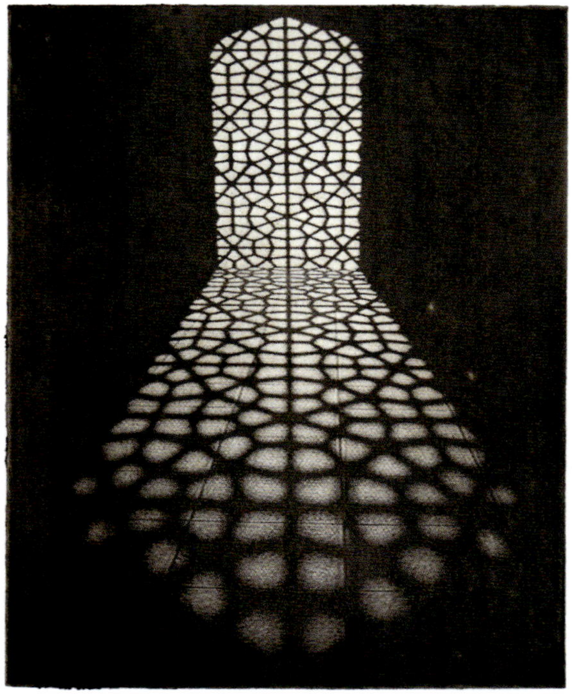

Let the Sun Shine, 20 x 15 cm
solar plate etching (edition of 10)

Words lead the viewer through the passage towards the light while the image reflects the influence of the words. The same poem is written in two languages on another image, English and Turkish, on an invisible circular line one after the other to express the idea of intertwined cultures in our life.

Handan uses architectural images taken on holiday or through her research, constructs them with Photoshop, then transfers them on to solar or zinc plate using a UVB light bed before etching and transferring on to hand-made paper.

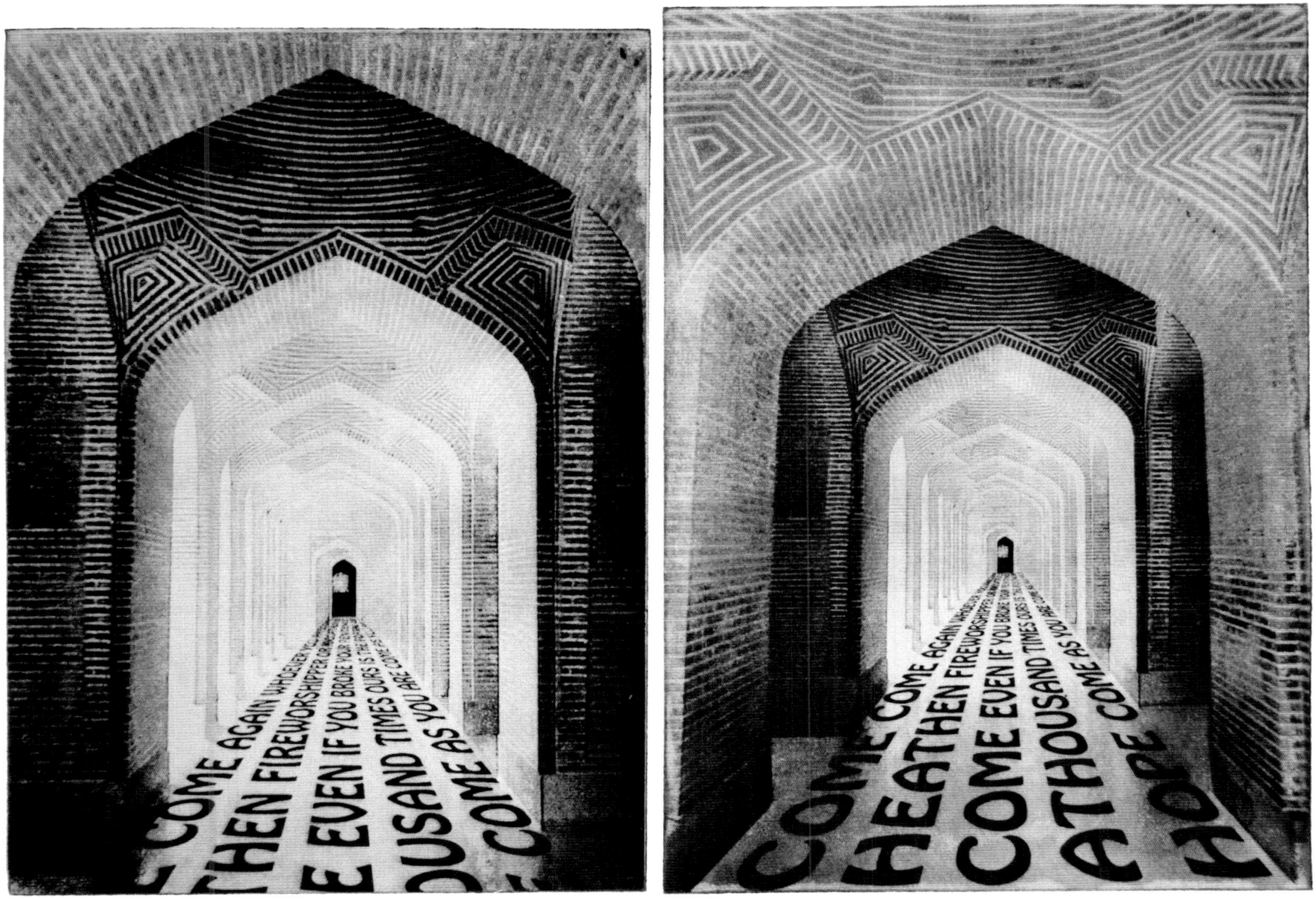

Portal of Hope, 20 x 20 cm, solar plate etching (edition of 10)

Ian Scaife

I first became interested in printmaking at school during a weekend etching workshop organised by a local college, then later, as an art student, I developed an interest in the German Expressionist printmakers, particularly Erich Heckel and Ernst Ludwig Kirchner. An enthusiasm for screen-printing was sparked after trying it at an evening class, and it has been my medium of choice ever since.

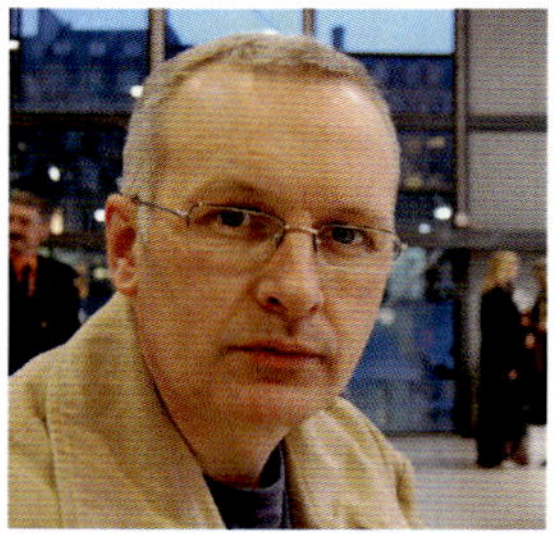

1960 Born Liverpool
1980 Fine Art Goldsmiths and Liverpool College of Art
1985 *Painting, Collage and Prints* School of Architecture, Liverpool. Exhibition with Margaret Carey and David Harrison
1985 Merseyside Arts Group Show, Lady Lever Art Gallery, Port Sunlight, Wirral
1986 Murdoch Lothian Gallery, Liverpool (curated group show)
1987 Mural, EPIC Leisure Centre, Ellesmere Port, commissioned by Merseyside Arts
1996 Site-specific painting commission, St Mary's Hospital, Paddington
1999 Solo show at The Warwick Leadlay Gallery, Greenwich
2008–09 Urban Art, Brixton
2011 Bicha Gallery, Gabriel's Wharf, London
2011 Bainbridge Open, Bainbridge Studios, West Norwood, London
2012 *Printathon*, Smokehouse Gallery, Hackney Wick
2013 *Going Underground*, Shoreditch Town Hall
2014 *Freshly Pressed*, London
2014 Bainbridge Open, Embassy Tea Gallery, Union Street
2014 *CMYK*, Pie Factory, Margate
2015 *Works on Paper*, Barbican Library, London
2015 *Style Cruise*, Canal Projects, London

Work held in private and public collections

In my work, I am interested in exploring the interplay between shape and colour, and I find screen-printing suits my intentions as it allows flat, hard-edged areas along with a reasonably large print size in comparison to other print methods.

My prints are made using paper stencils, which effectively means that the editions are very small – 5–10 is about maximum before the moisture in the ink begins to break the stencil down. The stencils themselves are cut from newsprint using a scalpel; a process I find very satisfying and which I think of as a means of drawing by cutting into the paper.

An idea for a print usually begins with making drawings, either in my sketchbook or on any scraps of paper that come to hand. I aim to find a combination of shapes or a means of combining areas of colour that I find engaging, and which allows further exploration of colour combinations and harmonies. I will often begin to think about the colour by writing on my sketches, then from there I use cut-out sheets of painted paper to arrange and finalise my composition, a process which can be quite short but which often takes several days.

Once the composition and colours are decided, a drawing is made to the finished print size (on the same size paper) which is used as a guide to cut out the stencils and for registration.

I find that mixing and testing the colours is one of the most enjoyable aspects of the process. I am drawn to the bright, synthetic colours used in manufacturing: colour used in car production, for example and (despite my prints being in small editions) I like the notion that screen-printing can be, and is often used as, a means of industrial production.

The writings of Johannes Itten and Josef Albers are influences on the way I think about colour and I admire the work of Ellsworth Kelly, Donald Judd, Marc Vaux and graphic designer Jean Widmer amongst others.

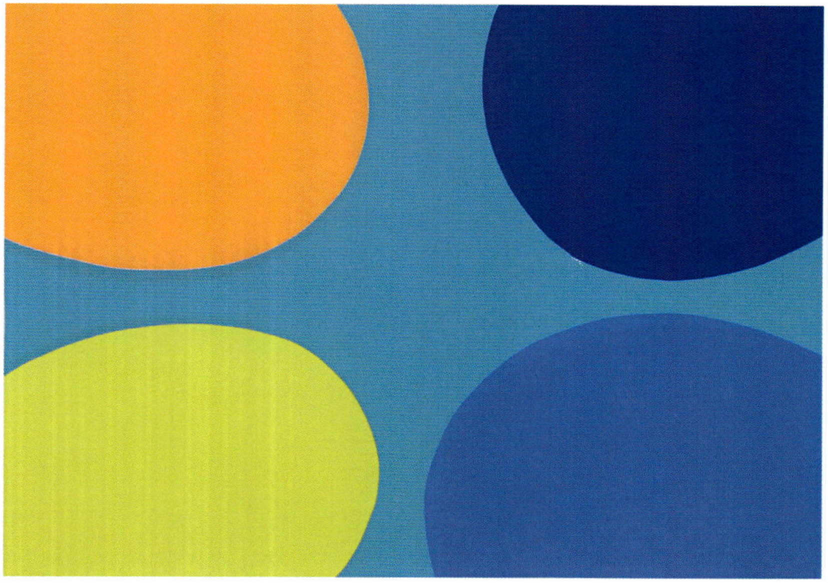

Blue Quartet, 57 x 38 cm, screen print (edition of 5)

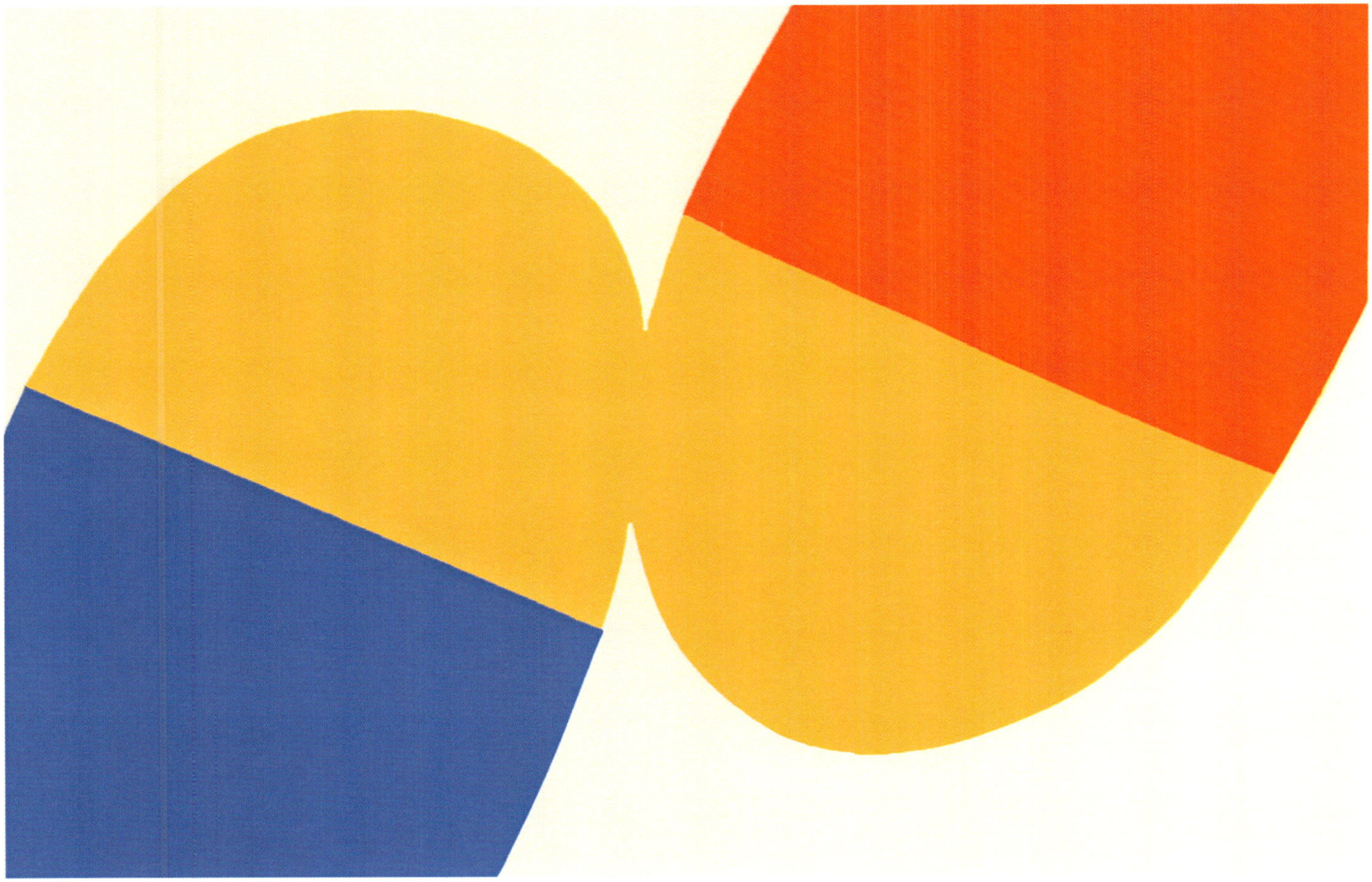

Yellow, Blue, Orange, 57 x 38 cm, screen print (edition of 5)

Margaret Sellars

My prints hover between the recognisably real and the abstract. The starting points are usually architectural and industrial structures within the contemporary environment. I concentrate on often-overlooked shapes and details, transferring, rearranging and changing their scale to discover new and unexpected forms, and alternative ways of considering space and depth.

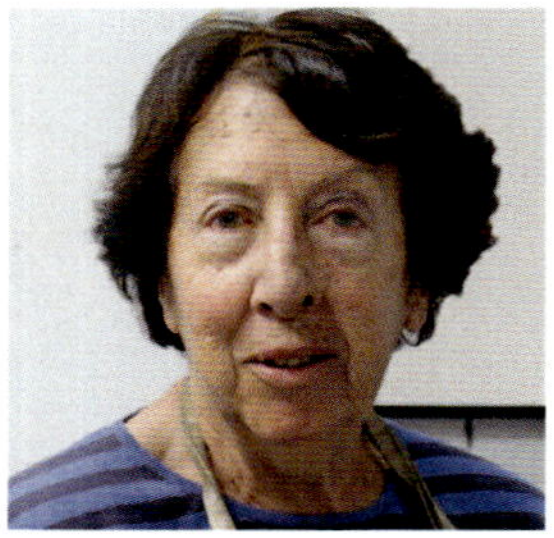

1937 Born Birkenhead, Merseyside
1953–58 Wallasey School of Art, Birmingham College of Art and Birmingham University
1958–76 Art teaching in Coventry, Fulham and Sutton
1973–74 Advanced Diploma in Art, Design and Printed Textiles, Goldsmiths College
1976–93 Head of Art, The Tiffin Girls' School
1993–99 Joined Printmakers Council and Richmond Printmakers
Elected to Royal Birmingham Society of Artists
Exhibited at Bankside Gallery, The Barbican, National Theatre, Kingston University, Chichester Open
1999 Solo exhibition at Riverside Gallery Richmond
2000 Joined Artichoke Print Workshop
Exhibited at Bankside Gallery, Clifford Chance, *Affordable Art Fair*
2009 *National Print Exhibition*, Mall Galleries, Arts Club Prize
Threadneedle Prize Exhibition
2010 RBSA Contemporary Print Show
Printmaking Today Prize
Featured artist in *Printmaking Today*
Royal West of England Exhibition
2012 Elected member, Royal Society of Painter–Printmakers
Curwen Studio Prize, RE Annual
2013 *Royal Academy Summer Exhibition*
London Original Print Fair at RA
2014 *Royal Academy Summer Exhibition*
2015 *National Original Print Exhibition*

I was brought up in Merseyside within sight of Cammell Laird's shipyard. This has had an ongoing influence on my way of seeing and choosing subjects. My initial training was as a painter; my interest in printmaking came later. Initially I avoided etching as I thought it required a fastidious, detailed approach. When I recognised that freer, more painterly, methods could be used, I began to warm to etching and to tap into its potential.

I work on a fairly large scale, often combining several plates to create a single image. By re-combining these plates, a considerable number of variations on a particular theme can be achieved. This method means I concentrate on mainly unique prints and thematically-related series, rather than large editions. My most recent series is of the interior of the Guggenheim Bilbao, in which I have used the play of light, through the irregular windows, as it falls across the curved walls.

Etching is now my preferred medium – soft ground on zinc; the line drawing and textures which can be achieved are remarkable. I add aquatint and often follow with monoprint. I have disciplined myself not to be overly critical at the early stages, instead responding positively to effects that occur along the way. Intriguing results can then become part of the print. All my powers of decision-making are used when I make prints. There is the obvious next step, problems to be solved along the way, and the elusive point of knowing when to stop. I have realised that there are no finite conclusions, only limitless possibilities.

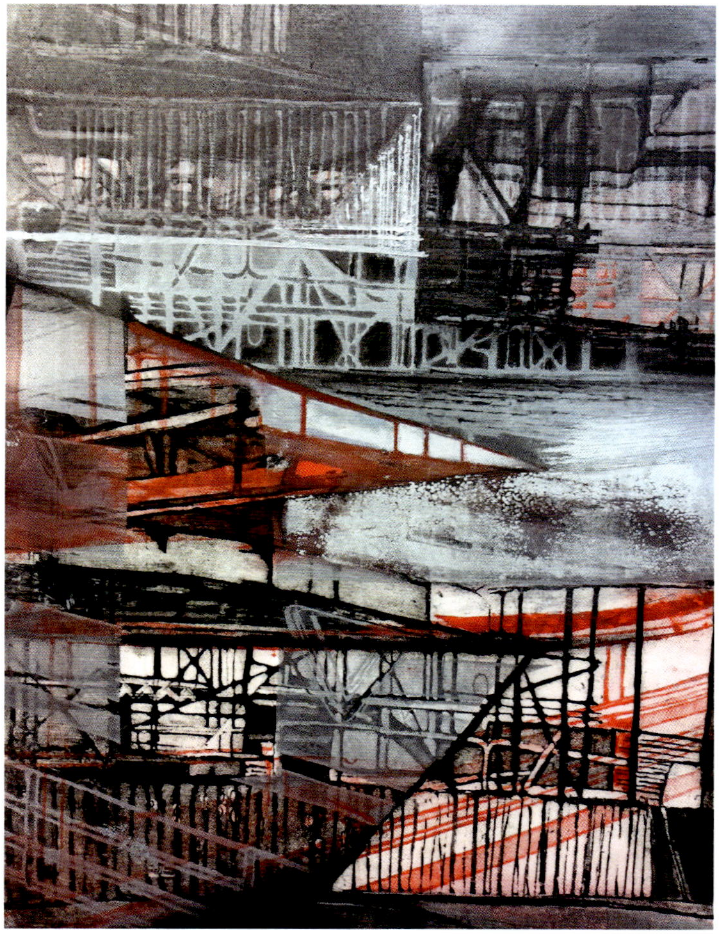

Terminus 4, 42 x 28 cm,
etching & monoprint (unique)

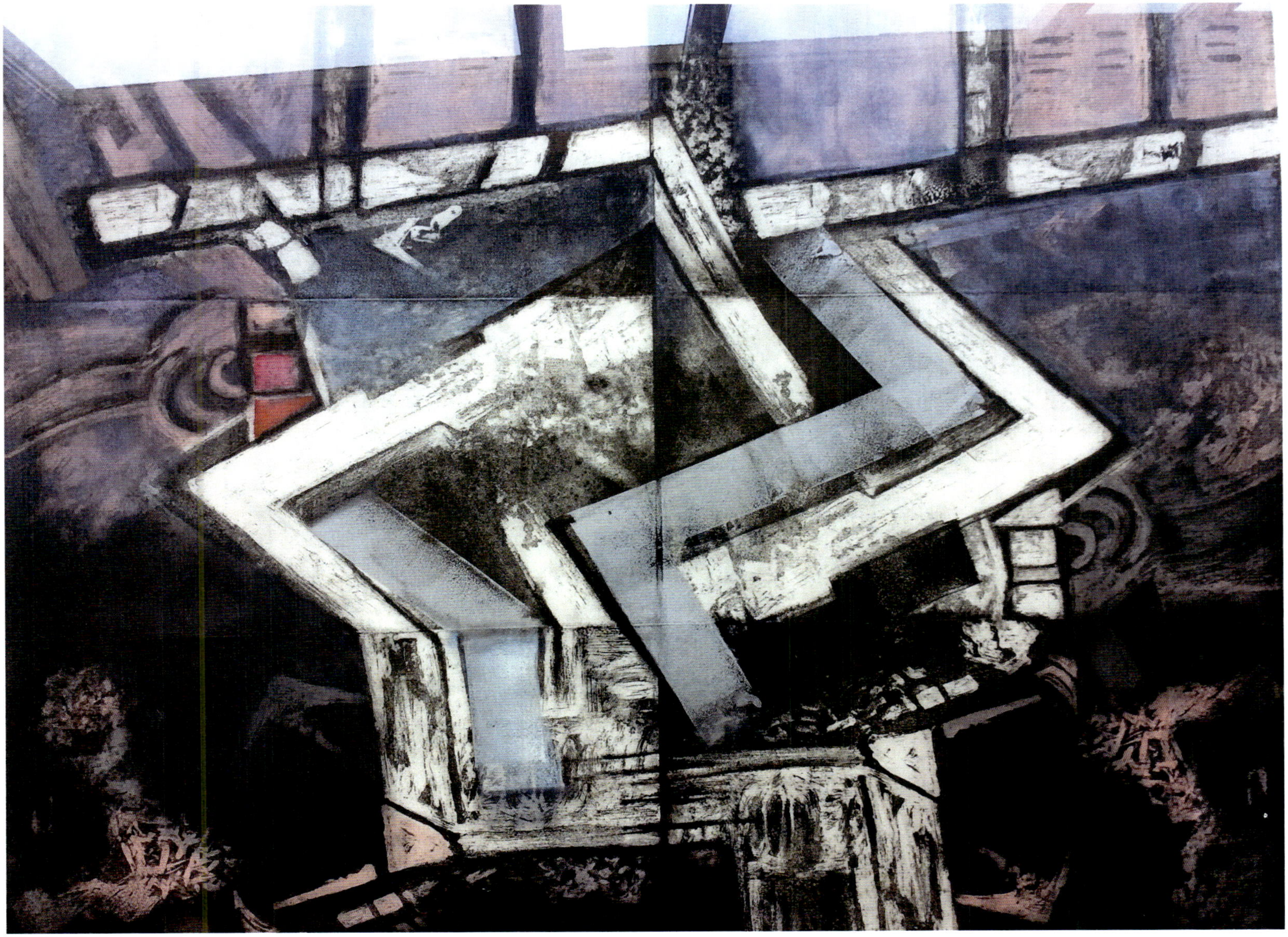

Diversion, 70 x 93 cm, etching & monoprint (unique)

Marilyn Simler

During my Fine Arts degree at the University of the Witwatersrand in Johannesburg, a section of the degree course was Printmaking. We had a wonderful teacher who made us aware of the endless and fascinating possibilities of printmaking. It was only when I emigrated to London in 1978 that I again explored printmaking at the Camden Arts Centre. I worked on screen-printing and etching which led on to my MA in Print at Middlesex, where all processes were available, many of which I still use today.

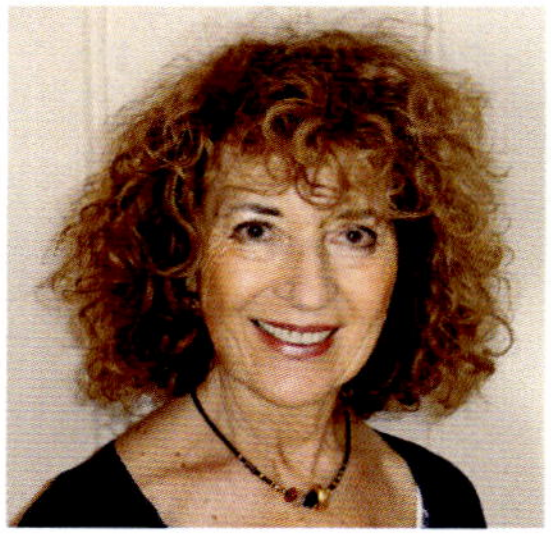

1947 Born Johannesburg
1965–68 BA (Hons) Fine Arts, University of Witwatersrand, Johannesburg, S.A.
1969 University Education Diploma, University of South Africa
1981 Diploma of Modern Art Studies, ICA London
1992–93 BA (Hons) Fine Arts, Middlesex University, London
1994–96 MA Fine Arts, Middlesex University, London

Solo Exhibitions

1989 The Hill Gallery London
1990 Charlotte Lampard Gallery London
1991 The Hopper Gallery london
1992 The Cadogan Gallery London
1997 The Pump House Gallery London
2002 Walton Gallery London
2005 West-Eleven Gallery London
2006 Royal Opera House, Covent Garden London
2009 Pyory Art at Popeck, London

Public Collections

Sandton Municipal Art Collection, South Africa. Middlesex University, Unilever plc Rolls building City of London

Commissions

Royal Caribbean Cruise Line
Corporate and private commissions

Publications include:

1995 Museum of Mankind Educational Service, *What is South African Art?*
1999 *Printmaking Today*
2000 *Art Review*, Northwest

Growing up in South Africa, with its wealth of natural beauty, different cultures, vibrant colour and intense light, has been formative and indelible, and a continuing source of inspiration to me.

Having lived in Britain now for more than half my life, I relish the constant exposure to so many wonderful contemporary artists and stimulating exhibitions.

I have been fortunate in being able to travel widely and am constantly fascinated and enthralled by the ethnic art of so many diverse cultures, which somehow find their way into my work. I always have my camera to hand for immediacy and a sketchbook if I have the time.

The art of past and present civilisations

Anything, from ancient petroglyphs through to African and Pre-Columbian carvings, and Byzantine mosaics can become part of my imagery.

Indian art and culture has been a particular favourite, as it is so diverse and abundantly sumptuous. I'm attracted to the exquisite colours and unusual perspectives of Indian miniature paintings as well as their architecture and craft.

A series on Indian Windows and Indian Quilts is still ongoing. The shapes, colours and complexity of the light reflections and cast shadows are endlessly fascinating to me.

The natural world

Vast deserts with their layers of mineral-enriched deposits creating exceptional swathes of colour and texture are thrilling experiences. The flora that survive in such spaces have become subjects of intense scrutiny.

The cycle of life from seed pod, germination, bud, full flower and back to seed pod is a continuing source being examined in my drawings, paintings and prints as all areas overlap constantly.

Flowers and plants and shells are central to me and I incorporate aspects of them in most of my work.

Images

Images sometimes overlap, partly concealing and revealing others.

I like to think of my work as containing images and colours that arrest the viewer's attention and challenge their perceptions. Images are often juxtaposed, having an aesthetic rather than a cerebral relationship. They may float or be grounded in an abstract or ambiguous space.

Working in mixed-media, I aim to create surfaces which are rich and varied and show the artist's hand rather than digital flatness. Because my work is quite painterly, I approach printmaking in a similar way to painting.

I have concentrated on the more immediate processes, such as various ways of monoprinting in layers and building up a rich surface of texture and colour. I include carborundum etching, lino, woodcut, and collage, enjoying the wonderful selection of paper available. I seldom do editions, preferring to work in series, or variations on a theme.

The natural world and the art of the past and present will hopefully provide endless and continuous development of my work.

Seaforms, 56 x 38 cm, screen print, monoprint

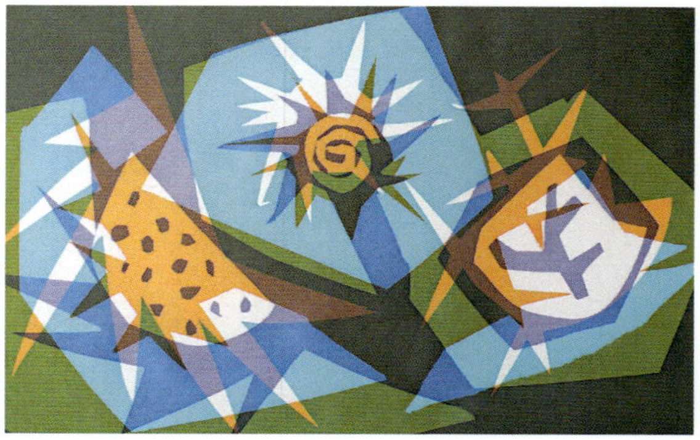

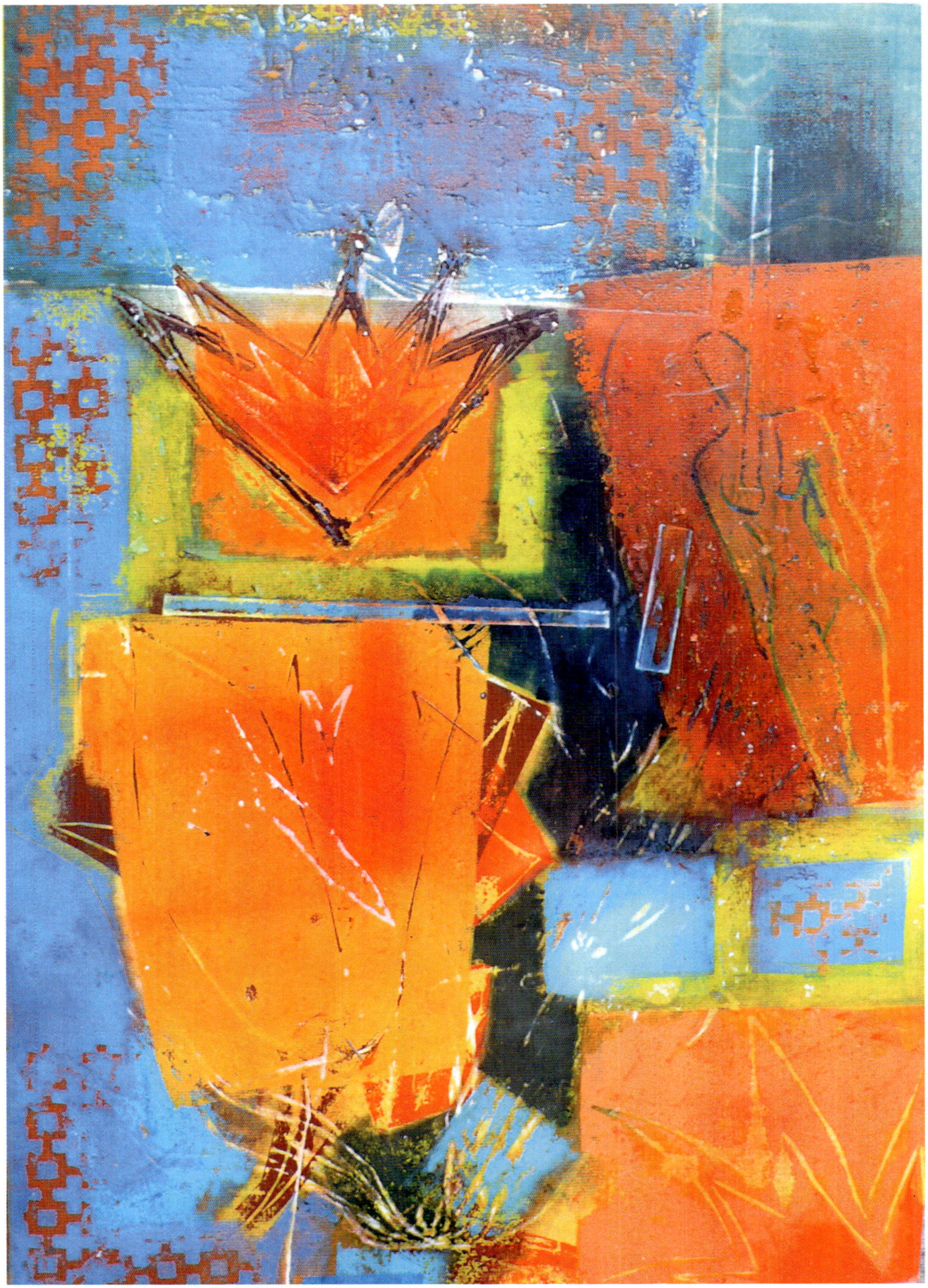

Figure and Flower
70 x 100 cm
mixed-media
monoprint

Ewelina Skowronska

I am a Polish illustrator, visual designer and printmaker and a recent graduate from the MA Illustration course at Camberwell College of Arts. Before I decided to move to London I worked successfully in advertising as a copywriter where I learned how to apply conceptual thinking in order to transfer ideas into visual language. However, after six good years there I have decided to start doing something different, something that I am really passionate about.

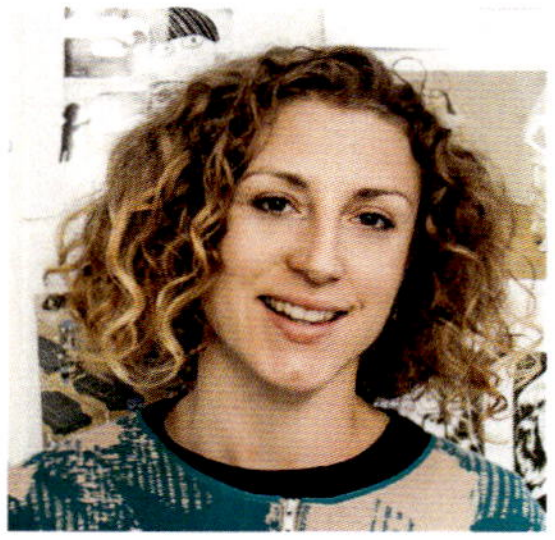

1980 Born Wrocław, Poland

1999–2004 MA Political Science, University of Wrocław, Poland

2013–15 MA Illustration, Camberwell College of Arts London

Exhibitions

2014 Group exhibitions: Camberwell Space, London & Brixton East Gallery, London

2015 Residency and show at Margate Resort Studio. Group exhibition London Transport Museum, *London Places* Group exhibition Chelsea Space, *Bestiary*. Group exhibition Chelsea College of Arts, *The piece may be fabricated*

Clients

University of the Arts London, Swiss Embassy, Hatalska.com, SLOW magazine, Gaga Magazine, Charaktery magazine, BORKO fashion, Helion Publishing House

Awards

2009 1st prize Złote Orły competition for poster *Lechu* design and concept

2010 1st prize Young Creatives Cannes Lions competition.

2011 Shortlist at Cannes Lions Festival for campaign *Sukiennice - Story Behind the Paintings*. Awards in KTR competition for campaign *Sukiennice - Story Behind the Paintings*

2013 Vice-Chancellor's Postgraduate Scholarships

2015 Shortlisted in KTR festival, Poland for *The Future Makers Today* project and The Best Portfolio
Shortlist for AOI Prize for Illustration

I tried screen-printing for the first time during my course at Camberwell. For me, it was an amazing discovery and the beginning of a great love. I am especially interested in the process of screen-printing and ways of pushing its boundaries. I wonder how the process of mark-making together with all the mistakes and limitations of screen-printing can influence the artwork and at the end tells the story or communicates certain subjects.

Even though I plan my work, I always leave room for spontaneity in the process and some decision-making that can apply only during printing. I like this uncertainty and constant problem-solving as well as the physical aspect of screen-printing.

I am also interested in everyday life observation, making my own comments on reality and translating the surrounding world into images. All of my work is focused on self-analysis and introspection as well as relationships between people and surroundings. My work is inspired by my life, and it changes as I evolve as a person and as an artist. Recently, even though I am not a religious person I got interested in the interpretation of some verses from the Bible, translating them into my own visual language with my own comment.

My goal is to fill the gap between design, illustration and art. I like to experiment with a variety of different effects, textures, overlapping colours and layers. I like putting elements in different contexts, giving them new meaning, creating new shapes. Thus I work mostly with photography, collage, typography and other traditional methods like painting and drawing.

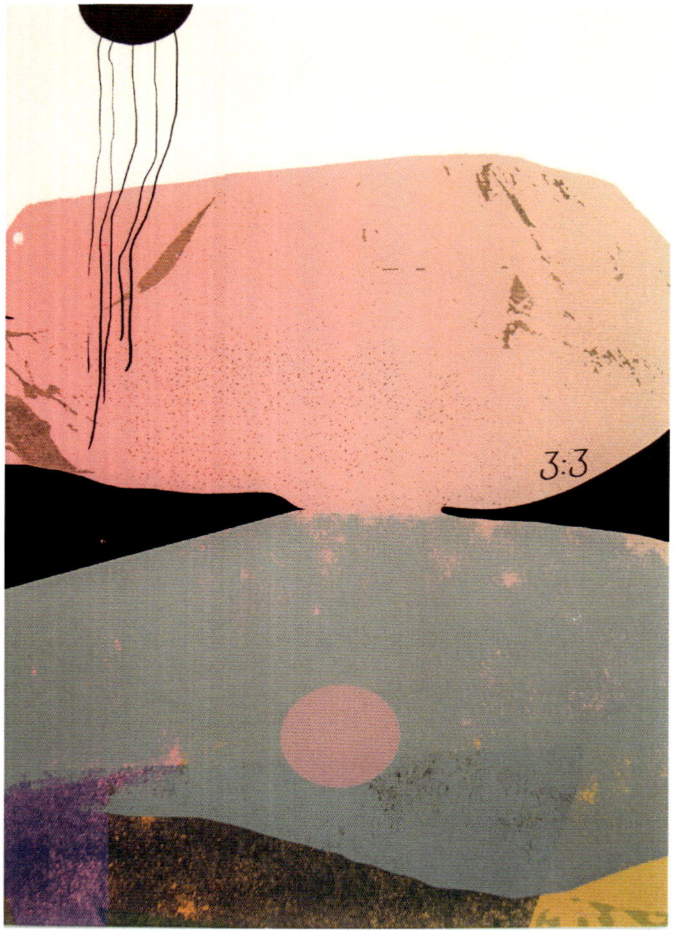

Ecclesiastes 3:3, 35 x 50 cm
screen print, (edition of 6)

Ecclesiates, 8 x 35 x 50 cm, screen print (edition of 5)

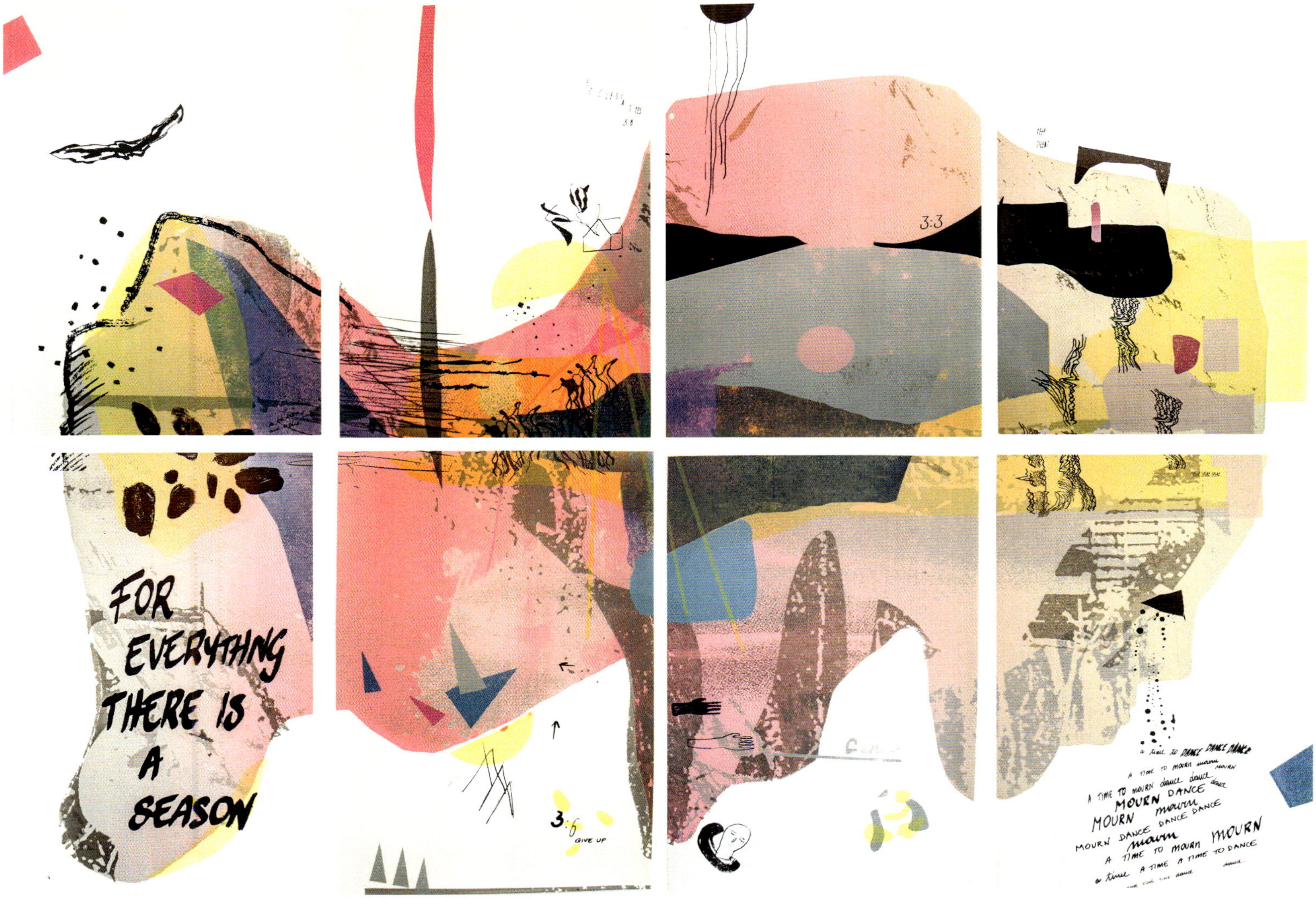

Carolyn Smith-Shaw

My first serious experience of printmaking was with lithography during Foundation and later with etching at evening classes, furthered during my time in Maidstone. Now I work predominantly with etching but it was whilst on Foundation that I discovered that I love the physical process of creating images on a plate.

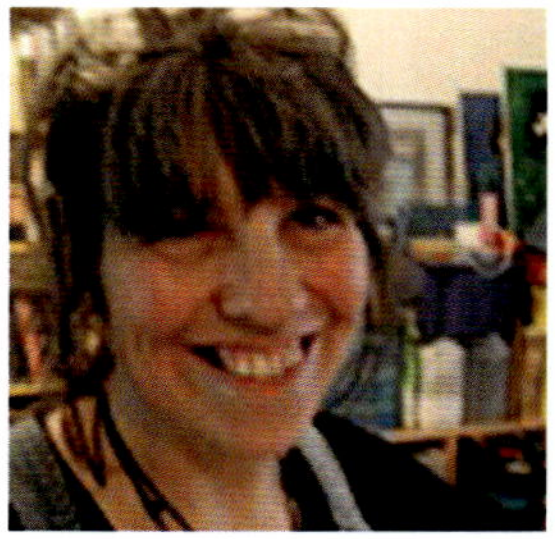

1982–85 BA Fine Art Printmaking
Maidstone College of Art

Exhibitions

1985 & **1986** Bankside Gallery
Rank Xerox
Tradition and Innovation in Printmaking Today

1986 108th Open Exhibition of Contemporary Prints

1986 Intaglio Printmaker, London
Printmakers Council 21st Birthday Show, Royal Festival Hall

1986 & **1987** Ayling Porteous Gallery
Christmas Show

1988 Norfolk Artists Cooperative Gallery
Christmas Show

1989 *Entirely Intaglio*, Royal Festival Hall

2010 Mall Galleries, London
A4 International Contemporary Printmakers Competition,
Penryn Cornwall
New Gallery Show

2014 *CMYK*, Pie Factory, Margate
ING Discerning Eye, Mall Galleries

Work in the Collections of
Epping Forest District Museum
Rank Xerox
Private Collections

Within my printmaking I work predominately with etching, using a mixture of line, open bite, coarse aquatint and sugar lift. I also work with lino and collographs. Recently I have been experimenting with colour using etching with chine collé and lino with cut line and the open bite of caustic soda. And I have rediscovered lithography, using zinc and polyester plates, and kitchen litho.

I enjoy the physical process of making the plate and the anticipation of the revealed print.

I enjoy the physical motion and actions of creating the plate – there is a satisfaction in the movement of filing edges, wiping scrim, rubbing in asphaltum.

My printmaking work evolves from sketches. I have always drawn what is around me. I draw what appeals to me, what I respond to – nature in the everyday world around me, reflections in glass buildings emphasising the vastness of sky, light effects, birds and trees, leaf forms, bare branches against an expanse of sky – articulating my emotional response with mark-making, lines, shapes, patterns, textures. Now I translate the mark-making into print.

Alongside nature in the everyday, I am intrigued by the human figure in a narrative and the archetypal echoes of myth and fairy tale that can glimmer through the drawing; both themes expressing the hidden within the everyday.

Experimenting in lithography with mark-making that responds to my drawn mark-making has been exciting and a nice change from my layered approach to etching. Whilst working with low-tech materials for kitchen litho and relief printing (tin foil, cola and vegetable oil, polystyrene party plates and a spoon) has been fun.

I am excited by the process of printmaking, the physical manipulation of the plate, the alchemical transformation, and the looking-glass effect of the mirror image and never quite knowing how it will be revealed once the paper is peeled from the plate.

OPPOSITE
Ravens in Eucalyptus, 36 x 28 cm, lithograph (edition of 4)

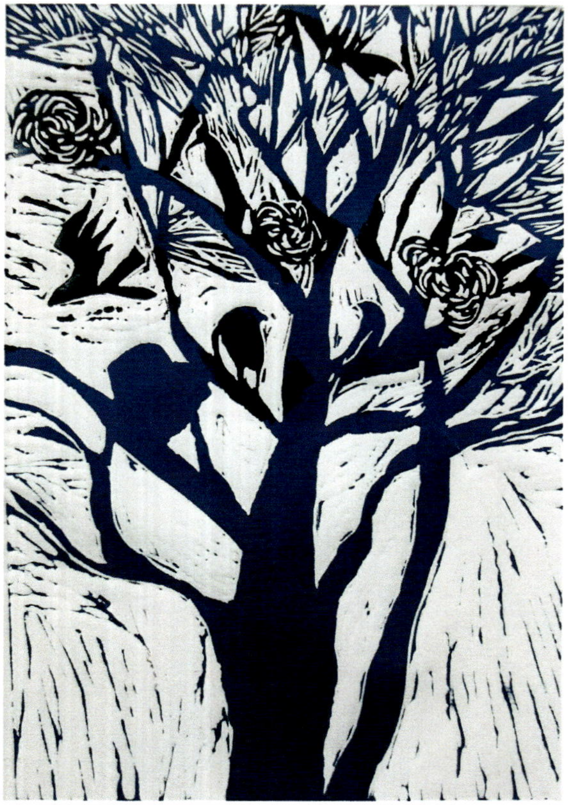

Ravens and Tree, 30.5 x 20.5 cm, lino (edition of 3)

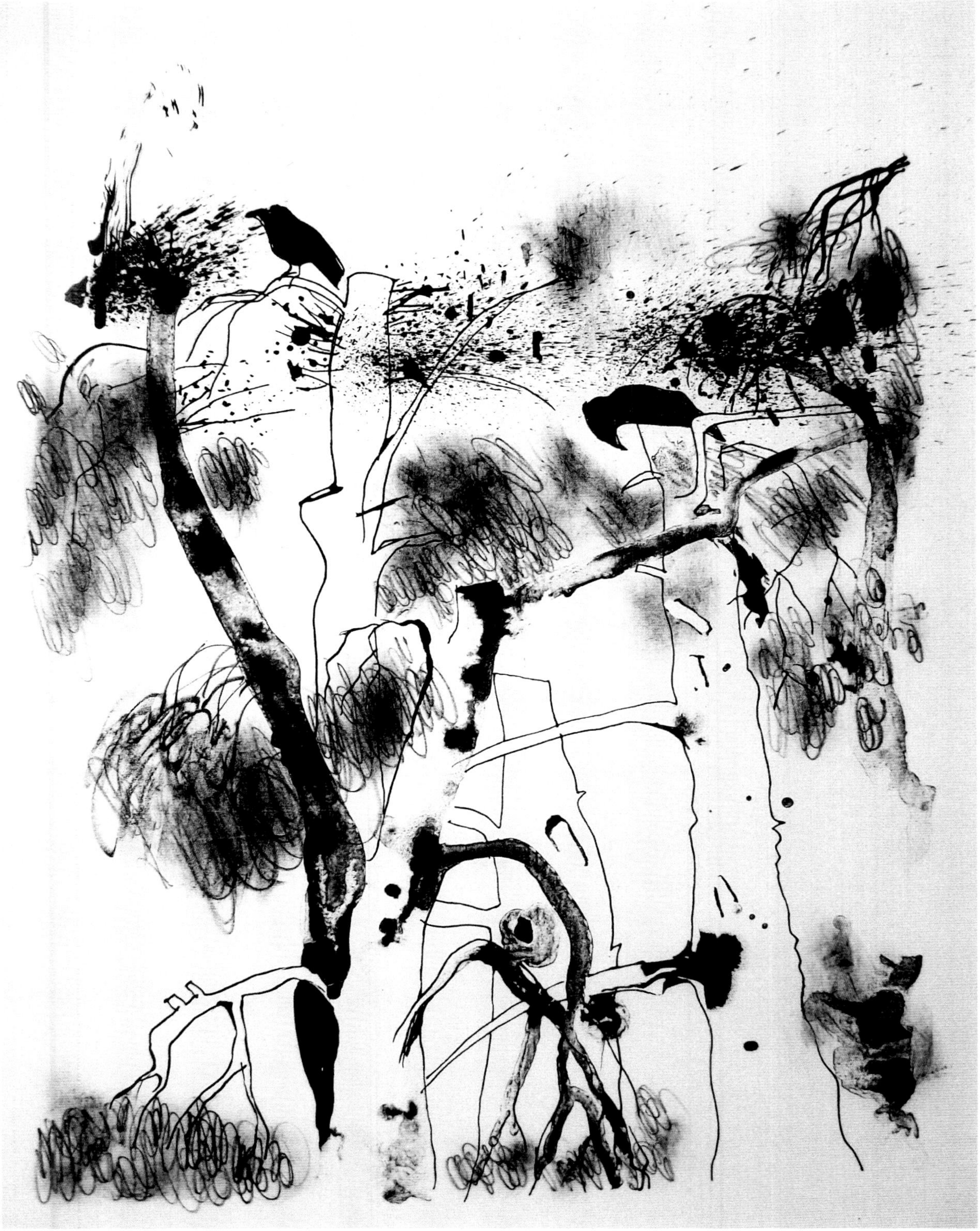

Tim Southall

Printmaking, in the form of etching, first captured my imagination in 1979 at what was then Newcastle Polytechnic. The magic of the 'reveal' when peeling the paper from an etching fresh from being taken through a press enthralled me. Since that first print 36 years ago I have continued to make etchings although these are now accompanied by silkscreen and monotypes.

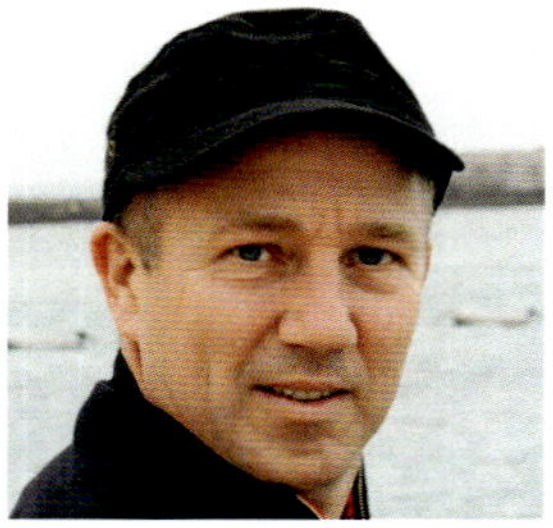

1961 Born Staffordshire, UK
1979–82 BA (Hons) Fine Art, 1st Class University of Northumbria
1982–85 MA (Henry Moore Bursary) Royal College of Art
1983 Ecole de Beaux Arts, Paris, Stone Lithography Studio
1985 The Creaser Gallery, London, inaugural exhibition
1986 Danziger-Miles Gallery, Dover Street, London, solo show
1987–97 Taught widely at University level in the UK
1993 Silver Paper Gallery, Milwaukee, solo exhibition
1997 Syndicated Arts, Wapping, solo exhibition
2011 The White Room, Bath, solo exhibition
2013 *Paintings & Prints*, Millard & Lancaster, Shrewsbury
2011 & **2013** *Royal Academy Summer Exhibition*
2011 *The Discerning Eye*, Mall Galleries, London
2012 The Royal Society of British Artists, Mall Galleries, London
2013 Royal West of England Academy Annual Open, Bristol
2013 BPM 30th Anniversary Exhibition, Birmingham Museum
2014 *Works on Paper*, The Science Museum, London
2015 The White Room, Leamington Spa, solo exhibition

I grew up on the very edge of the heavy industrial heartlands of the Black Country in the West Midlands. From the nucleus of my childhood home, I could walk one way and be engulfed by an endless, urban chaos; a colourless and man-made jungle. But walk in a different direction and I was embraced by the pastoral landscape of the English countryside. I always chose to walk into the natural world and this is where my journey as an artist began.

From the Midlands I moved to Newcastle, studying Fine Art at what is now Northumbria University, moving on to take my Master's in printmaking at the Royal College of Art. I then spent some time in the stone lithography studios at L'Ecole des Beaux Arts in Paris before settling back in London, then moving to Spain in 2001. Today I am lucky enough to spend most of my time at my house and studio in the beautiful countryside of Cádiz Province in southern Spain, just three miles from the Atlantic coast, which is where I find most of my inspiration and the starting points for my work.

I describe myself as a representational painter and printmaker. Both media are equally important to my creative expression and output, and both have their starting points at the same place. The base upon which I build my work is metaphysics: existence, objects and their properties, space and time, cause and effect, and possibility; and through my work I try express how I see and experience the world. Today I mostly do this through the landscape or the figure in the landscape. Previously I have also explored this through the animal kingdom and portraiture.

Over and above the metaphysical, I strive to make work which is delicate and shows a lightness of touch along with an eye for detail and nuance. At the same time I use the language of drawing and mark-making in an attempt to describe emotional depth and atmosphere. I also delight in using visual devices or narratives to convey some of the great classical themes and hopefully create something new and fresh with a modern voice. The resulting works are rarely direct representations or specific places but distillations of various places and experiences. Here I hope to pose the two basic questions of metaphysics: What is ultimately there? and, What is it like?

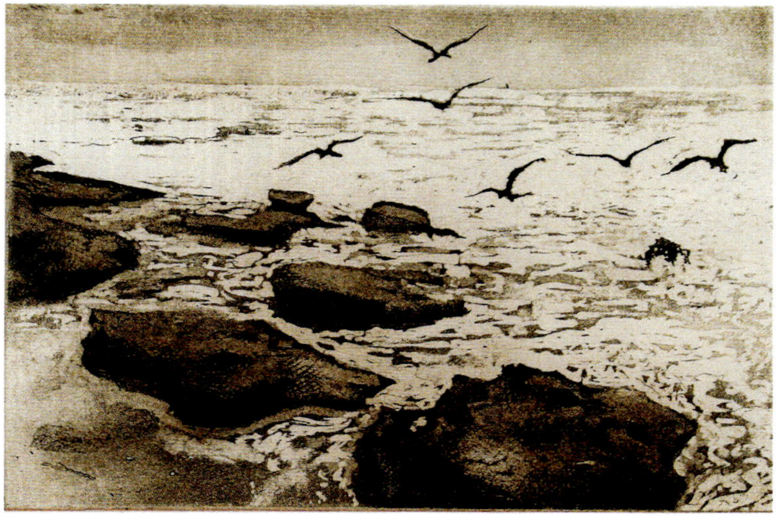

Sea Birds, 10 x 15 cm, etching & aquatint (edition of 75)

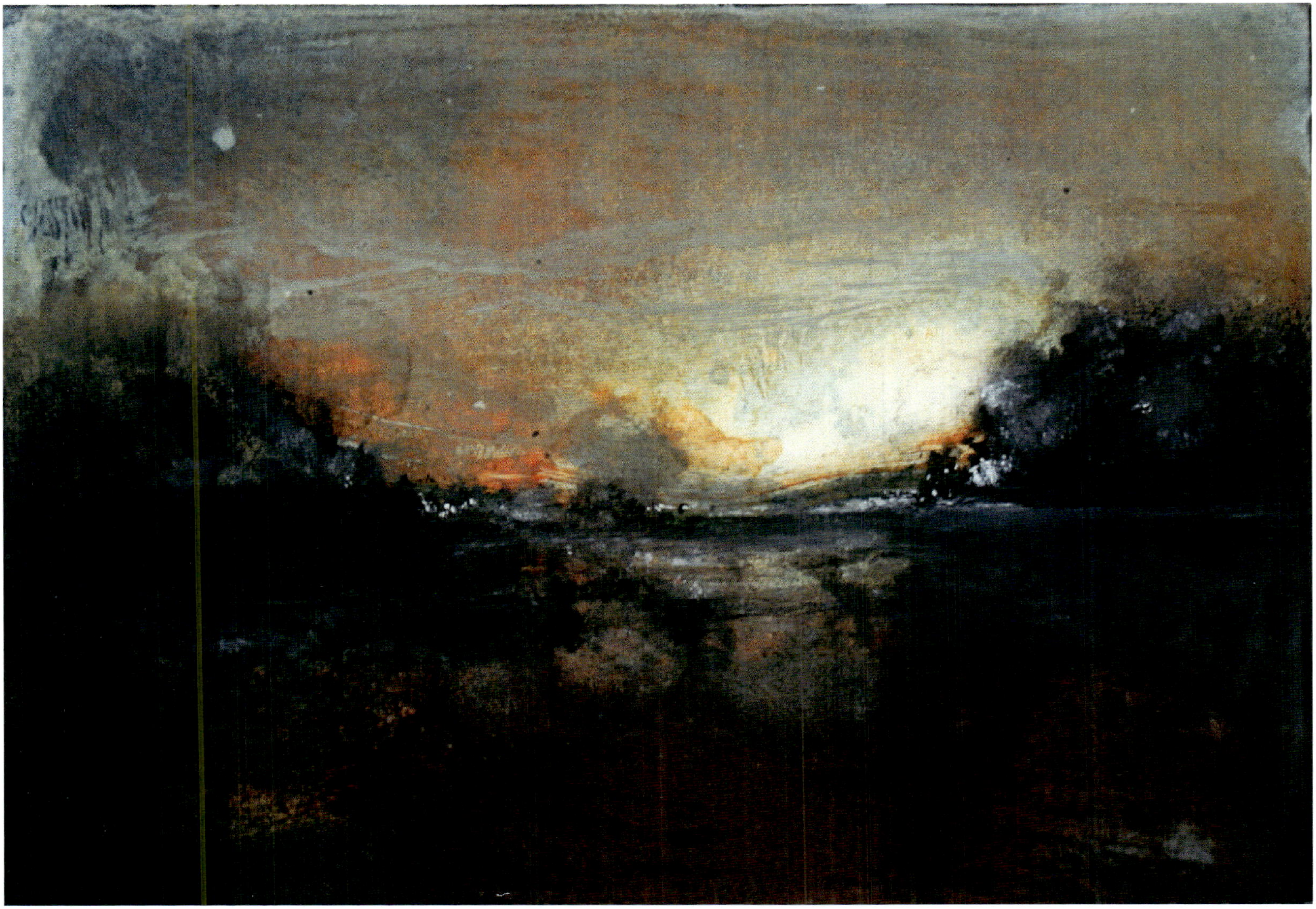

Glimmering End, 20 x 30 cm, monotype (unique)

Francesca Souza

Beginning with lino, monoprint and screen-printing from an early age, printmaking has continued to form an aspect of my practice as an artist. After focusing on screen-printing as part of my art school training, I went on to study lithography. Attracted and intrigued by the sensitivity of the medium, I found I could draw, paint and colour in a direct manner, while producing multiple versions and variants of my image due to the mechanical reproduction involved.

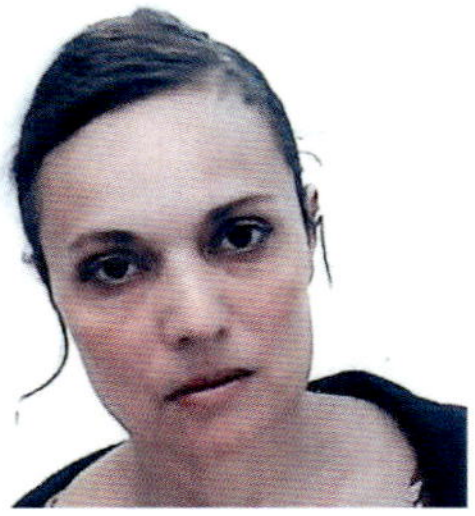

1978–79 St. Martins School of Art, London
1979–83 BA (Hons) Goldsmiths College of Art, University of London
1995–97 Postgraduate Degree, Painting, CSSD, University of London
2008 PGCE Institute of Education, University of London

Selected Exhibitions:

1983 *Women and Textiles: Their Lives and Their Work*, Battersea Arts Centre, London
1984 Printmakers Council Fair, Royal Festival Hall, London
New Contemporaries, ICA, London, UK
Making and Meaning, Brixton Art Gallery, London
1985 *Material Evidence*, Camden Arts Centre, London
ZG Gala, Riverside Studios, London
Multi-Dimensionality, Artist in Residence, Eastern Arts Association, UK
1992 *Printmakers: Making Marks*, The National Theatre, London
1998 *London Art Fair* (Julian Hartnoll Gallery), Islington, London
Camden Open, The Roundhouse, London
1999 *Souza, Glavurtic and Devine*, Hoxton Bibliotech Gallery Shoreditch, London
2000 *Waves*, Touring Exhibition Alexandra Palace, London, RDS, Dublin, International Halls, Harrogate
2013 *Drawing*, The Graphic Art Studio, Dublin, Ireland
The International Postcard Show, The Surface Gallery, Nottingham
2014 Lowes Cato Dickinson Award, The Ruskin Gallery, WMC, London (prize winner)

Because of the experimental way in which I work, etching as an intensely technical medium has only recently seemed compelling. Current work utilises a mixed-media approach, predominantly, chine collé and photo etching. When combining slow and traditional etching techniques with fast, direct methods such as chine collé, possibilities provoked allow me to capture ideas, generating visual representations or embodiments before they disappear.

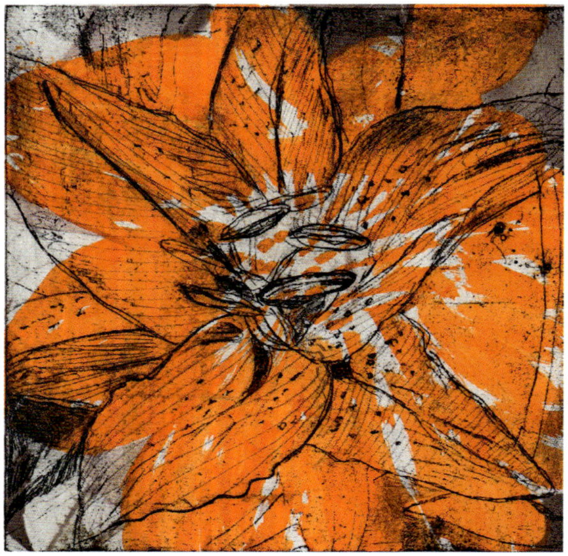

ABOVE

Toxic Lily, 12.5 x 12.5 cm, markerpen on chine collé etching (unique)

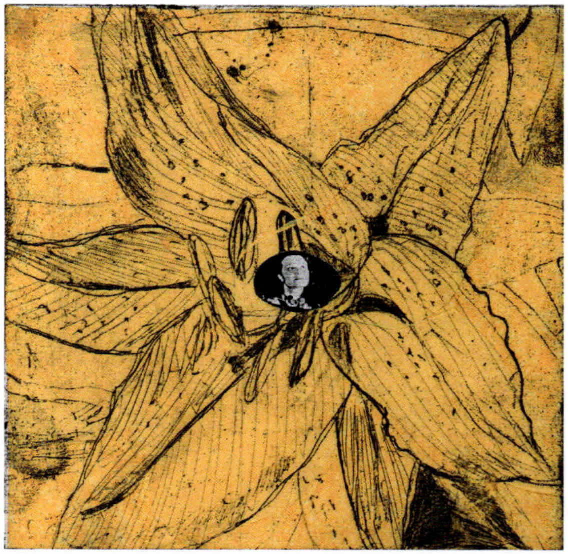

ABOVE RIGHT

Mother, 12.5 x 12.5 cm, chine collé etching (unique)

I place value on the pleasure of 'making' – experienced through the hands and fingers – in the sense that etching or printmaking manifests and displays the core principles of the 'craft of art' as espoused by the Arts and Crafts movement. The very crafting of the image on the plate involves a slow and labour-intensive intaglio process of incisions and revisions where physical and artistic stamina is called upon. This is the antithesis of when I create giclée prints by means of digital processes.

The work here forms part of a body of prints, condensing autobiographical memory with everyday metaphorical triggers.

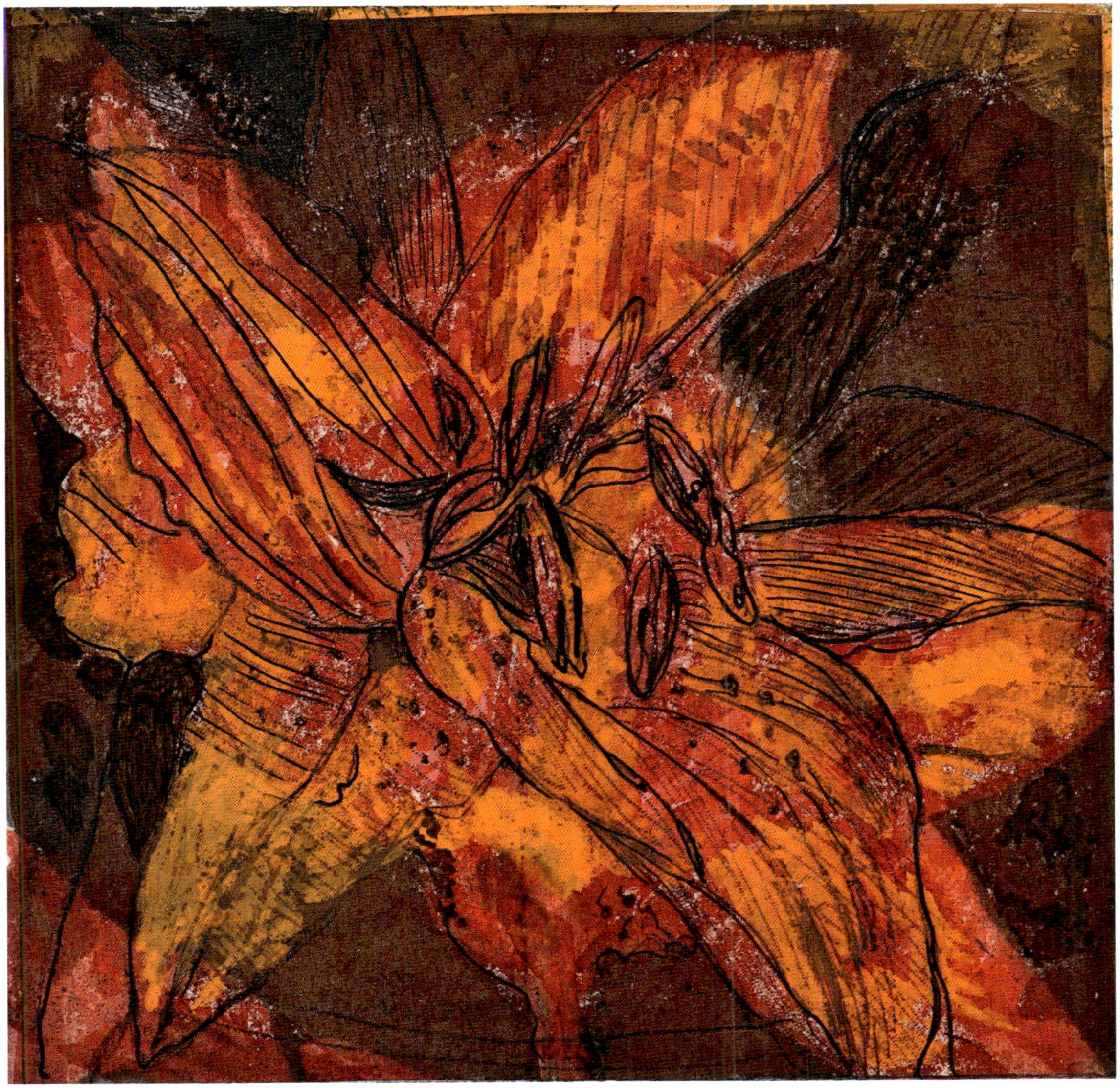

Gilding the Lily, 12.5 x 12.5 cm, markerpen on chine collé etching (unique)

Carolyn Stafford

I have been making prints since attending Bolton Art School, starting with silkscreen for textiles and also some block printing. Then at Manchester, while studying Fine Art and Textiles, I did my first litho and etching with Robin Jaques. At the Slade I did etching with Anthony Gross, and then spent a year with his friend S.W. Hayter in Paris.

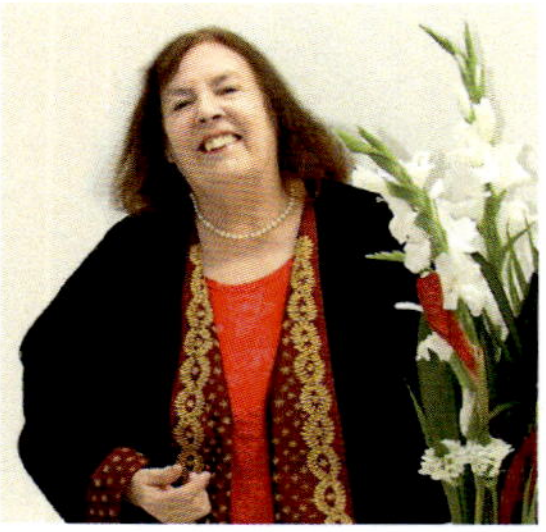

1935 Born Bolton, Lancs
1951–53 Bolton School of Art
1953–55 NDD, Manchester College of Art Bronze Medal for Painting, DA Manc
1954 Proctor Memorial Travelling Scholar to Paris
1955–57 Slade School of Fine Art, Slade Diploma in Fine Art (Very highly commended). First prizes in figure painting and drawing, landscape, plant and still-life drawing, Steer Landscape Prize
1956 Winifred Smith and Maud Foster Travelling Scholar
1957–58 Esmond Scholar of British Institute in Paris; etching with S.W. Hayter at Atelier 17
1958 Salon des Réalités Nouvelles, Musée d'Art Moderne, Paris
1959 John Moores, Liverpool
1959 London Group
1959 Bradford Biennale (invited artist)
1959 Work toured by Arts Council
1960 AIA Gallery
1963 Whitechapel Art Gallery
1964 Belfast Gallery
1966 WIAC Greece
1976 Joined the PmC
1980 Ben Uri Gallery, London and Tel Aviv
1989 *A Northern School*, Bristol and Touring
1990 *Royal Academy Summer Exhibition*
1996 Greek Cruise Ship, *Musica*
2000 Bankside Open Painter-Printmakers
2013, 2014 Margate
2014 Retrospective, Menier Gallery, London

I am 80, so have a very long career behind me. As well as lecturing in Art and Design in South London and for Surrey University, I also had four children, one of whom had special needs, so my time for exhibiting was somewhat limited for many years. However, I managed to do some etching in the 1960s at Birgit Skiöld's Print Workshop, Charlotte Street, taking my children with me!

My work in public and private collections includes the Government Art Collection, Slade School, University College, V&A, Bolton School, Bolton Art Gallery, Scarborough Print Archive, Lvov Ukraine and Landau Germany.

Throughout my career, I have exhibited in many galleries in England and abroad, in solo and group shows, especially with the Printmakers Council. I have been a member since the 1970s – not quite a founder one! I have been on the committee as Secretary, Vice Chairman and Treasurer. I organised an exhibition for the PmC to Paris, and others locally at Battersea, Clapham Common and Waterloo. We had several successful exhibitions at Whiteleys where we were hanging large works until midnight! Other PmC exhibitions that I was very much involved with were the Contemporary Art Fair Olympia, Royal Festival Hall, Paris (two exhibitions), US/UK Print Connection, Barbican and the Curwen Gallery. I have also exhibited more recently with the PmC in France, Germany, New Zealand, Bankside, Battersea, Vyner Street Gallery, and Margate.

I have been a member of several art societies including The National Society of Painters, Sculptors & Printmakers, The Contemporary Portrait Society and the Free Painters and Sculptors.

I have recently moved from Wandsworth to Lambeth and am still involved in my local community organising exhibitions. I teach a printmaking class every week in my studio and also run many workshops in galleries. Now I tend to do quite large lino and woodcuts – printing them by hand or by foot. I recently won the National Society Matthew White Printmaking Prize for my woodcut *Man with Arms Folded*.

I have been very influenced by the Lancashire moors where I grew up, and I am currently working on paintings and prints for a Northern exhibition. My retrospective, *From North to South* at the Menier Gallery last year, included over 100 works, many reflecting my Northern roots.

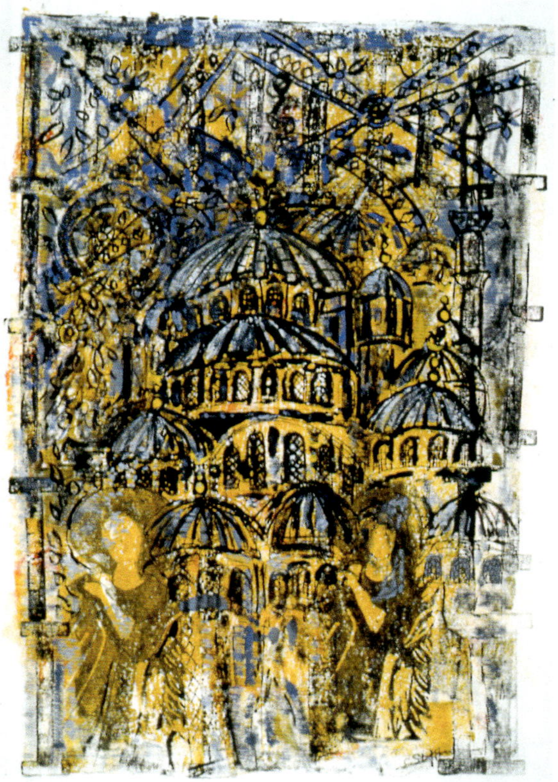

Istanbul, 53 x 34 cm, monoprint (unique)

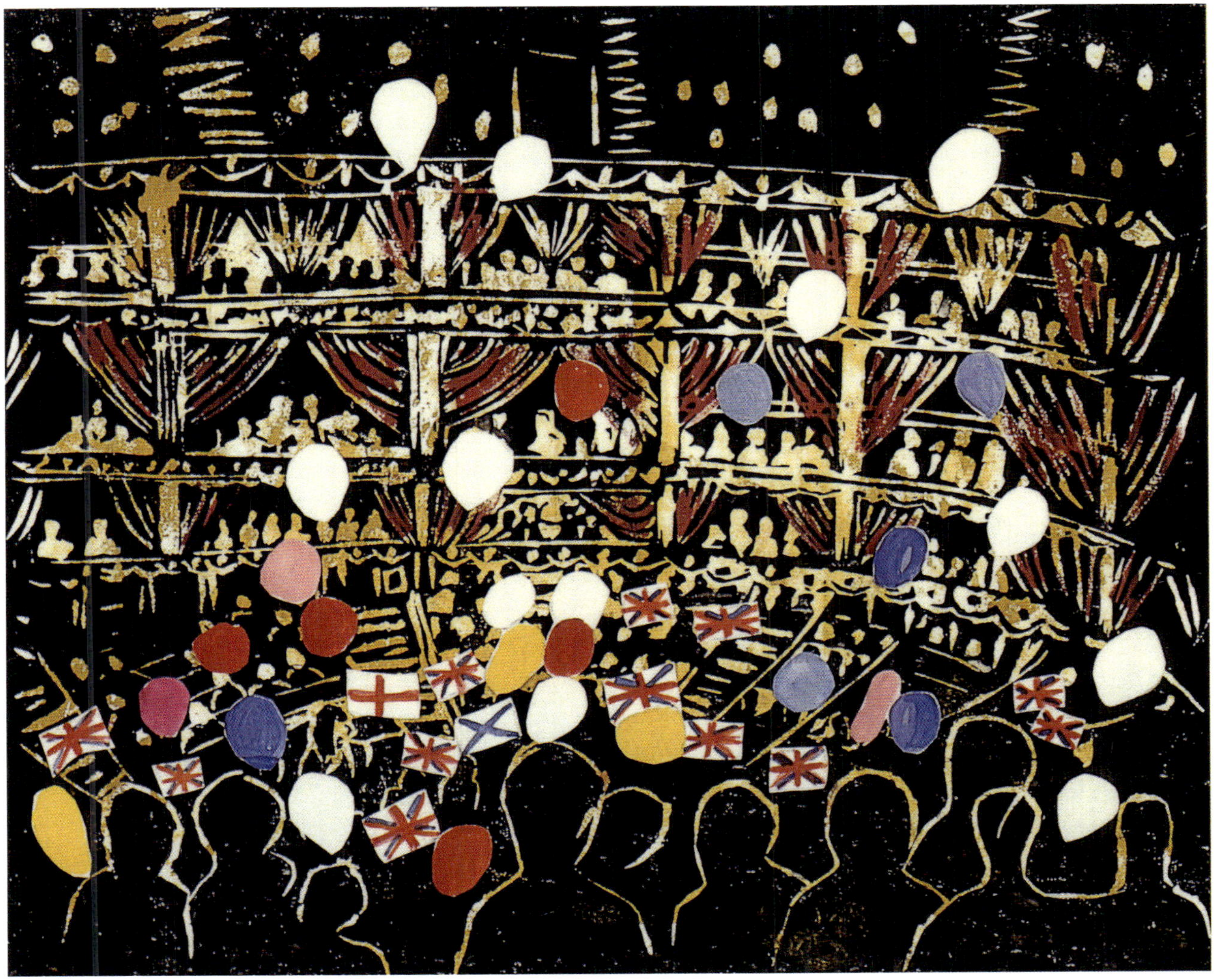

Last Night of the Proms, 41 x 46 cm, lino & collage (edition of 30)

Louise Stebbing

I have been mesmerised by printmaking techniques since attending an Art Foundation course in Cambridge taught by Walter Hoyle. I draw inspiration from my environment using the inherent qualities of printmaking techniques to capture the essence of my subjects.

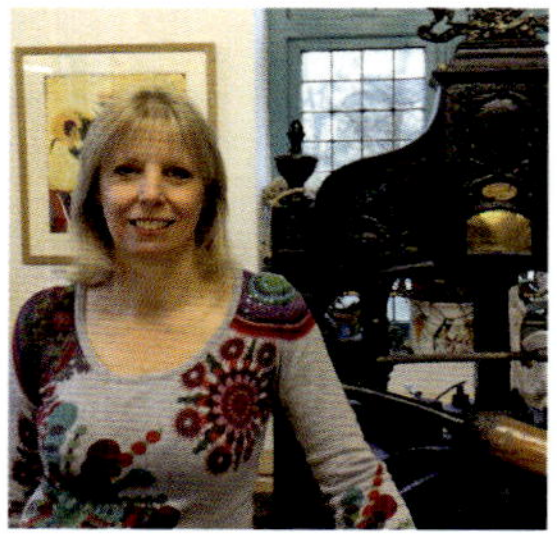

1961 Born Tydd, Cambridgeshire
1979–80 Art Foundation Cambridge
1980–83 BA (Hons) Fine Art Sheffield
1984–85 Postgraduate in Printmaking, Camberwell School of Arts and Crafts
1995–97 PGCE, Nottingham Trent University
2011 *Royal Academy Summer Exhibition*, London
2013 Article in *The Artist* magazine Feb Issue 2013 on linoprinting
Affordable Art Fair, Hampstead with PmC
2013/14 La Calacas Press including Eugenius Gallery, Australia; Casa de los Tres Mundos, Nicaragua; Atelier International Art Gallery, Texas.
2014 Solo Show, Bridewell Theatre Bar Gallery, London.
Cambridge Original Printmakers Exhibition, Pitt Building, Cambridge
2015 *Royal Academy Summer Exhibition*, London
Highly Commended Artist of Year exhibition, Mall Galleries London.
Affordable Art Fair, Hampstead with PmC

Awards:

1999 Won Best Print in the Show, Eastern Open, Kings Lynn
2005 Won title Artist of the Fens
2012 Artists Category at Patchings, Notts.
National Print Open, Ropewalk, North Lincs
2013 Artists Category at Patchings, Notts.

Since leaving college I have continued creating original prints and for many years I have also taught a wide range of art skills to both adults and children in different colleges and schools as well as in my own studio.

It is the processes of printmaking that I love: printmaking requires a lot of patience with elements of risk and surprise.

I have used a variety of printmaking techniques but recently my preferred printmaking medium is linocuts. Lino printing captivates me because of being able to use vibrant colour and the variety of bold expressive cuts that can be made with the gouges.

My images usually start with a sketch, often drawn whilst out cycling in the local landscape. I might pass the same scene several times before being attracted to it by the way the light is affecting the landscape or maybe just because my own mood is different.

Back in my studio I like the print to evolve as I create it – not working out too much detail in advance. I use my experience to let the image develop on the lino block and to keep the energy of the image flowing in the direction it happens to take me at that particular time. I believe that an original print should not be a reproduction of something else but should express the textures and qualities characteristic in the method used.

I usually use the reduction method of lino printing – using one block to print the different layers of colour – printing one colour, cutting more of the lino and overprinting the next colour. I can spend more than a day just cutting one stage of the lino, but the inking of the block is a much quicker process depending on the size.

I have exhibited my work extensively throughout the UK in mixed shows and solo exhibitions. I have been accepted twice into the Summer Exhibition at the Royal Academy and won several awards for my work. I am a member of the Printmakers Council and Cambridge Original Printmakers.

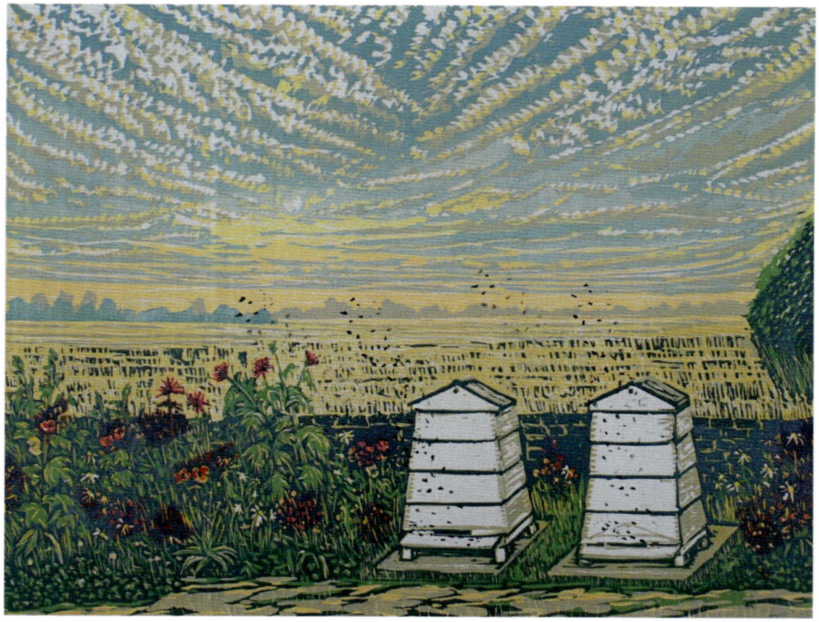

Bringing it Home, 39 x 50 cm, linocut (edition of 16)

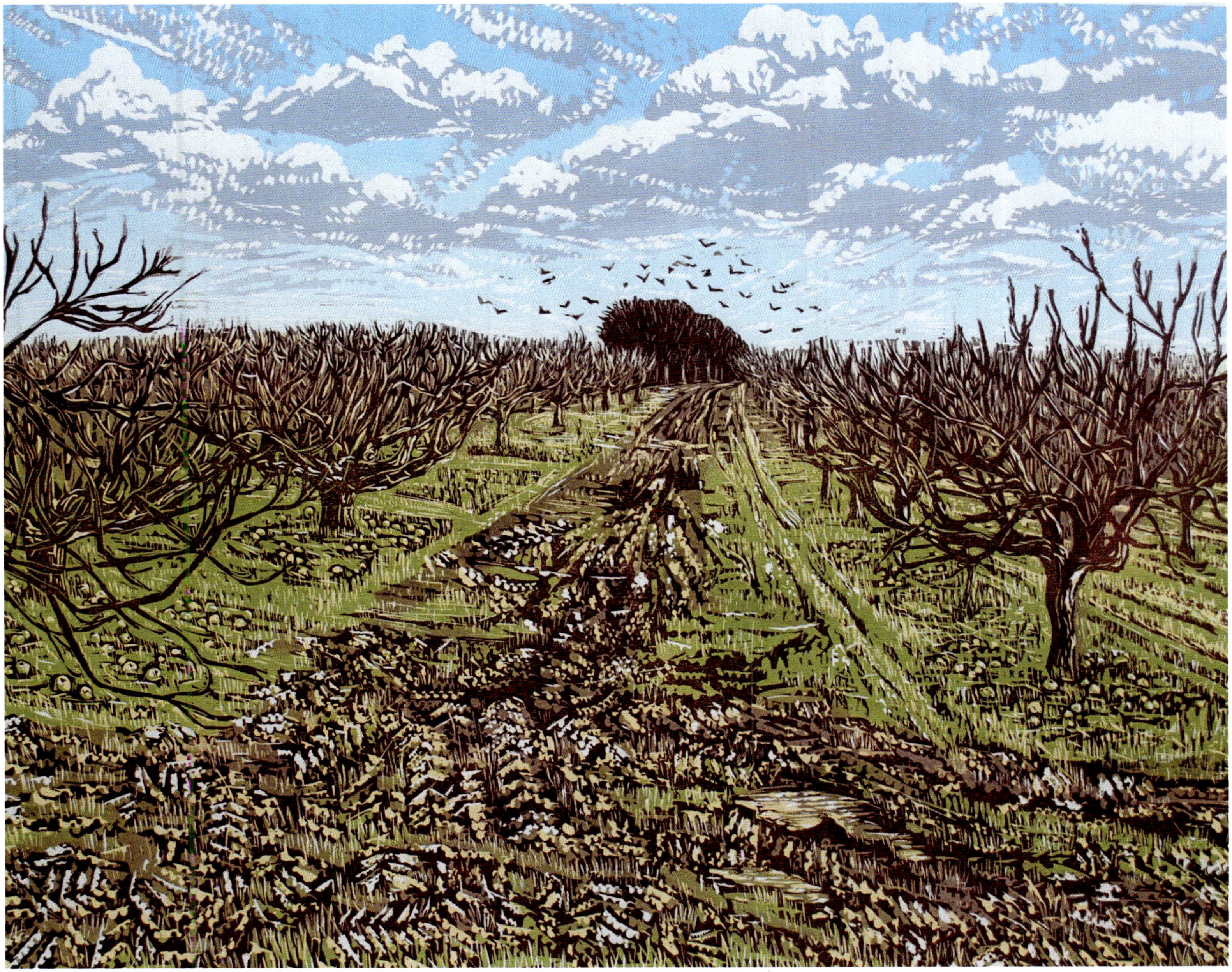

Waiting for Spring, 71 x 57 cm, linocut (edition of 12)

Euan G Stewart

I was brought up in Ayrshire in Scotland and have lived and worked in London following the completion of an MA in Sequential Design and Illustration at the University of Brighton in 1999. A sequential element has remained integral to my work ever since, by using repetition or progression to illustrate my desired narrative or concept.

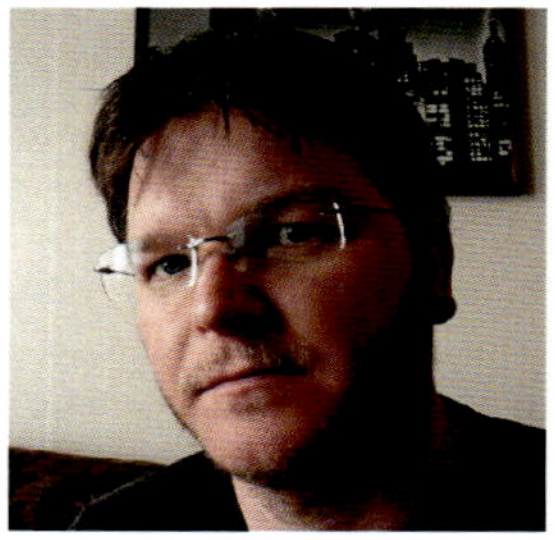

1975 Born Glasgow
1993–97 BA (Hons) Drawing and Painting, Edinburgh College of Art
1998–99 MA Sequential Design and Illustration, University of Brighton

Recent Exhibitions
2009 Lady Charlotte Stevenson Award, Café Gallery Projects, London
2011 *Bite*, Mall Galleries, London (Printmaking Today prize) *The London Group Open*, Cello Factory, London. National Open Art Competition Minerva Theatre, Chichester
2012 *The Pastel Society Open*, Mall Galleries, London. *Pushing Print*, Old Pie Factory, Margate (prize). *Canvas and Cream Open*, Canvas and Cream Gallery, London
2013 IMG–TXT–MSG, Studio 1.1 Gallery, London. *The Big Draw*, Tokarska Gallery, London. ELP, Shoreditch Town Hall, London. *Art Lacuna* Prize Exhibition, Art Lacuna Space, London
2014 *North Lincolnshire Print Open*, Ropewalk Gallery, Barton upon Humber. *Half Cut*, Stour Space, London. *This Year's Model*, Studio 1.1 Gallery, London. *Royal Academy Summer Exhibition*, London. neo:Print Prize, neo:gallery 22, Bolton. *Artists' Art from Artichoke*, Bankside Gallery, London. ELP, Embassy Tea Gallery, London. *Pushing Print: 5 Years On*, Old Pie Factory, Margate. *Derwent Art Prize*, Mall Galleries, London

Collections
2012 Wellcome Collection, London.

My work lies in the area between drawing and printmaking. In addition to traditional disciplines of relief and intaglio, I use experimental materials such as leather and rubber to maintain the immediacy of drawing in printmaking and bring some of the technical process of printmaking to drawing. I invite the viewer to see the evidence of the hand, through the pencil, pen, finger or the relief line in my finished work. The spirit of experimentation is central to my practice and most recently, I have been embracing this through monoprint. This allows me to use a wide variety of line and texture, through using different types of plate and new methods of mark-making. A natural product such as leather is similar to wood and even lino in some cases, but has unique characteristics that offer both variety and versatility. This can produce sometimes unexpected results that lead to new ideas and areas of exploration.

I feel that experimentation is best served by collaboration and discourse. Through working with studios such as Artichoke and East London Printmakers, I have found the feedback and support of the printmaking community has been invaluable in the progress of my practice.

My first encounter with print was Goya's etchings and this remains a constant influence. These prints are an exceptional example of the sequential as a tool to relay an uncompromising message and create a powerful impression that stands the test of time. I try to emulate this in my own way through exploring the themes of anatomy and identity.

Institutions such as the Hunterian Museum and Wellcome Collection have provided rich source material and constant inspiration for these themes. My time spent drawing in such environments is where I feel most at home, but translating the results of these sessions into larger work and longer sequences in the studio is where the challenge begins.

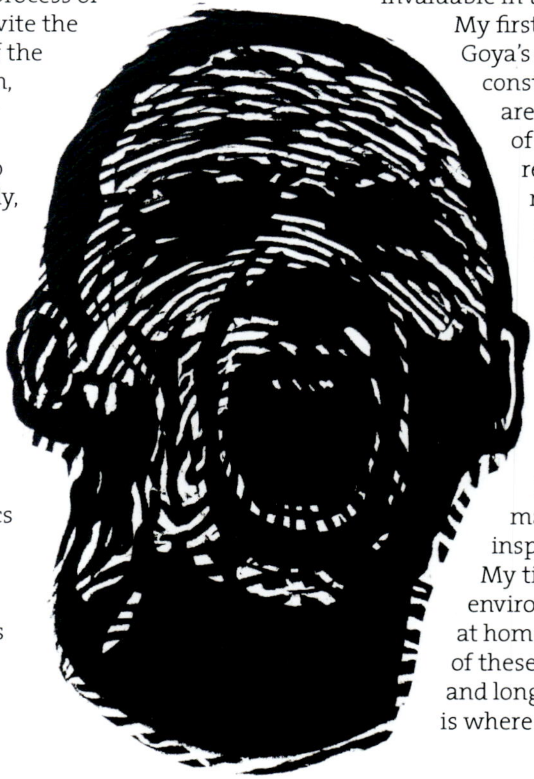

Identity Crisis V, 40 x 50 cm, woodcut (edition of 15)

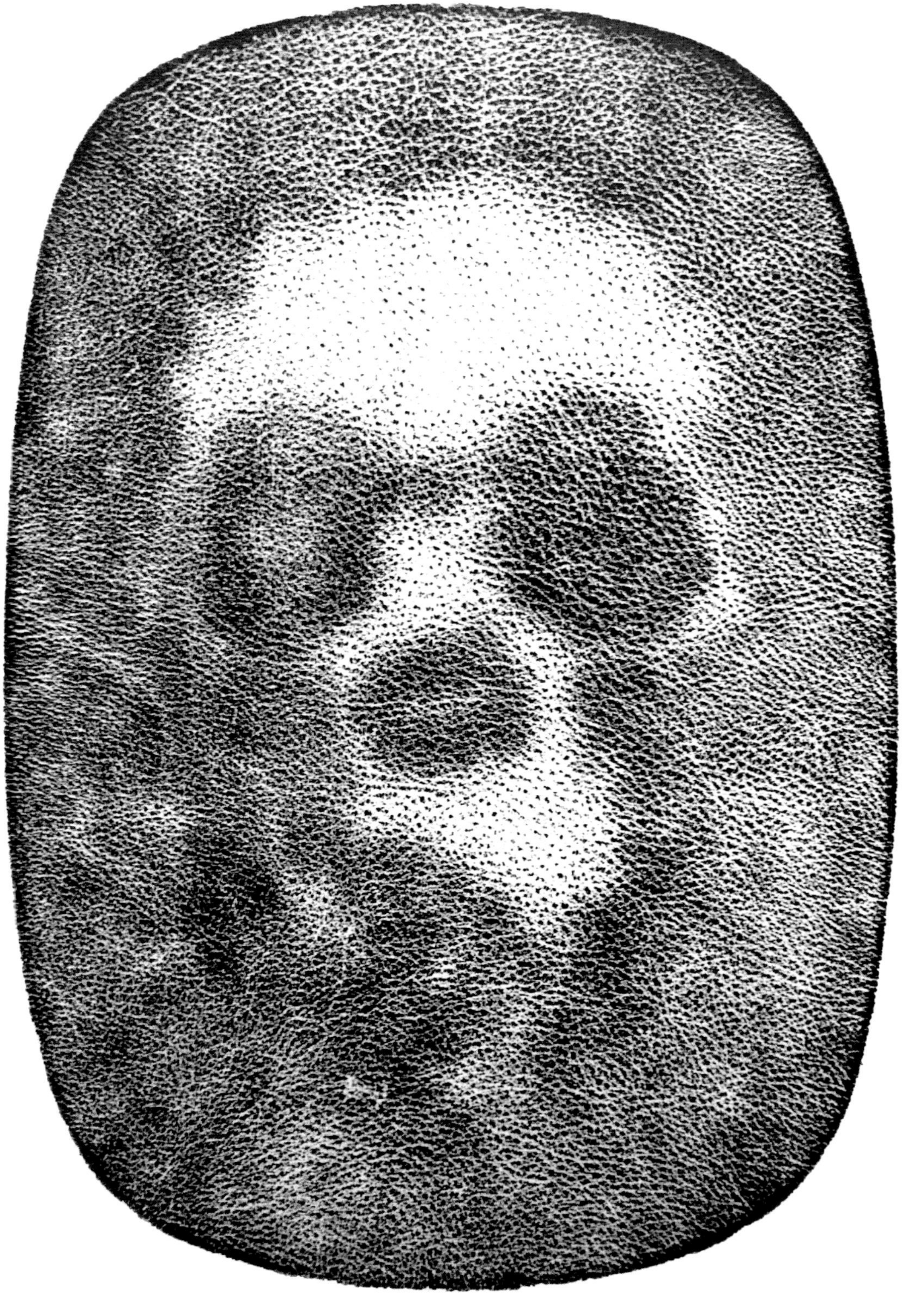

Presence I, 40 x 50 cm,
monoprint (unique)

Jane Stothert

I have always wanted to screen-print. My opportunity came when I finished at Cheltenham School of Art and discovered a screen-printing course at Putney School of Art and Design. My prints are influenced by my time as a graphic designer, which is where I became interested in simplifying my images into colourful geometric, hard-edged shapes. I am a big fan of Bridget Riley, Ittens and Albers.

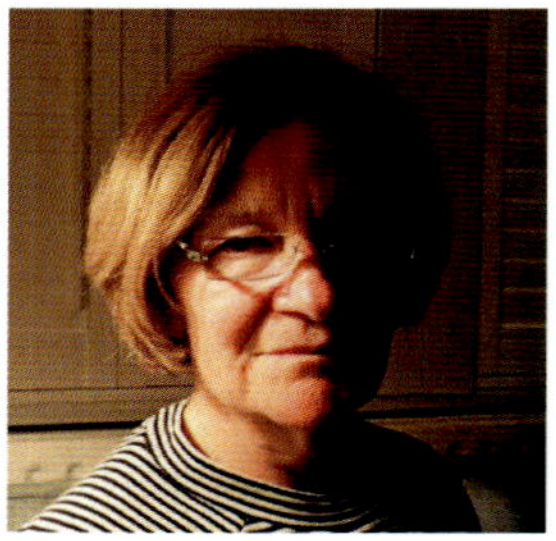

1952 Born in Manchester, but brought up in Warrington
1970–73 Trained as a teacher at Brighton University
1973–81 Taught at Croft Primary School and Cransley School
1981–84 Studied Graphic Design at Kingston University
1984–92 Worked as a graphic designer at Minale Tattersfield
1992–93 Foundation, Byam Shaw
1993–96 BA Fine Art Cheltenham School of Art
1997 Moved into a studio in Lavender Hill
1997–2008 Screen-printing course at Putney School of Art
1999, 2000 Exhibited with Polar Press at the *Contemporary Print Show* at the Barbican
2000 Joined Southbank Printmakers
2007 Collaborative exhibition with SBP at the Kunstverein Villa Streccius in Germany
2009–14 Chair of Southbank Printmakers
2010 Tenth Anniversary of Southbank Printmakers at the Crypt
2011 First solo show at the Crypt Gallery at St Martin in the Fields
2012 Joined Espacio Gallery
Joined South London Women Artists
2012–14 Showed in the *Original Print Fair* at the Espacio Gallery
2012 Selected to show in *Bite* at the Mall Galleries
2013 Rejoined Printmakers Council
2013 Joined The New Constructivists

Art has always been at the root of all my career decisions. I chose teaching because of the opportunities of working with young children creatively through art. Wanting to work more in the world of art, I studied graphic design. This resulted in working as a graphic designer for Minale, Tattersfield and Partners, a top international design group in London. A further interest led to a foundation course at the Byam Shaw School of Art, after which I studied fine art at Cheltenham College of Art. I didn't start printing until I left Cheltenham.

As for my working practice, to prepare a print I make lots of drawings, simplifying them as I go along. Recently I have started to make blind drawings, which results in unexpected shapes that would not happen from an observed drawing. From my drawings I create colour collages which can be manipulated until the desired effect is finalised. To create my shapes for print I still like cutting out my stencils using light-blocking Amberlith film.

I like images of the city because of the geometric shapes created by the buildings, but I also like anything to do with water and light having spent many summer holidays sailing in Anglesey. Images from my travels also inspire me. I was commissioned to make a rowing print for the Olympics, which encouraged me to include figures in my prints. Dorney Lake was the result.

When people see my work I would like them to enjoy the colour, shapes and rhythm.

I have taken part in many group exhibitions, but the exhibition that stood out for me was a collaborative exhibition with Southbank Printmakers and printmakers from the Palatinate at the Kunstverein Villa Streccius in Landau e. V. in 2007.

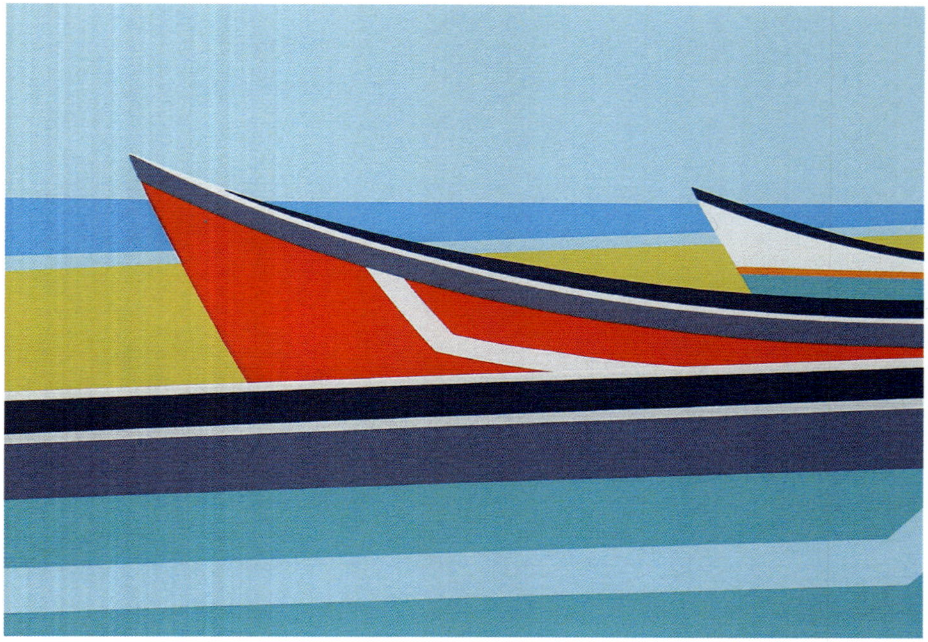

Ashwen Beach Goa,
19 x 27 cm,
screen print
(edition of 13)

Dorney Lake I, 28 x 38 cm, screen print, (edition of 12)

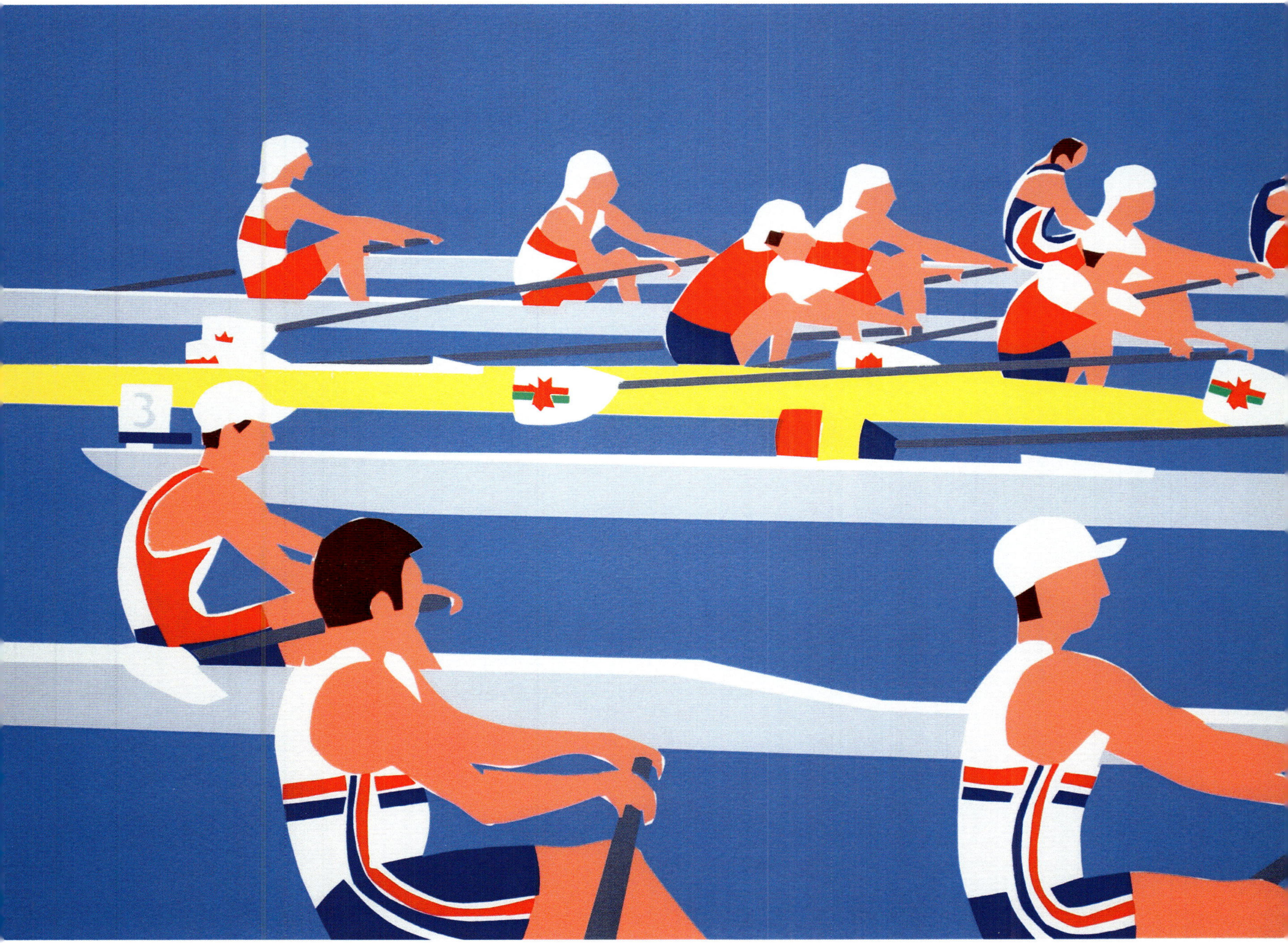

Nicola Styan

I am a London-based artist and my images are an imaginative response to a changing cityscape involving new constructions, historic buildings, bridges and locations. My work explores London icons from various positions and lighting conditions. The screen-printing process is used in my work to integrate photographic and drawn imagery to create a realm of recognition and abstract reflection.

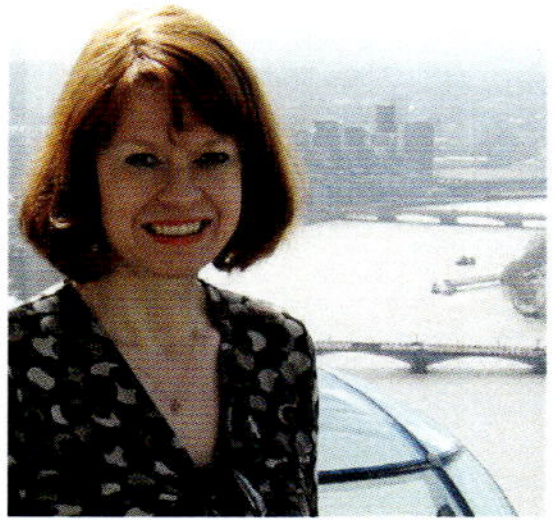

Born Romsey, England

1985–89 BA (Hons) Fine Art Printmaking, Winchester School of Art

1989–91 Postgraduate Diploma in Printmaking, University of Brighton

1991–92 MA Fine Art Printmaking, University of Brighton

1992–93 Graphic Design Diploma, London College of Printing and Distributive Trades

1993–95 Freelance Graphic Designer Commissions for Royal Mail Headquarters, Old Street, London and Royal National Institute for the Blind, London

1995–97 Certificate in Digital Origination at London College of Printing and Distributive Trades (Distinction)

1997–99 PGCE, Institute of Education, University of London

1999–2010 Printmaking lecturer, including head of printmaking and screen-printing department and moderator of art and design courses at the Working Men's College, Camden Town, London

2000–10 Exhibitions including solo shows at M&S Headquarters, Baker Street, London and BBC Television Centre, London. Group shows at the Business Design Centre, London

2010–present Exhibitions in London and regionally. Printmakers Council committee member and East London Printmakers member. Author of published work *Fingerprint Remembers London* in 2012

2010–present Victoria and Albert Museum, London Print Collection

Nicola Styan has studied printmaking and digital media, both contributing to her work. The orchestration of imagery through the screen-printing process and revisiting locations over time have helped formulate her ideas.

Sketches and photographs of the locations are taken at different times of the day. Digital media then integrate the images that are recombined through the process of screen-printing, establishing the forms and colours. In her compositions she often includes more than one viewpoint to relive the experience of exploring the locations and constructions. Her final images promote the fusion of a complex environment into dynamic colour and form.

Styan's imagery captures London icons in various contexts and environments. Her work portrays how atmospheric conditions can dominate locations to present an impressive visual spectacle. As London moves from day through dusk to night, a very different visual dynamic occurs. Her body of work encapsulates the transformation of a natural backdrop into a theatre of light.

Many of the recognisable structures of London are sometimes taken for granted and her prints document the juxtaposition of some of these structures against old and newer buildings to accentuate a changing cityscape. Her work celebrates new infrastructure that empowers the identity of London's historical icons and locations. Bridges are often included in her imagery to identify location and distinguish new developments. Also, the loss of an historic building is recorded, as shown in the screenprint *Ghost of Battersea Power Station*.

Styan was a printmaking lecturer, head of department and moderator at the Working Men's College in Camden Town for over ten years. She is a Printmakers Council committee member and makes limited edition screen prints. Her body of work includes a Fingerprint Series of limited edition prints, and she has published books of her work including *Fingerprint Remembers London* in 2012 that represents the artist at the scene of iconic London locations. Her work has been bought by a variety of people in the media and is in print collections held by the V&A.

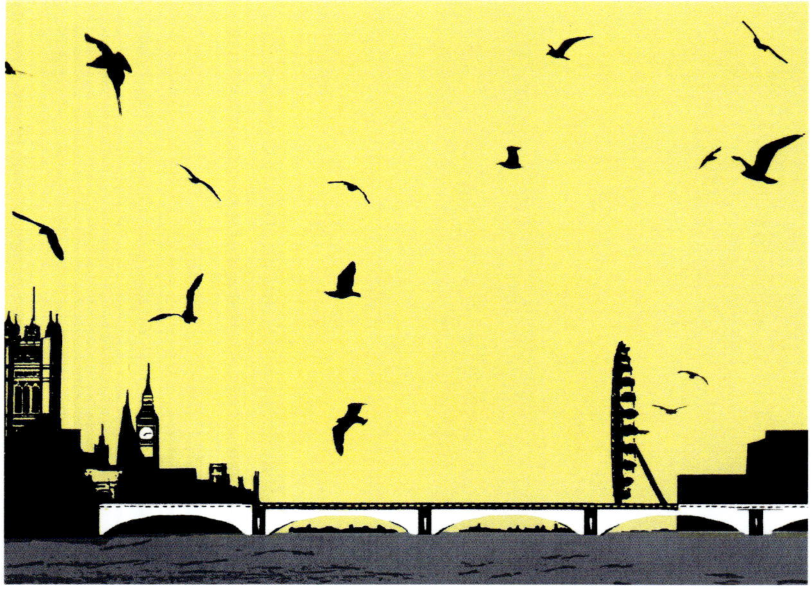

The Birds, Embankment
24 x 30 cm
screen print
(edition of 70)

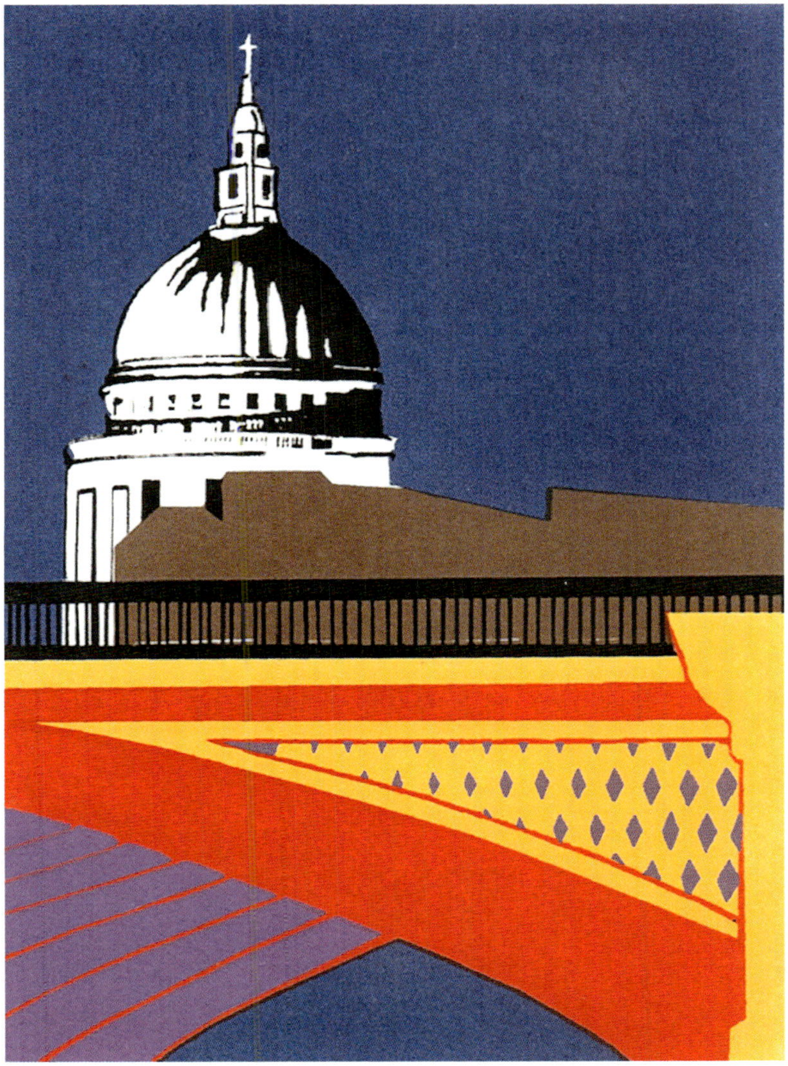

Blackfriars Bridge, 8.59pm
24.5 x 19.5 cm
screen print
(edition of 20)

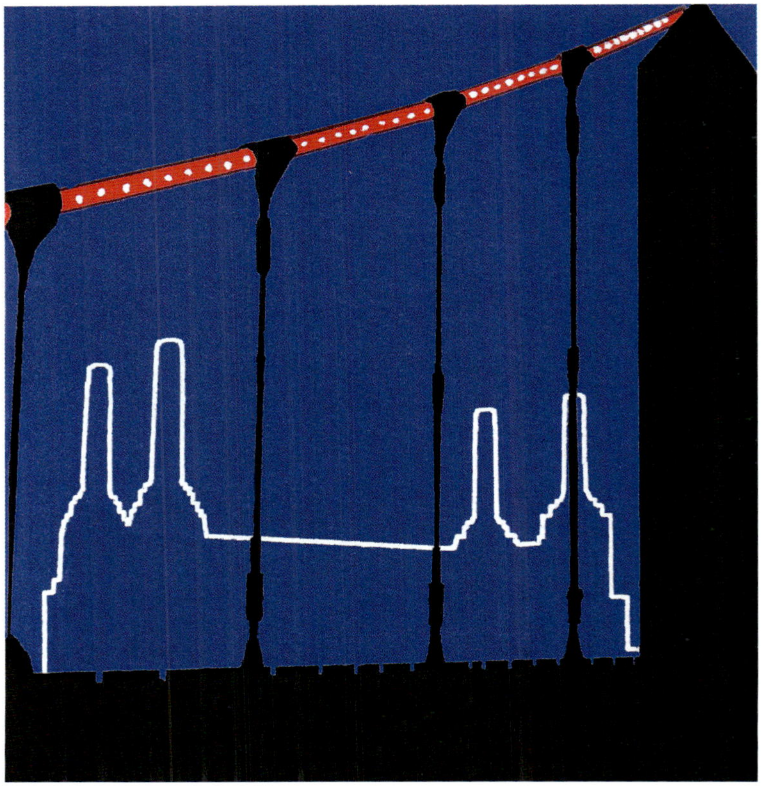

Ghost of Battersea Power Station
18 x 18 cm, screen print, (edition of 5)

Julie Sullock

I studied Fine Art at St Martin's School of Art after completing a foundation course at Central School of Art. It was at Central that Moy Keightley introduced me to the process of reduction lino printing, which I enjoyed enormously. I love the excitement of printmaking, as it is always partly a surprise when peeling off the paper from the block or etching plate.

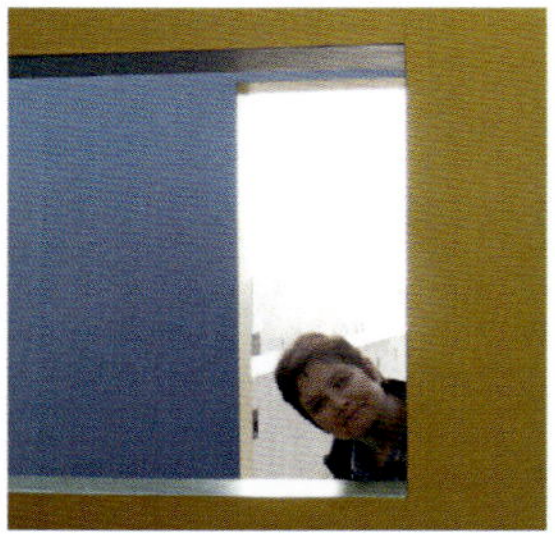

1962 Born Clapham, London

Education

1982–83 Foundation Course, Central School of Art & Design

1983–86 Fine Art, St. Martin's School of Art

1986–88 MA Printmaking, Brighton Polytechnic

1994–95 PGCE, Institute of Education

Employment

1987 Taught Lithography, Working Men's College, Camden Town

1989–90 Screen-printing tutor, Morley College

1990–99 Artist-led workshops during holidays, Geffrye Museum

1996–98 Art teacher, Putney High School for Girls

1989–2013 Taught Art, South Thames College

2014–present Craft Workshops, RHS Wisley Garden, Surrey

Exhibitions

1989–2013 Open Studios, Stockwell Studios London

2010 10 years on SBP, Crypt Gallery London

2014 Lambeth Open, Brixton East Gallery *Drawn to Abstraction*, Stables Gallery, Twickenham

2015 *50:50*, New Ashgate Gallery, Farnham Print Open, Art Hub Gallery, Deptford, *Works on Paper*, Barbican Library

Awards

2007 Juliet Gomperts painting award based in Tuscany

Professional Membership of Societies

1991–2002 Greenwich Printmakers

2000 Southbank Printmakers

2014 Printmakers Council

Although I spent most of the time during my degree at St. Martin's painting, I also worked in the printmaking department. Norman Ackroyd used to send us off on a trip to Wales with soft-ground etching plates, fastened together with slivers of card edging, which protected the plates while travelling. Drawing directly onto the plate in front of the Welsh countryside was always thrilling.

I enjoy the possibilities of screen print, chine collé, monoprints, and painting into the print. The combinations seem endless, yet there is always a constraint with print, which is imposed by the physical plate, wood or lino block.

Learning more about printmaking, especially lithography, when studying for a Master's in Printmaking at Brighton Polytechnic gave me a comprehensive grounding using several different print techniques.

My prints often combine the different mediums of etching, screen print and collograph to build up layers of colour to create different perspectives and atmospheres within the work.

Prints that I produce are concerned with colour and mood and I enjoy working from nature.

I am a member of the Printmakers Council and Southbank Printmakers at Gabriel's Wharf where more of my prints can be viewed.

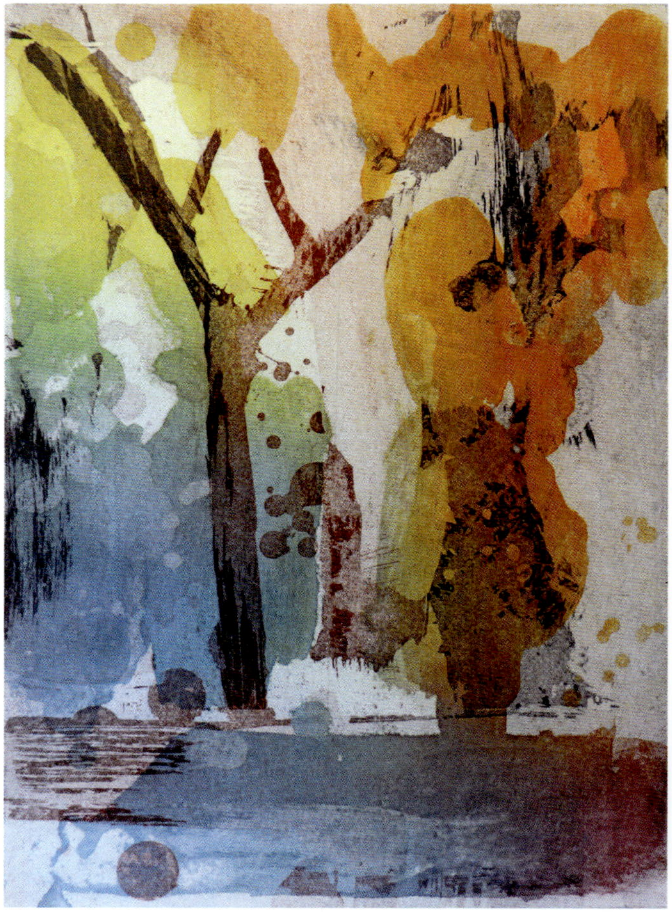

Autumn Tree, Richmond, 12 x 18.5 cm, etching (edition of 10)

OPPOSITE
Spring,
16 x 18 cm,
collograph with watercolour
(edition of 1)

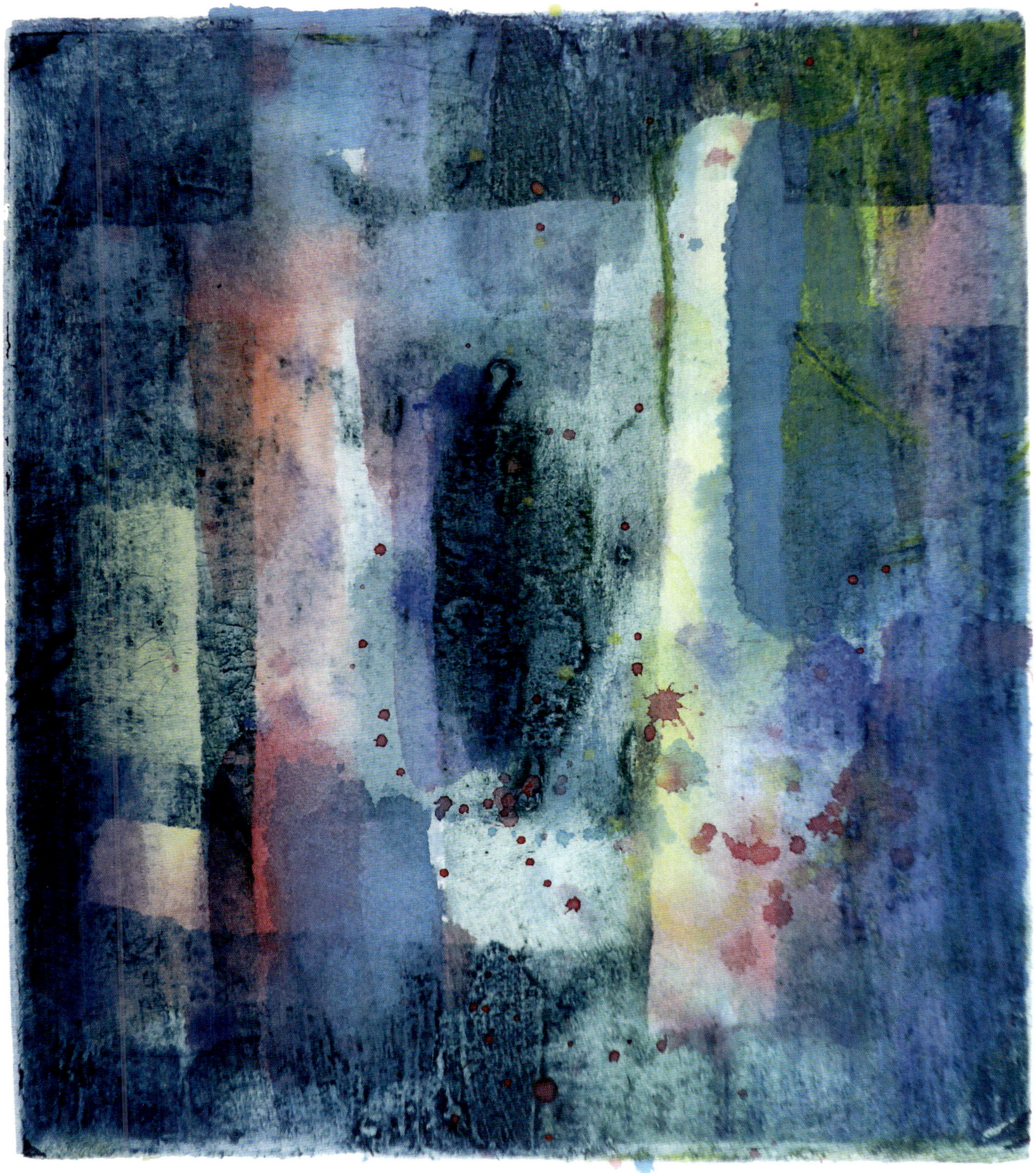

Anne Sumpner-Evans

I have always been excited by my surroundings and visualise them in a particular medium – poster paint when small and later watercolour. The most exciting day of my life was walking into Camberwell Art School. Life started from then on and I have enjoyed experimenting with many different media since. After painting my great joy was printmaking and then I was introduced to monoprinting and linoprinting and can't stop.

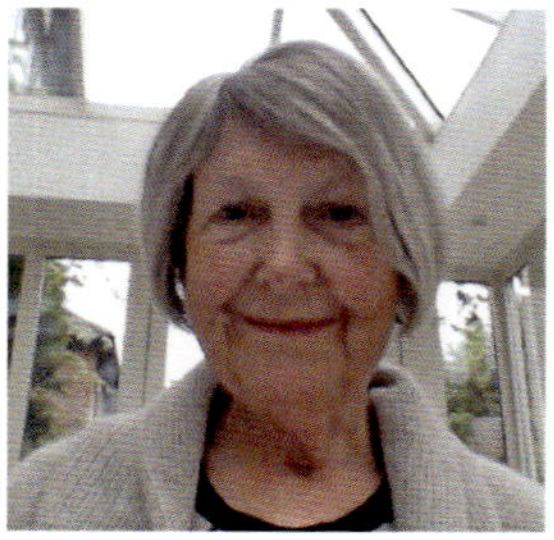

1937 Born London
1957 Camberwell School of Art
1960 NDD, St Martin's School of Art
1961 Freelance book jackets, illustration etc.
1971 Part-time teaching adults at Clapham
1980 Worked at Streatham and Tooting AEI
1992 Artists & Illustrators Award at United Artists Westminster Hall for best painting - accepted as a member
1993 Member, Ridley Art Society, with the Ridley Horniman Museum Exhibition, National Society. Smiths Gallery, Chelsea Arts Club, Battersea Arts Fair
1994 Ridley Art Exhibition
United Artists at Westminster Hall
Liquitex award for best painting in exhibition
1995 Battersea Arts Exhibition
Pastel Society, Mall Gallery
1996 National Society Bayern-Versicherung Munich
1997 Lesley Gore's Original Arts Gallery, Harrogate
1998 Alexander Llewellyn Gallery
1998 National Society Aya Broughton Prize
2000 Bedford Park Summer Exposition
National Society Commendation award
2010 National Society Matthew White Award
2011 National Society Mathew White Award prize for a print.
Accepted as a member of the PmC
2012 Merton Arts Trail Solo Exhibition
2013 The Upstairs Gallery
2014 Merton Arts Trail; National Society; PmC, Pie Factory, Margate
2015 Bedford Park Gallery
Llewellyn Alexander Gallery

With a background in figurative painting and drawing, I've noticed over time that every ten years or so the things I'm interested in, and the media I work in, change. An interest in boats, the harbour and seaside from frequent visits to Southwold, have provided plenty of painting and image-making inspiration. Other phases included still lifes of flowers from the garden, sometimes abstracted, and landscapes. Media have gone from drawings, watercolour and pastels to monoprints in oil, acrylic paintings and linoprints

After Art School I took a lot of work designing book jackets and illustrating various magazines (including *Vogue*), often doing the finished designs as lino and monoprints I also made some hand-printed relief prints on zinc for Harrods.

To make a change from working at home I attended pottery classes, something I missed out on at Art School.

I spent 20 years as a part-time instructor in drawing and painting and later pottery at Clapham and Tooting. To my surprise this proved very exhilarating and fun.

I came across a course in monoprinting at Putney Art Institute in the holidays which proved to be very inspiring and the start of a new method of working. It started off with oil-based images and led to lots of work in my studio the following year. Another course was silkscreen printing which taught a method of monoprinting which was very appealing, a very immediate painterly approach. This new method uses acrylic paints and led to lots of experiments. The skill in this sort of work involves working very fast and memorising exactly where all the images are to go on the screen. It is very exciting to discover how it all works out when new image is revealed as the paper is removed!

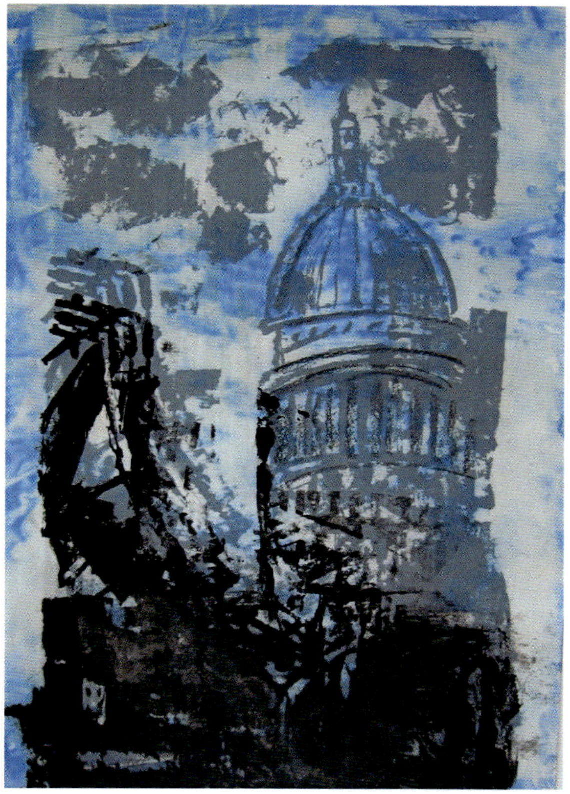

St. Paul's and the Wiggly Bridge, 54 x 35, media-monotype photographed on silkscreen and printed (edition of 3)

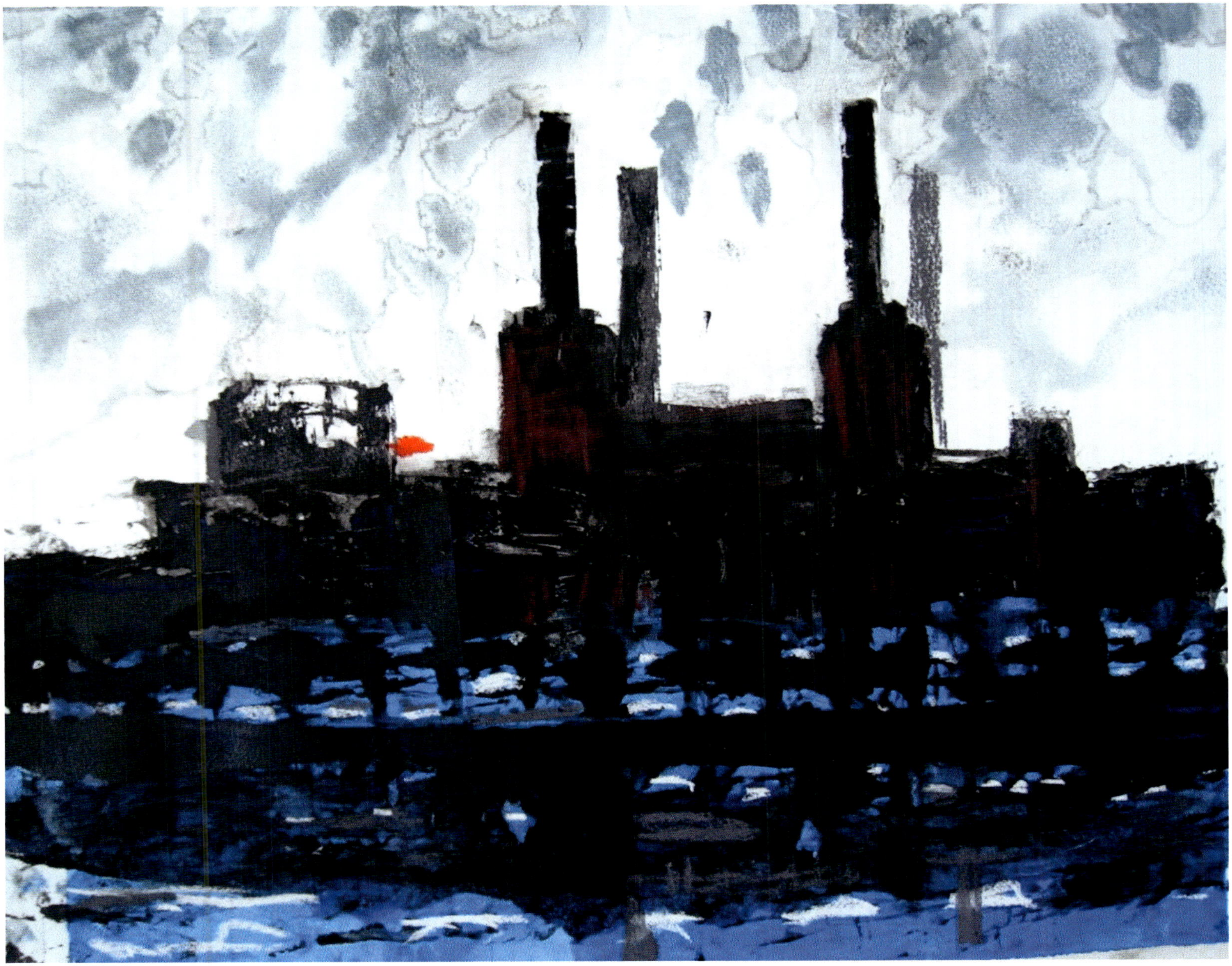

Battersea Power Station, 34 x 44 cm, silkscreen with monoprint background (unique)

Annette Elizabeth Sykes

I received my first real watercolour box at age ten, to keep me amused on our first holiday to Scotland. I will never forget – the caravan was on the very bank of Loch Lomond and each night dozens of ducks would waddle up to settle beneath us. So began my first clumsy attempts at water and birds.

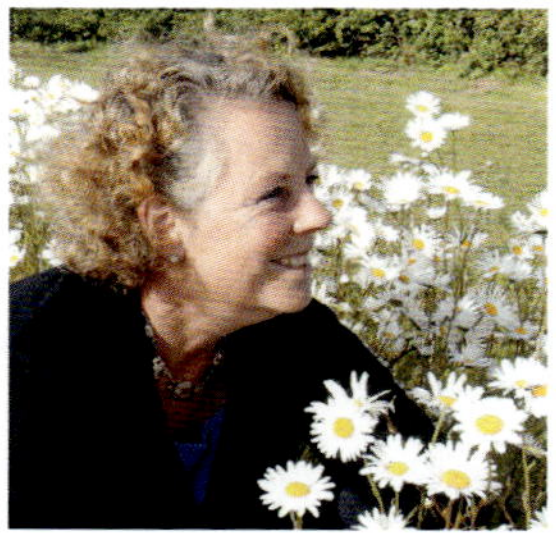

1952 Born Northamptonshire
1970 Studied Art and Sculpture, Coventry College
1972 Worked as a screen print designer
1990 FHE, Northampton
Taught in Adult Education
1998–2001 Studied Textile Design and Embroidery then 2 years design study with Mr John Allen
2008 SWA at the Mall
2009 Joined PmC
Exhibited with SWLA at the Mall
Birdscapes Gallery, Cley, Norfolk
2010 Bankside, London and Birdscapes Gallery
2011 Featured artist in *Imprint*
Work published in *Collograph – A Journey Through Texture*
2012 The Mall, *Cork Street Open*
8th International Print Exhibition
Solo show, Needhams, Cambs
2013 *Cork Street* Open
FPS Menier Gallery
Solo show, Moulton, Northants
Best Print in Show, Northampton Town and County
Work published in *Art of Poetry*
Began quarterly articles on printmaking in FPAA newsletter
2014 Menier Gallery, twice
Work published in *Art of Poetry* and ibooks: *101 Animals* and *101 Abstract Works*. Co-founded the SWAN Group of Artists
2015 New Ashgate Gallery, Farnham, Surrey
Alfred East Gallery, Kettering
Burnham Deepdale, Norfolk
The Hare and Hen Gallery, ongoing

This holiday was followed by many happy times in Norfolk in our own caravan, which embedded birds and water into my soul, in particular their flight and their perceived freedom, the patterns, shapes and colours. This was and is more important to me than 'what type of bird it is'.

Pattern, shape and colour also surrounded me at home as my mother worked in textiles, teaching needlework and pattern cutting amongst other things. These aspects of my work are 'in my blood' and I was encouraged to draw, cut, knit and sew. These skills have necessarily been my touchstone throughout my career.

My schooling took me to Wellingborough High School for Girls where I was lucky to have two art tutors; one who emphasised drawing and art history, the other who was a Sculptor at heart, I owe him loads, although I didn't realise it at the time.

After A-levels I went to Coventry College specialising in paint and sculpture, but left after a while to work in industry designing for screen print, where I stayed until my husband and I had a family.

As my two boys grew up I needed more and I returned to Tresham College for four years, studying textile design and embroidery, where I was re-introduced to printmaking: at the time they had a great print room which was fully equipped. From this beginning I now have my own workspace, Blue Frog Studio, which is equipped with a mangle doubling as an etching press and a relief press.

My inspiration still comes from the world around me. I draw upon the experiences of my immediate surroundings, my travels, and most importantly the coast, which I visit as often as possible; Norfolk, Scotland and the Orkneys being my favourite places to sketch, walk and photograph. Birds and people are my main interests along with ancient culture.

Whatever my subject matter, my designs need to flow; to show the way energy moves between everything in nature. I choose reduction linocut as my favourite print method, allowing my colours to be semi-transparent, allowing each layer to shimmer through and play its part in the whole production, a part which may peek through or be more dominant. Maya (illusion) is a vital element in what the eye sees and I hope to convey in a simplistic manner this interplay of illusion to build up a complexity of design.

My monochrome work follows the same philosophy, relying upon great design and cutting skills to give a flow to my pieces. Occasionally I have worked with drypoint, collograph and solar plate, mixing these genres, but I always seem to return to lino as my natural printmaking medium.

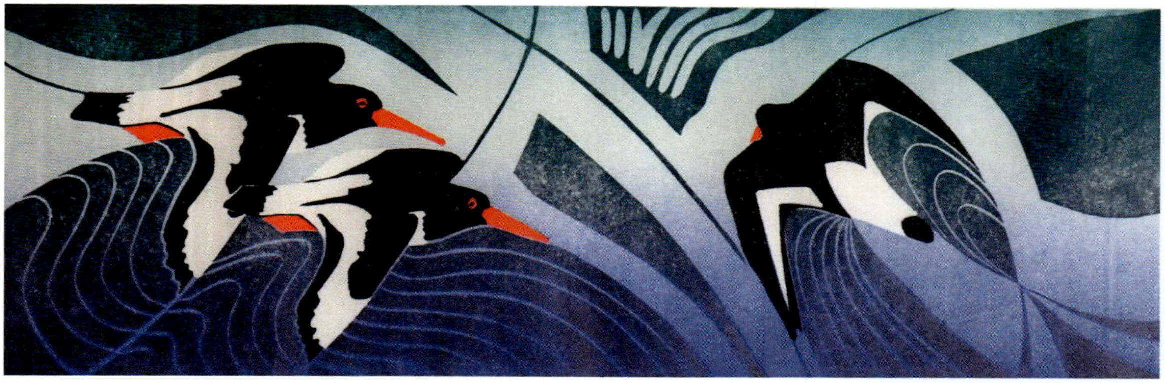

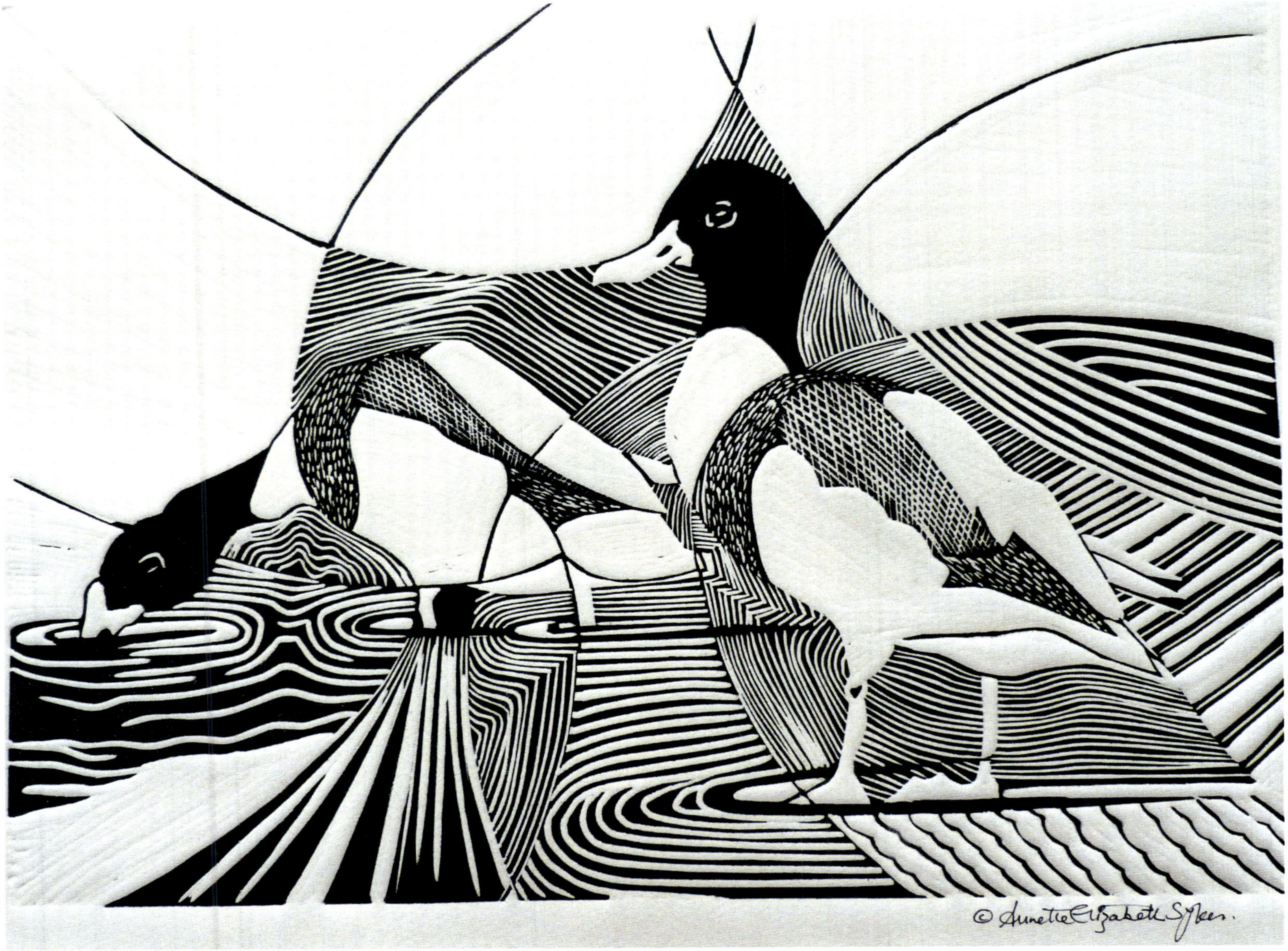

Shelducks, 24 x 32 cm, linocut (edition of 25)

LEFT: *Flight*, 13 x 36 cm, reduction linocut (edition of 9)

Despina Symeou

After the study of art forms primarily focusing on Printmaking, Photography and Life Drawing I specialised in Jewellery Design, gaining a BA (Hons) degree from Middlesex University. In recent years I have returned to the two-dimensional formats which had originally fired my imagination.

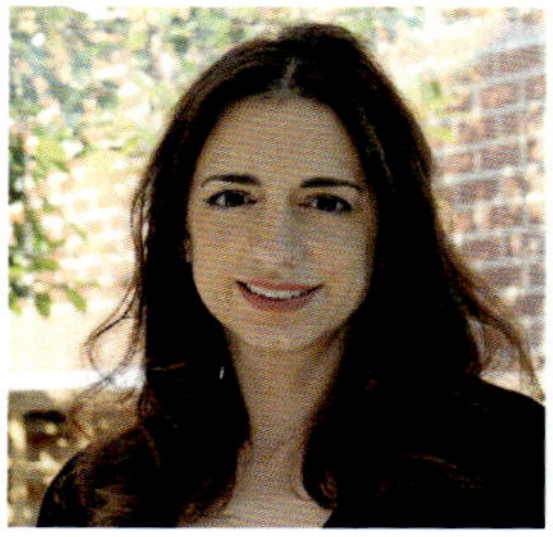

1960 Born London
1979 Art Foundation and Printmaking, Barnet College
1984 BA (Hons) Jewellery Design, Middlesex University
1985–2001 Fashion and Accessories marketing including window display design
2010 *Skin Shapes*, solo exhibition of paintings from the model at The Britannia Centre London
2010 & **2014** Two group shows at Britannia Centre London
2012 Member, Printmakers Council
2012–2013 Exhibited with the PmC many times including the Barbican Centre, Margate Gallery, The Framers Gallery London
2014 The Bainbridge Open
2014 *National Print Exhibition* at Bankside Gallery London
2015 New Ashgate Gallery, Surrey
2015 *Affordable Art Fair*, Hampstead
2015 *Transformation - Trees and Abstract*, The Cyprus High Commission, London multi-media group show
2015 Selected for the Royal Society of Marine Artists, Mall Galleries, London

The human form has been my preferred image but an eye for the interesting and occasionally quirky elements find their way into my style of work, be it representational or abstract.

A variety of printmaking media are applied to frequently capture a figurative form, often juxtaposed with man-made scenes surrounded by the beauty of nature.

Photography is used in much the same way as sketching, to collate information as a starting point or even to evolve into the dominating medium of the process. The use of colour introduces a vibrant and playful element into what can sometimes be a sombre image, evoking a feeling or mood which is as individual as the viewer.

The printmaking process can at times range from tedious to challenging but most times will lead on to creative satisfaction.

In any creative field, the path taken from inspiration to the end product is the most fascinating and instructive period.

Unconscious thought rhythms occur within the creative process that lead to 'happy accidents' resulting in a very pleasing image which has evolved from its original shape and format.

The traditional square or rectangle plate governs presentation, as do paper and canvas. Experimenting outside the embossed edge of the plate also appeals to me, as it brings another facet of possibility into play.

The years spent designing and making jewellery have begun to influence my printmaking. There are similarities between the two which at the beginning had not occurred to me. For example, both media involve the use of metal, be it precious or otherwise, that is worked to obtain a final piece.

As a follow-on from my current work I have begun using a collection of small plates to make a whole image.

I see the next body of work following this theme, where the two creative practices will meet and a hybrid version may evolve.

But as is the nature of this process the end result may in fact be something completely different.

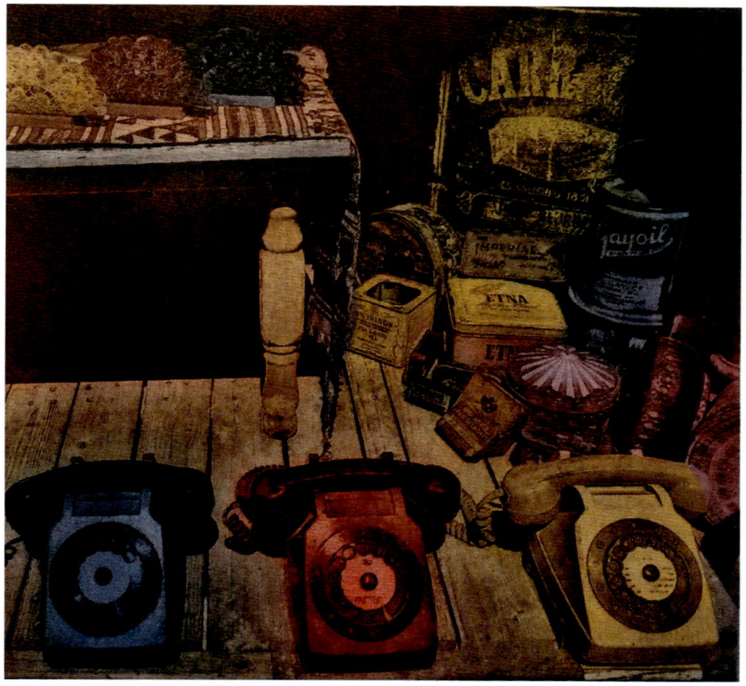

Colour Exchange, 40 x 40 cm, solar plate etching, (varied edition of 30)

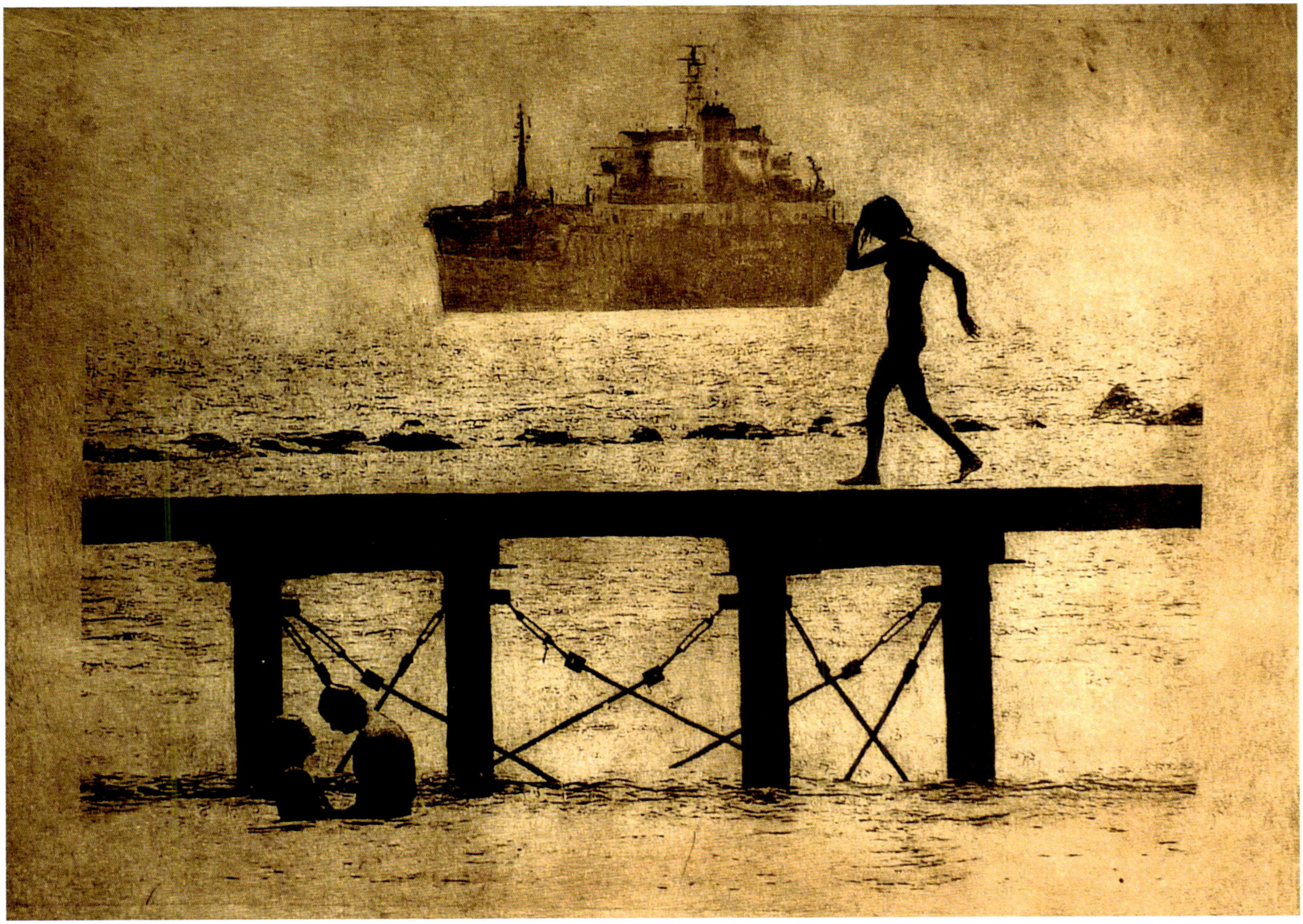

Walking The Pier, 40 x 50 cm, solar plate etching, (edition of 30)

Jasia Szerszynska

Born in Leicester, Jasia drew from an early age and first experimented with printmaking during her degree at Manchester Polytechnic and then further at Goldsmiths College in London where she made monoprints and large scale one-off screenprints. Since then Jasia has attended printmaking courses at Leicester Print Studio, Curwen Study Centre, East London Printmakers, Ochre Print Studio and the Art Academy, London.

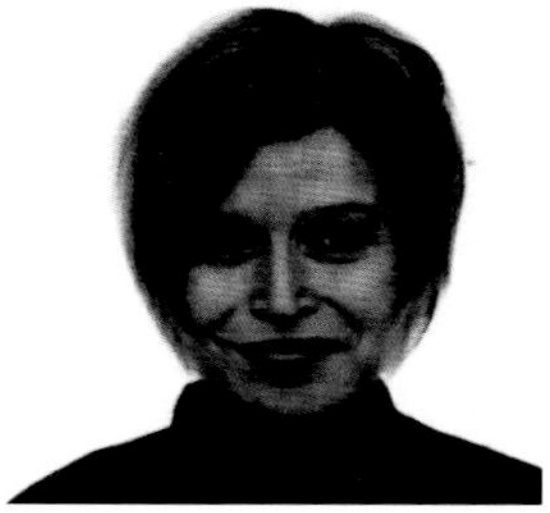

Education

(BA Hons), Manchester Polytechnic
Postgraduate, Goldsmiths College

Solo Exhibitions

1992 Techno UK, Bond Street, London
1994 Open Studio Exhibition, Hong Kong
1998 Gallery Maronie, Kyoto
2002 Gallery Omotesando, Tokyo
2005 The Tea Building, London
2006 The Seedprint Series, Box Gallery
2008 *Kitchen Utensils of a Spitalfields House*, Box Gallery, London

Joint Exhibitions

2010 *Observations*, Art and Architecture Gallery, London
2014 *Printworks*, Hampstead, London

Selected Group Exhibitions

1998 *Lodz Triennale*, Poland
1998 *Tracks, Lines, Circles and Grids*, John Batten Gallery, Hong Kong
1999 *Art Futures*, Contemporary Art Society
2002 British Council Exhibition, Scandinavia
2004 *British Art Now*, Tokyo, Japan
2005 *Images in the City*, Geffrye Museum
2006 *Royal Academy Summer Exhibition*
2010 *Contemporary Art Fair*, San Diego
2012 *Verge Art Fair* and *Art Brooklyn*, New York
2012 *Royal Academy Summer Exhibition*
2012 Arcane Gallery, Bethnal Green
2010–15 *Modern Works on Paper*, London
2012–15 AAF Hong Kong, New York & Milan
2014–15 *British Art Fair*, RCA, London
2015 *Envelope*, Peninsula Art Gallery

Born in Leicester, Jasia drew from an early age and first experimented with printmaking during her degree at Manchester Polytechnic and then further at Goldsmiths College in London where she made monoprints and large scale one-off screen prints. Since then Jasia has attended printmaking courses at Leicester Print Studio, Curwen Study Centre, East London Printmakers, Ochre Print Studio and the Art Academy, London.

Jasia's prints and drawings have been exhibited widely, including solo shows in Kyoto, Tokyo and London. She has taken part in The Royal Academy Summer Exhibition and recent exhibitions in London and New York.

Her work is held in the collections of: Manchester Art Gallery, Bank of England, Courtaulds plc, Curwen Studio Archive, Conquest Hospital, Hastings, Galileo UK and British Council Japan.

Jasia's work is inspired by her drawings and her working practice alternates between drawing projects, including residencies and experimental print projects in her London studio.

"Originally I used graphite and charcoal as the medium for mark-making on paper, because I love the quality of line and texture that it gives. I then began experimenting with brush and ink which released a new boldness and spareness when creating drawings out in the landscape. I sometimes use a mixture of these media, often working on squared paper."

When it comes to making prints Jasia often works directly from her sketchbooks, having half a dozen open in front of her. Her minimal drawings of room interiors and sparse landscape sketches give her a huge resource of visual material for her printmaking. Printmaking techniques used include: intaglio with textured plates, drypoint, lithography and screen-printing. Jasia usually makes prints in series which can be as many as twelve works. *The Encounters* series is the largest in scale so far and is a set of nine.

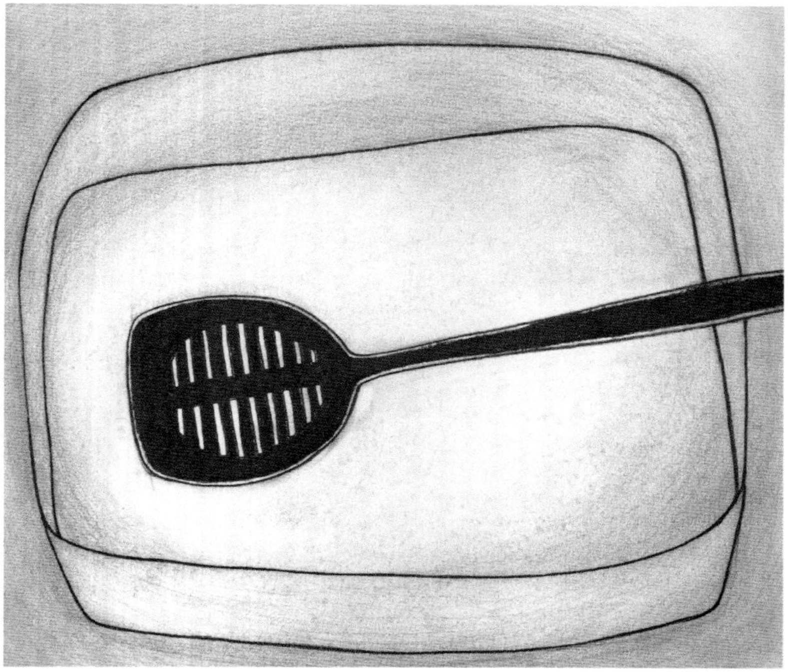

Utensils IV,
36 x 29 cm, lithograph,
(edition of 30)

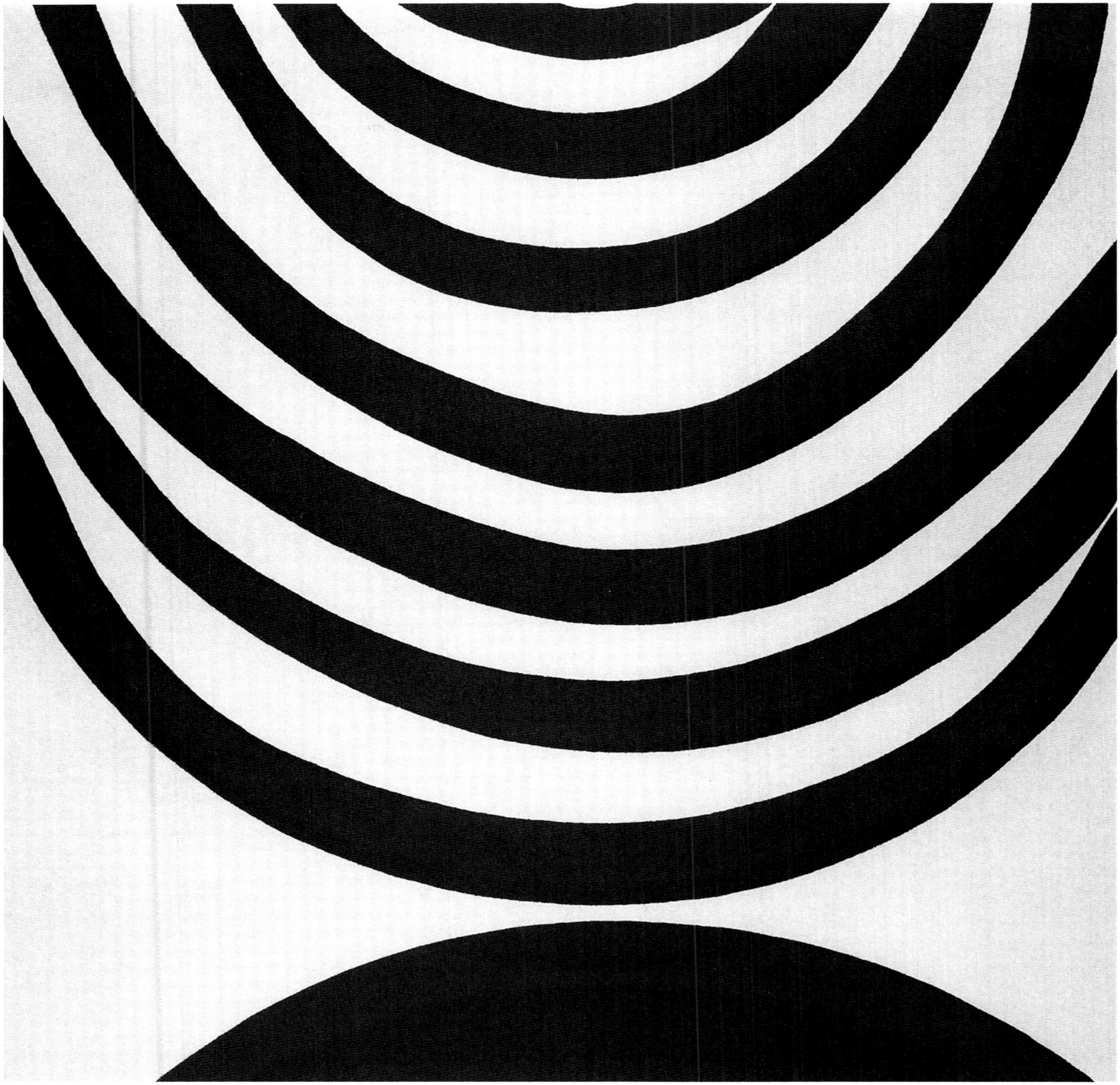

Seventh Encounter I, 48 x 48 cm, lithograph, (edition of 50)

Emma C Tabor

I have always been fascinated by patterns both natural and man-made; they can be intriguing and mesmerizing. Our eyes can be tricked by patterns because of the limitations in our visual perception; our experiences influence how we look at images and interpret them. These are the ideas that I look to investigate through drawing and printmaking.

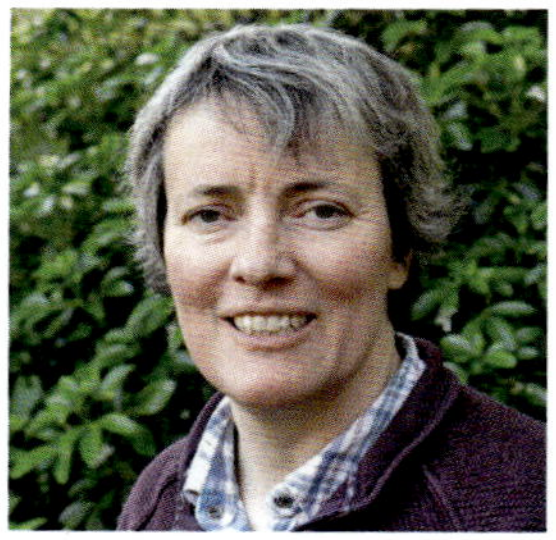

1967 Born Frimley, England

1986–90 MEng (Hons) Loughborough University of Technology, Manufacturing Engineering

1990–94 PhD Nottingham University, Manufacturing Engineering

1998 Chartered Engineer, Institution of Mechanical Engineers

1994–2002 Lecturer, Product Design, Brunel University

2002–05, & 2008–10 BA (Hons) Fine Art (part-time), University for the Creative Arts, Farnham

2005–07 Living in Gurgaon, India

2011–12 Artist in Residence, Ochre Print Studio, Guildford, Surrey

2011 Selected Exhibition *smallprint: big impression*, Leicester Print Workshop travelling exhibition

2012 Joined the Printmakers Council

2012 Group Exhibition: *Turn, Turn, Turn*, The Margate Gallery, Margate

2012 Group Exhibition: *The Contemplative Eye*, Othona, Dorset

2012 Selected Exhibition: Surrey Open, The Lightbox, Woking, Surrey

2013 Appointed Treasurer, Ochre Print Studio, Guildford, Surrey

2013 Selected Exhibition: *Open Space*, Mottisfont Abbey, Romsey

2014 Selected Exhibition: *Ochre Originals*, New Ashgate Gallery, Farnham, Surrey

2014 Selected Exhibition: *Open Print*, Salisbury Arts Centre, Salisbury

2014 Group Exhibition: *Glimpsing Wholeness*, Othona, Dorset

2015 Group Exhibition: *Quinquennial*, Guildford Cathedral, Surrey

My drawings are explorations in pattern, experimenting with line and forms, investigating the visual language that develops. I have an initial starting point but then each drawing grows in a unique way to find its final form and reveal itself. I am continually investigating the drawing to see what is happening and where interesting developments occur and seeing how I can stretch these further in the next drawing and the next and so on.

Often within the drawings and the prints it is the spaces between the lines and forms that have the most importance. Varying these spaces is what develops the sense of movement on the surface. It is not my aim to draw anything recognisable; part of the process of continual re-evaluation is to hear what other people see in it. It is not only our physiologies that affect what we see but our cultural perceptions and experiences too. There is something within all of us that needs to identify and name what we see in the abstract.

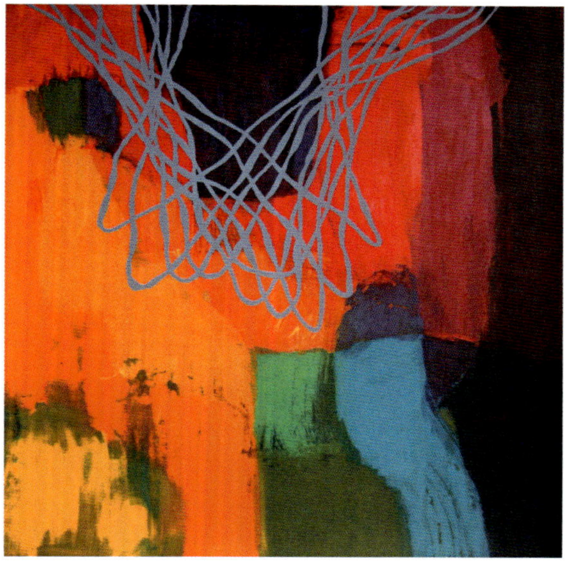

Since studying art I have enjoyed printmaking, probably as the processes link with my engineering background. There is endless scope for experimentation and development. While initially working with intaglio methods, as my drawings developed I discovered a greater synergy in the work with screen-printing. While my drawings are all single-layered, with the prints there is the opportunity to freely create multiple layered images.

Screen-printing is particularly suited to this as it is easy to experiment with the order and orientation of layers to achieve the most interesting effects. While printing I am looking for certain results but along the way the unexpected can happen which will lead to a new direction of investigation. When printing I also freely experiment with colour, particularly exploiting the thin application of ink, that enables optical mixing of transparent colours. Monoprinting with the screen also provides the chance to have some painterly qualities incorporated in imagery, providing a contrast to the drawn line.

Printing can seem to some a rather process-led technique which might prove restricting, but I have found the opposite; it provides methodologies that allow me to experiment and explore in depth the images I am trying to create. Each print offers something new and another direction to head in and will challenge me for a long time to come.

OPPOSITE

Imaginary Site I, 40 x 40 cm, screen print, (edition of 5)

#795, 30 x 30 cm, screen print, (unique)

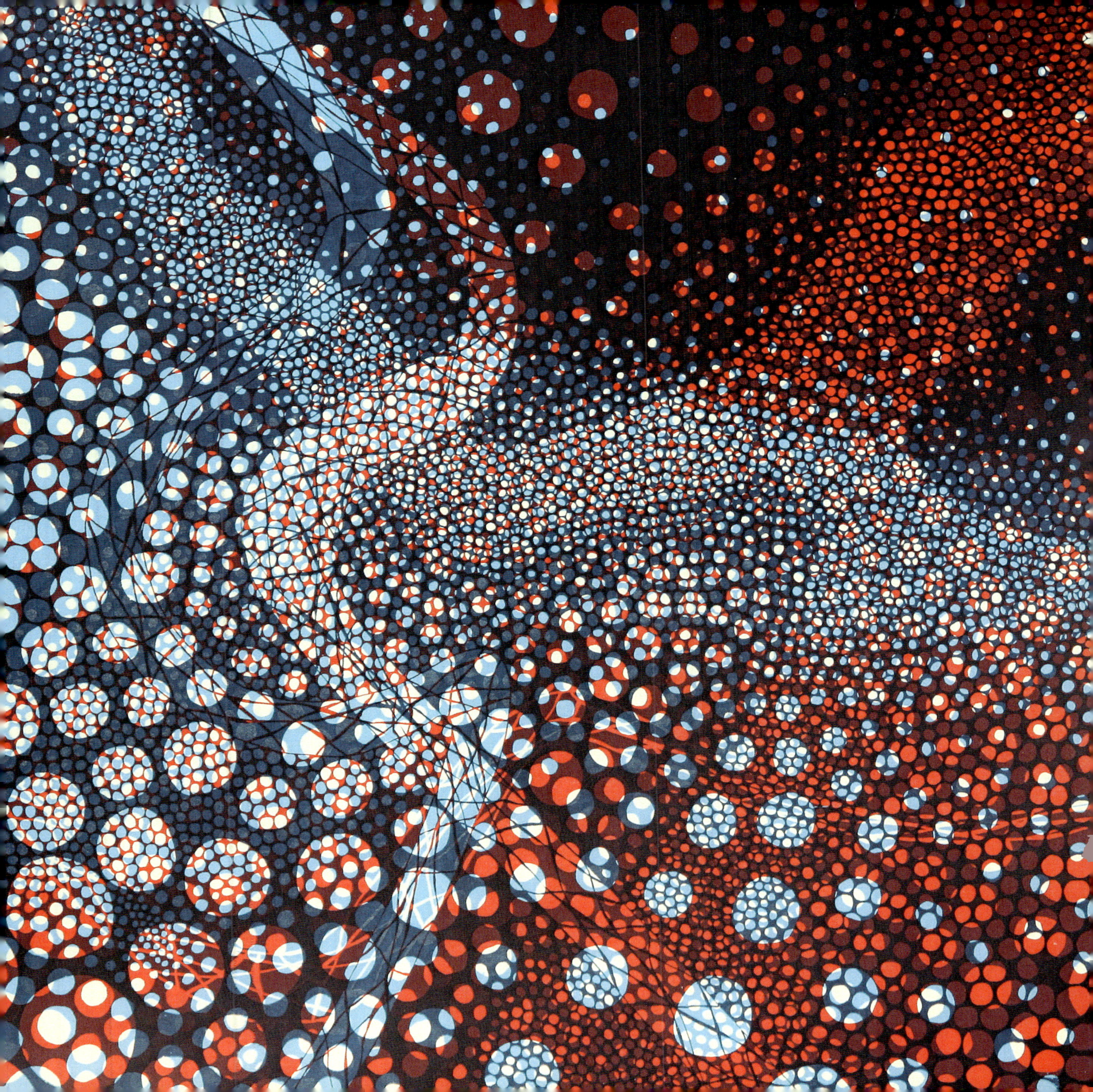

Peter Tingey

Interested in painting and drawing since childhood, I left a career in Surveying to attend Camberwell School of Arts and Crafts in the late sixties. I then went on to work as a teacher and designer in Education, also making prints, books, paintings and constructions.

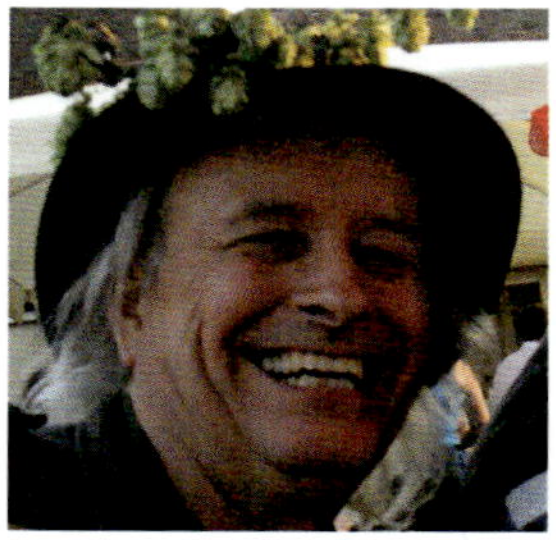

1945 Born Bromley, Kent
1953–63 St. Dunstan's College, Catford
1968–72 Camberwell School of Arts and Crafts
1971 Printer at White Ink intaglio editions
1972 South London Gallery mixed show
1973 Whitechapel mixed show
ILEA as Art Teacher and Printmaker
1973 Purchased a Harrild Albion Press
Established Peter Tingey Editions
1975 Papermaking
1975 Graphic and Educational Designer
1980 Media Resources Officer in Adult Education
1983 Produced book covers for The Many Press
1994 Woodlands Art Gallery
1998 Retired from Lewisham Education
2000 Bookbinding at The London College of Printing
2002 Visited America
2005 Established www.tingey.info
2008 Visited Japan
2011 Studio with Second Floor Studios Association
Exhibitions at NoFormat Gallery & Open studios
2012 Made in Greenwich Art Gallery
2014 Printmakers Council exhibitions

I was educated at Camberwell School of Art and Crafts under the liberal regime of the Graphic Design Department in the late sixties. There was a comfortable mix of the disciplines of the movement from which the School took its name plus contemporary ideas drawn from the worlds of Fine and Commercial Art. Tutors such as Peter Weaver, Frank Martin, John Henn, John Lawrence, Peter Woodcock and Michael Rothenstein came from a range of backgrounds and disciplines which enabled students to find an empathetic ear and eye in a department which provided access to lithographic, intaglio and relief presses, together with silk screen, typographic, photographic and bookbinding sections. We were encouraged to develop our ideas in a freely imaginative way without being bound by the conventions of the print industry on one hand or the dogmas of contemporary fine art movements on the other.

The emphasis on printmaking and the ability to move between these techniques encouraged a multi-media response to projects and a sensitivity to materials which has remained with me, and assisted in avoiding the trap of shoehorning a promising image into an unsuitable medium or format.

It seems so important that art schools, whilst teaching the technical means to interpret experiences in graphic terms, should also provide that momentum which enables artists and their work to keep evolving. I have tried throughout my professional career to adhere to those basic Art and Craft disciplines and obey Peter Woodcock's oft-heard exhortation through a haze of Gauloises: "Go away and make it better". So whether walking in a wood, visiting a gallery or travelling across a strange land, the thought process is the same. Here is a stimulus which can be the start of an adventure, which might well produce something interesting and unforeseen and may even be appreciated by a friend or stranger.

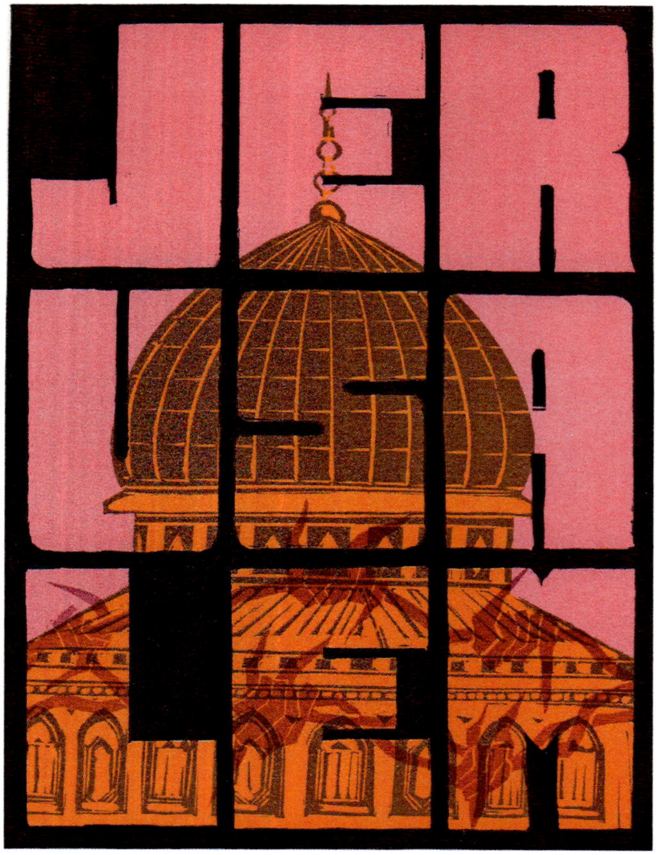

Jerusalem the Golden,
15 x 20 cm, linocut (edition of 100)

Two Turtle Doves, 38 x 38 cm, linocut (edition of 25)

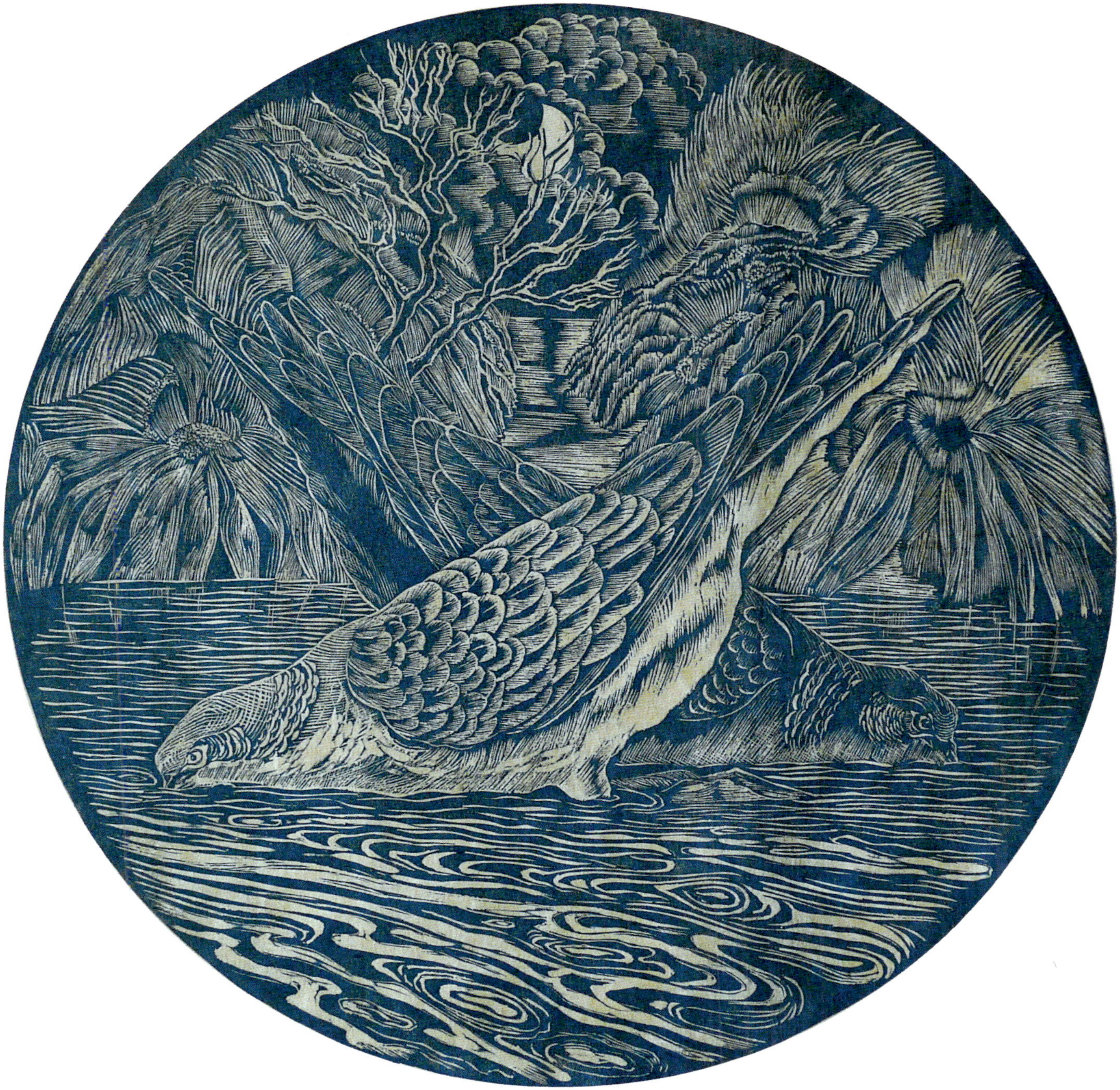

Susie Turner

I studied Fine Art Printmaking at Cambridge School of Art and Camberwell College of Arts. Based in Cambridgeshire, I work as a professional artist-printmaker and educator, delivering talks and demonstrations about traditional and contemporary methods of fine art printmaking.

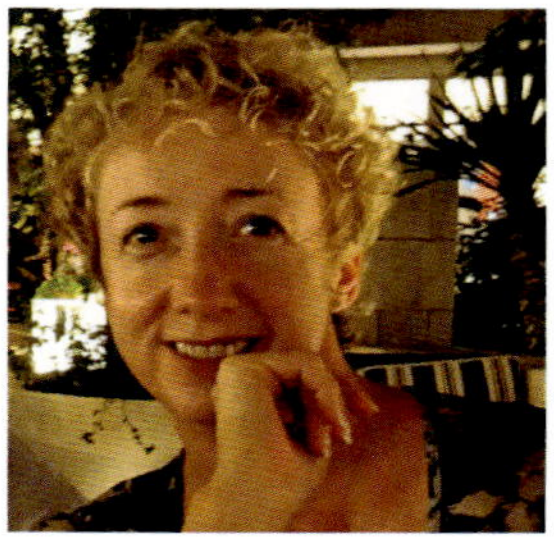

1965 Born Lichfield

1985–87 Higher Nat Dip Graphic Design & Illustration, Bournemouth & Poole College of Art & Design

2003–06 BA (Hons) Fine Art Printmaking, Cambridge School of Art

2007–09 MA Fine Art Printmaking, Camberwell College of Arts, London

Educational workshops

2004–12 Curwen Print Study Centre

2012 *Arts and Minds*, National Trust, NHS Croft, Ida Darwin Hospital

2013 *Red Hot Press*, West Yorkshire & Leicester Print Workshops

2011–15 Fermynwoods Contemporary Art, William Knibbs Complementary Education

2012–15 Sedgwick Museum of Earth Sciences, *Festival of Ideas*, Cambridge University Botanic Garden

2012–present Printroom, Cambridgeshire

Recent exhibitions

2012–15 *LOOP*, Bankside Gallery

2013 Leicester Print Workshop, Eleven Gallery, Hull

2014 Hoardings Commission, Nuffield Hospital, Cambridge

2014–15 Street Gallery, UCLH

2015 *50:50*, New Ashgate Gallery, Surrey

2015 Addenbrookes Hospital, Cambridge

Collections

Camberwell College
Clare College Cambridge,
Addenbrookes Hospital
Nuffield Hospital

My artistic practice is an investigation of our relationship to an ever-changing natural world. I am particularly interested in the impermanence of natural processes and the idea that nothing is static or fixed in time – everything is in continual and relative motion. This has led me to explore the shifting symbiotic relationship between humankind and nature through the use of transient material and natural phenomena. Both offer the potential for change and an exchange between prediction and chance. Cameraless and lens-based photography are also used as a means of capturing or fixing in time the very act of change. The local landscape is a constant source of visual ideas and I often work with objects of nature that change state over time or bear visual reminders of past activity. The ephemeral nature of material is an important element – used to draw intimate connections between the transient state of nature and our own existence. The aim is to create imagery that is informative and reflective – enhancing our perception or experience of nature. I tend to work with methods of printmaking that allow accuracy in capturing detail. The idea of making a real trace or a visual footprint of the original is most appealing. Over the last eight years I have been extensively exploring the potential of printmaking with photopolymer plates, otherwise known as solar plate. This method of printmaking offers fine detail and versatility in image-making using photographic elements, hand-drawn originals and the direct use of found material.

Much of my recent work is informed by the creative approaches and methodologies of both art and science. In particular, how collaborations between contemporary art practice and the physical and biological sciences can invite new ways of seeing or imagining and encourage a greater concern for how we relate to each other, the environment and nature.

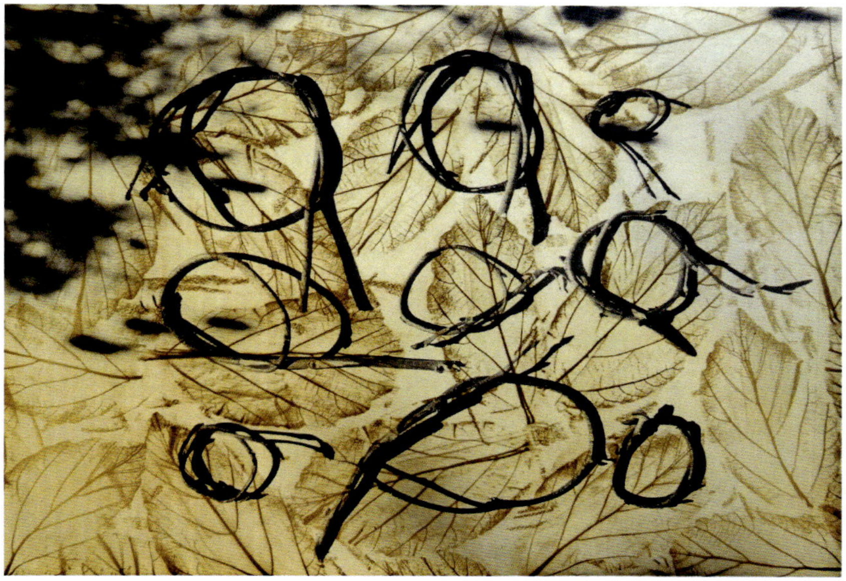

OPPOSITE
Light in Darkness,
30 x 42 cm,
solar plate etching,
(edition of 20)

Wisdom and Learning,
42 x 30 cm,
solar plate etching,
(edition of 20)

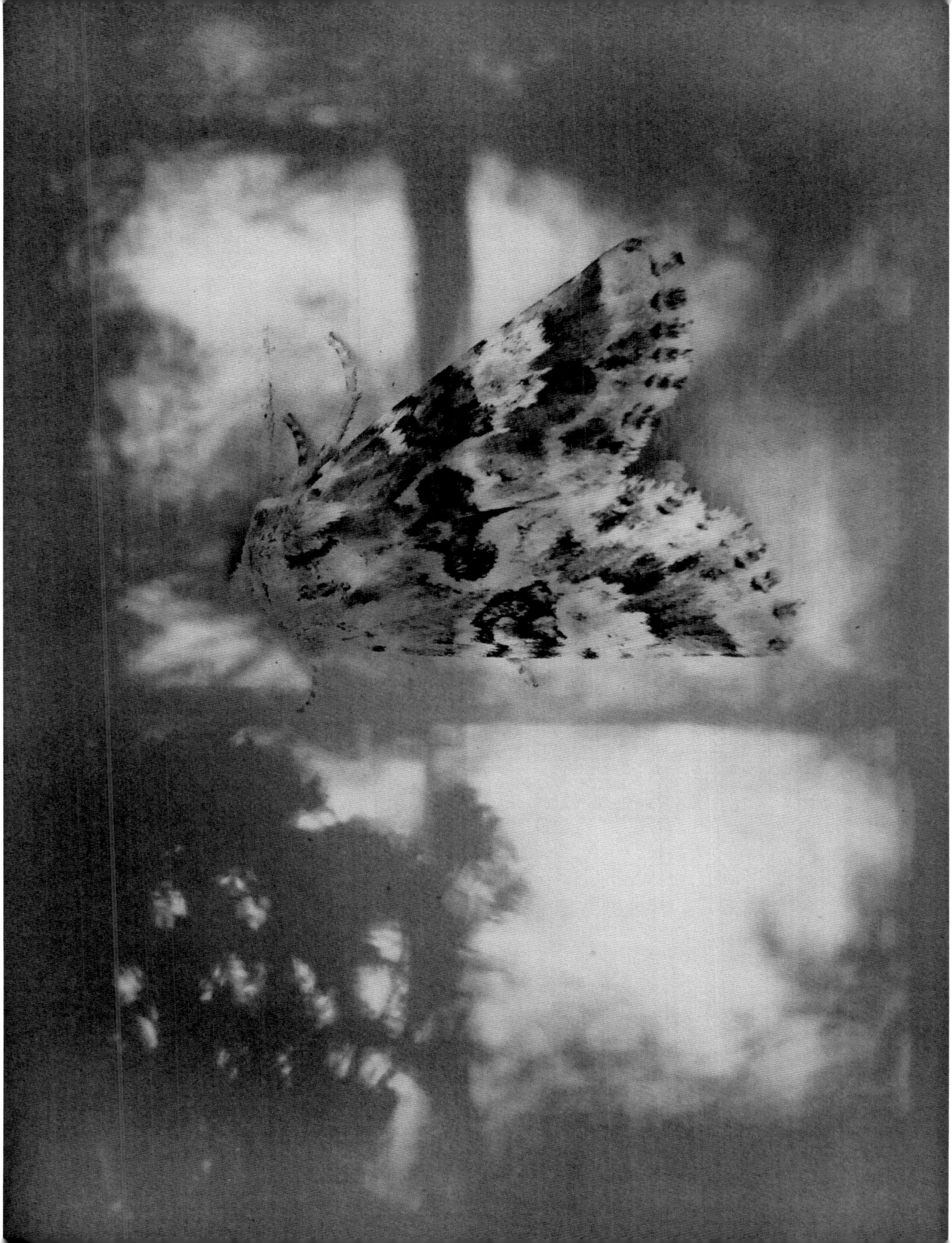

Maggie Warwick

I first discovered and became enchanted with etching at Morley College. Most of my working life has been involved with celluloid film, both in a commercial and fine art context, and for me there are similarities between the two processes. Both involve the chemical development of the image and the 'frisson of discovery' at the print stage.

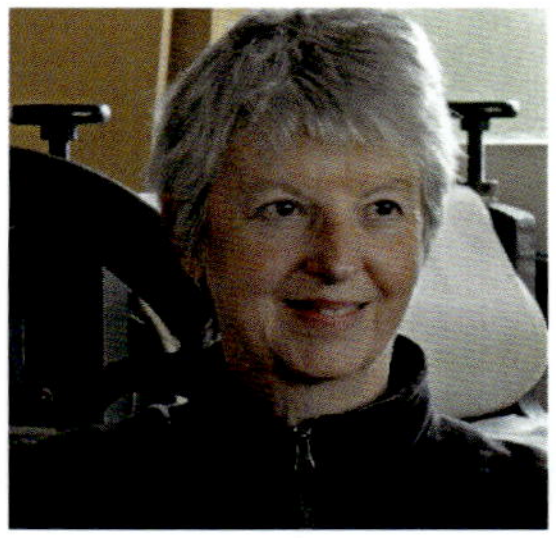

1953 Born Stockport
1982–84 MA Fine Art Film and Media, Royal College of Art
1984–86 London Filmmakers Co-op
1984–90 Moving image work shown nationally and internationally
1986–2012 Film director/producer
2010 Etching course, Morley College
2010–13 Print studio, City and Guilds School of Art
2013 Joined East London Printmakers
2015 Joined Printmakers Council

Exhibitions
2013–14 *LOPF*, Royal Academy of Art
2013–15 East London Printmakers Summer Exhibition, Shoreditch & Southwark
2013 Shortlisted, *Guanlan Print Biennale*, China
2014 *Print Jam 2014*, Art Bermondsey
2014 *Art Academy Summer Show*, Art Academy, London
2014 Museum of Childhood Designer Market, London
2015 *5 Artists from East London Printmakers*, AGIP, London
2015 ELP Boxed Set, Xylonite Arts, London
2015 E11 & E17 Art Trail, London
2015 Ochre Print Studio Summer Exhibition, Guildford
2015 Moka East View Tube, London
2015 *50 Years of Artists Prints*, Printmakers Council, Bankside Gallery, London

Collections
Victoria & Albert Museum
EndFragment

I love the alchemy of etching, the richness of the mark and the infinite permutations it offers. As my work developed I wanted to incorporate more colour in my images and became a little frustrated by the fact that colours do not remain true when printed from zinc and copper plates. Recently I've been using steel (which holds colour pure), exploring overlays and viscosity printing, sometimes combining etching with collograph. This has opened up a world of possibilities that's very exciting and full of potential for a new body of work.

My inspiration comes mostly from the natural world, maps, museum and art collections. I like bold shapes, textures and colours that evoke the atmosphere and history of a place or time.

My work is not always a literal interpretation of the world but comes out of memories, thoughts and emotions often long-forgotten until they appear on the page. As part of my film career I travelled extensively from the deserts of Jordan to the snowy wastes of Outer Mongolia and this experience of different cultures and landscapes also feeds into my art. I draw and take photographs but mostly I experiment until I have something I think is worth showing.

Being creative sometimes keeps me awake at night but most of the time it brings me a lot of joy: if my work allows me to share some of this with other people then that's a real pleasure.

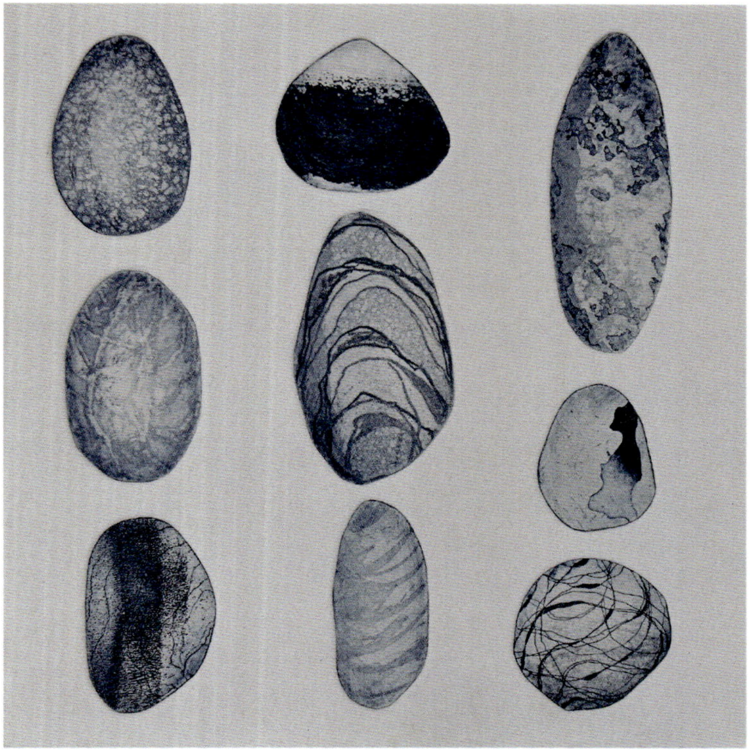

Box Set, 21 x 21 cm, multi-plate etching, (edition of 30)

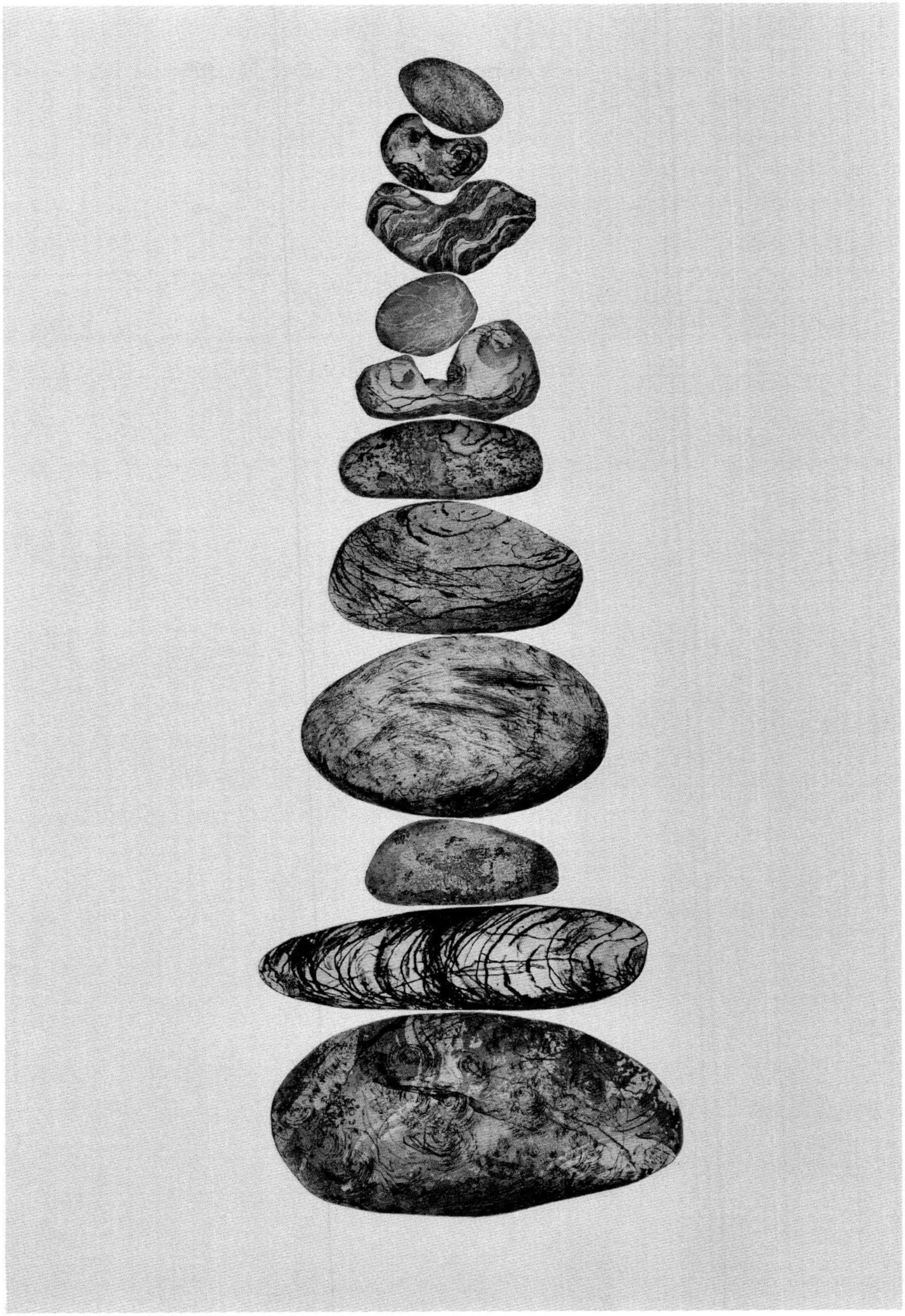

A Fine Balance, 40 x 75 cm, multi-plate etching, (edition of 30)

Felicity Weaver

Felicity Weaver creates interesting compositions using various print techniques with collage. Felicity has exhibited widely and her prints are in various public collections.

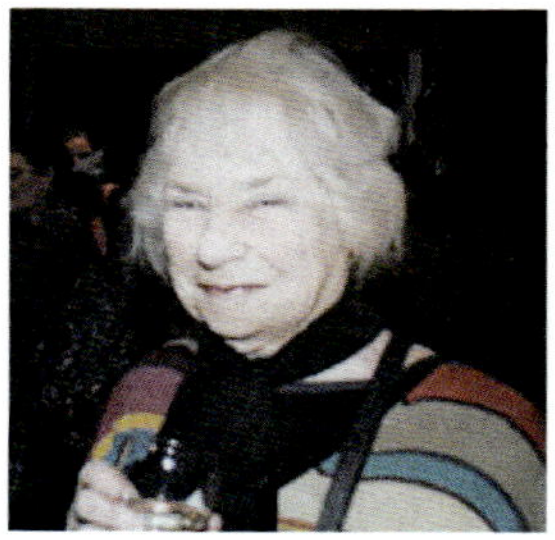

1930 Born Leeds
1948–50 Harrow School of Art
1950–52 Royal College of Art
1952–54 Camberwell School of Art
1953 City & Guilds Embroidery
1954 National Diploma in Design (Embroidery and Weaving)
Taught Embroidery Camberwell School of Art & Watford School of Art
Joined the Printmakers Council
Joined the National Society of Painters, Sculptors and Printmakers
1998–2002 Solo Shows at Greenwich Printmakers Gallery
Exhibited in many group exhibitions including Paris, Moscow, Landau, Germany, Belize
In London (National Theatre, Festival Hall, Curwen Gallery, Studio Voltaire) Manchester, Birmingham, Oxford, Cambridge, York, Brighton etc

Selected Exhibitions
Royal Society British Artists
National Print Exhibition
London Group
Royal Society of Portrait Painters
Contemporary Portrait Society
Royal West of England Academy
Small Print Exhibition

Public Collections
Birmingham Museums and Art Gallery
Scarborough Archive
Lewisham Council

Private Collections
England
Germany
America
Australia

One of my earliest inspirations was when living almost in the City of London, walking around the bombed-out ruins of the area of the Barbican, a strange romantic area of shattered buildings – then later watching it being built up again. This I think may be seen in my work and with it, but rather later, a Japanese flavour. This came about when catching a glimpse of my husband's architectural models – constructions, fanciful and eccentric, inspired by Japanese temples. Light catching the glass cases that contained them – reflections, shadows of fading light becoming abstract – made for me a point of departure and one which was reminiscent of the destruction of a city. I am inspired by the edge of cities where buildings, wrecked cars, abandoned posters, the remains of fences, roads leading nowhere come together, – and I like to add figures often very different from the described landscape.

I aim to give my prints an arresting pattern and colour scheme but with more realistic detail when looked at closely. I also like to contrast scale and techniques in the same print. In my etching I use both fine lines (bitten with Dutch mordant) and aquatint. The etching provides the subject, the detail, the drawing – in other words in many ways the complete work. But in other cases another print element is added – the colour. In some cases it will be by monotype, or by use of an offset press; in others, 'transfer rollings', taken from any of many textured and battered surfaces that I keep in my studio for the purpose. My usual procedure is to lay down the colour image first and print the etched plate over it. So I combine what may be called expressionist colour with clarity and detail. I also use collage, mainly using my own prints to create layers.

Edge of the City, 25 x 34 cm, etching & monotype (edition of 1)

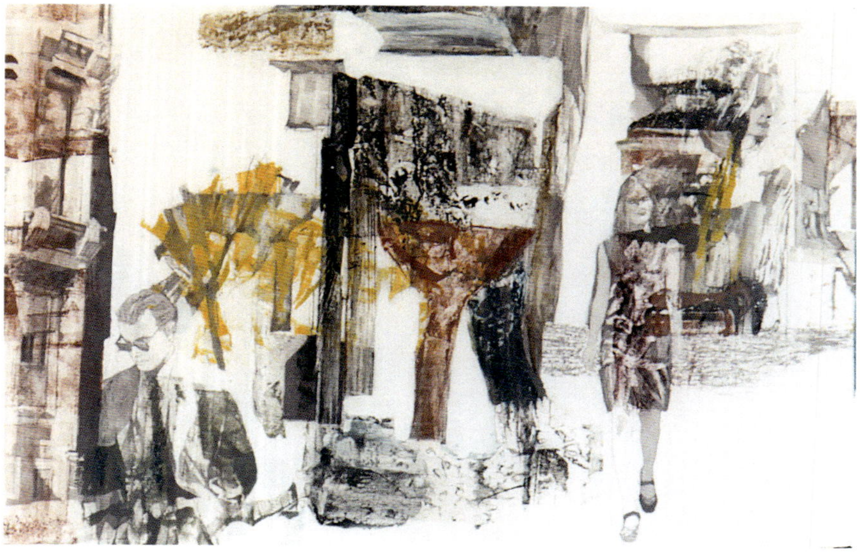

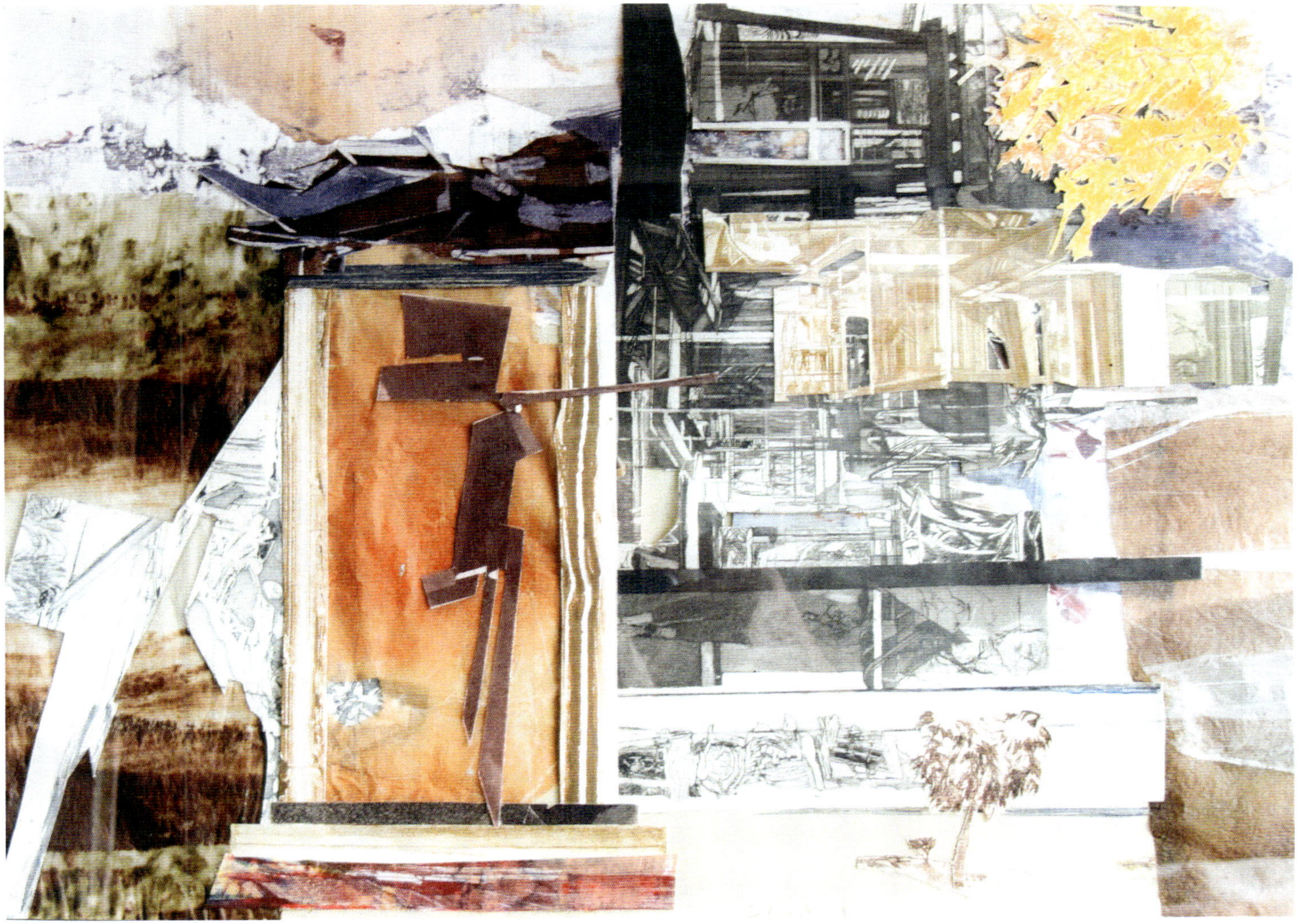

Looking Over The City, 30 x 44 cm, etching, collage & monotype (edition of 1)

Caroline Whitehead

Most of my recent prints are the result of many hours spent drawing specimens – preferably moth-eaten and crumbling – of anteaters, aardvarks, warthogs and all types of birds, in natural history museums. As well as the specimens themselves, I am also intrigued by the strange and incongruous juxtapositions created by the reflections that appear in the glass windows of display cases.

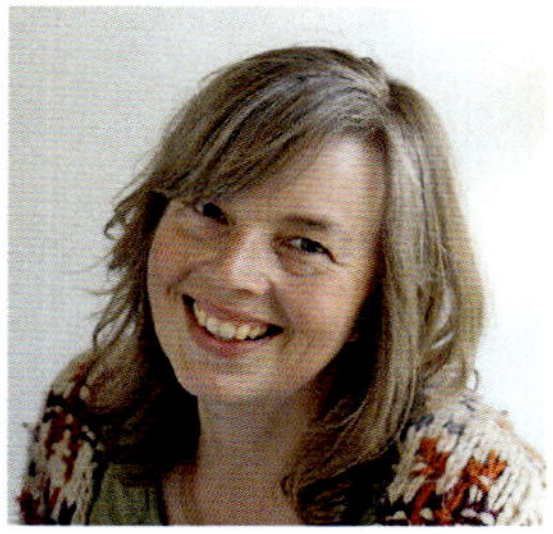

1963 Born London
1982 Byam Shaw School of Art
1982–85 Bachelor of Fine Art (Distinction) Ruskin School of Drawing and Fine Art, University of Oxford
1990–91 Litho for Artists, London College of Printing
1998–2000 MA in Sequential Design, University of Brighton

Selected exhibitions

1994 Royal West of England Academy National Drawing Exhibition
1998 Society of Wood Engravers
1996 & **1999** National Print Exhibition
1999 *Books by Artists*, Halifax Contemporary Artists' Book Fair
2000 *Lucky Dip*, University of Brighton
2001 Llewellyn Alexander Fine Paintings, Summer Exhibition
1997, 1998, 1999, 2000, 2001 London Artists' Book Fairs
2002 Illustratørene, Grafill Gallery, Oslo
2005 Hellviktangen Kunstkafé, Nesodden, Norway (solo exhibition)
2007 Primrose Hill Library, London
2013 *Unending*, Westminster Reference Library
Autumn Exhibition, Aubrey Art Gallery, Great Dunmow, Essex
2012, 2013, 2014 East London Printmakers' Summer Exhibition
2015 *Ghost*[ed.], Dean Clough, Halifax

Collections

Victoria and Albert Museum
Winchester School of Art
Manchester Metropolitan University
Royal Free Hospital

I first discovered printmaking at school, where I had the luck to encounter the Australian printmaker Katie Clemson, who was working in the art department. Katie taught us to make complex reduction linocuts using transparent inks and the excitement of revealing the colours created by successive printings remains with me to this day. Around the same time, the printmaker Mark Cheverton (later a founder of the Leith School of Art) showed me how a humble material such as cardboard could be used to make subtle and beautiful prints.

At Oxford, where I specialized in sculpture and printmaking, I spent days exploring the cabinets and drawers in the Pitt Rivers Museum, drawing all sorts of strange artefacts that later found their way into my prints. Rejecting the idea of making editions of identical prints, I instead explored the use of intaglio and screen-printing techniques to make series of related images with no predetermined result.

After Oxford I embarked on a short-lived legal career, but eventually returned to drawing full-time. Following completion of an MA at Brighton, I moved to Norway and joined Illustratørene, a collective of nine illustrators. During this period, using the collective's screen-printing workshop, I wrote and illustrated three children's picture books – the third of which, *Big Black Dog*, was illustrated entirely with screen prints.

In 2007 I moved back to London and joined East London Printmakers. After experimenting for a while with screen-printing and collographs, last year I discovered mokulito at a workshop run by Ewa Budka. Mokulito is a lithographic technique that uses a wooden plate instead of the traditional stone or metal. Using a wooden plate means that editions are small and variable, and I also very much enjoy the freedom of drawing on wood and the subtle veils of colour that arise during printing. Currently I am experimenting with combining mokulito with screen-printing and have also started to work with etched lino.

Children's picture books
(as Caroline Glicksman)

2003 *Eric the Red*, Random House Children's Books
2004 *Eric and the Red Planet*, Random House Children's Books
2006 *Big Black Dog*, Walker Books

Sea Sentinel, 10.5 x 15 cm, etched & cut lino on Somerset paper, (edition of 20)

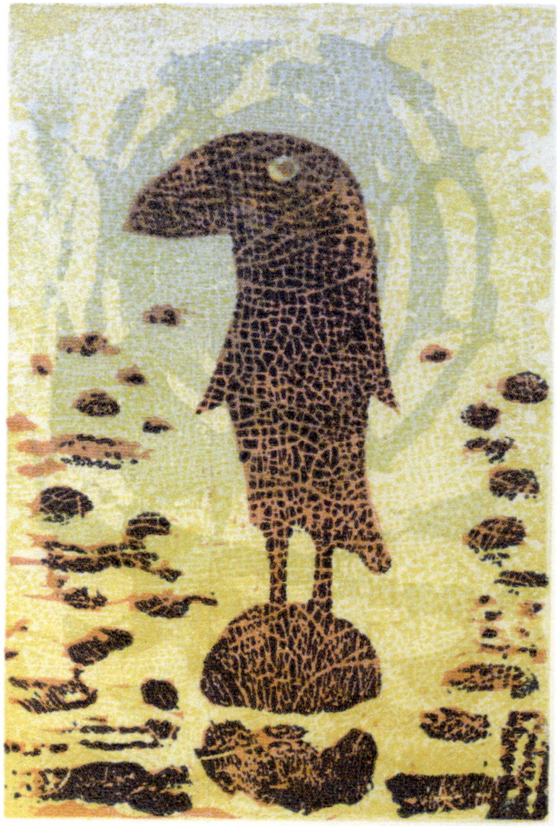

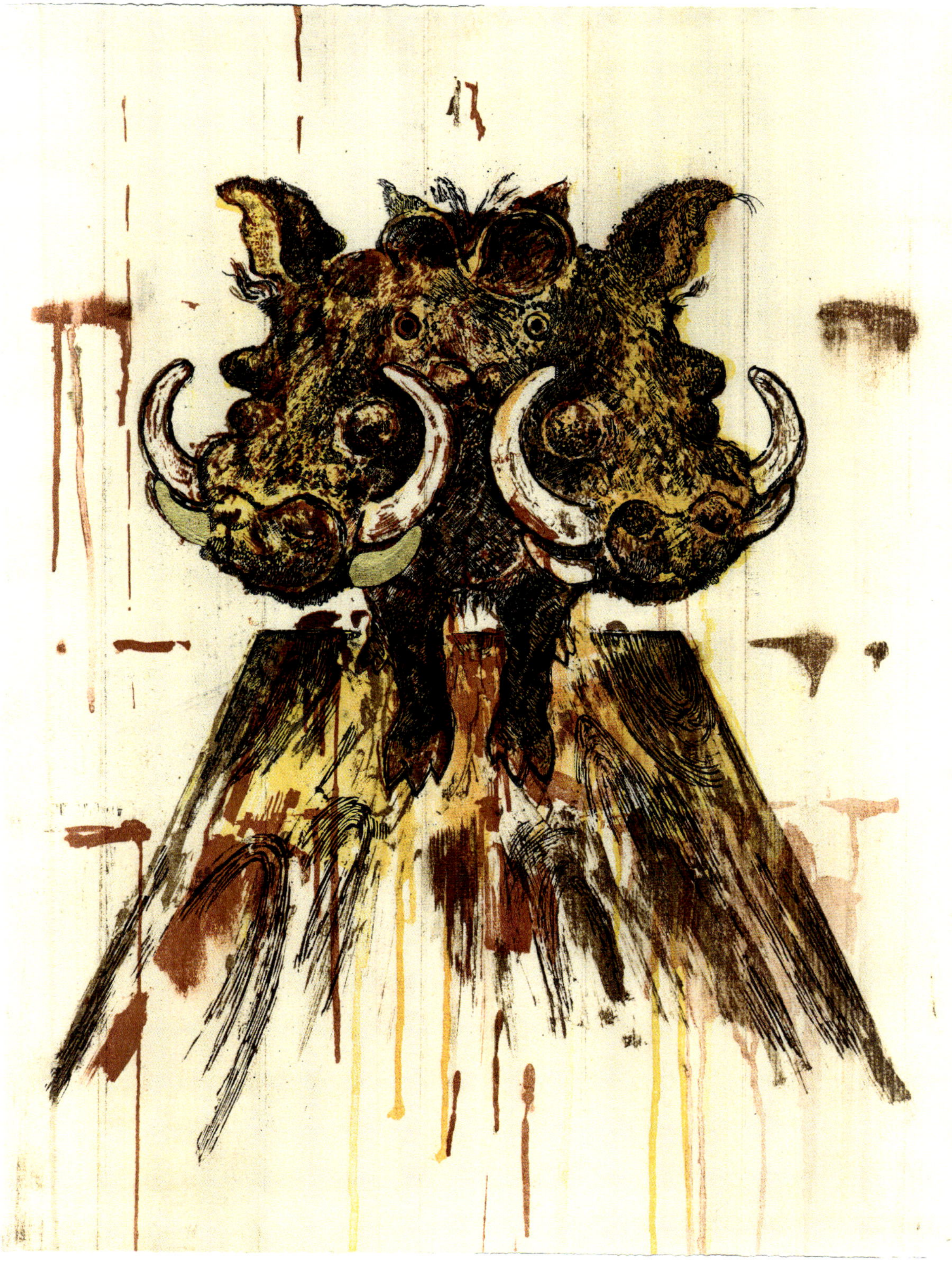

Inner Beast II, 56 x 76 cm, mokulito (litho on wood) with woodcut and applied gold leaf on Somerset paper, (variable edition of 10)

Patrick Whitehead

I started out as a painter, acquiring the skills and craft of etching and lithography in my second and third year at Norwich School of Art where I had access to two enormous printmaking studios. Invariably I had the studios to myself and I became hooked on printmaking! I found the whole printmaking process and techniques totally absorbing, seductive and enormously satisfying.

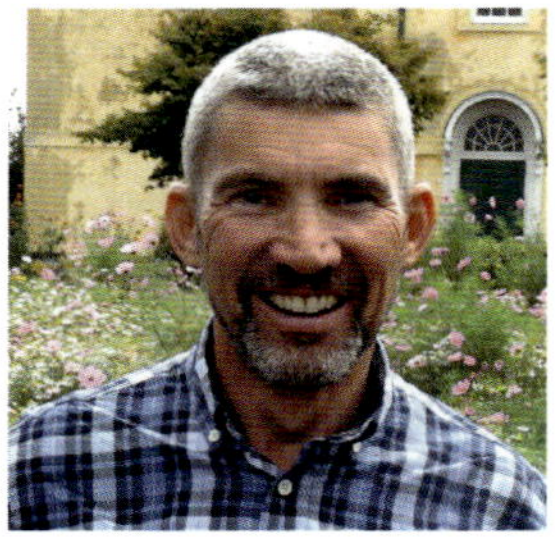

1957 Born Bradford
1974–75 Art Foundation Course, Lincoln College of Art
1975–78 BA (Hons) Fine Art, Norwich School of Art

Solo Exhibitions
1982 Canaletto Restaurant, Little Venice
1984 Travels in India, Wakefield Arts Centre
1985 Doncaster Technology College, Doncaster, Travels in India, York College of Art
1986 Fairburn House Gallery, Leeds
2007–08 The Westgate Business Centre & Technology College, Slough

Group Exhibitions
1976 *Stowell's Trophy Award Exhibition*, Chelsea
1978, 1986 *Open Annual Exhibition*, RE
1982 The Central Institute, London
1986–87 The Art House and Grape Lane Gallery, Leeds, and Leeds Art Fair
2007–08 *The Magic of Christmas*, Obsidian Gallery, Stoke Mandeville
2008 Open Exhibition, Café Gallery, Dilston Grove
2009 *The Candid Arts Fair*, Islington
2013 La Colorida Gallery, Lisbon
2014 *Parallax Art Fair*, Chelsea Town Hall
2014 *Art Below Exhibition*, Candid Arts
2014–15 Poole Printmakers Workshop Gallery, Shaftesbury Arts Centre, Durston Castle, Russell-Cotes Museum
2008–14 Various PmC Exhibitions

Collections
UK, France, Germany, Holland, Australia and the US

Although I specialised in etchings, aquatints and lithography at Art College and continued to develop these skills, I have extended my printmaking repertoire in recent years to include mezzotints, collographs, linocuts and solar etchings. Each printing method has its own particular attributes and qualities that I find appealing. As a printmaker I am fascinated by the fact that one never knows how an image will turn out until the plate is inked up and printed. Currently, I am exploring the technique of solar etching and working into the plates with a scraper, burnisher and a Dremel engraver to manipulate and enhance the images in order to achieve the effect I desire.

Primarily, I am inspired and motivated by my experiences gained through travel. I record what I see in the form of sketches, notes and photographs which I then use as a starting point for a series or set of prints to illustrate my travel experiences. Crowds, groups of people, landscapes, architecture (colonial buildings, temples, ruins etc) form the basis of my subject matter.

My work is figurative and representational and I have a strong interest in detail – the line, form, shape, texture and patterns in an image. Also, the type of marks that can be achieved with the different printing methods is important to me when deciding which printing method and techniques I will employ. The lighting in an image is crucial too, as I am fascinated by the effect of light and how it can be employed to create drama and effect. Ultimately, I aim to create a timeless quality in my work, a particular moment in time and to share that with the spectator. Printmaking has endless possibilities and is so diverse. This is especially true with the introduction of new methods such as solar etching and new materials that come onto the market. I feel that I am constantly learning and that the whole process is a voyage of discovery. Recently, I have acquired the skills for wood engraving and this method appeals to me greatly due to the fine detail, visual quality and wide range of marks that can be achieved with the different hand tools.

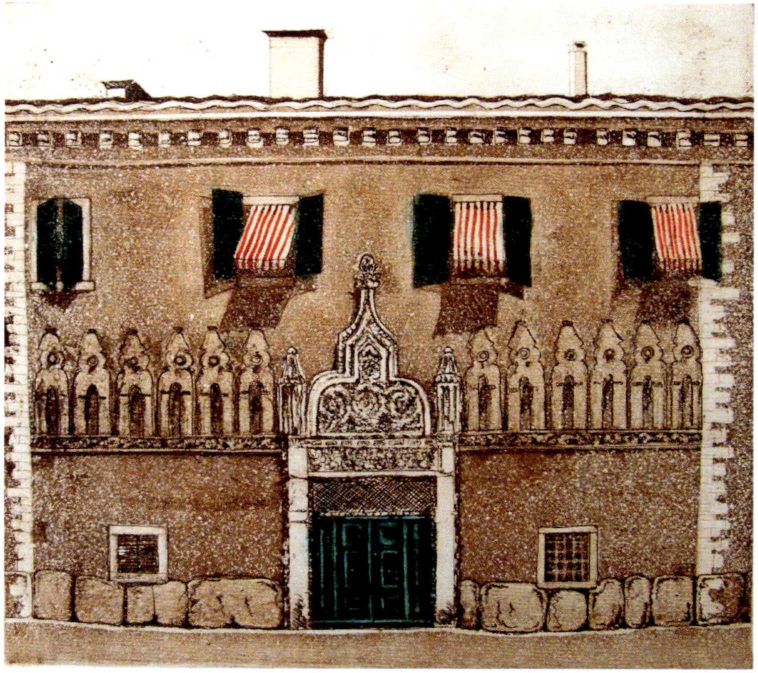

Venetian Facade,
23.5 x 26 cm,
etching and aquatint,
(edition of 40)

Women Crossing Ubein Bridge, Amarapura, 29 x 40 cm, collograph (edition of 15)

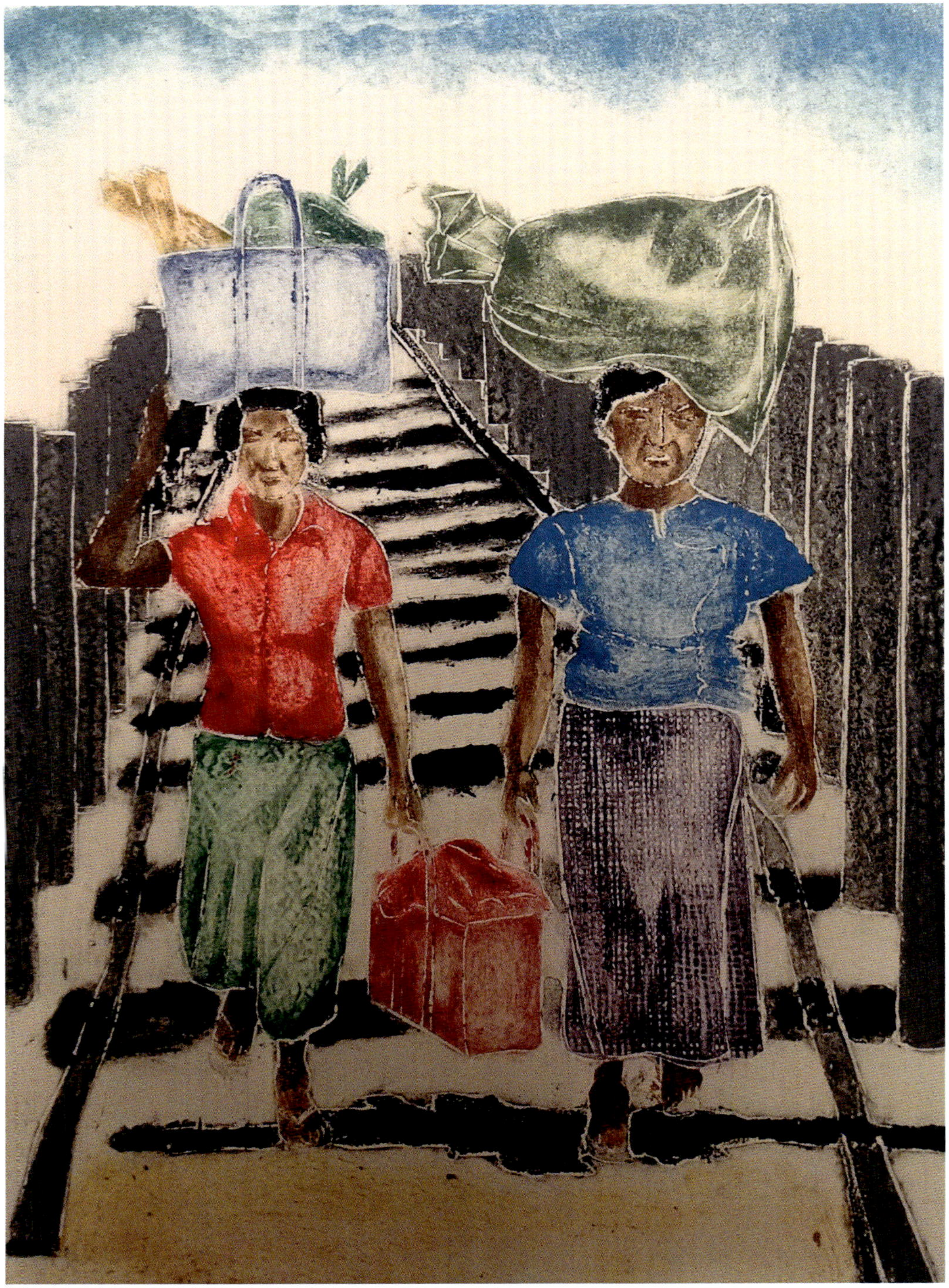

Cleo Wilkinson

From the outset I wanted to study classical sculpture – however it was not offered at art school. After stumbling into printmaking I discovered an ancient almost forgotten technique called mezzotint – it spoke to me immediately. I love nursing the life of an image out of its pitch black, dark womb and into the light – it has a primordial magic.

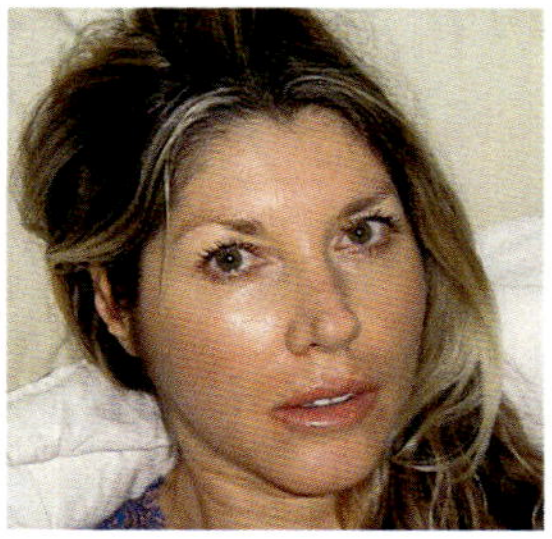

1959 Born Melbourne, Australia

1978–82 Bachelor of Fine Arts (Honours), Auckland University, New Zealand

1983–86 Graduate Diploma information Science, Queensland University of Technology, Australia

Further studies: Oxford University – Ruskin School of Drawing and Fine Art, UK; New York Academy of Fine Art NYC, The Art Students League of New York, Grand Central Academy of Art, NYC USA

2000–15 exhibited in over 200 international print shows and many International Art Residencies.

Selected Awards

2007 Purchase Prize *International Biennial of Engraving*, Acqui Terme, Italy

2007 Grand Prize *Guanlan International Print Biennale*, Shenzhen – China

2008 Jurors Award, *1st Biennial Footprint International*, Center for Contemporary Printmaking USA

2010 Jamie Evrard Prize, Biennial International Miniature Print Exhibition VI, Canada

2011 Ist Prize *8th International Miniature Print Biennial*, USA

2012 Printmakers Council Award *8th British International Mini Print*, London

2014 Finalist 2014 Print Council of Australia (PCA) Print Commission, Australia

2014 Honorary Medal *15th International Triennial of Small Graphic Forms*, Lodz Poland

My interest lies in the power to evoke disquieting and elusive moments with subtle nuances of hope in the form of light that the richness and halftones of the mezzotint can uncover. I am an explorer of twilight zones and ambiguous spaces. Much of my recent work explores ambivalence – suspended – the struggle with insight and doubt, hesitation and commitment – the difficulty of existence. Moments of isolation and dislocation, stillness and silence where introspection and alienation are consciously engaged and interrogated. People waiting in darkness caught between expectation and anxiety creates the most haunting imagery. I try to emphasize the singularity, silence and loneliness of a form – transforming it from ordinary to something more profound, into the realm of dreams and poetry; to translate the emotion and atmosphere around it. My source of inspiration comes from memory and subconscious which is rearticulated into my own visual language. I like to suggest, not prescribe – what is missing in the shadows and is suggested provides the greatest potential for me.

Recently I have been exploring the miniature format and have become fascinated by the power of the small print – it is a more intimate, quiet, private experience, demanding control and focus and creating visual impact out of proportion to its size. The viewer is invited into an intimate and immense universe, creating a very private experience as the viewer must come close and experience it alone.

The mezzotint is known as *manière noire* (black method) and demands patience, consequence, and precision. It is an extremely labour and time-consuming process; an intensely intimate one engaging the artist in a long arduous inward journey during the many solitary hours spent preparing the plate – the image tends to reflect this depth and distance of thoughts. The technique is contradictory – you create the relief and then eliminate it, working from pitch darkness, painstakingly and carefully nursing the image out of the shadows and into the light. It has a primordial mystery. The tiny dots created are the ancestors of the pixel. My journey is to raise my awareness and consciousness of light and understand it more deeply.

Inception III, 5 x 5 cm, mezzotint (edition of 50)

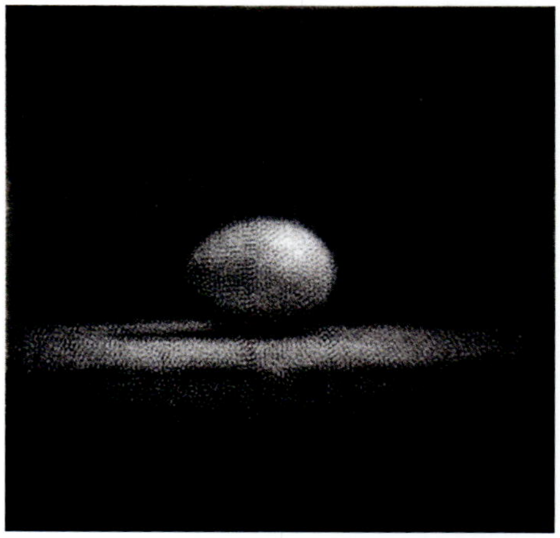

Murmur, 5 x 5 cm, mezzotint (edition of 50)

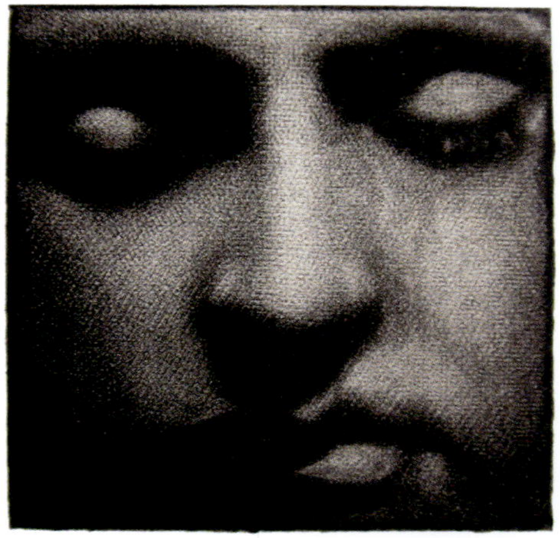

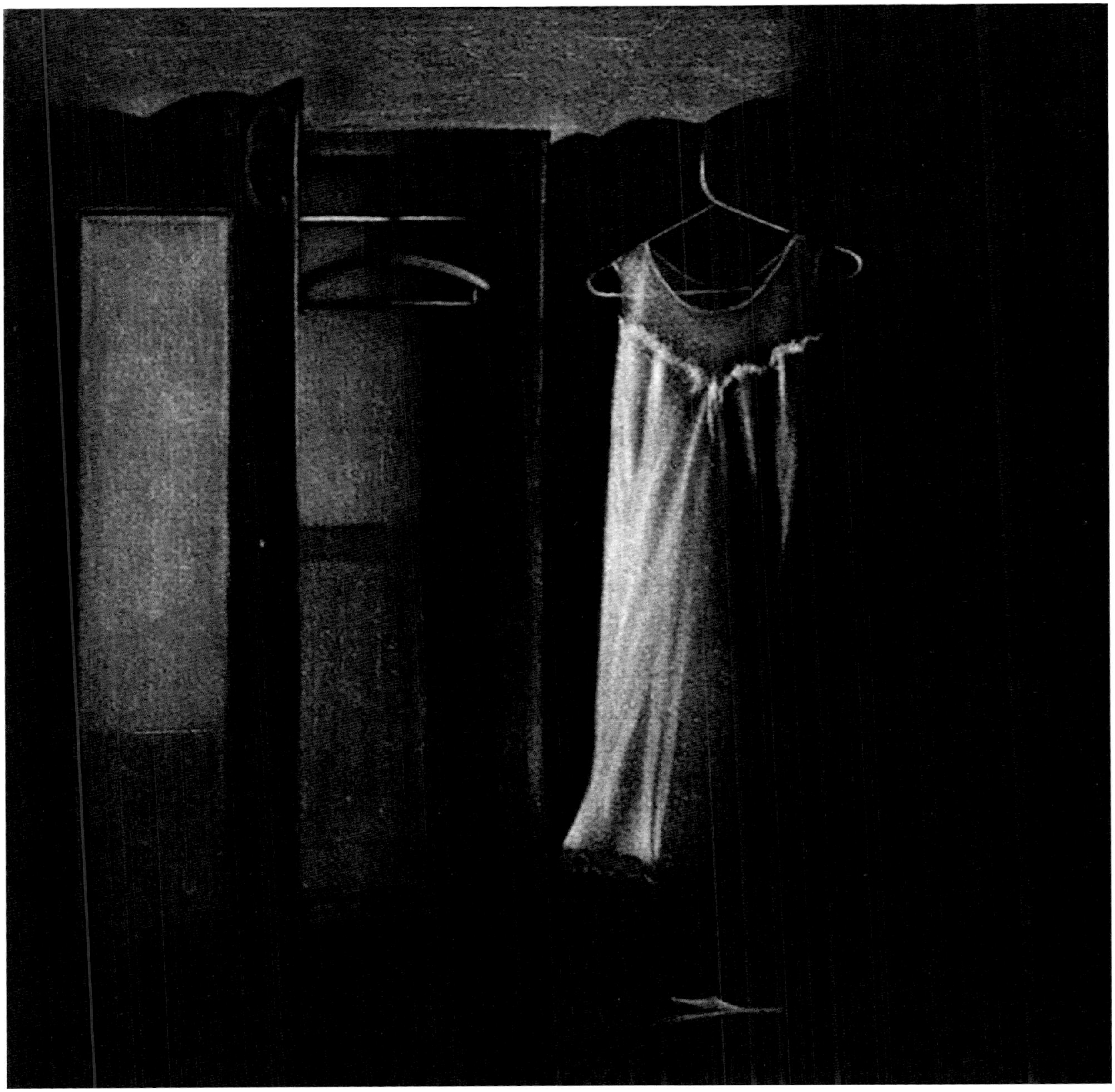

Abeyance, 30 x 30 cm, mezzotint print (edition of 30)

Roy Willingham

As I have worked full-time since I left college, my art-making has had to fit into the time left after work and family have made their demands. This has led to me working at a small scale; I can achieve results in short periods of time and I can take work with me if I am travelling.

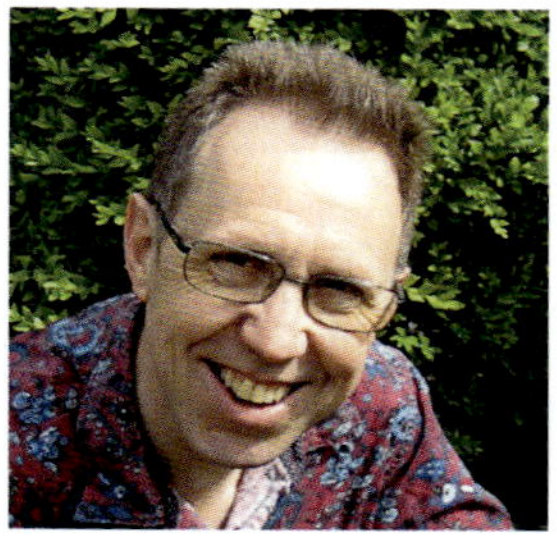

1976–79 BA Painting & Printmaking, Central School of Art & Design, London (CSAD)
1979–80 Advanced Studies in Printmaking, CSAD
1980 Taught life drawing at Sir John Cass School of Art
1982/83/84 Work selected for the Whitechapel Open Exhibition
1984-96 Served on the Committee of the Printmakers Council (PmC), Treasurer 1992-96
1987 *Xylon Print Triennale*, Switzerland
1989 Visiting lecturer at Byam Shaw School of Art
1990 Invited Artist, PmC Exhibition, Lvov, Russia
1991 PmC Exhibition, Valetta, Malta
1992 *Anne Desmet, Roy Willingham & Eric Gill*, Duncan Campbell Art, London *Contemporary Avant-garde Printmakers*, Plymouth
1994/97 *International Miniature Print Exhibition*
1994 *12 Contemporary British Printmakers*, Karelian Republic Art Museum
1995/2001/02/05/08-10 Work shown in Mall National Print Exhibition
2000/01/11 *The Discerning Eye*, London
2002 *1+1+1*, De Ploeg Gallery, Gröningen, Holland
2007/13 Wrexham Print International
2013 Elected Full Member of RE
2014 Invited to exhibit in *Wood Engraving - Developing the Medium*, Brook Gallery, Budleigh Salterton

I make prints for the sheer pleasure that the act of creating them gives me and as a means of expressing ideas I find easier to convey as images rather than in words. I am aware that they say things to me that they couldn't possibly to other people yet I delight in the idea that other people may also take from them concepts and expression that I may never have recognized.

I have always had an interest in landscape and this has remained the main subject matter of my work all my life, but I am also intrigued by work which sits on the borderline between figurative and abstract. I like to see how far towards abstraction I can push a landscape and still retain some sense of place.

My printmaking is usually either wood engraving or linocutting, both black and white and in colour. I will also combine other techniques such as digital print, stencils, monoprinting and collage. Most of my work is printed using oil-based inks on an Albion press in my home studio but I will also print small engravings by hand. My colour works will often involve printing many layers to build up an image and can take months to complete. I use a relatively limited range of traditional cutting tools but I am also interested in exploring unorthodox techniques, tools and materials to extend the ways in which I can create printed images and I like to allow fortuitous events in the process to influence the final results.

I have never been a purist who regards the print medium as complete in itself and have always been curious about how it might be used in conjunction with other media. I will print onto different supports, use it in combination with paint or collage, and manipulate the surface of prints to explore the possibilities for expanding its potential. I feel that there is scope to use its distinctive mark-making and ability to create rich texture on a small scale in combination with other media to create images which allow the formal aspects of the medium a more dominant role.

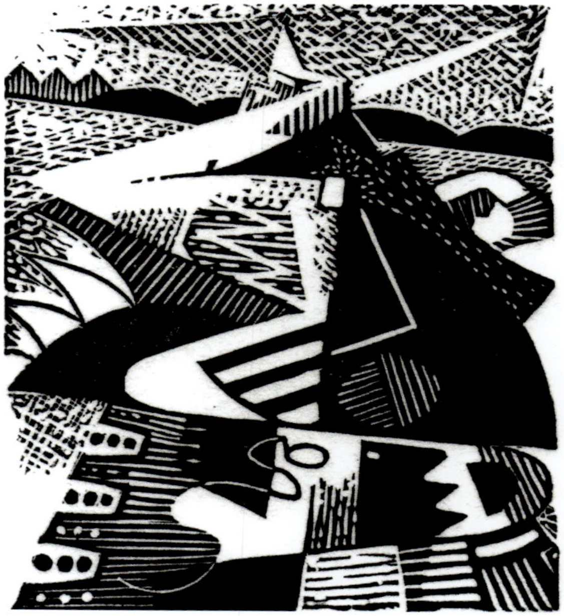

ABOVE
Calascibetta, 45 x 39 cm, wood engraving (edition of 15)

OPPOSITE TOP
Travelogue No.8 ~ Recondito Ad Ogni Ora
100 x 150 cm, linocut & collage (edition of 4)

OPPOSITE BOTTOM
Postprint No.9 ~ L'Esposizione
100 x 150 cm, linocut & laserprint (edition of 10)

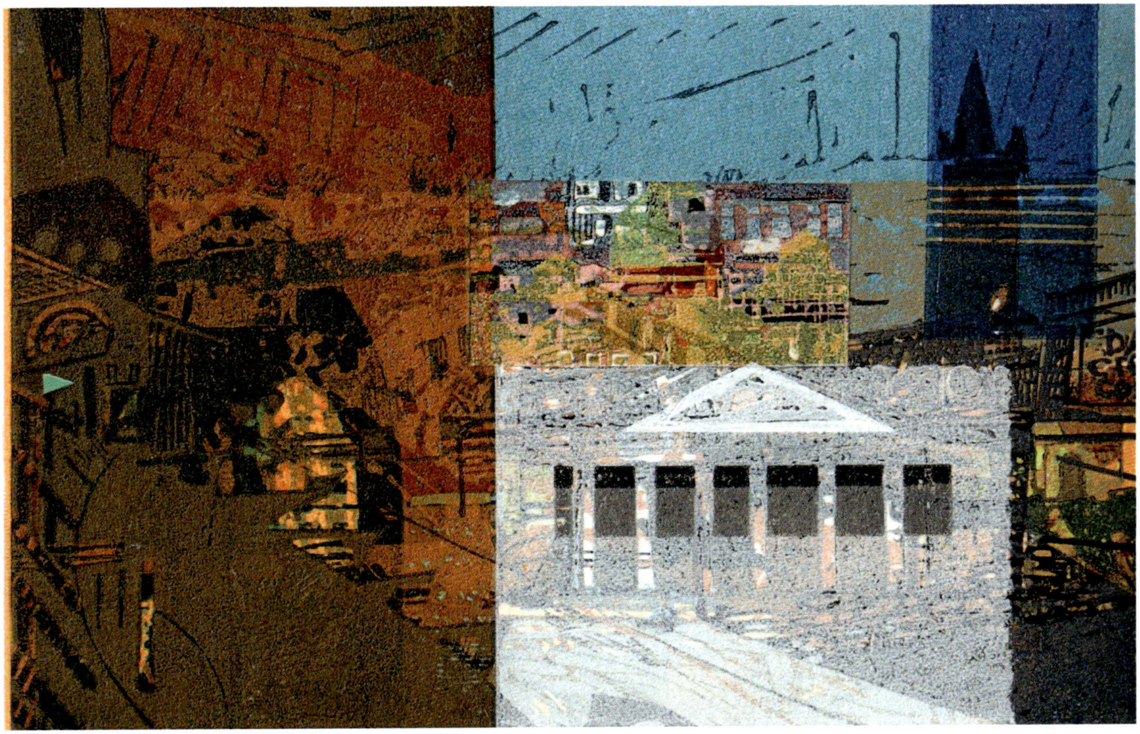

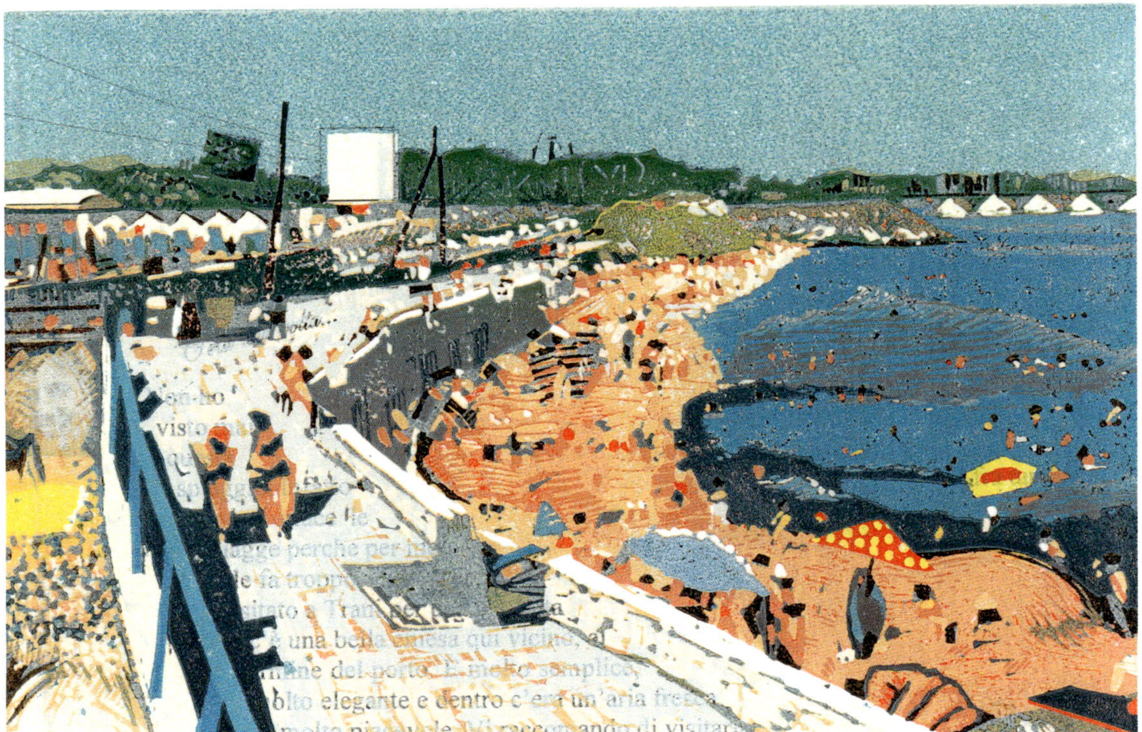

Kate Willows

During my foundation course, one of my tutors noted my interest in graphic art and drawing and suggested I might enjoy printmaking. Out of curiosity, I signed up for a short course at the Hampstead School of Art under the tutelage of Theresa Pateman. I enjoyed the course so much, I continued printmaking at the school for several more years. Theresa taught me the full range of printmaking processes, including drypoint, soft- and hard-ground etching, linocutting and chine collé.

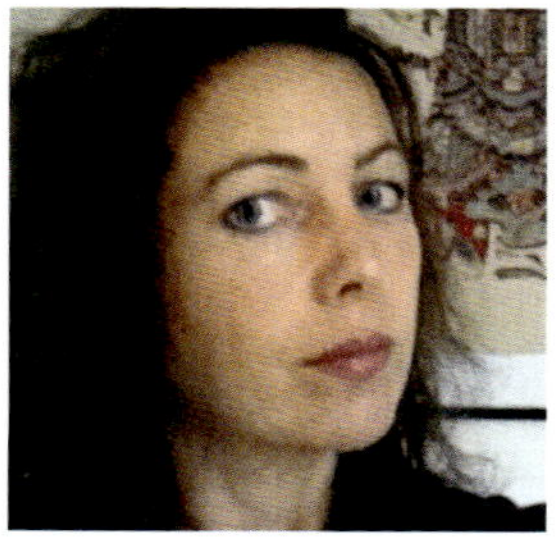

1967 Born St Albans
2005–06 Foundation Course, The Institute, Hampstead Garden Suburb
2006–13 Printmaking Classes at Hampstead School of Art under tutelage of Theresa Pateman

Exhibitions
2007 Tavistock Clinic, Belsize Park
2009 Sable D'Or, Muswell Hill
2009 Artsdepot Open, Barnet
2010 Hampstead School of Art and Institute Students, Burgh House, Hampstead,
2012–14 Kingsgate Workshops, West Hampstead
2013 *A Reflection in Print*, Highgate Literary and Scientific Institution
2011 *smallprint: big impression*, Leicester Print Workshop, Touring Exhibition
2014 *CMYK*, Pie Factory, Margate
2014 The Taproom, Islington
2015 The Maynard Arms, Crouch End
2015 Stephens House, East Finchley
2015 Chelsea Art Society 2014

Memberships
2011 Member PmC
2014 Member of the North London Artist Network (NLAN)

My printmaking practice began with experimental drypoint images from my imagination. I then progressed to hard-ground etching and aquatint, enjoying the task of creating clear lines and then gradually adding contrast through the etching process. At first, my prints were printed in monochrome, but I gradually began to experiment with different techniques and inks to create a variety of effects on the final image. Much of the learning procedure was through trial and error and could be incredibly frustrating. However, the moment when the perfect print finally rolled off the press made it all worth it!

I particularly enjoy working with soft-ground etching, which I enjoy for its immediacy: it allows me to transfer the spontaneity and energy of drawing to the printed image. I have found that this technique is well suited to drawing images of birds and I have produced a set of prints of peregrine falcons as a result.

Most recently, I have been exploring the possibilities of linocut prints. I began by making single block monochrome linocuts, moving on to reduction linocuts and multi-block linocuts. My linocut images are much stronger and brighter than my etching work. I also work as a sculptor and painter and I find that the physical aspect of linocutting fits in very well with the tactile and three-dimensional nature of my sculptural work and oil painting.

My linocuts allow me free reign to express my offbeat sense of humour and quirky take on life in a bold, graphic way.

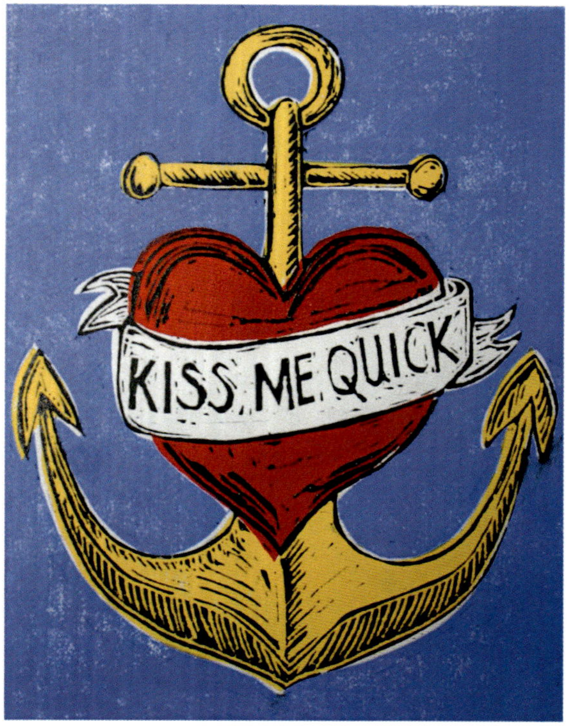

Kiss Me Quick, 15 x 20 cm, multi-block linocut (edition of 30)

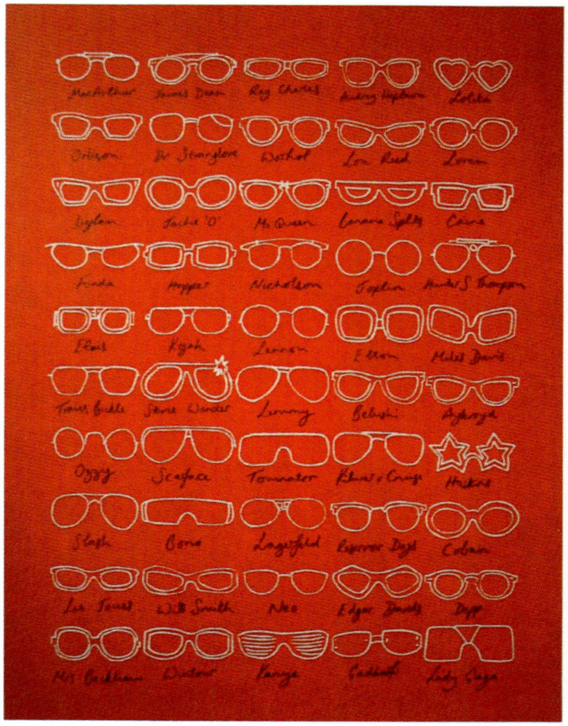

Fifty Shades, 30 x 40 cm, single block linocut (edition of 50)

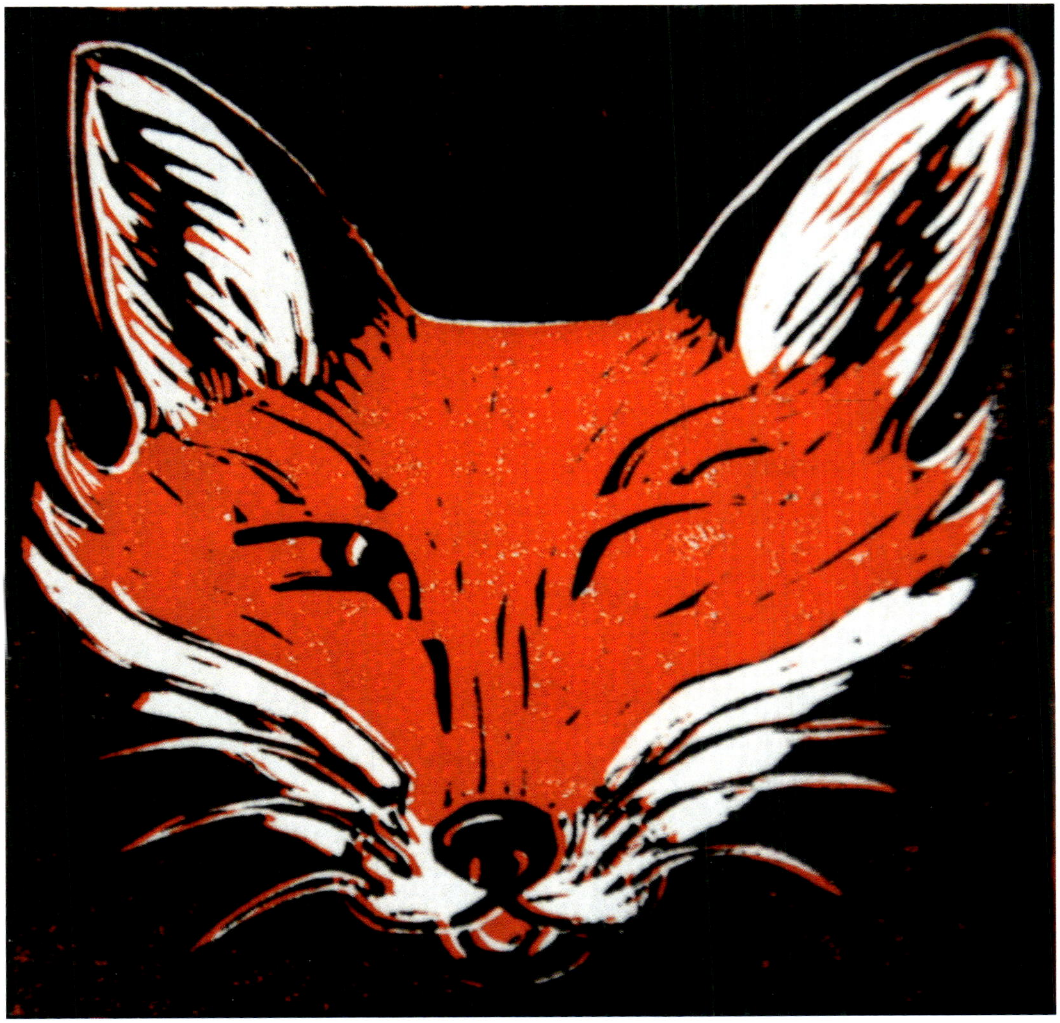

Well Hello There!, 10 x 10 cm, reduction linocut (edition of 6)

Joseph Winkelman

Rembrandt's etchings seen in books at the Public Library so captivated me as a child that I thought it would be wonderful to be able to make prints of such powerful expression and clarity one day. It was not until I was 25 that I made my first etching at the Philadelphia Print Club in an evening class, when I determined that it must be my profession.

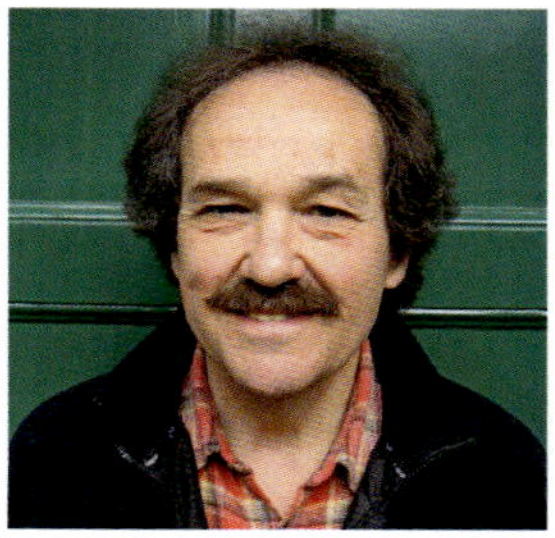

1941 Born Keokuk, Iowa
1964 BA English, University of the South, Sewanee
1967 University of Pennsylvania: Wharton School of Finance
1971 Certificate in Fine Art, Ruskin School of Drawing, University of Oxford
1989–95 President of the RE
1996 Honorary Fellow of the RWS
1987 Honorary Fellow of PmC
2004 Artist in Residence, St John's College, Oxford

Exhibitions

Royal Academy Summer Exhibitions. Newington House Gallery, Charlbury. Callahan Gallery, Boston. International School of Graphic Art, Venice. Oxford Gallery, Oxford. Taler Galeria Fort, Cadaqués.

Awards

1982 *Second International Miniature Print Exhibition*, Cadaqués, Spain
Second International Miniature Print Exhibition, Seoul, Korea
1985 The Royal West of England Academy, UK
1999 The Print Club of Albany, New York, USA
2000–03 *International Miniature Print Show*, Connecticut Graphic Arts Center

Public Collections

Ashmolean Museum, Bodleian Library, Fitzwilliam Museum, National Museum of Wales, Royal Collection, Tate Gallery, V&A, Museum of London, Science Museum, London Guildhall Library, British Library, Library of Congress, Washington

It was not obvious to me how entry is gained into a profession in which making a living is so difficult and many of the successful artists seem deranged. My family emphasized the importance of getting a broad education, circumspectly entering a line of work that would be stimulating yet would earn a decent income. Young Americans born after WWII also had to consider the prospect of two years' conscription into the military between ages 18–26 being reckoned into planning, although full-time education and teaching provided deferments.

With a wide range of interests, I kept my options open through school, entering a liberal arts course at university where I read English, with some basic instruction in studio art, and spending much of my free time designing and editing student publications. Still uncertain of direction after college, I volunteered to teach secondary school in Tanganyika where I had responsibility for the Fifth Form English A-level course and supervised O-level art. What little I knew about drawing and painting rapidly prompted me to improve my own skills which convinced me that I had a lot to learn.

While I was in East Africa during 1965–66, the Vietnam war flared up which I strongly opposed. When returning to America, I began graduate study towards an MBA degree but discontinued it to teach secondary school to have pause to find a full-time art course. A social anthropologist from Oxford whom I knew in East Africa informed me about the Ruskin School of Drawing where I was fortunate, with his help, to be offered a place in 1968.

The course was based on drawing and painting from life and the antique in the Ashmolean Museum, with exercises in basic relief and lithographic printmaking. We had short terms and were given much independence. This suited me perfectly as a mature student when I married, had two daughters, and acquired a Columbian Press from an engineers' scrap yard in Yorkshire for my Charlbury studio in 1971. I began teaching myself block-printing technique by trial and error using manuals, minding the children with help from au pairs when my wife worked in biochemical research at the University.

I painted portraits on commission, exhibited prints in solo and group shows, fostered a network of gallery links and friendships with others printmakers through organisations, and taught part-time. In summer 1974 I attended a print workshop at the Ruskin for instruction in intaglio processes from Chris Orr and Tom Piper that enabled me to broaden my scope and acquire a copper-plate press. Since then I have drawn and painted from observation, inspired by the natural and built environment and that continues to provide the basis of my prints today.

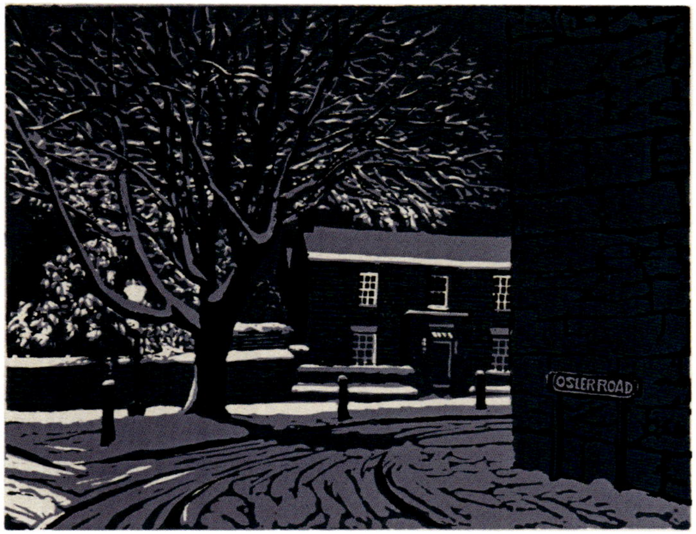

Osler Road, 18 x 23 cm, linoleum cut relief (edition of 100)

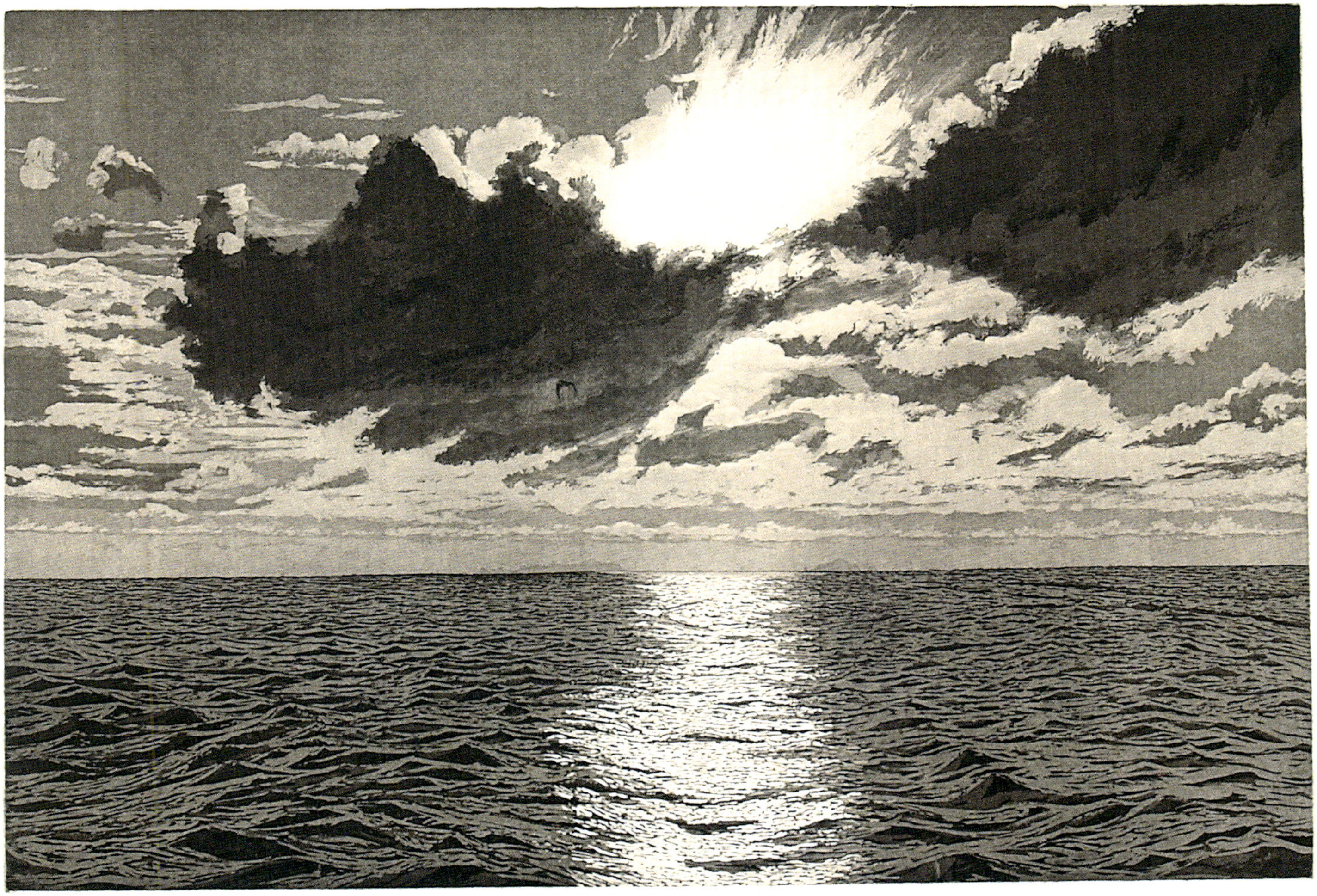

Approaching St Kilda, 38 x 54 cm, aquatint (edition of 150)

Mary Yazhari

Mary Yazhari is an artist who has combined her classical fine arts training with her experiences of studying and working in Iran, Japan, Belgium and the UK. Her printmaking combines her diverse studies of the classical techniques and different styles such as Japanese sumi–e (watercolours).

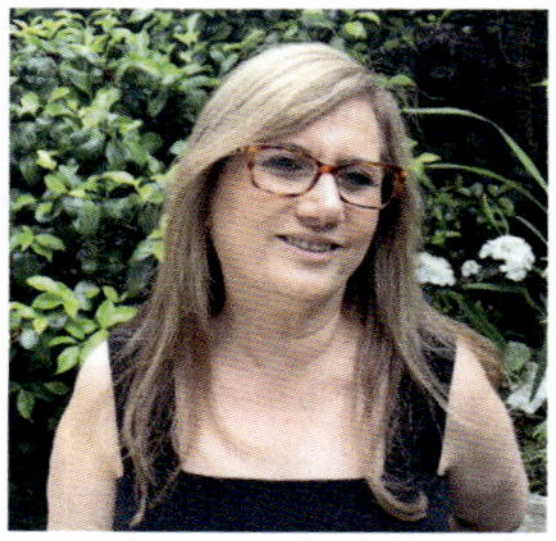

Born Tehran, Iran
1969–73 BA Fine Art, Tehran University
1981–87 Sumi–e (Japanese Watercolour) Studies Tokyo

Membership
2011 Joined Printmakers Council

Exhibitions
1989 *Europalia Japan* in Belgium Arts Festival, Brussels (Cultural exhchange between Japan and Belgium)
2008 *Originals 08*, Mall Galleries
2012 *8th British International Mini Print Exhibition*
2012 *Chino Tane*, International Museum, Tokyo
2012 *Chino Tane*, Museum of Kyoto
2012 *Chino Tane*, Museum of Hiroshima
2011 Society for Persian Arts and Letters, Hilton, Watford
2012/14 Society for Persian Arts and Letters, Hilton Terminal 5
2014 *National Original Print Exhibition*, Bankside Gallery
2014 *Microtopia*, Kingsgate Gallery
2015 *Works on Paper*, Barbican Library
2015 *50:50*, New Ashgate Gallery
2015 *Fifty Years of Artists Prints*, Bankside Gallery

I am an artist with an interest in nature which I see as an endless source of ideas. I spent my formative years in Iran surrounded by wonderful and spectacular scenery: such a beginning has been a crucial influence on the development of my body of work.

I have also been fortunate enough to have lived, studied, and worked in a number of other countries, and have been strongly influenced by their cultural and artistic landscapes. My early career was spent in Tokyo where I studied Japanese Watercolour with local artists and teachers. Later in Europe the powerful visual impact of printmaking attracted me, and has become my focus since the 1990s.

My work today is a mixture of different influences which I have absorbed through being immersed in varied cultures and communities. The ideas appearing in my prints are a blend of different styles and many are a reflection of the natural world around me. Many of the themes that pervade my work revolve around the seasons, and the powerful imagery that they can invoke. The bleak beauty of midwinter, the renewed hope of early spring and the rich decadence of midsummer are consistent themes running through my work. I want my work to have a lasting impact on the viewer, and believe the muscular simplicity of printwork is a very effective tool for achieving this.

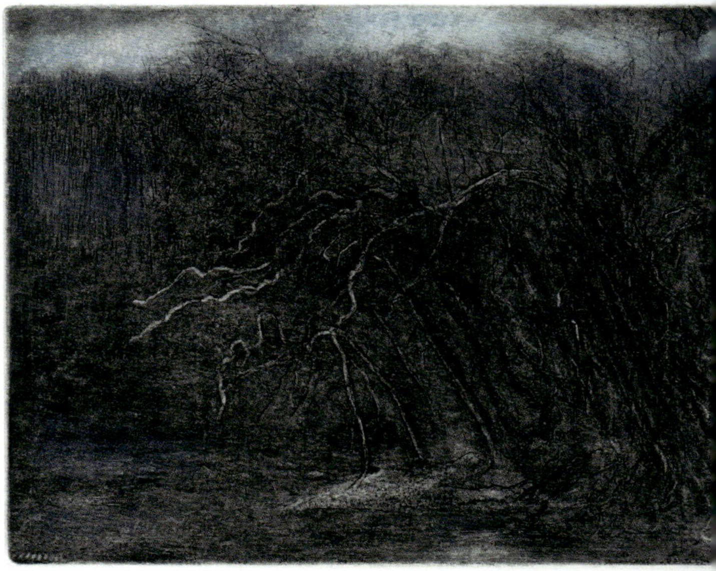

Black Wood, 20 x 15 cm, etching (edition of 80)

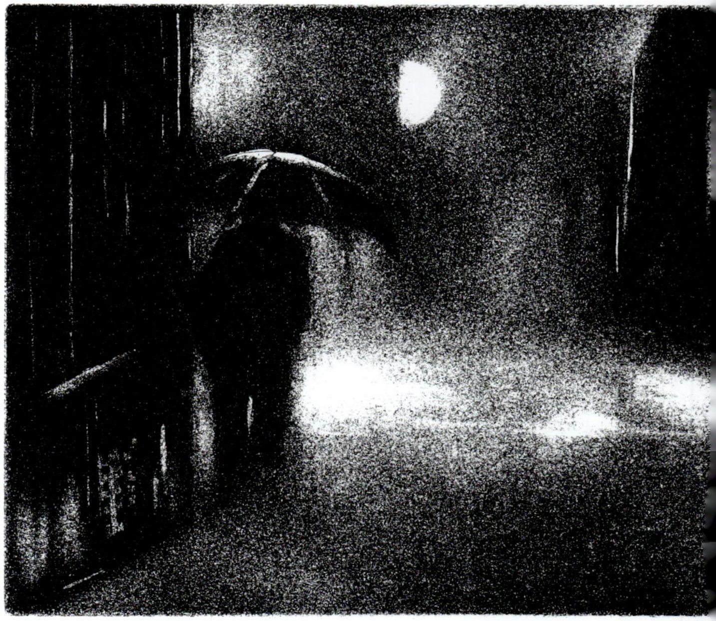

Rain II, 22 x 18 cm, etching (edition of 80)

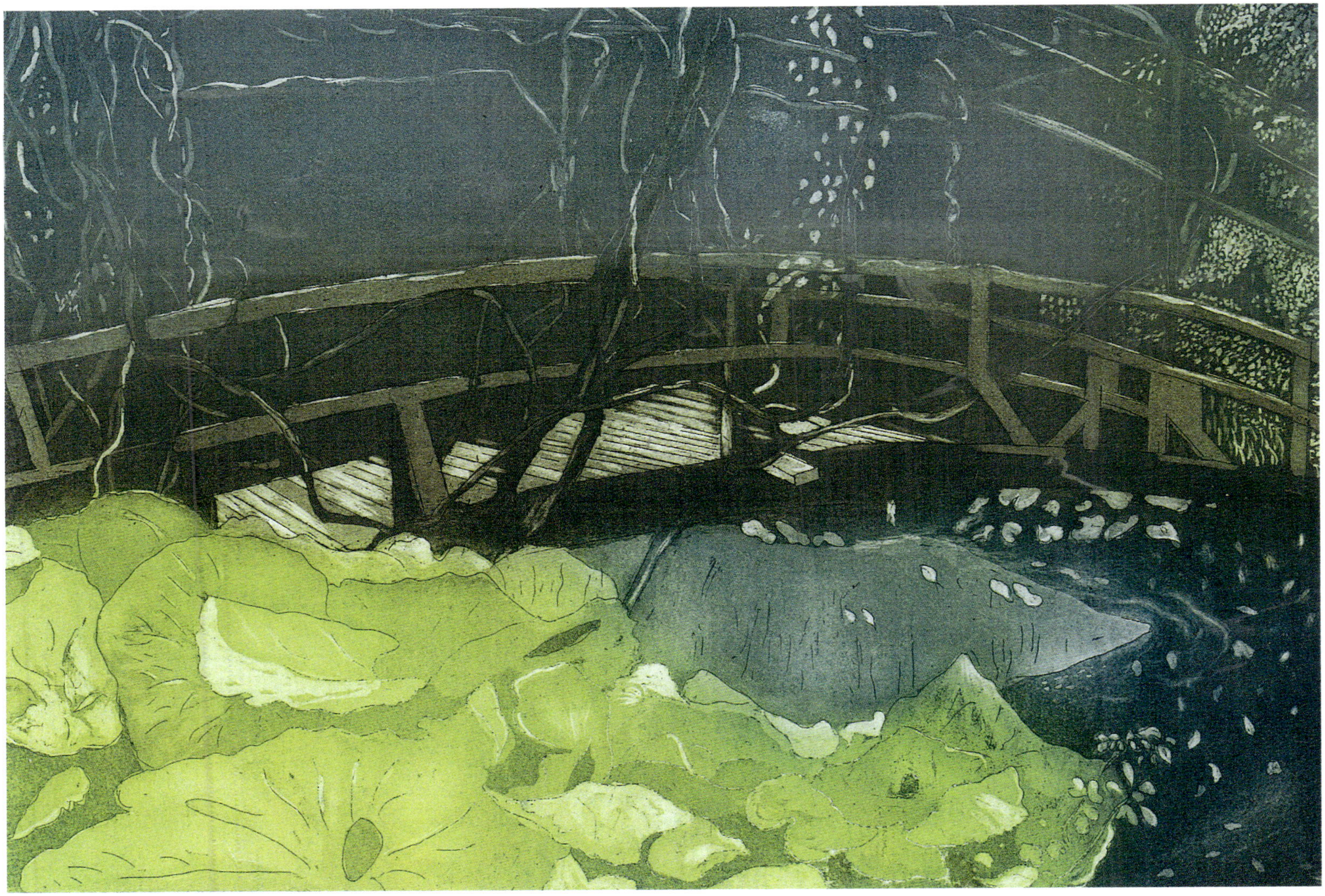

Japanese Bridge, 30 x 20 cm, etching (edition of 80)

Fouzia Zafar

After a series of challenging life events, I decided life was too short and embarked on fulfilling a lifelong ambition to complete an MA in Fine Art at City & Guilds of London Art School. It was on my MA that I discovered the print room. Printmaking not only suited my subject matter, but also provided me with infinite possibilities to manipulate plate, acid and drawing tools to create artwork in a vibrant medium.

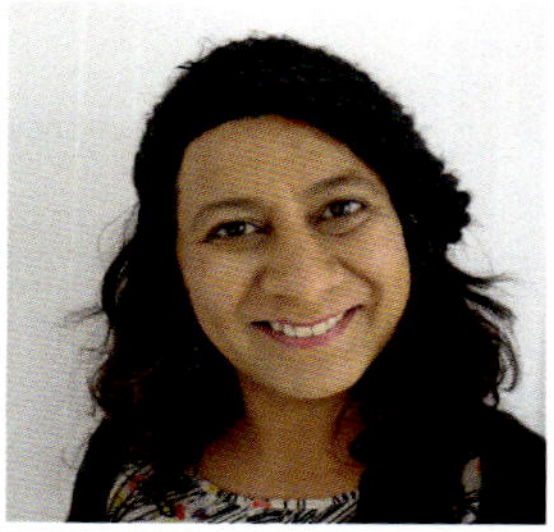

1971 Born Glasgow, Scotland
1991–94 B. Arch, Glasgow School of Art
1995–96 PGCE Goldsmiths College, London
1997–2007 Secondary Design & Technology Teacher
1998–2002 BA (Hons) Fashion Studies, London College of Fashion
2009–11 Diploma Fine Art, Putney School of Art, London
2011–13 MA Fine Art (Distinction) City & Guilds of London Art School
2012 Shortlisted for Clifford Chance Post-graduate Printmaking in London Prize
2012–13 MA Degree Interim and Final Show, City & Guilds of London Art School
2013 *Play*, London Print Studio
Gwen May RE Student Award, Royal Society of Painter–Printmakers, London, included associate membership
2014 Publication: *Printmaking Today* Volume 23, 2014, Issue 1, Spring
2014 Exhibitions
Atkinson Gallery, Somerset
East London Printmakers, Embassy Tea Gallery, London. Summer Show, Dulwich Picture Gallery, London.
Zillah Bell Gallery, Yorkshire. *Lessedra World Art Print Annual*, Sofia, Bulgaria.
Bainbridge Open 2014, London.
National Original Print Exhibition, London: received Curwen Studio Award
2014 Joined Printmakers Council
2012–15 Exhibited at *London Original Print Fair*, Royal Academy of Arts,
Stand at *Printfest*, Cumbria: awarded Printmakers' Printmaker
Canns Down Press Award received at RE Originals, London

There seemed to be no end to 'playing' with the possibilities that this offered. I use the concept of play to describe my work as it encompasses the various dimensions of my practice, from selection and use of materials, methods and processes to the themes I work with: the strangeness of memory, family histories, migration and absence. My images flicker between reality and fiction, but also flicker in the use of pictorial language and processes.

My background in architecture and fashion influences my fascination with objects occupying interior space and pattern within my practice. Objects acquire histories through being owned but also through being discarded. In my practice I conduct 'acts of play' by finding objects, staging and deconstructing them to create narratives using the processes of photography, collage and printmaking. Play involves repeatedly finding, composing and constructing new tools and processes to make images. Within this repetition, I extract creative outcomes, which invite the viewer to continue to play.

Each act of play invites the element of chance to enter the practice but also provides the opportunity to push each medium whilst embracing what it offers by accident. Crafting collages in a childlike manner allows movement to generate the composition. Soft-ground etching is another key element to the practice. Collages are pressed into soft-ground etching plates to literally create 'fossils' by allowing the acid to selectively erode the metal. Each preliminary act of play contributes to creating a nostalgic ghostly atmosphere in the final image, leaving traces of the process that made them and the human presence that existed.

I am drawn to the work of Dexter Dalwood, who paints his fictional interiors as 'portraits of people' from collaged materials, but devoid of human presence; Henri Matisse for his use of pattern and composition and Stephen Chambers for his use of domestic objects to create an 'otherly' world. Veils, screens, layering and peeling are all devices that artists like Sigmar Polke, Robert Rauschenberg and Ross Bleckner all use, and they also fuel my work.

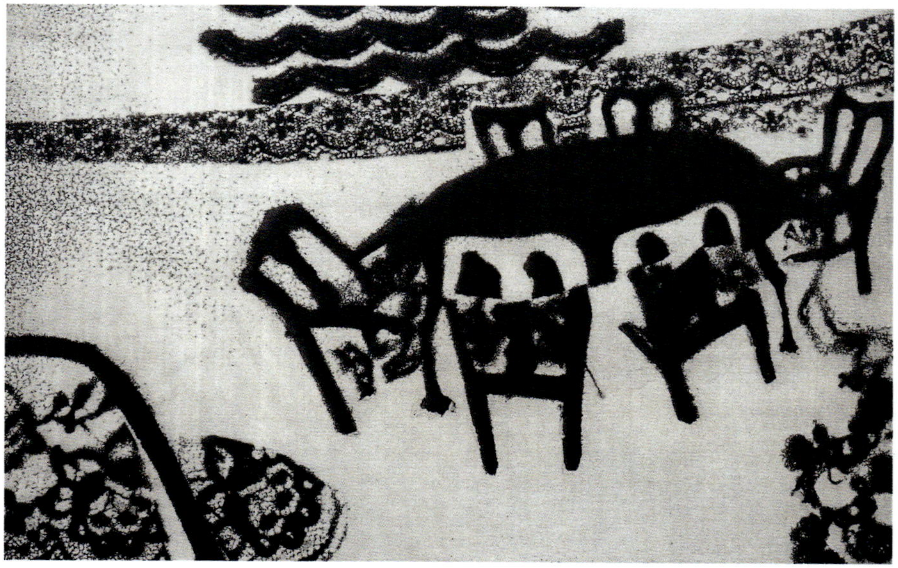

Dinner 7.00pm,
29 x 38 cm,
etching
(edition of 15)

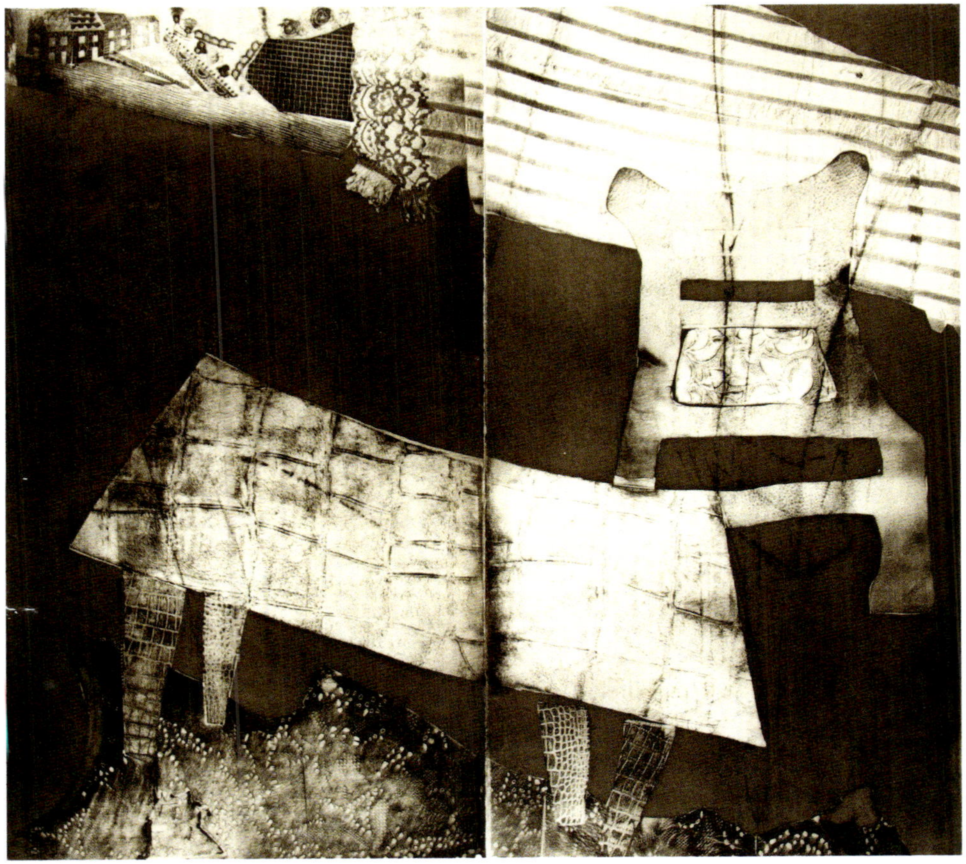

At Play, 90 x 97cm, etching, edition of 15

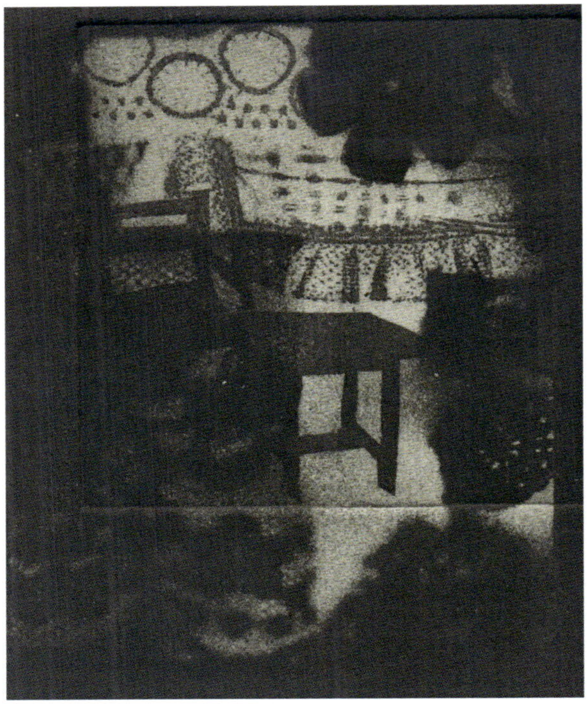

Screen Saver 2, 18 x 15cm, etching, edition of 15

Sisetta Zappone

Born in 1984, I am a professional printmaker and my favourite techniques are etching and engraving in all their variations. Finding inspiration from medieval iconography and ancient symbolism, I re-invent stories and legends very far away from us in terms of time and space, seeing mythology as a universal language by which to decode contemporary human culture and being.

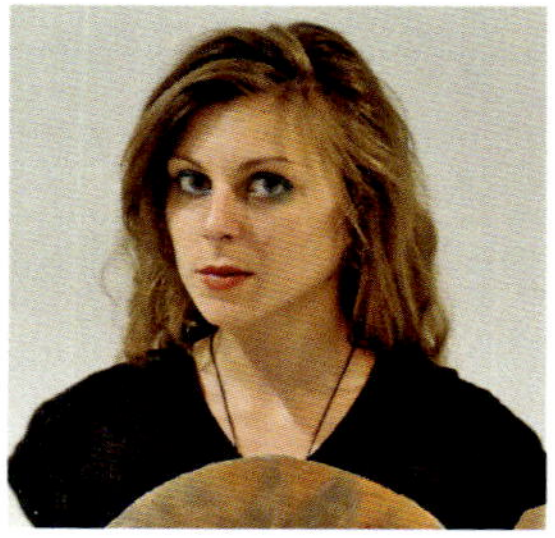

1984 Born Aspromonte
2007 BA Painting and Drawing (highest honours) Florence Fine Arts Academy, Italy
2008 Winner Printmaking Competition organized by Magnani paper mill in Pescia, Italy
2009 MA as a master printmaker Florence First solo exhibition at Florence's Natural History Museum
2011 Moved to London and worked as an intern printmaker and teaching assistant at The Royal Drawing School and Lazarides editions
Became a member of East London Printmakers, taking part in ELP shows
2012 DTTLS teaching qualification, London
Keyholder and tutor at Thames Barrier Print Studio
Print acquired by the National Italian Print Collection through Leonardo Sciascia prize
2013 *Unending Exhibition*, Westminster Reference Art Library
Un Mare D'Inchiostro, Florence Fine Art Academy Drawing Gallery
2014 Solo exhibitions
Mythical Creatures, Wien Culture Institute Austria
Playing the Alchemist, Westminster Reference Library
2015 Featured in V&A print collection with ELP boxset
Winner of public choice at Lubomirov-Easton Gallery Limited Editions Show
Winner of *Art Clash* competition
Member of Printmakers Council
Shortlisted for RA Summer Exhibition

I am from a village in Aspromonte, Southern Italy, land that was once Greek, but also in contact with Arabian culture and Spanish influences, that had French and Swedish kings and local brigands. This corner of the Mediterranean is full of stories, history and syncretism, the mix of religions and languages being still evident in our dialects and folklore. I grew up there, absorbed its legends and looked at its relics, developing a fascination for narrative and archetypes (which are still present in my current work).

I moved to Florence in 2002 and practised and studied in a traditional institution, where contemporary art knowledge and experimentation were frowned upon.

In 2005/6 I won an Erasmus Grant and I lived in Granada (Spain), blending into a different artistic environment. When back in Florence, I struggled and my painting teacher used to denigrate my experimentations. It was then that I had my vital encounter with printmaking.

I gave up painting the same year of my graduation and decided to study at Bisonte International School of Graphic Arts, where my passion for printmaking blossomed on a two-year intensive course focused mainly on etching and engraving, but covering also lithography on stone, screen-print and wood-cut.

Till 2009 I worked as an assistant at Bisonte and as a freelance printmaker for various studios, but I wanted to step away from Italian tradition and unadventurous taste so I moved to London.

About my aesthetic

I would call myself a Jungian neo-surrealist: my favourite artists are Perugino, Blake, Bosch and Sutherland, to name a few.

My style is characterized by a solid arcane background. My prints are detailed, obsessive and technically achieved and I still prefer traditional techniques and materials. Their subjects disclose a dense imagery of both the painful and the humorous: creatures which seem ferocious are often revealed to be ultimately pathetic or impotent, a darkly funny view of our inner lives and psychology.

From meticulous observation of reality, I look to produce shapes that are rooted in the first millennium's art but also in everyone's subconscious.

My aesthetic embraces the idea of the microcosmos being the macrocosmos' mirror, where nature nurtures our mind and thoughts, teaching us how to observe and how to wonder, through its metamorphosis.

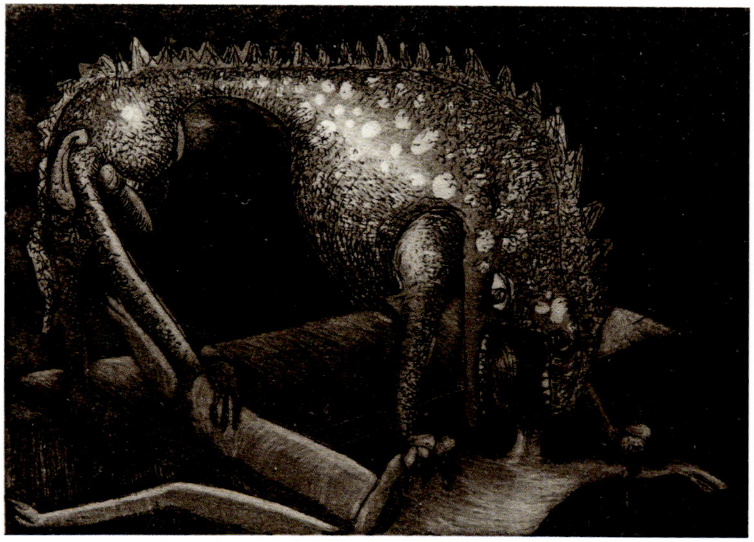

Hermaprodite Hyena, 27 x 30 cm, etching & aquatint (edition of 15)

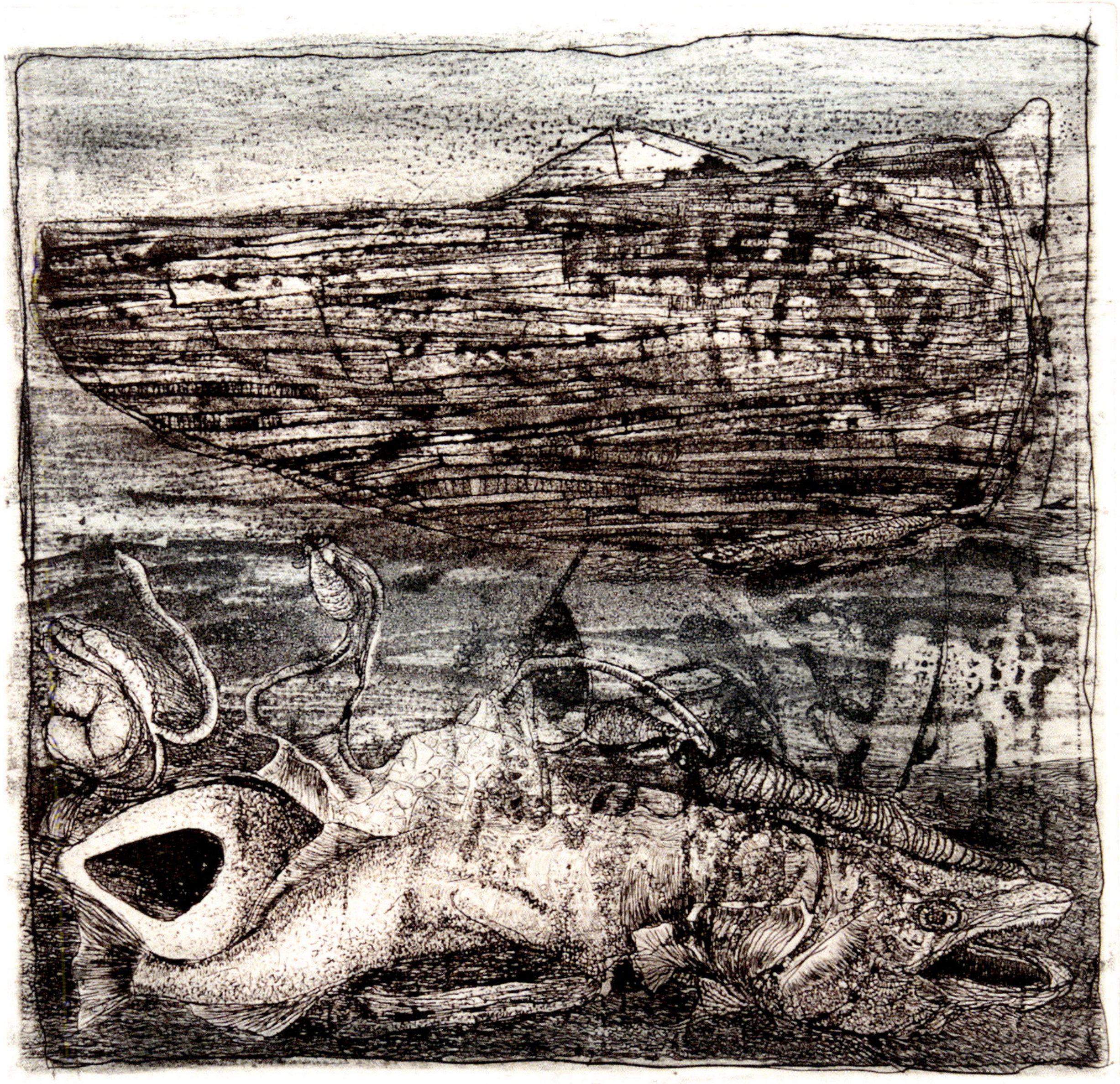

Sharksucker and fertility, 50 x 50 cm, etching & craqueleure, (edition of 15)